1982

RELIGIOUS TRENDS
IN ENGLISH POETRY

RELIGIOUS TRENDS

IN ENGLISH POETRY

By HOXIE NEALE FAIRCHILD

PROFESSOR OF ENGLISH

HUNTER COLLEGE OF THE CITY OF NEW YORK

VOLUME III: 1780-1830

ROMANTIC FAITH

IN LITTERIS
LIBERTAS

1754·1893

New York and London

COLUMBIA UNIVERSITY PRESS

FOR

Mary Tanner Fairchild

BELOVED WIFE AND COMRADE

PREFACE

AFTER SIX YEARS OF WORK I EMERGE WITH THE THIRD VOLUME OF A SERIES OF studies in which trends of religious thought and feeling are to be traced through English poetry from the beginning of the eighteenth century to the present.[1]

In scope and method the present volume differs markedly from its predecessors in the series. Instead of discussing a large number of writers, many of them justly unknown to fame, I here examine rather closely the religion of seven major poets: Burns, Blake, Wordsworth, Coleridge, Shelley, Byron, and Keats. In the first two volumes I attempted to establish an historical thesis by presenting a mass of evidence drawn from numerous and varied sources. Brick by brick, a foundation was laid on which I now feel emboldened to erect a more freely critical, less rigidly inductive treatment of a much smaller number of figures who deserve intensive study. This change may be welcome to readers who have not been able to share my enthusiasm for representatively atrocious verse. It is certainly refreshing to me, for although I enjoyed writing Volumes I and II I really prefer good poetry to bad.

This volume, however, presents difficulties and dangers of its own. What can one hope to add to the innumerable studies which have already been devoted to these poets? Even my special concern with their religion does not ensure an original contribution, for in relation to each of them the subject has frequently been glanced at and in some cases discussed elaborately. My sense of the fundamental importance of a religious frame of reference for the study of romanticism is substantiated by the fact that few scholars have felt able to grapple with the thought of a major romantic poet without considering his religion. Yet there is some encouragement in remembering that the last word about such figures has not been said, and never can be said. The men about whom most has been written are

[1] The two volumes of *Religious Trends in English Poetry* which have already appeared are: Vol. I:1700–1740, *Protestantism and the Cult of Sentiment* (Columbia University Press, 1939); Vol. II:1740–1780, *Religious Sentimentalism in the Age of Johnson* (Columbia University Press, 1942).

precisely those whose works offer inexhaustible opportunities for investigation and interpretation. It is always conceivable that even the humblest scholar who has devoted thirty-odd years to the study of Wordsworth and his contemporaries may bring to light a hitherto unnoticed fact or draw a new idea from facts already known but imperfectly understood. I should like to believe that my familiarity with the eighteenth-century precursors of these poets and with the general movement of English religious and ecclesiastical thought will add a certain freshness to the examination of familiar material. This is, furthermore, the first book in which a twentieth-century historical critic has treated the religion of all the major romantic poets in a single continuous discussion dominated by a unifying point of view.[2] From such a conspectus, if its execution were worthy of its aim, might emerge fruitful generalizations as to the religious implications of romanticism.

But although this book is based primarily upon a fresh first-hand study of all the work of the poets concerned, its preparation has also entailed reading and inwardly digesting a crushing amount of secondary interpretative material. To read everything that has been written about the great romantics would be no less impossible than unnecessary, but I hope I have not neglected many of the books and articles which offer important information or ideas about my subject. My obligations to the researches of other scholars are so great that I have often regretted the necessity of expressing disagreement with their opinions. At other times limitations of space have forced upon me the opposite sort of ingratitude—that of seeming to ignore views which I have carefully weighed before arriving at my own divergent conclusion.

This volume might be described in old-fashioned terms as a cluster of "spiritual biographies" describing the religion of each poet as it develops throughout his career. The method seemed desirable because the religious experience of poets, like that of other men, is a continuous but ever-changing stream. The *Immortality Ode* implies different beliefs from *Tintern Abbey,* and *Ecclesiastical Sonnets* from both. We must begin where the poet began and follow the movement of his mind as it responds to the circumstances of his life.

Since Robert Burns so clearly exemplifies the eighteenth-century cult of sentiment, the opening chapter will give readers who now join me for the

---

[2] In 1924 S. F. Gingerich, in *Essays in the Romantic Poets,* more briefly discussed Coleridge, Wordsworth, Shelley, and Byron with a similar but not an identical aim.

first time some notion of what has gone before. As this series progresses, however, it becomes increasingly difficult to make each volume an independent unit which will also subsume the findings previously arrived at. Those who are interested in the curve of the entire subject should therefore consult Volumes I and II.

Even after the lapse of several years my gratitude to the many generous and perceptive critics of the earlier volumes remains warm. I regret, however, that a few scholars should have regarded the definiteness of my personal religious views as a distorting influence on my treatment of the subject. A study in the history of ideas by a man who had no ideas of his own would be neither very interesting nor very fruitful; and surely these are times when a scholar who has arrived at conclusions on a subject of large human importance is not only entitled but obligated to express them as vigorously as possible. In some quarters, however, the possession of religious opinions is more culpable than the possession of aesthetic, political, or economic opinions. All I actually expect of any man who claims to have a religion is that he should believe in something other than the impulses of his own beautiful soul—a demand so modest that anyone who regards it as bigoted must himself be a trifle intolerant. Here, for better or worse, is a third opinionated book; but I trust that the opinions are legitimate deductions from facts. Readers who disagree with my interpretation will find plenty of objective material from which they are invited to draw whatever conclusions they may prefer.

In Volume IV, which will deal with religion in English poetry from about 1830 to about 1880, I plan to devote separate chapters, rather shorter than those of the present book, to a few major Victorians; but I shall also draw upon minor poetry to provide material for several topical chapters. Even with the proviso of "God willing," I hardly dare to guess when Volume IV will appear; for it will entail getting up a period in which I am at present by no means an expert. Probably the reader will have to stifle his impatience for seven or eight years.

H. N. F.

Hunter College of the City of New York
January, 1948

ACKNOWLEDGMENTS

THE AUTHOR GRATEFULLY ACKNOWLEDGES THE KINDNESS OF THE FOLLOWING publishers for permission to quote from copyright material:

George Bell and Sons, for permission to quote from Coleridge's *Aids to Reflection;* Clarendon Press, for permission to quote from Burns's *Letters,* Coleridge's *Biographia Literaria* and *Complete Poetical Works,* Keats's *Poetical Works,* Robinson's *Correspondence with the Wordsworth Circle,* Wordsworth's *The Convention of Cintra* and *The Prelude* (ed. Ernest de Selincourt), William and Dorothy Wordsworth's *Letters;* Houghton Mifflin Company, for permission to quote from Amy Lowell's *John Keats;* Macmillan Company (London), for permission to quote from F. Warre Cornish's *The English Church in the Nineteenth Century;* Oxford University Press (American Branch), for permission to quote from *Henry Crabb Robinson on Books and Their Writers* (ed. Edith J. Morley) and C. D. Thorpe's *The Mind of John Keats;* Oxford University Press (London), for permission to quote from Keats's *Letters* and John Middleton Murry's *Keats and Shakespeare;* Random House, Inc., for permission to quote from Blake's *Poetry and Prose;* Charles Scribner's Sons, for permission to quote from Byron's *Works* (ed. Coleridge and Prothero), George Santayana's *Character and Opinion in the United States,* and Shelley's *Works* (Julian Edition).

CONTENTS

RELIGIOUS TRENDS
IN ENGLISH POETRY

Chapter I

PRELIMINARIES

FOR SOME YEARS I HELD THE OPINION THAT ROMANTICISM COULD MOST FRUIT-fully be defined as the attempt to achieve, to retain, or to justify that emotional experience which is produced by an imaginative interfusion of real and ideal, natural and supernatural, finite and infinite, man and God.[1] It might have been simpler to say, "Romanticism means in art what pantheism means in theology." Although "pantheism" is perhaps too slippery a term to be relied upon in explaining a still more slippery one, this shorter version gives a fair equivalent of the original if pantheism be understood as the ascription of numinousness to a feeling of cosmic unity and interfusion. Either version implies that romanticism, at its deepest and most intense, is essentially a religious experience.

For me this definition remains useful in the study of the romantic spirit and its expression in art. Further reading and thinking, however, have gradually drawn me toward the conclusion that the interfusion-experience is the flower of romanticism but not its root. It is the culminating exploit of that imaginative power which Coleridge describes as "a repetition within the finite mind of the eternal act of creation in the infinite I AM." [2] And the romantic faith in this power stems from a deeper, broader faith in the natural goodness, strength, and creativity of all human energies. The taproot of romanticism, then, is an eternal and universal and primary fact of consciousness: man's desire for self-trust, self-expression, self-expansion. That is why the interfusion-experience is so precious to the romanticist: by effacing all distinctions and boundaries it permits unlimited outward projection of personal energy.

A completely original definition of romanticism offered in the year 1948 would be an absurdity. Although in matters of this sort nothing can be proved by counting noses, it is heartening to remind oneself that this in-

[1] For an expanded statement of this position see my *Romantic Quest*, pp. 237–256.
[2] *Biographia Literaria*, I, 202.

terpretation is not a personal crotchet. A few of many possible examples must suffice. According to Crane Brinton, the essential element in the revolutionary changes which occurred in England between 1750 and 1850 was a great expansion of human energy. For him, romanticism is the expression in art of "that energy which drives us all to expand our own activity, to get more goods, more power, more consideration from our fellows, to live, in short, a richer life." Faith in the natural goodness of man is the appropriate means of transcending whatever in the external world or in society threatens to check this impulse.[3] For Professor Barzun, the romantic assertion of human strength does not exclude recognition of human weakness; but he finds that romanticism "expresses and exalts Western man's energetic, creative, expansive tendencies, by recognizing that although he is but a feeble creature lost in the universe, he has unpredictable powers which develop under stress of desire and risk."[4] Here one may interject that to define romanticism in terms of belief in human energy is not to deny that the best poetry of the romantic period frequently laments the difficulty of being romantic in the modern world.

Mrs. Campbell speaks of "the true Romantic spirit—the belief in man."[5] Mr. Muirhead cites her approvingly, but he would add "that what to the romantic spirit is the chief value in human life is the sense of the Infinite which is implicit in it, and is the source of all man's deepest experiences."[6] Paul Elmer More associates romanticism with "our sense of an infinite, insatiable personality." This illusion was born in Alexandria, where "we can actually see the Occidental sense of the Ego merging with the Oriental sense of vastness and vagueness, of infinity as akin to the mere escape from limitation."[7] Similarly, T. E. Hulme asserts that romanticism is grounded on belief in man's natural goodness and his consequently limitless potentialities. "The Romantic is always talking about the infinite, because he believes that man is infinite."[8] We may infer that this line of interpretation is used both by friends and by foes of romanticism.

According to Professor Saurat, a growing "identification of the powers of man and the powers of God" characterizes the intellectual history of Europe from Milton onward.

---

[3] Crane Brinton, *The Political Ideas of the English Romanticists*, pp. 1, 45, 46–47.
[4] Jacques Barzun, *Romanticism and the Modern Ego*, p. 193.
[5] O. W. Campbell, *Shelley and the Unromantics*, p. 274.
[6] J. H. Muirhead, *Coleridge as Philosopher*, p. 26.
[7] *The Drift of Romanticism*, p. 26.
[8] *Speculations*, p. 116.

But the complete change came with the positive phase when man, having displaced God from the throne of the Creator, tried to hoist himself into that Supreme Seat. This was to lead to the idealism of the nineteenth century: the doctrine that it was the mind of man that created the world.[9]

To Albert Guérard, however, this generalization would seem oversimplified. He holds that the fundamental romantic illusions are "the myth of man's natural goodness, the myth of the Promethean individual, and the myth of a vital correspondence between man and nature." But he finds it hard to reconcile "Promethean individualism" with something equally romantic—"the pervasive longing for loss of self in an animate whole larger than self, . . . the impulse to self-immolation." This paradox he explains by suggesting that "both impulses offer means of escape from responsibility."[10] He provides a more significant clue, however, when he observes that "Fichte's myth of a nation really independent of the interests of its citizens . . . demands self-immolation and permits a projection of one's individual ego onto an enormous screen existing eternally, a large reward indeed."[11] We shall see that when "the impulse to self-immolation" implies anything more than the Promethean individual's intermittent despair it becomes his most effective means of self-assertion.

To define romanticism as faith in human energy is therefore not obviously eccentric or perverse. Some confusion arises, however, if we apply the term to every kind of vigorous and confident activity. Brinton regards romanticism as the literary aspect of the whole ferment of expanding energies—romantic in the broadest sense—which included the American and French Revolutions, the Industrial Revolution, the Evangelical Movement, nineteenth-century reform, nationalism, imperialism, the development of science and invention—everything, in short, from *Lyrical Ballads* to the Crystal Palace. No doubt all the characteristic activities of the age were tinged to a greater or less extent by the romantic spirit. But the true romanticist must be self-determining, creative, subjectively emotional, and central in the affairs of the cosmos. He arises not as the spokesman but as the antagonist of his environment when political and social thought becomes too coldly rationalistic or too drably utilitarian for his idealism; when a revival of traditional dogma denies his natural goodness; when science depicts a mechanistic and determined universe hostile to his vision

[9] Denis Saurat, *Blake and Modern Thought*, p. x.
[10] "Prometheus and the Aeolian Lyre," *Yale Review*, XXXIII, 484, 485.
[11] *Ibid.*, p. 483.

of free and dominant personality; when material progress burdens his imagination with a heavy weight of machinery and money-grubbing. Let us hear Shelley in *The Defense of Poetry:*

We have more moral, political and historical wisdom than we know how to reduce into practise; we have more scientific and economical knowledge than can be accomodated to the just distribution of the produce which it multiplies. The poetry in these systems of thought, is concealed by the accumulation of facts and calculating processes. . . . We want the creative faculty to imagine that which we know; we want the generous impulse to act that which we imagine; we want the poetry of life: our calculations have outrun conception; we have eaten more than we can digest. The cultivation of those sciences which have enlarged the limits of the empire of man over the external world has, for want of the poetical faculty, proportionately circumscribed those of the internal world; and man, having enslaved the elements, remains himself a slave.[12]

The applicability of this remarkable passage to our own day indicates the historical importance of our subject. In the so-called Romantic Period, human self-confidence totters as it reaches its climax. Man asserts mastery more strongly than ever before—and begins to feel more strongly than ever before that he is the slave of matter and mechanism. Greatly encouraged and greatly threatened, at once triumphant and desperate, the romantic impulse for the first time organizes itself into an *ism*. Prometheus raises his voice in a song of confident power, but he cracks on the top note.

Especially in dealing with the major *English* poets of the period we should avoid exaggerating the romantic elements in their general environment and should duly emphasize those anti-romantic pressures which impelled them to defend their vision—the post-Revolutionary conservative reaction, the mechanistic and materialistic temper of the Industrial Revolution, the Utilitarian-Evangelical compromise, the pervasive pre-Victorian spirit of smug indifference or hostility to art. The poets to be discussed in this volume are exceptional persons, more influential for later generations than for their own. The historian who examines them is studying the history of great Englishmen rather than the history of the English people between 1780 and 1830. To be sure, the thoughts and feelings of these men may be observed, in varying degrees of dilution, in the verse of their minor contemporaries. But if the present study were as hospitable to bad writing as the two preceding volumes of this series the run-of-the-mill

---

[12] Julian Edition, VII, 134.

poetry of the 1780–1830 period would reveal, on the whole, a rather timid continuation of eighteenth-century sentimentalism—a romanticism not fully aware of the glory and the peril of its status in a rapidly changing world. More frequently than in the Age of Johnson, however, we should find a blending of sentimental hankerings with a softened, half-romanticized Evangelicalism in a poetry which neither boldly affirms nor boldly denies the dominant tendencies of the *milieu*.

The major romantic poets reject this yea-and-nay compromise. "We want the poetry of life." They mean, of course, that they want religion. If human creativity is to elude the threat of mechanism, a downright naturalistic humanism is unthinkable: the pure Renaissance tradition has been taken over by the enemy. Nature—including of course human nature—must be supernaturalized. Some sort of Divine Spirit is therefore a necessity; and while the immanence of this Spirit is of primary importance for the romantic experience, Its supernatural status must be safeguarded by ascribing to It some measure of transcendence. Consequently this Spirit of the Universe, or Nature, or Love, or Beauty, may be endowed with several of the traditional attributes of God—creative power, wisdom, benevolence, sometimes even providential care. More or less personified for the uses of poetry, this deity may be loved, worshipped, addressed in prayer, mystically contemplated.

The romantic God, however, exists for the purpose not of transforming a weak and sinful creature into a being worthy of salvation, but of authenticating the natural goodness of man and lending divine sanction to his expansive impulses. "In remembering that one is mortal," says Mrs. Campbell, "there is no romance." [13] More drily, Professor Bush observes that "A romantic has been succinctly defined as a person who does not believe in the fall of man." [14] Although God represents ideals which the romanticist in his less sanguine moments may feel to be unattainable, there can be no essential disharmony between the spirit of God and the spirit of man. The difference is of degree, not of kind. For all his detestation of anthropomorphism, the romantic poet shapes a deity who is the supreme romantic genius, thus erecting a much more formidable rationalization of human self-sufficiency than a flatly non-religious naturalism could provide.

[13] O. W. Campbell, *Shelley and the Unromantics*, p. 258.
[14] D. N. Bush, *Mythology and the Romantic Tradition in English Poetry*, p. 155. The original source of this definition is unknown to me.

The essays of Ralph Waldo Emerson will enable us to sample romantic religion without stealing thunder from the following chapters. There are moments when he sounds very much as if he believed in God. "I am constrained," he writes, "to acknowledge a higher origin for events than the will I call mine." But this higher will can be described only in pantheistic terms as "that great nature in which we rest as the earth lies in the soft arms of the atmosphere; that Unity, that Over-Soul, within which every man's particular being is contained and made one with all other." Thanks to this romantic interfusion man exists within "the eternal ONE," but "Meantime within man is the soul of the whole." The ostensibly suprapersonal "higher origin for events" cannot really be distinguished from the human will in a universe in which everything is intertwined with everything else. "And this deep power in which we exist and whose beatitude is all accessible to us is not only self-sufficing and perfect in every hour, but the act of seeing and the thing seen, the seer and the spectacle, the subject and the object, are one." [15] The identity of the Over-Soul with the soul within us insures the deification of man:

We know that all spiritual being is in man. . . . There is no bar or wall in the soul, where man, the effect, ceases, and God, the cause, begins. . . . Revelation is the disclosure of the soul. . . . Ineffable is the union of man and God in every act of the soul.[16]

Like the English romantic poets, Emerson retains much of the eighteenth century's reverence for external nature as the all-sufficient medium of communication between man and God, combined with a large tincture of anti-intellectualism and sentimental primitivism: "We can never see God from the catechism: from the pastures, from a boat in the pond, from amidst the songs of wood-birds we possibly may." [17] But since the God revealed in nature is the Over-Soul, within whose unity it is impossible to say where humanity ends and divinity begins, to behold God in nature is to behold one's own creative power raised to cosmic proportions. With some malicious exaggeration but with no essential inaccuracy, Santayana explains the romantic blend of naturalism and transcendentalism as it appears in Emerson: "Nature, for the transcendentalist, is precious because it is his own work, a mirror in which he looks and says (like a poet relish-

---

[15] Emerson, *Essays. First Series*, pp. 252–253.   [16] *Ibid.*, pp. 255, 265, 274.
[17] *Ibid.*, p. 292.

ing his own verses), 'What a genius I am! Who would have thought there was such stuff in me?' " [18]

Emerson further resembles the English romantics, who in this as in the former case develop a well-established eighteenth-century tradition, by substantially equating the Over-Soul with genius. "The same Omniscience flows into the intellect and makes what we call genius." [19] That genius is the common property of all men who will recognize and lay hold upon it is strongly emphasized in the essay on *Self-Reliance,* where we find a completely undisguised expression of that primary romantic urge which *The Over-Soul* drapes in more elaborate philosophical robes. "To believe in your own thought, to believe that what is true for you in your private heart is true for all men—that is genius." Great men have always lived by the maxim, "Trust thyself." [20] Such greatness is available to everyone. "When we inquire into the reason of self-trust" we finally arrive at

that source, at once the essence of genius, of virtue, and of life, which we call Spontaneity or Instinct. We denote this primary wisdom as Intuition, whilst all later teachings are tuitions. In that deep force, the last fact behind which analysis cannot go, all things find their common origin.[21]

Thus the Over-Soul, genius, and instinct are alternative terms for the creative power of the universe.

The motto of *Self-Reliance* is a passage from the epilogue to Beaumont and Fletcher's *Honest Man's Fortune* beginning "Man is his own star." If traditional religion denies this assertion, so much the worse for traditional religion. With considerable satisfaction Emerson remembers a retort which he made

when quite young . . . to a valued adviser who was wont to importune me with the dear old doctrines of the church. On my saying, "What have I to do with the sacredness of traditions, if I live wholly from within?" my friend suggested,—"But these impulses may be from below, not from above." I replied, "They do not seem to me to be such; but if I am the Devil's child, I will live then from the Devil." No law can be sacred to me but that of my own nature.[22]

This is the upshot of Emerson's acknowledgment of "a higher origin for events than the will I call mine." There is really no will in the universe other than a magnified reflection of his own.

[18] *Little Essays Drawn from the Writings of George Santayana* (ed. L. P. Smith), p. 202.
[19] *Op. cit.,* p. 270.   [20] *Ibid.,* p. 47.   [21] *Ibid.,* p. 64.
[22] *Ibid.,* p. 52.

But despite Emerson's scorn of "the dear old doctrines of the church," such beliefs as he expresses took form in a civilization at least nominally Christian. How are Christianity and the romantic religion of self-trust related? The question cannot be answered dogmatically in days when the former term is often applied to anyone who regards the universe with approval and believes in persuading the less attractive young people of the community to dance with one another in drearily wholesome surroundings. For the theologically precise, the problem is simple enough: the religion of Emerson and of the romantic poets is a tissue of heresies. On the other hand, those who interpret Christianity as a religion of human self-sufficiency will naturally assert that romanticism is the embodiment in art of the Christian spirit. Thus Mrs. Campbell describes Jesus as "the great romantic"—greater even than Shelley—because He established that "Christian belief in man" which is the essence of romanticism.[23] Professor Barzun associates romanticism with a more historical conception of Christianity:

The judgment of Mme. de Staël, aided by Schlegel's, that the romantic view of life is basically Christian seems fully justified, for it combines the infinite worth of the individual soul in its power and weakness, the search for union with God and the gospel of work for one's fellow man.[24]

But here some would plead for a closer analysis of terms, which might show that worth of the soul, power and weakness of the soul, union with God, and human brotherhood do not mean for the romantic quite what they mean for the Christian.

No conclusion can be drawn from what the romantic poets thought of their own beliefs. Burns, Blake, and Coleridge regarded themselves as good Christians. So did Wordsworth throughout most of his long career, though for a brief but important period he probably deemed himself a deist. Shelley and Keats were avowedly non-Christian. Byron at times repudiated Christianity and at other times wished to be thought a better Christian than the shocked readers of *Cain*. Of course anyone can call himself a Christian. On the other hand, if romanticism expresses that pure Christianity toward which the first seventeen centuries of the Christian era had been groping through the fogs of superstition and bigotry, then the more emphatically a poet repudiates traditional Christianity the more strikingly he exemplifies what Christianity *ought* to be. One might

[23] *Op. cit.*, pp. 252, 253.   [24] *Romanticism and the Modern Ego*, p. 133.

suppose that belief in God, not belief in oneself, is the starting-point of the Christian experience. But since Mrs. Campbell regards Christianity and romanticism as equivalent terms for the cult of self-sufficiency, she need not hesitate to describe Shelley as a Christian:

The most important of his beliefs, the motive power of his life and work, was his immense *faith in man*. . . . It seemed to spring in the first place from that sense of his own divinity with which all geniuses are endowed. He extended this to all the world.[25]

Here is the pure Emersonian gospel.

The tendency to identify romantic religion with Christianity will be especially strong among those who, brushing aside the distinction between religion and ethics, trace romantic benevolism back to the Sermon on the Mount. It will probably be useless to remind them that there is nothing peculiarly Christian about humanitarianism unless it is the humanitarianism of Christians. The following chapters may indicate that romantic benevolism implies quite as much self-regard as self-sacrifice. The Good Samaritan was not actuated by "that sense of his own divinity with which all geniuses are endowed."

It is at all events a little confusing, for history no less than for theology, to apply the same title to a religion of human insufficiency, which offers redemption at the cost of humility and self-surrender, and to a religion of human sufficiency, which denies the necessity of redemption and offers man limitless self-expansion at no greater cost than the will to affirm his own goodness as part of a good universe; to a religion in which grace descends to man from a great outward Reality completely independent of his desires and imaginings, and to a religion in which grace is the echo of man's pride; to a religion which says, "Be it unto me according to thy word," and to a religion which says, "No law can be sacred to me but that of my own nature." Some will prefer to regard these as two stages in the gradual purification of Christianity. For me, however, the difference is so radical that I must continue to affront certain critics by restricting the term "Christianity" to the former kind of religion. The latter I call "religion of sentiment" in its preliminary eighteenth-century phases and "romantic religion" when it comes to full bloom in the period under discussion. Although my personal preference for Christianity is unconcealed,

---

[25] *Op. cit.*, p. 279. Throughout this volume italics are always those of the author cited unless otherwise noted.

the distinction is drawn not in the spirit of Torquemada but in that of an historian who is trying to avoid muddle.

This terminology by no means denies the possibility of tracing a line of descent from Christian to romantic belief. The spiritual genealogy of Emerson is clear enough: Puritanism sloughs down into Unitarianism; Unitarianism sloughs down into a romantic transcendentalism partly indigenous and partly fabricated from English, German, and Oriental materials. This movement will be familiar to readers of the earlier volumes of this series, which have tried to show that seventeenth-century Protestantism, especially of the Puritan type, is the father of that eighteenth-century sentimentalism which becomes romanticism on attaining maturity. The host of witnesses—some 380 poets of the eighteenth century—cannot be recalled to the stand; but, as above in describing my general conception of romanticism, I shall venture to remind the reader that the thesis is not the unique product of one student's personal bias. The scholars to be cited are not the lobbyists of any single religious faction. In matters of detail their accounts of the historical process sometimes differ widely from mine. We agree, however, on the major point that romantic religion descends from an essential element of the Protestant ethos.[26]

In *The Funeral Elegy and the Rise of English Romanticism,* J. W. Draper sometimes gives the impression that melancholy and romanticism are almost synonymous, and that all the melancholy of the eighteenth century derives from the elegies of the seventeenth-century Puritans. But occasionally, responding to the broader implications of his subject, he offers generalizations which would be highly significant if supported by material of ampler scope. He sees the eighteenth century as a transition leading from a seventeenth-century doctrine of Original Sin to a nineteenth-century doctrine of Original Genius.[27] The main factor in the shift was "the rise of the trading classes to wealth, their consequent return to artistic patronage and their re-interpretation of Protestantism on a Sentimental, instead of a Calvinistic basis." The sense of sin became an emotional luxury and the sense of election the basis of the cult of genius.[28]

According to Professor Cazamian, the psychology of the Puritan middle class largely determines the course of modern English literature. In the eighteenth century the upper middle class accepted the standards of neo-

---

[26] The following sketch of the "literature" of the subject adds fresh material to remarks repeated with slight changes from Volume I of *Religious Trends.*
[27] *Op. cit.,* p. 314.   [28] *Ibid.,* pp. 22, 152.

classicism but in so doing impressed upon them a puritan stamp. "Elle conserve en elle le germe vivant du sentimentalisme." [29] Evidence for this view is furnished by A. A. Perdeck's *Theology in Augustan Literature,* which shows that the chiefly puritanical religious verse of the Queen Anne period preserves more of the non-classical qualities of seventeenth-century poetry than does the secular verse of that period.

To move further into the eighteenth century, the Methodist Revival has often been described as a romantic movement in religion,[30] and Umphrey Lee has traced the history of "enthusiasm" from the Puritans to the Methodists.[31] The kinship between religious and literary enthusiasm throughout the same period has been discussed by Sister M. Kevin Whelan, S.S.J.[32]

No reader of William Haller's *The Rise of Puritanism* can fail to be impressed by the boldness with which the more radical Puritan thinkers anticipate the governing ideas of the romantics. In the Introduction to his collection of *Tracts on Liberty in the Puritan Revolution,* the same scholar explicitly recognizes the romanticism of the sectarian mystics. Of William Walwyn, for example, he writes: "He had . . . effected for himself that transposition of the Christian myth into romantic revolutionary images which held so much of significance for the future." [33] Blake's politico-religious thought is described by Mark Schorer as an example of precisely the same transposition:

The myth is of man's native goodness, a vision of the liberated individual progressing into dignity when released from the most crushing forms of authority. . . . This is the chiliastic hope of seventeenth-century Protestantism given specifically political form.[34]

"The zest of romanticism," says Santayana, "consists in taking what you know to be an independent and ancient world as if it were material for your private emotions." [35] As it appears in post-Kantian German idealism, this "Absolute Egotism" is "the form which Protestantism assumed at a moment of high tension and reckless self-sufficiency." Protestantism,

---

[29] Louis Cazamian, *L'Evolution psychologique et la littérature en Angleterre, 1660–1914,* pp. 28, 64, 86–87.

[30] See especially F. C. Gill, *The Romantic Movement and Methodism.*

[31] *The Historical Backgrounds of Early Methodist Enthusiasm.*

[32] *Enthusiasm in English Poetry of the Eighteenth Century.*

[33] *Op. cit.,* I, 40.   [34] *William Blake: The Politics of Vision,* p. 42.

[35] *Little Essays Drawn from the Writings of George Santayana,* p. 379.

as he sees it, is only externally a form of Christianity. Essentially it is a quite distinct religion, Teutonic in origin, which "mistakes vitality, both in itself and in the universe, for spiritual life." [36] To place Luther wholly beyond the Christian pale seems a trifle exclusive, and to make the human desire for self-trust a Nordic monopoly is tempting but rash. Nevertheless it is difficult to disagree with Santayana when he writes:

The Reformation did not reform this belief in the cosmic supremacy of man, or the humanity of God; on the contrary it took it (like so much else) in terrible German earnest. . . . The human race, the chosen people, the Christian elect were like tabernacle within tabernacle for the spirit; but in the holy of holies was the spirit itself, one's own spirit and experience, which was the center of everything.[37]

In this respect Emerson and the romantic poets are the heirs of the Reformation. Once romantic religion has fully evolved, it may fabricate an essentially Protestant reinterpretation of Catholicism. But while Catholicism as imperfectly embodied in the Church Visible has its own peculiar snares, its insistence on the corporate character of Christian life, its authoritarian discipline, and its devotion to a completely objective spiritual reality mediated down to man through grace-giving outward forms provide unfriendly soil for the romantic impulse. Before reaching the goal of his spiritual wanderings, the hero of Newman's *Loss and Gain* is told by a Roman Catholic priest that men

will not be blessed, they will effect nothing in religious matters, till they begin by an act of unreserved faith in the will of God, whatever it be, till they go out of themselves; till they cease to make something within them their standard.[38]

For better or worse, that statement touches the very core of Catholicism. Contrast Emerson's "No law can be sacred to me but that of my own nature," which would have shocked Calvin but which nevertheless seems to be the ultimate historical consequence of the Protestant position. Doubtless some Catholic communicants are essential Protestants, while some members of Protestant denominations are essential Catholics. Individual Catholics have their romantic hankerings like other men; conversely, many individual Protestants retain a deep sense of the outwardness and otherness of God. To become a thorough-going romanticist, however,

[36] *Ibid.*, pp. 80, 82.   [37] *Character and Opinion in the United States*, p. 21.
[38] J. H. Newman, *Loss and Gain*, p. 386.

one must break sharply away from Catholicism; to reach the same goal, one need only continue to the end of the road on which Protestantism set its feet.

It is not surprising, then, that the warmest admirers of the great romantics should frequently emphasize their Protestantism. Mark Schorer, as we have seen, associates Blake with "the dissenting myth." From the pages of Professor Harper's biography, Wordsworth (before his apostasy) emerges as a hero of Protestant liberalism. Of Byron, Mr. Marjarum declares: "His individualism is essentially Protestant; he is the descendant of the English nominalists who broke ground for the separatist tendencies of the Reformed faiths." [39] Shelley, hailed by Mrs. Campbell as a great Christian, is more specifically described by Mr. Barnard as "the essential Protestant," who "follows the Protestant principle of individualism to its logical end in the denial of the need, in religion, of any organization whatever." [40] Professor Grabo warmly agrees that Shelley

is the greatest of Protestants among modern poets and thinkers. . . . The moral system which Shelley proposes is, as we should expect, individualistic, Protestant in character. The seat of authority resides in the individual heart.[41]

The same scholar finds it only natural that Shelley should gradually have been drawn toward a more favorable view of Christ:

For Christ is one of the moral leaders of individualists, one of the greatest of Protestants, akin to the mystics and Platonists and all others who believe that our perception of divinity is an intuition of the heart. Such men—Socrates and Christ—and their followers, such as Shelley, are inevitably rebels.[42]

This jumbling of Christ with "the mystics and Platonists" and with intuitionalists of every sort characterizes both romantic religion and present-day romantic criticism. Shelley would, of course, have filled Socrates with amused astonishment. The comparison between the poet and Christ must be set aside for the present. We may more profitably wonder how Shelley and Bunyan's Christian would get along as fellow-pilgrims. The incongruity of the picture warns us not to identify romantic religion with

[39] E. W. Marjarum, *Byron as Skeptic and Believer*, p. 21.
[40] Ellsworth Barnard, *Shelley's Religion*, p. 4.
[41] Carl Grabo, *The Magic Plant: the Growth of Shelley's Thought*, pp. viii, 151.
[42] *Ibid.*, p. 159.

any phase of Protestantism which preserves more than a vestige of original Reformation theology. The faith of the Reformers had to undergo an astonishing metamorphosis as it moved down the long road from Calvin to Shelley.

The history of this change has been glanced at more or less suggestively by several of the scholars cited in the foregoing paragraphs. The subject receives fuller treatment in two valuable but not wholly satisfactory German monographs. In Herbert Schöffler's *Protestantismus und Literatur* the preromantic tendencies of the eighteenth century are said to have resulted from the secularization of Protestantism under the influence of the Enlightenment. The believing spirit of the seventeenth century and the reasoning spirit of the eighteenth flowed together in a compromise, each giving something to the other. The clergy developed secular literary interests, while secular literature took over some of the clergy's characteristic themes and moods. Unfortunately Schöffler's attempt to associate preromanticism as closely as possible with the work of clerics or sons of clerics narrows and warps his view of a very broad subject. His acquaintance with eighteenth-century secular literature is not rich or intimate, nor does he seem thoroughly at home in the history of English philosophical and religious thought. In particular he makes the shift from the seventeenth to the eighteenth century much too abrupt by exaggerating the ascetic temper of seventeenth-century Anglicanism.

A more searching study in *Geistesgeschichte* is H. O. Wilde's *Der Gottesgedanke in der englischen Literatur. Das Problem der Entwicklung von puritanischer zu romantischer Literatur.* The author's treatment is Hegelian. The severe rationalism of Puritan theology, he says, created a sightless chasm between man and God. The emotionalism of the Puritan temper, on the other hand, aroused a strong desire for union with God. The antithesis between these factors achieved synthesis toward the close of the eighteenth century, when the chasm between man and God was bridged by an interfusion of Methodist enthusiasm and the Deistic religion of nature. Like Schöffler, Wilde stops short of the romantic poets. His trump card is William Cowper, in whose poetry

beginnt der Frühlingshymnus der Romantik von der Liebe zu allem lebendigen Sein—zu Mensch, Tier, Erde, Pflanze und Stein, zu allem, denn alles ist göttlich! Die puritanischer Kluft zwischen Gott und Mensch, Gott und Natur, und Mensch und Umwelt ist überwunden. . . . Gott ist die Seele, die alles durchglühet—das ist der Gottesgedanke der Romantik, den wir bei Wordsworth finden. Cowper war das stolze Glück zuteil, das weltanschauliche Problem der Romantik zu lösen.[43]

This passage gives an excellent statement of romantic nature-feeling, but it ignores the relatively undiluted Evangelical Protestantism which gives *The Task* a distinctly reactionary position in the development of pre-romanticism. Though Wilde thinks harder than Schöffler, his materials are even less adequate: the only eighteenth-century poets besides Cowper whom he discusses are Pope and Gray. Christopher Smart would have given him an earlier and more striking example of the tendencies which he overemphasizes in *The Task;* and of course poets like Thomson and Akenside are much more closely akin to Wordsworth than is Cowper. Shaftesbury is mentioned only to be swept aside as if extraneous to the thesis. Nor is Wilde's treatment of seventeenth-century Puritanism entirely valid. Perhaps misled by his greater familiarity with the German Lutheranism of the period, he overestimates the rationalism of the English Puritans—or at least he underestimates the subjective and intuitive quality which pervaded it. Hence he makes far too much of the chasm between man and God, which, thanks to the Inner Light, was for many Puritans no chasm at all. He mentions the Sects, but does not seem fully aware of the romantic implications of their antinomian enthusiasm.

My own rather different interpretation of what Wilde calls *die Entwicklung von puritanischer zu romantischer Literatur* is already available to anyone who has the considerable patience required for reading it. Of course man's desire to feel self-sufficiently good, strong, and creative is much older than any form of Christianity. It is as old as human nature. In ancient times, it seizes upon selected aspects of Platonism, Stoicism, and Epicureanism—traditions which continue to be directly or indirectly influential throughout the history of the theme. In the Middle Ages, drawing much encouragement from Neoplatonic thought, it appears most clearly in the Pelagian heresy and in various expressions of "pre-Protestant" mysticism. In the sixteenth century, the romantic impulse is partly encouraged and partly threatened by the Renaissance, by the new science, and by the official formularies of the Reformation; but it draws immense nourishment from deep-rooted elements in Protestant psychology which are soon to transform the theologies of Luther and Calvin—or perhaps to reveal their essential meaning. In the seventeenth century, romantic self-

[43] *Op. cit.,* p. 150.

trust becomes the principal factor in the disintegration of Protestant Christianity. Uncurbed by Catholic or classical restraints, it goes far toward substituting a religion of justification by self-esteem for a religion of justification by faith.

In the eighteenth century the romantic urge receives a satisfying rationalization in the sentimental deism of Shaftesbury and in the poetry which flows from it. God, man, and nature are pantheistically interfused. In this system of universal benevolence, man shares immanent divinity with nature. Self-love, social love, and divine love are indistinguishable. Nature's God has confirmed man's longing to find goodness, wisdom, and creative power in the depths of his own heart. With rare exceptions, however, the religion of sentiment as expressed in eighteenth-century poetry retains a considerable amount of neoclassical nothing-too-muchness, common sense, utilitarianism, objectivity, and respect for the mechanical laws of Newtonian science. At last the accelerating tempo of social change renders this compromise inadequate for a few unusually sensitive and perceptive spirits. Then it is that the great poets of the 1780–1830 period, building upon the romantic elements in their eighteenth-century heritage, burst forth in songs of strangely mingled triumph and despair.

In this volume, however, we are concerned not with the historical background of the religion of self-assertion but with its culmination in the poetry of the Romantic Period. Our proper task has been too long delayed. The romanticism of Robert Burns, the first poet to be considered, is too rudimentary to make him a thoroughly satisfying example of these preliminary generalizations; but as a transitional figure he may serve to link the eighteenth-century phase of the subject with maturer expressions of romantic belief.

Chapter II

BURNS

I

PROBABLY NO PASSAGE IN THE NON-LYRICAL WORK OF BURNS IS MORE FAMILIAR than the description of family worship in *The Cotter's Saturday Night*. The poet knew the scene at first hand; he could hardly have portrayed it without thinking of his own fireside and his own father. Sometimes, indeed, the reading of the Bible on such occasions was delegated to young Robert, for he was early recognized as the best reader in the household.[1]

Family worship is not the only religious element in the poem. Before supper the guidman admonishes his children to obey their parents, to perform their daily tasks with sober industry, "to fear the Lord alway" and to ask His help in resisting temptation. When the guests have gone home and the bairns are in bed, the father and mother pray that He who feeds the raven and bedecks the lily

> Would, in the way His wisdom sees the best,
> For them and for their little ones provide;
> But, chiefly, in their hearts with Grace Divine preside.

Religion, indeed, was the all-important factor in the rearing of Scottish children. We know, although the poem does not tell us so, that religious and secular education were inseparable. Elementary schooling was based on the Bible and the Catechism, for every member of the Kirk should be able to read the Scriptures for himself and to listen to the sermon critically no less than devoutly. In William Burnes, the piously motivated Scottish respect for book-learning was unusually strong. When he discussed religion with Robert and Gilbert, as he did every day at Mount Oliphant, the father and his sons avoided Scotticisms as much as possible.[2]

---

[1] Dudley Wright, *Robert Burns and Freemasonry*, p. 9.
[2] Catherine Carswell, *The Life of Robert Burns*, p. 51.

The Bible was a well, not merely of heavenly wisdom, but of English undefiled.

Despite the studied artificiality and derivativeness of this poem, one need not doubt the sincerity of the assertion that "From scenes like these, old Scotia's grandeur springs." Only two years before his death Burns writes to Mrs. Dunlop: "With all my follies of youth, and I fear a few vices of manhood, still I congratulate myself on having had in early days religion strongly impressed upon my mind."[3] He always remained, according to his own peculiar lights, a son of the Kirk. Except perhaps toward the end of the Edinburgh sojourn and during the disturbed and bitter days which followed, he was a regular churchgoer throughout his life. At Mossgiel, becoming head of the household on the death of his father, he himself presided at family prayers and catechized "wee Davoc" the herd-boy so searchingly that

> He'll screed you aff "Effectual Calling"
> As fast as onie in the dwalling.[4]

When at last the poet could say "I hae a wife of my ain," he regularly conducted family worship at Ellisland. Biblical quotations and allusions often appear in his poems and letters. "It is really a glorious book," he tells Margaret Chalmers.[5] References to official Kirk documents such as the Westminster Confession are also rather numerous.

When he alludes to specific doctrines of the Kirk, however, the tone and context are usually whimsical, mocking, or seriously hostile. This fact implies a departure from the soberly devout spirit of his father's teachings but not a complete reversal of their matter. That the theology of William Burnes, regarded from a strictly Calvinistic point of view, was somewhat heterodox may be gathered from the *Manual of Religious Belief* which he prepared for the instruction of his sons.[6] We do not know whether it superseded or incongruously supplemented the official catechism, but it was certainly used in his household. Even the form of this dialogue holds liberal implications; for the Son, instead of being quizzed on matters

---

[3] *The Letters of Robert Burns*, II, 281. (Referred to hereafter as *Letters*.)
[4] *The Complete Poetical Works of Robert Burns*, p. 114. (Referred to hereafter as *Poems*.)
[5] *Letters*, I, 144.
[6] *A Manual of Religious Belief, in a Dialogue between Father and Son, compiled by William Burnes, farmer at Mount Oliphant, Ayrshire, and transcribed, with grammatical corrections, by John Murdoch, teacher.* I quote it from the Chambers-Wallace edition of *The Life and Works of Robert Burns* (New York, 1896), I, 455-459.

beyond his understanding, asks all the questions. In the Father's answers the frequent occurrence of "reason" and "rational" suggests the parental approach to religious problems.

To most present-day Protestants the theology of the *Manual* would seem stiff enough, but as representing the beliefs of a mid-eighteenth-century Ayrshire farmer it is decidedly broad and mild. At the outset strong emphasis is laid upon the natural revelation, for in answer to the question, "How shall I evidence to myself that there is a God?" the Father replies, "By the works of creation: for nothing can make itself; and the fabric of nature demonstrates its Creator to be possessed of all possible perfections, and for that cause we owe all that we have to him." This omits the essentially Christian part of the answer given to the same question in the *Larger Catechism*: "The very light of nature in man, and the works of God, declare plainly that there is a God; but his word and spirit only do sufficiently and effectually reveal him unto men for their salvation." [7]

In several other respects the *Manual* fails to strike the distinctive notes of Calvinism. The Father says not a word about predestination or total corruption. The aid of the Spirit is necessary for saving faith, but apparently this aid is available to all. God will save those who win His love by loving Him and by trying to imitate His goodness:

We ought to serve him out of love, for his perfections give us delightful prospects of his favour and friendship, for if we serve him out of love, we will endeavor to be like him, and God will love his own image, and if God loves us, he will rejoice over us to do us good.

In strict Calvinism, of course, these blessings would be only for the elect, but here there is no such restriction.

Perhaps the most striking passage in the *Manual*, while thoroughly Christian, breathes an unpuritanical spirit which Robert in later days may have interpreted more freely than his father intended:

Setting the rational part above the animal, though it promote a war in the human frame, every conflict and victory affords us grateful reflection, and tends to compose the mind more and more, not to the utter destruction of the animal part, but to the real and true enjoyment of it, by placing Nature in the order that its Creator designed it, which in the natural consequences of the

[7] *The Confessions of Faith, Catechisms, etc., of Public Authority in the Church of Scotland*, p. 327.

thing promotes Spiritual Life, and renders us more and more fit for Christ's spiritual kingdom; and not only so, but gives to animal life pleasure and joy, that we never could have had without it.

Where did William Burnes get his liberal ideas? That solemn young pedant John Murdoch may have been helpful, though there is no reason to doubt the statement on the title page that the *Manual* was merely "transcribed, with grammatical corrections," by Robert's early teacher. Murdoch was a leftish sort of Whig who may have acquired a tinge of French philosophism on his travels. Probably his religious views were a little too broad for William, though not for the growing Robert.

A stronger personal influence on the theology of William Burnes was exercised by the Reverend William Dalrymple, who, as first minister of the parish of Ayr, was the pastor of the Burns family until their removal to Lochlie. Dalrymple's gentle, uncontroversial, ethical rather than doctrinal sermons won William's heart soon after his migration to Ayrshire. The good minister, who was admired even by those who disliked his principles, did not openly attack predestination but left his hearers free to hope that the pearly gates would be opened to any repentant sinner. Though hardly a Socinian, he was not a very ardent Trinitarian. He held that the passions of men are sinful only when used for sinful ends. For such teachings Robert, no less than his father, admired the minister who had baptized him, and in later days came to his defense in *The Kirk's Alarm*:

> D'rymple mild! D'rymple mild!
> Tho' your heart's like a child,
> An' your life like the new-driven snaw,
> Yet that winna save ye:
> Auld Satan must have ye
> For preaching that three's ane and twa.[8]

On the whole, then, we may say that the ideas of William Burnes's *Manual* are those of Dalrymple's sermons.[9] Possibly there are other sources in

[8] *Poems*, p. 111. The orthodox party in the Kirk had attacked Dalrymple for commending a work by his much more radical assistant minister, William M'Gill.

[9] According to its title-page the *Manual* was written at Mount Oliphant—hence between 1766 and 1777. In the former year Burns was only seven—too young to absorb such advanced teachings, though William expected much of his son. It was in 1766 that Dalrymple published his first book, a volume of sermons. His other works all appeared after he became Moderator of the General Assembly of the Kirk in 1781. On the whole 1770 is a likely conjectural date for the composition of the *Manual*.

the theological literature of the day. For us, however, the important fact is that the views of Robert's father represent, in their mild and temperate way, a stage in a long evolution which we must examine in order to understand the religious thought of the son.

Far from being a solid rock of belief and practice, the Kirk at this time was perhaps the most fluid element in a rapidly changing culture. This fluidity, as I tried to show in the concluding chapter of my first volume, is inherent in the very nature of Calvinism. On the surface it appears as an anti-Calvinistic reaction, but its underlying relationship with the thought of the Reformation is evolutionary rather than revolutionary. Here, however, we must not attempt to go back to the roots of the change: we can only review the development as it pertains to eighteenth-century Scotland. After the Act of Union of 1707, a tolerant, sensible, Whiggish latitudinarianism of the sort typified by Archbishop Tillotson exerted an increasingly strong influence on Scottish thought. In certain quarters its anti-enthusiastic, easy-going cheerfulness undermined the dourness of Calvinism. Its utilitarian emphasis on the moral virtues as the essence of religion diminished the traditional respect for theology. Much later, William Wilberforce criticized the latitudinarians from a point of view which would have been understood by loyal Scottish Calvinists of the Queen Anne period:

Towards the close of the last [seventeenth] century, the divines of the Established Church . . . professed to make it their chief object to inculcate the moral and practical precepts of Christianity, which they conceived to have been too much neglected; but without sufficiently maintaining, often without justly laying, the grand foundation of a sinner's acceptance with God, or pointing out how the practical precepts of Christianity grow out of her peculiar doctrines, and are inseparably connected with them. By this fatal error, the very genius and essential nature of Christianity was imperceptibly changed.[10]

But in Scotland, where the contrast between old and new ideas was sharper than in England, the change was perceptible enough. By glorifying works, latitudinarianism weakened the solifidian foundations of Calvin's creed. Its reliance on the environmentalism of Locke made against original sin and pointed toward natural goodness. Its fondness for drawing teleological evidence from Newtonian science emphasized the

---

[10] William Wilberforce, *A Practical View of the Prevailing Religious System of Professed Christians in the Higher and Middle Classes of Society, Contrasted with Real Christianity*, p. 359.

natural revelation at the expense of the supernatural and encouraged the paradox of a this-worldly religion. Latitudinarianism is not a fixed theological position, but a very unstable attitude of mind. Its pragmatic outlook may become toughly positivistic, or tenderly illusioned. It may move through the Arianism of Samuel Clarke to outright Socinianism. It may pass beyond the haziest boundaries of Christianity to a negatively rationalistic sort of deism, or to the sentimental deism of Shaftesbury, or to the radical scepticism of Hume.

As was suggested a moment ago, these changes constituted a rebellion against certain external manifestations of Calvinism rather than against its essential genius. Let us hear the *Larger Catechism* on the great question of assurance of election:

Such as truly believe in Christ, and endeavour to walk in all good conscience before him, may without extraordinary revelation, by faith grounded upon the truth of God's promises, and by the Spirit enabling them to discern in themselves those graces to which the promises of life are made and bearing witness with their spirits that they are the children of God, be infallibly assured that they are in the estate of grace, and shall persevere therein unto salvation.[11]

There was nothing, then, to prevent any man from feeling within him the intoxicating sense of personal goodness and power possessed by God's elect. This infallible assurance could easily become identified with the Inner Light of the antinomian enthusiast, the universal reason of the rationalist, the natural goodness of the sentimentalist, the imagination of the romantic poet, or the creative ego of the transcendental philosopher. In the eighteenth century, influences which had long been operative in England caused the latent seeds of Scottish Calvinism to bear their natural fruit, and a religion of total human corruption rapidly revealed itself as a religion of human self-sufficiency.[12]

The literary reflections of these developments in Scotland have been well described in H. W. Thompson's *A Scottish Man of Feeling*. As the title indicates, his central figure is Henry Mackenzie. The earlier volumes of my own work, though chiefly concerned with poetry south of the border, have treated a number of Scottish poets who illustrate various

[11] *The Confessions of Faith, Catechisms, etc.*, p. 347.

[12] This refers to the eighteenth century. A strong Evangelical reaction which set in at the time of the French Revolution rendered the Scottish Presbyterianism of the first half of the nineteenth century more conservative, on the whole, than that of Burns's day.

stages in the sentimentalizing of Protestantism.[13] The case of James Thomson is especially clear. The son of a rural Presbyterian minister of the old school, he comes to Edinburgh to prepare himself for the study of divinity. At the university he becomes a Newtonian and a disciple of Shaftesbury. His beliefs grow more deistic, his imagination more secular, his pen more active, until at last he drops theology, leaves Edinburgh for London, and makes an important literary contribution to the cult of sentiment.

The changes which I have been describing are connected with social and economic as well as with intellectual history. The development of commerce which began in Scotland soon after the Act of Union contributed to closer relations with England and to the growth of a secular-minded urban culture. Sixty leading Scottish gentlefolk and nobles, representatives of their nation in the British parliament, now resided in England with their families and helped to give prestige at home to English speech, manners, and ways of thought. The sons of Scottish gentry were studying at Leyden or making the grand tour. All this furthered a relaxation of the austerity of the Kirk. Naturally the newer ideas were at first held chiefly by prosperous or blue-blooded folk in the larger towns; but gradually they were spread more widely by ambitious young rustics who came to the universities to quaff the pure springs of orthodoxy and who returned home laden with heretical bacteria.

The secularizing, rationalizing, sentimentalizing movement which takes place in Edinburgh is so closely intertwined with trends of English —and later in the century, of French—thought that it can hardly be regarded as a separate Scottish development. The movement in the West of Scotland, on the other hand, has a stronger indigenous quality, displays clearer lines of personal influence, and seems less dependent upon imponderable elements in the *Zeitgeist*. It is especially significant for us because it helped to condition the religion of Robert Burns.

Most ministers of Ayrshire, as of the western Lowlands in general, received their theological training at the University of Glasgow. Like the city itself, the university was extremely conservative and pious—distinctly more so than Edinburgh. In the 1720's, however, a serpent named John Simson raised his head amidst this Eden. He could cite Scripture for his

[13] In Volume I: Jean Adam, Robert Blair, Ralph Erskine, William Hamilton, David Mallet, William Meston, Joseph Mitchell, Alexander Nicol, Allan Ramsay, James Thomson. In Volume II: John Armstrong, James Beattie, Thomas Blacklock, John Cunningham, William Falconer, James Graeme, James Grainger, William Julius Mickle, William Wilkie.

purpose, for he had been Professor of Divinity at Glasgow since 1708. A disciple of Samuel Clarke, he had a taste for large philosophic speculations and was suspiciously ready to ascribe independent value to merely secular culture. "He was supposed to be doubtful about punishment for original sin and to have believed in Free-will and the possibility of the salvation of the heathen." [14] In 1717 he had been cautioned by Assembly against teaching Arminianism. Proceeding to darker heresies, he was tried for Arianism in 1726. A decision was not reached until three years later, when Assembly deprived him of his chair but not of his salary nor of his status as a minister of the Kirk.

Simson is less important in himself than as the teacher of Francis Hutcheson, the chief influence in the sentimental movement within the Kirk. He was born of Scottish parents in Ulster, where his father was a Presbyterian minister. Like most Scotch-Irish candidates for the ministry, young Hutcheson obtained his theological degree at Glasgow and, returning to Ireland, began to preach the ideas of Professor Simson in the parish to which he had been ordained. He made much of the moral virtues, the possible salvation of the heathen, and the benevolence of a God who wants us all to be happy. By most students of the history of thought Hutcheson is regarded as a philosopher who championed the system of Shaftesbury with some variations of his own. Primarily, however, he was an heretical Presbyterian parson who used philosophy for a parson's ends. As Scott observes,

It was the theological heresies, learnt from Simson, that, in all probability, prepared the way for the reception of the philosophy of Shaftesbury, a further indication that even here, as elsewhere with Hutcheson, the didactic, practical, and religious interests precede and dominate the speculative.[15]

Apparently his attention was directed toward the *Characteristics* by Lord Molesworth, a disciple of Shaftesbury, whom he met in Dublin.

Inspired by Shaftesbury's theory of moral taste, Hutcheson produced in 1725 his most famous work, *An Inquiry into the Original of our Ideas of Beauty and Virtue.*[16] This treatise, together with his *Essay on the Nature*

[14] W. R. Scott, *Francis Hutcheson*, p. 15.   [15] *Ibid.*, p. 20.
[16] The complete title is full of historical implications: *An Inquiry into the Original of our Ideas of Beauty and Virtue; in two treatises, in which the principles of the late Earl of Shaftesbury are explained and defended, against the Author of the Fable of the Bees; and the Ideas of Moral Good and Evil are established according to the Sentiments of the An-*

and Conduct of the Passions (1728), won him the chair of Moral Philosophy at Glasgow in 1730. Hutcheson proved an immensely popular and influential teacher. Some of his colleagues objected that he taught theology rather than ethics, but to him there was little difference. In any case Dr. Leechman, in whose election as Professor of Divinity he had been instrumental, was hardly less liberal than he.[17]

The general character of Hutcheson's system is probably familiar to most readers of this book. He taught Shaftesbury's moral-sense theory with special emphasis on the idea that the quality singled out by this faculty for approval in any virtuous act is benevolence. But though very enthusiastic about the beauty of virtue he distinguished the sense of beauty from the moral sense, and in his later works he offers a complicated hierarchy of "internal senses." He diminishes the aristocratic dilettante element in Shaftesbury's thought by granting intuitions of ethical value not merely to the moral virtuoso but to all men.

But Hutcheson could never have popularized the gospel of Shaftesbury in Scotland if he had not endeavored to show that it was consistent with Christianity. Christianity was essentially benevolence; hence Shaftesbury, great teacher of that virtue, must have been a Christian. Hutcheson was never quite certain, however, about the relation of his system to revealed religion. He regards the moral sense as independent of Revelation, but thinks that Revelation may be necessary to remove the selfish corruptions which have obscured man's innate benevolence. His picture of the beauty of human nature clashes with the doctrines of predestination, original sin, and total corruption. Hutcheson was nevertheless a minister of the Kirk, like his father and grandfather before him. He was not an anti-puritan, but a puritan in a state of decay. "However thorough he imagined his revolt to be," says Scott, "it was still Puritanism modified from within, not revolutionized from without, and this fact probably explains the leverage that gave him much of his influence in Scotland."[18] Hutcheson's teachings aroused some opposition among the orthodox, but

---

cient Moralists: with an attempt to introduce a Mathematical Calculation in subjects of Morality. The mathematical formulae, which suggest the influence of Clarke and Wollaston, were withdrawn in the fourth edition.

[17] The Presbytery of Glasgow charged that Leechman's published sermons on prayer were "Christless" and merely "moral" because he "did not specifically state that all our prayers to God must be offered in the name and for the sake of Christ." He was finally exonerated by Assembly, but not to the satisfaction of the conservatives. (John Cunningham, *The Church History of Scotland*, II, 322–323.)

[18] W. R. Scott, *Francis Hutcheson*, p. 259.

his personal popularity, his avoidance of any frontal assaults upon Kirk doctrines, and his amiable eclectic vagueness kept him out of hot water. That he had rebuked the cynic Mandeville was no longer of much importance, but a man who could provide an answer to David Hume was not to be condemned too hastily. If reason was of no avail there was something to be said for the feeling heart, and Hutcheson was extremely good at saying it.

One of Hutcheson's pupils at Glasgow was Adam Smith. He succeeded to his master's chair of Moral Philosophy in 1752 and occupied it until 1763. His *Theory of Moral Sentiments* (1759) is of interest to us because Burns mentions it with admiration in the common-place book which he began to keep in 1783.[19]

In a critical review of ethical theories comprising Part VII of his treatise, Smith places Hutcheson's theory among "those Systems which make Virtue consist in Benevolence." With considerable insight he finds the origin of this position in the Neoplatonists and observes that it was adopted "by many ancient fathers of the Christian church" and by the seventeenth-century Cambridge Platonists. Then, not quite ingenuously, he skips over Shaftesbury in silence and declares that "of all the patrons of this system, ancient or modern, the late Dr. Hutcheson was . . . the most acute, the most distinct, the most philosophical, and what is of the greatest consequence of all, the soberest and most judicious." [20] But although this is "a system which has a peculiar tendency to nourish and support in the human heart the noblest and the most agreeable of all affections," Smith cannot but think that it is a little too flattering to human nature, for "so imperfect a creature as man . . . must often act from many other motives" than a pure benevolence which excludes any tincture of self-love.[21] He doubts, too, whether Hutcheson's favorite concept can accurately be regarded as a *sense*.[22] He would prefer to attain his old teacher's ends by using a psychology which will enable us to cultivate the virtues of the feeling heart within a more scientific framework.

The solution, probably arrived at with the aid of Hartley, is a doctrine of sympathy. Man has an innate capacity to put himself in the place of others and to feel the same emotions as they feel in a given pleasing or painful situation. This faculty is entirely consistent with self-interest,

---

[19] *Common Place Book,* p. 7.
[20] *The Works of Adam Smith,* I, 531–532. The last clause is probably a disapproving sideglance at Shaftesbury.   [21] *Ibid.,* pp. 537, 539.   [22] *Ibid.,* pp. 571–582.

which, far from being reprehensible, is the chief means by which Nature promotes human welfare. Thanks to sympathy, the more deeply we are concerned about ourselves the more deeply we are concerned about others —a very convenient arrangement.

But enjoyment of the sympathetic glow, Smith hastens to assure us, can give no satisfaction to him who does not believe that this arrangement is supervised by "that great, benevolent, and all-wise Being; who directs all the movements of nature; and who is determined, by his own unalterable perfections, to maintain in it, at all times, the greatest possible quantity of happiness."[23] God, however, works in Neoplatonic-Cambridge Platonist-Shaftesbury fashion through a providential force called Nature, which takes care that the workings of the human mind and of the physical universe shall cooperate to produce "the happiness and perfection of the species."

Smith's style, unworthy of its optimistic message, is dry, wordy, and crushingly platitudinous. He learned much about the art of writing between this book and *The Wealth of Nations*. But a few purple passages, though not to be praised on literary grounds, must have struck a responsive chord in the young heart of Burns:

How amiable does he appear to be, whose sympathetic heart seems to re-echo all the sentiments of those with whom he converses, who grieves for their calamities, who resents their injuries, and who rejoices at their good fortune! When we bring home to ourselves the situation of his companions, we enter into their gratitude, and feel what consolation they must derive from the tender sympathy of so affectionate a friend.[24]

In 1764, Smith relinquished his chair of Moral Philosophy to Thomas Reid, who had just published his *Inquiry into the Human Mind on the Principles of Common Sense*. At Aberdeen, where he had served as Regent of King's College since 1751, Reid had been active in a "Philosophical Club" of professors of King's and Marischal colleges, whose discussions centered upon the difficulties raised by Hume. He is remembered as the only solid thinker of that Common Sense school which was briefly described in Volume II in connection with James Beattie.[25] Reid sees the necessity of attacking Hume's basic principle, that the primary data of experience are separate internal sensations. To this view, which he takes to be the result of idealism, he opposes a theory of "Natural Realism." The

[23] *Ibid.*, p. 413.   [24] *Ibid.*, p. 30.   [25] *Religious Trends*, II, 250.

real units of knowledge are not sensations, but judgments combining objective and subjective, passive and active. Seth summarizes the position as follows:

We do not have sensations first, and refer them afterwards to a subject and an object; our first having of a sensation is at the same time the knowledge of it as objective and the knowledge of it as mine. . . . We are never restricted to our own ideas; at the very first step we pass beyond our sensations into a real and permanent world on which they depend, and of which they are merely the signs.

These judgments cannot be proved by logic: they are intuitive principles of common sense—in Reid's phrase, "judgments of nature . . . immediately inspired by our constitution." [26] They affirm precisely what Hume denies—a real external world, free will, and causation. Except as regards free will they do not controvert, but seem rather indifferent to, the creed of Calvin and Knox. Reid never intended to give the heart prescriptive rights over the head; but his philosophy could be, and often was, interpreted in a loosely sentimental way.

One of Reid's pupils at Glasgow was Dugald Stewart, whose facile style later did much to popularize his master's theory of intuition. He succeeded his father as Professor of Mathematics at Edinburgh, but in 1785 he exchanged this chair for the more congenial one of Moral Philosophy. Thus through his connection with Reid and in his own career he unites currents of thought associated with Aberdeen, Glasgow, and Edinburgh. Burns idolized Stewart, who was the first Scottish intellectual and aristocrat to befriend him.

It is clear, then, that from about 1715 onward into the time of Burns theological students at Glasgow University were being exposed to ideas inconsistent with the creed which they were preparing to preach. Instruction in divinity was somewhat less heterodox than that in ethics, but it avoided specifically Calvinistic doctrine and stressed the moral virtues in a way which implicitly supported the legalism so passionately abhorred by the saints. Young men who went out from Glasgow to take parishes were ripe for heresy. It was whispered among the orthodox that large numbers of Ayrshire ministers were rank Socinians. These reports were exaggerated, but not wholly baseless.

A note appended by Burns to *The Ordination* states that " 'New Light'

[26] Andrew Seth, *Scottish Philosophy*, pp. 77–79.

is a cant phrase in the West of Scotland for those religious opinions which Dr. Taylor of Norwich has so vigorously defended." [27] John Taylor was an English dissenting minister, but his writings were highly influential in Scotland—perhaps because they expressed ideas which many ministers of the Kirk shared but hesitated to voice so boldly.[28] In *The Scripture Doctrine of Original Sin* (1740) he combatted the Calvinistic view of human nature. His inaugural sermon as minister of the Octagon Chapel in Norwich "disowned all party names, . . . claiming that of Christian only." Even this inclusive title was questioned by John Wesley, who described Taylor's notions as "old deism in a new dress." [29] The author of the article on Taylor in the *Dictionary of National Biography* grants that he followed Samuel Clarke to the extent of Arianism, but denies that he was a Socinian. In *A Narrative of Mr. Joseph Rawson's Case* (1737),[30] however, Taylor declares that the doctrines of the Trinity and of the divinity of Christ have no warrant in Scripture and should not be made the test of any Christian minister's orthodoxy.[31]

He advocates unlimited freedom and toleration. In the "Discourse in Defence of the Common Rights of Christians" prefixed to the *Narrative,* he gives a severe description of "Romish Popery." But the Whore of Babylon holds no monopoly on bigotry, for the Reformers made the "grand mistake" of supposing that the "Schemes of Faith" which they drew from the Scriptures were absolutely final and perfect. In refusing to tolerate "a free and peaceable study of God's word," they fell into "Protestant Popery." After the Revolution of 1688, "men began freely to use their Understandings; the Scriptures were examined with more Attention and Care, and their *true* Sense . . . was sought after." Since then, however, some dissenting congregations have grown unwilling to allow such freedom. This final perversion of religious liberty is "Dissenting Popery," for it implies "human Infallibility and Persecution." [32]

In the precious autobiographical letter to Dr. John Moore, Burns says that he read Taylor's *Scripture Doctrine of Original Sin* at about the age of sixteen—doubtless with the approval of his father, for the book appears in a list which includes such estimable works as the *Spectator,* Locke's

---

[27] *Poems,* p. 333.

[28] In New England his *Scripture Doctrine of Original Sin* drew 460 wrathful pages from the pen of Jonathan Edwards. Taylor was also an eminent Hebraist.

[29] *D.N.B.,* article, "Taylor, John, 1694–1761."

[30] Rawson had been excluded as a heretic from communion with a Congregational chapel in Nottingham. Taylor champions his cause.

[31] *A Narrative of Mr. Joseph Rawson's Case,* p. 14.   [32] *Ibid.,* pp. 1–10, *passim.*

Essay on the Human Understanding, Stackhouse's *History of the Bible,* a collection of *Boyle Lectures,* and Hervey's *Meditations.*[33] A work by an outright foe of Calvinism had found a place among the books chosen by William Burnes for the rearing of his sons.

Burns's use of "New Light" in connection with Taylor demands some explanation of the terminology of the movement. The conservative party was labelled "Evangelical." [34] Sometimes it was styled "Popular" because its members believed in appointing ministers by a democratic call from the people of the parish. Their enemies termed them "Highflyers." [35] The liberals referred to themselves as "Moderates." In Burns's youth, "Old Light" and "New Light" were slangy equivalents used in the West of Scotland for "Evangelical" and "Moderate" respectively. The same terms were also applied to two factions within a particular branch of the much-subdivided Secession Kirk, but as employed by Burns "Old Light" and "New Light" simply describe the two parties of the Established Church of Scotland.

It is not to be supposed that all Moderates were flaming disciples of John Taylor. Their title suggests the temper of the majority—broad, flat, sensibly optimistic purveyors of ethical platitudes like Dr. Hugh Blair, Edinburgh's most eminent preacher, the great authority on rhetoric and the deluded champion of Macpherson. Samuel Rogers, on a visit to Auld Reekie, heard him preach a soothing and elegant sermon against "Censoriousness." [36] This type of Moderatism was dominant in the General Assembly as early as 1740. By no means all of the Evangelicals, on the other hand, were wild-eyed enthusiasts. They included tolerant and cultivated men who had considerably softened the grimness of their ancestors. Hume could number among his friends not only Moderates like Blair and Robertson, but Evangelicals like Dr. Jardine.[37]

[33] *Letters,* I, 109. Observe that Burns gives Taylor's title exactly, though without the capitals.

[34] No connection with the English movement of the same name. The mildly Calvinistic English Evangelicals had nothing to teach the Scottish saints. As for the Methodists, Wesley's Arminianism prevented his gaining a foothold in Scotland. Free from this handicap, Whitefield went to Scotland in 1741 on the invitation of the Erskine brothers. But they offended him by trying to make a proselyte of him, by wishing him to give up his Episcopal orders, and by urging that he confine his preaching to their Secession Kirk. He finely said that even if the Erskinites were the Lord's people, as they asserted, the Devil's people also needed his ministry. (John Cunningham, *The Church History of Scotland,* II, 312–314.)

[35] Another ambiguity, since in England of the Queen Anne period this term was applied to Nonjurors and other very "high" Anglicans with Jacobite leanings.

[36] H. G. Graham, *The Social Life of Scotland in the Eighteenth Century,* p. 363.

[37] *Ibid.,* p. 358.

Between advanced Moderates and old-fashioned Evangelicals, however, there was bitter controversy and much politico-ecclesiastical chicanery. The Old Lights were shocked at the leniency with which Assembly regarded the heresies of Simson, Leechman, and Campbell,[38] and indignant at the severity which that body was showing toward Calvinists of impeccable orthodoxy. A striking instance of the latter tendency appeared as early as 1720. Though published in 1645, Edward Fisher's compendium of Calvinistic theology, *The Marrow of Modern Divinity,* was still in high favor with the devout. Thomas Boston, Old Light minister and author of the immensely popular *Fourfold State of Man,* hit upon the scheme of reissuing, with notes, Fisher's repository of saving truths. He was assisted in this good work by one Drummond of Crieff, who had previously been charged by his presbytery with preaching antinomian sermons. To the dismay of the editors, the General Assembly denounced the *Marrow* as "unsound and dangerous" because of its antinomianism.

Fisher had made such statements as these:

A believer is not under the law, but is altogether delivered from it. . . . A believer doth not commit sin. . . . The Lord can see no sin in a believer. . . . The Lord is not angry with a believer for his sins. . . . A believer hath no cause, neither to confess his sins, nor to crave pardon at the hand of God for them.[39]

Burns was perhaps too hasty in turning his back upon these consoling doctrines, which follow with perfect logic from the basic postulates of Calvin. But they were excessively strong meat for the milder Evangelicals in the Assembly, and of course detestable to the New Lights. This vulgar enthusiasm must be suppressed.

It was not, however, suppressed without a struggle. The judgment of Assembly was protested by Thomas Boston and eleven other ministers, including the brothers Ebenezer and Ralph Erskine.[40] In 1722 Assembly rebuked the rebels and refused to rescind its condemnation of the *Marrow;* but the controversy continued to smolder, and the bulk of the common people supported the "Marrow Men."

[38] Campbell was Professor of Ecclesiastical History in the University of St. Andrews. He was investigated by the Assembly in 1736 for printing four heretical propositions, the most startling of which was "that the law of nature was sufficient to guide rational minds to happiness." He convinced his inquisitors that he meant no harm and was let off with a warning. (John Cunningham, *The Church History of Scotland,* II, 302–303.)

[39] Quoted by John Cunningham, *The Church History of Scotland,* II, 251.

[40] Ralph Erskine's religious verse is described in *Religious Trends,* I, 283–287.

Such disputes were closely related to the question of parochial patronage.[41] The system whereby a lay patron, usually the chief landed proprietor of the locality, had the right to present a minister to the parish was established by law: it had been forced upon Scotland by a British Act of Parliament in 1712. This act, however, simply restored a medieval practice which had been cast aside in favor of free democratic choice in early Reformation days, revived in 1592, abolished in 1649, revived in 1660, and abolished with some reservations in 1690. The chequered career of the question left room for an appeal to earlier, more liberal precedents; and this opportunity was seized upon by the Evangelicals, since popular election would certainly favor ministers with Old Light principles. The Moderates, on the other hand, were warm partisans of patronage as a means of keeping down ill-bred enthusiasm. Hence as the Moderates became more powerful, the principle of patronage was more and more strictly applied. In 1732 the Assembly implemented the Act of 1712 with an act of its own which left no room for the wishes of the parishioners. Ebenezer Erskine and three other ministers were deposed for protesting and formed the "Associate Presbytery" in 1733. Four years later they established the "Associate Synod" or "Secession Kirk" when joined by Ralph Erskine and others. This schism drained away from the Kirk of Scotland a good deal of bigoted fanaticism—also a good deal of deep piety and honest conviction.

The patronage issue involved a strange paradox. Moderate ideas were supported by persons of quality, prosperous and cultivated folk, men of the world; Evangelical ideas were supported by the common people. Moderate ideas were forward-looking, liberal, and, viewed in the perspective of subsequent history, "democratic"; Evangelical ideas were obsolescent, narrow, and harsh. In order to keep down fanaticism, however, and to get as many parishes as possible into the hands of "nice" people, the Moderates espoused a thoroughly undemocratic ecclesiastical system. The resultant dependence of the New Light clergy upon the upper class was unwholesome. It estranged the ministers from their humbler parishioners and often immersed them in an atmosphere of worldliness, bootlicking, and dirty politics. Such democracy often compared unfavorably with the democracy of orthodox Calvinism, according to which all

---

[41] For a full account of this complicated subject, see Vol. II of John Cunningham's *Church History of Scotland*. He thinks that patronage was a more fundamental issue than theology, but this is carrying the economic interpretation of history pretty far.

men were on the same level in the eyes of God. The Kirk, too, had fought for its own civil and ecclesiastical liberties, as Burns himself recognizes when he associates Scottish piety with Scottish freedom in *The Cotter's Saturday Night*. Less familiar is his epigram:

> The Solemn League and Covenant
> Now brings a smile, now brings a tear.
> But sacred Freedom, too, was theirs:
> If thou'rt a slave, indulge thy sneer.[42]

Burns, however, departed far indeed from the religious principles of the Covenanters, and though never a slave he often sneered at those principles. In taking up the New Light cause, he separated himself from his own peasant tradition and in some respects denied his own democratic sentiments.

In saying this we look too far ahead. Our longish raid into "background" has prepared us to understand the religious and ecclesiastical conditions which surrounded Burns as he grew up. Of all regions of Scotland, Ayrshire was most loyal to orthodoxy, yet most affected by the new Glasgow teachings. With a few such exceptions as William Burnes, lowly folk were usually Evangelicals; but there were plenty of New Lights among the gentry and professional men who possessed so much that the ploughboy of Mount Oliphant desired. Even the Evangelicals, on the whole, were a softer lot than their covenanting ancestors. The clergy were much divided. Taking rural and town parishes together, the Old Lights could claim a majority. New Light ministers, however, were numerous. They held key positions and had influential contacts. They might be outvoted in the local presbytery, but they could count on being upheld by the General Assembly, and probably by their regional synod.[43]

2

In the Alloway cottage, of course, little Robert knew nothing of these matters, but he had his own childish problems. His father was an intelligent, upright, pious man who knew in his heart that he was a failure and

---

[42] *Poems*, p. 191.

[43] The Kirk Session—the minister with two or more elders—formed the lowest ecclesiastical court and conducted the affairs of the parish. A Presbytery consisted of clerical and lay delegates from several contiguous parishes. From two to eight adjacent Presbyteries combined to form a Synod. Lay and clerical delegates were sent from each Presbytery, from the universities, and from royal burghs to the all-powerful General Assembly in Edinburgh.

who concealed his bitterness in a cloud of cold reserve through which there burst occasional gleams of tenderness and occasional flashes of anger. His almost morbidly strong sense of paternal responsibility aroused respect, but discouraged affectionate intimacy. Though Robert and Gilbert loved him, they shrank from his unending efforts to ensure them a better lot than he had known. The nobility of the father's dreams for his children was somewhat marred by his feeling of national, social, and economic inferiority. He was originally a gardener, not a farmer, and he remembered, too vividly for Robert's future good, glimpses of an easier life which he had seen through Edinburgh windows and for which his proud independence was not a perfectly satisfying compensation. He treated his sons with a yearning strictness quite unrelieved by the theoretical easiness of his theology. There is a sort of religious liberalism which makes a narrow application of broad principles.

Robert's mother, the loyal descendant of a line of Ayrshire covenanters, had more orthodox opinions and a more liberal heart. Until hard work wore her down, her eye was quick and her step was light. Contentedly illiterate, she was full of ballads and folksongs and old saws.[44] Although she had no official status in her son's rearing, her unofficial influence, especially in the first few years, must have been considerable. Perhaps the child was puzzled by the fact that his parents were hard and soft in exactly opposite areas of experience. At all events there is fairly good evidence that he was "a nervous and temperamental child, alternating between wild high spirits and moody sullenness." [45] There would be a strong temptation to seek relief from his father's unattainable standards once that unyielding back was turned. He remembered, however, that he "was a good deal noted for . . . an enthusiastic, idiot piety.—I say idiot piety, for I was then but a child." [46]

All the biographers of Burns have described his schooling under John Murdoch and his reading in Arthur Masson's anthology. This prototype of *McGuffey* included, along with greater things, a typical example of sentimentalized piety in Mrs. Rowe's letters and excerpts from more nearly pure sentimentalists—Thomson, Akenside, Shenstone, Gray, Mackenzie.[47] Since we may be sure that Murdoch's approach to this material

---

[44] The early influence of folk-literature on Burns was also furthered by old Betty Davison, a poor relation of his mother who was especially well versed in superstitions.

[45] De Lancey Ferguson, *Pride and Passion*, p. 34.   [46] *Letters*, I, 106.

[47] Mrs. Rowe and Thomson are discussed in *Religious Trends*, I; the others, with the exception of Mackenzie, in Vol. II.

was moralistic rather than aesthetic, the relation between the softened theology of the *Manual* and the ideals expressed in sentimental *belles lettres* was firmly established in Burns's mind at an early age. Response to poetry as poetry was a different matter. The undefinable thrill was first aroused by Addison's hymn, "How are thy servants blest, O Lord."

Seeds of unhappiness which had hardly sprouted in Alloway began to bear fruit at Mount Oliphant. Life was harder now. The new farm was lonely, stony. His father's ill health was aging him prematurely. There was less money than ever. Before the close of this period, the attempt to do a grown man's work had given Robert the heart lesion which finally caused his death. Ferguson observes that not only the dizzy headaches but the fits of melancholy and "vapours" of which the poet often complains in later life are traceable to this organic cause.[48] But if the body affects the mind, the mind also affects the body, especially the heart, the stomach, and the sex glands. The heart disease would be none the less actual for being partly hysterical—at long last a more efficacious means of escape than whiskey or women, or even than song.

The summer quarter of 1772, during which Robert and Gilbert attended the parish school of Ayr in alternate weeks, was pleasant enough. Robert especially enjoyed the friendship of several lads of means and parts, who in typical Scottish fashion were beginning their education together with the sons of cotters. As Burns wrote some years later, "It takes a few dashes into the world to give the young Great Man that proper, decent, unnoticing disregard for the poor, insignificant, stupid devils, the mechanics and peasantry around him." [49] Even at this time, however, he began to envy their books, their clothes, their easy assured manners, and to cultivate a touchy pride in peasanthood which he expressed more aggressively than his stoical father. "He had always," Gilbert remembered, "a particular jealousy of people who were richer than himself, or had more consequence." [50] The return to bleak Mount Oliphant after these glimpses of ease and comfort was doubly hard, and he grew restive under the curb. Shortly before or shortly after the removal to Lochlie, he insisted on joining a dancing class against his father's wishes, and from that time to his death William Burnes feared that his firstborn would come to no good.

At Kirkoswald, where he was sent for a few weeks in the summer of 1775 to study surveying, Burns learned to know people of a very different

[48] *Op. cit.,* p. 54.   [49] *Letters,* I, 107.
[50] H. G. Graham, *Scottish Men of Letters in the Eighteenth Century,* p. 394.

sort from the young lairds of Ayr. This centre for smugglers gave him a taste, though merely as a spectator, of a wild, roistering, socially defiant, *Jolly Beggars* way of living. These shady folk were splendidly alive, and the life in him welled up in response. His hankerings toward gentility were always to be tempered by a warm appreciation of the disreputable. What he could never bear was the shabby, stupid, negatively virtuous mediocrity which lay like a layer of cold mutton fat[51] between the two.

At Mount Oliphant, Burns read a number of solid books, including, we remember, Taylor's *Scripture Doctrine of Original Sin*. Hervey's *Meditations among the Tombs* showed him the possibility of sentimentalizing a mildly melancholy Calvinism. The piously teleological use of Newtonian science was illustrated by Derham's *Physico-Theology* and *Astro-Theology* and by Ray's *Wisdom and Goodness of God in the Creation;* but Burns's poems and letters do not suggest that this aspect of latitudinarianism had much influence upon his religious thinking. At Kirkoswald his reading, as might be expected, was strictly secular. Smollett fitted the atmosphere of the place. Less appropriate, but more admired by Burns, were Thomson, Shenstone, and Mackenzie, bits of whom he had formerly read in Masson's collection. Hence, as Ferguson observes, "the foundations for the weakest elements in his work, as well as for the magnificent zest of 'The Jolly Beggars' and 'Tam o' Shanter,' were laid at Kirkoswald." [52] And finally, it was during the Mount Oliphant period that he wrote his first song for his first sweetheart. Years later he correctly describes *O, Once I Lov'd a Bonie Lass* as a poor poem, but says that he likes it because it reminds him of his boyhood innocence.[53]

Lochlie was a pleasanter place than Mount Oliphant, and closer to the town life which he loved. His first four years there were in many ways his happiest. He was eighteen when the family moved to the new farm. His full-blooded vitality, his intelligence, his humor, his wonderful command of language, his personal beauty, his power to make himself liked by men and loved by women were coming to bloom. Although taciturn and brusque in the presence of strangers, especially gentlefolk, he was the unquestioned leader among village lads of his own sort. His pursuit of the girls, though increasingly bold and ardent, was probably still innocent. The Tarbolton Bachelors' Club which he founded was slightly tinged with adolescent rakishness but was by no means a hellfire organization.

---

[51] I borrow a phrase from H. G. Wells's *Tono-Bungay*.
[52] *Op. cit.*, p. 59.   [53] *Poems*, p. 266; *Letters*, I, 108.

Debates were held on moral topics (religion was barred as too controversial), and every member was supposed to be hopelessly in love. Out-
side of the club, Burns began to be known as a champion of the New
Light, or at least as a scorner of the Old.

But in 1781 his father's financial difficulties made it seem best to send
Robert to the dreary town of Irvine to work as a flax-heckler. The confined, unwholesome labor was bad for a country lad, and his heart trouble
flared up. For a short time the melancholy related to this condition made
him more conventionally devout than at any other time in his life. In an
astonishing letter to his father he declares: "My only pleasurable employment is looking backwards and forwards in a moral and religious way."
He is "transported" at the possibility of leaving this world for a better one,
and thanks his father for his pious teachings.[54] The boy is ill in body and
mind, and eager to placate his father in the hope of being summoned
home. He also writes, perhaps mainly for the parental eye, several self-
consciously pious poems—two psalm-paraphrases, and *Stanzas Written in
Prospect of Death, A Prayer on the Prospect of Death, Prayer Under the
Pressure of Violent Anguish,* and *Winter, A Dirge.* These bits of devout
gloom are so completely uncharacteristic of the mature Burns that we had
better pass them by.

Improved health relieved this onset of saintliness and turned the rest of
his Irvine sojourn in a very different direction. He had received a warning
against enthusiasm from the vagaries of Mrs. Buchan. This daughter of
a Highland innkeeper created a stir in Irvine by convincing Hugh White,
minister of the Relief Kirk,[55] that she was the Holy Ghost. The excitement
and curiosity thus aroused had a large erotic element, for "Friend Mother,"
as she was called by her disciples, preached free love on the most wildly
antinomian basis. The Buchanites were communists in sexual relations as
in economics, and the cult proved especially attractive to women. When at
last Mrs. Buchan and White were driven out of town with some of the
faithful, they left behind them an unwholesome ferment. "This, my dear
sir," Burns gravely informs his cousin James,

is one of the many instances of the folly of leaving the guidance of sound
reason, and common sense in matters of Religion. Whenever we neglect or

[54] *Letters,* I, 4.
[55] The Relief Kirk was a body which, like the Seceders, had divided from the insufficiently
orthodox Kirk of Scotland. All Scottish schisms are in the direction of *more* orthodoxy.

despise these sacred Monitors, the whimsical notions of a perturbated brain are taken for the immediate influences of the Deity.[56]

A less sacred monitor was his seafaring friend Richard Brown, who showed Burns the lower pleasures of Irvine and encouraged him to make affairs of the heart affairs of the body as well. Burns implies that he was a virgin before he met Brown in 1781; but according to Brown his companion "was already fully initiated" by that time.[57] Our ignorance on this point should prevent us from equipping Brown with horns and tail. The worst that can be said of him is that he gave Burns a push along the path on which the lad had already set his feet. It is to Brown's credit that he praised some of Burns's verses and urged him to seek publication for them.

On returning to Lochlie from Irvine, Burns found the farm a failure, the landlord exigent, his father far gone in consumption. In revolt against a way of life which had become intolerable to both the highest and the lowest aspects of his nature he grew wild and bitter, and began to acquire a reputation as a village buck.

Beginning with this period, Burns was an active and enthusiastic Freemason to the end of his life.[58] The craft included local New Light ministers such as Dalrymple and M'Gill; Mauchline gentry and professional men like Gavin Hamilton and Dr. John Mackenzie; and great ones of Edinburgh whom Burns admired and who were to be of direct or indirect service to him—the poet Blacklock, Dugald Stewart, Henry Mackenzie, Henry Erskine, Hugh Blair. The proudest day of the poet's career was January 13, 1787, when, at a meeting of the illustrious St. Andrews Lodge of Edinburgh, the Grand Master proposed, amidst loud applause, a toast to "Caledonia and Caledonia's bard—Brother Burns." In both volumes of the Bible which Burns gave Highland Mary as a pledge of deathless love he inscribed his personal masonic sign.[59] Burns liked the secret ritual of masonic meetings, richer in emotional appeal than the dry services of the Kirk. He liked the democracy which enabled common folk to rub elbows with the gentry. But most of all he liked the combination of very hearty conviviality with a benevolism which hovered on the borderline between New Light religion and sentimental deism. The fusion of social and

[56] *Letters*, I, 19.

[57] *Ibid.*, p. 113; De Lancey Ferguson, *Pride and Passion*, pp. 137–138.

[58] His occasional verses relating to masonry are numerous and feeble. There are also masonic allusions in longer poems, as in stanza xiv of *Address to the Deil*. See Dudley Wright, *Robert Burns and Freemasonry*.

[59] R. T. Fitzhugh, *Robert Burns, His Associates and Contemporaries*, p. 57.

alcoholic glow was irresistible. But although Freemasonry provided one of the less harmful ways of externalizing his thwarted impulses, it was too completely a reflection of his own nature to lift him above his present self.

Did ideals found in literature provide an equivalent of what the Kirk and the lodge failed to give him? In 1783 he is writing to Murdoch:

My favorite authors are of the sentimental kind, such as Shenstone, particularly his Elegies, Thomson, Man of Feeling, a book I prize next to the Bible, Man of the World, Sterne, especially his Sentimental Journey, Macpherson's Ossian, etc. These are the glorious models after which I endeavour to form my conduct, and 'tis incongruous, 'tis absurd to suppose that the man whose mind glows with sentiments lighted up at this sacred flame—the man whose heart distends with benevolence to all the human race—. . . can he descend to mind the paultry concerns about which the terrae-filial race fret, and fume, and vex themselves? O how the glorious triumph swells my heart! I forget that I am a poor insignificant devil, unnoticed and unknown, stalking up and down fairs and markets, reading a page or two of mankind, and "catching the manners living as they rise," whilst the men of business jostle me on every side, as an idle encumbrance in their way.[60]

Observe the paradox that while these "glorious models" make him glow with benevolence they also give him a sense of superiority to the common herd and prevent him from feeling "insignificant." They make him feel so brotherly that they flatter his self-esteem. Such is the mood in which he begins, in the same year as this letter, the very artificial and selfconscious *Common Place Book:*

As I was placed by fortune among a class of men to whom my ideas would have been nonsense, I had meant that the book should have lain by me, in the fond hope, that some time or other, even after I was no more, my thoughts would fall into the hands of somebody capable of appreciating their value.[61]

We have just seen the chief sources of his "thoughts." By this time he knows Adam Smith's *Theory of Moral Sentiments,* and he will soon have personal contact with Dugald Stewart; but the belles-lettristic influences, enforced by the New Light elements in his immediate ambience, are much more important. The tendency of the Moderates to identify Christianity with benevolism was congenial to Burns's temperament. As early as 1781 he had written to Alison Begbie: "I grasp every creature in the arms of universal benevolence. . . . This, my dear, is a passion, at least

[60] *Letters,* I, 14–15.   [61] *Common Place Book,* p. ii.

in my view, worthy of a man, and I will add worthy of a Christian." [62]

But now he is ranting and drinking and clasping entirely too many creatures in those benevolent arms. This hater of hypocrisy was no hypocrite. His readers rightly love him for a warmth of human sympathy which extends from the louse to the Devil, and which is more authentic than that of his "glorious models." Too often, however, his artificially cultivated literary benevolism interfered with the true benevolence of his heart. It made him feel superior. Still worse, it showed him a way of justifying the life of unrestrained impulse which his own frank nature might otherwise have inclined him to reject. The boyish little essay "on the various species of men" in the *Common Place Book* passes from an adverse description of "the Grave" to

The Merry, . . . the jovial lads who have too much fire and spirit to have any settled plan of action; but without much deliberation, follow the strong impulses of nature: the thoughtless; the careless; the indolent; and in particular he who, with a happy sweetness of natural temper, and a cheerful vacancy of thought, steals through life, generally indeed, in poverty and obscurity; . . . and lastly, to grace the quorum, such are generally the men whose heads are capable of all the towerings of genius, and whose hearts are warmed with the delicacy of feeling.[63]

This, Burns adds, is the class to which he belongs. He wants to be a combination of Tom Jones, Parson Yorick, and young Annesley.[64]

This is not a mere adolescent pose, unless we choose to say that Burns maintained an adolescent pose to the end of his life. As late as 1790 he tells William Dunbar that their correspondence must not be allowed to lapse, for

We are not shapen out of the common, heavy, methodical Clod, the elemental Stuff of the plodding, selfish Race, the sons of Arithmetick and Prudence; our feelings and hearts are not benumbed and poisoned by the cursed influence of riches, . . . which are no friends to the nobler qualities of the heart; in the name of random Sensibility, then, let never the moon change on our silence any more.[65]

[62] *Letters*, I, 6.   [63] *Common Place Book*, pp. 20–21.

[64] The hero of Mackenzie's *Man of Feeling*. The resemblance between Burns and Fielding's Tom is startlingly close. As for Parson Yorick, has not the influence of Sterne been somewhat underestimated by Burns's biographers? In particular the more elaborate of the letters owe much more to the *Journal to Eliza* than to Mrs. Rowe. In sending a song to Thomson, Burns says of Clarinda, "The Lady on whom it was made, is one of the finest in Scotland; and . . . is in a manner to me what Sterne's Eliza was to him." (*Letters*, II, 265.)

[65] *Letters*, II, 1.

If "the strong impulses of nature" are good, there is a peculiar distinction in obeying all sincere promptings of random Sensibility, especially in defiance of the unco' guid.

Readers of my first two volumes will recognize in Burns a well-established eighteenth-century tradition which I have called "libertine sentimentalism." [66] This form of the cult of sentiment combines the moralistic type of benevolism with the libertinism which descends through the seventeenth century from a perversion of Renaissance humanism, the psychological common denominator being reliance on inward impulse. Libertine sentimentalism was at work among the more worldly New Light laymen of Mauchline—Gavin Hamilton is a perfect example. It permeated the atmosphere of the masonic lodge. Burns had spurned the antinomianism of the Evangelicals for antinomianism of a more attractive sort—the glorious freedom of the children of sensibility. Thus by the close of 1783 Burns's religion has taken form. In the remaining thirteen years of his life he did not change it in any essential respect. The work of those years will simply enable us to examine it more closely.

At Mossgiel the house was more comfortable than at Lochlie. It even boasted an attic, part of which could be used by Robert and Gilbert as a bedroom. Still better, the new home was only a mile down the Kilmarnock road from Mauchline, a larger and livelier place than Tarbolton. It was easier to enjoy the society of witty, cultivated, easy-going people like Robert Aiken, Gavin Hamilton, and John Mackenzie. But there was hardly time to savor these pleasures before William Burnes died. Almost his last words expressed a fear as to the future of *one* member of his family, and in answer to Robert's needless question he nodded his head.

Burns made an effort to fulfill his unwelcome responsibilities as head of a peasant family, but the impulse to escape was irresistible. He was soon swaggering about as leader of a group of street-corner gallants who called themselves "The Rebel Four." Their general aim was to shock the righteous in every respect, but they prided themselves chiefly on their amorous exploits. For the delectation of Richmond, Smith, and Hunter, Burns wrote such pornographic pieces as *The Fornicator* and *The Court of Equity*.[67] In the spring of 1785 Betty Paton, servant to his mother at

[66] See "sentimentalism, libertine," in the topical indexes of Vols. I and II.

[67] The latter poem is printed as an appendix to Catherine Carswell's *Life of Robert Burns*. From this time onward Burns wrote a large amount of pornographic verse. He was also a connoisseur and collector of the work of other writers in this genre. See De Lancey Ferguson, "The Suppressed Poems of Burns," *Modern Philology*, XXX, 53–60.

Lochlie and Mossgiel, bore him a daughter. "The rantin' dog, the daddie
o't" greeted the bairn in his first fully characteristic poem, *A Poet's Welcome to His Love-Begotten Daughter.* From the first he uses the situation
as a means of defying the Kirk:

> As dear and near my heart I set thee,
>   Wi' as guid will,
> As a' the priests had seen me get thee
>   That's out o' Hell.[68]

It is no part of my duty to account for Burns's eleven illegitimate
children or to trace his career as an amorist from Betty Paton through
Jean Armour and Mary Campbell to Jenny Clow, Anne Park, and the
rest. A few remarks here will serve to cover the whole subject. Burns was
a man of the eighteenth century, not of our immaculate twentieth. He
was very attractive to women, very susceptible, and very strongly sexed—
"Our Robert should have had two wives," said Jean reminiscently in her
widowhood.[69] He had an earth-spirit's delight in sheer fecundity; for
him the begetting of children was a good in itself. Often, too, he used
sexual indulgence as a means of escaping from unpleasant actualities, or
of relieving his sense of inferiority through acts of conquest and domina-
tion. The coarse physical realism of the peasant which he was and the
gay irresponsibility of the person of quality which he aspired to be entered into a disastrous combination. The selfishness and lack of chivalry
which marked his relations with women are not surprising in a man
of impulse who was almost always able to convince himself that his impulses were good.

Betty Paton's misfortune occasioned public scandal, public penance
on the cutty-stool. The Jean Armour incident followed so rapidly that
it is difficult to disentangle the literary results of the two affairs. The
Epistle to John Rankine, however, pertains entirely to the former. The
first four stanzas praise his neighbor as a foe of orthodox hypocrisy;
the remainder, following a submerged but natural path of association, describe the Betty Paton affair in pornographic symbolism based on par-
tridge-hunting. Here, and in the closely related *Reply to a Trimming
Epistle,* Burns is still mainly on the defensive: "Already the holy beagles,
the houghmagandie pack, begin to snuff the scent, and I expect every

---

[68] *Poems,* p. 113.
[69] R. T. Fitzhugh, *Robert Burns, His Associates and Contemporaries,* p. 5.

moment to see them cast off, and hear them after me in full cry." [70] His first chance to carry the war into the enemy's camp was provided by a quarrel about parish boundaries between two Old Light ministers, Moodie of Riccarton and Russell of Kilmarnock. In *The Twa Herds,* Burns abandons his uneasy libertine swagger and ironically laments this division in the Evangelical fold. He found, however, an even better opportunity in the unsuccessful proceedings of the Kirk Session of Mauchline against Gavin Hamilton. With the satiric masterpiece *Holy Willie's Prayer* Burns's career as a poet is in full swing.

In this poem, and in his best work as a whole, the pressure of genuine feeling submerged those "glorious models" to which he had paid homage and brought to the surface his essential Scottishness. By the end of 1784 he was well versed in native folksong. He knew something of the old "makaris," and had read Allan Ramsay and Robert Fergusson. The example of local village rhymers like John Lapraik, David Sillar, and Saunders Tait showed him that the vernacular tradition, though fallen on evil days, was not quite dead. He was now mature enough to recognize that this was *his* tradition. Its rugged closeness to reality suited his love of earthy life and his present rebellious mood. Since the Kirk had endeavored to suppress it, its revival would be a defiance of orthodoxy and smug respectability. Allan Ramsay was a somewhat remote figure; but Fergusson, in whom Burns recognized much of himself, was almost his contemporary. What Fergusson had done in Edinburgh, Burns could do in Mauchline. The resultant satires shocked and angered the rigidly righteous, and their disapproval increased his eagerness to flout them in daily conduct as well as in poetry. Wits like Hamilton and Aiken, on the other hand, were delighted by his clever strokes. The New Light clergy, while they might shake their heads over his wild behavior, passed his manuscripts from hand to hand with chuckles of glee. Rab of Mossgiel was a sad dog, but he was also a very useful party writer. The great ones of Edinburgh must hear about him. Both praise and blame gave Burns a sense of freedom and power. He tasted a sweeter triumph than even the consciousness of universal benevolence could give.

[70] *Letters,* I, 30.

3

Burns's career as a poet can hardly be said to have begun before 1784, and except for the songs written or revised for the collections of Johnson and Thomson it virtually ended with the Edinburgh edition of 1787. *Tam o' Shanter* is the one major non-lyrical poem produced within the last nine years of his life. We may therefore consider the poems as a whole, exclusive of the song-lyrics, as representing the period between 1784 and 1788. Of his New Light satires, *Holy Willie's Prayer* stands in a class by itself. The marvellous skill with which he makes Elder Fisher open his obscene soul before the eyes of God forces the admission that the other polemic pieces—even the delightful *Holy Fair*—are comparatively hasty and uneven. In such poems as *The Twa Herds, The Ordination,* and *The Kirk's Alarm,* the irony is rather broad and flat; and it is mingled, in a way always harmful to ironic satire, with direct attack. All of his work in this genre, however, is witty, vigorous, and refreshing. Its broader, more positive implications rise so far above topical pamphleteering as to justify Henderson's statement: "No one ever asserted more convincingly man's inherent right to the fulness of his humanity, or more vehemently denied the innate accursedness of present happiness and joy." [71]

It is easy to exaggerate the boldness of his defiance. Several of his strongest satires written in 1785 and 1786 did not appear in the Kilmarnock *Poems,*[72] and *Holy Willie's Prayer* was first published three years after his death. *The Kirk's Alarm,* composed later than the other satires on behalf of the heretic M'Gill, was never published during Burns's lifetime because the case was under discussion while the poet was hoping to be placed on active duty in the Excise service.[73] We also know that Burns's views were those of a large and increasingly powerful party. Bigotry and hypocrisy are eternal, but so far as specific conditions are concerned, Burns was beating a dead, or certainly a dying, snake. With the New Light clergy and gentry at his back the mocker of Calvinism can describe himself as the champion of *true* religion:

[71] T. F. Henderson, *Scottish Vernacular Literature,* p. 431.

[72] For example, *Epistle to John Goldie, The Twa Herds, Holy Willie's Prayer, Address to Beelzebub, The Ordination,* and *Address to the Unco' Guid.*

[73] A shortened version appeared in 1789 as an anonymous broadside, but probably not at Burns's desire. (F. B. Snyder, *Life of Robert Burns,* p. 338.)

> O Ayr! my dear, my native ground,
> Within thy presbyterial bound
> A candid lib'ral band is found
> Of public teachers,
> As men, as Christians too, renowned,
> An' manly preachers.[74]

Other poems, though bearing less directly on contemporary ecclesiastical issues, are closely related to them—*Address to the Deil, Address to the Unco' Guid, The Jolly Beggars*. On the great subversive cantata one agrees with Millar:

Here . . . is the mood which Burns expresses more adequately, more completely, than any other—the spirit of rebellion against "law, order, discipline," the reckless self-assertion of the natural man who would fain, if he could, be a law unto himself.[75]

Surely Burns speaks for himself in the lines,

> A fig for those by law protected!
> Liberty's a glorious feast,
> Courts for cowards were erected,
> Churches built to please the priest![76]

He speaks for himself even when he is apparently most objective, for he writes almost all of his New Light verse with the yapping of the "houghmagandie pack" in his ears. Besides attacking his enemies he must justify himself—in his own eyes no less than in the eyes of others. Hence the assumptions, particularly clear in *To the Reverend John M'Math* and *Address to the Unco' Guid,* that the sincerity of the good-hearted sinner is better than the pretended virtues of the saint, and that people of strict beliefs and precise conduct are almost invariably hypocrites. Burns has won deserved praise as enemy of hypocrisy and champion of tolerance. He is not, however, a wholly disinterested authority on the difference between real and pretended decorum, and readers of Volume II will recall that the contrast between sincere rakishness and hypocritical virtue is part of the defensive tactics of such libertine sentimentalists as Hall-Stevenson and Churchill.[77]

---

[74] *Poems,* p. 127.
[76] *Poems,* p. 107.
[75] J. H. Millar, *A Literary History of Scotland,* p. 425.
[77] See "hypocrisy" in the topical index of *Religious Trends,* II.

When we sift Burns's poems for indications of personal religious belief we find very little. Without denying Jamieson's assertion that the poet's "religious and moral vein is just as sincere as his defiant and ironic one," [78] we must observe that this vein is weak and thin, that its content is trite, and that with the dubious exception of *The Cotter's Saturday Night* it is not an important element in any of his best poems. It is likely to appear in poems composed in standard English rather than in Scottish dialect, and especially in occasional pieces written with a desire to please the recipient.[79]

When all goes well with us, says Burns, we may forget religion; but when the storms of life blow hard,

> A correspondence fix'd wi' Heav'n
> Is sure a noble anchor.

The safest anchorage lies between "the preaching cant" of the enthusiast and the profane wit of the atheist. "The great Creator" should be revered by His creatures.[80] He is "Nature's God," and He provides in "Nature's law" a "Universal Plan" which protects all who would assert "the dignity of Man." [81]

Burns does not, however, concern himself with the philosophical aspects of the sentimental tradition. He does not talk about the universe as an aesthetic harmony or identify social love with the law of gravity. It is significant, too, that this poet of nature almost never thinks of scenery or natural objects in religious terms.[82] He simply draws from the cult of sentiment the doctrine of the benevolent heart and makes it the foundation of his belief that

> The social, friendly, honest man,
> Whate'er he be,
> 'Tis he fulfils great Nature's plan,
> And none but he.[83]

Burns, indeed, has no supernaturalistic religion whatever, but he has an ethics according to which

---

[78] A. B. Jamieson, *Burns and Religion*, p. 110.
[79] For example, the unusually pious *Prayer: O Thou Dread Power*, for the New Light minister George Lawrie; and the trite "retirement" piece *Written in Friars Carse Hermitage*, for the Riddells.   [80] *Poems*, p. 40.   [81] *Ibid.*, pp. 21, 23.
[82] The very early *Winter* is a trivial exception.   [83] *Poems*, p. 47.

> The heart benevolent and kind
> The most resembles God.[84]

He himself possesses a heart of this godlike sort. "I am sometimes pleased with myself in my grateful sensations," he informs Robert Aiken, "but I believe, on the whole, I have very little merit in it, as my gratitude is not a virtue, but simply the instinctive emotion of my heart." [85] Such humility is the sweetest pride. Even when remorseful over his conduct to Jean Armour, he is happy in retaining "an enthusiastic, incoherent Benevolence." [86] And after all, as his Muse assures him in *The Vision,*

> ... the light that led astray
> Was light from Heaven.[87]

Thus conscience—that is, amiable impulse—is a better moral guide than the fear of Hell,[88] and man's noblest pleasure is

> . . . the self-approving glow
> Of conscious honor's part,[89]

the enjoyment of the

> ... tender feelings dear!
> The smile of love, the friendly tear,
> The sympathetic glow! [90]

As the first *Epistle to John Lapraik* shows, he wishes to rely on natural impulse in art as well as in conduct.

We need hardly remind ourselves that the "sympathetic glow" of Burns's heart sheds its light upon flowers and birds, beasts of field and farm, simple and lowly folk, the poor and oppressed. Here also, however, his poems display a mixture of genuine and fabricated feeling which suggests a lack of spiritual integration. He plainly sympathizes with suffering animals, but no less plainly he is anxious to say all the proper things about the wounded hare. He appreciates the genuine virtues of the cotter, but he knows what sentiments a bard of nature will be expected to utter on this theme. This self-division is particularly clear in his innumerable flings at the rich and great. Though Millar is almost blasphemous in

---

[84] *Ibid.,* p. 68.   [85] *Letters,* I, 46.   [86] *Ibid.,* p. 35.   [87] *Poems,* p. 23.
[88] *Ibid.,* p. 40.   [89] *Ibid.,* p. 149.   [90] *Ibid.,* p. 33.

describing *Is there for honest poverty* as a "spirited piece of inverted snobbery,"[91] the authentic democracy of Burns is certainly marred by his
longing to escape from the class which he glorifies and by envious resentment against the class which he admires even more deeply than he scorns
it.

The poems bear only a few indications of the sources of Burns's opinions. "Twa sage philosophers" are

> Smith wi' his sympathetic feeling,
> An' Reid to common sense appealing.[92]

Henry Mackenzie and Dugald Stewart are hailed as a pair unrivalled in
ancient Rome.[93] In *The Vision,* Stewart and his father appear as students
of "Nature's law" and worshippers of "Nature's God."[94] But Burns's religious and ethical concepts are simply commonplaces of eighteenth-century sentimentalism, expressed too conventionally to encourage a search
for specific documentary origins.

The poetry of Burns, in short, is curiously divided between Mackenzie
and Fergusson. When he casts his sentimentalism aside or, without abandoning it, gives its libertine element full rein, he is usually at his best.
When he suppresses the libertine element in serious efforts to glorify the
tender heart, he is usually at his worst. This fact has been obscured by
a critical sentimentality which itself descends from the most spurious
aspects of his own thought. An American Protestant minister addresses,
as a brother of the craft, a late nineteenth-century Scottish lodge of Free-
masons on "The Spirit of Robert Burns":

Surely no one, since the Son of Man lodged with the fishermen by the sea,
has taught more clearly the brotherhood of man and the kinship of all breathing things. That which lives in Robert Burns . . . is his love of justice, of
honesty, his touch of pathos, of melting sympathy, his demand for liberty, his
faith in man, in nature, and in God.[95]

The reverend gentleman might have been deterred from suggesting,
even so delicately, a comparison between Burns and Incarnate Deity by

[91] J. H. Millar, *A Literary History of Scotland,* p. 425.   [92] *Poems,* p. 143.
[93] *Ibid.,* p. 119.   [94] *Ibid.,* p. 21.
[95] Quoted by Dudley Wright, *Robert Burns and Freemasonry,* p. 111.

a glance at some of the less edifying letters written by the poet to his cronies during this period,[96] or at such passages as

> The Kirk an' State may join, an' tell
> To do sic things I maunna:
> The Kirk an' State may gae to Hell,
> And I'll gae to my Anna.[97]

That is the honest core of the matter, and there is nothing very Christlike about it. At times, indeed, Burns's libertine sentimentalism divides in a way which predicts Byron, one element satirizing the other. An example is *Nature's Law,* addressed to Gavin Hamilton when "Armour has just brought me a fine boy and girl at one throw." Nature has commanded mankind to increase and multiply, and Burns, "all devout," has obeyed:

> He felt the powerful, high behest
> Thrill vital thro' and thro';
> And sought a correspondent breast
> To give obedience due.
> Propitious Powers screen'd the young flow'rs
> From mildews of abortion;
> And lo! the Bard—a great reward—
> Has got a double portion![98]

The same readiness to parody the lingo of the earnestly moralistic kind of sentimentalism—somewhat as Fergusson parodies Mackenzie in *The Sow of Feeling*—appears in a letter which praises

a friend who has more of the milk of human kindness than all the human race put together, and what is highly to his honor, peculiarly a friend to the friendless as often as they come in his way; in short, Sir, he is without the least alloy, a universal Philanthropist; and his much beloved name is—a BOTTLE OF GOOD OLD PORT.[99]

Such material is seldom used in liberal clergymen's addresses on "The Spirit of Robert Burns."

[96] For example, *Letters,* I, 26–30.
[97] *Poems,* p. 309. This is Anne Park, who bore him a child.
[98] *Ibid.,* p. 116.   [99] *Letters,* I, 117.

4

Burns wrote song-lyrics from time to time throughout his adult life, but the great majority of them were composed during the last eight years. They are so completely secular and so nearly devoid of conceptual ideas of any sort that for the period between 1788 and 1796 our chief reliance must be the letters. Although they contain little that is unfamiliar to students of the eighteenth-century cult of feeling, some of them betoken a closer grappling with religious problems than is found in any of the poems.

According to Henry Mackenzie, Burns's association in Edinburgh with "dissipated men of high rank . . . flattered his vanity and in some degree unsettled his religious faith, which, however, he never abandoned." [100] There is no explicit evidence on this point, but certainly his stay in the metropolis was thoroughly bad for him. The spiritual life of the once pious city ran the gamut from a stodgy Moderatism to flagrant libertinism. Of the innumerable clubs several were bawdy and rakish, with a tinge of "hellfire" quality. From the gutter to the judge's bench, drunkenness was almost a social obligation.

To the sedater Brahmins of the Blair-Robertson-Mackenzie type, the plebeian Burns was a literary curiosity to be regarded with amiable superciliousness. They had no real understanding of him, nor he of them. As their enthusiasm for the poetical ploughboy cooled, his excessively snobbish sense of their snobbishness became acute. He found that there were few men of eminence who, like Dugald Stewart, could "keep a friendship properly alive with one much their inferior." [101] "His contempt of rank," Mackenzie coolly reports,

was a little affected, for he sometimes was rather more than enough flattered with the notice of great men, yet he put on the opposite feeling. . . . He indulged in sarcastic humour in talking of men, particularly if he thought them proud or disdainful of persons of inferior rank.[102]

The fine ladies, too, puzzled and tantalized him. Beneath their pretty gowns they had bodies like Jean Armour's, and they had hearts which plainly fluttered when he came near. But he could never come near

---

[100] Quoted by H. W. Thompson, *A Scottish Man of Feeling*, p. 230.
[101] *Letters*, I, 135.   [102] Quoted by H. W. Thompson, *op. cit.*, p. 230.

enough for any practical purposes: there was a gulf between them which he could not leap. Gradually he drifted off into lower, looser, easier company—best of all, company which granted him preeminence, if not as a great poet, at least as a master of bawdy wit. But in his heart he knew the cheapness of such triumphs, and he left Edinburgh a disillusioned man.

Further disillusionment awaited him on his return to Mauchline in June, 1787, at the close of the Border tour. Whereas in Edinburgh he had been no gentleman, in Mauchline he was fawned upon, by old foes hardly less than by old friends, as a famous poet and a prosperous man who had rubbed elbows with gentility. "I never thought mankind very capable of anything generous," the benevolist writes in his bitterness,

but the stateliness of the patricians in Edinburgh, and the servility of my plebeian brethren, who perhaps formerly eyed me askance, since I returned home, have nearly put me out of conceit altogether with my species.—I have bought a pocket Milton, which I carry perpetually about with me, in order to study the sentiments—the dauntless magnanimity; the intrepid unyielding independence; the desperate daring, and noble defiance of hardship, in that great personage, Satan.[103]

A less majestic source of consolation at this time was his elegant correspondence with Clarinda. Here he is trying his hardest not to be his real self, and the result is distressing to all who love the true Burns. Sensibility, he assures her in verse, is "charming," but its emotional luxuries are "dearly bought":

> Chords that vibrate sweetest pleasure
> Thrill the deepest notes of woe.[104]

For Clarinda, however, the pleasure is worth the price. Her own verses on the subject are not much worse than Burns's:

> Sensibility! sweet treasure,
>   Still I'll sing in praise of thee!
> All that mortals know of pleasure
>   Flows from Sensibility.[105]

But for Mrs. M'Lehose sensibility could not attain its full sweetness without the support of piety. Combining a languishingly sentimental tem-

[103] *Letters*, I, 96.   [104] *Poems*, p. 234.
[105] Quoted by Catherine Carswell, *The Life of Robert Burns*, p. 329.

perament with a strictly Evangelical creed, she tortured Burns with a sort of spiritual strip-tease. "These 'nameless feelings,'" she assures him,

I perfectly comprehend, tho' the pen of a Locke could not define them. Perhaps *instinct* comes nearer their description than either "Principles" or "Whims." Think ye they have any connection with that "heavenly light which leads astray?" One thing I know, that they have a powerful effect upon me, and are delightful when under the check of *reason* and *religion*.[106]

Reason and religion, then, as well as sensibility, should be ingredients of any philtre to be used in the wooing of Clarinda. Burns must promise to think of her every Sunday at eight o'clock during evening service, thus combining two kinds of adoration.

So far as their substance is concerned, the abundant observations on religion in the letters to Clarinda are not necessarily spurious. Beneath the affected language one perceives his attempt to say what he really thinks in a way which will please her without falsifying his own position. Nevertheless the artificiality of the whole Burns-Clarinda situation must enter into our judgment of his remarks.

He "reveres" her religion, but suggests that very precise beliefs are not always unattended by bigotry and Pharisaic pride.[107] She must not think him a mocker. He has many faults, but he has risen from his knees, "eased and strengthened," after repeating the penitent words of the Prodigal Son. "I despise the superstition of a fanatic, but I love the Religion of a Man." Indeed religion is his favorite topic, as it is hers, "but mine is the Religion of the bosom.—I hate the very idea of controversial divinity; as I firmly believe, that every honest, upright man, of whatever sect, will be accepted by the Deity." [108]

God, then, agrees with Pope: "Worth makes the man." As defined by Burns, "Worth" consists in

Truth and Humanity respecting our fellow-creatures; Reverence and Humility in the presence of that Being, my Creator and Preserver, and who, I have every reason to believe, will one day be my Judge.—The first part of my definition is the creature of unbiassed Instinct; the last is the child of after Reflection.[109]

---

[106] Quoted by F. B. Snyder, *The Life of Robert Burns*, p. 266. The second sentence is a provocative allusion to Burns's *The Vision*:

> But yet the light that led astray
> Was light from heaven.

[107] *Letters*, I, 153.   [108] *Ibid.*, p. 161.   [109] *Ibid.*, p. 154.

Observe that Burns reverses the order of the two basic injunctions of the Judaeo-Christian tradition, and that he assigns love of neighbor wholly to feeling and love of God wholly to reason. Since his own religion is "of the bosom," his preference for humanitarian goodwill is patent.

Nevertheless in another letter to his devout inamorata he sketches "the outlines of my belief. He who is our Author and Preserver, and will one day be our Judge, must be—not for His sake in the way of duty, but from the native impulse of our hearts—the object of our reverential awe and grateful adoration." Our complete dependence on His almighty power justifies "prayer and every other sort of devotion." God desires to save all men. "Consequently it must be in every one's power to embrace His offer of 'everlasting life;' otherwise He could not, in justice, condemn those who did not." The good will attain everlasting life; the bad "exclude themselves from eternal bliss, by their unfitness for enjoying it." God has entrusted "the immediate administration" of these matters to "Jesus Christ—a great Personage, whose relation to him we cannot comprehend, but whose relation to us is [that of] a Guide and Saviour; and who, except for our own obstinacy and misconduct, will bring us all, through various ways, and by various means, to bliss at last." [110] Thus Burns frankly denies predestination in the teeth of Clarinda's orthodoxy. We have just seen a letter in which "great Personage," here applied to Jesus, is applied to Milton's Satan. But although his Christology, as one would expect of an admirer of John Taylor, falls a trifle below the requirements of the Athanasian Creed, it places him on the Christian side of the vague boundary which separates latitudinarianism from deism.

On February 3, 1788, he writes: "I have just been before the throne of my God, Clarinda; according to my association of ideas, my sentiments of love and friendship, I next devote myself to you." This Sunday evening letter reaches a climax in the prayer:

Thou Almighty Author of peace and goodness and love! Do Thou give me the social heart that kindly tastes of every man's cup. . . . Clarinda, the dear object of my fondest love; there, may the most sacred, inviolate Honor . . . ever watch and animate my every thought and imagination.[111]

Burns doubtless meant all this at the moment of composition. On the twenty-third of the same month, he confesses that he has seen "a certain

[110] *Ibid.*, p. 159.
[111] *Ibid.*, p. 180. For parallels to "social heart," see "social" in the topical index of *Religious Trends*, II.

woman"—Jean Armour—but only to be made more appreciative than
ever of Clarinda's perfections. As for the vulgar Jean, "I am disgusted
with her; I cannot endure her." After an elaborately caddish comparison
between the two women he concludes: "Remember tomorrow evening at
eight o'clock: I shall be with the Father of mercies, at that time, on your
account." [112] This letter represents Burns's moral nadir, for on returning
to Mauchline he had been able to "endure" Jean to the extent of rendering
her pregnant for the second time.

Soon after writing this letter, to Clarinda's not wholly unjustifiable
rage he acknowledged the disgusting Jean as his wife. He was about to
establish himself at Ellisland; a farmer needed a helpmate, and Jean, for
whom he had a real affection, was the obvious choice. Her parents having
cast her out in her pregnancy, she was utterly dependent upon him. Here
was a chance to enjoy what Goldsmith calls "the luxury of doing good."
Was not this kindness a practical application of his religious principles?
He informs Bishop Geddes that in marrying Jean "I have secured myself
in the way pointed out by Nature and Nature's God." [113] To Mrs. Dunlop
he writes that his action has given him "conscious Peace in the enjoyment
of my own mind, and unmistrusting Confidence in approaching my
God." [114] We should not be revolted by our knowledge of the discrepancy
between these sentiments and his actual conduct at Ellisland and Dumfries. He simply had "the religion of the bosom," and as one of the heart's
elect could approach God with confidence at any time, no matter what
he was doing.

Mrs. Frances Dunlop, who now becomes a favorite correspondent, was
a well-born and well-to-do widow in her late fifties. She admired Burns's
poems with a taste not quite impeccable, for she thought *The Cotter's
Saturday Night* his masterpiece. But she was more than a fine lady to be
flattered: she had a mind and a heart, and the poet genuinely liked her.
She was a quietly loyal Presbyterian, but no bigot. When addressing her
on religious topics Burns is on his good behavior but is freer from the
temptation to be insincere than in his letters to Clarinda.

"Religion," he tells her, "has not only been all my life my chief depend-

---

[112] *Ibid.,* p. 194.
[113] *Ibid.,* p. 299. The Right Reverend John Geddes was the Roman Catholic Bishop of
Dunkeld. Elsewhere Burns describes him as "the first [*i.e.,* most admirable] cleric character
I ever saw" (*ibid.,* p. 135). He should not be confused with the Reverend Alexander Geddes,
the eventually unfrocked Roman Catholic priest who was a pioneer in the higher criticism.
[114] *Ibid.,* p. 234.

ence, but my dearest enjoyment." Here, to be sure, he pulls a rather long bow. "A mathematician without Religion," he continues, "is a probable character; an irreligious poet, is a monster." [115] To her, as to Clarinda, he says that he cares nothing for sects and creeds, but thinks any man fortunate who believes in the providential guidance of "Infinite Wisdom and Goodness." [116]

"We can no more live without Religion, than we can live without air; but give me the Religion of Sentiment and Reason." In this phrase sentiment is a constant and reason a variable. In relation to his own faith, reason is itself a form of believing emotion; in relation to "sects and creeds," it implies sceptical brainwork. When defending sentimentalism he is thoroughly anti-intellectual:

What a poor, blighted, rickety breed are the virtues and charities when they take their birth from geometrical hypotheses and mathematical demonstration! And what a vigorous offspring are they when they owe their origin to, and are nursed with the vital blood of a heart glowing with the noble enthusiasm of Generosity, Benevolence, and Greatness of Soul! [117]

The heart can defy the doubter by asserting something very like the will to believe. Even if religion is

a meer phantasm, existing only in the heated imagination of Enthusiasm— "What Truth on Earth so precious as the Lie!" My idle reasonings sometimes make me a little sceptical, but the Necessities of my heart always give the cold philosophizings the lie.[118]

Armed with this cardiac pragmatism, he is "in perpetual warfare with that doctrine of our Reverend Priesthood," the total corruption of human nature. On the contrary, "we come into this world with a heart and disposition to do good for it," but we are corrupted by a selfishness which wears the mask of prudence.[119]

He believes himself "accountable" to "an incomprehensible Great Being"; and he infers, "from the sublimity, excellence, and purity of His doctrine and precepts," that "Jesus Christ was from God." [120] But immortality, which seems to be assumed without question in the letters to Clarinda, becomes a difficult problem in the letters to Mrs. Dunlop.

[115] *Ibid.*, p. 184.   [116] *Ibid.*, II, 281.   [117] *Ibid.*, I, 342–343.
[118] *Ibid.*, p. 246. Burns is quoting Young's *Night Thoughts*, Night VII, l. 638.
[119] *Ibid.*, p. 242.   [120] *Ibid.*, p. 342.

"Would to God I as firmly believed it, as I ardently wish it!" Trusting
that Jesus, "amiablest of characters," is "no Imposter," he trusts also in
His promises of everlasting life.[121]

In another letter he argues that since "God is good, which is, I think, the
most intuitive truth in Nature," He would not have deluded us by im-
planting the belief in immortality in our hearts.

Though I have no objection to what the Christian system tells us of another
world, yet I own I am partial to those proofs and ideas of it which we have
wrought out of our own heads and hearts.—The first has the demonstration of
an authenticated story, the last has the conviction of an intuitive truth.

The phrase "intuitive truth," twice used in this letter, suggests the thought
of the Common Sense school, possibly as interpreted to him by Dugald
Stewart. Its usefulness in rationalizing the cult of feeling is obvious. Burns
goes on to say that his own "favorite proof" is: "Except our Existence *here,*
have a reference to an Existence *hereafter,* Virtue and Vice are words
without a meaning." [122]

The same argument is used in an interesting criticism of the moral system of such worldlings as Lord Chesterfield, who control their vices
merely as a means of achieving practical success. The best antidote to
Chesterfied, however, is Burns's boyhood favorite, Mackenzie's *Man of
Feeling*:

From what book, moral or even pious, will the susceptible young mind receive impressions more congenial to humanity and kindness, generosity and
benevolence—in short, all that ennobles the soul to herself, or endears it to
others?

His only fear is that such teachings may be too lofty for this selfish world:

Among the few favored of Heaven in the structure of their minds . . . there
may be a purity, a tenderness, a dignity, an elegance of soul, which are of no
use, nay in some degree, absolutely disqualifying for the truly important business of making a man's way into life.[123]

Unfortunately we may be sure that Burns includes himself among these
unhappy chosen ones.

To the correspondence with Mrs. M'Lehose and Mrs. Dunlop we may

---

[121] *Ibid.,* pp. 373-374.   [122] *Ibid.,* II, 26, 27.   [123] *Ibid.,* pp. 19-20.

add four letters addressed to Alexander Cunningham, one of the closest and most loyal of Burns's Edinburgh friends. Though a lawyer of good character, he was neither one of the rigidly righteous nor a person whose favor required cultivation. With a diminishing bottle at his elbow, Burns begins a letter to his crony in mock-enthusiastic jargon, breaking off with, "But of all Nonsense, Religious Nonsense is the most nonsensical." Growing more serious if not more sober, he asks

why a religioso turn of mind has always a tendency to narrow and illiberalize the heart? They are orderly; they may be just; nay, I have known them merciful: but still your children of Sanctity move among their fellow-creatures with a nostril snuffing putrescence, and a foot spurning filth.

They have the "conceited dignity" shown by "Scots Lordlings" to "humble folk." [124] The implied connection between his religious and his social uneasiness is worth noting.

In discussing the question of immortality with Cunningham, he is more sceptical than in his letters to Mrs. Dunlop:

I hate a man that wishes to be a Deist, but I fear, every fair, unprejudiced Enquirer must in some degree be a Sceptic.—It is not that there are any very staggering arguments against the Immortality of Man; but, that like Electricity, Phlogiston, etc. the subject is so involved in darkness that we want data to go upon.—One thing frightens me much: that we are to live forever, seems too good to be true.[125]

In Burns's mind, the incertitude rather than the certitude of science is associated with religious doubt.

Another letter displays the tendency, common in eighteenth-century poetry but rare in Burns, to view external nature with religious emotion. He hopes that his son may grow up to be religious, which would mean that

He looks abroad on all nature, and through nature up to nature's God. His soul, by swift delighting degrees, is rapt above this sublunary sphere, until he can be silent no longer, and bursts out into the glorious enthusiasm of Thomson [Here he quotes a passage from the *Hymn* appended to *The Seasons*]. . . . These are no ideal pleasures, they are real delights. . . . And they have this precious, vast addition, that conscious virtue stamps them for her own, and

[124] *Ibid.*, p. 120.   [125] *Ibid.*, p. 13.

lays hold on them to bring herself into the presence of a witnessing, judging, and approving God.[126]

Thus natural objects are links connecting the "conscious virtue" of the human benevolist with the divine beneficence.

A fourth letter to Cunningham contains the most nearly philosophical observation on religion in all of Burns's work, verse or prose. He finds that in an attack of hypochondria he is supported by "a certain noble, stubborn something in man," and by

those feelings and sentiments which, however the sceptic may deny them or the enthusiast disfigure them, are yet, I am convinced, original and component parts of the human soul; those *senses of the mind* . . . which connect us with, and link us to, those awful obscure realities—an all-powerful and equally beneficent God, and a world to come, beyond death and the grave.[127]

The almost Coleridgean tone of this passage hints at a definite source. "Senses of the mind" sounds like Hutcheson, though the intuitional position more strongly suggests Reid or Stewart. Under some such influence Burns here engages in the romantic attempt to enlist psychology on the side of transcendentalism.

On the whole the Cunningham letters are not radically inconsistent with those addressed to the pious ladies. They show, however, some relaxation of the effort to think in specifically Christian terms and a sentimentalism which, though Burns would deny the allegation, is more obviously deistic.

5

Soon after the removal to Dumfries, however, these serious reflections begin to disappear from his correspondence, which, except for the critical interest of the notes on Scottish song, becomes thin and trivial. Probably the truth about the Dumfries period lies somewhere between the older view, that Burns died a physical and moral wreck, and the view more recently defended by Snyder and Ferguson, who insist that in his last years he was neither better nor worse than he had ever been, but that his reputation suffered merely because of his short-lived and not very courageously abjured enthusiasm for the French Revolution. Let us compare him to Falstaff in Part II of *Henry IV*—the same man as in Part I, but with less

---

[126] *Ibid.*, p. 236.   [127] *Ibid.*, p. 235.

of the wit, magnetism, and dash which had made his human faults delightful. As an excise officer he was conscientious and efficient, but not happy. The work was alien to the free spirit of poetry, and it diminished the self-respect which was always so precious to him. As he well knew, these snooping little bureaucrats were detested both by the humble folk from whom he had tried to escape and by the gentlemen whose charmed circle he had vainly tried to enter and whom he now regarded with increased bitterness.

But now, thanks to his work for Johnson and Thomson, there was added to wine and women the third proverbial avenue of escape—the way of song. Burns's pure lyrics are of no religious significance. In post-Reformation Scotland, sacred song consisted almost wholly of metrical versions of the Psalms. Even the rare hymns were seldom more than paraphrases. The folksongs which descend to Burns are almost invariably secular. They give voice to a Scotland which is happily unconscious of Old Light and New Light. Despite what has often been said about the Scot's devotion to theology and metaphysics, the arid intellectualism of the Kirk did not take full account of the complexities of man's nature. There was a wild, free, tender, gross, partly good and partly bad human life which its abstract formulas did not touch, or touched only to breed hypocrisy or to enkindle mockery and rebellion. In the rich tide of human feeling which pulses through Scottish song there existed the potentialities of spiritual life, but Burns was not the man to develop them. He used folksongs as Keats used the Grecian Urn and the Nightingale: they were the happiest way of forgetting.

The final unconscious solution of Burns's difficulties was strictly aesthetic. He was sufficiently a man of the eighteenth century to believe that "poems" were written to satirize persons or institutions, to celebrate an occasion, or to derive a concept from some fragment of experience. "Songs," however, were almost entirely non-instrumental. Their usual purpose was to embody in words the emotional suggestiveness of a tune. The themes and materials of his song-lyrics are often related to his earlier environment, but they are remote from the disillusionment of Edinburgh and the drudgery of Ellisland and Dumfries. Even when written in the first person most of the songs are completely objective, and even those which respond to personal circumstances derive a kind of impersonality from being merged with a tradition and set to some old reel or strathspey or coronach. Thus the pains of life sang and danced themselves away.

Here was peace and solace—"The Deil's awa' wi' th' Exciseman." Here also was a more legitimate pride than his deep sense of inferiority had hitherto been able to achieve. What for most of his contemporaries would have been a job of hackwork was for him a patriotic duty for which he would accept no payment. He had indeed become "Caledonia's Bard."

This turning toward pure song did not, however, provide a wholly satisfactory solution. The relief was fragmentary and fitful; between songs, there was a hard life to be lived and urgent questions to be answered. Nor did aesthetic escape satisfy an element in Burns's character to which we have not yet done justice. Let us call it "spiritual realism." Though often too deeply buried, this quality lay, a stratum of solid rock, beneath his libertinism, his sentimentalism, and his snobbery. It is related to his peasant inheritance and to the best aspects of Calvinism. It largely accounts for the affection which we feel for him in spite of all his faults, and which Mrs. Carswell expresses so finely when she says that "to lack sympathy with Burns is to lack sympathy with mankind." [128]

This trait manifests itself from time to time throughout his whole career. As early as 1780 he describes human life as "one continued up-hill gallop from the cradle to the grave." [129] Well he knows that

> ...mankind are unco' weak
> An' little to be trusted.[130]

With apparent approval he quotes "a piece of devotion commonly known in Carrick, by the title of the 'Wabster's grace,'" which is wholesomely remote from the flaccid optimism of Mackenzie:

> Some say we're thieves, and e'en sae are we,
> Some say we lie, and e'en sae do we!
> Gude forgie us, and I hope sae will he!
> —Up and to your looms, lads.[131]

The dispossessed mouse is "blest, compared wi' me," because it lives only in the present, neither remembering the past with sorrow nor anticipating the future with dread.[132]

Burns can apply this knowledge to himself as well as to others. Deli-

---

[128] Catherine Carswell, *Life of Robert Burns*, p. ix.   [129] *Letters*, I, 2.
[130] *Poems*, p. 40.   [131] *Letters*, I, 139.   [132] *Poems*, p. 32.

cately but clearly, the conclusion of *Death and Doctor Hornbook* suggests his awareness of facts which are quite independent of his desires:

> I took the way that pleas'd mysel,
> And sae did Death.[133]

He admits his frailties and expresses remorse for them: "No sooner are the tumultuous doings of the wicked deed over, than, amidst the bitter native consequences of folly, up starts conscience and harrows us with the feelings of the damned." [134] When lust becomes habitual, its consequences are less painful but more dangerous to the spirit:

> I waive the quantum of the sin,
> The hazard of concealing;
> But och! it hardens a' within,
> And petrifies the feeling.[135]

He applies to himself the words of Young:

> Heaven's Sovereign saves all beings, but Himself,
> That hideous sight—a naked human heart.[136]

In one rare moment of insight he describes his benevolence not as an expression of natural goodness, but as an attempt to atone for his sins:

I have such a host of Peccadillos, Failings, Follies, and Backslidings (anybody but myself might perhaps give some of them a worse appellation) that by way of some balance, however trifling, in the account, I am fain . . . to do any good I can to my fellow-creatures, merely for the selfish purpose of clearing a little the vista of Retrospection.[137]

At times, then, he could be perfectly honest about his own soul. His final estimate of himself is only a little, or perhaps not at all, too charitable: "I was never a rogue, but have been a fool all my life." [138] The same self-judgment is elaborated in *A Bard's Epitaph*:

> The poor inhabitant below
> Was quick to learn and wise to know,
> And keenly felt the friendly glow

[133] *Ibid.*, p. 59.   [134] *Letters*, I, 78.   [135] *Poems*, p. 40.
[136] *Letters*, I, 138. Young is, rather unexpectedly, one of the poets most frequently quoted by Burns.   [137] *Ibid.*, II, 60.   [138] *Ibid.*, I, 102.

And softer flame;
But thoughtless follies laid him low,
And stain'd his name.

Reader, attend! whether thy soul
Soars Fancy's flight beyond the pole,
Or darkling grubs this earthly hole
In low pursuit;
Know, prudent, cautious self-control
Is wisdom's root.[139]

Observe, however, that just at the close of this manly confession he winces away from the sharp edge of truth. He knows his Bible quite well enough to be aware that the root, or beginning, of wisdom is not self-control, but the fear of the Lord. The cotter had taught his children to "fear the Lord alway" as the only means of resisting temptation. But Burns, associating that fear with a theology which he detests, invokes on a merely ethical basis the virtues in which, as Fielding admits, Tom Jones was deficient. Again like Fielding, however, Burns distrusts the prudential, fish-blooded morality of the unco' guid. Surely "cautious" is half ironic? In his heart he scorns to be one of "the sons of Arithmetick and Prudence." [140]

Limited though it was, Burns's spiritual realism might have provided the starting point for an adequate religion, but environmental and personal circumstances stood in the way. Instead, he seized upon New Lightism at its point of liquefaction into the cult of sentiment. Here was a faith which would sanction all his impulses, both good and bad. As Angellier remarks, however, Burns did not firmly believe even in such religion as he possessed.[141] It was a self-approving indulgence of the emotions, not a discipline of the spirit. It had no influence upon his conduct, for it exerted no upward pull. It flattered the lower aspects of his nature and tinged the higher aspects with affectation, confirming the egotism which tarnished his amiability. The religion of the bosom, except when its polemic and libertine aspects were strongly emphasized, was irrelevant or definitely unfavorable to his art. In the last analysis, its soft mendacity was unable to give him a quiet conscience. He never did anything for his religion, and it never did anything for him.

Especially when placed against the background provided by the first two

---

[139] *Poems*, p. 55.   [140] *Vide supra*, p. 42.
[141] Auguste Angellier, *Robert Burns*, I, 554–556, gives an admirable summary of the limitations of Burns's religion.

volumes of this series, Burns is a perfectly clear example of the transformation of Protestant Christianity into the religion of sentiment. It may be objected, however, that he is too completely of the eighteenth century to provide valid materials for interpreting romantic belief and unbelief. There is something to be said for the contention that "the most fruitful criticism of his work can come from regarding him not as a 'Romantic' at all, but as the last great figure of the earthy, racy, and not infrequently bawdy Scots Vernacular Tradition." [142] Nevertheless this approach should be combined with recognition of the fact that he made an important contribution to the early stirrings of the Romantic Movement. Burns is a transitional figure, but for that very reason he helps to establish historical continuity between eighteenth-century sentimentalism and the religion of poets whom nobody hesitates to describe as full-fledged romantics. Certainly he exhibits that basic desire for self-sufficiency which more sophisticated romanticists will drape in richer garments of illusion.

[142] R. T. Fitzhugh, *Robert Burns, His Associates and Contemporaries*, p. 12.

Chapter III

BLAKE

I

WILLIAM BLAKE LEAPT INTO THIS DANGEROUS WORLD[1] AT AN AUSPICIOUS TIME, for Swedenborg had proclaimed that the year 1757 was to begin a new Age in which mankind would regain moral freedom. The poet, however, was aware of a counter-prophecy:

> The Angel that presided o'er my birth
> Said, "Little creature, form'd of Joy and Mirth,
> Go love without the help of any thing on Earth." [2]

The long struggle to preserve the divine vision within the limits of the false vegetative world began in a lower-middle-class Nonconformist household. The hosiery business of James Blake was moderately successful. There is no evidence for the legend that he was Irish; in any case his mind was untouched by Celtic magic. Apparently he was one of those persons who, without being in the least mystical, are prone to accept, in a passively unimaginative way, the revelations of seers and mystagogues. His beliefs, however, were such as would have a very different effect upon a stranger, more passionate mind. He and his wife are said to have attended a Moravian chapel for a while; but by the time of William's birth he had developed strong Swedenborgian leanings and had probably become a practicing adherent of the New Church.[3] His son inherited the Nonconformist tradition in a form which retained a good deal of the enthusiasm of the seventeenth-century sects. This fact is important for an understanding of Blake's interwoven religious and political radicalisms and provides a striking illustration of my thesis concerning the Protestant origins of the

---

[1] *Poetry and Prose of William Blake* (ed. Geoffery Keynes, 1927), p. 90. Referred to hereafter as *Poetry and Prose*.
[2] *Ibid.*, p. 124.　　　　[3] Margaret R. Lowery, *Windows of the Morning*, pp. 13–15.

romantic faith. The point would receive more attention in this chapter had not Mr. Schorer emphasized it so strongly in his excellent book.[4]

To the little circle of admirers who gathered about him in his old age Blake said little or nothing about his father or mother, though he often spoke of his brother Robert.[5] The only external evidence of an unhappy relationship with his parents is the fact that they disapproved of his early visions. To believe in the visions of Swedenborg was one thing; to see angels of one's own was quite another. But since Blake's poems are often most self-revealing when they aspire to be most universal, it is significant that he uses the father, along with the priest and the king, as a symbol of oppressive authority. Tiriel, himself a tyrannical parent, blames his faults upon his father in a thoroughly modern spirit:

> The father forms a whip to rouse the sluggish senses to act
> And scourges off all youthful fancies from the new-born man.[6]

But although Mona Wilson asserts that "the Oedipus complex . . . positively prances through his pages," [7] Blake likes mothers no better than fathers. Generation imposes the bondage of the senses upon the child's free spirit.[8] Tirzah, the symbol of Natural Religion, indirectly represents the woman who draws each man down from Eternity:

> Thou, Mother of my mortal part,
> With cruelty didst mould my Heart,
> And with false self-deceiving tears
> Didst bind my Nostrils, Eyes, and Ears.[9]

Perhaps the pressure of Blake's doctrines warped his memories of his own Tiriel and Tirzah. They understood him well enough to encourage his early efforts as an artist and enrolled him in a drawing academy rather than in an ordinary school. They knew that their proud, moody son, who

---

[4] Mark Schorer, *William Blake: The Politics of Vision.* See especially pp. 16, 17, 25, 42, 60–63, 135, 140, 141, 441. No critic has detected in Mr. Schorer the slightest taint of Romanist or Anglican bias.

[5] Alexander Gilchrist, *The Life of William Blake,* p. 97.

[6] *Poetry and Prose,* p. 166. In *The First Book of Urizen* and in *The Four Zoas,* though not in the poem which bears his name, Tiriel is identified as the eldest son of Urizen. (*Ibid.,* pp. 256, 385.)

[7] Mona Wilson, *The Life of William Blake,* p. 67.

[8] In the final stage of Blake's thought, generation is a tragically necessary step in the total process of regeneration, but in itself it is always an evil.

[9] *Poetry and Prose,* p. 80.

had somehow been "born with a different face," would never brook the discipline of the rod or the drudgery of rote-learning. For him, Urizen would be not merely priest, king, and father, but "Schoolmaster of souls, great opposer of change." [10] Blake never identified himself more closely with his hero Los than when he made the Eternal Prophet declare:

> I must create a System or be enslav'd by another Man's.
> I will not Reason and Compare: my business is to Create.[11]

Blake's lonely, brooding boyhood and his lack of schooling, combining with his fiercely independent character, contributed much to the honesty and originality of his work. Unusually ignorant of how he *should* see the world, he was free to see it in his own strange and often delightful way. This freedom, however, incurred heavy penalties. It increased the solitude of a man who, though naturally benignant and loving, singularly lacked the ability to enter into happy social relationships. It enhanced his egotism, giving his sense of personal dignity a tinge of grotesqueness. He who wished to annihilate selfhood was completely shut up within himself. Those who disagreed with him or failed to appreciate his genius were simply wicked. Hence arose much of his intellectual and aesthetic eccentricity.

The question of Blake's sanity has grown wearisome. To a considerable extent his wilder extravagances of thought and speech were a reaction against contemporary tendencies which he detested. William Cowper says to him in a vision: "You retain health and yet are as mad as any of us all—over us all—mad as a refuge from Bacon, Newton, and Locke." [12] He was certainly a neurotic whose mind, for better and for worse, deviated widely from the norm; but he never lost control of his faculties, and his behavior was never perilous or even troublesome to himself or to society. In short he was a sane though extremely queer person. His belief in the actuality of his visions was natural enough. As a poet, he had the power to form vivid images, sometimes with and sometimes without the immediate stimulus of external objects. As an eccentric, he formed images which were often very strange, but not so strange that he could doubt their reality. As a mystic,[13] he knew that these images were symbols of eternal truths which the Divine Humanity had revealed to him. He advised a

---

[10] *Ibid.*, p. 428.　　　[11] *Ibid.*, p. 564.　　　[12] *Ibid.*, p. 1020.
[13] I use the term in a loose popular sense pending later discussion of the question of whether Blake was a genuine mystic.

young painter, "You have only to work up imagination to the state of vision, and the thing is done." [14] The latter was simply the highest degree of the former.

In Blake's childhood, of course, these traits were merely latent; but they developed considerably during his apprenticeship to the engraver Basire between 1771 and 1778. This kind master taught him a firm, dry, conscientious style of workmanship and a devotion to incisiveness of outline which Blake continued to champion even after he had developed his own manner. On the other hand Basire, who engraved for antiquarians, strengthened Blake's love of mystery and his sense of the spiritual significance of art by having him make drawings in Westminster Abbey and other old Gothic churches. Thus Blake early developed a tendency not merely to see the invisible but to render it in a wiry, clean-cut, realistic manner. This naturalizing of the preternatural appears in his poems as well as in his drawings. For Professor White, "the most impressive thing about the spiritual of Blake's 'Prophetic Writings' is its substantiality. . . . There is often beauty to it, but it is never ineffable." [15] The explanation may be that the artist and the mystic in Blake were never perfectly harmonized. He had been taught to detest smudgy lines even in the interests of ineffability.

Ideas cannot be given but in their minutely appropriate words, nor can a design be made without its minutely appropriate execution. . . . General Knowledge is remote knowledge; it is in Particulars that Wisdom consists and Happiness too. Both in Art and in Life, general masses are as much Art as a pasteboard Man is Human. . . . All Sublimity is founded upon Minute Discrimination.[16]

In the later Prophetic Writings, deepest damnation is the lapse into nonentity through loss of outline, and the redemptive work of the Eternal Prophet lies in imposing particular form upon spirit.

At the close of his apprenticeship Blake undertook to make a living by his craft. He became acquainted with such artists as Stothard, from whose fashionable drawings he made engravings and whose popularity he soon began to resent; Flaxman, an enthusiastic Swedenborgian and an admirer of Taylor the Platonist; and Fuseli,

[14] Gilchrist, op. cit., p. 339.
[15] Helen C. White, The Mysticism of William Blake, p. 209.
[16] Poetry and Prose, pp. 814, 836, 980.

> The only Man that e'er I knew
> Who did not make me almost spew.[17]

In 1780 or thereabouts he began to experience those "torments of love
and jealousy" which, enlarged to cosmic proportions, were to form the
theme of *The Four Zoas*. Unsuccessful in his courtship of "a lively little
girl" named Clara Woods, he responded to Catherine Boucher's pity with
an emotion which at the time he identified with love. In 1782 he married
this lowborn, illiterate, loyal, loving woman. Because Blake's father disapproved of the match the pair set up housekeeping for themselves on
nothing a year, with Robert, now William's pupil, as a third member of
the menage. Wishing to help his struggling friend, Flaxman introduced
him to Mrs. Mathew, one of the minor bluestockings of the day. Her
husband was an Evangelical minister, but she was distinctly the man of
the family. A strange young genius, until the full extent of his strangeness
had been disclosed, was a pleasing curiosity in her pseudo-Gothic drawing room. There Blake not only read his poems, but may even have sung
them to tunes of his own. He had been writing verses and bits of Ossianic
and Herveyesque prose since the age of ten or eleven; but in 1777, as the
end of his apprenticeship drew near, practical motives had caused him to
lay aside the pen for the burin. Hence the poems which Mrs. Mathew
heard were less mature than the mind of the man who now confronted
her. Eager to enjoy the pleasures of patronage, she urged her husband and
Flaxman to get Blake's verses into print. The benevolent trio would pay
the expenses. *Poetical Sketches,* a privately published, badly printed volume of seventy-four pages, appeared in 1783.

These are the poems of a talented youth of preromantic tastes who has
not yet established a style of his own or found a personal centre. But the
four season poems, with *To the Muses, My silks and fine array,* and *How
sweet I roamed,* are admirable in themselves and in their prediction of
better things to come. As regards content, one detects here and there the
seeds of his maturer thought. In personifying the seasons he employs an
abused eighteenth-century device in a way which faintly suggests his
later habit of seeing all things in human form. "Our love-sick land" in *To
Spring* foretokens the sick rose, the yearning sunflower, and the priest-
blighted garden of love; while *To Summer* and *To Autumn* hint the
remedy:

[17] *Ibid.,* p. 855.

The narrow bud opens her beauties to
The sun, and love runs in her thrilling veins.[18]

But the series ends with the oppression of *Winter:*

... I dare not lift mine eyes,
For he hath reared his sceptre o'er the world.[19]

This "direful monster" who "withers all in silence" and "freezes up frail life" will become Urizen. There are glimpses, too, of the fate of love in the Urizenic world. *How sweet I roamed*—doubly remarkable if written before the age of fourteen—is the first of many poems on love-bondage; and the theme of *Samson,* "how he was foiled by woman's arts, and by a false wife brought to the gates of death," [20] will become a favorite. In *Fair Elenor, Mad Song,* and *Gwin, King of Norway* we hear that "howling" which resounds through the Prophetic Writings.[21] Finally, Blake will devote his life to restoring the "antient love" for divine inspiration which modern bards have lost.[22] The butterfly has not yet emerged, but the chrysalis is beginning to crack.

Mrs. Mathew cooled toward her protégé when she found him lacking in the grateful humility which is necessary for a patron's enjoyment of the luxury of doing good. A passionate anti-feminist, Blake hated to be patronized by a woman who thought herself clever. The good lady is remembered, perhaps, in the squib:

Her whole Life is an Epigram, smart, smooth, and neatly pen'd,
Platted quite neat to catch applause with a sliding noose at the end.[23]

Blake refused to applaud the chatter of this coterie of learned females:

Is this the Female Will, O ye lovely daughters of Albion, to
Converse concerning Weight and Distance in the Wilds of Newton and
Locke?[24]

There was no open break, but the difficult man's visits grew less frequent and finally ceased entirely.

An Island in the Moon was written, probably in 1787, to satirize the confusion and empty pretentiousness of intellectual society, chiefly as he

---

[18] *Ibid.,* p. 4. [19] *Ibid.,* p. 5. [20] *Ibid.,* p. 44.
[21] *Ibid.,* pp. 7, 12, 15. [22] *Ibid.,* p. 14. [23] *Ibid.,* p. 101.
[24] *Ibid.,* p. 615.

had observed it at Mrs. Mathew's salon. Blake had no intention of publishing it, but was merely relieving his mind with an extravagance which betokens a rather deep agitation. Mingled with a great deal of wild nonsense are some keen thrusts at cocksure philosophical systems, pedantic antiquarianism, the glorification of mathematics and experimental science, the vanity and spleenfulness of savants. Professor Damon credibly suggests that Sipsop the Pythagorean is Thomas Taylor and that Inflammable Gass the Windfinder is Joseph Priestley.[25] In the madness of this work, then, there is much method. The impression of hopeless muddle is part of Blake's satirical intent. Already an anti-intellectual, he wishes to expose the chaos which underlies the eighteenth century's neatly associated ideas. The conversation is a medley of monologues: everybody rides his insane hobby, and nobody listens to anyone else. Although we cannot accept Miss Hamblen's opinion that *An Island in the Moon,* taken as a whole, directly expresses Blake's disappointment in his wife,[26] this feeling may have inspired the bitter song in praise of "Matrimony's golden cage." [27] But through the darkness which enwraps the island one discerns a few bright stars. Drafts of three of the *Songs of Innocence* appear,[28] and the scheme of illuminated printing is set forth.

One may conjecture that when he wrote *An Island in the Moon* Blake was approaching an emotional crisis in which his resentment toward the Mathew set lay nearest the surface of his mind and therefore provided him with a means of expressing a more general ferment of feeling. But before the work was completed an event occurred which helped him to see that the best solution lay not in satirizing the world which was thwarting him but in seeing it through the innocent eye of vision—in being a believing child rather than an angry man.

> Father, O Father! what do we here
> In this land of unbelief and fear?
> The Land of Dreams is better far,
> Above the light of the Morning Star.[29]

That event was the death of his brother Robert—the only being in the world whose spirit was wholly in tune with his own. William saw that

[25] S. F. Damon, *William Blake, His Philosophy and Symbols,* p. 33. It is unlikely, however, that such eminent figures were guests of the obscure Mrs. Mathew.
[26] Emily S. Hamblen, *On the Minor Prophecies of William Blake,* p. 8.
[27] *Poetry and Prose,* pp. 880–881, 9.
[28] *Holy Thursday, Nurse's Song, The Little Boy Lost.*
[29] *Poetry and Prose,* p. 114.

spirit escape from the body and pass through the ceiling, "clapping its hands for joy." "Thirteen years ago," wrote Blake in 1800, "I lost a brother, and with his spirit I converse daily and hourly in the spirit, and see him in my remembrance, in the regions of my imagination. I hear his advice, and even now write from his dictate." [30] Within William's imagination, which was the true location of Eternity, the departed Robert communicated to him not only the secret of illuminated printing but other secrets even more precious. It was as if a part of Blake's own soul had gone to dwell in Jerusalem. The stimulus to poetry, to belief, to a kind of mysticism, was powerful. From now on, the visionary life, hitherto sporadic, would be continuous and habitual. He would not always enjoy it in complete "fourfold" perfection, but he had been saved forever "From single vision and Newton's sleep." [31] Songs of Innocence, the firstfruits of this enlightenment, appeared in 1789.

"You certainly mistake," Blake writes to the Reverend John Trusler, "when you say the Visions of Fancy are not to be found in this world. To me this world is all one continued Vision of Fancy or Imagination." His visions, which Trusler has found incomprehensible, "have been elucidated by children, who have taken a greater delight in contemplating my pictures, than I even hoped. . . . Some children are fools and so are some old men. But there is a vast majority on the side of Imagination or Spiritual Sensation." [32] Songs of Innocence, then, is an attempt to enjoy the bliss of spiritual sensation by viewing the world through the eyes of the sort of child who is not a fool—that is, a child with the mind and heart of William Blake. Thus beheld, the world is a place of "mercy, pity, peace, and love"; of freedom and tolerance; of beauty and laughter and fun. The woolly lamb, the lamblike child, and the Lamb of God who made Himself a child play together within the Divine Humanity. The creation is beheld with a joyous brotherly affection which recalls St. Francis. Natural objects, however, are never quite what they seem. Almost always the illustrations, and frequently the poems, indicate their symbolic character. The more nearly complete the vision, the more readily the natural melts into the preternatural which is the sole source of its beauty and spiritual value.

> Farewell, green fields and happy groves
> Where flocks have took delight.

[30] Ibid., p. 1043.   [31] Ibid., p. 1068.   [32] Ibid., p. 1039.

Where lambs have nibbled, silent moves
The feet of angels bright;
Unseen they pour blessing
And joy without ceasing,
On each bud and blossom,
And each sleeping bosom.[33]

Professor Babenroth has argued that these best-loved of Blake's poems
are related to familiar eighteenth-century tendencies.[34] As he reminds us,
in *Divine and Moral Songs for Children* Isaac Watts had written religious
poetry for young people in simple language, sometimes employing symbols
drawn from nature, and in his Preface he had expressed the hope that
"some happy and condescending genius" would perform the same task
with greater skill. Between Watts and Blake juvenile literature had developed greatly in response to the growing interest in education. Blake
himself was to make other contributions to it in his children's emblem
book, *The Gates of Paradise,* and his engravings for Mary Wollstonecraft's translation of Salzmann's *Elements of Morality.* As in the latter
case, much of this literature, though almost always didactic, tended increasingly toward the rationalistic, the scientific, and the secular; but,
largely because of the Evangelical interest in Sunday Schools and charity
schools, much of it remained religious or more or less piously moralistic.

The sentimental movement, adopting and often distorting the theories
of Rousseau, had already used the uncorrupted child as a means of expressing naturalistic, primitivistic, and humanitarian ideas.[35] According
to Babenroth, Blake's children are associated with these concepts, especially with the doctrine of universal benevolence and the Rousseauistic
cult of freedom from institutional restraint.[36] "He is in the direct line
of development from Shaftesbury and Thomson, and, moreover, shows
the more daring phrasings of the Revolutionary period in which he
lived." [37] It would be more accurate to say that in this early volume Blake
still retains much of that Christianity of which sentimental benevolism is
the bastard offspring. Philosophically, though not chronologically, he is
the ancestor of Shaftesbury and Thomson rather than their descendant.
What would Thomson make of *A Cradle Song* or *The Lamb?* For Blake,
religious values do not depend upon the natural revelation. He is always

[33] *Ibid.,* p. 60.
[34] A C. Babenroth, *English Childhood: Wordsworth's Treatment of Childhood in the Light
of English Poetry from Prior to Crabbe.*
[35] *Ibid.,* pp. 15ff.   [36] *Ibid.,* p. 268.   [37] *Ibid.,* p. 291.

a passionate foe of the religion of nature, and the benevolism here expressed is not naturalistic or deistic, but Christian. *On Another's Sorrow* begins:

> Can I see another's woe,
> And not be in sorrow too?
> Can I see another's grief,
> And not seek for kind relief?

This might be a paraphrase of Adam Smith's *Theory of Moral Sentiments.*[38] Here, however, the basis of benevolence is not a theory of associative psychology, but quite simply God's love:

> He doth give his joy to all;
> He becomes an infant small;
> He becomes a man of woe;
> He doth feel the sorrow too.[39]

This is what the eighteenth century has been drifting away from, not what it has been working toward. In Blake's day that drift had to some extent been checked, or in some quarters even reversed, by the Evangelical Movement. *The Chimney-Sweeper, Holy Thursday,* and *The Little Black Boy* might well have been used as leaflets in support of three favorite Evangelical causes. In fact the *Songs of Innocence* often breathe forth a piety which is either that of the Evangelical Movement or of the earnestly emotional Protestantism of which the Movement was a continuation as well as a revival.

But the *Songs* can assuredly not be interpreted in terms of Evangelical Protestantism pure and simple. Even in this early work Blake has begun to remould Christianity nearer to his heart's desire. He did not lack precedents for doing so. John Wesley would recognize in *The Divine Image* that pseudo-mystical identification of God and man which had shocked him in the works of William Law.[40] Mr. T. S. Eliot, although he admires Blake's originality, laments that, unlike Dante, he lacked the advantage of inheriting a "continuous religious history." Rather too superciliously, the modern critic likens Blake's philosophy to

an ingenious piece of home-made furniture: we admire the ingenuity of the man who has put it together out of odds and ends about the house. England

---

[38] *Vide supra,* p. 29.   [39] *Poetry and Prose,* p. 64.
[40] See *Religious Trends,* II, 149–161.

has produced a fair number of these resourceful Robinson Crusoes; but we are not really so remote from the continent, or from our own past, as to be deprived of the advantages of culture if we wish them.[41]

These highly cultivated remarks have been sufficiently answered by Professor Percival:

But the Blakean heterodoxy was equally traditional with Dante's orthodoxy. The Orphic and Pythagorean traditions, Neoplatonism in the whole of its extent, the Hermetic, Kabbalistic, Gnostic, and alchemical writings, Erigena, Paracelsus, Boehme, and Swedenborg—here is a consistent body of tradition extending over nearly twenty-five hundred years.[42]

The trouble was not that Blake lacked a tradition, but that the tradition which he did inherit tended to exaggerate, rather than to curb, his egotism and eccentricity.

In *Songs of Innocence,* of course, Blake's philosophy has by no means reached its final form. We do not know how deeply he was versed in mystical and occult thought by 1789; probably he had much further to go in this direction. He may well have heard some or all of the twelve lectures on Plato and his followers delivered by Thomas Taylor at Flaxman's house.[43] But if Taylor is Sipsop the Pythagorean in the *Island,* we must suppose that this mystagogue at first merely amused him. In any case there is nothing particularly Neoplatonic in the *Songs.*

A letter written in 1800 to Flaxman contains the lines:

Now my lot in the Heavens is this, Milton lov'd me in childhood and shew'd me his face.
Ezra[44] came with Isaiah the Prophet, but Shakespeare in riper years gave me his hand:
Paracelsus and Behmen appear'd to me, terrors appear'd in the Heavens above
And in Hell beneath, and a mighty and awful change threatened the Earth. The American War began.[45]

Blake's chronology was sometimes faulty. The passage provides evidence, however, that even as a child he knew Milton, the great exemplar of the

[41] *The Sacred Wood,* p. 142.
[42] M. O. Percival, *William Blake's Circle of Destiny,* p. 1.
[43] S. F. Damon, *op. cit.,* p. 32.
[44] Emily S. Hamblen, *op. cit.,* p. 5, suggests that "the reference is to the Ezra of the Apochryphal books, Esdras i and ii, inasmuch as there we have the visionary and the prophet, while in the Old Testament Ezra functions mainly as priest."
[45] *Poetry and Prose,* p. 1046.

religious conception of poetry, and prophetic portions of the Bible. "In riper years," but still apparently before 1776, came the imaginative world of Shakespeare and the wisdom of two famous masters of the occult.

By the time when Blake wrote this letter he felt that he had passed beyond Swedenborg, but in 1789 he was quite definitely a Swedenborgian. So apparently was his wife, for in 1789 the names of William and Catherine Blake are among the eighteen signatures in the minute book of the Great Eastcheap Swedenborgian Society. They were lending their support to a plan to make a regular Swedenborgian congregation of a group which had been meeting informally since 1783. Although we may be sure that Blake's connection with this or any other society of worshippers would be brief, the marginal notes which he scribbled in a translation of Swedenborg's *Divine Love* at about this time are respectful and generally approving. Some of the thoughts suggested to him by the text are worth noting:

He who loves feels love descend into him and if he has wisdom may perceive it is from the Poetic Genius, which is the Lord. . . . Man can have no idea of anything greater than Man. . . . To think of holiness distinct from man is impossible to the affections.

When Swedenborg writes, "The Negation of God constitutes Hell, and in the Christian World the Negation of the Lord's Divinity," Blake adds his paraphrase, "The Negation of the Poetic Genius." [46] The identification of God, man, and poetic genius, constantly stressed in Blake's later works, is usually implicit rather than explicit in *Songs of Innocence;* but *The Divine Image* combines the first two members of the triad, and *The Voice of the Ancient Bard* adds the third. We recall that Blake composed the former poem while sitting in the New Jerusalem Church in Hatton Gardens. Other Swedenborgian elements in *Songs of Innocence* are the symbolic view of nature and the idea, probably derived from the *Arcana Cœlestia,* that words should be used in poetry as in the Scriptures, not to make truths clear, but to veil them from profane eyes in a sort of code.

To what extent such a code is employed in *Songs of Innocence* is a matter of dispute. These lyrics give most delight when read most naively. In the state of innocence it is not necessary to assert, as Blake does in the marginal notes on Lavater's *Aphorisms* which he wrote about 1788, that "All Life is Holy. . . . Active Evil is better than Passive Good. . . . All

[46] *Ibid.,* pp. 934, 935.

Act is Virtue. . . . Human nature is the image of God. . . . The female
lives from the light of the male." [47] The child happily plays within the
freedom which such propositions seek to defend. He is not under the
necessity of "striving with Systems to deliver Individuals from those Systems." [48] One sympathizes with Miss Wilson's complaint that students of
the Prophetic Writings "impose too systematic and definite a meaning
upon the lyrics in the light of their own interpretations of the details of
his other works." [49] Nevertheless even a very innocent reader of *Songs of
Innocence,* especially if he examines the illustrations along with the text,
becomes aware that the child through whose eyes Blake looks at the
world already possesses some of the ideas which will be expressed more
openly in *The Marriage of Heaven and Hell* and in the Lambeth Books.
Blake's conception of innocence is not fully revealed until it is contrasted
with experience in the combined volume of 1794. Since the tyranny of experience consists largely in the thwarting of the sex impulse, it follows
that sexual liberty is a major element in the innocent freedom offered by
the "Ancient Bard" to the "youth of delight." [50] Hence Wicksteed may
well be right in contending that the wild beasts in *The Little Girl Lost,
The Little Girl Found,* and *Night* represent sexual passion, harmless in
the eyes of innocence, and that the illustration for *The Blossom* "is a poetic
and symbolic rendering of the phallus prone and erect." [51]

We do not know to what extent the *Songs of Experience* were fermenting in Blake's mind while he was engraving *Songs of Innocence.* In the
earlier volume, however, the happy freedom of the child is already menaced. Several of the lyrics point forward to *Songs of Experience,* and *The
Voice of the Ancient Bard,* at the close of the former volume, is echoed
by the *Introduction* at the beginning of the latter. The contrast between
the two divisions of the 1794 volume is too familiar to be elaborated here,
but perhaps not all of my readers have considered the implications of the
subtitle: "Shewing the Two Contrary States of the Human Soul." Is life
a Manichaean struggle between two equally real forces? Or is the world
of experience a mere illusion of the senses, while the world of innocence
represents eternal truth? Is the mind to render evil nonexistent through
a heightening of visionary power, or use it as the necessary counterpart
of good?

[47] *Ibid.,* pp. 913, 917, 924, 925, 932.   [48] *Ibid.,* p. 566.
[49] Mona Wilson, *The Life of William Blake,* p. 40.   [50] *Poetry and Prose,* p. 68.
[51] J. H. Wicksteed, *Blake's Innocence and Experience,* pp. 115, 125, 129.

Blake can be cited in support of either view. On the one hand he asserts that "without Contraries is no progression. Attraction and Repulsion, Reason and Energy. Love and Hate, are necessary to Human existence."[52] As late as 1826 he is talking pure Gnosticism to Crabb Robinson, "asserting everything to be the work of God or the Devil—that there is a constant falling off from God—angels becoming devils. Every man has a devil in him, and the conflict is eternal between a man's self and God."[53] More than once Eternity, the realm of perfect vision, is described as a place of intense intellectual strife between complementary opposites. "Our wars," says Jesus in *Jerusalem*,

> . . . are wars of life, and wounds of love
> With intellectual spears, and long winged arrows of thought.
> Mutual in one another's love and wrath all renewing
> We live as One Man.[54]

From all this one would infer that experience is quite as real and quite as necessary as innocence.

On the other hand, Blake declares that "Everything is Atheism which assumes the reality of the natural and unspiritual world."[55] Surely this assumption is the very essence of the state of experience, the root of its unbelief, deceit, and cruelty. To destroy belief in the reality of this world is to build Jerusalem in England's green and pleasant land. "All things exist in the Human Imagination, . . . of which this World of Mortality is but a Shadow."[56] Are not "World of Mortality" and "State of Experience" synonymous terms, and will not the shadow vanish when imagination attains to fourfold vision? At the Last Judgment "the whole creation will be consumed and appear infinite and holy, whereas it now appears finite and corrupt. This will come to pass by an improvement of sensual enjoyment"—that is, by development of the ability to see through, rather than with, the eye. "If the doors of perception were cleansed every thing would appear to man as it is, infinite. For man has closed himself up, till he sees all things thro' narrow chinks of his cavern."[57] Here the only possible inference is that the state of experience is a mere delusion

---

[52] *Poetry and Prose*, p. 191.
[53] Henry Crabb Robinson's *Diary* in Arthur Symons, *William Blake*, p. 268.
[54] *Poetry and Prose*, p. 620; see also pp. 526, 632, 640.
[55] Robinson, *op. cit.*, p. 259.   [56] *Poetry and Prose*, pp. 688, 692.
[57] *Ibid.*, p. 197.

of the senses, while the state of innocence represents the imaginative truth which exists in Eternity.[58]

In *Milton* and *Jerusalem* Blake will try to reconcile this inconsistency by distinguishing between "Contraries," which are real and necessary, and "Negations," which have no actual existence because they can never be organized into particular forms. Negations are "Exceptions and Objections and Unbeliefs." They pertain to "meer Reasoning, . . . Malice and Envy." [59] Affirmation makes Contraries, denial makes Negations; therefore "the Negation must be destroyed to redeem the Contraries." But since the most inclusive symbol of Negation is Satan, the Universal Spectre, "the Reasoning Power in Man," [60] and since the world of experience is obviously Satan's world, one is led to the conclusion that the two states of the human soul are not a genuine pair of Contraries: innocence is a Contrary, while experience is a Negation. Here is one of many inconsistencies which make Blakean exegesis as difficult as it is fascinating.

Songs of Experience, especially when read together with the early section of the Rossetti Manuscript, raises another problem which is so closely intertwined with Blake's spiritual life that we cannot ignore it. How is Blake's absorption in sex—or rather, in ideas concerning sex—to be interpreted?

2

The fact that Blake is constantly talking about love does not necessarily imply that his physical passions were ardent. It might imply exactly the reverse. "Our Robert should have had two wives," said Burns's Jean;[61] but Catherine Blake told Kirkup, "I have very little of Mr. Blake's company; he is always in Paradise." [62] Wicksteed believes that "he had intensely strong passions, but all on the psychic rather than the animal plane. What he calls 'the torments of love and jealousy' were fierce and personal, but not carnal or sensual." [63] Probably his capacity for mating hung in a delicate equilibrium which depended on the state of his warm

---

[58] In the Prophetic Writings, Eternity is often called "Eden," suggesting that it is the realm of innocence.

[59] *Poetry and Prose,* p. 580.   [60] *Ibid.,* p. 546.   [61] *Vide supra,* p. 44

[62] Mona Wilson, *The Life of William Blake,* p. 214. At the time of this anecdote Blake was in his fifties, but he had begun to frequent Paradise much earlier.

[63] J. H. Wicksteed, Blake's *Innocence and Experience,* p. 214.

and idealistic but extremely neurotic imagination. He who asserted that "The lust of the goat is the bounty of God" [64] apparently made very moderate use of the divine largesse. In his poems the abundant passages relating to sexual passion are often specific in imagery but almost disquietingly impersonal in feeling. The love which he champions is "spiritual sensation."

Not a line of Blake's poetry overtly addresses Catherine in words of love. She is seldom even alluded to. At the Last Judgment in *Milton,* "My sweet Shadow of Delight stood trembling by my side." [65] Earlier in the same poem he asks the maiden Ololon to comfort his "Shadow of Delight, . . . for she is sick with fatigue." [66] There is the heart-warming line, "I've a Wife I love and that loves me," but to the same period (about 1810) belongs the bitter epigram,

> Grown old in Love from seven till seven times seven,
> I oft have wish'd for Hell for ease from Heaven.[67]

In Blake's letters she appears as the faithful housekeeper and amanuensis, now ailing and now improving in health, and wishing to be remembered to his correspondents. Once, however, he looks upon her with an artist's if not with a lover's eye: she "is like a flame of many colours of precious jewels" in her joy at leaving Lambeth for Felpham.[68]

It has been suggested that Blake was influenced by the radical notions of Mary Wollstonecraft,[69] and that Catherine may have been jealous of that brilliant and attractive woman.[70] Unfortunately there is not a scrap of evidence that he knew Godwin's consort. They would have disagreed hotly in their views on the rights of women; for no advocate of liberty was ever a more passionate anti-feminist than Blake, who believed that "The Man who respects Woman shall be despised by Woman," and that "She who adores not your frowns will only loathe your smiles." [71] In *The Four Zoas,* Urizen rages at Ahania, his rebellious emanation:

[64] *Poetry and Prose,* p. 193.

[65] *Ibid.,* p. 548. "Shadow" is occasionally used as a synonym for "Emanation" (female aspect of a divided spirit). Catherine is also referred to as his "Shadow" in a letter, *Ibid.,* p. 1052.

[66] *Ibid.,* p. 537. Probably an allusion to Mrs. Blake's illness at Felpham. Ololon's symbolism is difficult, but I think she represents the best aspects of Fancy, the highest degree of Imagination of which the separated feminine nature is capable.

[67] *Ibid.,* pp. 128, 125.

[68] *Ibid.,* p. 1048. Is alchemy, one of Blake's many occult interests, the basis of this simile?

[69] S. F. Damon, *William Blake, His Philosophy and Symbols,* p. 99.

[70] Mona Wilson, *op. cit.,* p. 47.   [71] *Poetry and Prose,* pp. 730, 744.

Shall the feminine indolent bliss, the indulgent self of weariness,
The passive idle sleep, the enormous night and darkness of Death,
Set herself up to give her laws to the active masculine virtue?
Thou little diminutive portion that dar'st to be a counterpart,
Thy passivity, thy laws of obedience and insincerity
Are my abhorrence. Wherefore hast thou taken that fair form?
Whence is this power given to thee? [72]

The fallen Urizen is the villain of the piece; but here, as often elsewhere, he is granted remembrance of the wisdom which he possessed in
Eternity. In that realm of fourfold vision,

> . . . Humanity is far above
> Sexual organization and the Visions of the Night of Beulah
> Where Sexes wander in dreams of bliss among the Emanations.[73]

Among the Eternals there is no marriage or giving in marriage.[74] Indeed,
there is no femaleness separate from maleness. "In Eternity Woman is the
Emanation of Man; she has No Will of her own. There is no such thing
in Eternity as a Female Will, and Queens." [75] Perfect man, the undivided
Human Form Divine, includes a masculine and a feminine element.
Imagination, vision, creative energy, inward feeling are male. Space, matter, nature, outward expression, the surface play of feeling, are female. A
union of both elements is necessary for the good life and above all for good
art. But the masculine must dominate the feminine, since "the consummation which the artist looks for is the entire subjection of the feminine
principle, its reduction to perfect malleability before the ardours of
imagination." [76] The potter needs clay, but he must be its master.

A terrible tragedy occurs when, as a result of mythological complications which need not concern us, the feminine principle, now an Emanation, separates from the masculine principle, now a Spectre, assuming its
own form and asserting its own desires. "As long as man's feminine
powers remain selfless, his perceptual powers remain flexible; when his
feminine powers develop a selfish will, his perceptions decline to an organic level" [77] and he loses the power to create truth through genius. Seeing "the female form now separate," the Eternals

[72] *Ibid.*, p. 325.   [73] *Ibid.*, p. 710.   [74] *Ibid.*, p. 614.
[75] *Ibid.*, p. 840.   [76] Basil de Selincourt, *William Blake*, p. 46.
[77] M. O. Percival, *William Blake's Circle of Destiny*, p. 110.

. . . shudder'd at the horrible thing
Not born for the sport and Amusement of Man, but born to drink up all
 his powers.
They wept to see their shadows; they said to one another: "This is Sin:
This is the Generative World;" they remember'd the days of old.[78]

Separated female spirits are jealous, secretive, deceitful. They have a
thirst for dominion. They subject themselves to "mystery" or to that Natural Religion which is the unacknowledged offspring of priestcraft. Their
morbid sense of sin makes them enforce the moral virtues and oppose all
unashamed delight. They have the ability

> To do unkind things in kindness, with power arm'd to say
> The most irritating things in the midst of tears and love.[79]

They torture their male victims, crying with ambiguous pity, "Shriek not
so, my only love." [80]

> They dance around the dying and they drink the howl and groan,
> They catch the shrieks in cups of gold, they hand them to one another:
> These are the sports of love, and these the sweet delights of amorous play,
> Tears of the grape, the death sweat of the cluster, the last sigh
> Of the mild youth who listens to the luring songs of Luvah.[81]

In the later Prophetic Writings, Blake more than half identifies himself
with Los, the spirit of imaginative energy, the "Eternal Prophet" who
"kept the Divine Vision in time of trouble." [82] Hence there is a sense in
which Enitharmon, Los's emanation,[83] who symbolizes woman as wife,
represents Mrs. Blake. She assists Los in his creative labors much as
Catherine assisted her husband, weaving garments for the spectres whom
Los has provided with forms in order to preserve them from complete
loss of identity.[84] On the whole, however, they are not a happy couple:

---

[78] *Poetry and Prose*, p. 450. Observe the vestige of Ossianic influence in the last line.

[79] *Ibid.*, p. 484. The passage refers to Satan, but the preceding pages of *Milton* show that
his irritating power, like most of his other traits, is characteristically feminine.

[80] *Ibid.*, p. 684.

[81] *Ibid.*, p. 518. Luvah, one of the Four Zoas, symbolizes sexual passion.

[82] *Ibid.*, p. 606. It has been noted that in Blake's designs the drawings of Los are self-
portraits. (Basil de Selincourt, *William Blake*, p. 8.)

[83] Her status, however, is unique, for while Ahania, Vala, and Enion, respectively the
emanations of Urizen, Luvah, and Tharmas, are "evanescent Shades," she is "the vegetated
mortal wife of Los, his Emanation, yet his wife till the sleep of Death is past." (*Poetry and
Prose*, p. 573.) [84] *Poetry and Prose*, p. 400.

Alternate Love and Hate his breast: hers Scorn and Jealousy
In embryon passions; they kiss'd not nor embrac'd for shame and fear.

        . . .

She drave the Females all away from Los,
And Los drave the Males from her away.[85]

When Los is most ardent, she is most frigid and timorous. His "jealous
lamentation" reveals much:

> Why can I not enjoy thy beauty, lovely Enitharmon?
> When I return from clouds of grief in the wand'ring elements
> Where thou in thrilling joy, in beaming summer loveliness,
> Delectable reposest, ruddy in my absence, flaming with beauty,
> Cold pale in sorrow at my approach, trembling at my terrible
> Forehead and eyes, thy lips decay like roses in the spring.[86]

Their essential difficulty is that Enitharmon, having divided from Los,
asserts a will of her own, whereas in Eternity "Males immortal live renewed by female deaths." [87] In the false world of generation, sexual union
draws man upward toward salvation only when the attitude of the female
is completely self-sacrificial—the utter surrender of the medium to the
artist.

Such are "the torments of love and jealousy" which constitute the declared theme of *The Four Zoas*. We can hardly doubt that similar torments were gnawing at Blake's heart when he wrote *Songs of Experience*.
It is much more difficult, at any rate, to accept Damon's view that Blake,
being "ideally married," produced these poems in order to convince the
world "that such felicity as his was the right—and the possible right—of
every living person." [88]

The reader who has begun to pity Blake should reserve a little sympathy
for his wife. Catherine had several qualities which Los would desire in
his Enitharmon. She was a pretty girl before hard work wore her down.
Her devotion to William was absolute. Illiterate at the time of their
marriage, she learned to read and write under his tutelage. She soon became not only an efficient housewife but a useful assistant, working off
William's engravings, coloring illustrations under his direction, and oc-

---

[85] *Ibid.*, p. 287.
[86] *Ibid.*, p. 373. Blake inserts well known characteristics of his own appearance. Notice
also the reminiscence of *Never seek to tell thy love.*
[87] *Ibid.*, p. 280.   [88] *Op. cit.*, p. 99.

casionally even designing in imitation of his manner. She believed unquestioningly in his visions, and was perhaps able to persuade herself that she saw some of her own. A loyal, loving, malleable woman. Even in his deepest unhappiness, Blake probably never ceased to regard her with affection and gratitude.

As the wife of such a man as Blake, however, she had her limitations. Though intelligent in a passively absorptive way, her mind could achieve no real companionship with his. Anti-feminist geniuses expect their wives to be stupid but are often indignant when their expectations are fulfilled. She was jealous of her husband's clever friends and perhaps especially of the beloved Robert. Blake found it hard to forget that pity—a womanly trait which became one of his prime aversions—had been a main factor in her acceptance of him. We do not know whether her barrenness was a partial cause or a result of their antagonism, but it deprived them of a means of rising above themselves.[89]

The quite possibly apocryphal anecdote of Blake and his wife, stark naked in imitation of Adam and Eve, reciting passages from *Paradise Lost* in their summer house, is entirely characteristic of William; but if Catherine took part in any such visionary game she was doing violence to some of her deepest instincts. Her plebeian puritanical "goodness" was unrelieved by any mystical antinomianism, and it was rendered acute by her jealousy, her sense of Blake's strangeness, and her awareness of his contempt for women. Her propriety partly accounts for Blake's detestation of the "moral virtues." Several passages in the poems suggest that she was priggish about her body and about William's—an ominous trait in the wife of an artist.

> And many of the Eternal ones laughed after this manner:
> "Have you known the Judgment that is arisen among the
> Zoas of Albion, where a Man dare hardly to embrace
> His own Wife for the terrors of Chastity that they call
> By the name of Morality? their Daughters govern all
> In hidden deceit! they are Vegetable, only fit for burning.
> Art and Science cannot exist but by Naked Beauty display'd." [90]

[89] Miss Hamblen's theory that *Songs of Innocence* was written as a compensation for childlessness is much too sweeping, but a sort of "Dream Children" feeling may have been one of several motives for its composition. (Emily S. Hamblen, *On the Minor Prophecies of William Blake*, p. 9.)

[90] *Poetry and Prose*, p. 618; see also pp. 93, 96, 98, 212.

Blake's radical theories about love, growing wilder with his mounting unhappiness, must have shocked her. We know that she was reduced to tears by his talk of introducing a concubine into the household.[91] Such incidents, however, were results rather than causes of their unhappiness.

I am inclined to believe, then, that a satisfactory physical relationship between William and Catherine soon became impossible, or possible only intermittently. If we may take literally the "exactly twenty years" in the letter to Hayley of October 23, 1804,[92] the situation had become painfully clear to Blake two years after marriage; but it is uncannily foretokened in the "seasons" series of *Poetical Sketches*.[93] The joys of matrimony are ironically hailed in *An Island in the Moon*. *Songs of Innocence* attempts to transcend frustration through the vision of childhood. By 1793, however, the problem has become crucial. "I say I shan't live five years," reads the pathetic memorandum, "and if I live one it will be a wonder." [94] *Songs of Experience* and the 1793 poems of the Rossetti Manuscript represent this phase.

Was the crisis induced by a particular incident, or was it an outburst of accumulated unhappiness? We do not know. *My Pretty Rose-Tree*[95] has been interpreted to mean that Blake was offered an extra-marital relationship, rejected it, but on returning faithful and ardent to the side of Catherine was met with jealous frigidity. This is what the poem seems to say, but the occurrence may have been invented to typify a less tangible emotional situation. Probably a very egotistical artist's distress at the world's unwillingness to recognize his genius was an important factor. Since his passions were more of the mind than of the body he tended to identify sexual with imaginative power. His physical inadequacy was therefore associated in his mind with aesthetic inadequacy, giving him a sense of twofold frustration.

[91] In 1789, while William and Catherine were members of the New Jerusalem Church, the society "withdrew from" six members who interpreted Swedenborg as approving concubinage. (Mark Schorer, "Swedenborg and Blake," *Modern Philology*, XXXVI, 158.) Mary Wollstonecraft fell in love with Blake's close friend Fuseli and "wished to join the Fuseli household as a spiritual concubine." (Mona Wilson, *The Life of William Blake*, p. 51.) In 1780 the Evangelical leader Martin Madan had disgraced himself and outraged his cousin William Cowper by publishing *Thelypthora*, an argument for the revival of Old Testament polygamy as a remedy for prostitution. As late as 1826 Blake shocked Crabb Robinson into the use of German by telling him "that from the Bible he has learned that *eine Gemeinschaft der Frauen statt finden sollte.*" (Robinson's *Diary* in Arthur Symons, *William Blake*, p. 269.)   [92] *Vide infra*, p. 116.

[93] *Vide supra*, p. 71. The only rational explanation is observation of his parents colored by precocious self-analysis.   [94] *Poetry and Prose*, p. 888.   [95] *Ibid.*, p. 74.

At the age of thirty-six Blake could not easily resign himself to this predicament.

> Thou hast a lap full of seed,
> And this is a fine country,
> Why dost thou not cast thy seed,
> And live in it merrily?
>
> Shall I cast it on the sand
> And turn it into fruitful land?
> For on no other ground
> Can I sow my seed
> Without tearing up
> Some stinking weed.[96]

The weeds must be destroyed, but first they must be distinguished from the flowers. Precisely what were the obstacles to happy love? It is never quite clear to us, nor perhaps to Blake, whether he wants freedom *of* the senses or freedom *from* the senses. Even when he seems to urge the former most ardently, his obvious detestation of the flesh makes him a very ambiguous advocate of unbridled passion. What was the real answer to the question which rings in the ears of Thel: "Why a little curtain of flesh on the bed of our desire?" [97] The answer was too deeply implanted in his own neurotic personality to be found and uprooted.

At this time he felt sure that the blame lay elsewhere than in himself. Women, for example, were obviously stinking weeds. He cries out against their jealousy, their false modesty, their false pity, their fear of frankness, their preference for "the look of soft deceit" and for "dark secret love," [98] their vested interest in monogamy:

> To a lovely mirtle bound
> Blossoms show'ring all around,
> O, how sick and weary I
> Underneath my mirtle lie.
> Why should I be bound to thee,
> O, my lovely mirtle tree? [99]

Mothers who deliver their children over to the bondage of the senses, and fathers who restrict their sexual liberty, are also to blame. Closely akin to

[96] *Ibid.*, p. 92. In *Ahania*, Urizen is said to have had a "lap full of seed" in Eternity before his fall. (*Ibid.*, p. 265.)   [97] *Ibid.*, p. 173.   [98] *Ibid.*, pp. 72, 74, 86, 100.
[99] *Ibid.*, p. 97. Another version is on p. 91 as part of *Infant Sorrow*.

the tyrannous father with his "holy book" are those "priests in black gowns" who have spoiled *The Garden of Love* by "binding with briars my joys and desires." [100] But the false restrictive morality of parents and priests is merely one aspect of a whole world of deceit, cruelty, and oppression, the experience-world of *London,* where "the chimney-sweeper's cry," "the hapless soldier's sigh," and "the midnight harlot's curse" sound in Blake's ears as the clanking of "mind-forg'd manacles." [101]

How has the mind, the source of true freedom, become the agent of tyranny? There can be no explanation in the language of reasoned discourse, but there can be a myth which will give symbolic form to the visionary and anti-visionary forces in life. Blake is already shaping that myth. Earth despairingly answers the summons of the Bard:

> Prison'd on wat'ry shore,
> Starry Jealousy does keep my den:
> Cold and hoar,
> Weeping o'er,
> I hear the father of the ancient men!
>
> Selfish father of men!
> Cruel, jealous, selfish fear!
> Can delight,
> Chain'd in night,
> The virgins of youth and morning bear? [102]

Here is Urizen—"your reason"—who has placed the mind in manacles and whose sworn enemy is Los, the champion of creative imagination.

3

Blake, indeed, had begun his myth-making immediately after, or even a little before, the completion of *Songs of Innocence.* The juxtaposition of the "two contrary states" in 1794 makes it easy to forget that a considerable amount of important work was produced between *Songs of Innocence* and *Songs of Experience.* For the adult, childhood innocence is impossible. "Instinct," Novalis was to say, "is genius in paradise;" but once paradise is lost it must be regained by "mental fight." The road ran from

---

[100] *Ibid.,* pp. 75, 80, 90.   [101] *Ibid.,* pp. 92–93.
[102] *Ibid.,* pp. 69–70; see also p. 93.

the innocence of the child through the darkness of experience to the mature innocence of the creative genius.

Issued in 1822, *The Ghost of Abel* is the poet's last published work, but after the date in the colophon come the words, "Blake's original stereotype was 1788." He now dedicates it "to Lord Byron in the Wilderness" as an explanation of the problem which Byron had failed to solve in *Cain*. The theme of Blake's mystery-play is that the imputation of sin is false religion, while the forgiveness of sin is true religion. This thought is so characteristic of the final stage of Blake's development that one wonders if the work may not have been reengraved with substantial revisions. But since Blake usually interprets "forgiveness of sin" to mean "denial of the existence of sin," *The Ghost of Abel* deviates from his early antinomianism in tone and emphasis rather than in fundamental belief.

Blake's first experiments in symbolic myth, *The Book of Thel* and *Tiriel,* were both engraved in 1789. *Thel* may be a trifle the earlier of the two, since all of it except the short final section is in the key of *Songs of Innocence,* while *Tiriel* takes place wholly in the state of experience. The maiden angel Thel, resident in a Neoplatonic paradise of preexistence,[103] is granted a view of what her life on earth would be. Her sense of transitoriness and uselessness is removed when she perceives through the eyes of innocence the spirit of love and service which pervades all things from cloud to clay to worm. Here Blake is close to the tradition of universal benevolence. In the last section, which contrasts harshly with the almost excessive tenderness of the main body of the poem, Thel sees the world with, rather than through, the eye, and shrieks at beholding the miseries imposed upon the spirit by the tyranny of the senses. That the poem is basically an allegory of spiritual *versus* sensual love is suggested by "Thel's Motto":

> Does the Eagle know what is in the pit?
> Or wilt thou go ask the Mole?
> Can Wisdom be put in a silver rod?
> Or Love in a golden bowl? [104]

Pit, rod, and bowl are erotic symbols. When we behold love with the piercing eye of the eagle (visionary genius) we see something much better

---

[103] Damon suggests that Thomas Taylor's influence is at work here. He also draws a helpful comparison with the Proserpina myth. (S. F. Damon, *William Blake, His Philosophy and Symbols,* p. 75.)   [104] *Poetry and Prose,* p. 168.

than when we behold it with the rudimentary eye of the mole (sense-bound humanity). But Blake's detestation of the mole makes the eagle rather less than a complete lover. In the question, "Why a tender curb upon the youthful burning boy?" the "burning" is a purely imaginative flame which has been smothered by "the little curtain of flesh." [105] If this deeply frustrated man's attempt to glorify the senses and to escape from them at the same time were fully understood, he would be less warmly idolized by genuine believers in free love.

Tiriel, very Ossianic and very noisy with cursing and howling, is less important for the exegesis of Blake and much less meritorious as a poem. It may best be interpreted as an allegory of tyrannous fatherhood and kingship which is in turn an allegory of imagination repressed by a decaying but still powerful system of creed and law.

Parallel with these experimental fumblings toward a mythical interpretation of his difficulties runs the attempt to convey his ideas through direct exposition. Somewhere between 1788 and 1790 he engraved the two-part tractate entitled *There Is No Natural Religion* together with its companion-piece, *All Religions Are One.* They may be regarded as a single work. Here he is concerned not so much with the inadequacy of natural revelation in the ordinary sense as with the impotence of reason (mere observation and inference) to apprehend spiritual truth. The only valid instrument of religious thinking is the imagination of the poet-prophet. This faculty, far from denying the data of experience, is genuinely experiential:

As the true method of knowledge is experiment, the true faculty of knowing must be the faculty which experiences. This faculty I treat of. . . . The Poetic Genius is the true Man, and . . . the body or outward form of Man is derived from the Poetic Genius. Likewise . . . the forms of all things are derived from their Genius, which by the Ancients were call'd an Angel and Spirit and Demon.[106]

The purpose of this idealistic interpretation of the experimental method is to burst the "mind-forged manacles" of a mechanistic and necessitarian conception of nature:

None could have other than natural or organic thoughts if he had none but organic perceptions. . . . If it were not for the Poetic or Prophetic character the Philosophic and Experimental [in the materialistic sense] would soon be

[105] *Ibid.,* p. 173.   [106] *Ibid.,* p. 148.

at the ratio of all things, and stand still, unable to do other than repeat the same dull round over again.

We can free ourselves from being "eyeless in Gaza at the mill with slaves" by affirming that

Man's perceptions are not bounded by organs of perception. . . . The bounded is loathed by its possessor. . . . The desire of Man being Infinite, the possession is Infinite and himself Infinite.[107]

Blake agrees with the deistic view that "all religions are one" in their origin; but he insists that they are derived, not from a primitive body of axioms universally acceptable to right reason, but

from each Nation's different reception of the Poetic Genius, which is everywhere call'd the Spirit of Prophecy. . . . As all men are alike (tho' infinitely various), so all Religions . . . have one source. The true Man is the source, he being the Poetic Genius.[108]

Thus by 1790 at the latest, Blake offers much that the romantic heart desires—absorption of experimental method by poetic vision, interpretation of experience in terms of transcendental idealism, identification of the transcendental faculty with the shaping spirit of imagination, the escape from necessity into freedom and from limitation into boundlessness, the glorification of the powers of the human mind. So far as fundamental ideas are concerned, there is hardly anything left for the other romantic poets to say.

Miss Wilson is probably correct in thinking that these neglected but deeply significant little pamphlets reflect the influence of Jakob Boehme as read in Law's translation.[109] Readers of Volume II of this series may remember that the same influence had an analogous effect on John Byrom.[110] But even in eighteenth-century writers who are comparatively untouched by the mystical tradition there are traces of a transcendentalism which appears as a sort of corollary of the cult of original genius.[111] Professor Damon illustrates Blake's belief in the identity of poetry and prophecy by referring to *The Age of Reason*,[112] where Paine declares that many parts of the Scriptures, especially the Prophets, are simply poetry:

[107] *Ibid.*, pp. 147, 148.   [108] *Ibid.*, p. 149.
[109] Mona Wilson, *The Life of William Blake*, p. 58.
[110] *Religious Trends*, II, 151–161.
[111] See "genius" and "transcendentalism" in the topical indexes of *Religious Trends*, I and II.   [112] *Op. cit.*, p. 61.

The imagery in those books called the Prophets appertains altogether to poetry. It is fictitious, and often extravagant, and not admissible in any other kind of writing than poetry. . . . The word prophet, to which later times have affixed a new idea, was the Bible word for poet, and the word *prophesying* meant the art of making poetry.[113]

Damon fails to observe, however, that Paine and Blake draw opposite inferences from the same fact. Paine concludes that prophecy, being *mere* poetry, need not be taken seriously. Blake concludes that if prophecy and poetry are one they must be taken very seriously indeed as a manifestation of inspired genius. Paine gives a sceptical twist to a religious conception of poetry which descends from the Renaissance through Milton. In the eighteenth century, as my earlier volumes have shown, it is cultivated chiefly by poets and critics of puritan-bourgeois background—Watts, Dennis, Blackmore, Aaron Hill, Young, Akenside, Collins. The idea that the loftiest poetry expresses religious enthusiasm enters into eighteenth-century theories concerning sublimity and original genius; and the glorification of genius, at its most extravagant, implies that the poet's mind is godlike in its creativeness. Blake, the son of a Nonconformist-Swedenborgian hosier, develops this puritan view of religious, original, divinely inspired, enthusiastic poetry in more or less Behmenistic terms. In so doing he goes to extremes which would startle Isaac Watts, but he is closer to Watts than to Paine.[114]

The comments which Blake, about 1790, wrote in the margins of Swedenborg's *The Wisdom of Angels concerning Divine Providence* are much less favorable than the earlier jottings in *Divine Love*. Probably Blake is learning to drink from more authentic sources of the occult. He particularly objects to Swedenborg's belief in predestination. Whether expressed in theological, philosophical, scientific, or aesthetic terms, the idea that the human mind is subject to any sort of external control is anathema to him.

It follows that political tyranny and social injustice were also among those stinking weeds which must be pulled up. Bronowski's slight but suggestive study and Schorer's more elaborate and penetrating work[115] advance the thesis that political radicalism supplied the primary motivation of Blake's art and of his mythological system. Certainly religious en-

---

[113] Thomas Paine, *The Age of Reason*, pp. 35–37.
[114] For Watts, see *Religious Trends*, I, 120–134.
[115] J. Bronowski, *William Blake: A Man Without a Mask;* Mark Schorer, *William Blake: The Politics of Vision.*

thusiasm and political enthusiasm are so closely intertwined in his thought that they are often hardly distinguishable. Which of them governs the other depends largely on which is the more interesting to the modern critic. I should prefer to say, however, that the source of both his political and his religious rebellions was the craving for personal imaginative freedom and power.⁻

The proofs of Book I of *The French Revolution* (1791)[116] are important for us only as introducing the question of Blake's personal contacts with the English Jacobins who consorted at the shop of Joseph Johnson—the "remarkable coterie of advanced thinkers" which included Godwin, Mary Wollstonecraft, Price, Priestley, Holcroft, and Paine.[117] The hypothetical probability that he was intimate with some of these radicals is fairly strong; but except for the apparently trustworthy anecdote of the warning to Paine the specific evidence is extremely tenuous. There is no reason to suppose that his reputation as a "liberty boy" aroused the alarm of William Pitt. On the other hand, Schorer, Bronowski, and Bruce[118] have refuted the formerly accepted opinion that Blake abjured his revolutionary principles in deference to the general conservative reaction. They have shown, indeed, that he retained those principles more firmly than most of his contemporaries.

Blake buried himself more and more deeply in the fastnesses of his myth not because of timidity or despair,[119] but because of his antipathy to the rationalistic aspect of contemporary radicalism. The mentality of the English Jacobin, as I have described it elsewhere,[120] was a curious blend of sentimentalism and *philosophe* rationalism, but between 1789 and 1794 the latter element was far too strong to suit Blake's dislike of cold logic. No names were more honored in the Godwin circle than those of Bacon, Newton, Locke, and (with some reservations) Voltaire and Rousseau; no names are more violently execrated in the poems of Blake.[121]

---

[116] Blake probably began the poem in the fall of 1789. It was to have been published by Johnson in six books in 1791, but there is no indication that it ever appeared or even that Blake completed it. Nothing remains but the proofs of "Book the First." That Johnson abandoned the project from fear of prosecution is a plausible conjecture.

[117] Alexander Gilchrist, *The Life of William Blake*, pp. 92–97 *passim*.

[118] H. L. Bruce, "William Blake and Gilchrist's Remarkable Coterie of Advanced Thinkers," *Modern Philology*, XXIII, 285–292; also his *William Blake in This World*, pp. 28–38.

[119] Here I take issue with Bronowski, *op. cit.*, p. 80.

[120] H. N. Fairchild, *The Romantic Quest*, pp. 24–49.

[121] For Bacon see *Poetry and Prose*, pp. 237, 239, 546, 574, 651, 968, 1020; for Newton, pp. 107, 137, 240, 244, 274, 469, 545, 546, 574, 615, 651, 679, 690, 845, 1010, 1020, 1068; for Locke, pp. 274, 469, 546, 574, 615, 651, 679, 690, 1020; for Voltaire, pp. 107, 274, 545, 648, 651; for Rousseau, pp. 107, 274, 545, 648, 651, 679.

They are the tools of Urizen and Satan. To be a Jacobin one need not, like Godwin and Holcroft, be an atheist. Price and Priestley were Unitarian ministers; Paine, the deist son of a Quaker, wrote *The Age of Reason* largely to dissuade his French friends from abandoning all belief in God. Mark Schorer has rightly emphasized the close relationship between Blake's political radicalism and his Nonconformist background.[122] But so far as contemporary conditions are concerned the Socinian or deistic beliefs held by the less irreligious radicals were too anti-visionary and naturalistic for the author of *There Is No Natural Religion*.[123] Blake could easily identify his personal hatred of restriction with the ideals of the French Revolution, but the Jacobin logic-choppers of his day themselves represented the "mind-forg'd manacles" which he aspired to burst. Like Carlyle, he found the rebellion glorious but did not think much of the rebels.

Songs of Experience provides ample proof that, for Blake, political, religious, and aesthetic rebellion are one. Bruce, Schorer, and Bronowski have also shown that to an extent almost unique in his generation he distrusted the Industrial Revolution as a cause not only of social injustice but of the mechanization of the human spirit. After the close of the Lambeth period he was less directly concerned with current mundanities, and his idea of salvation through anarchic revolt gave place to a theory of regeneration which we must examine later. Nothing indicates, however, that he became more conservative. In late additions to *The Four Zoas* he is still a foe of kingcraft and priestcraft, and the Last Judgment includes the release of the oppressed from their tyrants.[124] As in the sectarian radicalism of the seventeenth century, the millennium is necessarily a political and social revolution. In *Jerusalem*, the last of the major Prophetic Writings, Los addresses to Jesus a prayer vibrant with indignant humanitarianism: "The praise of Jehovah is chaunted from lips of hunger and thirst." [125] Urizen is held personally responsible for the Industrial Revolution:

> First Trades and Commerce, ships and armed vessels he builded laborious
> To swim the deep; and on the land, children are sold to trades

[122] *Vide supra*, p. 13.

[123] In *The Everlasting Gospel*, Priestley is listed with Bacon and Newton as a teacher of doubt and experiment. (*Poetry and Prose*, p. 137.)

[124] *Poetry and Prose*, pp. 425–426.

[125] *Ibid.*, pp. 606–607. In Blake, Jehovah almost always signifies the real Satan, whom deluded men have accepted as their God.

Of dire necessity, still laboring day and night till all
Their life extinct they took the spectre form in dark despair.[126]

Blake's attitude toward the "dark Satanic mills" [127] is precisely that of a
modern critic of technology, who, like Lewis Mumford, combines strong
social consciousness with strong aesthetic interests. "A machine," Blake
insists, "is not a Man nor a Work of Art; it is destructive of Humanity
and Art." [128] Economic injustice, uncreative labor, enslavement by the
machine, and bad art are all one hateful thing:

> The hour glass contemn'd because its simple workmanship
> Was as the workmanship of the plowman, and the water wheel
> That raises water into cisterns, broken and burn'd in fire
> Because its workmanship was like the workmanship of the shepherd,
> And in their stead intricate wheels invented, wheel within wheel,
> To perplex youth in their outgoings and to bind to labour
> Of day and night the myriads of Eternity, that they might file
> And polish brass and iron hour after hour, laborious workmanship,
> Kept ignorant of the use that they might spend the days of wisdom
> In sorrowful drudgery to obtain a scanty pittance of bread,
> In ignorance to view a small portion and think that All,
> And call it demonstration, blind to all the simple rules of life.[129]

The last two lines are especially remarkable for their sensitiveness to the
influence of the machine age upon intellectual life.

But just as Blake could not look upon a grain of sand without seeing
a world, so he could not look upon a human problem without seeing the
conflicts of Eternity. For him, as Berger reminds us,

the world of matter has no existence of its own: it is only a symbol of the
invisible universe. . . . History is a symbol: revolutions are symbols of some
great change actually taking place in the invisible world.[130]

They are also, it is extremely necessary to add, symbols of his internal
struggles. His attitude toward the French Revolution was at once more

[126] *Ibid.*, p. 386.

[127] It is characteristic of Blake that the phrase should symbolize both the mechanism of
the Newtonian heavens and that of the factory.   [128] *Poetry and Prose*, p. 823.

[129] *Ibid.*, p. 393. This passage from Night VII(b) of *The Four Zoas* is repeated with minor
changes in Book III of *Jerusalem* (*ibid.*, p. 675). Perhaps "wheel within wheel" was suggested by "worlds within worlds," a phrase often applied in the eighteenth century to the
system of Blake's pet aversion, Isaac Newton.

[130] Pierre Berger, *William Blake, Poet and Mystic*, p. 92.

cosmic and more personal than that of his contemporaries. He was never aware of any difference between the universe and his own tortured spirit.

In 1793 Blake moved from Poland Street to Hercules Buildings, Lambeth, and entered upon a seven-year period of agonized creative struggle. His personal revolution is fully expressed for the first time in *The Marriage of Heaven and Hell*,[131] although one cannot accept the statement of Sloss and Wallis that with this work "the study of Blake's teaching begins." [132] The prophetic poems known to students as the Lambeth Books follow in rapid succession. They may be divided into two groups. The first, which expresses in verse the anarchic revolt against political and moral restriction which *The Marriage of Heaven and Hell* expresses in prose, consists of *A Song of Liberty* (appended to the *Marriage*), *Visions of the Daughters of Albion* (1793), *America* (1793), and *Europe* (1794). In the second, Blake "evolves an uncompleted myth which aims at correcting the Hebrew, Christian, and Miltonic views of the origin of the earth, man, sex, and sin." [133] The poems are *The First Book of Urizen* (1794), *The Song of Los* (1795), *The Book of Los* (1795), and *Ahania* (1795).[134] *Vala*, probably begun in 1795, stands by itself as the first draft of *The Four Zoas*, which will be considered in the next section of this chapter. To what extent the myth of the Lambeth Books is "uncompleted," and to what extent incompletely revealed to the reader, is hard to say. I am inclined to agree with Professor White that Blake had an extensive myth in the back of his head as early as 1789. She says of *Tiriel*: "It is as if the author had been trying a piece of his myth out. . . . With the first book of *Urizen* the ground plan for all the stories is completed." Henceforward there are developments and changes, "but one feels it all as an unfolding rather than a building-up. It is as if Blake were letting the reader more fully into the

---

[131] This work, undated on the title page, is often assigned to 1790 on the strength of Blake's statement that thirty-three years have passed since Swedenborg's announcement of the new dispensation in 1757. But Sloss and Wallis, Damon, Plowman, Wicksteed, and Keynes prefer 1793, partly because Blake, who here mocks and parodies Swedenborg, was a member of a Swedenborgian society in 1789, and because the thought of the *Marriage* is so closely related to that of the Lambeth Books. The latter argument is more impressive than the former: the marginal annotations to *Divine Providence*, usually assigned to 1790, are also unfavorable to Swedenborg, though less so than the *Marriage*. This work is a miscellaneous collection of thoughts which may well have been begun in 1790 and finished about 1793.

[132] *The Prophetic Writings of William Blake*, edd. D. J. Sloss and J. P. R. Wallis, II, 5. Referred to hereafter as Sloss and Wallis.   [133] *Ibid.*

[134] The division, though useful, is somewhat artificial. The first group contains symbols which imply the myth of the second, and the second gives a more systematically mythological interpretation of many ideas contained in the first.

story, rather than elaborating his story." [135] Since the Lambeth myth is never given to us in its entirety, we cannot be sure that it was so markedly different from the myth of the later Prophetic Writings as Sloss and Wallis suppose.

A detailed examination of *The Marriage of Heaven and Hell* and the Lambeth Books would be impossible in the space at our disposal, and to describe them briefly would merely be to repeat what has already been said by others. It will be more profitable to use these works, together with the earlier material already discussed, in a general summary of Blake's religion as it existed shortly before his removal to Felpham in 1800.

For Blake, all the things which we suppose to be objects of sense-perception are merely symbols. These symbols are the product of Imagination or Genius, the sole faculty which can perceive or create truth. Imagination is the only ultimate reality—a universal spiritual energy from which the forms of all things are derived. Since humanity can imagine nothing higher than the human, the real as distinguished from the merely symbolic forms of all things are human forms, and nature is the creation of the human spirit. For the same reason the form of God is a human form. But "the Poetic Genius is the true Man," [136] and it is also the ultimate reality, the creative spiritual force of the universe. God, then, is perfect man, and perfect man is God. Thus true nature, true man, and true God are the same imaginative energy, and the true form of all three is "the Human Form Divine." "All deities reside in the human breast," and "The worship of God is: Honouring his gifts in other men, each according to his own genius, and loving the greatest men best." [137] But if the worship of God is the worship of human genius, Blake could not have found it easy to confine his adoration to the gifts of *other* men. Looking forward for a moment to *The Everlasting Gospel*, we see the inevitable conclusion:

> Thou art a Man, God is no more,
> Thine own Humanity learn to adore. [138]

From this idealistic anthropopantheism—to coin a fearsome but accurate term—it follows that

> ...everything that lives is holy, life delights in life;
> Because the soul of sweet delight can never be defiled. [139]

[135] Helen C. White, *The Mysticism of William Blake*, p. 167.
[136] *Vide supra*, p. 90.　　　[137] *Poetry and Prose*, pp. 195, 202.
[138] *Ibid.*, p. 136.　　　[139] *Ibid.*, p. 220; see also pp. 204, 215.

The good life consists in the freest possible expression of imaginative energy in art, religion, politics, sex, and all other aspects of conduct. "All act is Virtue." [140] To the great unhappiness of mankind, these truths have been denied and suppressed by the geometric formalism of classical art; by rationalism, with its hatred of imagination; by science, which accepts mere symbols as real and rejects the truths which they symbolize; by political tyranny and industrial mechanization, which crush the free spirit of man; by Natural Religion, which betrays creative faith into the hands of rationalism and science; and by the moral system of repression and denial which a perverted Christianity has fabricated.

The last-named enemy is his principal object of attack in *The Marriage of Heaven and Hell*. Although Blake never ceased to regard himself as a Christian, he felt free to interpret Christianity in terms of his Inner Light. Herein, of course, he was by no means disloyal to his Nonconformist ancestors. In *De Doctrina Christiana* Milton, "a true Poet and of the Devil's [*i.e.*, God's] party without knowing it," [141] writes:

We possess, as it were, a twofold Scripture, one external, which is the written word, and one internal, which is the Holy Spirit. That which is internal, and the peculiar possession of each believer, is far superior to all, namely the Spirit itself. . . . On the authority of Scripture itself, everything is to be referred finally to the Spirit, and the unwritten word.[142]

Aided by the Holy Spirit, which[143] for him means his imagination, and probably by some acquaintance with Gnosticism, Blake has persuaded himself that he is the only genuine Christian extant in the year 1793. Everyone else has made a serious mistake. The Jehovah of the Old Testament is really Satan; and the being whom other Christians call Satan is really Christ, the rebellious human genius who is the only God. Angels, who believe in restraint, are evil; devils, who believe in unbridled energy, are good. Heaven is really hell; and hell, where Blake walks "delighted with the enjoyments of Genius," [144] is really heaven.

These ideas are reflected in the Prophetic Writings of the Lambeth period. Urizen, by whom "the fiery joy" was "perverted to ten commands," [145] is the equivalent of Jehovah. On the other hand Orc, "the

---

[140] *Vide supra*, pp. 77–78.   [141] *Poetry and Prose*, p. 192.

[142] Quoted in a similar connection by Denis Saurat, *Blake and Milton*, p. 134.

[143] "Who" would be inapplicable even to Milton's conception of the Holy Spirit, and still more so to Blake's.   [144] *Poetry and Prose*, p. 192.   [145] *Ibid.*, p. 220.

fires of Eternal Youth within the vegetated mortal nerves," [146] bound by
the chain of jealousy, and Fuzon, "first begotten, last born" son of Urizen,
nailed by his father upon "the accursed Tree of Mystery" (the Cross), are
clearly related to Jesus.[147] Both are "youthful burning boys" who fight for
political and sexual freedom.

Even Blake's upside-down version of Christianity, however, becomes
pretty thoroughly obscured in the myth which he invents to explain, or
at least to represent in poetic form, the enslavement of man's spirit. Urizen
is not merely Jehovah in a new mask: he represents all the evil consequences of attempting to achieve, by non-visionary reason, what can be
achieved only by the higher reason of imagination. Cast out by the
Eternals for asserting independent powers, this "primeval Priest" organizes a world of his own—the sense-bound world in which we think we
live—and proceeds to impose his laws upon men and nations. His chief
opponent is Los, "the Eternal Prophet." Since prophecy is poetry, or art
in general, in the fallen state of mankind Los represents Man as Artist.
He is commissioned by the Eternals to isolate Urizen's world from
Eternity by walling it in (the imagination struggles to preserve a free
space for vision). This task he performs in fear and horror, but also in
pity. His pity divides from him in the form of Enitharmon, the first
separate female. Orc, the passionate young rebel against Urizen's laws, is
the fruit of their painful love. To a large extent Enitharmon becomes the
tool of Urizen, and the eternal life of Los himself is marred by his efforts
to curb the "Father of Jealousy." Gazing upon the monstrous labors of
Urizen, "he became what he beheld." In order to restrict Urizen, he must
himself become restrictive—must create a system of his own. Here was
a dilemma which harassed Blake's life as an artist. The hater of codes
must codify; he must become a sinner—a bad artist—by attacking the
sinfulness of imputing sin.

In the later Prophetic Writings, Blake's increasing desire to emphasize
the redemptive function of imagination makes what might be called the
Urizenic aspect of Los's creative struggles considerably less prominent.
One cannot say with Sloss and Wallis, however, that even in the Lambeth
Books Los is a fallen being in the same sense as Urizen.[148] From the very
beginning of the myth he is the Eternal Prophet. In the Lambeth Books,
to be sure, the only hope of escape from Urizen's "Philosophy of Five

---

[146] *Ibid.*, p. 522. Here I look ahead to *Milton* for Blake's most explicit identification of
this symbol.   [147] *Ibid.*, pp. 219, 256, 262.   [148] Sloss and Wallis, II, 259.

Senses" [149] lies in the wild revolt of "red Orc." His fierceness shows what
lustful, bloodthirsty excesses are caused by subjecting "the fires of Eternal
Youth" to the bondage of the world of generation. Nevertheless his fires
are "thought-creating," his voice makes dead things "begin to awake to
life," and he can defy Urizen in the words, "My fierce fires are better
than thy snows." [150] This destroyer and preserver—for one thinks of
Shelley's *West Wind*—is the child of Los, and as long as the son struggles
against his chains the poetic spirit of the father is still at work in the
world. [151]

Meanwhile Blake rages in his own chains. His efforts to "prove to the
Abstract Philosophers that Enjoyment and not Abstinence is the food of
Intellect" become furiously extravagant in their advocacy of any sort of
impulsive energy against any sort of restraint. "Energy is the only life.
. . . Energy is Eternal Delight." [152] "Pale religious letchery" is confronted
by "Love! Love! Love! happy happy Love! free as the mountain
wind!" [153] Blake's energy-worship has been likened to that of Nietzsche. [154]
Certainly some of the "Proverbs of Hell" sound startlingly modern:

The road of excess leads to the palace of wisdom. . . . If the fool would per-
sist in his folly he would become wise. . . . Prisons are built with stones of
Law, Brothels with bricks of Religion. . . . Every thing possible to be believ'd
is an image of truth. . . . Damn braces. Bless relaxes. . . . He who desires
but acts not, breeds pestilence. [155]

Of course it would be equally accurate to say, not that his rebellion is
modern, but that ours is very old.

4

In 1799 or 1800 Flaxman, who had opened the doors of Mrs. Mathew's
salon for Blake, did his friend an even more disastrous favor—he introduced him to William Hayley. The Hermit, as he loved to call himself,

---

[149] *Poetry and Prose*, p. 274.   [150] *Ibid.*, pp. 274, 255, 368.
[151] In *The Four Zoas* and *Milton* (*ibid.*, pp. 396, 401, 438, 493), we find that Orc is also
the generative-world aspect of Luvah, the Zoa who represents Love. These relationships
suggest how closely imagination and sex are associated in Blake's mind.
[152] *Ibid.*, p. 191.   [153] *Ibid.*, pp. 204, 213.
[154] One need not enlarge upon a comparison which has already been drawn by Irving
Babbitt, Pierre Berger, E. J. Ellis, Charles Gardner, Emily S. Hamblen, P. E. More, Denis
Saurat, Arthur Symons, Helen C. White, and doubtless by others.
[155] *Poetry and Prose*, pp. 192–195 *passim*.

was planning to write his life of Cowper. It was arranged that Blake, accompanied by his wife, should come to Felpham in Sussex, rent a cottage near Hayley's villa, execute the engravings for the Cowper volume, and help Hayley in other projects with which that trivially fertile mind was teeming. The Blakes were overjoyed at the prospect of a substantial period of profitable work in a pretty rural village by the sea. A change of scene was always stimulating to Blake's art, and he tended to invest moving-day with visionary meaning.

Shortly before leaving London he tells George Cumberland, "I begin to emerge from a deep pit of melancholy, melancholy without any real reason for it." [156] In a grateful letter to Flaxman he inserts lines of verse some of which have already been cited, but the remainder of the passage is now pertinent:

Paracelsus and Behmen appear'd to me, terrors appeared in the Heavens above
And in Hell beneath, and a mighty and awful change threatened the Earth.
The American War began. All its dark horrors pass'd before my face
Across the Atlantic to France. Then the French Revolution commenc'd in thick clouds,
And my Angels have told me that seeing such visions I could not subsist on the Earth,
But by my conjunction with Flaxman, who knows to forgive Nervous Fear.[157]

It is possible, then, that the *Sturm und Drang* of the Lambeth period was largely an attempt to convince himself that his weak nerves were strong. But can one suppose that horrible visions arising from the French Revolution were the sole cause of his "nervous fear"? Two months earlier, he had told George Cumberland that "melancholy" had oppressed him "without any real reason for it." Flaxman was a closer and more mystical friend than Cumberland, but the mixture of agreement and disagreement between the two letters is curious. A letter written four years later will suggest in due course that Blake's domestic situation was a main factor in the uneasiness which he now hopes to shake off.

However this may be, the first weeks at Felpham were delightful. He informs Flaxman that

Mr. Hayley received us with his usual brotherly affection. . . . Felpham is a sweet place for Study, because it is more Spiritual than London. Heaven opens here on all sides her golden Gates; her windows are not obstructed by vapours;

[156] *Ibid.*, p. 1044.   [157] *Ibid.*, p. 1046.

voices of Celestial inhabitants are more distinctly heard, and their forms more distinctly seen. . . . And now Begins a New Life, because another covering of Earth is shaken off. I am more famed in Heaven for my works than I could well conceive. In my Brain are studies and chambers filled with books and pictures of old, which I wrote and painted in ages of Eternity before my mortal life; and those works are the delight and Study of Archangels.[158]

For more than a decade he had granted fragmentary glimpses of these works to mortal men of his own era, and for the past four or five years he had been struggling to combine the whole mass of visionary experience in a single great poem. At Lambeth the task had proved surprisingly difficult for one who wrote from heavenly dictation, but in the new life at Felpham everything would be easier.

Although Blake's Prophetic Writings are obviously examples of allegorical mythology he was never willing to concede the fact. "Allegories," he insisted, "are things that relate to Moral Virtues"—sugar-coating for a didactic pill. His work, on the contrary, "is Visionary and Imaginative."[159] The symbols, no less than the truths they convey, are apprehended in Eternity. Blake could get whatever he wanted from any culture by piercing through the fables which had obscured the true genius of its makers. The *Descriptive Catalogue* explains that

The two pictures of Nelson and Pitt are compositions of a mythological cast, similar to those apotheoses of Persian, Hindoo, and Egyptian Antiquity, which are still preserved in rude monuments, being copies from stupendous originals now lost or perhaps buried till some happier age. The Artist having been taken in vision into the ancient republics, monarchies, or patriarchates of Asia, has seen those wonderful originals.[160]

From such original sources flow the very words of his prophecies. At the close of the Felpham period he informs Thomas Butts that he has written a great spiritual epic

from immediate Dictation, twelve or sometimes twenty or thirty lines at a time, without Premeditation and even against my Will; the time it has taken in writing was thus rendered non-existent, and an immense Poem exists which seems to be the Labour of a long life, all produc'd without Labour or Study.[161]

---

[158] *Ibid.*, pp. 1048–1049.   [159] *Ibid.*, pp. 841, 830.   [160] *Ibid.*, p. 780.

[161] *Ibid.*, pp. 1073–1074. Although he abandoned *The Four Zoas* in an unfinished condition he must be referring either to that poem or to some work now lost. Not much if any of *Milton*, and probably none of *Jerusalem*, was written before 1804.

Since Blake was a very honest man, we must ascribe such claims to his astonishing power of self-deception. The Prophetic Writings bear many marks of premeditation and conscious craftsmanship. In the Preface to *Jerusalem* he has hardly said that the poem was "dictated to me" when he defends his choice of free verse as against blank verse. "Every word and every letter is studied and put in its fit place." [162] Near the end of Night IV of *The Four Zoas* he scribbled the reminder, "Bring in here the Globe of Blood as in the B. of Urizen." [163] The Eternals never told him to do that, nor did they dictate to him two different versions of Night VII of this poem. Blake worked like any other poet except that his belief in the reality of his images approached hallucination.

The Four Zoas was never brought to completion or engraved. The text, with its remarkable drawings, exists only in Blake's manuscript. Three stages in the development of Blake's thought are here discernible: one identical with that of the Lambeth Books, one which looks partly backward and partly forward, and one which agrees in most respects with the later works, *Milton* and *Jerusalem*. In this section we are concerned with those elements of Blake's final myth which are common to the three major prophecies. Special distinguishing features of *Milton* and *Jerusalem* will be considered later.

It was probably in 1795 that Blake began a poem which he first entitled: "Vala/or/The Death and Judgement of the Eternal Man/A Dream/of Nine Nights." Judging from a note on the back of a drawing, he also considered calling it "The Bible of Hell, in Nocturnal Visions collected." In *The Marriage of Heaven and Hell* he had stated, "I have also The Bible of Hell, which the world shall have whether they will or no." [164] Later "Eternal" was replaced by "Ancient," and "A Dream of Nine Nights" was crossed out. In 1797, when he had finished perhaps seven books, he began to rewrite the whole work in the light of ideas slightly different from those of the Lambeth period. He now adopted a new title: "The Four Zoas/The Torments of Love and Jealousy/in/The Death and Judgment/of Albion the/Ancient Man." But "Vala" remains as the title at the head of each "Night." [165] The poem was further revised and enlarged at Felpham, and reached its present state either just at the close of the Felpham period or soon after the return to London in the autumn of 1803.

---

[162] *Ibid.*, p. 551.   [163] *Ibid.*, p. 340.   [164] *Ibid.*, p. 202.
[165] Observe the suggestion of Young's influence: *Night Thoughts* is divided into nine "Nights."

Blake probably abandoned it in 1804 when he decided to complete *Milton* and *Jerusalem*.

"Blake," says Wicksteed, "was burning with a great message which he could not leave unuttered, even though he found his contemporaries almost entirely unready for it. He seems, therefore, to have deliberately chosen to hide it in a precious casket, even at the risk of its remaining for ever unlocked." [166] But of recent years the casket has been opened and its contents so thoroughly inventoried by various scholarly Pandoras that one more detailed exegesis of Blake's mythology would be a work of supererogation. I shall merely discuss certain aspects of it which are especially important for an understanding of Blake's religion.

At a time when the unifying elements of mental behavior were greatly emphasized, Blake was interested not only in the association but in the dissociation of ideas. His inward conflicts drew his attention to the latter subject as early as *An Island in the Moon*. During the Lambeth period integration was to be achieved simply by defiance and revolt, for all his foes were conceived of as external to him. In *The Four Zoas, Milton,* and *Jerusalem* this idea is not decisively abandoned, but it is greatly tempered by recognition of the fact that some of the stinking weeds grow in his own mind. Man is now to win release from bondage not merely by rising up against the oppressor, but by undergoing inward changes which will make him worthy of freedom. Here was a possible starting-point for the development of a religion of sin and salvation.

The general shape of Blake's myth is described by Percival as a "Circle of Destiny." The term appears twice in Night I of *The Four Zoas*,[167] and the idea which it expresses is thoroughly traditional:

A circular movement of the soul in its absence from God is all but incumbent upon mystical religions. A wheel of birth, a cycle of destiny, a ring of return— these conceptions, foreign to Greek classical religions, came in through the Mysteries, and were basic in the Gnostic systems. In this type of thinking the soul has its origin in a supersensible world, incurs a fall, undergoes expiation and purification, and returns at last to its primal source.[168]

Undoubtedly something of this sort happens in the Prophetic Writings. But does the wheel forever continue to revolve both in the universal

[166] J. H. Wicksteed, *Blake's Vision of the Book of Job*, p. 23.
[167] *Poetry and Prose*, pp. 280, 281. Sloss and Wallis also recognize the importance of this symbol for Blake, although unlike Percival they do not regard it as the main unifying idea of the myth.   [168] M. O. Percival, *William Blake's Circle of Destiny*, p. 242.

macrocosm and the human microcosm, or is there some escape from it into eternal unity and peace? Will the scattered elements of Albion's nature begin to fall apart again as soon as they have been drawn together? In that case there is no possibility of a "judgment" in Blake's sense of the term. We are reminded of Shelley's "Circle of Destiny" in *Hellas*, where the Chorus shrinks from the thought that the return of "the world's great age" will merely begin a repetition of man's endless agony. Neither Sloss and Wallis nor even Percival can draw from Blake a consistent answer to this question,[169] and I have been no more fortunate than they. Blake's thought on the subject mingles "passionate hope and . . . equally passionate despair."[170] One may add that Blake's undiminished love of energy seriously conflicts with his hope that the wheel will either cease to turn or that certain redeemed spirits will be granted escape from its revolutions. He desires release from evil, but he identifies peace with torpor and struggle with the happy agony of the artist. Even in Eternity there must be intellectual warfare, endless attraction and repulsion between the "contraries." Here perhaps is foretokened the nineteenth-century heaven of human insatiability—Browning's heaven of striving and thriving and speeding and fighting.

The phrase "Circle of Destiny" raises a question as to the relation between fate and free will in Blake's system. Sloss and Wallis assert that in *The Four Zoas* "the necessitarianism of the earlier writings gave place to a belief in the existence of a beneficent Providence."[171] But are the Lambeth Books unqualifiedly necessitarian? What divine, natural, or human law can quench the fires of Orc? Waiving this point, one may still object that, if Providence now controls man's life in the shape of *destiny*, Blake has conceded much to one form of necessity. Further, if he means to say that the powers of Providence or destiny arise from any other source than the human imagination he is denying a belief which remains precious to him from the very beginning to the very end of his career. That which needs to be redeemed is the only conceivable redeemer.

But we must not discuss man's redemption before considering his fall. "You have a tradition," Blake informs the Jews near the close of Book I of *Jerusalem*, "that Man anciently contain'd in his mighty limbs all things in Heaven and Earth. This you receiv'd from the Druids."[172] Albion, the

---

[169] Sloss and Wallis, II, 205; Percival, *op. cit.*, pp. 237–249.
[170] Percival, *op. cit.*, p. 238.   [171] Sloss and Wallis, II, 6–7.
[172] *Poetry and Prose*, p. 597.

context indicates, is this cosmic man. Percival observes that Albion can be regarded as "the one character in the myth." He is

the last of a long line of primordial cosmic figures with which the Platonizing imagination filled ancient speculation and which came down along esoteric by-paths through the Middle Ages and emerged again into the main highway of knowledge in the Grand Man of Swedenborg.

As the passage just quoted from *Jerusalem* implies, he is the Adam Kadmon of the *Cabala*, and he is "the heavenly man of Philo, ideal, incorporeal, incorruptible, not yet sexually divided, the first of the two Adams of the Book of Genesis." [173] By combining this tradition with Druidism, Blake is also able to think of Albion as England, but only because England itself is an image of the cosmos. Albion means more than man in general: he means the universe revealed to perfect vision as human. The symbol covers the whole range of Blake's anthropopantheism.

"Four Mighty Ones are in every Man," [174]—the Four Zoas. In agreement with the conception of the human universe, they exist not merely in every man but in every atom of star and stone and beast. They are Urizen (analytical reason), Luvah (the emotions, but principally the emotion of love), Tharmas (instinct, the "vegetative power," the blind impulse to live and grow), and Urthona (the creative imaginative energy which pervades and unites all things). But even when Blake is speaking of Eternity, the names Urthona and Los are used interchangeably to signify "the fourth immortal starry one." In man's fallen state Los is sometimes called the spectre of Urthona and Urthona is sometimes called the spectre of Los. Sloss and Wallis are too severe in saying that "there seems to be no possible rational explanation" of this anomaly. The original idea, as they have observed, was probably that Urthona should represent "spiritual energy" in Eternity, while Los should represent the same force "in relation to the life of man, the temporary severance from Eternity." [175] But spiritual energy in the life of man expresses itself in prophetic poetry, or poetic prophecy. Blake was very fond of poetry and he was very fond of Los, his personal representative in the myth. While the Circle of Destiny is moving downward, poetry is an imperfect vestige of the eternal creative force. Hence Los is the spectre of Urthona. While the Circle is moving upward, poetry may be thought of as the higher aspect of a crude

[173] Percival, *op. cit.*, p. 13.   [174] *Poetry and Prose*, p. 278.
[175] Sloss and Wallis, II, 193.

primitive energy which cannot fulfill its potentialities until it is expressed in art. Hence Urthona is the spectre of Los, a sort of Vulcan assisting the Eternal Prophet at the forges of creation. Blake's personal preference for the latter conception is strong.

The "death" of Albion occurs when the harmony of the Zoas which compose his nature is disrupted by "selfhood." Each of the principles works for itself instead of for the whole, and the result of this struggle for dominion is the complete disintegration of man and hence of the universe which his mighty limbs contain. This cosmic disaster is of course the personal predicament of William Blake. In the fully developed myth the conception of the fallen state is much what it was during the Lambeth period with one important difference. In *Songs of Experience* and the Lambeth Books, the ultimate curse is enslavement to sense. Man can fall no lower than the world which is seen with, not through, the eye. But in *The Four Zoas, Milton,* and *Jerusalem,* the deepest pit is not sense-bondage, but complete absence of being—the loss of energy and outline which results from utter denial of the Divine Vision. The Circle of Destiny never quite reaches this theoretical extreme; but the lowest actual level of human existence, called Ulro, swings only a hair's-breadth above it. Everything which lies between Eternity and Ulro—visible nature, human institutions, relations between the separated sexes, the creative labors of the artist, the Incarnation of Jesus—may be looked at in two ways according to whether destiny's elevator is going up or down. In so far as they represent negation and doubt, they point toward Ulro. In so far as they represent man's endeavors to shape and organize and unify, they point toward Eternity. Even Urizen's hideous system of moral laws is better than nonentity. It has achieved a particular form; it has been engraved in the manner of Basire.

In attempting to explain Blake's changed conception of the fall, we have indicated the clue to his scheme of redemption. When man can see nothing below him but the void, he looks upward in his despair and begins to climb. In some respects Blake's myth aptly symbolizes the ambiguity which divides the life of man, so glorious and so abhorrent. It also enables Blake not to reconcile, but at least to juxtapose in an interesting pattern, some of the conflicting elements of his own character. Unfortunately Blake's whole scheme of salvation is vitiated by a basic inconsistency which is much more destructive than the obscurity of his symbolism.

Who or what turns the Circle of Destiny? Does Albion integrate himself by his own efforts, or does he receive help from some external force? Logically, the question should answer itself: there cannot possibly be anything external to this cosmic symbol. He is the universe conceived of as Man; he "contains in his mighty limbs all things in Heaven and Earth." The Human Form Divine, he includes all of nature, all of man, all of God. His "death" can only be the death of the pantheistic universe, and his resurrection—granting it to be conceivable at all—can only be the result of his own will to rise.

But the fallen Albion does not pull himself up by his own bootstraps. His fortunes, with those of the spectres and emanations who spawn from his dissolution, are watched over and to some extent guided by the Eternals, a "Council of God" exercising providential functions.[176] Percival, though seldom daunted by such problems, finds it "impossible to say" who the Eternals are.[177] The status of transcendent divinity in a pantheistic universe is naturally difficult to define. Sloss and Wallis must be mistaken in their assertion that Albion "is merely one of the Eternals";[178] such a limitation would deprive his fall of the cosmic significance which it is clearly intended to possess. In Eternity, as a passage in *Jerusalem* informs us, he was "the Image of God surrounded by the Four Zoas."[179] Originally, I believe, the Zoas themselves were the Eternals, united in the Divine Image which was Albion.[180] But once the Zoas, falling with the fallen Albion, have lost their places in Eden, the personnel of the Divine Council is never clearly explained. It is their corporate unity, not their separate individualities, which Blake considers important. Beheld through contracted senses, they appear as a "multitude" of spiritual beings. Beheld through expanded senses, they appear as one man, and that man is Jesus.[181] It is He who places the "pale limbs" of the fallen Albion "Upon the Rock of Ages, watching over him with Love and Care." [182]

The later Prophetic Writings draw much more of their symbolism from Christianity than do the Lambeth Books. This change is the natural consequence of Blake's growing interest in regeneration. For man's fall,

---

[176] *Poetry and Prose*, pp. 285, 298, 398. The phrase "to some extent" is necessary because while the Eternals usually possess providential powers, they are sometimes shocked and alarmed by events which they have not foreseen and which they seem unable to control. No *absolute* power, divine or otherwise, is ever congenial to Blake—except the power of imagination.

[177] *Op. cit.*, p. 45.   [178] Sloss and Wallis, II, 48.
[179] *Poetry and Prose*, p. 628.   [180] *Ibid.*, p. 278.
[181] *Ibid.*, pp. 278, 298, 321, 398, 407.   [182] *Ibid.*, p. 297.

a myth of warring psychological principles would do well enough; but a writer of Blake's background, however original, would find it almost impossible to symbolize man's rise to bliss without using images provided by the Christian tradition. Judging from the "washed in the Blood of the Lamb" tone of some of the letters of this period,[183] he may also have seen in the increasingly influential Evangelical Movement elements which could be reinterpreted in the light of his personal ideas. He remains, however, unswervingly hostile to all restriction of the human spirit by theological dogmas and moral codes. Jesus, though regarded with a deeper reverence than before, is still the antinomian Jesus of *The Marriage of Heaven and Hell,* as He will be the Jesus of *The Everlasting Gospel.* For a detailed account of the part played by Jesus in Blake's myth the reader should consult Sloss and Wallis. Here it is enough to say that when Los has learned from his own sufferings to carry on his tasks of imaginative creation in unselfish pity and love rather than in fear and hatred, the spirit of Jesus automatically becomes operative in the broken heart of man. The Saviour shares with man the great curse of sexual generation in order that brotherhood and forgiveness may enter the struggling vegetative world and lift it toward Eternity.

So far we are edified, but perhaps a little confused. We must reconcile ourselves to abandoning the pantheism of the Albion symbol in favor of the idea that man is saved by transcendent divinity. Further difficulties, however, are in store for us. One may find in Blake's poems a few vague and ambiguous references to a God the Father who is not the Jehovah worshipped by Urizen's slaves and yet is perhaps not quite identical with God the Son.[184] Blake's real belief, however, is simply that "God is Jesus" and that "God is Man."[185] It follows that Jesus is Man—not true God *and* true Man, since Blake can conceive of no divinity apart from humanity, but true God *because* true Man. From *Songs of Innocence* to the conversations with Crabb Robinson, Blake's conception of Christ is unchanging: "He is the only God—and so am I and so are you."[186]

Blake's belief that to perfected vision all natural objects have human forms, and that the universe as a whole is one cosmic Man, draws his completely human Christ back toward pantheism. Jesus is "the Divine Vision"—mankind unified in Him as the Human Form Divine. He is

[183] *Ibid.,* pp. 1119–1121. [184] *Ibid.,* p. 278 ("the Heav'nly Father").
[185] *Ibid.,* pp. 766, 1023.
[186] Robinson's *Diary* in Arthur Symons, *William Blake,* p. 270.

"the Universal Man," "Universal Humanity, Who is One Man," "the Eternal Great Humanity," "the Universal Humanity," "the Divine Humanity," "the Eternal Man."[187] These epithets, however, would apply equally to Albion, who is referred to repeatedly as "the Eternal Man,"[188] once as "the four-fold Man, the Humanity,"[189] and once as "the Image of God."[190] Accepting Blake's presuppositions, is there any discernible difference between Albion, the cosmic man, and Jesus, the cosmic man who saves him?

Jesus is Man. But "the true Man," as we already know, is the Poetic Genius, or Imagination.[191] Imagination is described as "the Holy Ghost in Man" and as "the bosom of God." It is "Eternity," the abode of those beings who collectively are Jesus. It is "the Divine Humanity," "the Divine Vision," "the Divine Body of Jesus."[192] Jesus then is Universal Humanity not merely as being all-inclusive, but as embodying that element in man and nature which is universal—imaginative energy. It is impossible, however, to disagree with the statement of Sloss and Wallis:

In the later writings, from the additions to *The Four Zoas* onwards, Los . . . is the dramatic personification of Blake's doctrine of the providential guidance of life to a good end: he is spiritual or imaginative impulse and energy in life.[193]

If this is true of Los and equally true of Jesus, how shall we distinguish between the Eternal Prophet and his Saviour?

Blake glories in these confusions as expressive of the highest wisdom. In Book IV of *Jerusalem,* the coda of the entire mythological composition, he brings together Jesus, Albion, and Los within the godhead of the human:

> Then Jesus appear'd standing by Albion as the Good Shepherd
> By the lost Sheep that he hath found, and Albion knew that it
> Was the Lord, the Universal Humanity; and Albion saw his Form
> A Man, and they convers'd as Man with Man in Ages of Eternity.
> And the Divine Appearance was the likeness and similitude of Los.[194]

---

[187] *Poetry and Prose*, pp. 57, 278, 285, 313, 339, 400, 407, 485, 525, 599, 601, 613, 653, 745, 838. [188] *Ibid.*, pp. 334, 354, 427. [189] *Ibid.*, p. 574.
[190] *Ibid.*, p. 628. [191] *Vide supra*, p. 90.
[192] *Poetry and Prose*, pp. 438, 464, 465, 466, 487, 529, 554, 556, 690, 703, 736, 769, 830.
[193] Sloss and Wallis, II, 190. [194] *Poetry and Prose*, p. 745.

Since Blake's drawings of Los are self-portraits we are furnished a clue to the appearance of Deity. Notice also that in this culminating passage both Albion and Jesus appear to be absorbed in Los, the Artist of Eternity.

Jesus was not merely human imagination: he was also the product of that faculty. Since "all Deities reside in the human breast," [195] there is a sense in which His very existence depends upon the mind of Los, and hence upon the mind of Blake. Miss Hamblen, who credits our poet with "profound insight into the nature of the Christian message," [196] admiringly cites Whitman as a parallel:

What do you suppose I would intimate to you in a hundred ways, but that
    every man or woman is as good as God,
And that there is no God any more divine than yourself; and that that is what
    the oldest and newest myths finally mean?

This is very close to the speech addressed by the regenerate Albion to Luvah and Vala at the Last Judgment in *The Four Zoas:*

If Gods combine against Man, setting their dominions above
The Human Form Divine, thrown down from their high station,
In the Eternal Heavens of Human Imagination, buried beneath
In dark Oblivion, with incessant pangs, ages on ages,
In enmity and war first weaken'd, then in stern repentance
They must renew their brightness, and their disorganiz'd functions
Again reorganize, till they resume the image of the human,
Co-operating in the bliss of Man, obeying his Will,
Servants to the Infinite and Eternal of the Human Form.[197]

There is nothing to suggest that Jesus is exempt from the omnipotence of human imagination.

Only one conclusion seems possible. In this myth of fall and salvation, the universe is saved by the universe, man is saved by man, imagination is saved by imagination, William Blake is saved by William Blake. When one who posits a godless universe asserts that man can rely only on himself, we grant that he has drawn the logical inference from his own premise. When from this basis he proceeds to a pseudo-religious glorification of man—"I am the captain of my soul," and so on—we feel that his bluster is absurd but psychologically credible. But when Blake brings us

---

[195] *Vide supra,* p. 97.
[196] Emily S. Hamblen, *On the Minor Prophecies of William Blake,* p. 25.
[197] *Poetry and Prose,* p. 438.

back to man-worship and self-worship after leading us through hundreds of pages full of Jesus, heaven, spiritual rebirth, and innumerable symbols ostensibly referring to supernatural realities—that is a very startling and disquieting experience.

Let us return to Blake's life at Felpham. As all the biographers tell us, Hayley's condescending benevolence combined with his utter failure to appreciate Blake's powers gradually became intolerable.[198] The Hermit wanted his protégé to drop his enthusiastic nonsense and cater to the gentry as a miniature painter.

O God, protect me from my friends, that they have not power over me.[199]
Thou hast giv'n me power to protect myself from my bitterest enemies.

Blake complains to his more understanding client, Thomas Butts, that he is so immersed in drudgery that he lacks time and energy to do his duty "as a soldier of Christ." The indignant Spirits whisper threats in his ear: "If you, who are organised by Divine Providence for Spiritual communion, refuse, and bury your talent in the earth, . . . sorrow and desperation pursues you thro' life, and after death shame and confusion of face to eternity." [200] By April, 1803, he is certain that Hayley, though a "corporeal" friend, is a spiritual enemy, and that only in London can he "see Visions, dream Dreams and prophesy and speak Parables unobserv'd and at liberty from the doubts of other Mortals; perhaps doubts proceeding from kindness, but doubts are always pernicious." [201] Blake's escape from the killing kindness of Felpham was arranged without any open breach. Indeed, Hayley's support in the absurd treason trial which followed the quarrel with the dragoon made Blake's feelings toward his patron just at the close of the Felpham sojourn a mixture of hatred and gratitude. By the middle of September, 1803, William and Catherine had established themselves in London at South Molton Street.

An understanding of Hayley's character will help to explain some of Blake's bitterest aversions in late additions to *The Four Zoas* and particu-

[198] To the obvious sources may be added H. N. Fairchild, "Unpublished References to Blake by Hayley and Lady Hesketh," *Studies in Philology*, XXXV, 1–10.

[199] *Poetry and Prose*, p. 478. These are Palamabron's words in *Milton*, but compare the epigram on Hayley, p. 850.

[200] *Ibid.*, pp. 1061–1062. Blake's hallucinations, though usually visual, were sometimes auditory. At this time Hayley had in his possession, and may well have shown to Blake, a diary kept by John Johnson during the last years of William Cowper, who was constantly threatened by "voices" in language of this sort. See H. N. Fairchild, "Additional Notes on John Johnson's Diary," *PMLA*, XLIII, 571–572.   [201] *Poetry and Prose*, p. 1073.

larly in *Milton* and *Jerusalem*. Though Hayley was not a churchgoer, he read Anglican morning prayer in his household, together with "devotional hymns of his own composition." [202] Blake, however, says that Hayley "is as much averse to my poetry as he is to a Chapter in the Bible." [203] The hymns are fortunately not extant, but we may infer from such poems as *The Triumphs of Temper,* vastly admired in their day, that his personal religion was a superficial and half-affected sentimentalism. He exploited the pleasures and pains of sensibility, felt quite at home within the female bosom, praised "simple" nature, and liked thè softer side of Rousseau. Most of all he was a benevolist, a connoisseur of the social smile and the social tear. Conceited and selfish, he avidly sniffed the incense of gratitude. Like many people of his type, however, he was not wholly devoid of real kindness; one of the most irritating things about him was that it was impossible to call him a bad man.

He may have possessed enough insight to feel a little jealous of his strange amanuensis; but his sentimentalism was much too thin and trivial to permit any real understanding of Blake's huge illusions. In a way very characteristic of the period, his soft empiricism was mingled with hard empiricism.[204] He thought himself a man of reason as well as of feeling, was a close friend of Gibbon and an admirer of Voltaire. In the presence of any strong emotional commitment he became uneasy and cynical. Hence his attitude of "Genteel Ignorance and Polite Disapprobation" [205] toward Blake's poetry.

> The idiot Reasoner laughs at the Man of Imagination,
> And from laughter proceeds to murder by undervaluing calumny.[206]

We may be sure that such a critic would be assigned to the lowest circle of Blake's *Inferno*.

Blake's detestation of what he calls "Natural Religion" was of long standing,[207] but in the later Prophetic Writings it becomes acute. The term includes deism, but has wider implications which cover any sort of belief in the reality of the world of the senses and especially in "the Selfish Virtues of the Natural Heart." [208] By this time he is even more strongly

---

[202] Alexander Gilchrist, *The Life of William Blake,* p. 199.
[203] *Poetry and Prose,* p. 1076.
[204] For the interplay of these tendencies in the latter part of the eighteenth century see "empiricism" in the topical index of *Religious Trends,* II.
[205] *Poetry and Prose,* p. 1076. [206] *Ibid.,* p. 528. [207] *Vide supra,* p. 90.
[208] *Poetry and Prose,* p. 647.

opposed to Natural Religion than to Urizenic Christianity, that earlier form of spiritual oppression from which, he believes, Natural Religion descends.

In Natural Religion, as Percival admirably explains,

the goodness of the natural man has its counterpart in the goodness of nature. Blake sees neither one as good. The nature which Enion spun[209] is in his eyes feminine, outward, passive, self-righteous, chaste, and cruel. . . . As man turned passive and feminine and holy and found himself plagued with a sense of sin, he sought to recover his old complacency. He turned for moral support to a nature made in his own image. To it he could look as the source of the morality on which he prided himself. He could bolster up his failing faith with a belief in natural goodness. Self-righteous man worshipping a self-righteous nature—that is the curse under which man and nature suffer together.[210]

In this citation we should particularly observe the close relationship between Natural Religion and femaleness. Since the masculine principle is spirit and the feminine principle is matter, to worship nature is to worship "the Maternal Humanity, calling it Nature and Natural Religion." [211] Blake may well have been influenced by Hancarville's theory, promulgated in England by Richard Payne Knight, that the ancient myths should be interpreted as allegories of procreation.[212] Little help was needed, however, in reaching a conclusion which was implicit in his personal obsession. Those cruel feminine agents of false religion, Rahab, Tirzah, and the Daughters of Albion, are all manifestations of Vala; and Vala, in the fallen state, signifies the natural vegetative sexuality whose tyrannous demands drain away the creative energies of the artist-male. Her "soft tears and sighs" and her "lovely form . . . drew the body of man from heaven into this dark abyss." [213] She is "Nature, Mother of all," [214] and though Blake does not say so she is the "little curtain of flesh on the bed of our desire." [215]

But Percival's phrase, "self-righteous man worshipping a self-righteous nature," is also a perfect description of William Hayley. The good Hermit

---

[209] Enion is the emanation of Tharmas (Instinct—an evil thing when separated from the other Zoas). Nature is sometimes symbolized by a web which she has spun.

[210] M. O. Percival, *William Blake's Circle of Destiny*, p. 174.

[211] *Poetry and Prose*, p. 736.   [212] E. B. Hungerford, *Shores of Darkness*, p. 11.

[213] *Poetry and Prose*, p. 343.

[214] *Ibid.*, p. 614. Some of the drawings in the *Four Zoas* manuscript indicate that Blake thought of the cult of Vala in terms of phallus-worship.   [215] *Vide supra*, p. 90.

was a model of the "selfish virtues." To the extent that Blake is Los, Hayley is Satan in Palamabron's description:

> ... You know Satan's mildness and his self-imposition,
> Seeming a brother, being a tyrant, even thinking himself a brother
> While he is murdering the just.[216]

It has been suggested by Damon and others that Hayley appears in *Milton* and *Jerusalem* as Hyle, who with the other Sons of Albion persecutes Jerusalem in the interests of Natural Religion. Professor Pierce has observed, however, that Hyle is an allegorical character in Henry More's *Psychozoia,* and that the phrase "this hyle or matter" is used, always pejoratively, in *Commentaries on Proclus* and other works by Thomas Taylor.[217] My guess is that Blake, with his flair for occult correspondences, was struck by the resemblance between Hayley's name, pronounced cockney-wise, and a term for "base matter."

One might suppose that Blake's dislike of Hayley would act as a lightning rod, deflecting his wrath away from womanhood toward his masculine patron. On the contrary, his feelings about Hayley were absorbed by his sex-neurosis. Satan's ways are woman's ways. The combination of soft sensibility and anti-visionary hardness which he found in Hayley could easily be regarded as one more example of the curse of the female will. Here was Mrs. Mathew all over again. The paradox was explained in the epigram,

> Of H[ayley]'s birth this was the happy lot,
> His Mother on his Father him begot.[218]

At this time Blake's growing interest in redemption is causing him to emphasize ideals of unity, brotherhood, and mutual service. In *Songs of Innocence* and in *Thel* he had rather closely approached the cult of universal benevolence; but even in those works, and still more watchfully thereafter, he had distinguished between a merely naturalistic benevolism (much cultivated by women) and a benevolism related to his reinterpretation of Christianity. Since his Christianity was merely a reflection of his personal impulses, no such distinction actually existed. He strongly be-

---

[216] *Poetry and Prose*, p. 474.

[217] F. E. Pierce, "Blake and Thomas Taylor," *PMLA*, XLIII, 1127. Although Blake knew something about the Hermetic philosophy, Taylor would seem to be a likelier source than More.   [218] *Poetry and Prose*, p. 847.

lieved in its existence, however, and his sense of its momentousness was enhanced by his perception of the selfish hardness which lurked behind Hayley's social smiles and social tears. Hence in *The Four Zoas, Milton,* and *Jerusalem* Blake's hatred of *false* benevolism rather confusingly parallels his glorification of *true* benevolism. We cannot doubt that Hayley is the "idiot Questioner" who

> ...smiles with condescension, he talks of Benevolence and Virtue,
> And those who act with Benevolence and Virtue they murder time on time.
> These are the destroyers of Jerusalem, these are the murderers
> Of Jesus, who deny the Faith and mock at Eternal Life,
> Who pretend to Poetry that they may destroy Imagination
> By imitation of Nature's Images drawn from Remembrance.
> These are the Sexual Garments, the Abomination of Desolation,
> Hiding the Human Lineaments as with an Ark and Curtains
> Which Jesus rent and now shall wholly purge with fire
> Till Generation is swallow'd up in Regeneration.[219]

At Felpham Blake felt himself smothered in these feminine, natural, Hayleyan garments.[220] In rage and terror, like one of his Zoas, he tore himself free and escaped to London.

5

On October 23, 1804, Blake sent Hayley a letter[221] which one would give much to be able to interpret. The passage in question is long, but too important for paraphrase.

I have entirely reduced that spectrous fiend to his station, whose annoyance has been the ruin of my labours for the last passed twenty years of my life. He is the enemy of conjugal love and the Jupiter of the Greeks, an iron-hearted tyrant, the ruiner of ancient Greece. I speak with perfect confidence and certainty of the fact which has passed upon me. Nebuchadnezzar had seven times passed over him; I have had twenty; thank God I was not altogether a beast as he was; but I was a slave bound in a mill among beasts and devils; these beasts and these devils are now, together with myself, become children of light

---

[219] *Ibid.*, p. 547; see also p. 737.

[220] Other symbols of the same concept are the web, net, veil, tent, and polypus.

[221] After Blake's return to London, Hayley continued to obtain commissions for him. In several letters Blake addresses Hayley in the most friendly and grateful terms, meanwhile privately abusing him in epigrams. No hypocrisy was involved: the corporeal friend and the spiritual enemy were two quite different persons.

and liberty, and my feet and my wife's feet are free from fetters. O lovely Felpham, parent of Immortal Friendship, to thee I am eternally indebted for my three years' rest from perturbation and the strength I now enjoy. Suddenly, on the day after visiting the Truchsessian Gallery of pictures, I was again enlightened with the light I enjoyed in my youth, and which has for exactly twenty years been closed from me as by a door and by window-shutters.[222]

What may be inferred from these statements? For "exactly twenty years"—that is, since 1784, two years after his marriage—something personified as a "spectrous fiend" has interfered both with his art and with "conjugal love." "Suddenly" the spectre has vanished. Blake has emerged from "perturbation" into "strength." He is now tingling with creative energy, and he and his wife are "free." It would be rash to interpret this experience as the threshold of a new life. Blake's spirits rose and fell at intervals. As he wrote in a friend's album, he was "born 28 Novr 1757 in London and has died several times since." Barely three years after the illumination here described he jots down, "Tuesday, Janry. 20, 1807, between two and seven in the evening—Despair;" but on May 23, 1810, he "found the Word Golden." [223] At the time, however, he regarded the 1804 experience as deeply and joyously significant both for himself and for Catherine.

The "perturbation" which he mentions reminds us of the "melancholy" and "nervous fear" in his letters of 1800 to Cumberland and Flaxman respectively.[224] Readers who have accepted my interpretation of Blake's domestic predicament and its influence on his work may leap to the conclusion that the barrier between William and Catherine had at last been broken down. On the contrary, I believe that the cause of Blake's relief was a decision, sudden so far as his conscious thought was concerned but the result of gradual subconscious growth, to abandon the "torments of love and jealousy" and to attempt a complete sublimation of the sex impulse through religious devotion to his art. This conjecture is supported by the final stanzas of *My Spectre around me night and day,* a poem which seems to give a definitely autobiographical statement of the relations between spectre and emanation:

[222] *Poetry and Prose*, pp. 1108–1109. Count Truchsess, an émigré, was exhibiting his unremarkable collection of paintings in the hope that a syndicate would buy them as the foundation of a permanent gallery. Blake does not, I think, mean to suggest any causal connection between the pictures and his sudden enlightenment; he is merely establishing the definiteness of the experience by dating it.

[223] *Ibid.*, pp. 897, 890, 893.   [224] *Vide supra*, p. 101.

Till I turn from Female Love,
And root up the Infernal Grove,
I shall never worthy be
To step into Eternity.

And, to end thy cruel mocks,
Annihilate thee on the rocks,
And another form create
To be subservient to my Fate.

Let us agree to give up Love,
And root up the infernal grove;
Then shall we return and see
The worlds of happy Eternity.

And throughout all Eternity
I forgive you, you forgive me.
As our dear Redeemer said:
"This the Wine and this the Bread." [225]

In 1793 this solution, even if subconsciously desired, would probably have been suppressed. In 1804, when Blake had reached the age of forty-seven, it began to have some claim to practicability. How Catherine felt about it we do not know.

At all events Blake, full of confidence and intellectual vigor, now embarked on important undertakings in art and poetry. *Milton* and *Jerusalem* have already been drawn upon in our general discussion of Blake's myth; but in some respects both poems differ from *The Four Zoas*, and in some respects they differ from each other. *Milton* is the earlier of the two, although there were several years during which Blake gave intermittent attention to both works. The date on the engraved title page is 1804, but the poem was not completed until 1808.[226] Portions of it may well have been written at Felpham—certainly it arises from the spiritual stress of 1800–1803. For that reason it supplanted *The Four Zoas*, which was so firmly rooted in the Lambeth period that Blake gradually abandoned the idea of revising it into agreement with his changing ideas.

[225] *Poetry and Prose*, p. 106. Keynes dates this poem "about 1800–1803," but the suggestion of Druid sacrifices in "infernal grove" and the thought that forgiveness is the essence of Christ's gospel associate it with *Jerusalem*, which was begun in 1804. Even if *My Spectre* was written a little earlier it may point forward to Blake's decision.

[226] I waive the bibliographical question as to whether the author originally intended *Milton* to consist of twelve books or two. The two books which were issued in 1808 reach what is, for Blake, a fairly definite conclusion.

Hayley thought himself a great authority on Milton. In 1796 he had published a life of the poet defending him against Dr. Johnson's strictures. A rather advanced Whig, he had more sympathy with Milton's politics than the Tory critic. While Blake was with him, he was at work on an edition of Milton's poems. Blake could not wholly have disagreed with Hayley's views on Milton, but we may be sure that he would regard them as inadequate. Since childhood, when "Milton lov'd me . . . and show'd me his face," his feelings toward the great poet had mingled admiration and disapproval. On the surface, Milton had justified the ways of the Urizenic Jehovah and preached the cruelties of the moral law. Blake also resented his classicism—and classicism implied intellectual and moral as well as aesthetic restriction. Like Shakespeare, Milton had been "curbed by the general malady from the silly Greek and Latin slaves of the Sword." [227] Blake had debated the matter with Milton's spirit: "I tried to convince him he was wrong, but I could not succeed. . . . His tastes are pagan; his house is Palladian, not Gothic." [228]

Nevertheless Milton "was of the Devil's party without knowing it." This statement did not arise from mere eagerness to enlist a famous poet on the right side. Blake had a real insight into Milton because the two poets represented different stages in the same tradition of human self-sufficiency. Saurat calls Blake "a wild brother of Milton";[229] but perhaps "undisciplined grandchild" would more accurately express the historical relationship. Looking back at his ancestor through the eighteenth-century cult of original genius, Blake found in him a view of poetry which implied the omnipotence of imagination; and intertwined with this glorification of the poet-prophet he found the titanic puritan pride which would eventually place man upon the throne of God.

The story of *Milton* is extremely complex, but its fundamental ideas are easily stated. The poet-hero is the "Awakener" of Albion through the religion which is art. In order to redeem man, however, he must redeem himself, descending from Eternity into the world of generation to struggle with his spectre—Satan, "the Great Selfhood, . . . worshipped as God by the Mighty Ones of the Earth." [230] Like Jesus, from whose function in the poem his own is indistinguishable, he must take upon himself the

---

[227] *Poetry and Prose*, p. 464.

[228] Alexander Gilchrist, *Life of William Blake*, p. 335.

[229] Denis Saurat, *Blake and Milton*, p. 7. Saurat draws a more elaborate comparison between the two poets than can be undertaken here.

[230] *Poetry and Prose*, p. 612.

body of death in order that it may be cast off forever. He proclaims his purpose in the great speech:

> The Negation is the Spectre, the Reasoning Power in Man:
> This is a false Body, an Incrustation over my Immortal
> Spirit, a Selfhood which must be put off and annihilated alway.
> To cleanse the Face of my Spirit by Self-examination,
> To bathe in the Waters of Life, to wash off the Not Human,
> I come in Self-annihilation and the grandeur of Inspiration,
> To cast off Rational Demonstration by Faith in the Saviour,
> To cast off the rotten rags of Memory by Inspiration,
> To cast off Bacon, Locke, and Newton from Albion's covering,
> To take off his filthy garments and clothe him with Imagination,
> To cast aside from Poetry all that is not Inspiration.[231]

Thus the two elements of Milton's program are the destruction of "Rational Demonstration" through a belief in Christ which is identical with imagination, and the annihilation of selfhood. These aims are linked by the fact that the essence of selfhood is intellectual negation, "the Reasoning Power." Such ideas would be implicit in the decision which, if my conjecture is valid, Blake arrived at after his visit to the Truchsessian Gallery. He must learn to think and to feel impersonally, and in order to do so he must consecrate himself to some ideal which transcended his selfish concerns. Being what he was, he could find this ideal only in art. In these lines from *Jerusalem* he speaks not through Milton's lips, but in his own person:

> . . . I rest not from my great task!
> To open the Eternal Worlds, to open the immortal Eyes
> Of Man inwards into the Worlds of Thought, into Eternity
> Ever expanding in the Bosom of God, the Human Imagination.
> O Saviour pour upon me thy Spirit of meekness and love!
> Annihilate the Selfhood in me: be thou all my life! [232]

But here again the movement of Blake's thought is circular, caught fast in the trap of pride. Over and over he has committed himself to belief in a Saviour completely different from the one invoked in these lines. A meek Christ would be the "Antichrist, Creeping Jesus" of *The Everlasting Gospel:*

[231] *Ibid.*, p. 546. These lines are followed by an angry, personal-sounding condemnation, quoted *supra*, p. 116, of the "idiot Questioner" of the Hayley type.
[232] *Ibid.*, p. 554.

Was Jesus Humble? or did he
Give any proofs of Humility?

. . .

God wants not Man to Humble himself:
That is the trick of the ancient Elf.

. . .

Humility is only doubt,
And does the Sun and Moon blot out,
Rooting over with thorns and stems
The buried Soul and all its Gems.[233]

Jesus was imagination, and for Blake, who thought of art as a ceaseless struggle between mind and matter, a meek imagination was inconceivable.

The identity of true Christianity and art was one of Blake's earliest ideas, but from 1804 onward he places more and more reliance upon it. "I know of no other Christianity and of no other Gospel than the liberty both of body and mind to exercise the Divine Arts of Imagination, Imagination, the real and eternal World of which this vegetable Universe is but a faint Shadow." [234] Probably Blake would wish us to infer—though he never plainly says so—that mankind would be united in the perfect brotherhood of Eternity if every man used the universal imaginative energy with complete freedom. What this actually means, however, is that everybody must share the visions of William Blake. Those who do not—Rubens, Newton, Hayley—are simply the tools of Urizen. "I certainly do thank God that I am not like Reynolds. . . . Inspiration and Vision is my Element, my Eternal Dwelling place; how can I hear it contemned without returning scorn for scorn." [235] His ideal of universal brotherhood was pugnaciously solipsistic. In Milton's declaration of his aims, selfhood is associated entirely with "the Reasoning Power." It is evil because it is a thing of doubt and restriction. But the unbounded seifhood of imaginative expansion was always precious to Blake. For him, self-annihilation means transcendence of sensuous limitations for the sake of increased personal imaginative power. It is not the suppression of self, but the removal of all that hinders self. Blake desires to be released from selfhood through limitless expansion of his ego.

It is noteworthy that this poem, so intensely opposed to selfhood, is

[233] *Ibid.*, pp. 135, 138. *The Everlasting Gospel* was written about 1818, but it may be cited here to show the unbroken continuity of Blake's thought on this subject.
[234] *Ibid.*, p. 703.   [235] *Ibid.*, pp. 1004, 1011.

much less objective in tone than *The Four Zoas*. The earlier work stands entirely on its own mysterious legs. In *Milton* he frequently speaks in the first person, interpreting his symbols or exclaiming, "Mark well my words! they are of your eternal salvation." He is a part of his own myth: "I also entered into Satan's bosom and beheld its desolations." Milton appears in the garden of the Felpham cottage and on another occasion enters Blake's left foot.[236] Blake is almost certainly the Bard whose song in Eternity impels Milton to set forth upon his redemptive mission, and who does not seem to be lacking in selfhood:

> ...I am inspired! I know it is Truth! for I sing
> According to the inspiration of the Poetic Genius
> Who is the eternal all-protecting Divine Humanity.

The Bard enters into Milton's bosom and accompanies him on his pilgrimage.[237] The association of Blake with Los is also more explicit than in *The Four Zoas*.[238]

In *Milton* the mythological apparatus of the Zoas becomes largely irrelevant. The functions of Urizen are now performed by Satan; those of Los, by Milton. Nevertheless the old figures still remain and create a superabundance of overlapping symbols. Blake was always reluctant to discard any of his inspirations. This applies even more strongly to *Jerusalem*, where symbols relating to the Four Zoas are buried beneath symbols drawn from the Scriptures, from Druidism, from European history, and from contemporary England.

Jerusalem, like *Milton*, bears the date 1804 on its title page; but in the *Descriptive Catalogue* of 1809 it is listed as not yet engraved, and 1820 is the earliest possible date for the completion of the engraving. Although much revised during the process of composition it never became an ordered whole: it is a collection of episodes illustrating an allegorical theme.

Again like *Milton*, *Jerusalem* is rooted in Felpham. In this case, however, the stimulus was provided not by the shortcomings of Hayley but by the treason trial. Blake invested this incident with cosmic significance. It symbolized the cruelty of accusation and judgment between man and

---

[236] *Ibid.*, pp. 466, 491, 540.

[237] *Ibid.*, pp. 487, 488.

[238] *Ibid.*, pp. 503, 537, and especially 549, where Los, like Blake, moves angrily from Felpham to London.

man, and the necessity of forgiveness. Eight of the twelve wicked sons of Albion bear the names of men who were associated with the case.[239]

The main theme of the poem is the conflict between Natural Religion and the gospel of brotherhood, forgiveness, and creative imagination. Natural Religion is represented by the fallen Albion—a much more active character than in *The Four Zoas* or *Milton*—with his sons and daughters. The members of this unpleasant family are Druids.[240] It is noteworthy that although the poem is much concerned with man's inhumanity to man, the Sons of Albion are under feminine influence. They worship Vala, the sexual nature-goddess, and are usually the tools of their sisters. The Daughters of Albion are sub-symbols of the "double female" Rahab and Tirzah—respectively false Christianity and Natural Religion proper, both being manifestations of Vala in the world of generation. Nothing in *Jerusalem* suggests that Blake's views on woman underwent any radical change after his visit to the Truchsessian Gallery. He may have rooted up the infernal grove, but he still regards it as an evil.

The Jerusalem symbol is as old as *The Song of Los* (1795), but although she is frequently mentioned in *The Four Zoas* and in *Milton* her full significance first emerges in the poem which bears her name. She may be described as the sum total of everything which Blake wishes to rebuild "in England's green and pleasant land." Often she is called the emanation of Albion, as Satan is called his spectre; hence in relation to art she is perfect form, the opposite of Satan's complete indefiniteness. But since Jesus, like Albion, is Universal Man, she is also the bride and garment of Jesus. Of course she is also a city, the antithesis of Babylon, the abode of Vala. London, which is the Los-built city of Golgonooza in the generative world, is Jerusalem in Eternity. During the course of the poem she is oppressed, and to a considerable extent corrupted, by the minions of Natural Religion. Even in her fallen state, however, she believes in Jesus, longs for Him, and retains glimmerings of the gospel of forgiveness. At last she is awakened by the redeemed Albion and becomes the consummation of Blake's vision—that liberty of creative imagination which is true religion, true art, true love, true human life.

[239] Sloss and Wallis, II, 232–233. Coban may seem to be an exception, but the name is an anagram for Bacon—not only a philosopher whom Blake detested but a dishonest judge. The Sons and Daughters of Albion are mentioned in *Milton* but play a much more important part in *Jerusalem*.

[240] Sloss and Wallis, I, 440: "Druid symbolism is rare in the latest additions to *The Four Zoas* and in *Milton*: it is in *Jerusalem* that Blake develops the symbolical possibilities of its rites of human sacrifice in order to express the complete negation of forgiveness."

Two closely related ideas which appear in late additions to *The Four Zoas* and in *Milton* are greatly elaborated in *Jerusalem*. Blake expresses them in the statements, "Brotherhood is Religion," and "The Spirit of Jesus is continual forgiveness of sin." [241] Here one is tempted to say that such assertions show Blake's grasp of the essential spirit of Christianity. Brotherhood, however, demands the casting off of selfhood, and we have seen that self-annihilation, for Blake, really means self-expansion. Furthermore, the attainment of brotherhood depends on forgiveness, and Blake interprets this idea as meaning that there is nothing to forgive. Christianity demands that we forgive those who trespass against us and refrain from judging our fellows. If, however, there is no distinction between man and God, even Deity is denied the right to impute sin. In explaining his painting, *The Last Judgment*, Blake says:

We do not find any where that Satan is accused of Sin; he is only accused of Unbelief and thereby drawing man into Sin that he may accuse him. Such is the Last Judgment—a deliverance from Satan's accusation. Satan thinks that Sin is displeasing to God; he ought to know that nothing is displeasing to God but unbelief and eating of the Tree of Knowledge of Good and evil.[242]

Jesus, then, is "the Friend of Sinners" [243] in a peculiar sense: He is the destroyer of that Satanic imposture, the moral law. At the Judgment He will not forgive the actual trangressions of believing and repentant sinners: He will simply release them from the fallacy of supposing that they have sinned at all. The only sin is to assert the reality of sinfulness. Here Blake stands in a straight line of descent from seventeenth-century antinomian perversions of the Pauline "liberty of the children of God."

No one, of course, perceives the evils of the generative world more clearly than Blake or struggles more vigorously against them. In order to reconcile the gospel of forgiveness with the necessity of "mental fight" he draws a distinction between "States" and "Individuals." [244] Evil may be imputed to the former, but never to the latter. Thus the fallen Albion commits no sin: he merely enters the State called "Satan." This idea recalls the familiar precept that we should hate the sin but love the sinner. For Christianity, however, loving the sinner does not exclude, but rather demands, recognition of the fact that in the sight of God he *is* a sinner, like everyone else. The notion that no individual can be accounted a sin-

---

[241] *Poetry and Prose*, pp. 658, 550.   [242] *Ibid.*, p. 842.   [243] *Ibid.*, p. 550.
[244] The idea first appears in *Milton* but is more strongly emphasized in *Jerusalem*.

ner by man or God denies all moral responsibility. Blake's antinomianism, though now expressed in terms of love rather than in terms of rebellion, is no less rampant in *Jerusalem* than in *The Marriage of Heaven and Hell.*

6

The spurt of creative energy which followed Blake's return to London brought him, of course, no recognition as a poet but provided a fair amount of employment as an engraver and even some commissions for original works. Before long, however, the Circle of Destiny again turned downward. The trouble with Cromek convinced Blake that the Sons of Albion were at their evil task of suppressing good art. In a desperate attempt to appeal to the British public over the heads of his "enemies," he opened in 1809 a "one-man show" at the house of his brother James. The great "fresco" of *The Canterbury Pilgrims* was exhibited along with *The Last Judgment* and other "poetical and historical inventions," many of them beautiful with a strangeness very bewildering to the Urizenic mind. In his pugnaciously visionary *Descriptive Catalogue* he undertook to elucidate these works and to point out their beauties with a naive egotism which was perfectly sincere but which gave an impression of megalomania. The only result of the exhibition was to establish his reputation as a madman. The unpublished prose notes on art criticism and the wildly scurrilous epigrams against his spiritual foes in the later portion of the Rossetti Manuscript show how deeply he was shaken by this defeat.

So dark was the obscurity into which Blake now fell that almost nothing is known about his life between 1810 and 1818. A few colorless references by contemporaries, some drawings and engravings which can be dated— that is all. *Jerusalem,* on which he was intermittently engaged during these years, shows that he "kept the Divine Vision," but the circumstances of the struggle are hidden from us. From 1810 to his death, indeed, he lived almost unknown to the world; but in 1818, a man of sixty-one, he emerged from total darkness into a little patch of autumnal brightness warmed by the affectionate admiration of youth.[245] Most of the intimate details concerning Blake's character, manners, way of living, and domestic situation are drawn from this final period. The likeness is not untrustworthy, but

---

[245] The necessity for compression causes some foreshortening. In 1818 he met Linnell, who soon introduced him to John Varley. It was not until 1824 that, through Varley, he met and became the "Master" of Tatham, Palmer, Richmond, and the other young artists who constituted the "Ancients." He had then only three years to live.

it is the portrait of an ageing man painted largely by young disciples. To accept it as a delineation of Blake as he lived, say, between 1793 and 1804 would be rash. Crabb Robinson's memories of Blake, which pertain to the same period, are cooler than those recorded by the "Ancients." He could never quite make up his mind as to whether Blake was a hopeless madman or an inscrutable genius. But although his scepticism casts a few shadows on the composite portrait, it does not greatly darken it.

The picture, then, is that of a loving and lovable old man, fresh-minded and energetic, unconscious of poverty, perfectly true to himself, industrious and temperate, contented in his home and in his work. Never forcing his visions on others, he was patient and courteous to all who sincerely turned to him for enlightenment. Only to the mocker or the wilfully stupid did he speak rudely or extravagantly. He treated people of all ranks as his equals, preserving always a simple, unaffected dignity. His scanty purse opened readily, especially to struggling artists. The company of youths and children was dear to him. He seemed very happy—so happy that he had forgotten many things. To a little girl he said, "May God make this world to you, my child, as beautiful as it has been to me." [246]

William and Catherine had grown old together in the spirit of "I forgive you, you forgive me." Painful tensions had slackened, leaving deep affection and the sweetness of long comradeship maintained through darkness and storm. After so many years of patient loyalty her limitations seemed much less important than her steady goodness. In all but one matter she had always subjected herself to him, and the pain of that cosmic tragedy had grown faint. He had not transcended it: it had simply moved away from him down the years, leaving him with the illusion of spiritual victory. Catherine was no longer a daughter of Vala: he had redeemed her for Jerusalem. Talking with a young artist who complains of a lapse of inspiration, Blake turns to his wife: "It is just so with us, is it not, for weeks together, when the visions forsake us? What do we do then, Kate?" And Kate quietly answers, "We kneel down and pray, Mr. Blake." [247]

Although his health began to fail in 1824, Blake was blessedly capable of work almost to the end. From his deathbed Los gazed up at Enitharmon: "You have been an angel to me." He burst into snatches of visionary song, of which he told her, "My beloved! they are *not mine. No!* they are *not* mine!" One of the "Ancients" reports that he "died in a most

[246] Alexander Gilchrist, *The Life of William Blake,* p. 328.
[247] *Ibid.,* p. 317.

glorious manner. He said he was going to that country he had all his life wished to see, and expressed himself happy, hoping for salvation through Jesus Christ." [248] If these words were actually used by Blake they should be interpreted in the light of his personal conception of Christ and of salvation. Certainly he believed that he was entering the Eternity of genius and that the creations of his mind would live forever:

> For above Time's troubled Fountains
> On the Great Atlantic Mountains,
> In my Golden House on high,
> There they Shine Eternally.[249]

In a letter to Gilchrist, Samuel Palmer gives his impression of Blake in the last years: "He was a man without a mask; his aim single, his path straight-forward, and his wants few; so he was free, noble, and happy." [250] Such praise might be accorded one of the great saints. Had Blake undergone some profound spiritual change? Nothing in his work from 1818 onward supports that hypothesis. In *The Everlasting Gospel* (ca. 1818), as in earlier writings,

> The Vision of Christ that thou dost see
> Is my Vision's greatest Enemy.[251]

The inscriptions on the *Laocoön* engraving (ca. 1818) express his old theory that Christianity is art and *vice versa*. The *Job* engravings (1821–1825), a Prophetic Book in pictorial form, convey much the same message as *Jerusalem. The Ghost of Abel,* stereotyped in 1788 but not issued until 1822, may, as has already been suggested, have undergone changes before its final appearance.[252] The dedication to Byron, which of course is of 1822, draws the familiar contrast: "Nature has no Outline, but Imagination has. Nature has no Tune, but Imagination has. Nature has no Supernatural, and dissolves: Imagination is Eternity." [253] Here is the basis of his well-known distrust of Wordsworth's naturalism. Neither in this nor in any other respect do the conversations with Robinson add anything essential to what Blake had written time after time.

[248] *Ibid.,* p. 382.
[249] *Poetry and Prose,* p. 127. Observe the association of Eternity with the Atlantis of the speculative mythologists.
[250] Gilchrist, *op. cit.,* p. 317.   [251] *Poetry and Prose,* p. 133.
[252] *Vide supra,* p. 89.   [253] *Poetry and Prose,* p. 769.

There are indications, however, that during the final period of his life Blake's doctrinaire pugnacity gave place to a rather Quakerish sweetness. He became more easy-going and tolerant. His late-found serenity is to be ascribed, not to any new spiritual experience but to the fact that, time having solved his most disturbing problem, the relaxation of nervous tension permitted what he had always desired—complete devotion to art. The clue to his twilight happiness is revealed in an interview with Robinson:

He spoke with seeming complacency of himself—said he acted by command. The spirit said to him, "Blake, be an artist and nothing else." In this there is felicity. His eyes glistened while he spoke of the joy of devoting himself to divine art. "Art is inspiration. . . . I should be sorry if I had any earthly fame, for whatever natural glory a man has is so much detracted from his spiritual glory. I wish to do nothing for profit. I wish to live for art. I want nothing whatever. I am quite happy." [254]

In this passage, "art" pretty certainly means painting, draughtsmanship, and engraving—not poetry. Several of Blake's writings are lost to us. Some were destroyed by Tatham, who became a bigoted Irvingite; others have simply disappeared. Besides works whose titles have been preserved,[255] there are the "six or seven epic poems as long as Homer, and twenty tragedies as long as *Macbeth*" which he mentioned to Robinson; but these, as Damon says, "may have been written in Eternity, and never committed to any material medium." [256] In the last ten years of his life, at all events, Blake used the pen much less than the brush or crayon. Knowing that nobody would read him, he no longer incurred the expense of illuminated printing. In his work as an artist, on the other hand, a trickle of half-charitable commissions, combined with hackwork, provided the little money that he needed. This relatively complete abandonment of poetry, whether voluntary or involuntary, probably contributed to his happiness. The Eternals might provide him with words, but when he tried to transfer them to paper they fell so far short of the truth that they pulled him down to the delusive earth. The picture, however, was the Divine Vision itself, free from any necessity for conceptual thinking.

[254] Robinson's *Diary* in Arthur Symons, *William Blake*, p. 257.
[255] Barry, *The Book of Moonlight, For Children—The Gates of Hell, Vision of Genesis, Titian, The Book of Enoch. Outhoun* is probably an alternative title for *Visions of the Daughters of Albion*, whose heroine is Oothoon.
[256] S. F. Damon, *William Blake, His Philosophy and Symbols*, p. 245.

Thus without recanting any of his old ideas, he could now live in an atmosphere of blissfully undefined spirituality provided by line and color. Innocence had been regained at last.

Possibly Blake's consecration to the unattainable ideal of perfection in art gave him in the end some inkling of a transcendent Deity. The conjecture is beyond proof. He had always adored his own humanity on his knees, enjoying simultaneously the pleasures of pride and of awe. The incongruity of bowing before a God who was indistinguishable from himself never daunted one who believed, like Whitman, that "Whatever satisfies souls is true." It seems more likely, then, that to the end he worshipped, with a serener reverence than in earlier years, the Christ of his genius.

7

This chapter has attempted the impossible. Blake's religion so deeply permeates every line of his poetry that a thorough treatment of the subject would demand a long book.[257] There is some solace in the fact that even a much more elaborate discussion would fail to reconcile the radically divergent views which are held concerning this poet. In venturing to criticize the thought of Blake one lays oneself open to the retort that Urizen's slaves cannot hope to apprehend the truths of Eternity. "Blake," says Damon, "does not cry 'Procul, profani!' but he baffles all such by requiring that first they put on intellect. No swine can ever reach his pearls." [258] Such warnings are most discouraging.

Many readers will continue to side with those authorities who regard Blake as a great poet of Christianity. Damon grants his early Gnosticism but insists that "at heart, Blake was one of the great Christians," and that he "steadily became more and more passionate, even dogmatic, over the essentials of the Christian faith." [259] From what point of view "essentials" is used it would be hard to say. In relation to Catholic doctrine Blake is obviously an utter heretic, nor would his beliefs be acceptable to any Protestant in whose mind the outlines of Reformation theology had not completely faded. Those who call Blake a Christian must mean that he

---

[257] I must particularly have disappointed one friend who urged upon me the interesting but impracticable task of discussing Blake's illustrations in relation to his text. The omission is not, I think, completely destructive. In the engraved volumes an illustration will sometimes help to elucidate a particular passage; but Blake's poetry, taken as a whole, provides a sufficient basis for the study of his ideas.

[258] *Op. cit.*, p. x.   [259] *Ibid.*, p. xi.

has pierced through creeds and empty forms to "the essence and principle"[260] of the religion of Christ. But the "spirit" of Christianity, torn from its doctrinal setting, may mean anything that one happens to like, including denial of everything that Christians believe. Thus Miss Hamblen, who credits Blake with "profound insight into the Christian message,"[261] declares also that "Our century, happy above any other of the Christian era, has had three forerunners of Superman—Blake, Nietzsche, and Whitman. Urizen is beginning to shed tears"[262]—tears, one supposes, of pardonable bewilderment. The happy century referred to is the twentieth, which has seen much of Superman. For other students, the "very essence of Christianity" revealed by Blake is something quite different— "the doctrine of the love of all men."[263] Only a bigot could think of this doctrine as peculiarly Christian, although those who entertain the fallacy are prone to regard it as a prime antidote to bigotry. Love of neighbor becomes Christian when it arises from love of the Christian God. We have seen that because of Blake's humanization of God and deification of man his idea of brotherhood, despite its verbal supernaturalism, circles back to the naturalistic level. It would seem impossible to deny Professor White's statement: "The center of Blake's universe is man rather than God."[264] Similarly Mr. Schorer, whose personal beliefs seem to be antipodal to those of Miss White, finds that "his intuitions do not have a religious but an ethical content, do not deal with man's relationship to God but with man's relationship to his total being and to other men." Blake is "a religious poet who is without either a theology or a proper God; for the first he substituted a mythology, for the second, the image of Man."[265] And the image of Man, we may add, was none other than the image of William Blake. His religion can be called Christianity; but it is, in Mallock's phrase, "a new firm trading under the old name." Blake emphasized the imaginative and aesthetic side of religion at a time when such emphasis was greatly needed. Here as always, however, his lack of measure and balance vitiates what might otherwise be a valuable contribution. There is a sense in which the Christian religion is a great poem, but when Blake declares that he knows no other Christianity than liberty of creative imagination he is simply saying that he is not a Christian at all.

[260] Basil de Selincourt, *William Blake*, p. 145.
[261] Emily S. Hamblen, *On the Minor Prophecies of William Blake*, p. 25.
[262] *Ibid.*, p. 361.   [263] Pierre Berger, *William Blake, Poet and Mystic*, p. 196.
[264] Helen C. White, *The Mysticism of William Blake*, p. 185.
[265] Mark Schorer, *William Blake*, pp. 47, 97.

It may be urged that even if Blake was not a Christian he was something much more important—a great mystic. Undoubtedly Blake was what is loosely and popularly termed a mystical sort of person, but in a stricter sense he was not a true mystic. The mystic path leads inward, but it ends in the discovery of a divine outwardness. The object of Blake's contemplation, on the contrary, is the glory of his own mind, not of the godhead. He is incapable of surrender; we have seen that his rejection of selfhood is merely a way of obtaining boundlessness. He had no humility, and scorned it in others. Quite meaningless to him is the *purificatio* which must precede *illuminatio,* for he detested all intellectual and spiritual discipline. On their way to God, the great mystics are sometimes granted visionary experiences, symbolic adumbrations of the ineffable to refresh them in the steep ascent. But these are not the ultimate union: the final goal is an experience far beyond sight, far beyond words. For Blake, however, the visions are the be-all and end-all of the process. He comes back from Eternity bursting with images and words, but with no indication that he has found anything greater than William Blake.

> Nought loves another as itself,
> Nor venerates another so,
> Nor is it possible to Thought
> A greater than itself to know.[266]

The author of those lines was an occultist and a mystagogue, but hardly a genuine mystic.[267]

Berger suggests that Blake would wish to be remembered not primarily as a mystic, but rather as a prophet-poet whose words reveal spiritual truth to mankind.[268] In this rôle he has been highly esteemed. To Wicksteed, "Blake in his later works appears no longer merely as a brilliant and stimulating eccentric among men of genius, but as one of our great and serious English prophets," [269] and to Percival "it is obvious that Blake is one of those who have caught God's secret." [270] Apparently he also had the power of communicating the secret to others, for Damon says: "He tried to solve problems which concern us, and his answers to

---

[266] *Poetry and Prose,* p. 78.
[267] For corroboration of these unfashionable views, see Helen C. White, *The Mysticism of William Blake,* and Mark Schorer, *op. cit.,* pp. 50–92. Mr. Schorer dislikes mysticism as warmly as Miss White reveres it, but they unite in denying that Blake was a true mystic.
[268] *Op. cit.,* p. 60.   [269] J. H. Wicksteed, *Blake's Vision of the Book of Job,* p. 14.
[270] M. O. Percival, *William Blake's Circle of Destiny,* p. 4.

them are such as to place him among the greatest thinkers of several centuries." It is not enough that he should have been crowned as poet and painter: "The modern Trismegistus must receive his third crown, that of Philosopher, before his place among the great of this earth can be determined." [271]

Speaking for myself—it is all one can do in such a case—I see Blake as a man of rare spiritual gifts. He was a staunch enemy of all forces which, seeking to identify truth with the fruits of sense-perception, spell the death of religion. More clearly and passionately than any other person of his time, he saw that since the days of Bacon man's brain had been shaping a world that was not fit for man's spirit to live in. He proclaimed that the Urizenic "Philosophy of Five Senses" was leading mankind not toward perfection, but toward the enslavement of personality, the loss of all ideal values, and the downfall of civilization. Herein, as history has too abundantly proved, Blake was a genuine prophet.

But the failure of Blake's attempts to think and even to feel coherently on religious questions makes it difficult to crown him as a philosopher. He has a keen intuitive perception of the malady of the age, but no ability to formulate a remedy which will not prove to be a more insidious form of the disease. His ideas are thrown together with an irresponsibility which even the pantheistic scorn of differences will hardly serve to explain. He cries, "Everything that lives is holy," and condemns nature as a sinister illusion. Although he seems to deny all distinction between good and evil, he is a persistent and angry moralist, and yet a moralist whose chief ethical principle is the abrogation of the moral law. Apparently a pure idealist, he denies the reality of matter but often describes it as a genuine and necessary "contrary" of spirit. He is simultaneously a worshipper of the Christian Saviour and a pantheist. He asserts that the essence of the Gospel is forgiveness of sin, and denies that there are any sins to be forgiven. Reverently he raises his eyes to a God whom he believes to exist only in himself. Preaching the casting off of selfhood, he is, not only temperamentally but on principle, an egotist and a solipsist. A precursor of Nietzsche, he is all for loving-kindness and universal brotherhood—among those who see as he does. Although he assails the cult of feeling, he relies much more completely than the detested Rousseau upon the outgush of impulse. He is a foe of Natural Religion who has no conception of the supernatural. Apostle of the untrammeled libido, he abhors sex with a

[271] *Op. cit.*, pp. ix, xi.

frustrated loathing. This prophet of the Divine Vision can contemplate nothing with impersonal detachment. Completely at home in Eternity, he makes the cosmos the mirror of his neuroses. Despite some shifts of emphasis with the passing years, all of these elements coexist throughout his career in sufficient strength to render his thought a tangle of incongruities. It may be urged that they represent the tension between contraries which moves the Circle of Destiny, the creative struggle which leads to perfect synthesis. Only if this characteristically modern justification of chaos appeals to us can we say that Blake possessed a religious philosophy.

Blake's title to the crown of laurel is unimpeachable.[272] His best poetry cannot be spoiled even by the enthusiasm of his devotees. It is sad, however that his immense talents, which were certainly fostered by his religion, should also have been marred and eventually ruined by his religion. The unevenness of his writing is caused by the fact that, believing all of it to be inspired, he regarded self-criticism, no less than criticism by others, as a form of blasphemy. The worst was as good as the best. Still more destructive was Blake's increasing immersion in prophetic propaganda, combined with the perverse notion that the saving truths which he wished to convey should be shrouded in impenetrable mystery.

Berger and De Selincourt stress the conflict between Blake's poetry and his mysticism. "It was the problem of Blake's life," says the latter authority, "that he never realised the discrepancy between them. His aim was to make art—which traffics in truth as it may be traced in the appearance of things—a vehicle for the kind of truth which is not reached by considering appearances at all." [273] This conflict would have been even more harmful had Blake been one of those genuine mystics whose experience is supersensuous. It is true, however, that his theories imposed upon him a doctrinaire suspicion and scorn of that world in which, as a poet, he warmly delighted. In the margin of Wordsworth's 1805 *Poems* he wrote: "Natural objects always did and now [1826] do weaken, deaden, and obliterate Imagination in me. Wordsworth must know that what he

---

[272] The same applies to his status as artist, which I shall not attempt to discuss. His work in painting, draughtsmanship, and engraving probably excels his work in poetry. Both are adversely affected by factors which the text will explain; but the former, being exempt from the curse of making statements, is more resistant to these influences than the latter. In short his art is better than his poetry except when he tries too hard to make line and color perform what he conceives to be the function of poetry.

[273] Basil de Selincourt, *William Blake*, p. 271.

writes valuable is not to be found in Nature." [274] This may be the triumph of Jerusalem, but it is the death of poetry. Wishing to derive his materials solely from Eternity, he withdrew more and more into the fastnesses of his own confused mind, his own divided spirit.

The final paradox is that he simultaneously wishes, and does not wish, mankind to share his vision. He explains to Butts that "Allegory addressed to the Intellectual powers, while it is altogether hidden from the Corporeal Understanding, is my definition of the Most Sublime Poetry." [275] In refusing to communicate thought and feeling to the corporeal understanding this great genius refused to be a poet. The complete edition of Blake's works referred to throughout this chapter contains some 750 pages of verse; but all of it which gives genuine poetic delight could be compressed within less than a tenth of that space. The Prophetic Writings add much to our understanding of Blake, but little to our admiration of him as a poet. Unless one confuses the pride of having solved a puzzle with the pleasure of reading poetry, this applies even to the initiate who, with infinite labor, has disentangled the threads of the system. The not infrequent gleams of beauty are inadequate compensation. We are especially distressed when, in *Milton* and *Jerusalem*, he falsifies his own theory of the sublime by nervous attempts to explain his symbols, not in poetic images but in the language of conceptual thinking. *The Four Zoas*, in its dignified impenetrability, is aesthetically superior, but without the clues provided by the two later poems no one could read it with understanding. To explain the symbols is to fall from poetry into rhetoric; to leave them unexplained is to remain unintelligible. Upon the horns of this dilemma Blake was impaled. "There can be few instances," say Sloss and Wallis, "in which men, of genius comparable with Blake's, have as deliberately and completely stultified themselves." [276]

As our study develops we may come to see that Blake, in his extravagant and eccentric way, voices aspirations which are expressed more temperately by other romantic poets. Such a conclusion has already been suggested,[277] but we are not yet prepared to test its validity. A comparison between Blake and Burns, for which the materials are now on hand, may seem at first glance to be absurd, so obvious and so immense are the differences. Nevertheless the religions of the two poets are far from anti-

---

[274] *Poetry and Prose,* pp. 1024–1025.
[275] *Ibid.,* p. 1076. "Intellectual" of course is used in his special anti-intellectual sense.
[276] Sloss and Wallis, II, 114.   [277] *Vide supra,* p. 91.

thetical. Both Burns and Blake illustrate the decay of Nonconformity into a cult of human self-sufficiency. Both say "Christianity" and mean "inward impulse." Both rely upon energy and spurn moral restrictions. *The Jolly Beggars* breathes the same anarchic spirit as *The Marriage of Heaven and Hell*, and Urizen is the father of Holy Willie. The egotism of Blake's ideal of brotherhood is like the selfishness of Burns's benevolism.

The fact remains that Blake would certainly regard Burns as an earthbound slave of Natural Religion, while Burns would regard Blake as a crack-brained enthusiast. This divergence between two contemporaries who in some respects are so closely akin is partly a matter of temperament but also a matter of intellectual background. The Nonconformity inherited by Blake is steeped in influences which affected Burns hardly at all. The sources of Blake's poetry have been amply discussed by other scholars, but it might be well to list those which are either indisputable or highly probable:[278] the Bible, especially the prophetic and apocalyptic portions; the *Bhagavad-Gita,* known either in translation or through some such work as Sonnerat's *Voyage to the East Indies;* Gnosticism, probably through the hostile but full account in Mosheim's *Ecclesiastical History;* Plato and Neoplatonism, chiefly Plotinus, as edited and interpreted by Thomas Taylor; the *Kabalah,* probably through the *Kabbala Denudata* of Knorr von Rosenroth; Paracelsus; Boehme, as translated and interpreted by William Law; the Hermetic nature-mysticism; Milton; Bishop Berkeley; Swedenborg; Jacob Bryant, William Stukeley, and probably other members of the eighteenth-century school of esoteric mythologists.

As readers of my earlier volumes are aware, Neoplatonism, largely through Shaftesbury, exerted a considerable influence upon the eighteenth-century cult of sentiment. It was, however, so greatly diluted by rationalism, empirical common sense, and naturalism that Blake regarded Natural Religion as an enemy rather than as a friend in disguise. He adhered instead to a purer form of the "mystical" tradition which had never wholly disappeared and which, as a result of the decay of rationalism, even enjoyed a sort of revival toward the close of the eighteenth century. These were the days of Joanna Southcott and Richard Brothers. Cosway, a miniature painter of the period, "kept a house for the practice and study of magic, and left behind him a considerable bundle of magic formu-

[278] Many other suggestions have been offered, but I believe that none of them would provide Blake with ideas which he might not more probably have drawn from one or more of the sources mentioned here. His background in mystical and occult literature was doubtless richer than this list would indicate, but specific evidence is lacking.

lae." [279] Were artists particularly liable to such vagaries? The astrology of John Varley is a case in point. Thomas Holcroft was told by an engraver named Sharp, a disciple of Brothers, that he "had been absolutely favored with a revelation, communicating to him personally, beyond all doubt, the revelations that are immediately to happen." There are to be revolutions and earthquakes, "and those who do not take up arms against their fellow men, are to meet at the Grand Millennium." [280] Our poet's personal environment abounded in such notions. Saurat declares that "the more we study Blake, the more persuaded we become that there was not one absurdity in Europe at the end of the eighteenth century that Blake did not know." [281]

It is natural that the visions of Swedenborg should have been attractive not only to sensitive artists but to sober Nonconformists like Blake's father. Although they were doubtless unconscious of the fact, the Dissenters possessed an inheritance which prepared them to receive the message. On the learned and indirectly on the popular level, Protestantism of the sixteenth and seventeenth centuries had been considerably influenced by the Plato of the *Timaeus* and by Neoplatonism. Especially among the more violently antinomian sects, but also among cultivated puritans like Milton, the ideas of Boehme and other "mystics" were at work. Blake's reading was part of a great ancient and medieval stream of thought which contributes to Protestantism elements too strong to be curbed by formal Reformation theology: personal and immediate revelation; pantheistic union of God, man, and nature in the dispensation of an all-pervading Holy Spirit which is identified with the Inner Light; an individualistic kind of brotherly love; antinomian freedom; the creative power of the elect; the implicit divinization of man. If we add the heritage of religious psychology to literary sources in the strict sense, Blake was the heir of Dionysius the Areopagite, John Scotus Erigena, Waldensians and Albigensians, medieval pantheistic mystics like Richard Rolle, the Brothers and Sisters of the New Spirit, the Friends of God, Eckhart, Tauler, Suso, the unknown author of *Theologia Germanica,* Wyclif, the Lollards, the Anabaptists, Familists and Seekers and Ranters and Levellers. Through Swedenborg, he was also the heir of German Pietism. Blake was one of a few men who received this inheritance in a form relatively untouched by the eighteenth-century compromise. He used it as a weapon against what

---

[279] Damon, *op. cit.,* p. 305.   [280] *Life of Thomas Holcroft,* II, 246.
[281] Denis Saurat, *Blake and Modern Thought,* p. 59.

he regarded as an unbelieving age. He did not realize that the cult of sentiment, having absorbed these quasi-mystical tendencies and harmonized them with the Bacon-Newton-Locke tradition, was more quietly performing precisely his own task—"the shifting of creative power from God to man." [282]

If Blake was an occultist who did not know that he was also a sentimentalist, Burns was a sentimentalist who did not know that he owed anything to the pseudo-mystical tradition. His philosophers were not Plotinus and Boehme, but Adam Smith and Dugald Stewart. To these he much prefers Henry Mackenzie, the perfect illustration of Blake's "polypus of soft affections." In reading *The Theory of Moral Sentiments,* Burns may have noticed that Smith traces Hutcheson's benevolism back to the Neoplatonists,[283] but such historical subtleties were quite beyond him. Probably he knew little or nothing about the Neoplatonic and Cabalistic roots of his Freemasonry. His intellectual background merely represents the collapse of Scottish Calvinism into latitudinarianism, and of latitudinarianism into sentimentalism. Historically and psychologically, his belief in natural impulse and Blake's belief in free imagination are first cousins, but neither poet would recognize the kinship.

These considerations may help to explain the externally antagonistic, fundamentally sympathetic relationship between the beliefs of Blake and of Burns. They may also prove useful as our study moves onward. Blake feared that Wordsworth was an atheist and Wordsworth regarded Blake as an interesting madman, but they had more in common than they knew.

[282] *Ibid.,* p. ix. [283] *Vide supra,* p. 28.

Chapter IV

WORDSWORTH

I

WHEN YOUNG WILLIAM WORDSWORTH ENTERED THE HAWKSHEAD GRAMMAR
School after his mother's death in 1778, he had received the elementary
religious training of an eighteenth-century Anglican child. John Wordsworth, in this as in other respects too busy to make much impression upon
his children, entrusted such matters to his wife. The poet's recollections
of his mother, "lost too early for the frequent tear," preserve only a few
details of her piety. As was customary in the rather old-fashioned Cocker-
mouth parish, she sent him off to Lenten catechism with a nosegay of her
own plucking.[1] When he told her that he had gone to church to see a
woman doing public penance in a white sheet, she expressed the hope that
he would always remember the lesson; but when he added that he had
gone merely in the mistaken expectation of receiving a penny for his
devout curiosity, she said that he deserved to be disappointed.[2] In *The
Prelude* such memories find no place: not until the period of *Ecclesiastical
Sonnets* did Wordsworth remember that he had begun his life as a High
Churchman. But Mrs. Wordsworth was "high" merely in the same sense
as her brother, the Reverend William Cookson, fellow of St. John's, Rector
of Forncett, and from 1791 a canon of Windsor. In a negative way he was
politically and ecclesiastically conservative, but he was hardly a precursor
of the Tractarians. There is no evidence that the boy had any contact with
those obscure stirrings of revived Anglo-Catholicism which had begun to
manifest themselves at about the time of his birth. In *The Prelude* he
honors his mother not for her orthodoxy but for having been a benign,
unworried woman with enough faith in his "innocent instincts" to let
him grow up without fussy interference.[3] Her guidance was too mild and

---

[1] *Poetical Works* (one-volume Oxford Edition, 1942), p. 465. Cited hereafter as *Oxford*.
[2] Edith C. Batho, *The Later Wordsworth*, p. 249.
[3] *The Prelude* (ed. Ernest de Selincourt, Oxford, 1926), V, 256–290. Cited hereafter as
Prelude. Throughout this chapter I use the original version unless I indicate an exception.

too soon cut short by death to have influenced the little boy very deeply.

At Hawkshead he had plenty of freedom and he revelled in it. "In sun and shower" he grew up wilful, moody, and hot-tempered, deriving from nature, unlike Lucy, a great deal of "impulse" and very little "law." Though not unsociable and not meanly selfish he was quick to resist whatever threatened to curb his self-expansion. Herein the child was father of the man. De Quincey reports that Wordsworth's great desire was "freedom—unlimited, careless, insolent freedom"; [4] and the less malicious Aubrey de Vere, observing the poet much later, says that

It was very necessary for him to do what he pleased; and one of his dearest friends [Miss Fenwick] said to me, with a smile of the most affectionate humour: "He wrote his 'Ode to Duty,' and then he had done with that matter." [5]

The uncurbed boy was happy—rather too happy for his future welfare. Everything conspired to make him believe that man and his environment were good, beautiful, and favorable to William Wordsworth. He was conditioned toward sentimentalism before he had any conscious understanding of the eighteenth-century heritage which would help him to rationalize his intuitive belief in himself as the centre of a beneficent universe. When in later years this faith was shaken by experience he too readily assumed that the remedy lay in preserving the scenes, feelings, types of character, and ways of life which he had known in those

> ... summer days, when we were young;
> Sweet childish days, that were as long
> As twenty days are now. [6]

Not to feel precisely as he had felt in childhood became, despite all his talk about philosophic recompense, the great tragedy of his life; and his preoccupation with his psychological development was less a study of growth than a means of returning to Hawkshead along the path of natural piety.

The Hawkshead Grammar School was a Church of England foundation under a clerical headmaster and many of the students were destined for the cloth, but Wordsworth tells us nothing about the religious side

---

[4] Thomas de Quincey, *Collected Writings*, II, 263.
[5] Aubrey de Vere, *Essays Chiefly on Poetry*, II, 294.   [6] *Oxford*, p. 106.

of the regimen. He remembers Dame Tyson, with her "clear though shallow stream of piety," dozing over her Bible on hot Sunday afternoons or marching off to church in her finery;[7] but although he admired the "gracious look" of the big white church on the hill,[8] he does not tell us that he ever accompanied the good woman. The simple piety of the dalesmen, nostalgically recalled in conservative days as an important element in their lives, did not impress him at this time.

To what extent was the development of his thought furthered by personal influences? Vainly we wonder how far Matthew and the Wanderer are the creations of the mature Wordsworth, and how far Wordsworth himself is the creation of their respective prototypes, William Taylor the schoolmaster and Drummond the pedlar. What of that "honored teacher" who "loved the poets," and upon whose tombstone, at his own wish, was incised "A fragment from the Elegy of Gray"?[9] Wordsworth's juvenile verse shows that he was saturated in the poetry of eighteenth-century sentimentalism by the time he entered Cambridge.

Unless *Matthew* and *The Two April Mornings* completely transform Taylor in describing him as "Nature's favorite child," who never goes astray in following the dictates of his heart, we may imagine that he was one of those broad, soft clerics who liked to talk to boys about benevolence, the harmony of things, and "Nature and Nature's God." Probably the more formal side of the religion of the school is represented by the lines which fourteen-year-old William wrote for the bicentenary of its foundation. The spirit of Industry explains to the rapt youth that Archbishop Sandys' generosity is an instance of the enlightenment produced by the Reformation, when

> Science with joy saw Superstition fly
> Before the lustre of Religion's eye,

and the philosophy of Bacon banished the "mazy rules" of "jarring monks." Thanks to this benign intellectual revolution, the Hawkshead students "follow Nature to her secret springs" and are guided in "the sacred paths of moral truth." But in perusing the book of human behavior they should

> Join to the rigours of the sires of Rome
> The gentler manners of the private dome;

---

[7] *Prelude*, IV, 207–221.   [8] *Ibid.*, 13–15.   [9] *Ibid.*, X, 490, 500, 511.

When Virtue weeps in agony of woe,
Teach from the heart the tender tear to flow.[10]

This latitudinarian Protestantism—Baconian, Newtonian, softly Stoical, benevolistic—is what the schoolboy Wordsworth would call the Christian religion. Readers of my first two volumes will recognize it as the soil from which the religion of sentiment most readily grows.

In seeking to draw factual information about the boy Wordsworth from *Prelude* I and II, the autobiographical portions of the *Recluse* fragment, and the account of the Wanderer's childhood in *The Excursion,* we must make some allowance for the mature poet's natural tendency to impose a good deal of his present upon his past. On the whole, however, Wordsworth makes an honest and successful effort to distinguish between the actual feelings of his boyhood and his later realization of their significance. There is no reason to doubt that in his schooldays his organic sensibility was exceptionally intense and that he responded to external nature not only sensuously, but emotionally and imaginatively, at an unusually early age.

The "stolen boat" scene in *Prelude* I and the conclusion of *Nutting* are the most striking of several passages which suggest that the boy Wordsworth sometimes regarded "the souls of lonely places" and the "Spirit in the woods" with the dread of a savage. His animism, however, has been taken rather too seriously. The gift of concentrated observation enabled him to be scared by particular mountains and trees, but it seems unlikely that the lad who had absorbed the lingo of sentimental latitudinarianism at the age of fourteen consciously entertained any animistic notions. Under the influence of classical and pseudoclassical poetry he might fancifully assign separate spirits to separate objects. Almost as soon as he could think about such matters at all, however, he must have learned that "All are but parts of one stupendous whole."

The fear aroused in him by the "presences of Nature" held less of reverence than of rebellious pride:

Deep pools, tall trees, black chasms, and dizzy crags,
And tottering towers: I loved to stand and read
Their looks forbidding, read and disobey,
Sometimes in act and evermore in thought.[11]

---

[10] *Oxford,* pp. 618–619.
[11] *The Recluse,* p. 47.

So strong was his sense of organic union with non-human nature that the dark power of the universe made him feel powerful rather than weak. Solitary—surely he speaks for the poet here—says that in youth it is a joy "To have a body . . ./And to the elements surrender it/As if it were a spirit." But this surrender is a triumph, for he soon adds that it is "a joy to roam/An equal among mightiest energies." [12]

Wordsworth's adolescence, which began probably in 1785, brought with it deeper, tenderer, more inwardly agitated feelings. He came to love nature for her own sake and not merely as the setting for his "glad animal movements." In particularly meaningful "spots of time" he felt what he was later to call "the visionary power." Then, he seems to remember,

> . . . such a holy calm
> Did overspread my soul, that I forgot
> That I had bodily eyes, and what I saw
> Appeared like something in myself, a dream,
> A prospect in my mind.[13]

In such moments, absorbed concentration of the senses on the object, attended by very strong emotion, induced something like a self-hypnotic trance in which the object itself faded out, leaving only the feelings which had colored the observation and a melting, interfusing blur of after-images. In 1840 the poet told the Reverend R. P. Graves

that, at a particular time of his mental progress, he used to be frequently so rapt into an unreal transcendental world of ideas that the external world seemed no longer to exist in relation to him, and he had to convince himself of its existence by *clasping a tree* or something that happened to be near him.[14]

Here is the basis of what has often been called Wordsworth's "mysticism." To debate the applicability of the ambiguous term is less important than to observe that in these experiences his mental state was not supersensuous, but so very sensuous that the senses, like those of Keats before the Elgin Marbles, failed to respond to the abnormal demands which had been made upon them. Nor did the schoolboy lose his little ego in a

---

[12] *Excursion*, IV, 508–532. Compare the skating scene in *Prelude* I, especially line 479, "When we had given our bodies to the wind."

[13] *Prelude*, II, 330, 367–371. But for the most explicit account of the "spots of time," too long for quotation here, see XI, 258ff.

[14] Christopher Wordsworth, *Memoirs of William Wordsworth*, II, 480. Italics in quotations are never mine unless I indicate the contrary.

reality greater than he: on the contrary, the outlines of the scene were lost in the glory of the visionary power and "Appeared like something in myself." How and why this happened he did not know, and the mystery doubtless gave him a feeling of quasi-religious awe which may be described as "mystical" by those who like to use the word very broadly and loosely. In any case, identification of his own creativity with that of "the one great Mind"—the logical extreme of romantic self-expansion—still lay in the future.

But adolescence also brought with it the claims of a world which was recalcitrant to the visionary power, a world for which the freedom of Hawkshead had not prepared him. He began to realize that in losing even a rather indifferent father he had lost a home.[15] The future seemed to forbid any permanent reunion with Dorothy. There was little hope that the Earl of Lonsdale could be made to disgorge the £4,700 which he owed to the otherwise almost non-existent Wordsworth estate. The uncongenial uncles regarded William no longer as a child but as a young man who must soon begin to support himself. The spoiled fledgling was very loth to leave the nest. From now on he would increasingly wish to enjoy liberty not on the open stormswept moors of life, but within some firm protective haven of peace and security.

Hence the affected and imitative melancholy of such adolescent effusions as *The Vale of Esthwaite* is mingled with genuine regret

> ... that full soon I must resign
> To delve in Mammon's joyless mine.[16]

His mature poetry shakes off this mawkish moping but not the retrospective longings which were associated with it. In the only portion of *The Vale of Esthwaite* published during his lifetime he has already begun to forge the chain of natural piety:

> Dear native regions, I foretell,
> From what I feel at this farewell,
> That, whereso'er my steps may tend,
> And whenso'er my course shall end,
> If in that hour a single tie

---

[15] *The Poetical Works of William Wordsworth* (edd. Ernest de Selincourt and Helen Darbyshire), I, 280. This edition will hereafter be cited as *Works*. I use it chiefly for poems not included in the one-volume *Oxford* and for bibliographical information.
[16] *Ibid.*, p. 282.

Survive of local sympathy,
My soul will cast the backward view,
The longing look alone on you.[17]

It was not David Hartley who first taught him to attach preeminent value
to early impressions. He began to yearn toward childhood before he became an adult.

In 1787 Dorothy informs Jane Pollard that William wishes to become
a lawyer "if his health will permit, but he is troubled with violent headaches and a pain in his side."[18] We are to hear much more of these and
similar symptoms. But even apart from the question of health, family
connections made the Church a more practical solution; and by March,
1790, she seems to assume, rather anxiously and uneasily, that he will
take Orders.[19] She doubtless sensed that her brother had no settled plan
for the future and did not want to have one.[20] When he entered Cambridge, however, he was probably not disposed to rebel against his Uncle
Cookson's wishes. The youth had no spiritual vocation, but how many
eighteenth-century parsons did? Only an Evangelical enthusiast would
have regarded him as anything but a sound Anglican. There was no reason why he should not become a nature-loving, Christian-sentimentalist,
versifying clergyman like the Reverend John Langhorne, whose poems
he was always to admire.

2

Looking back upon his college days in *The Prelude,* Wordsworth seems
uncertain as to whether they constituted a period of advance or of dete-
rioration. A gain in the creative as opposed to the merely receptive side
of his dealings with the world about him was almost, but never completely, submerged by the frivolities of student life. During the summer
vacation of 1788 the old joy returned with a more "Wide-spreading,
steady, calm, contemplative" quality than before, and with a new "hu-
man-heartedness."[21] This happy sojourn provided what De Selincourt
refers to as "that unforgettable experience when at sunrise, on the moors

---

[17] *Oxford,* p. 1.
[18] *The Early Letters of William and Dorothy Wordsworth* (ed. Ernest de Selincourt), p.
7. Cited hereafter as *Early Letters.*   [19] *Ibid.,* p. 28.
[20] *Prelude,* VI, 29–48. But see also the 1850 text, which is even more explicit on this
point.   [21] *Ibid.,* IV, 131, 225.

above Hawkshead, he had vowed his life to poetry." [22] But as a glance at the passage will show, Wordsworth "made no vows" at this time: it is merely in *remembering* this leaping up of the heart that he believes

> ...vows
> Were then made for me, bond unknown to me
> Was given, that I should be, else sinning greatly,
> A dedicated Spirit.

This experience occurred after an all-night dance, with "Slight shocks of young love-liking interspersed." [23] Wordsworth was still an adolescent. Despite such moments of elevation, on the whole "There was an inner falling-off" [24]—too much of the college boy preening his sophisticated plumage among the rustics.

On returning to Cambridge, however, he "settled . . . into habits/More promising" [25] than those of his freshman year. He even derived emotional satisfaction from geometry—not as a means of self-discipline through devotion to objective truth, but as a demonstration of the godlike functions of the human intellect. He never studied the subject hard or deeply, but merely to think about it gave him a feeling of "paramount endowment in the mind" and opened up the possibility of shaping "an independent world" without grappling with objects of sense-perception.

> ...Mighty is the charm
> Of those abstractions to a mind beset
> With images, and haunted by itself.[26]

Wordsworth loved images, but sometimes their distinctness resisted his desire for interfusion.

As the poet told De Quincey in 1804, "The manners of the young men were very frantic and dissolute at that time"; [27] but there is no reason to doubt the usual assumption that the libations to Milton represent Wordsworth at his most frantic. Evidence as to his religious opinions is lacking. When he graduated he must have signed the statement: "I, William Wordsworth, do declare that I am *bona fide* a member of the Church of England as by law established." [28] With the probable exception of a brief

[22] Ernest de Selincourt, *Dorothy Wordsworth*, p. 21.
[23] *Prelude*, IV, 316–345—the whole passage in question. [24] *Ibid.*, 278.
[25] *Ibid.*, VI, 22–25. [26] *Ibid.*, 135–142, 178–187. [27] *Early Letters*, p. 369.
[28] D. A. Winstanley, *Unreformed Cambridge*, p. 313.

period which will be discussed later, there was never a time when so roomy a formula would have violated his conscience. Curiosity is piqued, however, by a discarded *Prelude* passage which hints at

> A less devout observance, visits paid
> Remissly, at chance seasons, to a friend
> Unsettled in the heart by cozenage
> Of new affections.[29]

Most Cambridge students were too indifferent to question the creed which they parroted; but this was probably not true of William Godwin's sole pupil, who like Wordsworth entered St. John's in 1787.[30] Although it would be gratuitous to suppose that this youth was the friend alluded to, his presence at Cambridge suggests that strong meat was available to any babes who chose to seek it. These "new affections" doubtless pertained to politics as well as to religion. In 1793, St. John's and Trinity were regarded as hotbeds of Jacobinism,[31] and the liberal trend which was so strong in England during the 1780's must have influenced the minds of many undergraduates in Wordsworth's student days.

But although his beliefs may well have shifted a little to the left at this time, they probably did not stray far. The official religion of Cambridge was too flat and colorless to stimulate much opposition. It was a clear, dry, shallow, unimaginative latitudinarianism rooted in Boyle, Newton, Locke, Clarke, Butler, and Paley—essentially the religion of the Hawkshead School in a more scholastic, less tender-minded form. From this centre individual minds could move in a more radical direction. In the late 1760's and the 1770's several prominent dons had supported the campaign headed by Archdeacon Blackburne to relieve clergymen from subscribing to the Thirty-nine Articles and had agitated to obtain the same privilege for students of the university. By the time Wordsworth entered, the close association of the anti-subscription cause with Unitarianism had led even the more liberal members of the faculty to fall back to a position of compromise.[32] There were exceptions, however. In 1788 the Reverend William Frend, fellow and tutor of Jesus College and a veteran of the subscription controversy, openly espoused Unitarianism, tried to convert the university, and was deprived of his tutorship. Many undergraduates and some dons

---

[29] *Prelude*, p. 81*n*.   [30] F. K. Brown, *The Life of William Godwin*, p. 22.
[31] E. Halévy, *A History of the English People in 1815*, p. 477.
[32] Winstanley, *op. cit.*, pp. 301–315.

sympathized with him. Wordsworth says nothing about these commotions, but he could not have been wholly untouched by them.

Whatever emotional quality the religion of Cambridge possessed was centered in the Newtonian reverence for the Great Artificer as revealed through the laws of nature. Wordsworth was already prepared to accept this type of devotion. The softer latitudinarianism which, blending Newton with Shaftesbury, emphasized moral sense, benevolism, retired contemplation, and sentimental deism in general, received little official encouragement; but it would surely be rife in any group of youngsters who had read plenty of preromantic verse. To judge from *An Evening Walk*, Wordsworth himself leaned in this direction.

Evangelicalism was a foreign body in the university—active, increasingly influential, but alien to the nature of the organism. From the pulpit of Trinity Church, Charles Simeon hammered away at a congregation consisting mainly of townsfolk and farmers but with a fair sprinkling of earnest, unattractive undergraduates. Isaac Milner held Newton's old chair and the presidency of Queen's. But a Christianity based on the need of redemption from sin held no message for one who had never dreamed of so enthusiastic a notion.

Wordsworth is honest and right in shouldering almost the whole burden of blame for neglecting his studies. As the example of his brother Christopher shows, he could have obtained an excellent education if he had wanted one. Cambridge was torpid and corrupt; but it was in much better condition than Oxford, and especially at William's college some wholesome reforms had been instituted.[33] St. John's had only recently been outstripped by Trinity in size, and it stood even with its rival in scholastic eminence.[34] Probably, indeed, *The Prelude* gives Cambridge somewhat less than full credit for its contribution to Wordsworth's intellectual development. He could hardly have obtained his B.A. without hearing something about Plato, Aristotle, Bacon, Newton, Locke, Shaftesbury, Clarke, Berkeley, Hume, Butler, Hartley, and Paley. The implications for "the growth of a poet's mind" are important. Wordsworth learned too little at Cambridge, but Coleridge was not the first man who had ever mentioned philosophy in his presence.

An Evening Walk, the only substantial poem of the Cambridge period, is a mournfully descriptive-reflective "region poem"[35] which shows that

---

[33] *Ibid.*, pp. 299ff.   [34] *Ibid.*, p. 185.
[35] R. A. Aubin, *Topographical Poetry in Eighteenth-Century England,* pp. 365–369.

the youth has too faithfully been reading Lady Winchilsea, Thomson, Young, Akenside, Gray, Beattie, Burns, Cowper, and Darwin. Dr. Meyer, however, has cogently urged that the poem is more genuinely related to Wordsworth's personal circumstances than its derivative affectations would indicate.[36] With this help we see that the young poet, as in the closely related *Vale of Esthwaite,* seriously laments the loss of those "Delights with whom my road begun," and hopes that he and Dorothy, reunited in a rural cottage, may some day regain them.[37]

The continental walking tour of the summer of 1790 is impossible to interpret with any hope of accuracy. *Descriptive Sketches* inextricably mingles thoughts and feelings of this vacation with thoughts and feelings of 1791 and 1792, when most of the poem was written. The account of the tour in *Prelude* VI adds other layers to the palimpsest. One gathers that he is still melancholy in a half-histrionic, half-genuine way, still longing for a cottage with Dorothy, and still a hazy believer in "Nature's God," but that his boyish approval of the French Revolution will soon mature into a deeper feeling.

Since the months spent in London, in Wales and at Forncett just after his graduation are also unrewarding for us, let us follow him as he recrosses the Channel in November, 1791, and watch his revolutionary enthusiasm burgeon under the influence of Michel Beaupuy. Not that Wordsworth's mind was passively moulded by his new friend: he already possessed much of the gospel which was preached to him. Beaupuy is set before us not as a materialistic *philosophe,* but as a sort of revolutionary Franciscan. His humility was that of a saint. Of noble birth, he loved and served all men, but especially the poor, as if he had taken the vows of some religious order. He believed in the rights of man as a child believes in a fairy tale. His seeming vanity was really "fondness, and a kind of radiant joy" in doing "works of love or freedom."[38] Such a man would not be an atheist or a devotee of the Goddess of Reason. The Supreme Being he would doubtless reverence, but less as a remote First Cause than as a personification of the naturally good impulses of man. He was a follower of Rousseau in everything that set his master apart from Helvétius and Holbach. A native of a country in which both Catholics and Protestants held definite notions about the meaning of Christianity, Beaupuy would probably have called himself a deist; English and Anglican Wordsworth,

[36] G. W. Meyer, *Wordsworth's Formative Years,* pp. 39–49.
[37] *Works,* I, 4–5, 37–38.   [38] *Prelude,* IX, 293ff.

holding much the same beliefs, could continue to call himself a Christian. Even at the height of his revolutionary ardor he was never a bigoted doctrinaire. After all, he was the lover of a Royalist girl. "In spite of those heart-bracing colloquies" with Beaupuy he often luxuriated in visions of the glamorous past of the Loire valley, gazing at old castles and even at old convents "with chivalrous delight." [39]

On the whole, however, dreaming forward was more delightful than dreaming backward. When Beaupuy pointed to a "hunger-bitten girl" and said,

> ... " 'Tis against *that*
> Which we are fighting," I with him believed
> Devoutly that a spirit was abroad
> Which could not be withstood.[40]

Of practical measures for cooperating with this stream of tendency we hear almost nothing. The "spirit" was simply the "noble nature" of man "as it is/ The gift of God and lies in his own power." Events were reopening "the natural inlets of just sentiment," [41] and when oppressive institutions had been swept away "the Godhead which is ours" would be free to do its beneficent work. It "was as an instinct" to believe

> That man was only weak through his mistrust
> And want of hope, where evidence divine
> Proclaimed to him that hope should be most sure.[42]

Such phrases as "gift of God" and "evidence divine" perhaps belong rather to 1804, when Books IX and X of *The Prelude* were written, but even as they stand these passages are full of human self-confidence.

One does not traduce the sincerity of this "pleasant exercise of hope and joy" in saying that, like all humanism, it was quite as useful in dilating the ego as in righting the people's wrongs. Wordsworth's boyhood feelings of freedom and mastery had been thwarted by the adult world. He had been a failure at Cambridge and had come to France aimless and discouraged. Suddenly, reason became an "enchantress," and "the very world" assumed "the attraction of a country in romance." In a sort of parody of the Incarnation, all the illusions of eighteenth-century senti-

---

[39] *Ibid.*, 443ff.   [40] *Ibid.*, 509ff.   [41] *Ibid.*, 361–362, 356.
[42] *Ibid.*, X, 171, 144–146.

mentalism had been made flesh. Ceasing to be literary fads, they had entered the bloodstream of history. It was really *true* that men—Wordsworth not excluded—possessed goodness, power, godhead. The stuff of life was "plastic" in his hands. The Hawkshead values lay not merely in the past but in the present and the future.[43]

He was also successful in love—at first that triumph must have loomed large in the whole glory of the time. Herein, however, his natural goodness overreached itself. Very soon after the birth of Caroline in December, 1792, he found that lack of funds would force him to return to England. It was when he paused in Paris on the way home that the revolutionary dream began to fade. At the moment there was no bloodshed, but the September massacres were a recent memory and the city seemed "Defenceless as a wood where tigers roam." Alone in his hotel at night, Wordsworth felt the chill of fear.[44] He makes little of this "spot of time," but it is not too fanciful to suppose that at this moment his old desire for peace and shelter awoke, never again to slumber. To be sure, he says that he banished these fears and that he would gladly have risked any danger for the good cause.[45] The original text of *The Prelude* explains that he had no money; otherwise

> I doubtless should have made a common cause
> With some who perished, haply perished, too.[46]

But this is extremely hypothetical, and the notion that Wordsworth played a dangerously active rôle in the Girondist party is a myth born of the purest democratic wishfulness. Incidentally, his description of Robespierre as wielding "the sceptre of the atheist crew"[47] does not suggest a very intimate knowledge of his prime aversion.

Let us make neither too much nor too little of the Annette Vallon affair as a cause of the distress felt by Wordsworth after his return to England. The political situation, in its implications for man in general and for Wordsworth in particular, was the dominant factor. But to suppose that he was quite untroubled by his conduct toward the girl is to set a very low value on his character. The moral traditions of his social class, if more easy-going than Richardson's, were much stricter than Fielding's. He would not have regarded an illegitimate child as the peccadillo of a

[43] *Ibid.*, 690–728. [44] *Ibid.*, 54–82. [45] *Ibid.*, 135–137.
[46] *Ibid.*, 189–197. [47] *Ibid.*, 458.

brisk young man. Gallic political idealism, not Gallic sexual realism, had appealed to him in France. It is no less unlikely that he had entertained conscientiously radical scruples against marriage. Such ideas belonged to the system which he was about to adopt, not to that which he championed during his courtship. What would Rousseau's St. Preux have thought of such conduct? At the height of his belief in natural goodness Wordsworth had behaved badly. While historic events were shaking his faith in the world, his personal conduct shook his faith in himself. The fact that as early as 1794 he was addressing love-poems—Wordsworthian love-poems—to Mary Hutchinson from Windy Brow[48] is not inconsistent with the supposition that his conscience was troubled about Annette. It is not likely, however, that his remorse was so poignant as to require any elaborately Freudian techniques of suppression.

Contrasting *The Prelude* with the trivial and on the whole fairly cheerful letters of the period, some scholars have refused to believe that he underwent a painful spiritual crisis between his return to England and his settlement at Racedown. Doubtless the desire to make his poetic autobiography tell a story of fall and redemption led him to darken the actual color of the period. Even *The Prelude* makes it plain that the darkness was illumined by flashes of happiness and that nature's lessons were at no time wholly forgotten. On the other hand, Wordsworth's letters were never the key with which he unlocked his heart. Indeed there were few men—Matthews and Wrangham were not among them—to whom he confided his deepest feelings in any medium. For several years Coleridge, addressed throughout *The Prelude,* was one of the exceptions. When Wordsworth tells his friend that for months and even years after England's declaration of war against France he suffered from nightmares, awaking with

> . . . a sense
> Of treachery and desertion in the place
> The holiest that I knew of, my own soul,[49]

he is either lying or presenting an aesthetically heightened version of the truth. The latter supposition is not only more charitable but more probable. Wordsworth had found in the French Revolution an answer to the deepest desires of his heart. We may well believe that he suffered a pro-

---

[48] Ernest de Selincourt, *Wordsworthian and Other Studies,* pp. 21ff.
[49] *Prelude,* X, 369–381.

found moral shock when his beloved country allied herself with the Coalition against the land of freedom and brotherhood and soon began to suppress the faintest stirrings of liberal thought within her own borders. Even more heart-sickening was his disillusionment when France herself turned to the guillotine and to nationalistic aggression. Good man, good world, good Nature and Nature's God hurtled in fragments at his feet. It would be absurd to describe him as living in a state of unrelieved despair from 1793 to 1796, but the deeper currents of his feeling were dark.

At first the remedy seemed to lie in cultivating illusions almost exactly opposite to those which he had cherished in France. He had looked for a speedy transformation of society; he would now attempt to retain his hopes by placing their fulfillment a comfortable distance in the future. He had been a man of feeling, with much enthusiasm for the concrete; he would become a man of cool, abstract reason. Had he not been fascinated by geometry at Cambridge? In place of "the Godhead which is ours," necessity; in place of communal ardor, the extremest individualism. We may accept "Godwinism" as the most convenient term for the panacea. Ideas like those of Godwin were of course pervasive in Wordsworth's environment. He could, without looking at *Political Justice,* have selected what he wanted from the French *philosophes* or from Price, Priestley, Fawcett, Holcroft, Thelwall, and Paine. It seems excessively sceptical, however, to reject the hypothesis that he was influenced by the famous work of the chief English exemplar of the rationalism which he now espoused. There is no evidence that he was personally acquainted with Godwin at this time, but he was on familiar terms with such members of the philosopher's circle as Montagu and Nicholson. Hazlitt's anecdote is not easily dismissed: " 'Throw away your books of chemistry,' said Wordsworth to a young man, a student in the Temple, 'and read Godwin on Necessity.' " [50] Coleridge in 1804 asserts that his friend—apparently until rather recently—has been "even to extravagance a necessitarian." [51] In 1796 Wordsworth, having just received from Montagu the second edition of *Political Justice,* tells Matthews, "I expect to find the work much improved"—[52] clear evidence of his acquaintance with the first edition. But although Wordsworth was influenced not only by the Godwinian way

[50] William Hazlitt, *Collected Works,* IV, 201.
[51] S. T. Coleridge, *Letters,* p. 454.
[52] *Early Letters,* p. 156. But here and at least twice elsewhere in his letters he spells the name "Godwyn."

of thinking but probably by Godwin, he was never a pharisaically orthodox disciple.

"Strict logicians," says Hazlitt, "are licensed visionaries."[53] He is speaking of Bentham, but the epigram can be applied to Godwin, whose rationalism, as his later works attest, was of the sort that is on the verge of collapsing into the warmest emotionalism. To his young admirers there was high excitement in reliance on "the human Reason's naked self":

> ... Tempting region that,
> For Zeal to enter and refresh herself
> Where passions had the privilege to work,
> And never hear the sound of their own names.[54]

His doctrinaire absurdities were enlisted in the service of a lofty ideal. Rereading *Caleb Williams* in 1827, Crabb Robinson testifies that

Godwin was in his early days an enthusiast of a high kind. There was a sort of religious and devotional spirit in his anti-religious prejudices, and while he disbelieved in a personal God, he worshipped a divine principle—the spirit of justice and truth.[55]

Of *Political Justice* he declares: "No book ever made me feel more generously."[56] Even in *The Prelude,* where Wordsworth writes of Godwinism with an abhorrence which he did not feel in 1793, one can see that he has not forgotten its appeal to a youth who wished to believe in man's power to become "Lord of himself, in undisturbed delight."[57]

The trouble was that Godwinism sought to achieve this aim "by such means/ As did not lie in nature"[58]—in Wordsworth's nature, at all events. The feelings which he had enjoyed with Beaupuy had been a more genuine reflection of his character than the violent antidote which he had seized upon to cure his disillusionment. When the exhilaration of the new drug wore off, he found himself more confused and hopeless than ever. One thing lacking in his Rousseauistic enthusiasm had been that organic union with non-human nature on which his happiness at Hawkshead had been based. In France he had been trying to love man without loving the *whole* of nature. Godwinism, far from supplying this deficiency, had led

[53] *Op. cit.,* p. 199.   [54] *Prelude,* X, 811–814.
[55] *Henry Crabb Robinson on Books and Their Writers* (ed. Edith J. Morley), p. 345. Cited hereafter as *Robinson*.
[56] *Ibid.,* p. 3.   [57] *Prelude,* X, 839.   [58] *Ibid.,* 843–844.

him much further away from the true sources of his being. He was a poet, as Dorothy kept reminding him through these troubled days; and poets are men of images, not men of syllogisms. Sometimes, fleeing from geometrical abstractions, he ranged the woods in fierce hunger for concrete reality. But his creative response to nature had been crippled by the Godwinian tendency "to sit in judgment rather than to feel," and "the eye was master of the heart." Hence these enjoyments, though "sought insatiably," were merely

> ...a transport of the outward sense,
> Not of the mind, vivid but not profound.[59]

This is how he felt "a few miles above Tintern Abbey" in the summer of 1793.

Somewhat over a year earlier, he had written Matthews from Blois: "It is my intention to take orders in the approaching winter or spring." [60] (Willing or unwilling, he would not have been eligible for ordination before the age of twenty-three.) But by February, 1794, he has decided that "I cannot bow down my mind to take orders." [61] The implications of this statement are elusive. There is not the slightest reason to suppose that he followed the atheist Godwin to the extent of believing that "Religion is in reality in all its parts an accommodation to the prejudices and weaknesses of mankind." [62] He may quite possibly, however, have agreed with Godwin's statement that the whole Church of England "is employed in support of a system of blind submission and abject hypocrisy," [63] and with his description of priests in general as "patrons of prejudice" and "enemies to freedom of inquiry." [64]

There is little anticlericalism, however, where we should most expect it—in the *Letter to the Bishop of Llandaff*. To some extent Wordsworth's opportunities were restricted by the fact that Watson was liberal in his theological and ecclesiastical views, as he had been in politics before the publication of Burke's *Reflections*. He exhibited the vices of apostasy rather than of orthodoxy: "While, with a servility which has prejudiced many people against religion itself, the ministers of the Church of England have appeared as writers upon public measures only to be the advocates of slavery civil and religious, your Lordship stood almost alone as

[50] *Ibid.*, XI, 165, 187–189.   [60] *Early Letters*, p. 75.   [61] *Ibid.*, p. 109.
[62] William Godwin, *An Enquiry Concerning Political Justice*, II, 230.
[63] *Ibid.*, p. 92.   [64] *Ibid.*, I, 29.

the defender of truth and political charity." [65] But now the Bishop laments the fate of the French clergy instead of rejoicing with all lovers of liberty that they have been "stripped of the rewards of their vices and their crimes." [66] On the whole, however, religious questions play a minor part in the not very rampant radicalism of the *Letter*.

The poems generally referred to as "Godwinian" are similarly inconclusive. There is nothing explicitly anti-religious, anti-Christian, or even anticlerical about *Guilt and Sorrow, The Ruined Cottage, The Convict, Incipient Madness,* and *Argument for Suicide.*[67] The same remark applies to *The Borderers*, although it differs from the rest of the group in important respects. Nevertheless these poems have a quality of horizonless gloom, of morbid psychological probing without hope, which betokens an unwillingness to think in religious terms. This mood, however, cannot be ascribed wholly to Godwin's influence, for it appears in two pieces which De Selincourt would place as early as 1791—the untitled fragments which look forward to *Guilt and Sorrow,* and the *Fragment of a Gothic Tale* which looks forward to *The Borderers*. Wordsworth begins his return to poetry by reworking melancholy juvenilia. There is now, to be sure, a more impersonal social indignation and a more authentic gloom, but as a poet he does not become wholly contemporary with himself until the Alfoxden period.

Coleridge's description of Wordsworth in 1796 as "at least, a semi-atheist" [68] should be observed with interest and heavily discounted: for Coleridge, atheism consisted in disagreement with his own peculiar ideas. We may infer, however, that Wordsworth was distinctly heterodox at this time. The poet himself tells us that in his Godwinian endeavors to "probe/ The living body of society" he even

> ...set foot
> On Nature's holiest places . . .
>   .   .   .
> Dragging all passions, notions, shapes of faith,
> Like culprits to the bar.[69]

Solitary, who is Wordsworth as well as Fawcett, was similarly seduced into "An infidel contempt of Holy Writ." [70]

---

[65] *Prose Works* (ed. William Knight), I, 4.   [66] *Ibid.,* p. 8.
[67] I refer, of course, to the original versions of the first two poems.
[68] S. T. Coleridge, *Letters* (ed. E. H. Coleridge), p. 164.
[69] *Prelude,* X, 875–879, 890–891.   [70] *Excursion,* II, 249.

But the solidest evidence is provided by Christopher Wordsworth's *Memoirs*. For a nineteenth-century clerical family biographer, Dr. Wordsworth was not a dishonest man, but he was certainly not inclined to exaggerate his uncle's divagations from the Book of Common Prayer. He goes far indeed when he says:

His mind was whirled round and round in a vortex of doubt, and appeared to be almost on the point of sinking into a gulph of despair. Not that he ever lapsed into scepticism. No! His early education, his love of the glories and beauties of creation, protected him from any approach to that. Yet at this period of his life, his religious opinions were not very clearly defined. He had too high an opinion of the sufficiency of the human will, and too sanguine a hope of unlimited benefits to be conferred on society by the human intellect. He had a good deal of Stoical pride, mingled with not a little of Pelagian self-confidence. Having an inadequate perception of the necessity of divine grace, he placed his hopes where they could not stand. . . . He sought for ideal perfectibility where he could not but meet with real frailty, and did not look for peace where alone it could be found. Hence his mind was ill at ease.[71]

In the second sentence of this statement "scepticism" must mean "atheism," since the rest of the passage indicates that Wordsworth was very sceptical indeed toward Christianity. The biographer is trying to tell us, in his mealy-mouthed way, that at this time his uncle was a deist.

There is no other single term which would not less accurately describe an inherently amorphous situation. In this confused period Wordsworth had no definite religious ideas. His deism was largely a corollary of his political views. The entire Church of England—High, Latitudinarian, and Evangelical—had risen in alarm against Jacobinism and Jacobin infidelity. Where then should he turn? Congregationalists and Baptists were hardly less conservative than Anglicans. Quakerism, though strongly tinged with deism at this time, would have been too mystical and quietistic for a devotee of reason. The necessitarian, materialistic, and pro-French Unitarianism of Joseph Priestley was so closely akin to Godwinism that it would have appealed to him, and he was doubtless influenced by it. Dorothy had been happily associated with prominent Unitarians at Halifax and at Norwich, the city nearest Forncett; and when William joined her at Halifax in 1794 he was warmly received by a circle of cultivated, liberal folk whom he found much more congenial than Canon Cookson. But if Wordsworth had ever definitely aligned himself with the Unitar-

[71] Christopher Wordsworth, *Memoirs of William Wordsworth*, I, 89.

ians, whom he later held in special detestation, we should probably hear
of the fact from Coleridge, Robinson, or Harriet Martineau. If, then, a
question which Wordsworth himself probably refused to answer must be
answered by the scholar, the only remaining choice is a deism more or less
like that of Thomas Paine.

Racedown brought no sudden and absolute release from Godwinism.
The return to nature was a gradual process not wholly completed before
1798. Clear foretokenings of the change, on the other hand, run back as
far as the tour of the Wye valley in the summer of 1793 and become more
marked in 1794 during the brief period when his hopes were rekindled
by the death of Robespierre. In that year, while happily sojourning with
Dorothy at the Calverts' Windy Brow cottage, he wrote several passages
which he contemplated adding to *An Evening Walk*. One of them describes

> A heart that vibrates evermore, awake
> To feeling for all forms that Life can take,
> That wider still its sympathy extends,
> And sees not any place where being ends;
> Sees Sense, through Nature's rudest forms betrayed,
> Tremble obscure in fountain, rock, and shade,
> And while a secret power those forms endears,
> Their social accents never vainly hears.[72]

The universality of something called "being" which animates with "a
secret power" all forms of life, the same power as it exists in man being
used to "endear" those forms; the active rather than passive response of
the senses to the unity of being made manifest in external nature, and conversely the possession by natural objects of something like sense; the
association of this union of man and nature with the doctrine of universal
benevolence—these ideas belong to the Wordsworthian "philosophy of
nature" in its fully developed stage.

Another passage contrasts the vulgar many, who are heedless of nature's charms, with

> ... those favoured souls, who, taught
> By active Fancy or by patient Thought,
> See common forms prolong the endless chain
> Of joy and grief, of pleasure and of pain;

[72] *Works*, I, 10.

But chiefly those to whom the harmonious doors
Of Science have unbarred celestial stores,
To whom a burning energy has given
That other eye which darts thro' earth and heaven,
Roams through all space and [   ] unconfined,
Explores the illimitable tracts of mind,
And piercing the profound of time can see
Whatever man has been and man can be,

                    .   .   .

And proud beyond all limits to aspire
Mounts through the fields of thought on wings of fire.[73]

Here again the "common forms" of nature are significant as reflections or symbols of human feelings. The chief emphasis, however, is laid upon the great man's aspiring, insatiable energy, expressing itself through a transcendental kind of science but still more satisfyingly through "that other eye," the creative imagination of the poet. Anticipating a much-disputed point, we note that neither of these passages is purely sensation-alistic. The pleasure-pain scale is accepted but absorbed and transformed by a doctrine of mental power, and this power in man is none other than the "secret power" or activating principle of all being.

These 1794 passages should be sufficient to cure anyone of the notion that Wordsworth possessed no philosophical ideas until Coleridge told him about Plotinus, Spinoza, Boehme, and Kant. Later I shall urge the importance of remembering that Wordsworth had begun to read preromantic poetry at an early age. Dorothy at this time compares her "strange and wayward" brother to the hero of Beattie's *Minstrel*.[74] She suggests a more interesting comparison, however, when she writes, "His pleasures are chiefly of the imagination." [75] Most of the ideas expressed in the Windy Brow lines can be found in Mark Akenside's philosophical poem.

When the fall of Robespierre failed to produce the millennium Wordsworth relapsed into restless dejection. The boon of Racedown, however, raised his spirits once more. In the "preamble" lines of *The Prelude*, written in September, 1795, he speaks of "Trances of thought and mountings of the mind." His response to nature is not merely passive, for the sweetness of the wind on his body has made him feel within himself

A corresponding mild creative breeze,
A vital breeze which travell'd gently on

[73] *Ibid.*, pp. 12–13.   [74] *Early Letters*, pp. 97–98.   [75] *Ibid.*, p. 52.

O'er things which it had made, and is become
A tempest, a redundant energy
Vexing its own creation.[76]

He was once more what he had been at Hawkshead—"A sensitive, and a creative soul." [77] But final victory was not to be won so easily. For some time his restored natural piety clashed with the rationalism to which he still clung. Much of the old morbidity remained. The preceding years had filled his mind with pictures of human misery which were hard to reconcile with his new-found personal happiness.

The transitional state of conflict finds expression in *The Borderers*. This drama is implicitly anti-Godwinian in that its "general moral . . . is to show the dangerous use which may be made of reason when a man has committed a great crime." [78] Oswald's pride of intellect might have become true visionary power had it been rooted in "solid principles of genuine benevolence" rather than in self-interested calculation. Godwin himself was a benevolist, but he regarded benevolence as the product, not the substratum, of reason. Dissatisfied with this idea, Wordsworth is uncertainly working his way back to a Shaftesburyan or Rousseauistic concept of innate goodness. Reason which denies the primacy of feeling is morally dangerous. He could not, however, have meant Oswald to be a typical representative of the Godwinian philosophy: as the preface shows, he was interested in him as a very special psychiatric case.[79] Hence it would be hasty to group *The Borderers* with such contemporary assaults upon Godwin as Walker's *The Vagabonds*. Another curious feature of the work is that if Oswald is a brainy monster, his chief victim is a sentimental fool. According to Dr. Meyer, Marmaduke's tragic fault is that, although essentially a pure benevolist, he rejects "the evidence of the feelings and of nature." [80] This in a way is true, but it ignores a paradox: Marmaduke rejects the evidence of his feelings because he is so complete a feeler that he does not use his brains at all and is therefore easily duped by the cerebral Oswald. *The Borderers* does not so much preach a sermon as pose a question of personal concern to its author. How could intellectual power and benevolistic feeling be harmonized in a single personality?

We may note in passing that the pious remarks made by various characters are merely dramatic. The strange fact that Oswald is not only a rationalist but an animist and a sun-worshipper is explained in the Preface:

---

[76] *Prelude*, I, 20, 41–47.   [77] *Ibid.*, XI, 257.   [78] *Works*, I, 348.
[79] *Ibid.*, pp. 345–347.   [80] G. W. Meyer, *Wordsworth's Formative Years*, p. 202.

"Having shaken off the obligations of religion and morality in a dark and tempestuous age, it is probable that such a character will be infected with a tinge of superstition." [81]

The Borderers offers no solution to the problem which it raises. But a solution is quietly, slowly being provided by the daily course of life at Racedown. Wordsworth's mind, weary of geometrical diagrams, is refreshing itself in a bath of sense-impressions. He is turning from Godwin back to Rousseau, and especially to the *Émile* with its healing gospel of "Come forth into the light of things." The old dream of a cottage in the country with Dorothy has at last come true. Before his eyes the wild, free energies of his own childhood reappear in little Basil Montagu. And in Coleridge he has found not only a friend but a man of genius who insists that he, William Wordsworth, is the greatest poet of the age.

3

The years 1797–1800 constitute so important a phase of Wordsworth's career that they deserve to be studied rather intensively. Of the two persons whom he thanks for helping him to return to his true self Dorothy is the less important for our purposes. Technically speaking, at this time she was a very broad Anglican with Unitarian leanings. In reality, however, her religion consisted in loving flowers, birds, children, men and women, Coleridge, and above all William. Throughout her life she would feel neither deep repugnance nor warm enthusiasm for any creed or form which could provide a garment for her affections. In such matters she was content to follow where her brother led. But although she did not directly influence his religious thought she greatly furthered its expression by providing an example of that union of observation and feeling, of "wild ecstasies" and aspen-leaf tenderness, which was essential for his poetry.

As regards the influence of Coleridge, the orthodox scholarly position is stated by Legouis:

Dorothy was all sensibility, with little or no need of thought. . . . In her society Wordsworth might be cured of Godwin, but he would also endanger his chances of ever arriving at a comprehensive philosophy of his own. Just at the right time, the counterpoise on the speculative side began to be provided by Coleridge.[82]

[81] *Works*, I, 347.
[82] Émile Legouis, *The Early Life of William Wordsworth*, p. 318.

This view cannot be accepted without qualification. Undoubtedly Coleridge did something to push his friend's mind in a transcendental, antinecessitarian, anti-materialistic direction. But as the Windy Brow additions to *An Evening Walk* bear witness, Wordsworth in 1794 possessed ideas of precisely the sort which he is often supposed to have derived from his friend. The "preamble" lines of *The Prelude,* also of philosophical significance, were written after Wordsworth had met Coleridge but before the latter's influence could have been felt.

Nowhere does Wordsworth provide a clear, firm statement of his intellectual indebtedness to Coleridge. In *Prelude* II he praises his fellow-poet as one who, knowing how to put science in its inferior place, is

> ...no slave
> To that false secondary power, by which,
> In weakness, we create distinctions.[83]

But the implication is that this insight is shared by the two on an equal basis, not that it is a gift from one to the other. Describing his redemption from the Godwinian *esprit de géometrie* in *Prelude* X, Wordsworth vaguely refers to Coleridge as a "most precious Friend" who helped "to regulate my Soul." [84] Coleridge receives three lines to Dorothy's thirteen, and drops out of sight in the 1850 version. When Wordsworth returns to this theme in *Prelude* XIII he couples Coleridge with Dorothy as a "loving Soul" who helped to soften the gloomy severity of his feelings toward nature.[85] This change, according to the subsequent lines, opened the way to a deeper wisdom, but there is nothing to suggest that the wisdom itself came from Coleridge. His function and Dorothy's was to revive the atrophied affections.

We may be sure that Coleridge talked to Wordsworth about "spy nosey" and other philosophers. William had learned a little about some of them at Cambridge, but their relevance to his own problems became more apparent when their ideas were refracted by his companion's shaping spirit of imagination. On the other hand we must remember that Wordsworth was always suspicious of systematic brainwork and never more so than in his reaction from Godwinian peeping and botanizing. He would be highly resistant toward ideas which he had not already sensed in his own less formal way. Nor is it certain that he always understood what

---

[83] *Prelude,* II, 215–224.   [84] *Ibid.,* X, 906–908.   [85] *Ibid.,* XIII, 246–253.

Coleridge was saying. Years later, Samuel Rogers told how he and Words-worth called upon Coleridge one afternoon in London. Coleridge talked steadily for about two hours,

during which Wordsworth listened to him with profound attention, every now and then nodding his head as if in assent. On quitting the lodging I said to Wordsworth, "Well, for my own part, I could not make head or tail of Coleridge's oration; pray, did you understand it?" "Not one syllable of it," was Wordsworth's reply.[86]

There were times when Wordsworth nodded his head and kept his own counsel. He was much fonder of intellectual and emotional privacy than Coleridge. The antagonisms which arise when two egocentric geniuses attempt to live as boon companions began to ferment very early. Words-worth soon discovered reasons for feeling morally superior to Coleridge, and, as Sperry observes, "It was Coleridge's misfortune . . . to become increasingly aware of his failings when in the company of the Words-worths." [87] This awareness led to injured feelings and defensive counter-criticism. In May, 1799, Coleridge writes to Thomas Poole:

My many weaknesses are of some advantage to me; they unite me more with the great mass of my fellow-beings—but dear Wordsworth appears to me to have hurtfully segregated and isolated his being. Doubtless his delights are more deep and sublime; but he has likewise more hours that prey upon the flesh and blood.[88]

Even a year earlier, Coleridge reports to Estlin that on the subject of religion he and Wordsworth "are habitually silent; we found our data dissimilar, and never revived the subject." [89] Since for both men religion and philosophy were closely intertwined, it seems clear that even in 1798 their intellectual communion had its limitations. What they chiefly talked about at Alfoxden was neither religion nor philosophy as such, but the writing of a joint volume of poems for fame and money—both of which, as unsuccessful drifters in their late twenties, they sorely needed. And as poets, after a few abortive attempts at actual collaboration, they went their extremely different ways.

One cannot describe in the same terms all of Wordsworth's contribu-

[86] R. E. Roberts, *Samuel Rogers and His Circle*, p. 164.
[87] W. L. Sperry, *Wordsworth's Anti-Climax*, p. 47.
[88] Coleridge, *Letters*, p. 297.   [89] *Ibid.*, p. 246.

tions to the first edition of *Lyrical Ballads*. A slightly morbid interest in the grotesque and the mentally abnormal carries over from the preceding period. More obvious and more important is the reaction against the abstract rationalism, the logical analysis, the glorification of learning, the scorn of the personal and domestic affections, the disapproval of private property, which were associated with Godwinism. To eradicate these from his mind by cultivating their opposites was a need which Wordsworth satisfied with vigor. On the other hand, even disregarding such pre-Alfoxden pieces as *The Female Vagrant* and *The Convict,* we find much of that social indignation which, though differently expressed, was common to both Beaupuy and Godwin. This spirit, indeed, runs back to Lonsdale's injustice and to glimpses of the aftermath of the American Revolution observed at Hawkshead.

Wordsworth's Jacobinism—I use the word in the contemporary English sense—had cooled considerably after reaching its climax in 1793, but throughout the period under discussion his political and social views were still radical for those times. Even in subject and diction, *Lyrical Ballads* was to some extent a piece of democratic propaganda. Christopher Wordsworth the younger is sound on this point:

The clue to his *poetical* theory, in some of its questionable details, may be found in his *political* principles; these had been democratical, and still, though in some degree modified, they were of a republican character. At this period he entertained little reverence for ancient institutions, as such; and he felt little sympathy with the higher classes of society. He was deeply impressed with a sense of the true dignity of the lower orders, and their sufferings. . . . He desired to impart moral grandeur to poverty, and to invest the objects of irrational and inanimate nature with a beauty and grace, of which, it seemed to him, they had been stripped by a heartless and false taste, pretending to the title of delicacy and refinement.[90]

This implies a movement away from Godwin toward the more Rousseauistic attitude of 1791 and 1792. But the failure of the Revolution had convinced him that the only sound basis for reform lay in a more genuine radicalism than that of Beaupuy. He must be radical in the strict etymological sense—must examine the roots of human nature in themselves and in relation to the soil of the universe. The best materials for this investigation would be provided by children and by uncomplicated

[90] *Memoirs,* I, 125. For exactly the same interpretation see Hazlitt, *Collected Works,* IV, 271.

peasants whose thoughts, words, and actions sprang directly from their physical environment. A letter of 1802 casts light upon the 1800 *Preface*. Defending *The Idiot Boy* against John Wilson's strictures, Wordsworth retorts that we can understand human nature only

by stripping our own hearts naked, and by looking out of ourselves towards men who lead the simplest lives, and those most according to nature; men who have never known false refinements, wayward and artificial desires, false criticisms, effeminate habits of thinking and feeling, or who, having known these things, have outgrown them. This latter class is the most to be depended upon, but it is very small in number.[91]

Obviously the experiment is not an experiment at all. Wordsworth is in search of the Hawkshead values and he knows perfectly well that he will find them. Furthermore, especially when he expresses his predetermined conclusions in poetry, his personal experience of those values is colored by the eighteenth-century naturalism which he had accepted since boyhood. It was simply axiomatic that the universe was a harmony of benevolence, that external nature was not only morally beneficial but in some sense numinous, that man's native impulses possessed a quality of goodness akin to the goodness of Nature and of Nature's God, and that the natural virtues could therefore most readily be discerned in simple, uncorrupted, rural folk. In 1795 Wordsworth had found that the peasants about Race-down "are wretchedly poor; ignorant and overwhelmed with every vice that usually attends ignorance in that class, viz. lying and picking and stealing etc. etc." [92] But now that he has escaped from Godwinian intel-lectualism and renewed his contact with the tradition which has moulded his mind, he remembers how peasants should be described.

The dice, though heavily loaded, would not roll in quite the proper way. Wordsworth fully accepted the doctrine of universal benevolence. "Love of nature leading to love of man" was a part of his inherited reli-gion and he usually tried to carry it into action. Yet although he loved Man, he did not really love or understand people. One can think of indi-vidual exceptions, but none of them were peasants. The Ambleside cotters were to remember him as "not a man as folks could crack wi', nor not a man as could crack wi' folks." [93] His pseudo-experiment was a psychologi-

---

[91] *Early Letters*, p. 295.
[92] *Letters of William and Dorothy Wordsworth. The Later Years*, p. 1334.
[93] H. D. Rawnsley, "Reminiscences of Wordsworth Among the Peasantry of Westmore-land," *Transactions of the Wordsworth Society*, VI, 182.

cal study of the association of ideas on the simplest and clearest level. But he could not get inside the minds of his subjects. They did not seem to think and feel as they should, and to credit them with "a pleasurable feeling of blind love" was not altogether satisfactory. Hence an investigation begun in an effort to be objective became more and more frankly what it had always been—a recital of personal experience. In the letter to Wilson quoted a moment ago, Wordsworth declares that "the class . . . most to be depended upon" in the study of human nature consists not of those who have never known civilized corruptions, but of those "who, having known these things, have outgrown them." To this small group Wordsworth himself belongs, and in all the most important poems of this period it is his own mind, not the mind of an excited rustic, with which he deals.

He has convinced himself, and wishes to convince others, of the cosmic significance of two very different kinds of pleasure. On the one hand, he took intense delight in the impact of the external world upon his senses. Even more than with most poets, his sensuous, emotional, and intellectual states were closely intertwined. The reverence which since adolescent days had tempered his self-trust inclined him to regard the physical sources of his joy with filial respect and even with a kind of awe. The ascent from sensation to emotion to intellect to worship could best be rationalized in terms of sensationalism and associationism.

The other pleasure cannot be explained on a sensationalistic basis. It was the enjoyment of the creative dominance of mind over the impressions of sense. Wordsworth possessed that desire for free, boundless self-expansion which we have observed on a rudimentary level in Burns and at its most rampant extreme in Blake. Even in childhood the power of nature had been felt as a power wielded also by himself. The flowering of his genius now inclined him to interpret those trance-like moments of over-concentration when "we are laid asleep/In body" as the highest triumph of the imagination, which confers upon nature the values which nature imparts to man. In relation to the pleasure of imaginative dominance, Wordsworth's religious impulses would lead him to relate his own mind to a universal Mind.

Both of these joys were so precious that he refused to surrender either of them for the sake of the other. The fact that the whole width of the Cartesian chasm lay between them made him all the more eager to assert that they were not two experiences, but a single experience which might be looked at in two ways,

> A balance, an ennobling interchange
> Of action from within and from without.[94]

The "high argument" of the great philosophical poem which Coleridge urged him to write is to show

> How exquisitely the individual Mind
> (And the progressive powers perhaps no less
> Of the whole species) to the external World
> Is fitted:—and how exquisitely too—
> Theme this but little heard of among men—
> The external World is fitted to the Mind;
> And the creation (by no lower name
> Can it be called) which they with blended might
> Accomplish.[95]

But even "blended might" fails to do complete justice to Wordsworth's intuition of the unity embracing and reconciling both aspects of the ennobling interchange. In the notes to his edition of *The Prelude*, De Selincourt printed for the first time an "isolated piece of blank verse" found by him in one of the poet's manuscript notebooks. I believe it to be a discarded draft of a portion of that section of *The Recluse* which Wordsworth used as the "prospectus" of *The Excursion* and from which the foregoing quotation is drawn. In this remarkable fragment he asserts that there can be no real difference between the passively receptive and the actively creative functions of mind, since they both take place within

> ... the one interior life
> That lives in all things, sacred from the touch
> Of that false secondary power by which
> In weakness we create distinctions, then
> Believe that all our puny boundaries are things
> Which we perceive and not which we have made;
> —In which all beings live with god, themselves
> Are god, Existing in the mighty whole,
> As indistinguishable as the cloudless east
> At noon is from the cloudless west, when all
> The hemisphere is one cerulean blue.[96]

---

[94] *Prelude*, XII, 376–377. It is interesting that the original version should sound more transcendental than the 1850 text, which reads "from without and from within."

[95] *The Recluse*, pp. 53–54.

[96] *Prelude*, pp. 512–513. De Selincourt shows that the fragment was probably written between the summer of 1798 and February, 1800. The former date seems preferable: the lines are too bold and adventurous to fit the quieter mood of 1800.

Here an extremely advanced and sophisticated psychology is enlisted in the service of the highest romantic aspiration: removal of all boundaries and limits which distinguish man from God. The thought is precisely that of Emerson: "Within man is the soul of the whole. . . . There is no bar or wall in the soul, where man, the effect, ceases, and God, the cause, begins." [97]

Perhaps Wordsworth discarded this passage because it reflected only imperfectly the quality of an experience which was beyond words. Or perhaps in the very act of expressing his deepest desire he was held back from self-deification by the caution and the reverence which never quite deserted him. This suppression of his boldest thoughts forced him to describe his nature-experience in inadequate terms of "balance" and "interchange." And so far as the published work of this period is concerned, the sensationalistic and associationistic side of the balance is weighted more heavily than the transcendental side. Wordsworth, who disliked sudden intellectual leaps, has not yet wholly abandoned the Godwinian position. Its definiteness and clarity made it much easier to express the influence of the external world upon the mind than the influence of the mind upon the external world. He also feels love and gratitude toward the concrete realities which are bringing peace to his spirit, and is inclined to emphasize the importance of wise passiveness. However vainly, he is trying to "look out of himself" toward nature and man.

Nevertheless the notion that Wordsworth at this time was a sensationalist pure and simple is obviously absurd. In considering this question it is unwise to lean too heavily on lyrics which dart at the nature-experience from a single point of view and skim quickly away. The only short poem of this period which approximates Wordsworth's complete thought is probably *To My Sister*. On this "first mild day of March" the vernal sweetness gives pleasure to William and Dorothy because there is pleasure *in* the scene itself. [98] "A blessing in the air" seems to impart "a sense of joy" to the trees and mountains and grass as well as to the human strollers. The explanation is that

> Love, now a universal birth
> From heart to heart is stealing,
> From earth to man, from man to earth.

[97] R. W. Emerson, *Essays: First Series*, pp. 253, 255.
[98] Compare *Lines Written in Early Spring*.

In this "hour of feeling"—universal feeling—

> Some silent laws our hearts will make,
> Which they shall long obey.

But these self-made laws are worthy of obedience because the mental force which shapes them is part of a cosmic force:

> And from the blessed power that rolls
> About, below, above,
> We'll frame the measure of our souls:
> They shall be tuned to love.[99]

In this little poem of 1798 Wordsworth for the first time says almost everything that he means, and perhaps he was never to say it more clearly. Here sensationalism is important, but only as one element in a harmony of benevolence and joy uniting God, nature, and man in one happy and loving wholeness of being.

In *Tintern Abbey* the associational element in lines 27–30 is obvious; but almost immediately Wordsworth describes a "more sublime" quasi-mystical experience which does not sound at all like Hartley's "theopathy." It may be more than coincidence that the phrase "power of harmony" in lines 47–48 echoes the title of John Gilbert Cooper's *The Power of Harmony* (1745), a poem expressing Shaftesbury's view of the universe as an aesthetico-ethical composition.[100] Later it is said that the senses "half create" the world which they "perceive," and the author's footnote refers us to a thoroughly transcendental passage in Young's *Night Thoughts* which goes on to declare that "Man makes the matchless image, man admires." [101]

Tintern Abbey does not quite deserve its reputation as "the *locus classicus* or consecrated formulary of the Wordsworthian faith." [102] Written in almost immediate response to the occasion, it is not an instance of "emotion recollected in tranquility." In a way very puzzling to a reader of *The Prelude,* Wordsworth brushes aside "the coarser pleasures of my boyish days" with scornful haste in order to contrast his present feelings with that superficial "transport of the outward sense" which provided relief from Godwinian abstractions in 1793. But if his present recognition of

---

[99] *Oxford,* pp. 482–483.
[101] *Ibid.,* pp. 147–148.
[100] *Religious Trends,* II, 323–324, describes this poem.
[102] F. W. H. Myers, *Wordsworth,* p. 33.

"something far more deeply interfused" in nature and in the human mind is really "abundant recompense" for the loss of the earlier sensuous delight, it is strange that he should desire to see his "former pleasures" in the "wild eyes" of Coleridge and should turn to Dorothy with the cry, "Oh! yet a little while/May I behold in thee what I was once." [103] One would say that these lines look forward to his lament for the loss of the visionary gleam in the *Immortality Ode* were it not for the fact that what has here been lost is not visionary at all, since the gleam is assigned not to child-hood or to youth but to maturity. The thought of this beautiful but hastily written poem has not been clearly defined.

Only the first two books of *The Prelude* were composed between 1797 and 1800. They are predominantly sensationalistic. Nevertheless he affirms that even in infancy "action from without" is blended with "action from within." The clearest of several pertinent passages is that beginning "Blest the infant Babe" in lines 237–280 of Book II. The infant is conditioned by his mother's love to look lovingly upon the world and thus to influence what he receives from it. This loving mental activity, being part of the cosmic love which pervades mother, babe, and external nature, makes the child "An inmate of this active universe."

> From nature largely he receives; nor so
> Is satisfied, but largely gives again.

Hence it may be said that

> . . . his mind
> Even as an agent of the one great mind,
> Creates, creator and receiver both,
> Working but in alliance with the works
> Which it beholds.

And this duplication within the infant's mind of the work of the Divine Mind is the beginning of poetry,

> By uniform control of after years
> In most abated or suppressed, in some,
> Through every change of growth or of decay,
> Pre-eminent till death.

[103] *Oxford*, p. 207.

This passage satisfyingly expresses the more positive side of Wordsworth's religion as it exists between 1797 and 1800. It is not avowedly anti-
Christian. Miss Batho, indeed, asserts that his conception of indwelling
Deity is simply "Catholic Christianity" [104]—the incarnationalism and sac-
ramentalism of his High Church childhood broadened to include the
altars of nature. But the child Wordsworth had never been a High
Churchman in any sense that would condition him toward a sacramental
interpretation of his response to nature. Eight-year-old Anglicans are not
deeply versed in such matters. Hawkshead had made him a complete
latitudinarian, and more recent influences had made him a deist. Even in
his later years of conservatism he was to maintain a stoutly Protestant distaste for "high" sacramental doctrine. During the period which we are
now examining, Wordsworth ignores the Christian scheme of redemption
so pointedly that one may as well say that he denies it. Having broken the
chain of natural piety, man in a sense has fallen; but he can regain paradise simply by recognizing his position as part of the universal goodness.
There is no room for the Cross. It is true that the central Angelican tradition emphasizes the Incarnation, but unless Incarnation *includes* Atonement it is not a Christian doctrine at all. Thanks to the Holy Spirit,
Christians can believe in immanent Deity. Divine immanence without
divine transcendence, however, is not Christianity but pantheism. As my
earlier studies have shown, in the eighteenth century the line between
sentimental latitudinarianism and sentimental deism was thin and wavering, and many people whom a modern historian would describe as deists
regarded themselves as broadly rational Christians.[105] But at this time
Wordsworth stands well across the deistic side of the boundary, and I
believe that he is aware of the fact. He does not talk of looking through
nature up to Nature's God. As Harper says, "He thought of nature as
having the Life of Life abiding in her." [106] The word "God" appears only
once in the first two books of *The Prelude,* and then merely in the tauto-
logical phrase, "With God and Nature communing." [107] In line 152 of
Tintern Abbey, using what he will one day refer to as "a passionate expression, uttered incautiously," [108] he declares himself "a worshipper of
Nature."

The nature-worshipping type of deism, at its deepest and most intense,

[104] Edith C. Batho, *The Later Wordsworth,* pp. 237–249.
[105] *Religious Trends,* II, 279–284, 335–337, 369–370.
[106] G. M. Harper, *William Wordsworth,* I, 4.   [107] *Prelude,* II, 446.
[108] *The Letters of William and Dorothy Wordsworth. The Middle Years,* p. 618.

is hardly distinguishable from pantheism. The particular trend here involved is that descending from Shaftesbury through many eighteenth-century poems. It tempers the more rationalistic sort of deism with an aestheticized Newtonianism and with chiefly Neoplatonic but partly Stoical ideas of the World Soul or Spirit of Nature to produce a divine Whole of beauty, love, goodness, and creative energy. Wordsworth's pantheism is not of the crude sort which deifies the sum-total of things. Nor is it the austerely abstract pantheism of Spinoza, though certain aspects of Spinoza's thought may indirectly have helped to form it. It is rooted in a deeply personal experience which corroborates his eighteenth-century heritage—the bliss of feeling "the sense sublime/Of something far more deeply interfused," the "sentiment of Being," [109] the "Wisdom and Spirit of the universe," [110] "the human soul that *through* me ran," [111]

> ...the life
> Of all things, and the mighty unity
> In all which we behold, and feel, and are.[112]

In short he "saw one life, and felt that it was joy." [113] This joy, both in the visible world and within himself, was Nature, and it was the only God which at this time he knew. Since the sense of a numinous cosmic unity and interfusion is what the Western world has usually meant by "pantheism," the use of such terms as "panentheism" or "panpsychism" to describe Wordsworth's position would seem to be a needless apologetic refinement.

One of the favorite assertions of eighteenth-century deism was that Jesus was a good deist. "He loves and venerates Christianity," writes Coleridge of his friend in 1798. "I wish he did more." [114] To do more, however, would be to deny his personal faith. In several poems he protects his nature-religion by almost explicit rejection of Christian supernaturalism. There is no spiritual realm apart from this earthly matrix of spirit, and hence no immortality. The dead Lucy is simply

> Rolled round in earth's diurnal course
> With rocks, and stones, and trees.[115]

At the death of his beloved teacher he addresses the Hawkshead schoolboys without the slightest hint of religious consolation:

---

[109] *Prelude*, II, 420.   [110] *Ibid.*, I, 428.   [111] *Oxford*, p. 482. Italics mine.
[112] *Prelude*, XIII, 253–255.   [113] *Ibid.*, II, 430.
[114] Coleridge, *Letters*, p. 246.   [115] *Oxford*, p. 187.

> Now stretched beneath his grass-grown mound
> He rests a prisoner of the ground.[116]

The traditional images of eschatology arouse in him something like scorn:

> Jehovah—with his thunder, and the choir
> Of shouting Angels, and the empyreal thrones—
> I pass them unalarmed.

These awaken less dread than that which he feels on contemplating the mysterious powers of the human mind—"My haunt, and the main region of my song."[117] But the most aggressively naturalistic poem of the period is *Peter Bell*, a tale of moral—not religious—conversion through a chain of completely natural occurrences which, interpreted as preternatural by the superstitious potter, awaken the atrophied goodness of his heart.[118]

In *Peter Bell* and other poems of 1797 and 1798 one finds such expressions as "God," "heaven," "a Christian psalm." But these are either placed with dramatic appropriateness in the mouths of rustics and children or are uttered by Wordsworth in his imagined character as a member of the rural community. When the arithmetically minded adult in *We Are Seven* says "Their spirits are in heaven," nothing is implied as to the poet's actual beliefs.

More noteworthy are several indications that Wordsworth is not wholly confident of the validity of his own position. *Lines Written in Early Spring* is sprinkled with little hesitancies—notably "If this belief from heaven be sent," which makes the concluding question hypothetical. He recognizes the possibility that the insight "into the life of things" recorded in *Tintern Abbey* may express "but a vain belief."[119] And one of the most strongly pantheistic passages in *The Prelude* is qualified by the statement that

> If this be error, and another faith
> Find easier access to the pious mind,

---

[116] *Ibid.*, p. 577. Contrast the pious observations added in 1842.
[117] *The Recluse*, pp. 51–52. This passage shocked Blake and Flaxman. (*Robinson*, pp. 156, 327.
[118] Lines 971–980, alluding to the ass of Palm Sunday, were not in the original MS of 1798. They were added when the poem was first published in 1819, removed in 1827, and restored in 1832.   [119] *Oxford*, p. 206.

he will still be grateful for nature's benign influence.[120] Cautious northerner as well as romantic genius, Wordsworth always kept an anchor out
to windward.

The cold, homesick, straitened sojourn in Germany threw Wordsworth
inward upon himself—always his most fruitful theme—and thus contributed to the maturing of his art. With some relief he discovered that
the great philosophical poem would require a very long running start, and
turned in *The Prelude* to the more congenial task of autobiography. In an
alien land the Hawkshead values appeared particularly precious, and the
disturbed state of Europe made him feel more keenly than before that
they were *English* values. The change inevitably pointed toward patriotic
nationalism; hence toward increased respect for traditional English institutions. The seeds were slow in germinating, and other influences would be
required to make them grow; but they were planted at this time.

Home in England at last! But where were William and his sister to
live, since the Alfoxden lease was not to be renewed for a radical and the
friend of such radicals as Thelwall and Coleridge? "It is William's wish,"
writes Dorothy to Thomas Poole, "to be near a good library, and if possible in a pleasant country." [121] Not infrequently, on turning from Wordsworth's poems to his letters or Dorothy's, one feels a slightly disquieting
gap between art and fact. We cannot, however, regard with cynicism the
joy which Wordsworth expresses in that portion of the *Recluse* fragment
which must have been written during the first spring at Town End. On
some ramble of the Hawkshead days, a "young and happy Being," he had
looked down into the wild but sheltered Vale of Grasmere and thought of
it as a place where he could enjoy the two great desires of his heart—perfect liberty and perfect security.[122] At last the prize, often dreamed of during the intervening years, was in his grasp. Best of all, this peaceful beauty
was to be enjoyed with "a younger Orphan of a home extinct," his beloved sister. The thought makes him look upward rather than outward
or inward:

> Aye, think on that, my heart, and cease to stir,
> Pause upon that, and let the breathing frame
> No longer breathe, but all be satisfied.
> Oh, if such silence be not thanks to God

---

[120] *Prelude*, II, 435–441.   [121] *Early Letters*, p. 228.
[122] *The Recluse*, pp. 1–5. Here the fallacies of retrospection are doubtless at work, but the
report is faithful to his present feelings.

For what hath been bestowed, then where, where then
Shall gratitude find rest? [123]

Other places have the usual charms of nature, but Grasmere uniquely
gives him "one sensation/Of majesty, and beauty, and repose." It is

A termination, and a last retreat,
A centre, come from whereso'er you will,
A whole without dependence or defect,
Made for itself, and happy in itself,
Perfect contentment, Unity entire.[124]

The "embrace" of the hills exerts a "guardianship" like that of "the
solemn shelter of the night." It can

. . . lap in pleasing rest, and bear us on
Without desire in full complacency,
Contemplating perfection absolute,
And entertained as in a placid sleep.[125]

This desire for sheltered repose, even for a snugness not far from the ideal
of Cowper, is natural in a homecoming wanderer considerably battered
by the storms of life. But the mood, although it will for some time be
blended with more vigorous assertions of imaginative energy, is destined
to become stronger.

Wordsworth's doubts as to the validity of the philosophy of nature are
now quieted by the hope that his feelings are reasonable:

That which in stealth by Nature was performed
Hath Reason sanctioned; her deliberate Voice
Hath said; be mild, and cleave to gentle things,
Thy glory and thy happiness be there.[126]

---

[123] *Ibid.*, p. 6. Here, however, we must consider the possibility of revision in more conservative days. The text of the *Recluse* fragment, first published as a whole in 1888, is something of a puzzle. I think with De Selincourt that the concluding lines which begin "On
Man, on Nature, and on Human Life," published in the Preface of the 1814 *Excursion*,
were written as early as 1798. They agree, even in punctuation and capitalization, with the
1888 text. The rest of the poem was doubtless written in 1800. But in 1836 Wordsworth
assigned the *Water Fowl* lines (published separately in 1823) to the year 1812. This may
imply a revision of the whole at about that time. Nevertheless the *Recluse* passages here cited
agree with other evidence as to the state of the poet's mind in 1800. Observe, above, the
typically deistic preference for *wordless* prayer.

[124] *Ibid.*, pp. 10–11.   [125] *Ibid.*, pp. 8, 21.   [126] *Ibid.*, p. 48.

This monitor is not the "most exalted" reason which will later be equated with imagination, but simply the reason of sober judgment, of common sense. William and Dorothy had begun to grow old. De Quincey regards them as prime examples of the fact that "Some people . . . live faster by much than others." His explanation, though somewhat Gothically expressed, is probably valid: "In the Wordsworths one part of the cause is, no doubt, the secret fire of a temperament too fervid; the self-consuming energies of the brain, that gnaw at the heart and life-strings for ever." In 1809, when Wordsworth was thirty-nine, he was taken by a whole coachful of passengers to be a man of sixty.[127] Looking back over the happiness of the Grasmere years in a letter of 1805, Dorothy inserts the ominous clause, "though the freshness of life was passed away even when we came hither." [128]

An idea extremely common in eighteenth-century poetry is that the contemplative pleasures of rural retirement are not to be enjoyed selfishly. If not the reward of services already performed for mankind, they should inspire benevolent emotions and actions. Herein the *Recluse* fragment is true to type:

> Yet 'tis not to enjoy that we exist,
> For that end only; something must be done.[129]

Grasmere Vale is not a solitude but a social organism. "Home of untutored shepherds as it is," it "swarms with sensation" which Wordsworth respects and desires to share. He is now part of an English community of precisely the sort which Hawkshead has conditioned him to think of as ideal. In sober fact, indeed, the dignified and independent "statesmen" were immensely superior to the squalid peasants of the south:

Towards the head of these Dales was found a perfect Republic of Shepherds and agriculturalists, among whom the plough of each man was confined to the maintenance of his own family or the occasional accommodation of his neighbour. . . . The Chapel was . . . the supreme head of this pure Commonwealth; the members of which existed in the midst of a powerful empire, like an ideal society or organized community, whose constitution had been imposed and regulated by the mountains which protected it. Neither high-born nobleman, knight, nor esquire was here; but many of these humble sons of the hills had a consciousness that the land, which they walked over and tilled, had for

---

[127] De Quincey, *Collected Writings*, II, 248–249.
[128] *Early Letters*, p. 555.   [129] *The Recluse*, p. 44.

more than five hundred years been possessed by men of their name and blood.[130]

Such a man is the shepherd Michael. In a sense he remains a Rousseauistic child of nature, but as a citizen of the "perfect Republic" he has had a sufficient elementary education for his needs, he is an hereditary land-owner, and he goes to church. Himself a member of this democratic but highly conservative commonwealth, Wordsworth in his great pastoral is definitely favorable to Michael's pride of property; and though he does not share the old shepherd's simple piety, he must vicariously sympathize with it in order to sympathize with his subject at all. The poem departs from the classical pastoral only to ally itself with Old Testament pastoral, and its spirit is different from that of the dramatically Christian elements in the Alfoxden poems. In that softer, slacker idyll, *The Brothers,* Leonard and James are good young Churchmen, and the old parson is drawn with a friendly pencil

Although in the gladness of this homecoming Wordsworth imagined himself to be a neighbor among neighbors, he was quite willing to accept the eighteenth-century opinion that a poet's benevolism is best exerted through the writing of poetry. His retirement is chiefly to be justified by using his talents and his vision—they amounted to the same thing—for the benefit of mankind:

> Possessions have I that are wholly mine,
> Something within which yet is shared by none,
> Not even the nearest to me and most dear,
> Something which power and effort may impart;
> I would impart it, I would spread it wide.[131]

In this deliberate "effort" to do men good through poetry lurks the snare of priggish didacticism. For a few years his genius will elude it, but forebodings are aroused by the assertion in the 1800 *Preface* that each of his poems "has a worthy purpose." [132]

The message is essentially the message of Alfoxden expressed with the greater steadiness and sobriety which he had begun to acquire in Germany. Here and there, however, one detects a few symptoms of more fundamental change. The two parts of *Hartleap Well* link the philosophy

---

[130] William Wordsworth, *A Guide to the District of the Lakes,* pp. 57–58.
[131] *The Recluse,* p. 44.   [132] *Works,* II, 387.

of nature with a medieval legend in a way which looks forward, though at a long distance, to *The White Doe of Rylstone*. Is it partly because of this association of the present with the past that Wordsworth's naturalism takes on a faint tinge of supernaturalism?

> This Beast not unobserved by Nature fell;
> His death was mourned by sympathy divine.
>
> The Being that is in the clouds and air,
> That is in the green leaves among the groves,
> Maintains a deep and reverential care
> For the unoffending creatures whom he loves.[133]

Creatures are things which have been created. In the three subsequent stanzas which conclude the poem, nature resumes her traditional sex, but for one moment the great Something has been thought of as "he." The divine Sympathy, the Being of Nature, is still primarily a pantheistic concept. But although *he* is *in* the material world, *he* is at the same time sufficiently personal and sufficiently detached from that world to observe, love, mourn, and care for his creatures. This mixture of immanence and transcendence raises problems which Wordsworth will not long attempt to solve by his own unaided powers. By the close of 1800, indeed, he would not have objected to calling himself a Christian provided the title did not demand acceptance of any particular Christian doctrine. He was about to recross the hazy boundary which divides sentimental deism from sentimental latitudinarianism.

4

The main spiritual turning-point of Wordsworth's life lies between the publication of the second edition of *Lyrical Ballads* in January, 1801, and the publication of *Poems in Two Volumes* in the spring of 1807. During this period the philosophy of nature attains its maturest form, but even before it has done so it begins to melt away. The two parts of this process must be examined separately. Books III–XIII of *The Prelude*[134] remain predominantly pantheistic—more confidently and enthusiastically so, indeed, than the mild retreatist mood of the first months at Grasmere might

---

[133] *Oxford*, p. 203.
[134] The reader is reminded that I cite the original version, which was divided into thirteen, not fourteen, books.

have led us to expect. "God and Nature's single sovereignty" [135] is proclaimed to be

> ...the life
> Of all things, and the mighty unity
> In all which we behold, and feel, and are.[136]

Wordsworth still believes, as Stallknecht says, "that all Nature is somehow one life, and that this life is a matrix of those values from which the human soul may derive all the inspiration that it requires." [137]

The divine unity of nature is not static: it is a series of events, a process of organic growth. The sensationalistic, or "action from without" aspect of the process remains highly important. "The speaking face of èarth and heaven" is still the "prime Teacher" of the mind.[138] Wordsworth is glad that throughout the uneasy affectations of adolescence "I still/At all times had a real and solid world/Of images about me." [139] No less than in *Three years she grew,*

> The mountain's outline and its steady form
> Gives a pure grandeur, and its presence shapes
> The measure and the prospect of the soul
> To majesty; such virtue have the forms
> Perennial of the ancient hills; nor less
> The changeful language of their countenances
> Gives movement to the thoughts, and multitude,
> With order and relation.[140]

Wordsworth's problem would have been simplified had he become a pure idealist; but he was never willing to surrender his belief in a world of real objective forms with whose workings the workings of the mind are mysteriously allied.

Nevertheless it is easy to agree with the majority of scholars that *The Prelude,* despite many veerings and inconsistencies, becomes increasingly transcendental as it approaches its conclusion. Since the theme is "the growth of a poet's mind," it is not surprising that the process should culminate in

---

[135] *Prelude,* IX, 237.   [136] *Ibid.,* XIII, 253–255.
[137] N. P. Stallknecht, *Strange Seas of Thought,* p. 4.
[138] *Prelude,* V, 11–12.
[139] *Ibid.,* VIII, 602–604.
[140] *Ibid.,* VII, 722–729.

> ... deepest feeling that the mind
> Is lord and master, and that outward sense
> Is but the obedient servant of her will.[141]

Sensation and association have done no more than lay the indispensable but humble groundwork for this creative rapture.

We observed, however, abundant transcendental implications in the poetry of 1787–1800. The differentiating feature of the present period is not so much the continuance of the shift from matter-over-mind to mind-over-matter as it is the intensified attempt to describe the all-pervading force which welds the two movements of the "interchange" into one Being. More frequently than in Books I and II this power is called "God," but the poet continues to prefer "Nature" or some such synonym as "principle of Being" or "Soul of all the worlds."

The harmonizing power may be described as "the sovereign Intellect," which diffuses through our images of external nature "A soul divine which we participate." [142] Its work is therefore the work of reason. But it has nothing to do with the reason of logical analysis or scientific induction—for that "inferior faculty" Wordsworth will always maintain a somewhat anxious scorn. The reason of Nature is purely synthetic and intuitive, a thing of power rather than of knowledge.[143] Its lower but important function—sometimes represented by "right reason"—is to provide the Stoical wisdom which comes from restraint and the recognition of suprapersonal law. Even in his most romantic moments, Wordsworth never quite forgets the importance of moral discipline:

> I had been taught to reverence a Power
> That is the very quality and shape
> And image of right reason, that matures
> Her processes by steadfast laws.[144]

But on its highest level reason is affirmative, expansive, creative. "In a soul sublime" it is indistinguishable from "passion." [145] And since the sublimest soul is the soul of the poet, this reason is identical with imagination, and imagination conversely

---

[141] *Ibid.*, XI, 271–273.   [142] *Ibid.*, V, 14–16.

[143] *Ibid.*, 449; VIII, 753–754.

[144] *Ibid.*, XII, 24–27. For an acute comparison between this view of reason and the "ethical imagination" of the present-day new humanists, see J. W. Beach, "Reason and Nature in Wordsworth," *Journal of the History of Ideas*, I, 341–344.

[145] *Ibid.*, V, 39–40.

> Is but another name for absolute strength
> And clearest insight, amplitude of mind,
> And reason in her most exalted mood.[146]

It is literally true, then, that

> ... Visionary Power
> Attends upon the motions of the winds
> Embodied in the mystery of words;[147]

for poetry, with its interweaving of object and subject, is the cosmic synthesizing force wielded by the mind of man. The plastic power of Nature over the material world is a "counterpart" of the imaginative faculty possessed by "higher minds" who

> ... from their native selves can send abroad
> Like transformations, for themselves create
> A like existence, and whene'er it is
> Created for them, catch it by an instinct.
>   .   .   .
> Such minds are truly from the Deity,
> For they are Powers.

The consciousness of sharing in the universal divinity is man's highest bliss. It is the source of faith, true reason, "sovereignty within and peace at will," passion that can most be trusted "when most intense," "truth in moral judgements," delight in the visible universe, and "genuine liberty." [148]

The rather undemocratically Shaftesburyan emphasis on "higher minds" is tempered by the belief that we should all be poets if we preserved the heritage of natural piety. Precisely as in Shaftesbury's system, also, the cosmos of universal imagination is the cosmos of universal benevolence. The "blest the infant Babe" passage in Book II has already identified "the first/Poetic spirit of our human life" with the spirit of love.[149] The great culminating passage of Book XIII returns to the same thought. In lines 166–167, imagination is prerequisite to that higher love which is both spiritual and "intellectual," but in lines 185–188 the two "are each in each, and cannot stand/Dividually." The growth of the reason which is imagi-

---

[146] *Ibid.*, XIII, 167–170.   [147] *Ibid.*, V, 619–621.   [148] *Ibid.*, XIII, 74–122.
[149] *Vide supra*, p. 169.

nation, and the imagination which is love, has been the theme of *The Prelude*. The final result is

> The feeling of life endless, the great thought
> By which we live, Infinity and God.[150]

As the orthodox revision in the 1850 text indicates, these lines of the original version do not refer to immortality and a transcendent personal Deity. They may be paraphrased: "The feeling of boundlessly expansive life in all things, the great thought by which we also live—the thought of a divine infinitude which is ours."

The benign poetic soul of the world is suprapersonal. Wordsworth regards it with awe and never pretends to understand its dark and sometimes fearsome mysteries. It is the source of control as well as of liberty. Its "goings-on" in external nature have helped to shape his mind through his senses. But in the last analysis the "one great Mind" is most clearly revealed in that which most closely resembles it—the human mind. The presence of mental qualities and activities in external nature is for Wordsworth a real fact, but the sole evidence for it consists of analogies drawn from human thought and feeling. Inevitably, then, man is "of all visible natures crown" in being "more than anything we know instinct/With Godhead." And since man must conceive of suprapersonal divinity in terms of personal divinity, man is the only God that man can surely know. Further, since the poet, even more than other men, must trust and love his own images, when Wordsworth glorifies man he glorifies himself as a creative force. "Thus we see," says Stallknecht, "that the mind which feeds upon infinity is really feeding upon itself, *i.e.* what it is and would become. In other words its energy is directed toward the reproduction of its own nature." [151] In those moments when his pantheistic faith is at its height, Wordsworth is not far from Blake's self-deification.

For the most thorough and sensible treatment of the endlessly disputed problem of Wordsworth's philosophical sources the reader should consult Joseph Warren Beach's *The Concept of Nature in Nineteenth-Century English Poetry*. Recognizing that Wordsworth's poetry grew not from systematic treatises at his elbow but from a complex of eighteenth-century assumptions which he used as a natural birthright, Professor Beach contents himself with distinguishing the elements which certainly,

---

[150] *Prelude,* XIII, 183–184.
[151] N. P. Stallknecht, "Wordsworth and Philosophy," *PMLA,* XLIV, 1125.

probably, or possibly formed part of the fertilizing compost-heap. Further than this one cannot profitably inquire. The case for Wordsworth's specific indebtedness to this philosopher or that must remain largely conjectural. His poetry is almost never sufficiently precise and technical in expression to provide reliable internal evidence. The meagre philosophical knowledge acquired at Cambridge was doubtless enlarged and illuminated by Coleridge, but guesswork as to what Coleridge *may* have said to his friend is slippery ground on which to base an argument. When we turn from the poems to the letters, prefaces, and other prose documents we are balked by the almost complete absence of allusion to philosophers—their personalities, books, systems, or particular ideas. One would think he had never read a philosophical book. Though usually a dull and unwilling correspondent, Wordsworth could write fully and eloquently on subjects which lay close to his heart. If he had felt much interest in technical philosophy it would sometimes have risen to the surface of his prose; but he is at his very warmest when he refers to Shaftesbury as "an author at present unjustly depreciated." [152] Hartley's *Observations on Man* is mentioned merely to illustrate the fact that a book is often a more valuable commercial property after an author's death than during his lifetime.[153] He declares that he has "never read a word of German metaphysics, thank Heaven!" [154] There is external evidence that he read Taylor's translations from Plato with some care, but all the Platonism in his poetry could as easily have come from the Shaftesbury tradition plus a little of Coleridge's spouting. The catalogue of the Rydal Mount Library omits many titles which were withheld from the sale by the poet's family. In 1819, furthermore, Wordsworth cheerfully confesses to Wrangham that he has never read "a fifth part" of the books which he owns.[155] And of course he must have read many books which were not on his shelves and of which no record has been preserved.

It seems probable that Wordsworth knew the main ideas of *Observations on Man* at first hand, or through Godwin or Priestley, or through the talk of Coleridge; but that Hartley is the sole or even the chief source of the associationism which blends so curiously with transcendentalism in

[152] *Works*, II, 418.
[153] *The Letters of William and Dorothy Wordsworth. The Middle Years*, p. 242. Cited hereafter as *Letters, Middle Years*.
[154] *The Correspondence of Henry Crabb Robinson with the Wordsworth Circle*, p. 401. Cited hereafter as *Robinson Correspondence*.
[155] *Letters, Middle Years*, p. 842.

the poet's philosophy of nature would be hard to establish. Professor Beatty refutes his own thesis when he quite correctly says:

The associationist doctrine . . . could not be fully accepted by Wordsworth, for by it the Imagination was given a very subordinate part to play in the mental life. He knew from his own experience that the poet's art is no mean one; hence he exalted the Imagination to the highest place. In Wordsworth's thought it takes the place of association in the system of Hartley.[156]

A faithful disciple would not have upset his master's applecart quite so completely.

As a matter of fact Hartley is rather unusual among eighteenth-century associationists for the lowly position which he assigns to imagination. From the time of Hobbes onward, this faculty was more respected by empiricists than by rationalists. Professor Welch reminds us that

In the Aristotelian doctrine of sense, Imagination merely presents or reproduces images to the intellect, whereas in the Associational doctrines of sense, Imagination not only Reproduces, but Produces. It matters little whether the psychological system be a logical or a materialistic one, provided it contains a doctrine of sense based on associationism. . . . As reason turned into mere analysis, or disappeared into the shadows of the laws of association, imagination was left as the sole active power of the human mind, and absorbed into itself more and more of the functions which the Divine Creator had once performed. From the artist's "fancy" it spread across the entire mind of man.[157]

Welch instances Thomas Reid as a thinker who combined associationism with great respect for the active powers of the imagination not only in poetry but in philosophy and religion.[158] From Reid's "Common Sense" or "Scottish" philosophy Wordsworth could have learned that, contrary to Berkeley, there is a real external world which we perceive directly and intuitively without any sort of idealistic mediation. But he could also have learned that, contrary to Hume, "the mind is, from its very nature, a living and active being."[159] Ideas are simply "the *acts* or *operations of our minds* in perceiving, remembering, and imagining objects."[160] These mental activities obey the laws of association, but they are not mechanically produced, as in Hartley's system, by the impact of

[156] Arthur Beatty, *William Wordsworth: His Doctrine and Art in Their Historical Relations,* p. 162.   [157] Livingston Welch, *Imagination and Human Nature,* pp. 68, 80.
[158] *Ibid.,* pp. 72–75.
[159] Thomas Reid, *Essays on the Intellectual Powers of Man,* p. 6.
[160] *Ibid.,* p. 127.

the external world upon the mind. "By the will of God, our power of perceiving external objects is limited to and circumscribed by our organs of sense"; but "we ought not to confound the organs of perception with the *being that perceives.* The eye is not that which sees; it is only the organ by which we see." [161] Here Blake and the Scottish philosopher are at one.

According to Reid the chief function of matter is the communication, through associative "trains," of mental qualities from mind to mind. Of course "we are . . . immediately conscious of the operations of our own mind," but

Other minds we perceive only through the medium of material objects, on which their signatures are impressed. It is through this medium that we perceive life, activity, wisdom, and every moral and intellectual quality in other beings.

This provides the basis for Reid's aesthetics, for he continues:

The signs of these qualities are immediately perceived by the senses; by them the qualities themselves are reflected to our understanding, and we are very apt to attribute to the sign the beauty or the grandeur which is properly and originally in the thing signified. Thus the beauties of mind, though invisible in themselves, are perceived in the objects of sense, on which their image is impressed. If we consider, on the other hand, the qualities in sensible objects to which we ascribe beauty, I apprehend we shall find in all of them some relation to mind, and the greatest in those that are most beautiful.[162]

In support of this theory Reid appeals to the authority of Plato, whose "opinion has been adopted by Lord Shaftesbury and Dr. Akenside among the moderns." [163]

Reid's combination of British empiricism and Platonism may be a philosophical monstrosity, but what other system available to Wordsworth could have done more to harmonize his sensationalism and his transcendentalism by giving an appearance of unity to the "ennobling interchange/Of action from within and from without"? Archibald Alison, whose *Essays on the Nature and Principles of Taste* Wordsworth is often supposed to have read with care, probably draws from Hartley much of his detailed information about associative processes. Primarily, however, he is a disciple of Reid, under whom he had studied at Glasgow University. His culminating idea, expressed almost in Reid's words, is "That the beauty and sublimity which is felt in the various appearances of matter,

[161] *Ibid.,* p. 34.   [162] *Ibid.,* pp. 473–474.   [163] *Ibid.,* p. 472.

are finally to be ascribed to their expression of mind; or to their being, either directly or indirectly, the signs of those qualities of mind which are fitted, by the constitution of our nature, to affect us with pleasing and interesting emotion." [164] His list of supporting authorities is also the same as Reid's except for a few embellishments: "the Platonic school, . . . all the philosophical systems of the East, . . . Lord Shaftesbury, Dr. Hutcheson, Dr. Akenside, and Dr. Spence." He loyally adds, however, that the mental origin of the beauty of nature "has no where been so firmly and so philosophically maintained as by Dr. Reid in his invaluable work *On the Intellectual Powers of Man.*" [165]

It would clearly be possible to flutter the dovecotes of scholarship with the novel and attractive theory that Wordsworth looked through Alison not to the mechanistic and anti-imaginative associationism of Hartley but to the much more congenial views of Reid. The only difficulty is formidable: there is not one scrap of scientifically respectable proof that Wordsworth's philosophy of nature was *directly* influenced by the writings of Reid, Alison, Hartley, Plato, Spinoza, Boehme, or any other philosopher. [166]

Let us, therefore, turn from hypothesis to demonstrable fact. I would suggest that our poet derived his most characteristic philosophical and religious ideas largely, though of course not entirely, from poetry—"matter wherein right voluble I am." And although the influence of Spenser, Daniel, Milton, Vaughan, and Herbert was assuredly important, the compost-heap consisted mainly of ideas which had been blended by poets of the eighteenth century. As a schoolboy Wordsworth saturated himself in these poets. Retrospective in his literary experience no less than in his feeling for nature, he continued to love them as a man:

> . . . the books which then I loved the most
> Are dearest to me now. [167]

From his earliest verses to the very close of his career, his poetry, his letters and those of his family, his prefaces and other prose works, furnish

---

[164] Archibald Alison, *Essays on the Nature and Principles of Taste,* p. 421.
[165] *Ibid.,* pp. 417–418.
[166] The sole almost certain exception is Godwin, but he influenced the philosophy of nature only antagonistically. The circumstantial-evidence case for Plato, Shaftesbury, and Rousseau is strong; but here I am demanding proof that Wordsworth expressed certain ideas because he had read certain books, not that he used ideas which were floating about in his intellectual ambience.   [167] *Prelude,* VI, 117–118.

unmistakable proof that he knew at first hand the poems of Addison, Akenside, Armstrong, Beattie, Blake, Bowles, Moses Brown, Bruce, Burns, Chatterton, Chesterfield, Collins, Cowper, Crabbe, Crowe, Darwin, Sneyd Davies, Dyer, Edwards, Gay, Gilbert, Goldsmith, Gray, Hamilton of Bangour, Johnson, Langhorne, Logan, Macpherson, Mason, Mickle, Percy (as poet as well as editor), Pope, Prior, Russell, Shenstone, Charlotte Smith, Sympson, Thomson, Tickell, Watts, Lady Winchilsea, and Young.[168]

It will be observed that, with obvious exceptions, these poets are more or less rich in preromantic tendencies. Wordsworth is sharply critical toward their powers of observation and their diction, but surprisingly ready to find in them that quality of imagination which for him is the prime essential of poetry and of life. Thus although Thomson "writes a vicious style," he has "genius as an imaginative poet." *The Seasons* "is a work of inspiration," [169] and at least one passage of *The Castle of Indolence* breathes "a strain of profound enthusiasm." [170] Dyer—and *The Fleece* is in question—receives more astonishing praise: "In point of *imagination,* and in purity of style, I am not sure that he is not superior to any writer in verse since the time of Milton." [171] Langhorne's picture of "common life" in *The Country Justice* is "philosophical and poetical," [172] and even Tickell is "a man of no common genius." [173]

At this point I must confess to some embarrassment. Nobody should be asked to read two other long books in order to evaluate this one. On the other hand I cannot review here the evidence brought forth in my earlier studies. Those who have accompanied me from 1700 to 1780 will be aware that Wordsworth could have derived every element of his naturereligion from the eighteenth-century poets whom he is known to have read with such close attention. His superiority to them is so great as al-

---

[168] Limitations of space forbid documentation. I can only assure the reader that I have confined myself to instances in which the poet is either directly quoted or referred to by name with remarks which prove Wordsworth's actual knowledge of one or more of his poems. Many of the poets mentioned were in the Rydal Mount library, but that has not been my criterion. The library also included the poems of Savage, Fergusson, and Hayley, various separately published poems by forgotten eighteenth-century scribblers, and several miscellanies, among them Ramsay's *Evergreen.* These have not been listed above, although there can be little doubt that Wordsworth read them. It is a fair assumption that he knew many other eighteenth-century poems, such as Fawcett's *Art of War,* Thelwall's *The Peripatetic,* and Cooper's *The Power of Harmony.*   [169] *Works,* II, 419, 421.
[170] *Letters, Middle Years,* p. 469.   [171] *Ibid.,* p. 478.
[172] *The Letters of William and Dorothy Wordsworth. The Later Years,* p. 829. Cited hereafter as *Letters, Later Years.*   [173] *Guide to the District of the Lakes,* p. 36n.

most to obscure the relationship. He is a sentimentalist who is almost never sentimental in the pejorative sense of the term. He has austerity and a deep sense of the mystery of things; he derives from experience and from the contemplation of world events a strong personal belief in the ideas which he inherits; he has lived the life which his precursors merely talked about; above all, he is a great poet. Nevertheless his ideas develop from the ideas of eighteenth-century sentimental poetry. Wordsworth's contemporaries recognize this fact. *The British Critic* places *The Excursion* in the familiar tradition of descriptive-reflective verse:

The shackles were burst by Thomson and Collins and Akenside, and, since their day, the works of nature have not wanted observers able and willing to deduce from them lessons, which Providence . . . intended them to convey. But none have ever entered so profoundly into this theory of their art as those commonly known by the name of the Lake Poets, particularly Mr. Wordsworth.[174]

Hazlitt declares that when Wordsworth rises to a lofty theme "his powers of description and fancy seem to be little inferior to those of his classical predecessor, Akenside."[175]

This perverse critical judgment at least serves to remind us that of all the eighteenth-century poets certainly known to Wordsworth,[176] it is Akenside who assembles in something like a system the largest number of congenial ideas. Both Reid and Alison, in passages cited above, mention "Dr. Akenside" along with Plato and Shaftesbury in listing precedents for their aesthetic position. Reid clinches the point by quoting from *Pleasures of Imagination* the thoroughly Wordsworthian statement:

> *Mind, mind alone!* bear witness earth and heaven,
> The living fountains in itself contains
> Of beauteous and sublime.[177]

In fact the weightiest positive objection to my Reid-Alison hypothesis is that Akenside, who antedates both of these thinkers, expresses in more

---

[174] Elsie Smith (ed.), *An Estimate of William Wordsworth by His Contemporaries*, p. 191.

[175] *Ibid.*, p. 150.

[176] For evidence as to Wordsworth's interest in Akenside see *Oxford*, p. 626, and *Letters, Later Years*, p. 906. It is noteworthy that Coleridge also admired *Pleasures of Imagination* as a "metaphysical poem" and made favorable mention of Akenside's odes. (Coleridge, *Letters*, pp. 163, 218.)

[177] Thomas Reid, *Essays on the Intellectual Powers of Man*, p. 473. The italics are Reid's.

appealing form what Wordsworth would have cared to draw from them.

Akenside is a bourgeois and a northerner; a political liberal and a deist with strong pantheistic leanings. Like other poets of his time, he is at once an associationist, a Newtonian, and above all a disciple of Shaftesbury. He is a benevolist and a lover of external nature. He aspires to combine beauty and truth, Plato and Bacon. The universe for him is an aesthetic and ethical harmony, the thought of a Divine Mind whose "eternal joy" is shared by men of "finer mould" and especially by poets. Poetic imagination is the reflection of divine creativeness in the human soul. Although our minds are moved by sensations emanating from the external world which the Divine Mind has thought into being, at their full development they are free and masterful. The highest beauty abides in those aspects of nature where the mind imaginatively apprehends qualities and powers like its own. Thus the poet is a seer who imparts "forms divine to mortal sense." Poetry is essentially religion, and religion is essentially poetry. Akenside's aim is the aim of Wordsworth: "to enlarge and harmonize the imagination, and by that means insensibly to dispose the minds of men to a similar taste and habit of thought in religion, morals, and civil life." His manner is sometimes as Wordsworthian as his matter:

> O ye Northumbrian shades, which overlook
> The rocky pavement and the mossy falls
> Of solitary Wensbeck's limpid stream;
> How gladly I recall your well-known seats
> Belov'd of old, and that delightful time
> When all alone, for many a summer's day,
> I wander'd through your calm recesses, led
> In silence by some powerful hand unseen.
> Nor will I e'er forget you. Nor shall e'er
> The graver tasks of manhood, or the advice
> Of vulgar wisdom, move me to disclaim
> Those studies which possess'd me in the dawn
> Of life, and fixed the colour of my mind
> For every future year.

Here are not only the thought but the personal background and even the cadences of Wordsworth.[178]

[178] This paragraph, including the passage quoted, paraphrases *Religious Trends*, II, 325–334. Three years later, C. T. Houpt independently quotes the same passage and compares it to Wordsworth in his *Mark Akenside*, p. 164.

Although Akenside is a particularly obvious precursor, Wordsworth could have found many of the same ideas scattered more loosely through the poems of Dyer, Collins, Langhorne, Beattie, and especially Thomson.[179] The well-known pantheistic passages in Pope's *Essay on Man* would also have been suggestive. This thesis does not deny that Wordsworth knew something about the philosophical background of these poets or that his knowledge was increased by conversations with Coleridge. But since the germs of all his fundamental ideas can be found in poets whom he read and admired it seems a waste of time to hunt for his immediate sources in treatises which he cannot be shown to have read or in his friend's misty oratory, much of which he did not like or understand.

We may now turn to the second main aspect of the 1801–1807 period—Wordsworth's gradual shift from the religion of nature toward more supernaturalistic views. Several factors combined to shake that confidence in the independent goodness and power of man and of himself in particular which had been the psychological foundation of his beliefs. The naturalistic-humanistic faith, first inflamed and then nearly quenched by the French Revolution, had been revived in a form made stronger than before by its closer relationship to his boyhood experience and to a congenial literary tradition. But it could meet this second attack only by accepting a compromise. The movement of history and of his own life forced Wordsworth to recognize the chasm between the nature of man and the nature of God.

As to the influence of Coleridge in this connection I remain a sceptic. It was all on the side of supernaturalism, but its weight is problematical. By 1804 Coleridge credits himself with having converted Wordsworth from necessitarianism to a state of illumination somewhat like his own,[180] but at times he still fears that his friend is a pantheist and a "semi-atheist." [181] Such remarks reveal less about Wordsworth than about Coleridge, who during these years is a particularly unreliable witness as to the relations between other minds and his own. Wordsworth had not been "even to extravagance a necessitarian" since 1796 at the latest. In order to get on with *The Recluse* he needed more technical knowledge than he

[179] Again I confine myself to poets whom Wordsworth demonstrably read and liked. My case will be strengthened if it is granted that he probably knew such Shaftesburyan "harmonious universe" poems as I. H. Browne's *Of Design and Beauty*, Brooke's *Universal Beauty*, and Cooper's *The Power of Harmony*. Akenside's *Pleasures*, however, is the culmination of this type.

[180] Coleridge, *Letters*, p. 454. [181] Coleridge, *Anima Poetae*, pp. 35–36.

possessed, and this he vainly hoped to obtain from his fellow-poet. But Coleridge—sick, vacillating, exigent, morbidly supersensitive—was not at this time a man to whom Wordsworth would turn for fundamental spiritual insights. Soon after the settlement at Grasmere the opium-taking was an open secret. Wordsworth became increasingly conscious of the gap between Coleridge's high-aspiring verbosity and the complete mess which he had made of his life, and Coleridge was increasingly pained by Wordsworth's "self-involution." [182] The breach widened in 1801,[183] and still further in 1803 during the Scottish tour.[184] When Coleridge returned from Malta in 1806 an utter wreck, little remained of the friendship except stubborn loyalty to old memories. William mourns his loss in *A Complaint*. He would fain believe that the "well of love" remains deep and full, but

> What matter? if the waters sleep
> In silence and obscurity.
> —Such change, and at the very door
> Of my fond heart, hath made me poor.[185]

This emotional impoverishment and the ominous spectacle of the downfall of a great genius constitute the chief "influence of Coleridge" during these years.

Marriage, parenthood, domestic obligations, were no more encouraging to Wordsworth's self-expansiveness than to that of other men. They enhanced the cautious, conservative side of his character. Dorothy's "wild ecstasies" were unknown to Mary Hutchinson. She was competent, loyal, unexciting, fecund, slightly cross-eyed, unlearned but quietly intelligent,

> And yet a Spirit still, and bright
> With something of angelic light.

Her placidity was not merely negative: it partook of the quality which old-fashioned folk call "recollectedness." She was at peace, and she wished peace for others. Sharp-eyed De Quincey agrees with Clarkson that she could say little more than "God bless you," but he finds in her "a sunny

---

[182] S. T. Coleridge, *Unpublished Letters* (ed. E. L. Griggs), I, 290–291.
[183] Coleridge was angered because Wordsworth had urged Poole to lend their friend money for a trip to the Azores.
[184] Coleridge, *Unpublished Letters*, I, 287.   [185] *Oxford*, p. 111.

benignity, a radiant graciousness." [186] The marriage was a happy one; we may be sure that after 1802 Annette, already half-forgotten, became no more than a budgetary problem. When Wordsworth, troubled about many things, inquired into the cause of his wife's serenity, he discovered no profound secret. Since childhood she had accepted, with unquestioning humility, the doctrines of Christianity as interpreted by the Book of Common Prayer.

Wordsworth always delighted in the animal vitality of children, and this feeling grew even stronger as the life ebbed from his limbs. But for his own children, like most other fathers, he wanted success and safety more than passionate adventure. Illegitimate Caroline was not excepted. As he walks with her on Calais beach in 1802, his mind brims with pious images which no "beauteous evening" of 1798 would have suggested: "The holy time . . . nun . . . adoration . . . Abraham's bosom . . . Temple's inner shrine . . . God being with thee." [187] Caroline was doomed to be a Papist, but better fortune was in store for John and Dora. "Today," writes Dorothy to Mrs. Clarkson on July 15, 1803, "we have all been at Church. Mary was *churched* and the Babe christened." [188] When the beloved second child, Dora, is a month old, Wordsworth is reminded that

> . . . In that Being's sight
> From whom the Race of human kind proceed,
> A thousand years are but as yesterday;

and from her first smiles, those exploratory "feelers of love," he gathers

> Tranquil assurances that Heaven supports
> The feeble motions of thy life.[189]

On De Quincey's first visit to the Wordsworths in 1807 he was awakened by the voice of four-year-old Johnny, who had slept in the same room: " 'Suffered under Pontius Pilate; was crucified, dead, and buried.' " [190] It was right that children should recite such formulas; and perhaps right that fathers, if only for their children's sake, should recite them too.

Wordsworth's marriage in 1802 was made possible by the fact that the

[186] De Quincey, *Collected Writings*, II, 236–238.   [187] *Oxford*, p. 258.
[188] *Early Letters*, p. 329.   [189] *Oxford*, pp. 172, 173.
[190] De Quincey, *Collected Writings*, II, 306.

new Earl of Lonsdale, on inheriting the title, had paid his father's debt with interest. The net share of William and Dorothy came to £3,825. To be sure it was not until 1816 that Richard Wordsworth, the pathological procrastinator, could be prevailed upon to draw up the documents assigning the Lonsdale money to the several heirs, but at least there were funds in London to be drawn upon. Marriage, children, a little money, are forces making for conservatism. So also are the friendship of men like Sir Walter Scott and the patronage of men like Sir George Beaumont. There is no reason to suppose that Beaumont consciously attempted to influence Wordsworth or that Wordsworth consciously toadied to him. One merely observes that Sir George and his lady were generous, amiable, cultivated, Torified, and extremely pious. On the whole Wordsworth's association with them was perhaps more a symptom than a cause of his changing views. When he visited London for several weeks in the spring of 1806, he divided his time between Sir George's very comfortable town house in Grosvenor Square and Christopher Wordsworth's equally comfortable rectory at Lambeth. Christopher was becoming a power in that revival of "high" Anglicanism which paved the way for the Oxford Movement. The brothers had drifted so far apart since the revolutionary days that their colloquies at this time could not have been very intimate, but their reunion played some part in Wordsworth's trend toward safe-and-sane respectability.

This trip to London, the poet tells Mrs. Clarkson, was taken "with an odd sort of hope that it may be of some use both to my health of body and mind: I am not quite so well as I was when I saw you last summer." [191] Wordsworth's medical history is something of a puzzle. There is plenty of testimony that, as with Michael, "His bodily frame had been from youth to age/Of an unusual strength"; and yet it was very easily put out of order. Coleridge, of all people, accused him of being a hypochondriac.[192] Like many vigorous and self-centered men whose womenfolk adore them, Wordsworth made much of any little ailments that came his way; but his most important physical difficulties were none the less genuine for being chiefly mental in origin. Hard thinking and feeling, and especially the effort to crowd his huge vague broodings into words and stanza-patterns, were an agony to him. The strain affected his nerves, and his nerves affected his body. Hence we hear much of pains in his side

---

[191] *Letters, Middle Years*, pp. 17–18.
[192] Coleridge, *Unpublished Letters*, I, 287, 291.

and sometimes in his stomach, heart, chest, or head. The reports of indigestion, colds, toothaches, earaches, piles, sleeplessness, and being simply "tired" are probably a part of the same psycho-physical nexus. Troubles of this kind begin as early as 1787,[193] probably because of his unwillingness to be uprooted from his boyhood environment. They are mentioned occasionally in the letters and journals of 1797–1799, but come thick and fast after 1802. In 1804 is first mentioned that inflammation of the eyelids which eventually damaged the eyes themselves. This handicap, which made reading and writing increasingly difficult, did not become serious until somewhat later. But even during the period which we are now examining the effort to write poetry wearied him, deranged his nerves, and made him ill. He was, as we have seen, beginning to age with abnormal rapidity. He felt a kinship with *The Small Celandine* in the storm:

> It doth not love the shower, nor seek the cold:
> This neither is its courage nor its choice,
> But its necessity in being old.
>
> . . .
>
> O Man, that from thy fair and shining youth
> Age might but take the things Youth needed not![194]

The primitive germ of Wordsworth's nature-philosophy was his childhood sense of physical vitality and freedom enjoyed in an environment which, as with the young man in *Ruth,*

> . . . seemed allied
> To his own powers, and justified
> The workings of his heart.[195]

As a sensationalist, Wordsworth was willing to grant that the source of his loftiest feelings was physiological; but as a transcendentalist, he was impelled to interpret the original pleasure as a movement of the "one great Mind" and therefore as a sign of the "visionary power" which his own mind derived from the "Wisdom and Spirit of the Universe." Even in the first two books of *The Prelude,* the latter interpretation looms almost as large as the former. Now, as the effort to express the inexpressible diminished his vitality, his sensuous delight in the world of eye and ear grew slack and feeble. With the impairment of his sensuousness, the

[193] *Vide supra,* p. 144.   [194] *Oxford,* p. 571.   [195] *Ibid.,* p. 193.

"visionary gleam" which depended upon that joy seemed correspondingly to grow dim. "Where is it now, the glory and the dream?" Inevitably, then, the rising scale of mental values was inverted: the highest insights belonged to childhood, not to maturity. Deteriorationism began to supplant perfectibilitarianism.

One consolation remains. The child, as the *Immortality Ode* declares, does not understand the insights and powers which he possesses, and perversely wishes to discard these precious gifts; while the adult can interpret, to himself and to others, the true significance of what he is losing, and lovingly cherishes the faintest glimmerings of the fading light. But the ability to rationalize an experience which he no longer deeply feels cannot be a satisfactory recompense for an anti-intellectualist whose whole philosophy was based upon the importance of vital emotion. The earlier transcendentalism which is the natural flower of Wordsworth's joy differs markedly from the later transcendentalism which ruefully seeks a substitute for that joy in explaining the mechanism of the process. The *Ode* gives no pertinent answer to Coleridge's *Dejection*. The only real consolation offered is that occasionally, "in a season of calm weather," something of the Hawkshead delight comes back in all its freshness. This *must* be true—"Or let me die!" Inevitably, however, the time approaches when nothing will be left but the didactic urge to talk about it and about it:

> Oh! mystery of Man, from what a depth
> Proceed thy honours! I am lost, but see
> In simple childhood something of the base
> On which thy greatness stands, but this I feel,
> That from thyself it is that thou must give,
> Else never canst receive. The days gone by
> Come back upon me almost from the dawn
> Of life: the hiding-places of my power
> Seem open; I approach, and then they close;
> I see by glimpses now; when age comes on,
> May scarcely see at all, and I would give,
> While yet we may, as far as words can give
> A substance and a life to what I feel:
> I would enshrine the spirit of the past
> For future restoration.[196]

[196] *Prelude*, XI, 329–343. The change from "my power" to "man's power" in the 1850 text is revealing.

In pursuance of this aim, many of the short poems of this period attach to the butterfly or the cuckoo or the sparrow's nest not the fading pleasure which they now actually give, but the untarnished pleasure of childhood. On a larger, more systematic scale, Books III–XIII of *The Prelude* use retrospection for the same purpose. Hence also his excessively meticulous interest in the psychological processes on which his poetry is based. But the remembrance of "visionary hours," no matter how vivid, is not vision, and the signposts of life point toward the dusty end of the journey, not toward its fresh beginning. He would "rather be a pagan" than lose the gleam entirely; the great sonnet, however, makes a despairing gesture without offering a solution. *The Green Linnet* and *The Waggoner,* in their different ways, seek relief in the contemplation of animal vitality for its own sake; but although they are delightful poems they do not satisfy Wordsworth's desire for an interfusion of matter and spirit. Only one choice remains, and it demands an unwelcome sacrifice of pride. If he can no longer soar with the skylark, he must remain on earth and gaze upward to a heaven which is not of his own making:

> I, with my fate contented, will plod on,
> And hope for higher raptures when life's day is done.[197]

His self-confidence thus shaken, Wordsworth looked out upon a world which gave scant support to belief in the natural goodness of man. He was still an adherent of Fox rather than of Pitt. It was French methods, not French principles, that he had abandoned. The French had abandoned their own principles, and the result was enslavement to Napoleon. And now this tyranny, the bastard child of revolution, was menacing the shores of England. The peril was no less spiritual than physical, for it was clear to his patriotic eyes that France had deserted the warm Rousseauistic naturalism of Beaupuy for the cold, unbelieving, mechanistic naturalism of Helvétius, Holbach, and Condorcet. His own naturalism was extremely different, but were the differences sufficiently black-and-white for a member of the Home Guard company which Beaumont had provided with uniforms?

As those who have grown to maturity during the twentieth century are aware, there is nothing like a war for making men talk about God. No time for metaphysical subtleties: what one needs is an omnipotent Chief of Staff. It is to be expected that Wordsworth should hail the English as

[197] *Oxford,* p. 160.

> A people, on their own beloved Land
> Risen, like one man, to combat in the sight
> Of a just God for liberty and right.[198]

To a considerable extent he is using patriotic ardor as a means of uplifting his imagination. The self-expansion which had been checked by the fading of the visionary gleam might be restored vicariously by sharing the communal emotions of the embattled fatherland and of oppressed European peoples who might make trouble for Napoleon if their nationalistic feelings could be aroused. In the patriotic sonnets of this period, Wordsworth feels the cloak of Milton about his shoulders:

> We must be free or die, who speak the tongue
> That Shakespeare spoke; the faith and morals hold
> Which Milton held.[199]

But although France was "far more abject," England herself was hardly an embodiment of loving imagination. Forgetful of Milton, she was "a fen of stagnant waters."[200] Her statesmen had no high principles, no large grasp of issues. The Tories wanted English victory, not human liberty. The Whigs advocated reform, but their patriotism was suspect and they spoke of freedom in rationalistic, utilitarian tones which menaced the religion of nature. In 1806 Dorothy reports to Mrs. Clarkson that "William seems to consider it almost indifferent what administration we have, that there is no true honour or ability amongst them."[201] At the height of his patriotism he is compelled to say to England, "Oh grief that Earth's best hopes rest all with Thee!"[202]

Since 1797 Wordsworth had regarded the philosophy of nature itself as the cure for the evils of the age. During this period, however, the doctor begins to lose faith in his own prescription. At times he expresses the view that although the world may reject it, it is still good for *him*. Looking out over Grasmere Lake in 1807 he seems to hear

> Great Pan himself low-whispering through the reeds,
> "Be thankful, thou; for if unholy deeds
> Ravage the world, tranquillity is here!"[203]

---

[198] *Ibid.*, p. 309.   [199] *Ibid.*, p. 307.   [200] *Ibid.*, pp. 309, 307.
[201] *Letters, Middle Years*, p. 10.   [202] *Oxford*, p. 309.   [203] *Ibid.*, p. 313.

But this private escapism denies the social feelings which are essential to his original theory—and when he was a real pantheist he did not talk about Pan.

The philosophy of nature was a religion, a metaphysics, an aesthetics, an ethics, and a psychology. It was also a sociology which glorified the ideal commonwealth of the Lake District. Whatever corruptions might exist beyond these hills, here was the true England—the England of his boyhood to which he had so joyfully returned. The good life of *Michael* and *The Brothers* must at all costs be preserved, he urges in the letter which he sent to Fox with a copy of the 1800 *Ballads*.[204] But how long could the last citadel of nature hold out against the Industrial Revolution? The Lake District was not a rich farming country. In the old days the agriculture and sheep-raising of the average dalesman had been supplemented by the weaving of his wife and daughters. But now, as cottage industry decayed with the development of weaving machinery, more and more of the natives were forced to sell their land or to take out mortgages which they often found themselves unable to pay. If the son of the family, like Michael's Luke, should go to the "dissolute city" to recoup the family fortunes, it was a foregone conclusion that he would be corrupted. The poverty of the dalesmen made it easy for superficial lovers of the picturesque to buy up land. Large properties were beginning to supplant the little independent farms. The beauty of the region was being defaced by inappropriate building and landscape gardening.[205]

As yet these changes would seem very slight to the ordinary observer, but to Wordsworth they were catastrophic. Everywhere he saw the work of a money-grubbing, mechanistic, unbelieving spirit.

> Plain living and high thinking are no more:
> The homely beauty of the good old cause
> Is gone; our peace, our fearful innocence,
> And pure religion breathing household laws.[206]

In the preceding century Thomson, Dyer, Young, and other poets had often glorified applied science and commercial progress as examples of human power. By this time, however, soft empiricism and hard empiricism were more definitely opposed. The great modern cleavage between poetry and life was well advanced. Bourgeois utilitarianism was busily

---

[204] *Early Letters*, pp. 260–262.
[205] Wordsworth, *Guide to the District of the Lakes*, pp. 6off.   [206] *Oxford*, p. 307.

shaping a world which was deeply repugnant to bourgeois sentimentalism. Like Blake, Wordsworth sees in "these dark Satanic mills" one of imagination's deadliest foes.

One cannot fully agree with De Selincourt's statement that the death of John Wordsworth on February 5th, 1805, marks "the beginning of the change from the naturalism and sensationalism of his early poetry to a more definitely orthodox attitude." [207] In the first place, as De Selincourt himself appears to say elsewhere, Wordsworth's naturalism had never been completely sensationalistic. Secondly, as this and the preceding sections have shown, the shift toward supernaturalism is in progress two or three years earlier than 1805. Unquestionably, however, the loss of the greatly loved brother struck a powerful blow at Wordsworth's self-sufficiency. Death was the great negation of the dignity of the human mind, and death was a law of that nature which he had been attempting to deify. Hence Wordsworth writes to Beaumont a little over a month after the disaster: "Would it not be blasphemy to say that, upon the supposition of the thinking principle being destroyed by death, however inferior we may be to the great Cause and Ruler of things, we have *more of love* in our nature than He has?" The only way to "get rid of" this "monstrous" thought is to posit *"another* and a *better world."* Throughout life John displayed the highest virtues, and yet "we see what has been his end! So good must be be better; so high must be destined to be higher." [208] The title "great Cause" smacks of deism, but "Ruler" seems to imply continuous providential control. The latter element is even stronger in letters written immediately after John's death:

I trust we shall with the blessing of God grow calmer every day. . . . It was the will of God that he should be taken away. . . . I trust in God that I shall not want fortitude, but my loss is great and irreparable.[209]

But the humble piety of these words is not reflected in the poems directly arising from the tragedy. Wordsworth is reluctant to express in poetry ideas which, if carried to their ultimate conclusion, would necessitate abandonment of the beliefs which have nourished his best work. This may explain why even those portions of *The Prelude* written after John's death remain, despite some inconsistencies, loyal to the original philosophy of nature. In his old age he explained to De Vere

[207] *Prelude,* p. 608.   [208] *Early Letters,* pp. 460–461.
[209] *Ibid.,* pp. 449, 452.

that when in youth his imagination was shaping for itself the channel in which it was to flow, his religious convictions were less definite and less strong than they had become on more mature thought; and that, when his poetic mind and manner had once been formed, he feared lest he might, in attempting to modify them, become constrained.[210]

Despite its title, *To the Daisy* is wholly devoted to relating, with an objectivity suggestive of Cowper's *Castaway,* the story of John's death. The flower will bloom "upon his senseless grave"[211]—a grave not very different from that of Lucy in *A slumber did my spirit seal.* The *Elegiac Stanzas in Memory of My Brother, John Wordsworth* try harder to assert that natural beauty is a source of consolation but finally turn from this idea to convey the warning:

> Oh do not Thou too fondly brood,
> Although deserving of all good,
> On any earthly hope, however pure.[212]

In the *Peele Castle* stanzas, the recent loss is described as a cause of that flagging of creative energy which the poet had lamented as early as 1802 in the *Immortality Ode.* Now, however, the fading of the gleam demands submission to "a new control" of Stoical "fortitude and patient cheer." After all his talk about "love of nature leading to love of man," Wordsworth begins to fear that the old nature-philosophy is egotistic and antisocial. "A deep distress hath humanized my soul. . . ./Farewell, farewell the heart that lives alone." [213]

In the third chapter of her dissertation on *Wordsworth's Reading of Roman Prose* Dr. Jane Worthington deals so efficiently with the Stoical strain in the poems of this period that those who seek light on this topic may be referred to her. She would not wish the reader to infer from her concentration on material relative to her subject that from 1802 to 1815 the poet was a thoroughgoing disciple of the ethics of Cicero and Seneca.[214] The graph of Wordsworth's thought cannot be so exactly plotted from year to year as to enable one to say that the line passes through an

---

[210] Aubrey de Vere, *Essays Chiefly on Poetry,* II, 282.
[211] *Oxford,* p. 580. [212] *Ibid.,* p. 581. [213] *Ibid.,* pp. 578–579.
[214] I believe she is right in saying that although there are interesting resemblances between Wordsworth's nature-religion and that of the Stoics the only direct influence is ethical, not metaphysical. Indeed, she might have made more of his failure to realize that the faith which he rejects in favor of the "new control" is hardly less Stoical than the ethics with which he now attempts to discipline himself.

exclusively Stoical stage before it rises, or descends, to dependence on supernatural omnipotence. Stoicism is one of the mingled elements in this period of transition, wholly absent from some poems, faintly suggested in others, and in still others strongly dominant. It is quite to be expected of a man who was educated in the eighteenth century and whose naturalistic self-confidence has been shaken, but who still hesitates to bow his head before any external moral guide conceived of as a divine personality. For a time the Stoical tendency was stimulated by the death of John, but it appears also in poems written before that disaster. There is a trace of it in the respect for a self-disciplinary "right reason" which we noted in the *Recluse* fragment and in *The Prelude*. It is strong in *Resolution and Independence* (1802) and in *The Small Celandine* (1804). As for the *Ode to Duty*, there now seems to be no doubt that it was composed several months earlier than the shipwreck. Wordsworth's Stoicism is primarily an attempt to adjust himself to the fading of the visionary gleam and only secondarily a response to the loss of John. There is no need to invoke the Categorical Imperative or the *schöne Seele* in order to interpret the *Ode*. Eighteenth-century poetry teems with prayers to half-deified personifications of ethical abstractions, and here is one more of them. Miss Worthington shows that the poem is rooted in Seneca rather than in Kant or Schiller.

Although the poems of Stoicism are ethical rather than religious, they possess a supernaturalistic element which deserves more notice than it has sometimes received. The Happy Warrior's virtues are those of a good Roman, but he dies "in confidence of Heaven's applause." Duty is not an independent power: she is "Stern Daughter of the Voice of God." *Resolution and Independence* ends with the prayer, "God, . . . be my help and stay secure," and the eighth stanza includes Wordsworth's first use of the term "grace" to mean a gift from above rather than a quality immanent in nature and the human heart.[215]

Both before and after John's death many of the less Stoical poems of this period betoken Wordsworth's increasing willingness to seek religious values in a transcendent God rather than in a pantheistically interpreted nature. Examples have already been instanced, but the point deserves further illustration. The *Immortality Ode* attempts to explain the basic emotions of the religion of nature by means of a supernaturalism which is inconsistent with Wordsworth's original beliefs. The visionary gleam is

---

[215] Elizabeth Geen, "The Concept of Grace in Wordsworth's Poetry," *PMLA*, LVIII, 695.

not a possession of nature: it is the glory which the child brings to this world from a higher realm. "God" and "heaven" are used in a mainly Platonic sense, but the thought of the poem is close enough to Christianity to be used in the lines on the death of Fox which were written in the same year that the *Ode* was completed:

> ... Man, who is from God sent forth,
> Doth yet again to God return.[216]

In the sixth stanza of the *Ode,* furthermore, the earth does its best to make the child "forget . . . that imperial palace whence he came." Professor Havens insists that in this passage "Wordsworth means by 'earth' not nature but the world." [217] In Book V of *The Prelude,* however, "old Grandame Earth" is a whimsical synonym for nature,[218] and Book I states that even in childhood Wordsworth

> ... felt
> Gleams like the flashing of a shield; the earth
> And common face of Nature spake to me
> Rememberable things.[219]

Here the earth is the abiding-place of the gleam, not its enemy. The *Ode* departs widely from the original doctrine; Beach is hardly too sweeping in calling it "virtually a recantation." [220]

Elsewhere one notices many little fragments of conventional piety which, taken together, suggest the direction in which Wordsworth's thought is moving: "For God took pity on the Boy[221] . . . From early converse with the works of God." [222]

> ... this I speak
> In gratitude to God, who feeds our hearts
> For his own service, knoweth, loveth us,
> When we are unregarded in the world.[223]

Something may also be learned from Wordsworth's choice of subjects even in poems where he is not ostensibly speaking for himself. More and

[216] *Oxford,* p. 581.   [217] R. D. Havens, *The Mind of a Poet,* p. 322.
[218] *Prelude,* V, 346.   [219] *Ibid.,* I, 613–616.
[220] J. W. Beach, *The Concept of Nature in Nineteenth-Century English Poetry,* p. 155.
[221] *Oxford,* p. 295. This poem, *The Blind Highland Boy,* also mentions guardian angels.
[222] *Prelude,* VII, 718.   [223] *Ibid.,* XII, 274–277.

more he cultivates the pious legends of the Border. *The Force of Prayer* concludes with lines which cannot be wholly impersonal:

> Oh! there is never sorrow of heart
> That shall lack a timely end,
> If but to God we turn, and ask
> Of Him to be our friend! [224]

The Horn of Egremont Castle is full of allusions to "Christ our Saviour ... my sinful soul ... all the saints in heaven ... good angels." [225] Here of course there is no question of belief, but Wordsworth would hardly have treated such material if he had lacked all sympathy with it. Nor would he have been likely to modernize Chaucer's *Prioress' Tale* before 1801. He still feels rather apologetic about it, but urges that "the mode in which the story is told amply atones for the extravagance of the miracle." [226]

Song at the Feast of Brougham Castle is more loyal to the religion of nature. Even here, however, there are signs of the coming change. In *Three years she grew,* Nature possessed the twofold power "to kindle or restrain" Lucy's emotions, giving her "both law and impulse" as equally desirable gifts.[227] In the *Song,* however, this equilibrium has been lost. Nature's influence is all on the side of restraint and humility; it prevents Clifford from becoming the proud and violent warrior mistakenly hailed by the minstrel, who

> ...did not know
> How, by Heaven's grace, this Clifford's heart was framed:
> How he, long forced in humble walks to go,
> Was softened into feeling, soothed, and tamed.[228]

These lines, corroborated by similar passages in other poems of this period, suggest that by 1807 Wordsworth wishes to derive from nature more "law" and less "impulse" than in 1799. Weary of "uncharted freedom," he needs centrality and permanence and a firm sonnet-like pattern at the core of a whirling world. He is losing his faith in the power of the divine wholeness to confer these values. Neither Clifford nor Wordsworth can be "soothed and tamed" by nature unless the influence of

[224] *Oxford,* p. 495.   [225] *Ibid.,* pp. 535–536.   [226] *Ibid.,* p. 552.
[227] *Ibid.,* p. 187.   [228] *Ibid.,* p. 205.

sense-experience upon the mind and the influence of the mind upon sense-experience are regarded as operations of "Heaven's grace."

The change is important, but let us not make too much of it. Nothing like a conversion has occurred: we are dealing with a gradual change which exhibits much wavering and inconsistency. Wordsworth is not yet thinking in specifically Christian terms. Such phrases as "Heaven's grace" imply no clear distinction between divinized nature and transcendent Deity—much less any recognition of the sinful soul's need of a Saviour. Wordsworth hopes to achieve the peace of humility without any thoroughgoing sacrifice of pride. He addresses Duty:

> Yet not the less would I throughout
> Still act according to the voice
> Of my own wish; and feel past doubt
> That my submissiveness was choice:
>
> . . .
>
> Denial and restraint I prize
> No farther than they breed a second Will more wise.[229]

We may be sure, however, that by 1807 Wordsworth regarded himself as a Christian and that he would indignantly have rejected any imputation of deism or pantheism. In the eighteenth century the cult of human sufficiency exhibits various degrees of deviation from the Christian norm. More cautiously than Akenside, Thomson describes a God who "ceaseless works alone, and yet alone/Seems not to work." [230] Other poets admired by Wordsworth, such as Beattie and Langhorne, are still more anxious to harmonize Nature's God with the God of Christianity. Hence Wordsworth, without wholly repudiating the influences which have formed his thought, can cultivate their less heterodox aspects. The poetry of the Age of Johnson displays a decline of overt deism and a growing tendency to identify a hazily benevolistic sentimental naturalism with Christianity.[231] The French Revolution encouraged a brief revival of straightforward deism, and Wordsworth responded to this trend. But the desire to preserve the satisfactions of the cult of feeling without quite losing the

---

[229] *Ibid.*, p. 492. This stanza was omitted from all editions subsequent to the first appearance of *Ode to Duty* in 1807. Miss Worthington, *Wordsworth's Reading in Roman Prose*, p. 63, observes that "To the Stoics there was nothing paradoxical in thus anticipating a freedom based upon obedience to law." She grants, however, that the stanza clashes with the submissiveness which pervades the rest of the poem.

[230] *Religious Trends*, I, 524.   [231] *Ibid.*, II, 369–370.

upward pull of Christianity was greatly enhanced by the post-revolutionary conservative reaction. The traditional faith, furthermore, was embodied in a stabilizing civic institution, an essential part of the British bulwark against Jacobinism, Bonapartism, and the new stirrings of popular discontent bred by the Industrial Revolution. As the vision faded, Wordsworth felt no sense of apostasy when he spoke of "Heaven's grace." At such a time, what Englishman would hesitate to call himself a Christian? What Englishman *need* hesitate to do so?

5

During the years 1807–1814 Wordsworth more definitely attempts to supernaturalize the religion of nature without surrendering its essential satisfactions. The Stoical asceticism of the *Ode to Duty,* which appears even more sternly in *Laodamia,* externalized the strain of rocky endurance in his character but could not satisfy his deepest desire. True to his boyhood experience and to his eighteenth-century precursors, he wished to be a joyous human being in a joyous universe—to "taste," like James Thomson, "the joy of God to see a happy world." [232] As late as 1812 he insists that he is "one of the happiest of men," and that "no man has completely understood him—Coleridge not excepted, who is not happy enough to enter into his feelings." [233] More and more frequently, however, come those unillumined moments when he must say with the Wanderer, "I daily lose what I desire to keep." [234] The self-reliance derived from pantheism no longer gives adequate assurance of free creativity, and "the self-reliance of despair" [235] blasphemes the gospel of universal happiness. He must therefore look to a supernatural Deity in order to authenticate and preserve the fading joy. On the other hand, the joy will disappear entirely unless the interaction of external nature and human imagination remains the chief agency through which divine grace operates.

As Dr. Comparetti has observed, *The White Doe of Rylstone* may be grouped with those other medievalistic narratives of 1807,[236] *The Song at the Feast of Brougham Castle* and *The Force of Prayer.*[237] But it received deeper thought and more careful artistry than the other poems of this

---

[232] *Ibid.,* I, 518.   [233] *Robinson,* p. 73.   [234] *Excursion,* IV, 612.
[235] *The White Doe of Rylstone,* 1056.
[236] Although Wordsworth did not publish *The White Doe* until 1815, he began to compose it in the fall of 1807 and had completed a first draft by the following February.
[237] *The White Doe of Rylstone, A Critical Edition by Alice Pattee Comparetti,* p. 19.

group, and it is a more interesting attempt to use the supernatural as a buttress for his naturalism. Specifically—the Dedication associates the poem with the death of John—it is a study in how to transform pain into peace through an imaginative sympathy conceived of as God's love at work in His creatures.

The bereaved Emily, endeavouring to follow the despairingly Stoical counsels of Francis, becomes "A joyless human being"—for Wordsworth, the ultimate paradox. With her own dutiful hands she has embroidered for her father a banner depicting the crucified Christ. But the nobly imaginative fervor with which the Catholic rebels regard this symbol is stained with popish fanaticism and superstition:

> To Durham first their course they bear;
> And in Saint Cuthbert's ancient seat
> Sang mass,—and tore the book of prayer,—
> And trod the bible beneath their feet.[238]

Emily, on the contrary, had learned at her Protestant mother's knee

> To worship in simplicity
> The invisible God, and take for guide
> The faith reformed and purified.[239]

These teachings, however, will not suffice, for in the cold impenetrability of her sorrow she lives "without one uplifted look." She is saved by a more Wordsworthian symbol than the Cross. If she cannot look up she can look down—down into the limpid eyes of one of God's "inferior creatures," which

> ... is spotless, and holy, and gentle, and bright;
> And glides o'er the earth like an angel of light.[240]

When she beholds the love in the doe's eyes, her own inhibited affections begin to stir, and gradually she regains her place in the universal benevolence. Her softened heart leads her from the wrong kind of melancholy to the pure contemplative melancholy in which she is "by sorrow lifted towards her God."

The doe is neither a mediatorial vehicle of the Holy Spirit nor a direct agent of Providence. She is simply an animal,

---

[238] *White Doe*, 711–714.   [239] *Ibid.*, 1039–1041.   [240] *Ibid.*, 240–241.

Who, having filled a holy place,
Partakes, in her degree, Heaven's grace.[241]

Despite the pious language and the supernaturalistic patina of the work, its action can be understood only in terms of the "ennobling interchange" of the original philosophy of nature—Emily's love sensationalistically awakened by, and then transcendentally enhancing, the doe's love. The laws of association are still at work. The animal is Emily's childhood playmate—"the very Doe of other years." By leading Emily into scenes where she was happy in earlier days the gentle beast revives "the memory of old loves" [242] and forges anew the chain of natural piety. All this is suffused with an atmosphere of legendary strangeness and besprinkled with "God," "grace," "heaven," "prayer," and similar drops of holy water. Nevertheless the doe is no more necessarily a gift of grace than the ass which softened Peter Bell's hard heart by thoroughly naturalistic means.

It is only fair to say that *The White Doe* meant more to Wordsworth than it ever meant to anyone else. In his old age he told Justice Coleridge that

The true action of the poem was spiritual—the subduing of the will, and all inferior passions, to the perfect purifying and spiritualizing of the intellectual nature; . . . the Doe, by connection with Emily, is raised, as it were, from its mere animal nature into something mysterious and saintlike.[243]

Emily's apparent self-abnegation strikes Professor Harper as culpably un-Protestant. For him the poem is "a confession of human failure so sweeping that the Western mind refuses to join in it. Behind our intellectual, no less than our material achievements, throbs the vital spark of self-trust." [244] Harper might have observed, however, that according to the poet's own statement the doe is rendered "mysterious and saintlike" not by her connection with God, but by her "connection with Emily." And "intellectual nature" means imagination, the "love more intellectual" of *The Prelude*. Wordsworth explains that the banner and the doe

derive their influence not from properties inherent in them, not from what they are actually in themselves, but from such as are bestowed upon them

---

[241] *Ibid.*, 1875–1876.   [242] *Ibid.*, 1659, 1754.
[243] Christopher Wordsworth, *Memoirs*, II, 313.
[244] G. M. Harper, *William Wordsworth*, II, 157.

by the minds of those who are conversant with or affected by those objects. Thus the Poetry, if there be any in the work, proceeds whence it ought to do, from the soul of man, communicating its creative energies to the images of the external world.[245]

The doe is a more potent symbol than the banner simply because it receives from the beholder a purer and loftier imaginative treatment. This subjectivism is asserted more clearly in Wordsworth's statements *about* the poem than in the text. The implication, however, is inevitable: the quasi-sacramental function of the doe is the work of Emily's imaginative human soul.

To a greater extent than in earlier poems the human soul, with its creative powers, is regarded as the gift of a transcendent God. As the motto from Bacon declares, "Man, when he resteth and assureth himself upon Divine protection and favor, gathereth a force and faith which human Nature in itself could not obtain." But the passage quoted by Wordsworth begins, "They that deny a God destroy Man's nobility." Bacon is saying that religion is the best means of safeguarding Renaissance "magnanimity"—not "force and faith," but faith for the sake of force, reverence for the sake of humanistic pride. *The White Doe* shows a diminution of Wordsworth's self-trust, but the new humility is used to validate the old faith in individual imaginative might. The poem, then, is not alarmingly un-Protestant. Professor Harper's throbbing spark has not wholly been quenched. With reverence Wordsworth bows his head before God. But he will not take the great contra-natural leap, and the doe remains a man-made sacrament.

As a sonnet of this period declares, man can be regarded as weak-willed and joyless only by him who lacks the "glorious faculty," the "sacred power" of

> Imagination lofty and refined:
> 'Tis hers to pluck the amaranthine flower
> Of Faith, and round the sufferer's temples bind
> Wreaths that endure affliction's heaviest shower,
> And do not shrink from sorrow's keenest wind.[246]

Does faith demand humility, or encourage pride? Is imaginative power conferred by faith, or is faith the creation of imaginative power? Words-

---

[245] *Letters, Middle Years*, p. 705. See also pp. 197–198.   [246] *Oxford*, p. 259.

worth was never fully to resolve this ambiguity in his thought. It perplexes us not only in *The White Doe* but in *The Excursion.*

The latter poem has a more specifically Christian flavor than the former, but by no means all contemporary readers approved of its theology. Shelley lamented that Wordsworth had become a hypocritical bigot,[247] while Lamb found in the work "the character of an expanded and generous Quakerism." [248] According to Jeffrey, the poet had obscured "a few very simple and familiar ideas" beneath "a tissue of moral and devotional ravings" comparable to "the mystical verbiage of the Methodist pulpit"; [249] and the *Monthly Review* agreed that "neither mysticism nor enthusiasm is the best conductor of misguided mortals back to the precincts of a calm and rational religion." [250] Evangelicals objected, not of course to Wordsworth's enthusiasm, but to his failure to emphasize the distinctive doctrines of a saving faith. The poet, said James Montgomery in the *Eclectic Review,* regards nature with so passionate a devotion "that it is sometimes difficult to distinguish the reverence which he pays to it, from the homage due to the Supreme alone." [251] Cargill thought the religion of the poem "merely subjective" and "no better than atheism" because it ignored "faith in redemption by Christ"; [252] and Mulock held the same opinion because Wordsworth lacked any sense of "the depravity of human nature." [253]

Such objections, however, were not peculiar to members of the Evangelical party. When Crabb Robinson reported Cargill's views to Julius Hare, that very broad Churchman "seemed willing to concur notwithstanding his love of Wordsworth." [254] A very high clergyman also considered *The Excursion* to be "altogether anti-Christian" in that it

represents faith *per se* as meritorious. Now faith independently of the *object of faith* I hold to be as worthless as the moral virtues. The only faith that is of any value, is *Christian* faith—faith in the *redeemer as such,* faith in that *connection between the redeemer and the redeemed* in which alone Christianity exists.[255]

At the opposite end of the theological scale the Unitarian Patty Smith considered Wordsworth a pantheistic nature-worshipper.[256] If allowance

[247] *Robinson,* p. 212.
[248] Elsie Smith (ed.), *An Estimate of William Wordsworth,* p. 170.
[249] *Ibid.,* pp. 160–161.   [250] *Ibid.,* p. 185.   [251] *Ibid.,* p. 175.
[252] *Robinson,* pp. 65, 490.   [253] *Ibid.,* p. 246.   [254] *Ibid.,* p. 495.
[255] *Robinson Correspondence,* p. 300. The speaker is not named.
[256] *Letters, Middle Years,* p. 618.

is made for the overstrained language of ecclesiastical partisanship, these criticisms still retain validity for persons to whom Christianity continues to mean anything in particular.

Crabb Robinson was Wordsworth's devoted admirer, but like many religious liberals he was quick to observe the heterodoxy of his supposedly orthodox friends. It seemed to him that the religion of *The Excursion* resembled that "of the German metaphysicians, a sentimental and metaphysical mysticism in which the language of Christianity is used." The poet's sincerity is unquestionable, "but perhaps he is himself not perfectly clear on the subjects on which his mode of thinking and feeling is anxiously inquired after by his religious admirers." [257] This judgment is not ungenerous, for in 1812 Wordsworth had told Robinson that the religion of Unitarians

allows no room for imagination, and satisfies none of the cravings of the soul. "I can feel more sympathy with the orthodox believer who needs a Redeemer and who, sensible of his own demerits, flies for refuge to Him (though perhaps I do not want one for myself) than with the cold and rational notions of the Unitarian." [258]

That parenthesis casts a shadow over the Pastor's references to "the faith derived through Him who bled/Upon the cross," [259] and reminds us of the Wanderer's assertion that he would prefer to accept the grossest superstitions rather than subject his imagination to

> The repetitions wearisome of sense,
> Where soul is dead, and feeling hath no place.[260]

Wordsworth's original plan was probably that the religion of the Wanderer should be reinterpreted and raised to a higher level by the Christianity of the Pastor. The collapse of this intention justifies Coleridge's disappointment in *The Excursion* as a philosophical poem.[261] The priest is but a decorative sycamore to the Wanderer's majestic oak.[262] His graveyard stories are feebly inconclusive. Even at the vicarage tea-table, where surely he might have been allowed to take the lead, he admiringly listens, in almost unbroken silence, to the Wanderer's oratory. Being after all the chaplain of the party, the Pastor offers prayer at the con-

---

[257] *Robinson*, p. 158.   [258] *Ibid.*, p. 87.   [259] *Excursion*, IX, 721–722.
[260] *Ibid.*, IV, 611–630.   [261] Coleridge, *Letters*, pp. 641–642, 647–648.
[262] *Excursion*, V, 455–461.

cluding picnic, but his half-hearted truisms are anticlimactic. One makes
the proper allowances for his profession and turns to the Wanderer as
Wordsworth's true spokesman.

The Wanderer is both a child of the Kirk of Scotland and a child of
nature in the purest Wordsworthian sense. The latter side of his heredity
is dominant. To be sure, his youthful moments of elevation in the presence of nature made him think of the Scriptures:

> O then how beautiful, how bright appeared
> The written promise! Early had he learned
> To reverence the volume that displays
> The mystery, the life which cannot die;
> But in the mountains did he *feel* his faith.
> All things responsive to the writing, there
> Breathed immortality, revolving life,
> And greatness still revolving; infinite!
> There littleness was not; the least of things
> Seemed infinite; and there his spirit shaped
> Her prospects, nor did he believe,—he *saw*.[263]

Obviously "the Bible of the Universe" [264] was the more inspiring volume.
Thanks to the contemplation of revolving infinitude, with the passing
years Calvinistic grimness

> Was melted all away; so true was this,
> That sometimes his religion seemed to me
> Self-taught, as of a dreamer in the woods;
> Who to the model of his own pure heart
> Shaped his belief, as grace divine inspired,
> And human reason dictated with awe.[265]

We may conjecture that Drummond, the retired Scottish pedlar of Wordsworth's boyhood who is in some measure the Wanderer's prototype, was
a "Moderate" who had gone far in the direction of Shaftesbury and
Hutcheson. The cooperation of divine grace and human reason is good
Arminianism, but it provides no basis for the idea that the "pure heart"
is a sufficient "model" for belief. The Wanderer has made up a superior
"self-taught" religion; but since he has done so "with awe" and under
the inspiration of "grace divine," he is the best of Christians. Wordsworth
insists on having it both ways.

[263] *Ibid.*, 222–232.   [264] *Letters, Middle Years*, p. 618.
[265] *Excursion*, I, 406–413.

The psychological root of *The Excursion* is the description of the Pastor's daughter, her younger brother, and his chum—so radiant with "pride and joy," so full of life in every limb.[266] The poet's neighbors remembered that "he was fond o' children like enough, but children was niver vara fond o' him."[267] Perhaps they sensed that his love was too hungry to be quite disinterested: they possessed so much that was slipping from his grasp. The Wanderer explains that in old age we yearn toward childhood because

> . . . there the Soul discerns
> The dear memorial footsteps unimpaired
> Of her own native vigour.[268]

But although we lose much with advancing years, we receive compensation in "Fresh power to commune with the invisible world,"[269] and the final result of this communion is a restoration of the old nature-experience in a form less exciting but more spiritual. No such recompense can be ours, however, unless we believe that our life

> . . . is ordered by a Being
> Of infinite benevolence and power;
> Whose everlasting purposes embrace
> All accidents, converting them to good.[270]

With deep reverence, then, the Wanderer pays homage to the

> . . . dread source,
> Prime, self-existing cause and end of all
> That in the scale of being fill their place;
> Above our human region, or below,
> Set and sustained.

All else is imperfect and transient. Our consciousness is but "the motions of thy will." Our apprehension is but

> . . . those transcendent truths
> Of the pure intellect, that stand as laws

---

[266] *Ibid.,* VIII, 493–499, 545–587.
[267] H. D. Rawnsley, "Reminiscences of Wordsworth Among the Peasantry of Westmoreland," *Transactions of the Wordsworth Society,* VI, p. 188.
[268] *Excursion,* IX, 36–39. [269] *Ibid.,* 86. [270] *Ibid.,* IV, 10–17.

(Submission constituting strength and power)
Even to thy Being's infinite majesty! [271]

Apparently, then, man is utterly dependent upon God. But the line, "Submission constituting strength and power," suggests that the motive for humility remains the same as in *The White Doe of Rylstone*. Man's spirit, says the Wanderer, is too weak to provide direct contemplation of the pure abstract intelligence which governs the world.[272] Since we cannot rise to Him, the God of perfect love descends to us. He makes His will known through

> . . . the law
> Of conscience—conscience reverenced and obeyed
> As God's most intimate presence in the soul,
> And his most perfect image in the world.[273]

Hence the seat of judgment is occupied not by the Incarnate Lord but by the Inner Light. Man is utterly dependent upon God—as found within himself.

The transcendent God, though constantly assumed to be the God of Christianity, reveals himself in a manner which smacks of pantheism. He permeates "every form of being" as "an *active* Principle" of loving energy —"the Soul of all the worlds, . . . the freedom of the universe." But the "most apparent home" of this cosmic force is "the human Mind." [274] Despite Wordsworth's recognition of human weakness and dependency, he asserts the godlike energies of the individual mind no less strongly in *The Excursion* than in *The Prelude:*

> Within the soul a faculty abides
> That with interpositions, which would hide
> And darken, so can deal that they become
> Contingencies of pomp, and serve to exalt
> Her native brightness.[275]

This faculty is the "love more intellectual," the perfect reason which is perfect imagination. "Access for you," Solitary is assured,

---

[271] *Ibid.*, 79–99. In line 81, observe the survival of the eighteenth century's "chain of being."

[272] *Ibid.*, 174–183.   [273] *Ibid.*, 222–227.   [274] *Ibid.*, IX, 1–20.

[275] *Ibid.*, IV, 1058–1062.

> Is yet preserved to principles of truth,
> Which the Imaginative Will upholds
> In seats of wisdom, not to be approached
> By the inferior faculty that moulds,
> With her minute and speculative pains,
> Opinion, ever changing![276]

Sensationalism and associationism, however, have not wholly been banished. The divine "active principle" is immanent in the world of sense-perception as well as in the mind. Hence if the doctrine of the Imaginative Will is too rarefied for Solitary, he can equally well trust to "Nature's humbler power." He can roam the woods,

> Where living things, and things inanimate,
> Do speak, at Heaven's command, to eye and ear,
> And speak to social reason's inner sense,
> With inarticulate language.[277]

By inserting a few such phrases as "at Heaven's command" Wordsworth can preserve all his favorite ideas about the benign influence of external nature and rural life. Strangely enough, there is more true humility in the naturalism than in the supernaturalism of the poem; for the former implies loyalty to a real objective world, while the latter sets no limits to egotistic expansion. In the last analysis, transcendentalism and belief in a transcendent God are incongruous. On the whole, however, the subjective emphasis in *The Excursion* is so strong that the ascription to nature of any control over the mind seems inconsistent with the general tenor of the work. The two halves of Wordsworth's philosophy are drifting apart. For the Wanderer, the essential element in all religion, Christian or non-Christian, is that "the imaginative faculty" should be "lord of observations natural."[278]

It has already been shown that the connection between the Wanderer's "self-taught" religion and that of the Pastor's rustic flock was clearer to Wordsworth than to many of his contemporaries. Certain critics of our own times, however, have met the poet's theology rather more than half-way. Miss Batho, who sees Wordsworth as a good High Churchman from the beginning to the end of his career, avers that in *The Excursion,* "like many of the greatest saints and theologians, he turned instinctively to that doctrine which sees in the Incarnation rather than in the Crucifixion the

---

[276] *Ibid.,* 1126–1132.   [277] *Ibid.,* 1187–1229.   [278] *Ibid.,* 707–708.

essense of the Atonement."[279] But it is difficult to see that Wordsworth feels any personal need of the Atonement at all. He wishes to regain, at whatever cost, the power which he is losing, but he does not know that he is a sinner. For Anglicanism high or low—for any sort of Christianity, indeed—God in *The Excursion* is too much like Wordsworth, and Wordsworth is far too much like God.

For Dean Inge, Wordsworth was a Christian and a Platonic pantheist or panentheist or panpsychist whose religion "rests the whole weight of its conviction on the testimony of the Holy Spirit, and maintains that this is sufficient."[280] It is true that the Imaginative Will may be traced back, through successive stages of disintegration, to the Holy Spirit as interpreted in terms of the World Soul by quasi-Christian Neoplatonists; but by the time it descends to Wordsworth the connection has become extremely tenuous. The best answer to Miss Batho and the Dean is John Sterling's epigram: "Wordsworth is not a Christian. He is nothing but a Church of England pantheist."[281]

Undoubtedly Wordsworth believes that he has presented the Christian answer to the otherwise unanswerable question,

> ...How shall man unite
> With self-forgetting tenderness of heart
> An earth-despising dignity of soul?[282]

At times, however, the basic ambiguity of Wordsworth's thought breeds festers of subconscious intellectual dishonesty. Hazlitt rightly protests that *Candide* should not have been called "dull":[283] to the spectator, a blow below the belt is all the more offensive for being impotent. The frequent scornful flings at science and analytical reason betray a timorous obscurantism. Even more distressing is the arbitrariness with which the Pastor selects his stories. The Wanderer, hard pressed by Solitary, turns to the wise priest. What, in his rich experience, is man actually like—strong or weak, good or bad?

> Give us, for our abstractions, solid facts;
> For our disputes, plain pictures.[284]

[279] Edith C. Batho, *The Later Wordsworth*, p. 283.
[280] W. R. Inge, *The Platonic Tradition in English Religious Thought*, p. 114.
[281] John Hunt, *Pantheism and Christianity*, p. 306.   [282] *Excursion*, V, 576–578.
[283] *Ibid.*, II, 484; Elsie Smith (ed.), *An Estimate of Wordsworth*, p. 151.
[284] *Excursion*, V, 637–638.

It is a fair question, and deserves a fair answer. But when the Pastor hints that he has seen much of the evil side of human nature, the Wanderer "somewhat eagerly" disclaims any desire

> ... that you, for such poor gain,
> (Gain shall I call it—gain of what?—for whom?)
> Should breathe a word tending to violate
> Your own pure spirit.[285]

"Thus sanctioned," the relieved parson assures his hearers in advance that

> ... I willingly confine
> My narratives to subjects that excite
> Feelings with these accordant: love, esteem,
> And admiration; lifting up a veil,
> A sunbeam introducing among hearts
> Retired and covert; so that ye shall have
> Clear images before your gladdened eyes
> Of nature's unambitious underwood,
> And flowers that prosper in the shade.[286]

The desirability of relieving Solitary's gloom hardly justifies such use of loaded dice in a philosophical poem.

In this connection the political and social thought of *The Excursion* requires some scrutiny. As the preceding section has shown, Wordsworth began in 1802 to seek in nationalistic feeling a vicarious means of preserving his sense of personal vitality through sharing in the collective ego of the fatherland. For a time his patriotism had been chilled by the absence of lofty imaginative principles from England's policy. But, as he asserts in *The Convention of Cintra* (written 1808), England's cooperation with Spain and Portugal in their struggle for independence soon placed her in the position of a "disinterested and generous" champion of liberty.

From that moment "this corruptible put on incorruption, and this mortal put on immortality." This sudden elevation was on no account more welcome . . . than by the returning sense which accompanied it of inward liberty, and choice, which gratified our moral yearnings, inasmuch as it would give henceforward to our actions as a people, an origination and a direction unquestionably moral.[287]

[285] *Ibid.,* VI, 579–584.   [286] *Ibid.,* 645–654.
[287] Wordsworth, *The Convention of Cintra,* pp. 10–11.

At such a time even the popery of the Spaniards can be forgiven, since it is a chief source of their patriotic ardor:

Even the very faith in present miraculous interposition . . . passes into a habit of obscure and infinite confidence of the mind in its own energies, in the cause from its own sanctity, and in the ever-present invisible aid or momentary conspicuous approbation of the supreme Disposer of things.[288]

The conception of miracle as validating the energies of man no less than the power of God is revealing. Simultaneously with such utterances, Wordsworth is writing letters urgently opposing the enfranchisement of Roman Catholics in his own country: "With the Methodists on one side, and the Catholics on the other, what is to become of the poor Church and people of England?" [289]

But the terms of the Convention of Cintra, drawn up between the English and French generals without regard to the interests and national sensibilities of the Iberians, "had degraded a heroic national struggle into a petty mercenary war of professional soldiers." [290] Wordsworth continued to prefer the Ministry to the Opposition because it was more actively anti-Bonapartist and anti-Catholic,[291] but after 1808 he could no longer find true loftiness of principle in either party. The underlying cause of the national decay was that

while Mechanic Arts, Manufactures, Agriculture, Commerce, and all those products of knowledge which are confined to gross—definite—and tangible objects, have, with the aid of Experimental Philosophy, been every day putting on more brilliant colours; the splendour of the Imagination has been fading—[292]

fading from society no less than from his own mind. With everything moving away from the Hawkshead values, he began to develop a panicky dread of any sort of change. Security looked even more desirable than freedom, though he was willing to surrender neither the one nor the other.

During the period which now concerns us we hear much of low spirits and ill health, and especially of that ominous inflammation of the eyelids.[293] In 1810 he had broken with Coleridge, and the ensuing reconcili-

[288] *Ibid.*, p. 117.   [289] *Letters, Middle Years*, pp. 250, 291.
[290] Alfred Cobban, *Edmund Burke and the Revolt against the Eighteenth Century*, p. 144.
[291] *Letters, Middle Years*, p. 569.   [292] *Convention of Cintra*, p. 166.
[293] *Letters, Middle Years*, pp. 260, 371, 420, 461, 585, 591.

ation was merely on the surface. The most influential reviewers had dealt savagely with his poems. His knowledge of how they could be placated in the future played some part, though probably a small one, in his increasing conservatism and in the priggishly edifying tone which suffuses his later work. Lack of appreciation, though it hurt and angered him, could be laid to the aesthetic and moral deficiencies of the critic; but the fact that his poems did not sell raised a practical problem. Wordsworth liked money,[294] and at this time he needed more of it because the enlargement of his family and the consequent removal from Dove Cottage to more expensive quarters—Allan Bank, the Rectory, Rydal Mount—placed a strain upon his income. In 1812 the poet asks Lord Lonsdale's help in obtaining some sinecure—his father and grandfather had loyally served his lordship's family.[295] The following year, thanks chiefly to the good offices of Samuel Rogers, Lonsdale secured for him the office of Distributor of Stamps for Westmoreland. It was a fairly lucrative post, and one which encouraged judicious views on matters of Church and State.

There were fresh burdens of sorrow—the loss of his daughter Catharine and his son Thomas in 1812. The death of the boy, the second blow within six months, was especially hard to bear, "for he was a child of heavenly disposition. . . . I trust that Almighty God has received him amongst the number of the blessed." [296]

All of these influences tended to sap his animal vitality, depress his spirits, and forge chains of obligation which bound him more and more firmly to that world which is too much with us. Thus *The Excursion* was written during a confused and troubled state of transition between the by no means wholly illiberal political feelings voiced in *The Convention of Cintra* and the much more timid and obstructive Toryism of his old age. Patriotism is an essential part of the Wanderer's religion.[297] In no jingoistic spirit he looks forward to the day

> ... when the righteous cause
> Shall gain defenders zealous and devout
> As they who have opposed her.[298]

He speaks for the liberties of Englishmen and of all mankind. His indictment of the dehumanizing effects of the Industrial Revolution, especially

[294] In 1846 the adoring but critical Miss Fenwick "talked freely, with great love and truth of the great poet's only fault, his love of money." (*Robinson*, p. 657.)
[295] *Letters, Middle Years*, pp. 485–486.   [296] *Ibid.*, p. 528.
[297] *Excursion*, VII, 891–901.   [298] *Ibid.*, IV, 310–319.

on factory children, and his plea for universal elementary education are eloquent. On the other hand, his proposals for reform are motivated by a desire to insulate the ideal commonwealth of the Lakes from the whole trend of the nineteenth century. His humane sentiments are tinged with fear. When he protests against regarding man as a means rather than as an end, he adds that this error breeds a desire for revenge among the oppressed.[299]

Crabb Robinson reports that in 1813 Wordsworth "strongly" shared Southey's expectation that the industrial proletariat would soon rise in a servile war.[300] Ever since that night of fear in his Paris hotel in 1792, dread of revolution had colored his political thought. One widely advocated means of averting such a catastrophe was Dr. Bell's scheme of education—a cheap monitorial technique by which a modicum of elementary instruction was to be combined with a dose of soothing Anglican piety. At first the Wanderer champions this system as a means of giving to all the opportunity of progressing from vital childhood to spiritually enlightened manhood.[301] But another reason soon emerges. Europe is in a state of upheaval. Unshaken England may well take warning:

> The discipline of slavery is unknown
> Among us,—hence the more do we require
> The discipline of virtue; order else
> Cannot subsist, nor confidence, nor peace.
> Thus, duties rising out of good possest
> And prudent caution needful to avert
> Impending evil, equally require
> That the whole people should be taught and trained.
> So shall licentiousness and black resolve
> Be rooted out, and virtuous habits take
> Their place; and genuine piety descend
> Like an inheritance, from age to age.[302]

While Dr. Bell is at work on the children, other agencies will take care of the adult population. In 1814, Wordsworth addresses Lord Lonsdale:

Every one knows of what importance the equestrian order was in preserving tranquillity and balance and gradation of power in ancient Rome; the like may take place among ourselves through the medium of an armed yeomanry; and surely a preservative of this kind is largely called for by the tendencies of

---

[299] *Ibid.*, IX, 114–126.   [300] *Robinson*, p. 127.   [301] *Excursion*, IX, 293–310.
[302] *Ibid.*, pp. 336–362.

things at present. . . . If the whole island was covered with a force of this kind, the Press properly curbed, the Poor Laws gradually reformed, provision made for new Churches to keep pace with the population, . . . order may yet be preserved among us, and the people remain free and happy.[303]

In the good cause of keeping the people free, happy, and above all tranquil, the Established Church is to add the blessings of religion to Ku Kluxism, the muzzling of the press, and palliative charity.

Hence Wordsworth, speaking in his own person, opens Book VI of *The Excursion* with a paean of praise to the English State and Church, but particularly to the latter. A footnote to this passage may be drawn from Robinson's diary for 1812:

He [Wordsworth] considers the combinations among journeymen, and even the Benefit Societies and all associations of men, apparently for the best purposes, as very alarming: he contemplates a renovation of all the horrors of a war between the poor and the rich. . . . Wordsworth spoke in defence of the Church establishment, and on the usual grounds said he would shed his blood for it. He declared himself not virtuous enough to be a clergyman. Confessed he knew not when he had been in a church at home—"All our ministers are such vile creatures"—and he allowed us to laugh at this droll concession from a staunch advocate for the establishment.[304]

Apparently Wordsworth became an ardent Church-and-State Anglican before he became a Christian.

6

The tendencies observed in the preceding section become still more strongly marked from 1815 to 1822. Wordsworth bids farewell to the visionary gleam, to poetry, almost to life itself, in the last stanza of the poem *Composed Upon an Evening of Extraordinary Splendour and Beauty* (1818). For a moment the lingering sunset makes his heart leap up as in the Hawkshead days, but the experience is now so rare that he asks,

> This glimpse of glory, why renewed?
> Nay, rather speak with gratitude;
> For if a vestige of those gleams
> Survived, 'twas only in my dreams.

[303] *Letters, Middle Years*, p. 585.   [304] *Robinson*, p. 90.

Dread Power! whom peace and calmness serve
No less than Nature's threatening voice,
If aught unworthy be my choice,
From THEE if I would swerve;
Oh, let thy grace remind me of the light
Full early lost, and fruitlessly deplored;
Which, at this moment, on my waking sight
Appears to shine, by miracle restored;
My soul, though yet confined to earth,
Rejoices in a second birth!
—'Tis past, the visionary splendour fades,
And night approaches with her shades.[305]

Here is no hint of philosophic compensation: the tragedy is firmly confronted, and the only solace lies in prayerful submission. In *The Convention of Cintra*, Wordsworth had wished "to recall to the reader his own knowledge, and to reinfuse into that knowledge a breath of appropriate feeling; because the bare sense of wisdom is nothing without its powers, and it is only in these feelings that the powers of wisdom exist." [306] Now that the sun of feeling has set, the wisdom amounts to very little. It is time, if only pride will permit, for more devout subservience to a Power which is not the power of Nature or of his own mind.

Wordsworth was a great poet from 1797 to 1807 and a very interesting one as late as 1814. But *The Excursion,* despite its noble passages, is mainly dull, and thereafter the descent is steep. In his post-1814 writings there are perhaps more good lines and even good poems than have been recognized by critics who refuse to credit him with saying well in 1820 what he would not have said at all in 1798. On the whole, however, the later work is not merely inferior to that of his best period but falls below a much less lofty standard. He himself has told us again and again the reason for this decline. The basis of his art, his philosophy, and his religion—they were all one thing—was the enjoyment of organic sensibility. Because a misleadingly happy boyhood was followed by a troubled and uncertain youth, the burgeoning of his vitality into great poetry was long delayed. When at last he laid hold upon his power he cultivated it with such intensity that the hot, sudden flame, after leaping to the heights, soon began to subside. As he lost his sensuous energy, he lost the emotions which had been produced by that force, retaining merely a wistful memory

---

[305] *Oxford*, p. 458.   [306] *Convention of Cintra*, p. 43.

of them and a knowledge of their value. The change in his religious views
was a result rather than a cause of this desiccation. Despite a good deal of
apparent evidence to the contrary, there is no inevitable causal nexus between Anglicanism and bad poetry. Nevertheless his politico-religious
conservatism, once established, probably furthered the process of decay
because it was so alien to the feelings and thoughts which had nourished
his best poetry.

Considering the occasion, the *Ode* written for the day of thanksgiving
after Waterloo is not offensively chauvinistic. This is a day when "The
very humblest is too proud of heart." The fifth and sixth stanzas represent the war as a general outburst of evil in which England has shared
and which God alone could have quelled. Much of *Ode. 1815,* however,
moves on a lower level. Wordsworth gives thanks to that "God of peace
and love" who is also the "Tremendous God of battles, Lord of hosts,"
and whose

> . . . most dreaded instrument
> In working out a pure intent
> Is Man—arrayed for mutual slaughter,
> —Yea, Carnage is thy daughter! [307]

But at the end of this poem Wordsworth turns from the national Moloch
to the "Just God of Christianised Humanity" who has granted peace at
last. England will be

> Blest, above measure blest,
> If on Thy love our Land her hopes shall rest,
> And all the Nations labour to fulfil
> Thy law, and live henceforth in peace, and pure good will.[308]

On Wordsworth as on other men, victory imposed the responsibility of
using the blessings of peace wisely and humanely. His endeavours to respond to this challenge were vitiated by the fact that he feared the English
reform movement, which was greatly stimulated by post-war conditions,
even more than he had feared Napoleon. The secular, utilitarian, materialistic temper of the reformers descended from an eighteenth-century
tradition hostile to that which had fostered his own thought. From 1815
onward, Wordsworth's Toryism rapidly became even more rigid than the

---

[307] *Oxford,* p. 328n. This passage was cancelled in 1845.   [308] *Ibid.,* p. 329.

work of the preceding period would have led us to expect. He still desired freedom and happiness for all men. He was by no means satisfied with the social callousness of the Tories. It fell far below his Burkian ideal of a non-competitive feudal society in which aristocratic privileges entailed paternal obligations toward the poor and lowly. But whenever the possibility of *doing* something arose, his dread of revolutionary change threw him into the Tory camp. At least he could not say of the Ministry, as he said of the Opposition, that not a man among them "is capable of looking at the subject of Religion with the eyes which an English Politician ought to possess." [309]

The practical bearings of that remark are revealed in the Preface to the 1815 *Poems*. At that time the Establishment was under fire not merely from anticlerical Benthamites but from loyal Churchmen who wished to make that torpid institution more effective. There were protests, for example, against pluralism and a system of promotion through patronage which depended largely on family connections.

Bishop Sparke of Ely, his son, and son-in-law, are said to have received among them more than £30,000 a year of church money. Archbishop Moore is reported to have died worth a million; his elder son had £12,000 a year of church preferment, his younger £3000. Archbishop Manners Sutton, "a mild but rapacious prelate," presented seven of his relations to sixteen benefices, besides cathedral dignities.[310]

Sutton was also extremely kind to Christopher Wordsworth, his chaplain and confidential friend.[311]

On all such issues the poet upholds the *status quo*. "Abolish pluralities," he writes in the Preface, "is a favourite cry, but . . . it may be asked what benefits would accrue from its *indiscriminate* adoption to counterbalance the harm it would introduce by nearly extinguishing the order of curates." [312] The equalization of clerical salaries would be no less unwise, because the profession would then offer no inducements to members of the class who, being pleased with their own status, are most concerned to teach their less fortunate brethren

the wisdom that blunts approaching distress by submission to God's will, and lightens, by patience, griefs which cannot be removed. . . . In a country so

[309] *Letters, Middle Years*, p. 734.
[310] F. Warre Cornish, *The English Church in the Nineteenth Century*, I, 102.
[311] J. H. Overton, *The English Church in the Nineteenth Century (1800–1833)*, p. 38.
[312] *Works*, II, 454.

rich and luxurious as that of England, the character of its clergy must un-
avoidably sink, and their influence be everywhere impaired, if individuals from
the upper rank, and men of leading talents, are to have no inducements to
enter into that body but such as are purely spiritual.[313]

The desideratum is not ecclesiastical reform, which smells of democracy,
but the building of more churches in order to extend the Establishment's
ministrations to the grumbling poor of the manufacturing towns. It is
true that churches were sorely needed in these districts, but not exactly
for Wordsworth's reason: "In quarters where there is not an attachment
to the Church, or the landed aristocracy, and a pride in supporting them,
there the people will dislike both, and be ready . . . to join in attempts
to overthrow them." [314] Meanwhile Wordsworth will dedicate his art
to the good cause, even to the extent of reinterpreting what he had earlier
written for wholly different purposes. He concludes his Preface by quoting
Prelude XII, 223-272, saying that the passage

turns upon the individual dignity which humbleness of social condition does
not preclude, but frequently promotes. It has no direct bearing upon clubs for
the discussion of public affairs, nor upon political or trade-unions; but if a
single workman—who, being a member of one of those clubs, runs the risk
of becoming an agitator, or who, being enrolled in a union, must be left
without a will of his own, and therefore a slave—should read these lines, and
be touched by them, I should indeed rejoice.[315]

Similar views are everywhere to be found in the letters of this period.[316]
Perhaps, however, the most striking example of the working out of
Burke's political philosophy in practical affairs is Wordsworth's champion-
ship of Lord Lonsdale (eldest son of the second Earl) against Henry
Brougham as a candidate for Parliament in 1818. The theme of the two
Addresses to the Freeholders of the County of Westmoreland is more
compactly expressed in a letter to Lonsdale:

It appears to a superficial observer, warm from contemplating the theory of
the Constitution, that the political power of the great landholders ought . . .
to be strenuously resisted; but I would ask a well-intentioned native of Westmoreland or Cumberland, who had fallen into this mistake, if he could point
to any arrangement by which Jacobinism can be frustrated except by the ex-

---

[313] *Ibid.*, pp. 456–457.   [314] *Ibid.*, p. 453.   [315] *Ibid.*, p. 461.
[316] *Letters, Middle Years*, pp. 782, 783–784; *Later Years*, pp. 33, 58, 69.

istence of large estates, continued from generation to generation in particular families, and parliamentary power in proportion.[317]

The grateful Stamp Distributor advises his patron, in order "not to exclude or give offence to dissenters, who are very powerful in Kendal," to substitute "King and Constitution" for "Church and King" in his election slogan.[318] This politic consideration may explain why, except for attributing the anticlericalism of the Whigs to "a repugnance on their part to associate with persons of grave character and decorous manners," [319] the *Addresses* avoid Church problems. The pamphleteer is content to remind his readers that "The Freeholders of past times knew that their rights were most likely to repose in safety, under the shade of rank and property," and to warn them that anyone who votes for Brougham, an advocate of annual parliaments and universal suffrage, will find himself in "the VANGUARD OF A FEROCIOUS REVOLUTION." [320]

Wordsworth's services in this election were not merely literary. He asks Lonsdale's opinion

as to the propriety of precautionary measures in augmenting the numbers of trustworthy freeholders. An offer has been made to me of an estate which would divide into *twelve* small freeholds; and, with your Lordship's sanction, I would purchase it, being able to reckon on as many persons,—gentlemen, my friends and relations,—who could be depended upon.[321]

It is unlikely that Lonsdale withheld his sanction—or the necessary funds. At all events he was victorious over the future Lord Chancellor of England, and before the year was out the useful bard had become a Justice of the Peace. One is reminded of Dion in Wordsworth's poem of 1816, who tragically descends from the heights of philosophy to the mire of politics.

Having observed that Wordsworth's Churchmanship was primarily political, we must now observe that his politics included an element of genuine religious feeling. Still retrospective, he regarded the roots of English culture with that reverence which he had formerly paid to the childhood roots which had nourished "the growth of a poet's mind." Like

---

[317] *Letters, Middle Years*, p. 804.   [318] *Ibid.*, p. 805.
[319] *Prose Works*, II, 293.   [320] *Ibid.*, pp. 312, 313, 329.
[321] *Letters, Middle Years*, pp. 805–806. See also p. 831 for what seems to be a second instance of the same device. De Selincourt, p. 806n, supposes that the two letters refer to the same estate, but the second letter speaks of a division into seven, not twelve, freeholds.

his master Burke, he recognized something mysterious, holy, and in the highest sense imaginative in the Constitution, the feudal loyalties, the Church-and-State nexus, of old England. Men like Brougham, who wished to disrupt this continuity of noble feeling, were essentially blasphemers. There might have been a fine poem in all this if Wordsworth could have approached the theme with energies unimpaired and with motives perfectly pure.

Inevitably he gravitated toward the High Church party because in its policies were mingled, much as in his own mind, a panicky self-interested Toryism and authentic religious feeling. The conception of Holy Church which had been the vitalizing force in the Anglo-Catholicism of the seventeenth century had never wholly disappeared. In the second half of the eighteenth century, indeed, it underwent an obscure but historically significant revival. The Evangelical Movement, by its earnest though lopsided emphasis on much that was essential to Christianity, impelled a slowly increasing number of High Churchmen to assert positively, as of deepest spiritual import, the Catholic implications of Prayer Book doctrines which they had long held negatively and defensively as party emblems. Clerics like William Jones of Nayland and Thomas Sikes, pious and learned laymen like Alexander Knox, would later be hailed as precursors by the Tractarians. These pioneers dwelt upon "Holy Catholic Church" as a neglected article of the Creed. "In Sikes's use of the word [Church]," says Warre Cornish, "is implied the whole theory of apostolical succession of divinely appointed pastors in the Church, of an authoritative guide to interpret Scripture and pronounce upon morals, and of an obedient laity." [322]

Until the days of Newman this movement was small and feeble compared to Evangelicalism, but it was encouraged by the conservative reaction which followed the French Revolution, and encouraged more strongly by the desire of post-Waterloo Tories to find loftier ground than mere expediency on which to defend the Church of England against the encroachments of secularistic liberalism. By the beginning of the period which we are now examining, the Evangelicalism of Clapham was challenged by the Anglo-Catholicism of Clapton and the neighbouring suburb of Hackney, where a cluster of devout High Churchmen had gathered. The activating members of a larger circle were the layman Joshua Watson, his brother John, Rector of Hackney, his uncle Archdeacon Daubeny, the

[322] F. Warre Cornish, *The English Church in the Nineteenth Century*, I, 66.

Reverend John Norris, curate to John Watson, and William Stevens, a rich London tradesman. Their views were shared by influential Churchmen at Oxford, where Martin Joseph Routh was president of Magdalen and William Van Mildert the Regius Professor of Divinity.[323]

Christopher Wordsworth was closely associated with the activities of this group. After his appointment as Master of Trinity in 1820 he combatted both the Evangelicalism and the Broad Churchism of the university, and was largely responsible for the fact that, until the Oxford Movement proper began, Anglo-Catholicism had made more progress at Cambridge than at Oxford. William from now on became much more intimate with his brother and was considerably influenced by him.[324] He was deeply impressed by the "eloquent and dignified conversation" of Alexander Knox, aged veteran of the eighteenth-century phase of the movement, whom he met on his tour of Ireland in 1829.[325] In the late 1820's he corresponded with the Reverend Hugh James Rose, a Cambridge theologian whose advice the Tractarians sought at the inception of their campaign, and in the 1830's with Joshua Watson. He regarded the latter as "perhaps the ablest supporter the Church has out of her own bosom." [326] Bishop Van Mildert he admired as warmly as he disapproved of the heretic Hampden.[327] By 1820, if not two or three years earlier, Wordsworth considered himself a High Churchman in the same sense as his brother.

The members of the "Hackney Phalanx" and their friends elsewhere in England were rigidly orthodox as regards the Trinity and most other doctrines of the historic faith. Their theology was anti-Calvinistic. Although they believed in redemption through the Incarnation as a whole rather than solely through the Blood of the Lamb, the notion that the Atonement did not matter would have shocked them to the core. The Holy Spirit was at work, not among the trees or in man's good heart, but in the Apostolic Succession, which conferred upon the Church and its priesthood the full authority of its Founder. Their respect for tradition was dogmatic and historical, without much emotional antiquarianism. They preferred the Liturgy to the Thirty-Nine Articles. Strict in all rites and observances, they did not luxuriate in ceremonial for its own sake.

---

[323] Routh was revered by Newman in his Anglican days. Van Mildert left his professorship to occupy the see of Llandaff in 1819 and became Bishop of Durham in 1826. He was probably the "highest" pre-Tractarian bishop.

[324] Letters, Middle Years, pp. 430, 641, 715, 722; Later Years, pp. 395, 461, 616.

[325] Letters, Later Years, p. 773.   [326] Ibid., p. 623.   [327] Ibid., pp. 786–787.

They advocated Dr. Bell's system of education and the building of new churches. They were active, indeed, in all forms of missionary work which did not entail cooperation with Evangelicals or Dissenters.

Their attitude toward the Church of Rome was somewhat ambiguous.

The new High Churchmen of the nineteenth century denied the Catholicity of the continental churches, and began by degrees to look for points of agreement with Rome. Rome had erred, but we too had declined from some points of primitive religion. . . . The inquirers turned their veneration from the first reformers to the later fathers of the English Church, who looked to the first four Councils for the interpretation of the Scriptures; Cranmer, Ridley, and Hooper gave place to the Caroline divines and the non-jurors, who showed how this decline from Catholic unity might be made up within the bounds of the English formularies.[328]

This spirit, however, did not fully develop until the days of the Tractarians. The Hackney Churchmen were almost as concerned not to be popish as they were to be Catholic. Their doctrines implied devotion to the Church as an end in itself, but their Tory Church-and-State policies saddled them with Erastianism. Those policies also necessitated opposition to the enfranchisement of Roman Catholics in England and the establishment of the Church of Rome in Ireland. Such views could not gracefully be combined with warm acceptance of the whole body of Catholic doctrine and cultus. Hence these High Churchmen, though sacramentalists in theory and to a considerable extent in practice, circled in a cautious and gingerly fashion about the fully Catholic view of the Eucharist, Holy Penance, and the Communion of Saints.

How much of all this Wordsworth actually understood is doubtful. Sharply defined ideas were as distasteful to him in theology as in philosophy. What he saw in the Hackney Phalanx was a group of devout Christians who loved the Church, revered tradition, believed in unity, order, and authority, worshipped in the finest English prose, and held exactly the right political opinions. That was sufficient for him. It was not, however, sufficient for good religious poetry.

Detailed analysis of *Ecclesiastical Sonnets*[329] is probably unnecessary and certainly impossible. With a few familiar exceptions, the sonnets are

---

[328] Warre Cornish, *op. cit.*, p. 68.

[329] The original title, of course, was *Ecclesiastical Sketches*. My remarks in this section concern only the sonnets which appeared in the first edition of 1822. Some of the more important subsequent additions will be glanced at later.

mildly agitated pieces of rhetoric rather than poems. They seldom reveal any personal religious emotion. So far as their ideas are concerned, they give the impression of being the result of collaboration between a humane Protestant who wishes to say all that can justly be said for Catholicism and a humane Catholic who wishes to be equally polite to Protestantism. The plus and minus signs in this travesty of the *via media* cancel out, leaving an intellectual and spiritual zero.

Primarily, of course, the work was intended to illustrate the history of the religious tradition in English culture, whose tranquil and stabilizing spirit had resisted both the fanaticism of Protestant enthusiasts and levellers and the tyranny and superstition of Rome. On specific issues related to this theme Wordsworth's views are those of a pre-Tractarian High Churchman. As a contribution to Church history, however, the sonnets are vitiated not only by their inevitable sketchiness but by the author's inability or unwillingness to grapple with theological principles. The unifying metaphor set forth in the opening sonnet is that the English Church, like the River Duddon, is a flowing stream; but Wordsworth does not pause to ask, "From whence then hast thou that living water?"[330] The Samaritan woman's question is irrelevant to his real subject—the spirit of the English people as interpreted by a good-hearted conservative. The fundamental problems concerning the nature of the Visible Church and the source of its authority are left untouched: we do not know whether it is the Mystical Body of Christ and the extension of the Incarnation or a man-made association of worshippers. Deprived of any such foundation, the yea-and-nay treatment of medieval Christianity in Part I is wholly inconclusive.

In Part II, nothing is said about the basic principles of the Reformation or about the bearing of that event upon the status of the English Church. Did the Church *in* England, upon becoming the Church *of* England, continue in communion with the one Holy, Catholic, and Apostolic Church? On this issue of cardinal importance to his own ecclesiastical party, Wordsworth offers no opinion. He prefers to balance, with all the caution of a freshman history textbook, the advantages and disadvantages of the dissolution of the monasteries. The seventeenth-century sectarians, though praised for their love of liberty, are blamed for disturbing British peace and quiet; but there is no religious standard from which their nobility or their excesses can be judged. While Charles I and Laud are hailed in

[330] John iv, 11.

proper High Church fashion as martyrs, one cannot see that they are martyrs to anything in particular except the English way of life. Part III, "From the Restoration to the Present Times," abandons all attempt at historiography. In the penultimate sonnet he exclaims:

> Glory to God! and to the Power who came
> In filial duty, clothed with love divine,
> That made His human tabernacle shine
> Like Ocean burning with purpureal flame;

but the connection between the Incarnation and the Church of England remains in darkness. The concluding sonnet derives hope for the future course of the river not from the witness of the Spirit in Holy Church, but from "the WORD . . . with unpresumptuous faith explored."

Closer inspection of the work would show that its fundamental purport accords with the Protestantism of this conclusion. It is not too paradoxical to say that even the author's Catholic sympathies are Protestant. He asserts that prayers for the dead, though consoling, are irrational; the practice, together with auricular confession, places too much power in the hands of the clergy.[331] Waldo is praised for spurning "the pompous mass," with its "rites that trample upon soul and sense," and for teaching his followers "To adore the Invisible, and Him alone," as enjoined by "the unadulterate Word." [332] The original version contains no sonnets on the sacraments; that on *The Liturgy* (III, xix) tepidly praises the Christian Year as a stimulus to "lofty thoughts." If Wordsworth's view of nature is sacramental, as some critics have asserted, it is strange that his view of Christianity is not. His half-hearted approval of monks and hermits smacks of the eighteenth-century cult of pensive retirement. Related to the same tradition, but with more admixture of religious feeling, is his affection for old abbeys:

> Once ye were holy, ye are holy still;
> Your spirit freely let me drink, and live.[333]

Still more exceptional is his tribute to "Our tainted nature's solitary boast," *The Virgin*. At the dissolution of the monasteries

---

[331] *Oxford*, p. 423.
[332] *Ibid.*, p. 431. So Emily was taught by her mother in *The White Doe*, Vide *supra*, p. 205.
[333] *Ibid.*, p. 449.

Thy Image falls to earth. Yet some, I ween,
Not unforgiven the suppliant knee might bend,
As to a visible Power, in which did blend
All that was mixed and reconciled in Thee
Of mother's love with maiden purity,
Of high with low, celestial with terrene.[334]

But although the apologetic "not unforgiven" is only a slight blemish, it arouses a suspicion which is increased by several other sonnets. Wordsworth leans toward certain Catholic doctrines and practices because he feels that, precisely in being superstitious, they contain a precious imaginative element which flouts that "false secondary power," the lower reason. The Crusaders wielded

...the mightiest lever
Known to the moral world, Imagination.

The medieval Church was the soil from which grew "the flowers of chivalry." The Reformation repudiated the cult of saints, but

Ah! if the old idolatry be spurned,
Let not your radiant shapes desert the Land.[335]

Wordsworth does not seriously believe in such trumpery, but he wistfully admires its power to ward off mental desiccation. It possesses a glow somehow akin to that which he has lost. There are times when he would almost be willing to substitute "I'd rather be a Catholic" for "I'd rather be a pagan" in *The world is too much with us*.[336] But while Catholic Emancipation threatens to destroy the Constitution such notions are not to be encouraged.

They may be indulged, however, when writing about the Middle Ages or when travelling in Roman Catholic countries. Many passages in *Memorials of a Tour on the Continent* (1820) take advantage of the latter opportunity. For German boatmen working their way through dangerous rapids he provides a thoroughly Catholic hymn. *Our Lady of the Snow* is a reverend address to the "Meek Virgin Mother." [337] A rural chapel in one of the Catholic cantons of Switzerland prompts the reflection that

[334] *Ibid.*, p. 435.　　　[335] *Ibid.*, pp. 427, 430, 434.
[336] For further evidence on this point see H. N. Fairchild, "Wordsworth's Doctrine of Creative Delusion," *South Atlantic Quarterly*, XLVI, 545–555.
[337] *Oxford*, pp. 336, 338. On the latter page see also *Engelberg, the Hill of Angels*.

> Doomed as we are our native dust
> To wet with many a bitter shower,
> It ill befits us to disdain
> The altar, to deride the fane
> Where simple Sufferers bend, in trust
> To win a happier hour.

In our travels we need

> ...Charity!—to bid us think
> And feel, if we would know.[338]

These sympathies, however, are not to be indulged unreservedly. He feels an almost sinister fascination in the spectacle of a religious procession "on a Sabbath morning in the Vale of Chamouni":

> Trembling, I look upon the secret springs
> Of that licentious craving in the mind
> To act the God amongst external things,
> To bind, on apt suggestion, or unbind;
> And marvel not that antique Faith inclined
> To crowd the world with metamorphosis,
> Vouchsafed in pity or in wrath assigned;
> Such insolent temptations wouldst thou miss,
> Avoid these sights; nor brood o'er Fable's dark abyss.[339]

In the shadow of Mont Blanc, this demonstration of an ecclesiastical power which a Protestant must regard as merely human reminds him that in earlier years his own chief delight had been "to act the God amongst external things." For a moment he sees in "Fable," Catholic or pagan, a means of restoring the lost joy, but he resists "that licentious craving."

This recantation of pride is echoed in many poems of the period which have no bearing on Catholic devotion. He is still inclined to regard faith as a way of enabling us to "feel that we are greater than we know," [340] but the tendency is less marked than in *The Excursion*. That he has Christianized the Stoical element in his thought is suggested by *The Pass of Kirkstone*. Toiling through the fog up the steep grade—symbolically "the hill of duty"—is weary work, but he is grateful

[338] *Ibid.*, p. 337.
[339] *Ibid.*, pp. 346–347.
[340] *Ibid.*, p. 384.

> For the rich bounties of constraint
> Whence oft invigorating transports flow
> That choice lacked courage to bestow.

The summit is gained; the fog soon lifts; everything is clear, fresh, joyous. Faith, from her cloud, proclaims:

> Whate'er the weak may dread, the wicked dare,
> Thy lot, O Man, is good, thy portion fair! [341]

Now, when he thinks of his childhood, he remembers pieties which had seemed unimportant when he wrote *The Prelude*. At Easter, in the old happy days, every "Cottage dame" put on a fresh woollen garment of her own making,

> And she who span it culled the daintiest fleece
> In thoughtful reverence to the Prince of Peace,
> Whose temples bled beneath the platted thorn.
> A blest estate when piety sublime
> These humble props disdained not! [342]

This reinterpretation of childhood is necessarily accompanied by a reinterpretation of nature. Precisely as in *Lines Written in Early Spring,* the little flowers among the rocks possess "Beauty, and life, and motions as of joy." But the poet immediately adds:

> Nor doubt but He to whom yon Pine-trees nod
> Their heads in sign of worship, Nature's God,
> These humbler adorations will receive. [343]

The idea that external nature worships "Nature's God" is expressed by Wordsworth's old favorite James Thomson and by several other eighteenth-century poets.

Natural objects not only worship God, but help us in our own worship of Him:

> Cliffs, fountains, rivers, seasons, times—
> Let all remind the soul of heaven;
> Our slack devotion needs them all;

[341] *Ibid.*, pp. 214–215.   [342] *Ibid.*, p. 255. See also *Decay of Piety*, p. 256.
[343] *Ibid.*, p. 337.

> And Faith—so oft of sense the thrall,
> While she, by aid of Nature, climbs,
> May hope to be forgiven.[344]

The last line recalls "not unforgiven" in the sonnet on *The Virgin*.[345] Wordsworth's attempt to harmonize his love of nature and his Christianity is hindered by his anti-sacramental adherence to "the Invisible God." In reacting against his early pantheism he seems not to realize that a complete Christianity would give him a God who is both transcendent and immanent. For him the only alternative to deified Nature is a God who cannot *really* be found in nature at all. Natural objects are images not altogether unlike the fallen but lovely image of the Virgin Mary. To use them devotionally is a little superstitious, but the practice is so dear to his heart that he "hopes to be forgiven." Since it will always be for him the most congenial mode of worship, one regrets that he could not more firmly believe in the validity of what he was doing.

Wordsworth had abjured the romantic way of uniting the visible and the invisible. The Catholic way tempted him, but he felt that it was superstitious. Hence the enjoyment of nature could be sanctified only by a constant shifting of tired eyes from earth to heaven. In his premature old age, he increasingly thought of this world in terms of the next. Just as the River Duddon reaches the great ocean at last, so he would move through the remainder of his life

> Prepared, in peace of heart, in calm of mind
> And soul, to mingle with Eternity! [346]

Such thoughts arise when he contemplates the young vitality of Dora. She is in her springtime, he tells her in *The Longest Day*, but from now on the hours of sunshine will diminish. "He, who governs the creation" has ordained a similar ebbing of human freshness. Even at thirteen Dora should "look . . . to Eternity." Let her learn early that the thistle of duty —the only sceptre of true queenhood—must be firmly grasped as a preparation for

> . . . those palms of honour
> Which selected spirits wear,
> Bending low before the Donor,
> Lord of heaven's unchanging year! [347]

[344] *Ibid.*, p. 341.   [345] *Vide supra*, p. 230.   [346] *Oxford*, p. 384.
[347] *Ibid.*, p. 90.

In *A little onward,* Wordsworth speaks as Dora's comrade rather than as her monitor. His eyes having recovered from one of their attacks, he summons her from her "orisons" to join him in gathering lessons of "reverential awe" from "Heaven-prompted Nature," chiefly from scenes where the sun-dappled birches suggest

> ...the living presences of nuns;
> A gentle, pensive, white-robed sisterhood,
> Whose saintly radiance mitigates the gloom
> Of those terrestrial fabrics, where they serve,
> To Christ, the Sun of righteousness, espoused.

As his eyes continue to grow stronger, he and Dora will read together "the page of classic lore." But best of all,

> ...the page of Holy Writ,
> Again unfolded, passage clear shall yield
> To heights more glorious still, and into shades
> More awful, where, advancing hand in hand,
> We may be taught, O Darling of my care!
> To calm the affections, elevate the soul,
> And consecrate our lives to truth and love.[348]

From such evidence one infers, much more clearly than from *Ecclesiastical Sonnets,* that Wordsworth in this period not only accepts the institutional formularies of Christianity but aspires toward the Christian ideal of self-surrender. All outward signs of pantheism have vanished, and the cult of personal imaginative creativity, though not wholly abandoned, has been greatly modified. His abnegation of selfhood would impress us more favorably, and it would certainly have produced better poetry, if he had achieved it in the fullness of strength and joy. He was offering up what had already been taken from him. To the end of his days, however, Wordsworth was a stiff-necked, self-centered man. It could never have been easy for him to discover that he was not the master of his soul or of the world in which he lived. That he should sometimes have tried to evade so unwelcome a conclusion is not surprising.

[348] *Ibid.,* p. 496.

7

Between 1822 and 1836 there is no marked change, but these years are rich in material illustrating the views which had taken form during the preceding period. At this time he had several reasons to be satisfied with his lot. His domestic life was tranquil. Though not affluent, he now had sufficient money for his needs. His literary reputation, which reached its height about 1830, had begun to improve as early as 1819. In that year the *New Monthly Magazine* saw in him "a firm friend to the constitution, which is the same as saying that he is a loyal subject of the king, and a sincere member of the Church of England"; while the *British Critic,* even in reviewing *Peter Bell,* declared that "His writings are devoted to the cause of religion and morality, and in that holy cause we scarcely know a more zealous, a more fearless, a more eloquent advocate." [349] It followed, of course, that he was an excellent poet. At a time when greatly inferior bards could win high praise by writing as patriots, pietists, and prudes,[350] it was not difficult for Wordsworth to sing down his past. He was now capable of addressing goldfish in a bowl with the words, "Cold though your nature be, 'tis pure." [351] "And as for his habits," the old cotter told Canon Rawnsley, "he had noan, niver knew him with a pot i' his hand, or a pipe i' his mouth." [352] There was sap in that withering oak: in *The Triad* the vividness of the three pretty girls is enjoyed with that love of life for life's sake which never quite deserted him. And yet he was to be remembered as "a man as had no pleasure in his faace." [353]

His nerves, after long experimentation with other parts of his body, had apparently fixed upon the eyes as their chosen victim. At increasingly frequent intervals, and for longer periods than before, the attacks of inflammation prevented him from reading and from writing without the aid of an amanuensis. Otherwise, except for petty ailments, he was so well and vigorous that Dorothy could not quite see why he did not get on with *The Recluse.*[354] It was in his mind rather than in his body that he felt the approach of actual old age. "I cannot get up my spirits," he complains;

---

[349] Elsie Smith (ed.), *An Estimate of Wordsworth,* pp. 284, 299.
[350] See W. S. Ward, "Some Aspects of the Conservative Attitude toward Poetry in English Criticism, 1798–1820," *PMLA,* LX, 386–398.   [351] *Oxford,* p. 526.
[352] H. D. Rawnsley, "Reminiscences of Wordsworth Among the Peasantry of Westmoreland," *Transactions of the Wordsworth Society,* VI, 174.
[353] *Ibid.,* p. 181.
[354] *Letters, Later Years,* pp. 443–444; *Robinson Correspondence,* p. 132.

"everything seems going against sober sense, patience, and justice."[355] "Non sum qualis eram," he writes in 1825 and again in 1830.[356] One by one, the personal ties which linked him with his past were snapping. Beaumont died in 1827, Scott in 1832, Lamb and Coleridge in 1834, Sara Hutchinson in 1835. Soon after Sara's death, Dorothy's mind gave way; she had been ill in body since 1829. Wordsworth did not give himself freely to those he loved, but he drew them so deeply into himself that to lose one of them was like losing a part of his body. In attempting to confront these sorrows with "trust in God's goodness,"[357] he leaned upon his wife's simpler, stronger faith:

> Peace settles where the intellect is meek,
> And Love is dutiful in thought and deed;
> Through Thee communion with that Love I seek:
> The faith heaven strengthens where he moulds the creed.[358]

His private distresses were interwoven with his worries about public affairs. Once the Test and Corporation Acts had been repealed in 1828 and the Catholic Relief Bill passed in 1829, he transferred his direst fears to the Reform Bill. "God of Mercy have mercy upon poor England!—to think of this glorious Country lacqueying the heels of France in religion (that is *no* religion), in morals, government, and social order!"[359] The passage of the bill distressed him so deeply that he envied those who, like his ailing sister, "are likely to be removed from the afflictions which God is preparing for this sinful nation. . . . I have witnessed one revolution in a foreign country, and I have not courage to think of facing another in my own."[360] Just as the French Revolution produced Napoleon, so the English Revolution will breed its own tyranny. "Despotism will be established, and the whole battle will have to be fought over by subsequent generations."[361] Hence, sincerely convinced that he is a champion of liberty, he fights every proposal pointing toward human freedom.[362] Abandoning the standpoint of *The Excursion,* he now distrusts the movement for national rate-supported education: "There is an officious disposition on the part of the upper and middle classes to precipitate the tendency of the people toward intellectual culture in a manner subversive of their own happiness

[355] *Letters, Later Years,* pp. 591, 680.   [356] *Ibid.,* pp. 219, 469.
[357] *Ibid.,* p. 748.   [358] *Oxford,* p. 112.   [359] *Letters, Later Years,* p. 554.
[360] *Ibid.,* pp. 616–617.   [361] *Ibid.,* p. 704.
[362] His approval of the Poor Laws illustrates the amiable side of his feudalistic paternalism, but his views on this issue are strongly influenced by his anxiety to throw a sop to Cerberus.

and dangerous to the peace of society." [363] As for the anti-slavery cause, he is less concerned for the freedom of the blacks than for the property-rights of their owners. "Slavery is not in itself and at all times and under all circumstances to be deplored," and in any case there is too much "fanaticism" abroad in the land. In the same letter he refers disapprovingly to a recent bill against cruelty to animals: "The best surety for an unedu-cated man behaving with care and kindness to his beast lies in the sense of uncontrolled property which he possesses in him." [364] It follows that the best means of safeguarding the rights of slaves and beasts is to safe-guard the institution of private property. He refuses the request of Mrs. Rawson, an abolitionist and social reformer, that he provide her with verses to use in propaganda against slavery and child labor, for he will not "add to the excitement already existing in the public mind upon these, and so many other points of legislation and government." It is the function of poetry to stir the feelings, whereas "what, at this period, we want above everything is patient examination and sober judgment." [365] For propa-ganda gladly devoted to the Tory cause, the reader may see *Sonnets Dedi-cated to Liberty and Order* and that all-around diatribe, *The Warning*.

At a time when the Church had some reason to fear the ultimate tragedy of disestablishment, Wordsworth's political and ecclesiastical views were more than ever inseparable:

Three great conflicts are before the progressive nations: between Christianity and Infidelity; between Popery and Protestantism; and between the spirit of the old *Feudal and Monarchical governments,* and the representative and re-publican system as established in America. The Church of England, in addi-tion to her infidel and Roman Catholic assailants, and the politicians of the anti-feudal class, has to contend with a formidable body of Protestant Dis-senters.[366]

Although pure feudalism is now merely a theoretical idea, its place in this alignment of good and evil forces has largely been filled by property, which "makes up for the decay of chivalrous loyalty and strengthens gov-ernments." On this institution depends the spiritual no less than the tem-poral welfare of the Church, for "religion . . . cannot be preserved from abuse of priestly influence, and from superstition and fanaticism, nor can

[363] *Letters, Later Years,* p. 461. See also pp. 327–334.
[364] *Ibid.,* pp. 647–648.
[365] *Ibid.,* pp. 650–651.
[366] *Ibid.,* p. 358.

honour be an operating principle upon a large scale, except through *property.*[367]

The Oxford Movement did not attract much general attention until almost the close of this period. Between 1822 and 1836 Wordsworth continued to express his rather limited and imperfect interpretation of the Churchmanship of the Hackney Phalanx. He remained a stout Protestant for whom "Catholic," in extra-liturgical usage, seldom meant anything but "popish." "I reprobate as of the most injurious tendency," he assures Sir Robert Inglis in 1825, "every Measure which does not point to the maintenance of Protestant ascendency, and to the diffusion of Protestant principles." These principles are by no means wholly political: "Papacy," he continues, "is founded upon the overthrow of private judgment—it is essentially at enmity with light and knowledge. . . . A sincere Romanist is by *duty* a persecutor."[368]

Several additions to *Ecclesiastical Sonnets* dating from this period indicate that Wordsworth should be called a High Church Protestant rather than an Anglican Catholic. The one exception is II, iv, which praises the social policy of monasticism, with its respect for every soul which Christ died to save. But this recognition of Catholic democracy is more than counterbalanced by *The Point at Issue* (II, xxx). Here Wordsworth tries to atone for the vagueness of the original version of the *Sonnets* by grappling with the central problem of the Reformation. The Protestant position, he now asserts, is

> . . . that the Soul, freed from the bonds of Sense,
> And to her God restored by evidence
> Of things not seen, drawn forth from their recess,
> Root there, and not in forms, her holiness.[369]

Certainly the medieval Church abused her forms, but the notion that she regarded forms as the *root*—not the divinely instituted vehicle—of holiness is absurd. After reading this sonnet we can attach no meaning to the new group on *Baptism* (with its appended *Sponsors*), *Confirmation,* and *Sacrament* (III, xx, xxi, xxiii, xxiv, xxv). These rites are described in tones of devout solemnity; but since God disapproves of forms, and does not work upon the human soul through objects of sense, they cannot possibly be sacraments. The last sonnet of the group is especially unsatisfying. The

---

[367] *Ibid.,* p. 321.   [368] *Ibid.,* pp. 209–210.   [369] *Oxford,* p. 436.

Eucharist is called "memorial Sacrament," "saving rite," and "armor divine," but nothing is said to suggest why it deserves these praises, how it operates, or what happens at the altar. The epithet "memorial" of course implies a Protestant position.

Wordsworth's Protestant beliefs, however, are still powerless to unweave the spell exerted upon him by the "bold credulities" of popery. As a great fabric of ideas, Catholicism means nothing to him; but as a fount of creative superstition it appeals strongly to his feelings. He likes the sentimental medievalism of Kenelm Digby's *Broad-Stone of Honour* and *Orlandus.* From the latter work he draws *The Armenian Lady's Love,* dedicating the poem to Digby "in acknowledgment, however unworthy, of pleasure and instruction derived from his numerous and valuable writings, illustrative of the piety and chivalry of the olden time." [370] This poem and *The Egyptian Maid* are very bad tales of chivalry in which a nambypamby, imitation-stained-glass piety is the chief element.

For some years Wordsworth had been quick to sympathize with any belief, Christian or non-Christian, which offered a refuge for imagination "though reason might say no." [371] In *The Wishing-Gate* he associates the superstitions which cluster about the spot with "the mystic yearnings" of "the ancient faith." No doubt "the land of Wishes" is a realm of

> ... fruitless day-dreams, lawless prayer,
> And thoughts with things at strife;
> Yet how forlorn, should *ye* depart,
> Ye superstitions of the *heart,*
> How poor, were human life! [372]

This theme is applied to Catholicism in *Stanzas Suggested in a Steamboat off Saint Bees' Heads.*[373] The founding of the monastery is related sympathetically:

> To aid the Votaries, miracles believed
> Wrought in men's minds, like miracles achieved;
> So piety took root; and Song might tell

---

[370] *Works,* II, 485.   [371] *Oxford,* p. 224.

[372] *Ibid.,* p. 223. The same note is struck in *Presentiments,* pp. 225–226.

[373] Wordsworth's note, *Ibid.,* p. 924, explains that the original monastery on the Cumberland coast was founded by St. Bega about 650. Shortly before the poem was written in 1833, an Anglican theological seminary had been established at the site "under the patronage of the Earl of Lonsdale," and the old conventual church had been repaired.

What humanizing virtues near her [Bega's] cell
Sprang up, and spread their fragrance wide around.

In this poem Wordsworth defends requiem masses and prayers for the dead as being at all events good for the living. Such a phrase as "priestly cunning" will not "best unlock the secrets of Saint Bees," for the monastery was a home of sincere devotion. Active as well as contemplative, the monks succoured the shipwrecked and entertained both pilgrim and minstrel. They not only prayed for the Crusades, but made

> . . . a Holy-land at home:
> The Star of Bethlehem from its sphere invites
> To sound the crystal depth of maiden rights;
> And wedded life, through scriptural mysteries,
> Heavenward ascends with all her charities,
> Taught by the hooded Celibates of St. Bees.

Their influence on the spiritual and social life of the neighborhood is warmly praised. "In Reformation's sweeping overthrow" they were driven out and their house was destroyed.

> But now once more the local Heart revives,
> The inextinguishable Spirit strives

in the seminary newly established on the old site. The concluding stanza reveals the feeling on which the entire poem rests:

> Alas! the Genius of our age, from Schools
> Less humble, draws her lessons, aims, and rules.
> To Prowess guided by her insight keen
> Matter and Spirit are as one Machine;
> Boastful Idolatress of formal skill
> She in her own would merge the eternal will:
> Better, if Reason's triumphs match with these,
> Her flight before the bold credulities
> That furthered the first teaching of St. Bess.[874]

But since Wordsworth cannot seriously accept this teaching, the "bold credulities," though more desirable than the fruits of unimaginative reason,

[874] *Ibid.*, pp. 465–468.

are merely a sort of noble nonsense. He told William Rowan Hamilton, the scientist friend of this period, that he revered the kind of science which "raised the mind to the contemplation of God in His works," but that he would rather be "a superstitious old woman" than subject himself to "all science which was a bare collection of facts for their own sake, or to be applied merely to the material uses of life." [375] Again one thinks of "I'd rather be a pagan." On his tour of Ireland he was much impressed by the unquestioning faith of a poor woman who came to bathe her sick child in the healing waters of St. Kevin's Pool. "What would not one give," he writes to Christopher, "to see among Protestants such devout reliance on the mercy of their Creator, so much resignation, so much piety, so much simplicity and singleness of mind, purged of the accompanying superstitions!" [376] These religious values had become precious to Wordsworth, but where could he obtain them? He did not find them in Protestantism, and he had no clear conception of any Catholicism other than that of the "superstitious old woman" from whose hands he was unwilling to receive them. There is a genuinely religious element in Wordsworth's High Churchmanship, but it is almost vitiated by his inability to solve this dilemma.

As we have observed, even his devotion to Christianized nature was marred by the fear that the use of the senses in the religious enjoyment of beautiful forms was inconsistent with the principles of *The Point at Issue*. Nevertheless it is in the woods, rather than at the altar-rail, that this High Churchman comes closest to satisfying his personal religious needs. The moon, though no longer worshipped as in pagan times, still plays its part in declaring the glory of God. From it both "sage and simple" may draw "moral intimations" of meekness, patience, and faithfulness to duty. Hence

> ...let us—without offence
> To aught of highest, holiest, influence—
> Receive whatever good 'tis given thee to dispense.[377]

In a less apologetic mood, Wordsworth can even declare that natural objects provide the most enduring *Devotional Incitements*. The heart-stirring ceremonies of the cathedral are, after all, man-made and transitory. They

---

[375] Hamilton's sister Eliza, quoted by Edith C. Batho, *The Later Wordsworth*, p. 30.
[376] *Letters, Later Years*, p. 395.
[377] *Oxford*, pp. 460–461.

change as creeds change, or may be swept away by storms of fanaticism, while from age to age

> Kind Nature keeps a heavenly door
> Wide open for the scattered Poor.
> Where flower-breathed incense to the skies
> Is wafted in mute harmonies;
>
>   . . .
>
> Where birds and brooks from leafy dells
> Chime forth unwearied canticles,
> And vapours magnify and spread
> The glory of the sun's bright head—
> Still constant in her worship, still
> Conforming to the eternal Will.[378]

In Wordsworth's original system, man's ability to discern moral qualities in nature was part of the divine imaginativeness of the universe. Now the patient sun and moon are given the more conventionally pious function of providing symbolic material for little sermons.

The poet does not utterly forsake his earlier belief that natural objects, since they are permeated by the one universal energy, are themselves "Powers." During the Scottish tour of 1831 he summons his Highland guide:

> ...Up, hardy Mountaineer!
> And guide the Bard, ambitious to be one
> Of Nature's privy council, as thou art,
> On Cloud-sequestered heights, that see and hear
> To what dread Powers He delegates his part
> On Earth, who works in the heaven of heavens, alone.[379]

Here Wordsworth preserves the less aggressively pantheistic side of the eighteenth century sentimental tradition. James Thomson describes the sun as a

> ...great *delegated* source
> Of light, and life, and grace, and joy below,

and his God

[378] *Ibid.*, p. 228.   [379] *Ibid.*, p. 389.

... ceaseless *works alone,* and yet alone
Seems not to work.[380]

In the later Wordsworth, however, the God who thus delegates His powers is often described in more specifically Christian terms than in Thomson. The sense of fellowship with the lower animals, for example, is sanctioned by the thought,

> For are we not all His without whose care
> Vouchsafed no sparrow falleth to the ground?
> Who gives his Angels wings to speed through air,
> And rolls the planets through the blue profound? [381]

The last line suggests the usefulness of Newtonianism as a link between Wordsworth's earlier and later thought.

Similarly the Shaftesburyan concept of the universe as a benevolent harmony receives a baptismal sprinkling. In *The Excursion,* Wordsworth used the "chain of being" [382] as a symbol of cosmic integration which did not necessarily imply a pantheistic interfusion of all levels of nature. The theme of *The White Doe* was not an absolute unity of love, but a graduated concatenation of

> ... sympathies
> Aloft ascending, and descending deep
> Even to the inferior Kinds.[383]

In two poems of the present period, *Humanity* and *The Primrose of the Rock,* the chain of being has become a Jacob's ladder on which the benevolent affections move up and down, establishing relationships between the lowest and the highest:

> ... Glorious is the blending
> Of right affections climbing or descending
> Along a scale of light and life, with cares
> Alternate; carrying holy thoughts and prayers
> Up to the sovereign seat of the Most High,
> Descending to the worm in charity.[384]

This revised version of the old "ennobling interchange" is wholly dependent upon the supernatural. The basis of the psychological process

---

[380] *Religious Trends,* I, 522–524. Italics mine.   [381] *Oxford,* p. 273.
[382] *Vide supra,* p. 000.   [383] *Oxford,* p. 395.   [384] *Ibid.,* p. 500.

which makes us feel hopeful in springtime is "God's redeeming love." The primrose is still something more than Peter Bell could see, but its present *moreness* is different from that of 1798. The flower is now "a lasting link in Nature's chain/From highest heaven let down." It is part of a hierarchy of dependence: flower, stem, root, rock, earth, solar system—"And God upholds them all." Thus although men are "sin-blighted" there descends from God through nature to the humble heart the "vernal" hope that the winter of this life will be followed by "one eternal summer." [385] This is

> The faith that elevates the just
> Before and when they die;
> And makes each soul a separate heaven,
> A court for Deity. [386]

In such poems Wordsworth is happily able to forget that this conception of the mediatorial function of nature is radically inconsistent with his distrust of the senses and of forms as vehicles of grace.

The faith described in the preceding paragraph is still not very firmly distinguished from the workings of poetic imagination, but Wordsworth does what he can to extricate himself from the snare of self-sufficiency. "You were not mistaken," he is glad to assure J. K. Miller in 1831, "that it is the habit of my mind inseparably to connect loftiness of imagination with that humility of mind which is best taught in Scripture." [387] The genius who tries to live by "passion craved for passion's sake" can never respond rightly to nature. He must learn

> . . . that meekness is the cherished bent
> Of all the truly great and all the innocent.

Then follows a couplet which seems to draw a firm line of demarcation between Wordsworth's earlier and later thought:

> But who *is* innocent? By grace divine,
> Not otherwise, O Nature! we are thine.

The beauty of the visible world in itself is spiritually worthless:

---

[385] Here Wordsworth remembers the *Hymn* which concludes Thomson's *Seasons*.
[386] *Oxford*, pp. 224–225.
[387] *Letters, Later Years*, p. 592.

> No perfect cure grows in that bounded field.
> Vain is the pleasure, a false calm the peace,
> If He, through whom alone our conflicts cease,
> Our virtuous hopes without relapse advance,
> Come not to speed the Soul's deliverance.[388]

If the older Wordsworth's supernaturalized naturalism does not unequivocally depend upon the basic doctrines of Christianity, it is by no means inconsistent with a sincere belief that "To save the contrite, Jesus died." [389]

8

Wordsworth was sixty-seven when Victoria ascended the throne; but except for the last few years of his life he remained the old man that he had been since 1815. Although positive joy had departed with the feelings of youth, the closing period was mainly contented and serene. The critical adulation and the official honors which now came to him so abundantly were deeply gratifying, and even the curiosity of trippers was not displeasing. He continued to worry about public affairs, but the long-cherished conviction that England was going to the dogs had become, like some familiar domestic inconvenience, almost one of the necessities of life. He no longer expected a bloody revolution within the next year or so. Except when confronted by new horrors, such as the Kendal and Windermere Railway and the proposal to abolish capital punishment, his Toryism mellowed and relaxed a little.

Beneath specific issues, however, he continued to see in the onward march of science and the extension of scientific method beyond the walls of the laboratory the arch-enemy of the believing imagination.

> ... True it is that Nature hides
> Her treasures less and less.—Man now presides
> In power, where once he trembled in his weakness;
> Science advances with gigantic strides;
> But are we aught enriched in love and meekness? [390]

In these lines the apparent antithesis of scientific pride and religious humility is somewhat misleading. The visionary power of Wordsworth's

[388] Oxford, p. 455.   [389] Ibid., p. 275.   [390] Ibid., p. 281.

original philosophy of nature expressed itself in a breaking down of boundaries and differences, an interfusion of man, nature, and God in one divine wholeness of loving imaginative life. This power was threatened by the rising power of science. Wordsworth never realized that it was no less completely denied, though for different reasons, by the Christian religion. Even his sincerest affirmations of "love and meekness" are partly motivated by the longing to authenticate the last vestiges of the romantic experience. He regrets that "Niebuhr and other modern historians" have deprived those who love ancient Rome's legendary glories of "Those old credulities, to nature dear." Men who were reared before these times of "severe research" at least know

> How, for exciting youth's heroic flame,
> Assent is power, belief the soul of fact.[391]

In Wordsworth the flame of youth has subsided, but Christian humbleness may help him to preserve a little of the power which lies in all assent.

Even more than in the preceding period, the poet looks toward Catholicism as a rich source of those "old credulities" which resist the encroachments of science. When that which is assented to is scientifically impossible, the reason of mechanistic materialism is most satisfyingly defied. Wordsworth's Catholic sympathies are especially evident in the *Memorials of a Tour in Italy, 1837,* though they are not confined to the fruits of this journey.[392] The most striking example is *Musings Near Aquapendente,* one of the Italian poems. Here, on the eve of his arrival at Rome, he anticipates the pleasures which he will enjoy in scenes associated with Horace and Virgil and with the "bold fictions"—scorned by Niebuhr—which cluster about the ancient Roman heroes. These will blend harmoniously in his mind with the city's "Christian Traditions," which do not disdain "Union with those primeval energies/To virtue consecrate." From the Catacombs he hopes to gain a glimpse of those who

> . . . of yore enclasped the Cross
> On knees that ceased from trembling; . . .
>
> . . . And thou Mamertine prison,
> Into that vault receive me from whose depth
> Issues, revealed in no presumptuous vision,

[391] *Ibid.,* p. 359.   [392] *Ibid.,* pp. 91, 352, 360, 362.

> Albeit lifting human to divine,
> A Saint, the Church's Rock, the mystic Keys
> Grasped in his hand; and lo! with upright sword
> Prefiguring his own impendent doom,
> The Apostle of the Gentiles.

These also are "bold fictions." In this poem the phrase "Christian Traditions"—observe the plural—means not the progressive unfolding of doctrine, but a body of inspiring stories. They deserve our belief as an antidote to science, whose tyranny has imprisoned us in

> ...a chilled age, most pitiably shut out
> From that which *is* and actuates, by forms,
> Abstractions, and by lifeless fact to fact
> Minutely linked with diligence uninspired,
> Unrectified, unguided, unsustained
> By godlike insight.[393]

The last phrase suggests that Wordsworth has not quite outgrown his old hankering for human self-deification. For him the faith of the historic Church is an escape from reason rather than the groundwork and pinnacle of reason. He wants the Catholic thrill without undergoing the Catholic discipline of intellect and spirit.

Nevertheless Wordsworth saw in Catholic respect for the past a stabilizing anti-revolutionary force which agreed with his own conservatism. In his picture of the Middle Ages, furthermore, the Church was the dominant factor in a benevolistic, non-competitive, feudal society. To a greater extent than in the 1820's, it was now possible for him to combine his Catholic sympathies with his Anglican High Churchmanship. Thanks to the Oxford Movement, the number of Anglicans who regarded themselves as no less completely Catholic than the Romanists had greatly increased. Wordsworth never adopted this position, but in his final period he advanced somewhat beyond the moderate and cautious Anglo-Catholicism of the Hackney group. This trend was encouraged by the influence of Miss Fenwick and of Professor Reed.[394]

After reading his nephew's *Theophilus Anglicanus,* the poet sends *To*

[393] *Ibid.,* pp. 352–358.
[394] Wordsworth's American correspondent was a pronounced Anglo-Catholic. His wife's grandfather, who lived with the Reeds for many years, was Bishop White, one of the two original bishops of the American Church. Several of the Catholic additions to *Ecclesiastical Sonnets* were written at Reed's request.

the Reverend Christopher Wordsworth his congratulations on showing the boys of Harrow

> ...the road
> That, in our native isle, and every land,
> The Church, when trusting in divine command
> And in her Catholic attributes, hath trod.[395]

The lines imply a more than merely nationalistic conception of the Church. In agreement with this view, the additions to *Ecclesiastical Sonnets* composed during this period emphasize the "Catholic attributes" of the English Church to an extent which mitigates, without unequivocally denying, the Protestantism of the first edition.[396] Wordsworth also revised several of the earlier sonnets. In *Sacrament* (III, xxv),[397] for example, "memorial Sacrament" becomes "mysterious Sacrament," but there is still no clue to the interpretation of the mystery.

Modern clergymen, pathetically grateful for belles-lettristic encouragement, are seldom inclined to scrutinize very closely the theology of poets whose general tone suggests that they are on the side of the angels. It is not surprising, then, that Newman and several of his associates regarded Wordsworth as a supporter and in some degree an inspirer of their cause. His influence on Keble is well known. But anyone who attempts to state with exactitude Wordsworth's opinion of the Oxford Movement finds himself in a thicket of conflicting evidence. He did not, in the first place, know very much about it. In January, 1840, he had read only one of the *Tracts*,[398] and as late as 1842 he is not sure that Keble is to be numbered among the Oxford group.[399]

Wordsworth's most explicit public utterance on the subject—a note of 1842 on the passage in *Musings Near Aquapendente* which we recently examined—is cautiously favorable. Reminding the reader that his "repugnance to the spirit and system of Romanism has been so repeatedly, and, I

---

[395] *Oxford*, p. 281. This course is Christopher junior, the poet's biographer, at this time (1843) Headmaster of Harrow, later Canon of Westminster, and finally Bishop of Lincoln. It is perhaps significant that Wordsworth was much less intimate with his nephew Charles, whose Catholicism was more aggressive than that of Christopher senior and junior.

[396] See especially II, i, ii, ix, xi; III, xxvi, xxvii, xxviii, xxxi. For further details on this point see Abbie F. Potts's edition of *Ecclesiastical Sonnets*, pp. 56–57.

[397] *Vide supra*, p. 239. This sonnet first appeared in 1827.

[398] *Robinson Correspondence*, p. 396. It was probably No. 80, *On Reserve in the Communication of Religious Knowledge*, for Robinson writes in September, 1839: "I fear I have heard Wordsworth speak favorably of this Tract." (*Robinson*, p. 576.)

[399] *Letters, Later Years*, p. 1137.

trust feelingly expressed, that I shall not be suspected of a leaning that way," he nevertheless refuses to join in the outcry against "a movement that takes, for its first principle, a devout deference to the voice of Christian antiquity." [400] But Gladstone's views on *The State in its Relations with the Church* were "too high for Wordsworth" [401] in 1839. In 1844, thanking Gladstone for his essay on "Present Aspects of the Church" in the *Foreign and Colonial Review,* he says that he agrees almost completely, "only felt some little dissatisfaction as to the limits of your Catholicity, for some limits it must have." He warns his correspondent of the perils of Romanism—"my horror of it, I will not use a milder term, notwithstanding all that I love and admire in that Church, is great indeed." [402] According to Yarnall, the American High Churchman, Wordsworth declared in 1849: "I foresaw that the movement was for good, and such I conceive it has been beyond all question." [403] But the Unitarian Crabb Robinson writes in the crucial year of 1845:

On my reminding him he had not executed his purpose of introducing in the new edition a note expressing his regret that he had ever uttered a word favorable to Puseyism, he said his only reason was that he was at last quite tired—a very insufficient reason. And I fear he will never do it.[404]

Another statement by Robinson gives what is probably an accurate summary of the matter:

The poet is a *high* churchman, but luckily does not go all lengths with the Oxford School—He praises the *reformers* (for they assume to be such) for inspiring the age with deeper reverence for antiquity, and to a more cordial conformity with ritual observances—as well as a warmer piety—But he goes no further.[405]

Catholicism appealed to Wordsworth's Burkian view of society and to his fondness for "bold credulities." This attraction, however, was weaker than the complex of political and religious feelings which gave him a "horror" of Romanism. He tells Robinson that Maitland's *The Dark Ages* "confirms, without alluding to any thing of mine, all that I had previously thrown out upon the benefits conferred by monastic institutions, and ex-

---

[400] *Oxford,* p. 907.
[401] *Robinson,* p. 564. See also *Robinson Correspondence,* p. 376.
[402] *Letters, Later Years,* pp. 1199–1201.
[403] Ellis Yarnall, *Wordsworth and the Coleridges,* p. 42.
[404] *Robinson,* p. 655.   [405] *Robinson Correspondence,* p. 472.

posing the ignorance of Robertson, Milner, Mosheim and others upon this
subject—repels most successfully their calumnies." [406] Nineteenth-century
English monasticism, however, was a different matter. Revisiting some of
his old haunts in 1841, Wordsworth "drove to a part of Charnwood forest
where they are erecting a monastery for Trappists." Lord Shrewsbury and
"other Romanist Grandees" are "no doubt" the financial backers.

Where are these things to stop, is a question which any one who has reflected
upon the constitution of the Romish Church will naturally put to himself with
such objects before him, and not without some apprehensions of mischief. Perhaps alarm may be needless, but surely it is too late in the day for such Institutions to be of much service, in England at least.[407]

His mind thus divided, Wordsworth could be neither a downright opponent nor a firm supporter of the Oxford Movement. He was never quite
able to conceive of a fully Catholic but non-Popish religion.[408] Even if he
had recognized the possibility of such a religion he would probably have
shrunk from it, for no less in his admiration than in his detestation of
Catholicism he remained a thorough Protestant.

Beneath his official Church-and-State opinions, the Christianized religion of nature remains his chief spiritual reliance. He now sets such
store by his orthodoxy, however, that the subjugation of nature to the
supernatural is even more strongly affirmed than in the preceding period.
He muses in the shady groves of Vallombrosa, near the cell

> Where our Milton was wont lonely vigils to keep
> For converse with God, sought through study and prayer.

But such respect for transitory places and forms as this tradition fosters
are blameless only

> ... if the Soul be intent on the day
> When the Being of Beings shall summon her hence.

> For he and he only with wisdom is blest
> Who, gathering true pleasures wherever they grow,

[406] *Ibid.*, pp. 579–580.
[407] *Letters, Later Years*, pp. 1082–1083. His objection is not to the Trappist rule, but to
modern monasticism in general.
[408] Of course Wordsworth was not unique in this respect: from the days of Newman to
the present the same difficulty has drawn many Anglicans from Canterbury to Rome. For
the poet, however, the question was how to preserve his Protestantism, not his Catholicism.

Looks up in all places, for joy or for rest,
To the Fountain whence Time and Eternity flow.[409]

By this time the cuckoo-clock and the actual "wandering Voice" are about equally efficacious in bringing back old memories which fill him with gratitude for God's goodness.[410] The cuckoo heard near the monastery of Laverna, however, reminds him chiefly of Saint Francis, in whom the poet now sees the perfect lover of nature:

> Rapt though He were above the power of sense,
> Familiarly, yet out of the cleansed heart
> Of that once sinful Being overflowed
> On sun, moon, stars, the nether elements,
> And every shape and creature they sustain,
> Divine affections.

We too must have "the power, the faith,/Of a baptized imagination" if we would

> ...catch from Nature's humblest monitors
> What'er they bring of impulses sublime.[411]

It may not be unfair to conjecture that, underneath the dews of baptism, the imaginative belief which imparts spiritual values to nature remains akin to the visionary power of Wordsworth's youth. So far as his explicit utterances are concerned, however, he now preaches a far more humble message than in the great poems of 1797–1807.

It was plainly incumbent upon him to set his literary house in order. Earlier work must be revised in the light provided by the baptized imagination; new poems like *The Westmoreland Girl* must be written to counterbalance *Three years she grew;* that completely non-religious elegy, *Address to the Scholars of the Village School of [Hawkshead]*, must be provided with a devout tag written "By the Side of the Grave Some Years After." He had tinkered with *The Prelude* at intervals since finishing the original version, but in 1838 and 1839 he undertook the task in earnest. A

---

[409] *Oxford*, pp. 364–365. But see *Letters, Later Years*, p. 1007, where it is said that Milton "has erred, and grievously," in matters theological. The letter was written in 1840, the poem in 1840 or 1841.

[410] *Ibid.*, p. 229.

[411] *Ibid.*, p. 362.

few of the many significant changes may be cited here. Their trend is too obvious to require comment.

1805:　　...Wonder not
　　　　　If such my transports were; for in all
　　　　　　　things now
　　　　　I saw one life, and felt that it was joy.

1850:　　...Wonder not
　　　　　If high the transport, great the joy I felt,
　　　　　Communing in this sort through earth
　　　　　　　and heaven
　　　　　With every form of creature, as it looked
　　　　　Towards the Uncreated with a counte-
　　　　　　　nance
　　　　　Of adoration, with an eye of love.[412]

1805:　　Nature's self, which is the breath of God.

1850:　　*adds:*　Or His pure Word by miracle re-
　　　　　vealed.[413]

1805:　　[*Man is*]
　　　　　...of all visible natures crown; and first
　　　　　In capability of feeling what
　　　　　Was to be felt; in being rapt away
　　　　　By the divine effect of power and love,
　　　　　As, more than anything we know, instinct
　　　　　With Godhead, and by reason and by will
　　　　　Acknowledging dependency sublime.

1850:　　...of all visible natures crown, though
　　　　　born
　　　　　Of dust, and kindred to the worm; a
　　　　　Being,
　　　　　Both in perception and discernment, first
　　　　　In every capability of rapture,
　　　　　Through the divine effect, *etc.*[414]

1805:　　God and Nature's single sovereignty.

1850:　　...presences of God's mysterious power
　　　　　Made manifest in Nature's sovereignty.[415]

[412] *Prelude,* pp. 62, 63.　　　[413] *Ibid.,* pp. 146, 147.　　　[414] *Ibid.,* pp. 294, 295.
[415] *Ibid.,* pp. 320, 321.

1805:   ...Great God!
            Who sends thyself into this breathing
                world,
            Through Nature and through every kind
                of life,
            And mak'st man what he is, Creature
                divine.

1850:   ...O Power Supreme!
            Without Whose call this world would
                cease to breathe,
            Who from the fountain of Thy grace
                dost fill
            The veins that branch through every
                frame of life,
            Making man, *etc.*[416]

1805:   Oh! Soul of Nature! that dost overflow
            With passion and with life.

1850:   O Soul of Nature! that, by laws divine
            Sustained and governed, still dost over-
                flow
            With an impassioned life.[417]

1805:   ...but there is higher love
            Than this, a love that comes into the heart
            With awe and a diffusive sentiment.

1850:   Unless this love by a still higher love
            Be hallowed, love that breathes not
                without awe;
            Love that adores, but on the knees of
                prayer,
            By heaven inspired.[418]

1805:   The feeling of life endless, the great
                thought
            By which we live, Infinity and God.

1850:   Faith in life endless, the sustaining
                thought
            Of human Being, Eternity, and God.[419]

[416] *Ibid.*, pp. 382, 383.   [417] *Ibid.*, pp. 430, 431.   [418] *Ibid.*, pp. 482, 483.
[419] *Ibid.*

But Wordsworth was too honest a man to revise *The Prelude* out of all relationship to its original principles, and even now too much the artist to discard work which he knew to be better poetry than the fruits of his orthodoxy. With a few discreet alterations, most of his early writings could stand if the reader were guided in the proper interpretation of them. This is the motive of many of the Fenwick notes and of several statements to correspondents and to visitors at Rydal Mount. To Henry Alford he explains that in his poems he has always been

averse to frequent mention of the mysteries of Christian faith; not from a want of due sense of their momentous nature, but on the contrary. I felt it far too deeply to venture on handling the subject as familiarly as many people scruple not to do. . . . Besides general reasons for diffidence in treating subjects of Holy Writ, I have some especial ones. I might err in points of faith, and I should not deem my mistakes less to be deprecated because they were expressed in metre.

How could he dare to walk the path from which "even Milton, in my humble opinion, has erred, and grievously?" [420] Similarly the Reverend R. P. Graves reports an interview with Wordsworth which occurred in 1840:

He expressed to me the feelings of reverence which prevented him from venturing to lay his hand on what he always thought a subject too high for him; and he accompanied this with an earnest protest that his works . . . should not be considered as developing all the influences which his own heart recognised, but rather those which he considered himself able as an artist to display to advantage, and which he thought most applicable to the wants, and admitted by the usages, of the world at large.[421]

As an explanation of why Wordsworth seldom wrote "sacred" poetry in the strict sense even in his High Church days, these remarks may be accepted at approximately their face value; but as an explanation of the absence of Christian supernaturalism in his earlier and greater poetry they must be taken with a grain of salt. Christopher Wordsworth strikes the note which would have been most gratifying to his uncle:

He had some doubts how far uninspired men are competent to write sacred poetry. But, however this may be, he considered it to be the mission of all

---

[420] *Letters, Later Years*, pp. 1006–1007.
[421] Christopher Wordsworth, *Memoirs*, II, 366.

poets, and he regarded it as his own vocation, to endeavour to elevate the mind to sacred things. . . . He endeavoured to prepare their minds to worship with more devotion in the outer court of the natural world, and thus to fit themselves for admission into the sanctuary, under the guidance of revealed religion.[422]

That is, even when he least seemed to be writing as a Christian he was deliberately leading his readers from the natural toward the supernatural revelation. For many years this was the official—and spurious—interpretation of the whole body of his work.

It has always been difficult to understand why Wordsworth, so deeply interested in the development of his own mind, should have spurned chronology in the perverse classification of his poems which he insisted upon in all collected editions from 1815 onward. One consequence—not the sole or perhaps even the partial conscious *motive*—of this arrangement was that poems representing a heterodox naturalism were mingled with poems which expressed varying degrees of more traditional piety. By readers who associated Wordsworth with Rydal Mount rather than with Alfoxden the resultant blur of earnest, elevated thought and feeling could easily be interpreted in the most edifying sense. In "Poems Referring to the Period of Childhood," "Poems Founded on the Affections," "Poems of the Fancy," and "Poems of the Imagination," it was impossible to follow his tracks. This remark does not apply to groups based upon an occasional rather than a topical concept, such as "Poems Dedicated to National Independence and Liberty" and "Memorials of a Tour on the Continent," or on more closely restricted themes, such as "Ecclesiastical Sonnets" and "Evening Voluntaries." It is significant, however, that the poems included under these and similar heads are almost always conservatively Christian. Thus the arrangement combined special groups of concentratedly orthodox impact with more general groups in which heterodoxy and orthodoxy were inextricably blended. We may also remind ourselves that the 1815 Preface, in which the beauties of this arrangement are explained on different but unconvincing grounds, is the first document in which the poet explicitly dedicates his art to the Tory ideals of Church and State. These considerations do not imply that the later Wordsworth was a hypocrite. They merely demand recognition of the fact that he was extremely anxious to rearrange his past for the easing of his own conscience, for the enhance-

[422] *Ibid.,* p. 356.

ment of his contemporary reputation, and for the spiritual benefit of posterity.

The household at Rydal Mount was a pious one; for Mrs. Wordsworth, in her serene unaggressive way, fully agreed with her husband's Churchmanship. The day began and ended with family prayers.

One of the images which recurs oftenest to his friends is that of the old man as he would stand against the window of the dining-room at Rydal Mount and read the Psalms and Lessons for the day; of the tall bowed figure and the silvery hair; of the deep voice which always faltered when among the prayers he came to the words which give thanks for those "who have departed this life in thy faith and fear." [423]

Strolling in the grounds after breakfast, the visitor would be confronted by a boulder on which had been inscribed:

Wouldst thou be gathered to Christ's chosen flock,
Shun the broad way too easily explored,
And let thy path be hewn out of the Rock,
The living rock of God's eternal Word. [424]

Since about 1820 the poet had been a regular churchgoer. Probably, however, he was seldom as happy on his knees in his pew as when musing in the churchyard, where he could lift his eyes from the inscriptions on the tombs to the fields and hills which lay beyond. De Vere relates an anecdote in which he quotes Miss Fenwick as saying:

"That rough old face is capable of high and real beauty; I have seen in it an expression quite of heavenly peace and contemplative delight, as the May breeze came over him from the woods while he was slowly walking out of church on a Sunday morning, and when he had half emerged from the shadow." A flippant person present inquired: "Did you ever chance, Miss F—, to observe that heavenly expression on his countenance as he was walking *into* church on a fine May morning?" A laugh was the reply. [425]

Although the correlation between the beliefs and the behavior of Christians is tenuous, certain details may be admitted in evidence. As the centre of his domestic firmament and of a large circle of admirers Wordsworth was treated with a deference which seemed to him not improper.

---

[423] F. W. H. Myers, *Wordsworth*, pp. 182–183.　　[424] *Oxford*, p. 626.
[425] Aubrey de Vere, *Essays Chiefly on Poetry*, II, 294.

It is doubtful if he often thought or felt beyond himself in human relationships, but the principle of benevolence had always been an essential
feature of the personality within which he existed. Despite the narrowness
of his views, he was not intolerant of anyone who possessed that authentic
vitality of being which was always so precious to him. Faber and De
Vere, much more enthusiastic Newmanites than Wordsworth, would
soon follow their leader into the Roman fold. Dr. Thomas Arnold, an
advanced Broad Churchman, "was a *good* man, and an admirable schoolmaster, but he would make a desperate bad bishop." [426] Crabb Robinson
was a Unitarian. Harriet Martineau had moved beyond Unitarianism to
a combination of agnosticism and complete faith in Mesmerism. Wordsworth agreed with none of these; from none of them did he withhold his
friendship. His tender and generous kindness to poor Hartley Coleridge
suggests a submerged capacity for love. When that wastrel of genius was
given his last Communion by his brother Derwent, Wordsworth also
received beside the deathbed. His humbler neighbors remembered him
as "a kind mon, there's no two words about that: if any one was sick i' the
plaace, he wad be off to see til 'em." [427] One anecdote strikes the authentic
note of Christian foolishness. When the cook, angry because a beggar had
thrown away her gift of food on reaching the gate, vowed she would never
again help those cheating rascals, her master protested: "O, don't say that,
Elizabeth! Go on giving, and some day the right beggar will come!" [428]
And yet the cottagers saw in him "a desolate-minded man. . . . Hartley
had always a bit of smile or a twinkle in his faace, but Wordsworth was
not lovable in the faace by no means." [429] He never got enough fun out of
being a Christian.

Beneath his rather too complacent exterior, the Wordsworth of the
1840's was not always satisfied with his spiritual condition. He writes to
Miss Fenwick:

Worldly-minded I am not, nor indifferent to the welfare of my fellow-creatures; on the contrary, my wish to benefit them within my humble sphere
strengthens, seemingly, in exact proportion to my inability to realise those
wishes, in any project which I may engage in. What I lament most is that
the spirituality of my Nature does not expand and rise the nearer I approach

[426] *Robinson Correspondence*, p. 704.
[427] H. D. Rawnsley, "Reminiscences of Wordsworth Among the Peasantry of Westmoreland," *Transactions of the Wordsworth Society*, VI, 168.
[428] Edith C. Batho, *The Later Wordsworth*, p. 45.
[429] Rawnsley, *op. cit.*, pp. 181, 182.

the grave, as yours does, and as it fares with my beloved Partner. The pleasure which I derive from God's works in his visible creation is not with me I think impaired, but no kind of reading interests me as it used to do, and I feel that I am becoming daily a much less instructive Companion to others.[430]

Perhaps the trouble was that although he now affirmed the Christian ideal of self-surrender his heart was not quite in agreement with his principles. This difficulty is of course universal among Christians, but Wordsworth would feel it very keenly because "the light/Full early lost, and fruitlessly deplored" had been so bright a flame of self-trust.

Near the end the old man's ability to say "Thy will be done" was tested beyond the breaking-point. He had opposed Dora's marriage to Quillinan chiefly because he could not bear to lose the companionship of the vivid child who, now that his sister's bright eyes were clouded, kept alive a little of his own youth.[431] When Dora died in 1847 her mother's faith rose to the challenge triumphantly, but her father was crushed by the blow. He took his sorrow morbidly and selfishly. Robinson tells of the lesson taught the poet by his servant James several months after the tragedy:

Expressing my sorrow that Mr. Wordsworth was unable to submit, he [James] said: "Ah, Sir, so I took the liberty to say to him, and then master said: 'Oh, but she was such a bright creature.' And then I said: *'But don't you think she is brighter now than she ever was?'* And then he burst into a flood of tears." [432]

When at last he rallied from the shock, the sands of his own life were running low. On April twenty-third, 1850, having received the Sacrament at the hands of his son John, he ended the earthly pilgrimage just as the treasured cockoo-clock was striking noon.

Not all of the inconsistencies in this study of Wordsworth's religion are to be laid at my door. His ideas on the subject were always hesitant and cloudy. He valued belief less as a means of shedding light upon darkness than as a means of preserving the inviolability of mystery. His early self-trust is tempered not only with cautious reservations but with genuine reverence for the suprapersonal; his late-learned humility is in some

---

[430] *Letters, Later Years*, p. 1223. See also p. 1212 for a slightly earlier letter to Miss Fenwick in which he seems to be contrasting her tendency to criticise his faults with his wife's willingness to accept and forgive them.

[431] It is true that Dora was an invalid and that Quillinan's financial circumstances and his rather shiftless character justified real doubts as to his ability to support her. He was also, in a half-hearted sort of way, a Roman Catholic. (Ernest de Selincourt, *Wordsworthian and Other Studies*, pp. 34ff.) But Wordsworth would not have been enthusiastic about *any* suitor for Dora's hand.   [432] *Robinson*, p. 855.

measure a new cloak for the old pride. His pantheism has hardly taken form before it begins to send out feelers toward transcendence; the outwardly rigid Anglicanism of his old age at times looks back wistfully at the heresies of his youth. On the whole, however, it is not extremely difficult to trace the curve of Wordsworth's beliefs from 1784 to 1802 and to explain it as a continuation of the sentimental naturalism of the eighteenth century. The changes which begin to occur about 1802, and which seem completely to have transformed his religious thought by 1820 are to me much harder to understand. It may be said that they are unimportant in the interpretation of the "true" Wordsworth's greatest poetry; but for the history of ideas, and perhaps even for literary criticism, the long twilight of romanticism is no less interesting than its brief noontide.

What did Wordsworth actually believe in the years when he regarded himself as a pillar of Anglican orthodoxy? In 1825 he wrote to Beaumont:

I have never had a higher relish for the beauties of Nature than during this spring, nor enjoyed myself more. What manifold reasons, my dear Sir George, have you and I to be thankful to Providence! Theologians may puzzle their heads about dogmas as they will, the religion of gratitude cannot mislead us. Of that we are sure, and gratitude is the handmaid to hope, and hope the harbinger of faith. I look abroad upon Nature, I think of the best part of my species. I lean upon my friends, and I meditate upon the Scriptures, especially the Gospel of St. John; and my creed rises up of itself with the ease of an exhalation, yet a fabric of adamant.[433]

The enjoyment of self in nature; gratitude to Nature's God; scorn of theological subtleties; sanguine views of the human heart, based on carefully selected evidence; finally a leap—over a considerable chasm—to St. John. Hence arises "my creed"—the pronoun is meaningful. Toward a less personal creed Wordsworth in 1838 takes an attitude which we should not expect of the author of a sonnet in defense of *The Commination Service*.[434] Talking with Robinson, he

apologized for making salvation depend on opinion, by the suggestion that only depravity of will could prevent that examination of evidence which must lead to the conviction of truth; but he would not affirm that such a principle applied to the Athanasian Creed, which he pretended not to justify, but wishes to remove.[435]

[433] *Letters, Later Years*, pp. 204–205.
[434] *Oxford*, p. 447. The sonnet, to be sure, was probably written four years later than the date of the reported conversation. [435] *Robinson*, p. 559.

As late as 1843 he "declared in strong terms his disbelief of eternal punishment." [436]

In 1826 the diarist summarizes "some scattered notes of talk with Wordsworth." What follows is presumably a half-quoted paraphrase of the poet's words:

"The Atonement is a doctrine which has its foundation in that consciousness of unworthiness and guilt which arises from an upright self-examination—as all the orthodox doctrines are warranted by a humble spirit and all that is best in our moral nature. There is internal evidence for all these doctrines, which are a source of happiness. And the difficulty of comprehending the mysteries of the Gospel is no sufficient reason for rejection. It is not necessary to define with precision the doctrines thus received, and the Church of England has encumbered itself by needless and mischievous attempts at explanation. The Athanasian Creed is one of these unhappy excrescenses. Nor does the idea of the personality of the Spirit come with such authority, or claim so imperiously our adoption, as the doctrine of the divinity of Jesus Christ. The thought that an infinitely pure being can receive satisfaction from the sufferings of Jesus Christ and accept them as a satisfaction for the sins of the guilty is declared by Coleridge to be an outrage on common sense. It is a hard saying, nor can I explain it to my satisfaction. . . . Coleridge used to declare that the belief in miracles is not a necessary part of a Christian's creed; but this is contrary to the express and uniform declaration of the Scriptures, and I have no difficulty in believing in miracles since I consider as superstition the imagined knowledge and certainty which men suppose they have as to the laws of nature." This [Robinson continues] I believe is all that Wordsworth can be said to believe, and it is little. It is quite clear that he does not place any weight in the historical evidence, and when I said that I tried to believe, he said, "That is pretty much my case." [437]

In this passage the most noteworthy features are the almost complete subordination of external to internal evidence and the pragmatic justification of doctrine in terms of "happiness," the dislike of all precise definition of belief, the Arian unwillingness to accept the full personality of the Holy Spirit, the uneasiness as regards the Atonement, and the acceptance of miracle as a rebuke to science. It seemed to Robinson that "Wordsworth's own religion . . . would not satisfy either a religionist or a sceptic." [438] The views here reported are of course wholly consistent with modern Christian liberalism. They seem very loose and vague, however, for a nineteenth-century High Churchman.

[436] *Ibid.*, p. 628.   [437] *Ibid.*, pp. 481–482.   [438] *Ibid.*, p. 481.

Even to questions which many readers will regard as more essential
Wordsworth does not give unequivocal answers. Miss Geen, who has carefully studied "The Concept of Grace in Wordsworth's Poetry," states:

Although references to Christ increase in frequency, Wordsworth's conception
of grace was never to have a marked Christological emphasis. . . . With a
due recognition of the poet's evident respect and love for the figure of Christ,
it might be said that his religion from 1814 on was more Platonic and theistic
than it was definitely Christian in the narrow sense of the word; Christ for
Wordsworth was never *the* way to the central peace of God.[439]

Ample allowance should probably be made for the High Churchman's
unwillingness to use the redemptive terminology of those offensive creatures, the Evangelicals. By 1820 at the latest, Wordsworth had surely
repudiated the notion that he did not need a Redeemer.[440] I am inclined to
agree, however, that belief in the Saviour was chiefly valuable to him as
providing a safe traditional wall within which he could cultivate a more
congenial kind of spiritual experience based upon the relationship between
nature and a half-impersonal Holy Spirit who—or which—was about as
closely related to the human imagination as to the Trinity. In short Wordsworth became a Christian, but not—to adopt Miss Geen's revealing phrase
—"in the narrow sense of the word." It is not surprising that his writings
were most deeply influential not in Tractarian circles, but among vaguely
and tenderly earnest Broad Churchmen—Arnold, Clough, the Hare
brothers, Maurice, Trench, Monckton Milnes, Tennyson, Arthur Hallam.
Nor is it surprising that today he is admired as a religious thinker chiefly
by clerics and scholars who represent a later phase of the tradition which
descended to the Victorian Broad Churchmen from the eighteenth century.

Through all the changes in Wordsworth's religion runs a flexible but
stubbornly consistent core of continuity. At heart he never strays very
widely from the Christian sentimentalism, or sentimental Christianity, of
the softer type of eighteenth-century latitudinarianism. During a few years
of exceptionally fervid self-trust, he devotes his highest powers to the most
extreme form of this tradition, accepting the pantheistic implications of
sentimental deism. As his vitality subsides, however, he returns with no
shock of incongruity to a safer, meeker, more ostensibly Christian expres-

---

[439] Elizabeth Geen, "The Concept of Grace in Wordsworth's Poetry," *PMLA*, LVIII, 708.
[440] *Vide supra*, p. 209.

sion of the religion of nature. Gradually, political and personal circumstances impel him to erect a still more solidly conservative stockade within which the "baptized imagination" might enjoy the last vestiges of the visionary power. At last he develops Protestant hankerings toward Catholicism and hesitantly clothes his latitudinarian feelings in Puseyite vestments. But the chain of natural piety, though strained and battered and changed in outward appearance almost beyond recognition, is never completely broken.

Chapter V

COLERIDGE

I

THE FRAGMENTS WHICH COLERIDGE LEFT BEHIND HIM ARE MATERIALS FOR A stately pleasure-dome of thought which, had it ever been built in air, would have embodied the romantic ideal of an all-embracing synthesis. They are also the fragments of a personal tragedy—a tragedy less of the Sophoclean than of the present-day clinical type.

Although S.T.C. could lie to himself as well as to others he perfectly understood the sickness of his soul. Readers of his letters know how he loves to talk about his infirmity of will, his craving to be esteemed by others and still more by himself, his flight from the concrete into the abstract in the hope of avoiding mental and physical pain, and his enslavement to opium as another means of attaining the same end. But Professor Bald has unearthed from one of the notebooks a more searching self-analysis than the poet confided to any of his friends:

It is a most instructive part of my Life the fact, that I have been always preyed on by some Dread, and perhaps all of my faulty actions have been the consequences of some Dread or other in my mind from fear of Pain, or Shame, not from prospect of Pleasure.[1]

This dread, as Coleridge goes on to show in revealing detail, assumed various forms at various stages, but beneath all its protean changes it remained a constant in his personality. In this romantic poet an exceptionally strong craving for imaginative dominance is shadowed by a frustrating realization of weakness. If he would satisfy the former he must find some means of escaping from the latter.

Whatever hereditary roots his fear may have had are hidden from us,

---

[1] Quoted by R. C. Bald in "Coleridge and *The Ancient Mariner*," *Nineteenth-Century Studies*, pp. 26–27.

but a well-known letter to Thomas Poole helps to explain the early environmental factors. The favor shown him by his parents aroused the jealousy of Frank, the next elder brother, and of Frank's old nurse. The other boys of the large family and his father's pupils scorned the little milksop, teased him, drove him from their play. There seems to have been no severe bullying, but this was an abnormally sensitive child. He found his own way of achieving superiority over his fellows:

So I became a *dreamer,* and acquired an indisposition to all bodily activity; . . . and because I could read and spell and had . . . a memory and understanding forced into almost an unnatural ripeness, I was flattered and wondered at by all the old women. And so I became very vain, and despised most of the boys that were at all near my own age. . . . Sensibility, imagination, sloth, and feelings of deep and bitter contempt for all who traversed the orbit of my understanding were even then prominent and manifest.[2]

Shrinking into himself, he created an unreal world of his own out of materials drawn from the fairy-tales in which he revelled. He was not incredulous when his father described to him the marvels of the Newtonian universe, "for from my early reading of fairy tales and genii, etc. etc., my mind had been habituated *to the Vast.*"[3] In later years his interest in science was never to be extricated from his interest in magic.

The delight of withdrawing from the actual into the imaginary was not unalloyed. What he read was so vivid to him that it sometimes seemed as real as that real world which he dreaded, but stranger and more disquieting. Just when poetic images became most delightful they took on an unendurable quality of truth and created a need of escaping even from the fairy-tale refuge. The nightmares began very early. At six or seven he was so deeply impressed by the *Arabian Nights* "that I was haunted by spectres, whenever I was in the dark."[4]

Against these terrors he possessed a charm:

> "Matthew! Mark! Luke and John!
> God bless the bed which I lie on.
> Four angels round me spread,
> Two at my foot, and two at my head."

This prayer I said nightly, and most firmly believed the truth of it. Frequently have I (half-awake and half-asleep, my body diseased and fevered by my

[2] S. T. Coleridge, *Letters* (ed. E. H. Coleridge, 1895), p. 12. Referred to hereafter as *Letters.*   [3] *Ibid.,* p. 16.   [4] *Ibid.,* p. 12.

imagination) seen armies of ugly things bursting in upon me, and these four angels keeping them off.[5]

It was many years before he rediscovered this method of soothing the pains of sleep. At Ottery he probably did not distinguish very clearly between the Scriptures and the *Arabian Nights*. His father's theology mingled eccentric speculation with half-mystical credulity, a combination which soon proved attractive to the son. But what the moping, timorous, conceited child needed was a faith that would take him out of himself and enable him to walk before the Lord *in the land of the living*. If his father possessed such a faith he did not impart it to Samuel.

A lonely schoolboy can be homesick even for an unsatisfactory home, but as time went on Coleridge grew happier at Christ's Hospital than he had been at Ottery. He always needed success, affection, praise, petting, as a flower needs sunlight; and in London he ultimately received enough of these boons to quiet, though not to eradicate, the fear in his heart. He was not enough of a rebel to be an exciting butt for his schoolmates, and his evident desire to be liked made some of them like him. Middleton and other older boys admired his gifts and granted him their protection. Boyer grumbled at the floweriness of his style but placed some of the lad's verses in his private album.

With one or two exceptions the poems of the Christ's Hospital period are too factitious to provide solid material for the interpretation of young Coleridge's thought. Practically all of the evidence used by biographers for this purpose was set down long after the fact in his own reminiscences and in those of Lamb and others. One gathers that he soared above Christian orthodoxy into a jumble of rationalism (Voltaire, Erasmus Darwin) and Neoplatonism (chiefly Taylor's translations from Plotinus). Now as later he desired both to dream and to find some demonstrable proof of his dreams. The Neoplatonism was far more congenial to his visionary, believing nature, it was more deeply secluded from actuality, and it provided a means of acquiring a reputation for Orphic wisdom among the boys. On the other hand, the rationalism was attractively daring and advanced. It was a distinction to be flogged by Boyer for declaring that he intended to be, not a parson, but an infidel shoemaker. The rationalistic side of the balance was strengthened by his interest in surgery and medicine (his brother Luke was in training at London Hospital), and, in 1789,

[5] *Ibid.*, p. 13.

by the revolutionary enthusiasm expressed in *Destruction of the Bastile.*
Let us not regard too solemnly the thought of the schoolboy Coleridge.
In both its aspects it included a large element of showing off. And though
he was to some extent genuinely in quest of truth he was also, despite
his comparative peace of mind, in flight from reality—a contradiction
which he would never be able to reconcile. From his reading he had
already begun to spin a protective cocoon of words-for-words'-sake: "My
eloquence was most commonly excited by the desire of running away and
hiding myself from my personal and inward feelings, *and not for the expression of them."* [6]

Since in later days Coleridge often describes metaphysics as a refuge
from life and even from poetry, one scents danger when he reports that
"Even before my fifteenth year, I had bewildered myself in metaphysics,
and in theological controversy. . . . History, and particular facts, lost all
interest," and poetry itself "became insipid." [7] But he was rescued from
this condition by the flatteringly affectionate hospitality of the Evans
family. Mary in particular stirred feelings which were not yet intense
enough to be alarming, and the poetry of Bowles suggested the possibility of expressing such feelings with a mild melancholy simplicity which
was a pleasanter remedy for Della Cruscanism than Boyer's astringent
common sense. At almost the same time the outbreak of the French Revolution promised to harmonize personal illusion with outward reality.
Hence during the last two years at school he was riding one of his crests.
In a poem entitled *Life,* written in September, 1789, just after a visit to
Ottery to see his ailing sister, he tells how the Devonshire landscape
roused him from his "torpid woe." At first he saw a succession of lovely
objects, but suddenly he combined the whole in a single act of synthesis:

> May this (I cried) my course through Life portray,
> New scenes of Wisdom may each step display,
> And knowledge open as my days advance!
> Till what time Death shall pour the undarken'd ray,
> My eye shall dart thro' infinite expanse,
> And thought suspended lie in Rapture's blissful trance. [8]

[6] Thomas Allsop, *Letters, Conversations and Recollections of S. T. Coleridge,* II, 136.
[7] *Biographia Literaria,* I, 9.
[8] S. T. Coleridge, *Complete Poetical Works* (Oxford, 1912), pp. 11–12. Referred to hereafter as *Poems.*

Here is the first hint of that "shaping spirit of imagination," or "esemplastic power," which will play so large a part in his aesthetics, his metaphysics, and his theology.

During his first year at Cambridge he maintained the healthy mood in which he had left school. He lived soberly and studied hard. Soon after entering Jesus College he was using opium as a remedy for a rheumatic attack, but the fact would not be ominous if we did not know the sequel. The drug was freely prescribed in those days, and a letter to his brother George implies that he had taken it previously—probably for a similar ailment at Christ's Hospital—with no "disagreeable effects." [9] Soon, however, he began to weaken. When he returned to Cambridge after the long vacation of 1792 he was in poor health and low spirits. He had carelessly piled up debts which he found himself unable to pay. In 1821, warning young Derwent against any similar folly, he says that he

can never forget that the stupefying effect of my first Term Bill . . . affected and infected my whole life following—and by pure terror and hauntings of mind brought about a cowardice as to mental pain, which has been the main source of all my real Misdoings and *Not*-doings, and the occasion of many and worse being attributed to me.[10]

Although this predicament was certainly not the originating cause of his dread, it produced a major psychological crisis. Instead of facing the music he indulged in hysterical evasions which plunged him into deepening misery. His love for Mary Evans, which he had probably declared to her in the previous summer, was corrupted by morbid terrors. He drank heavily and sought relief in sexual debauchery. If we may believe him—though on the whole we may not—he seriously contemplated suicide.[11] A less drastic way out was provided by the military fiasco, which ended when he returned to Cambridge in April, 1794, free of debt thanks to his brothers, and full of good resolutions.

Coleridge told Thelwall in 1796 that for some time after entering the University he was an "infidel," [12] but what meaning should be attached to this term is uncertain. He was never an atheist—his childish boast at Christ's Hospital should be discounted—and according to *Biographia*

---

[9] S. T. Coleridge, *Unpublished Letters* (ed. E. L. Griggs, 1932), I, 3. Referred to hereafter as *Unpublished Letters*.

[10] *Ibid.*, II, 278.   [11] *Ibid.*, I, 13–14.   [12] *Ibid.*, p. 51.

Literaria he was so far from being a deist at Cambridge that he was "decried as a bigot by the proselytes of French Phi (or to speak more truly, Psi-)losophy."[13] A letter to Mrs. Evans in which he signs himself "Samuel Taylor Coleridge, Reverend in the future tense"[14] is of uncertain date but should probably be assigned to February, 1792. Apparently he neither strongly believed nor disbelieved anything in particular until his association with William Frend, which began in January, 1792, led him to espouse Unitarianism.

Frend, of whom something has been said in the preceding chapter,[15] was so uncompromising a Socinian that in defiance of the Blasphemy Act he published such manifestoes as the following:

I daily and openly do deny the divinity of our Lord Jesus Christ. . . . For I consider Jesus as a man, in all things like myself, sin only excepted, but I firmly believe that he was a chosen messenger and servant of Jehovah, his father and our father, his God and our God. I do deny the personality of the Holy Ghost. . . . The person . . . whom ye worship under the name of the Holy Ghost, is a non-entity, an ideal being, a phantom of your own imaginations. I do also say, that our Lord Jesus Christ and the Holy Ghost are not proper objects of a Christian man's worship; for there is no command in scripture for Christians to worship either.[16]

We may be sceptical of Coleridge's assertion that he was converted to these views as a result of profound study.[17] Young Cambridge liberals who shrank from outright deism were quite likely to be Unitarians, though not always so outspokenly as Frend. Nor was Coleridge by any means unique in combining his Unitarianism with the sensationalism of Locke, the materialistic associationism of Hartley and Priestley, a good deal of Godwinian perfectibility, and a fairly strong tincture of youthful Jacobinism. He was simply following a current left-wing fashion.

If he did not wholly forsake the Neoplatonic interests which had mingled with his rationalism at Christ's Hospital, here again he did not stand alone. The young intellectuals of Cambridge, no less sentimental in their rationalism than rationalistic in their sentimentalism, required a philosophy for their looser reveries. At this time the translations of Thomas Taylor, with which Coleridge already had some acquaintance, were stim-

---

[13] *Biographia Literaria*, I, 49n.   [14] *Letters*, p. 41.
[15] *Vide supra*, p. 146.
[16] William Frend, *An Account of Some Late Proceedings of the "Society for Promoting Christian Knowledge,"* p. 8.   [17] *Unpublished Letters*, I, 51.

ulating a slight revival of Platonic studies. It was probably at the University, also, that he began to read the Cambridge Platonists. He is not thinking of Frend or Hartley when he confesses to George:

I have little faith, yet am wonderfully fond of speculating on mystical schemes. Wisdom may be gathered from the maddest flights of imagination, as medicines were stumbled upon in the wild processes of alchemy.[18]

On the whole, however, the main trend of his thought during the Cambridge years moved in the opposite direction from "mystical schemes."

The letter just cited was written in March, 1794, shortly before his discharge from the cavalry. Coleridge was always most pious, metaphysical, and mystical when most anxious to evade some unpleasant circumstance; at such a time the gospel according to William Frend seemed rather too negative to meet the needs of the situation. In February and March of this year it was also necessary to placate his orthodox and disgusted brother:

I long ago theoretically and in a less degree experimentally knew the necessity of faith in order to regulate virtue, nor did I ever seriously disbelieve the existence of a future state. In short, my religious creed bore, and perhaps bears, a correspondence with my mind and heart. Fond of the dazzle of wit, fond of subtlety of argument, I could not read without some degree of pleasure the levities of Voltaire or the reasonings of Helvetius; but, tremblingly alive to the feelings of humanity, and susceptible to the charms of truth, my heart forced me to admire the "beauty of holiness" in the Gospel, forced me to *love* the Jesus whom my reason (or perhaps my reasonings) would not permit me to worship,—my faith, therefore, was made up of the Evangelists and the deistic philosophy—a kind of *religious twilight*.[19]

In such a crisis he feels the need of prayer and penitence: "Pray for me, my brother. I will pray nightly to the Almighty dispenser of good and evil, that his chastisement may not have harrowed my heart in vain." [20] To interpret these words as politic hypocrisy would be to oversimplify the complexity of Coleridge's mind. His morbidly acute self-knowledge frequently conflicted with his craving for self-esteem. He is now genuinely disgusted with himself, although he is also quite consciously saying the proper thing to the Reverend George. But penitence demands that we lay hold on pain and use it, and the dread of pain was the master passion

---

[18] *Letters*, p. 64.   [19] *Ibid.*, pp. 68–69.   [20] *Ibid.*, p. 61.

of Coleridge's life. Not until much later does he learn to transform his sense of sin into a subtly luxurious kind of pride. At present its reality is unbearable. Hence in another letter he tells George that the satisfactions of penitence have been exaggerated. It may bring calm,

> but it cannot restore to the mind that inward sense of Dignity, which is the Parent of every kindling energy! I am not what I was:—*Disgust*—I feel, as if I had jaundiced all my Faculties.[21]

Creative energy authenticated by an inward sense of Dignity—it is the primary romantic desire, and it does not thrive on penitent self-scrutiny. Not to his brother but to his friend George Cornish he writes on March 12, 1794:

> I have been, deeply do I feel that I have been, the dupe of my Imagination, the child of Error and Imbecility—yet when I look back on the numbers and characters of those, who have honoured me with their Regard, I am almost reconciled to myself, and half listen to the whispers of self-adulation.[22]

He blames his weakness not upon himself, but upon a cluster of eighteenth-century personifications. By the time he met Southey at Oxford in June, 1794, the whispers of self-adulation had swelled into a shout, and his inward sense of dignity was fully restored.

2

An important phase of Coleridge's career runs from his meeting with Southey in June, 1794, to his settlement at Nether Stowey on the last day of 1796. The period comprises the inflation and collapse of the pantisocratic balloon; the rise and fall and imperfect restoration of his friendship with Robert Southey; the loss of Mary Evans, the reluctant marriage to Sara Fricker, and the birth of his first child; ventures in politico-religious lecturing, preaching, and journalism; the publication of his first volume of poems; the preliminary stages of the opium habit.

"In the book of pantisocracy," Coleridge informs Southey, "I hope to have comprised all that is good in Godwin, . . . (I think not so highly of him as you do, and I have read him with the greatest attention)." [23] S.T.C.

[21] *Unpublished Letters*, I, 13.
[22] *Ibid.*, p. 18. See p. 20 for the same thought in practically the same words.
[23] *Letters*, p. 91.

was always a hero-worshipper, but none of his heroes ever said precisely the right thing in precisely the right way. He never approved of Godwin's atheism, his sexual radicalism, or his scorn of the private affections; but in December, 1794, he is still grateful for Godwin's "holy guidance,"

> For that thy voice, in Passion's stormy day,
> When wild I roam'd the bleak Heath of Distress,
> Bade the bright form of Justice meet my way—
> And told me that her name was HAPPINESS.[24]

Unquestionably the basic conception of pantisocracy was Godwinian. In the spring of 1794 Coleridge and Southey were sentimental rationalists with strongly republican views. They were anti-war, anti-Pitt, and pro-French so far as the abstract ideals of the Revolution were concerned. The excesses of the Terror, however, had shocked and disillusioned them. In *The Fall of Robespierre,* they tried to persuade themselves that France shall "liberate the world" now that the Jacobin dictator has fallen,[25] but they had little real hope for immediate large-scale reform. Too discouraged to think in "global" terms, and yet unwilling to surrender their ideals, they naturally turned to *Political Justice.* As Coleridge explains in *The Friend,* they hoped to demonstrate the benign workings of necessity upon a small, carefully selected group in an environment which would automatically stamp impressions of reason and virtue upon the *tabulas rasas* of their children.[26]

But the rationalism of these youngsters, like that of the age in which they lived, was thin and fragile. Beneath it, and frequently breaking through to the surface, was the sentimental naturalism which has become so familiar to my readers. From one point of view, retirement to the wilderness was merely a device for providing proper laboratory conditions; yet from another, it was less a retreat to a necessitarian incubator than a pseudo-Rousseauistic quest for primitive goodness and simplicity on the beautiful banks of the Susquehanna. The latter element is naturally prominent in the poems which Coleridge composed in 1794 and the early months of 1795. Except when he is pamphleteering in verse on men and issues of the day, he usually writes as a youth of tremulous sensibility, a

[24] *Poems,* p. 86.
[25] *Ibid.,* p. 517. The lines are Southey's, but Coleridge doubtless approved.
[26] S. T. Coleridge, *Complete Works* (ed. W. G. T. Shedd, 1878), II, 203. Referred to hereafter as *Works.*

"Child of Nature" [27] whose main spiritual reliance is a benevolism which, in the notorious lines *To a Young Ass,* extends very far indeed.

At the outset, however, the official religious position of pantisocracy was mainly negative. The prime essential was to be "right orthodox in the heterodoxy of Unitarianism." [28] Coleridge was still a disciple of William Frend, whose credo consisted almost wholly of incredulity. The experiment will be ruined if Mrs. Fricker joins the colonists: "We shall have her teaching the infants *Christianity*—I mean, that mongrel whelp that goes under its name,—teaching them by stealth in some ague fit of superstition." [29] And what of "the little Frickers"—will they not also corrupt the pantisocratic children-to-be? "How can we insure their silence concerning God, etc.? Is it possible *they* should enter into our *motives* for this silence?" [30]

But as early as the autumn of 1794 there are signs, not that Coleridge is becoming more orthodox, but that he has begun to view his heterodoxy more warmly and affirmatively. We have already observed that his piety rose as his self-approval diminished. He was no longer as happy and confident as in June. Doubts of pantisocracy and of Southey were gathering into thunderheads. He had hardly become engaged to Sara Fricker when he knew that he loved Mary Evans—but with a desire so real that it was inevitably a source of pain and fear. Mary rejected his desperate proposal in November, and there was no honorable escape from Sara. Meanwhile he was neglecting his Cambridge studies, and George was frowning. Such troubles were especially painful to Coleridge because he so clearly understood his inability to cope with them:

> To me hath Heaven with bounteous hand assign'd
> Energic Reason and a shaping mind,
> The daring ken of Truth, the Patriot's part,
> And Pity's sigh, that breathes the gentle heart—
> Sloth-jaundic'd all! and from my graspless hand
> Drop Friendship's precious pearls, like hour-glass sand.
> I weep, yet stoop not! the faint anguish flows,
> A dreamy pang in Morning's feverous doze.[31]

Contemplation of his own weakness suggested that the evils of the age were to be cured, not by any general adoption of man-made systems, but

[27] *Poems,* p. 66.
[28] *Unpublished Letters,* I, 31. In the same letter he asks George Dyer to present his "most grateful respects" to William Frend—"God almighty bless him!"
[29] *Letters,* p. 98.　　　[30] *Ibid.,* p. 102.　　　[31] *Poems,* p. 77.

by the gradual inward enlightenment of one individual after another. By preaching the dependence of external upon inward reform he might restore the creativity of his "energic reason"; the best means of forgetting his inadequacy was to become a prophet. Hence the Bristol lectures of 1795. Here he expounds the beauties of pantisocracy (he is still vaguely trying to raise money for the expedition), attacks the Pitt ministry, and opposes the war. But he departs from Jacobinism in recommending a quiet trust in the inevitability of progress. "For this subdued sobriety of temper a practical faith in the doctrine of philosophical necessity seems the only preparative." [32] And although he is very severe against bigotry and intolerance as agents of tyranny, he departs from the unbelieving spirit of French philosophism in insisting that the doctrine of necessity must be united in the heart of every man with the religion of love taught by Jesus Christ, the supreme benevolist.

Technically speaking, the gospel preached by Coleridge in 1795—and with slight variations in 1796—was that of contemporary Unitarianism:

For I was at that time and long after, though a Trinitarian (i.e. ad normam Platonis) in philosophy, yet a zealous Unitarian in Religion; more accurately, I was a *psilanthropist,* one of those who believe our Lord to have been the real son of Joseph, and who lay the main stress on the resurrection rather than on the crucifixion.[33]

This, being interpreted, means that he believed philosophically in the Platonic triad:

> Where'er I find the Good, the True, the Fair,
> I ask no names—God's spirit dwelleth there!
> The unconfounded, undivided Three,
> Each for itself, and all in each, to see
> In man and Nature, is Philosophy.[34]

But although he recognized Christianity as the embodiment of these values, he cared nothing for "the Platonisms of John, or the Rabbinisms of Paul." [35] Spurning also any Arian compromises, he affirmed the Socinian doctrine of the simple humanity of Jesus.[36]

[32] *Works*, II, 307. [33] *Biographia Literaria*, I, 114–115.
[34] *Poems*, p. 1011. The date of this fragment is unknown. [35] *Table Talk*, p. 290.
[36] Some of those who called themselves Unitarians, notably Richard Price, held the Arian view of Jesus as a sort of demigod created in heaven before the creation of the world; but simon-pure Unitarians were of course Socinians, and they often regarded their Arian cousins as heretics and idolaters.

Coleridge would wish us to regard the last clause of his statement as particularly important. At this time the doctrine of the Atonement was deeply repugnant to him, for he interpreted God's love in terms of sentimental benevolism. To stress the resurrection rather than the crucifixion was to glorify the human but godlike powers of perfected man as manifested in the son of Joseph and to minimize the propitiatory sacrifice of the Lamb. Coleridge's admired friend and correspondent, the Unitarian minister J. P. Estlin, concedes that "The doctrine of the *Atonement* . . . is admitted in some sense by some Unitarian Christians," but he adds that presumably they all believe in *"at one-ment."* More specifically,

They consider the death of Christ as the *Effect* and not the *Cause* of the Mercy of God. . . . an important part of the Divine plan to save or redeem us, *from our sins;* and thus to reconcile—not *God to man,* a mode of expression never used in Scripture, but—*Man to God.*[37]

As a matter of fact Estlin's interpretation, though perhaps a trifle lopsided, does not radically conflict with the teachings of the historic Church. But Coleridge detested the Evangelical-Calvinistic view of the Atonement and did not realize for several years that a more enlightened view of the mystery could also be found elsewhere than in Unitarianism.

"The religion which Christ taught," as described to the unbelieving Thelwall,

is simply, first, that there is an omnipresent Father of infinite power, wisdom, and goodness, in whom we all of us move and have our being; and secondly, that when we appear to men to die we do not utterly perish, but after this life shall continue to enjoy or suffer the consequences and natural effects of the habits we have formed here, whether good or evil. This is the Christian *religion,* and all of the Christian *religion.*[38]

But this slightly Christianized version of the more affirmative sort of deism was far too simple for Coleridge's subtle mind. To him a religion was a philosophy and a philosophy was a religion. Unitarianism was especially attractive to him because it had become firmly linked—at least among the more intellectual members of the sect—with the associationism and necessitarianism of David Hartley.

[37] J. P. Estlin, *A Unitarian Christian's Statement and Defence of His Principles,* pp. 28–29. The pious pun, *"at one-ment,"* is nowadays so popular that it is interesting to find it in use as early as 1815, when Estlin's address was published. Has anyone studied the origin and history of this phrase?   [38] *Letters,* p. 199.

Hartley is hailed in *Religious Musings* as

> ...he of mortal kind
> Wisest, he first who marked the ideal tribes
> Up the fine fibers through the sentient brain;[39]

and he is also "that great master of *Christian* philosophy" after whom the poet named his firstborn son.[40] Even to such wisdom as Hartley's there were limitations, for in December, 1794, Coleridge writes to Southey: "I am a complete necessitarian, and understand the subject as well almost as Hartley himself, but I go further than Hartley, and believe the corporeality of *thought,* namely, that it is motion." [41] The statement is puzzling, since it would scarcely be possible to "go further" than Hartley's own views on this point. The philosopher states in *Observations on Man:* "External Objects impressed upon the Senses occasion, first in the Nerves on which they are impressed, and then in the Brain, Vibrations of the small, and as one may say, infinitesimal medullary Particles." [42] Although the "infinitesimal" character of these particles is strongly emphasized they are unquestionably tiny solids, and their vibratory motion weaves the entire fabric of our mental life. But even if Coleridge misinterprets the master on this point, he was certainly an enthusiastic disciple of Hartley from 1794 through 1796 and regarded him highly for three or four years thereafter.

It was Joseph Priestley, described by Coleridge as "the author of the modern Unitarianism," [43] who amalgamated the Socinian gospel with the psychology of Hartley. He proclaimed himself "an Unitarian, a Necessarian, and even a Materialist," [44] thus establishing a model for Coleridge's statement, "I am a Unitarian Christian, and believe in the automatism of man." [45] Not only as a philosopher, theologian, and scientist but as a persecuted champion of civil and religious liberty Priestley ran a close second to Hartley in Coleridge's esteem.[46] His emigration to Northumberland, Pennsylvania, was an inspiration to the pantisocrats. On the banks of the Susquehanna, according to *Sonnets on Eminent Characters,*

> Meek NATURE slowly lifts her matron veil,
> To smile with fondness on her gazing Son,[47]

the discoverer of oxygen.

[39] *Poems,* p. 123.　　[40] *Letters,* p. 169.　　[41] *Ibid.,* p. 113.
[42] *Observations on Man,* I, 11–12.　　[43] *Table Talk,* p. 290.
[44] Joseph Priestley, *Defences of Unitarianism for the Year 1787,* p. 53.
[45] *Letters,* p. 127.　　[46] *Poems,* p. 123.　　[47] *Ibid.,* p. 82.

In December, 1795, Coleridge began his oratorical tour to secure subscribers for *The Watchman*. As a married man he was in need of money, and he hoped to combine this practical aim with the more congenial one of edifying his fellow-men. Only the latter purpose appears in *Reflections on Having Left a Place of Retirement,* which presents the familiar conflict between retired contemplation and benevolistic action. The poet has been happy in the Clevedon cottage, where the view of the Bristol Channel seemed like a temple of the Omnipresent. But the call of duty is insistent. He must not be one of those selfishly indolent Men of Feeling

> Who sigh for Wretchedness, yet shun the Wretched,
> Nursing in some delicious solitude
> Their slothful loves and dainty sympathies!
> I therefore go, and join head, heart, and hand,
> Active and firm, to fight the bloodless fight
> Of Science, Freedom, and the Truth in Christ.[48]

On these lips, "active and firm" are ominous words: *The Watchman* died in May, 1796, after a life of less than three months. It had advanced the same views as *Conciones ad Populum* and the other Bristol lectures of the preceding year, but in more emotional, less rationalistic tones and with even stronger emphasis on personal philosophic-religious enlightenment as the prerequisite for reform. The "book of pantisocracy" had turned into a no less shadowy "book on Godwin" which would "compare the two systems, his and Jesus' ",[49] to the demolition of the former.

Students of poetry will turn from *The Watchman* to *Religious Musings* and other poems which express the governing ideas of this period. So far as our subject is concerned, the most important problem which they raise is that of the relationship between the Hartleyan philosophy and the more transcendental and mystical influences which prepared Coleridge's mind for the reception of German idealism. In later years he described his necessitarianism as a Babylonian captivity from which he was rescued by a succession of Neoplatonic and other "mystics" who showed him how to accord mind its rightful dominance over matter; and he became unwilling to grant that Hartley had ever furnished the slightest satisfaction to the transcendental side of his nature. Thus he created a black-and-white

[48] *Ibid.,* pp. 107–108.
[49] *Letters,* p. 210. See also pp. 161–162; *Unpublished Letters,* I, 65; Lawrence Hanson, *The Life of S. T. Coleridge. The Early Years,* p. 455.

contrast between the influence of Hartley and the influence of (for example) Plotinus and Boehme, which some scholars have too trustingly accepted. When they examine the philosophical poems of this period, therefore, they find abundant evidence that Neoplatonic and other mystics are supplanting Hartley in Coleridge's thought. This evidence by no means vanishes, but it shrinks very considerably, when one realizes that at this time[50] Hartley was valued by Coleridge as providing a scientific basis for his transcendental impulses and a mysticism which was validated by the mechanism of the universe. The system satisfied both the desire to believe and the desire to prove.

For Coleridge the Hartleyan philosophy was inseparable from Unitarianism. Beneath its dry intellectualistic crust, Unitarianism preserved that faith in human goodness, wisdom, and power which had always been its vitalizing principle. Historically, the doctrine of a merely human Jesus was not the basis of this faith, but its corollary.[51] It was inevitable that the transcendental lava should break through the thin temporary surface. The curve of Coleridge's thought, indeed, is precisely the curve more tardily followed by Unitarianism in general.[52] Many readers will draw the obvious parallel between old England and New England, where Unitarianism emerges from Puritanism, and transcendentalism from Unitarianism.[53]

Thanks to Hartley, herein faithfully interpreted by Priestley, the term "Unitarian" had come to imply not merely a heterodox view of the Trinity, but a theory of cosmic oneness. All our associations originate from, and ultimately lose themselves in, the loving, all-necessitating mind of God. On the other hand, as we rise in the scale of pleasures and pains, the higher levels permeate and govern the lower levels; and if we attain theopathy, the highest level of all, our entire mental experience from crude perception up through the moral sense is divinized. It was quite proper for a poetically gifted disciple of Hartley to speak of God both as "Na-

---

[50] That is, in 1795 and increasingly in 1796. Throughout much of 1794 the negative implications of Hartley's materialism remained influential, as they had been under Frend's leadership at Cambridge. *Religious Musings* was begun on Christmas Eve, 1794, but it did not reach anything like its final form until 1796.

[51] A. C. McGiffert, *Protestant Thought before Kant*, p. 109.

[52] But see John Stoughton, *Religion in England from 1800 to 1850*, I, 227, for the fact that even before the close of the eighteenth century such Unitarians as Mrs. Barbauld were displaying "a tone of religious feeling, different from the dry heterodoxy of Dr. Priestley."

[53] See John Hunt, *Religious Thought in England in the Nineteenth Century*, pp. 242–246, for the similar development in England, where the influence of Channing was a potent factor.

ture's essence, mind, and energy," and as "one omnipresent Mind,/Omnific" whose "most holy name is Love," and to insist that

> ... 'Tis the sublime of man,
> Our noontide Majesty, to know ourselves
> Parts and proportions of one wondrous whole!
> This fraternizes man, this constitutes
> Our charities and bearings. But 'tis God
> Diffused through all, that doth make all one whole.[54]

At various points the language in which these ideas are expressed takes on some Platonic coloration—for example, "Supreme Fair" in line 56 of the same poem. But the prominent Unitarian, Theophilus Lindsey, aspires

to lead others out of the mazes of impenetrable mystery, and polytheism, to this *Parent Mind*, "To the First good, First perfect, and First fair," alone worthy of the highest love, adoration, and gratitude.[55]

Even the Johannine view of Christ could, with some little violence, be adjusted to Unitarian doctrine. Coleridge's friend Estlin explains that "It is the opinion of some [Unitarians], that the *logos* or *word* does not mean a *person*, but a *character* or *quality*, and that this character or quality is *Reason, Wisdom*, or *Intelligence*." Christ, he continues, was not the Logos, but the Logos or Divine Intelligence was manifested in his humanity.[56] For the time being this would satisfy Coleridge perfectly.

As a test case let us take the most obviously mystical passage in *Religious Musings*, where the poet declares that Christ's manifestation of Divine Love dispelled the idolatrous fears of the soul,

> Till of its nobler nature it [the soul] 'gan feel
> Dim recollections; and thence soared to Hope,
>
> . . .
>
> From Hope and firmer Faith to perfect Love
> Attracted and absorbed; and centered there
> God only to behold, and know, and feel,

[54] *Poems*, pp. 111, 112, 113.

[55] Theophilus Lindsey, *An Historical View of the State of the Unitarian Doctrine and Worship*, p. vii. The Platonic line is quoted from the great opening passage of Epistle II of *Essay on Man*. What Pope writes in mockery of human pride, Lindsey accepts as true and edifying.

[56] J. P. Estlin, *A Unitarian Christian's Statement and Defence of His Principles*, pp. 34–35.

Till by exclusive consciousness of God
All self-annihilated it shall make
God its Identity; God all in all!
We and our Father one! [57]

Hanson supposes that the idea of the self-annihilation of the loving soul in the Divine Love must be drawn from Plotinus.[58] But as Miss Waples has pointed out, and as any reader of Coleridge's footnotes can see for himself, the passage comes straight from Hartley.[59] The more important of the two passages in *Observations on Man* which Coleridge cites must be quoted:

Since God is the Source of all Good, and consequently must at last appear to be so, *i.e.* be associated with all our Pleasures, it seems to follow, even from this Proposition, that the Idea of God, and of the Ways by which his Goodness and Happiness are made manifest, must, at last, take place of, and absorb all other Ideas, and He himself become, according to the Language of the Scriptures, *All in All*.[60]

Far from being inconsistent with his psychology, Hartley's mechanized mysticism is firmly based upon it:

If we suppose Creatures subject to the Law of Association to be placed in the midst of a Variety of Pleasures and Pains, the Sum total of the first being greater than that of the last, and to connect God with each as its sole Cause, Pain will be overpowered by Pleasure, and the infinite Number of compound Pleasures resulting from Association be at last united intirely with the Idea of God.[61]

But for Coleridge in *Religious Musings,* as for Blake, "self-annihilation" is another way of saying "boundless self-expansion." What sounds like humility is really a casting-off of earthly restrictions in order that man

... by sacred sympathy might make
The whole one Self! Self, that no alien knows!
Self, far diffus'd as Fancy's wing can travel!

[57] *Poems*, pp. 110–111. Observe Coleridge's notes and those of the editor.
[58] Lawrence Hanson, *The Life of S. T. Coleridge. The Early Years*, p. 302.
[59] Dorothy Waples, "David Hartley in *The Ancient Mariner*," *JEGP*, XXXV, 342. Miss Waples does full justice to the Hartleyan influence in the poems of this period. For more extensive comment on the implications of this passage see also my article, "Hartley, Pistorius, and Coleridge," *PMLA*, LXII, 1010–1021.
[60] David Hartley, *Observations on Man*, I, 114.   [61] *Ibid.*, II, 313.

> Self, spreading still! Oblivious of its own,
> Yet all of all possessing! This is Faith!
> This the Messiah's destined victory! [62]

Before long Coleridge would come to feel that materialistic necessity was hostile to his craving for "energic reason and a shaping mind." But he never perceived any fallacy that contributed to his mental comfort. By this time his transcendental impulses were strongly developed, but he was still quite sufficiently a man of the eighteenth century to be unwilling to make a fool of himself. In a letter of December 31, 1796, he concludes a sketch of various interpretations of the term "life" with the words: "Plato says it is *harmony*. He might as well have said a fiddlestick's end; but I love Plato, his dear, *gorgeous* nonsense." [63] In the necessitarian system, however, *amor intellectualis* and the Beatific Vision—or close equivalents of those luxuries—were rooted in the inevitable mechanisms of nature. As a disciple of Hartley, who taught that "The intellectual Pleasures and Pains are as real as the sensible ones," [64] Coleridge could be mystical and scientific at the same time. As early as January, 1795, he writes to George Dyer:

> The pleasures, which we receive from rural beauties, are of little Consequence, compared to the Moral Effect of these pleasures—beholding constantly the Best possible we at last become ourselves the best possible. In the country, all around us smile Good and Beauty—and the images of this divine Καλοκαγαδόν are miniatured in the mind of the beholder, as a Landscape in a Convex Mirror. [65]

Here Coleridge redeems the "gorgeous nonsense" of the Platonic tradition by translating it into the technical language of Hartley's theory of vibrations and vibratiuncles.

A famous passage in *The Eolian Harp* raises the question:

> And what if all of animated nature
> Be but organic Harps divinely fram'd,
> That tremble into thought, as o'er them sweeps
> Plastic and vast, one intellectual breeze,
> At once the soul of each, and God of all? [66]

[62] *Poems*, p. 115.   [63] *Letters*, p. 211.   [64] *Observations on Man*, I, 83.
[65] *Unpublished Letters*, I, 33.
[66] *Poems*, p. 102. But observe that Coleridge immediately retracts this notion in order to avert the "mild reproof" of his more orthodox spouse. His troubles with Sara did not begin in the Lake Country.

"Plastic" smacks of Neoplatonism or Cambridge Platonism.[67] Professor Stallknecht, who likes to read a maximum amount of technical mysticism into his romantic poets, quotes from Boehme's *Signature of All Things* a passage which, he says, "makes it hard to doubt that both the idea and the basic metaphor of Coleridge's poem are derived from Boehme." [68] The parallel is close. Professor Gingerich, on the other hand, is certainly right in contending that in this poem Coleridge "conceives universal life as automatous." [69] "Was it then Boehme," Stallknecht asks, "who transcendentalized Hartley in Coleridge's mind? I believe that it was." [70] If my contention is valid, however, it would be much safer to speak of "Boehme as necessitated by Hartley" in interpreting any poem of this period.

Both Hartley and Priestley eagerly denied that the doctrine of necessity deprived man of all freedom of action or absolved him from moral responsibility.[71] Limitations of space forbid an analysis of their arguments, which seem to me utterly spurious. All we need to know is that they were temporarily satisfying to Coleridge. His reforming efforts would especially be justified by Priestley's idea—it is also Godwin's—that the motives which govern men's behavior can be improved indefinitely by persuasion and education. An advocate of this system could easily forget that the teacher was no less an automaton than the pupil.

Necessitarianism gave ostensibly scientific approval to everything that an eighteenth-century sentimentalist could desire. It made perfectibility a law of nature. "I would ardently," writes Coleridge to Southey, "that you were a necessitarian, and (believing in an all-loving Omnipotence) an optimist." [72] Tolerance and universal benevolence are corollaries of the system.[73] The moral sense stands only just below theopathy in the hierarchy of pleasures. Although Hartley, as a disciple of Locke, cannot describe the moral sense as innate, he treats Shaftesbury's position with surprising politeness, granting that

some Associations are formed so early, repeated so often, riveted so strong, and have so close a Connexion with the common Nature of Man, . . . as, in a

---

[67] See *Ibid.*, p. 84, for a similar use of the word in the sonnet to Bowles.

[68] N. P. Stallknecht, *Strange Seas of Thought*, pp. 106–107.

[69] S. F. Gingerich, *Essays in the Romantic Poets*, p. 25. On pp. 25–26 he makes the same point concerning *The Destiny of Nations*.   [70] *Op. cit.*, p. 43.

[71] Hartley, *Observations on Man*, I, vii–viii, 500–501; II, 53–56. Priestley, *A Free Discussion of the Doctrines of Materialism, and Philosophical Necessity*, pp. 177–178.

[72] *Letters*, p. 126.

[73] *Ibid.*, p. 160; *Unpublished Letters*, I, 51; Hartley, *Observations on Man*, I, 510; Priestley, *A Free Discussion of the Doctrines of Materialism, and Philosophical Necessity*, p. xxiii.

certain way of speaking, to claim the Appelation of original and natural Dispositions and to appear like Instincts.[74]

To the empiricism which constantly vitiates his rationalism the issue is unimportant, since "the Moral Sense is Part of the Light of Nature, and of our natural Faculties, whether it be considered as an Instinct, or as the general Result of external Impressions and our natural Frame taken together."[75] Hence in *Conciones ad Populum* Coleridge is not disloyal to Hartley when he appeals to "that moral taste which derives our most exquisite pleasures from the contemplation of possible perfection, and proportional pain from the perception of existing depravity."[76] Here Shaftesbury and Hartley lie down together, though the latter would grumble a little at "taste."

According to the *Observations,* when a man achieves the virtues which flow from the moral sense, "a pleasing Consciousness and Self-approbation rise up in his Mind, exclusively of any direct explicit Consideration of Advantage likely to accrue to himself, from his Possession of these good qualities."[77] The eighteenth-century cult of disinterested goodness was not genuinely anti-utilitarian: it had the highly practical aim of enjoying the bliss of self-esteem. The Man of Feeling, like Johnson's Dick Minim, "feasts upon his own beneficence." To imitate Christ, one infers from *Religious Musings* and *The Destiny of Nations,* is to be admitted to this banquet. But if we possess the moral sense in full perfection we also possess the even loftier joys of theopathy: the summit of the system is the sense of being godlike. Hence Coleridge is still a good Hartleyan when he concludes the second of the *Conciones* with one of Akenside's most transcendental passages on the kinship between man and God:

> ... We feel within ourselves
> His energy divine: he tells the heart
> He meant, he made us to behold and love
> What he beholds and loves, the general orb
> Of life and being—to be great like him,
> Beneficent and active.[78]

It is easy to say that this philosophy is riddled with inconsistencies; that it is based upon an immature psychology; that while it agrees with the

[74] *Observations on Man,* I, 498–499.   [75] *Ibid.,* II, 45.   [76] *Works,* II, 302.
[77] *Observations on Man,* I, 493.   [78] *Works,* II, 303.

natural religion of Hartley and Priestley it has no logical connection with the *revealed* religion in which they profess to believe. But the fallacies of the system did not trouble Coleridge until what had appeared to be its main advantage—the authentication of sentimentalism and transcendentalism by means of a "scientific" psychology—became its main disadvantage. Once the increasing unhappiness of his actual life made him wish to escape from the senses entirely, the Hartleyan philosophy was no longer a source of self-confidence but a source of fear. As soon as he felt that it was repugnant he began to see that it was intellectually spurious. If this process had been completed within the period now under discussion Coleridge would not have named his son "David Hartley" as late as September, 1796. Nevertheless there are signs that a change is imminent.

The collapse of *The Watchman* was a severe blow both to Coleridge's finances and to his prophetic ambitions. Sara's difficult pregnancy was made no easier for her husband by her "unintermitting dyspathy." It must already have been clear to him that his marriage was a failure. The news of his son's birth gave him no joy, but only confused feelings of bewilderment and dread.[79] By this time opium had become a favorite means of avoiding both mental and physical pain, though he was not yet a full-fledged addict.[80] Since he cannot approve of himself as a politico-religious journalist, he now seeks to approve of himself as a saintly recluse. He announces his withdrawal from propaganda in *Ode to the Departing Year*:

> Now I recentre my immortal mind
>   In the deep Sabbath of meek self-content;
> Cleans'd from the vaporous passions that bedim
> God's Image, sister of the Seraphim.[81]

This retirement is accompanied by an increase of "practical" piety. The following letter of November, 1796, reveals the psychological motive of the change:

I am seriously ill. The complaint, my medical attendant says, is nervous—and originating in *mental* causes. I have a Blister under my right ear and I take Laudanum every four hours, 25 drops each dose. God be praised for all things! A faith in goodness *makes* all nature good.[82]

[79] *Poems*, pp. 152–153.
[80] All due weight should be given to the neuritis, neuralgia, septic teeth, and so on, and to the close connection between Coleridge's mental and physical states. The utmost charity, however, will not justify the notion that he began to take opium to quiet unbearable physical pain. See *Letters*, pp. 173, 175; *Unpublished Letters*, I, 46; II, 112–113.
[81] *Poems*, p. 169.   [82] *Unpublished Letters*, I, 59.

In a sonnet of 1794 the simon-pure necessitarian had expressed disapproval of petitionary prayer,[83] but on March 20, 1796, he addresses a Unitarian minister in language which is probably more whimsical than his real feeling:

I know you do not altogether approve of direct petitions to Deity—but in case there *should* be any efficacy in them, out of pity to the Guts of others pray for the Brains of your friend.[84]

On Hartley's birth in September the father attempted to pray, but with such "confuséd thought/And shapeless feelings" that "no heavenly visitation" was vouchsafed; he is determined, however, to try again.[85] By November he is able to report to Thelwall, "I am daily more and more a religionist." [86]

Although England as a whole has proved unworthy of his message, he delights more than ever in the rôle of personal spiritual adviser to such less enlightened friends as Thelwall and Lloyd.[87] When Charles Lamb, crushed by his hideous tragedy, begs for "as religious a letter as possible," Coleridge is in his element:

I approve altogether of your abandoning what you call vanities. I look upon you as a man called by sorrow and anguish . . . into quietness, and a soul set apart and made peculiar to God! We cannot arrive at any portion of heavenly bliss without in some measure imitating Christ. . . . You are a temporary sharer in human miseries that you may be an eternal partaker of the Divine nature. I charge you, if by any means it be possible, come to me.[88]

This to a man who had more grace in his little finger than Coleridge was ever to possess!

Although still a Unitarian, Coleridge now turns toward a more personal, inward, Evangelical type of piety. Hartley and Priestley gave small encouragement to this kind of religious experience.[89] On revealed religion they were wholly inadequate, and natural religion was not enough for a

---

[83] *Poems*, p. 79.   [84] *Unpublished Letters*, I, 48.   [85] *Poems*, pp. 152–153.
[86] *Unpublished Letters*, I, 60.   [87] *Poems*, pp. 157–158; *Letters*, p. 170.
[88] *Letters*, pp. 171–172.
[89] Hartley makes an unconvincing attempt to show that prayer is consistent with his philosophy (*Observations on Man*, I, 508; II, 331–332). More frankly, Priestley regards the practices of "popular" religion as "a system calculated for the *bulk of mankind*," which, in the perfectibilizing process, will gradually be superseded by the "higher" sentiments of pure necessitarianism (*A Free Discussion*, p. 298).

man on his knees. Coleridge now withdraws from pantheism so precipitately that he seems to equate it with atheism. As early as March, 1796, he inquires:

How is it that Dr. Priestley is not an atheist? He asserts in three different places that God not only *does*, but *is* everything—But if God be everything, everything is God: which is all that the Atheists assert.[90]

Three months later he writes to Thelwall: "We have a hundred lovely scenes about Bristol, which would make you exclaim, O admirable *Nature!* and me, O Gracious *God!*" [91] The distinction has become important.

That *any* philosophy insinuates a corrupting pride into "the deep Sabbath of meek self-content" is suggested by a letter of December:

I have been myself sorely afflicted, and have rolled my dreary eye from earth to Heaven, and found no comfort, till it pleased the Unimaginable High and Lofty One to make my Heart more tender in regard of religious feelings: My philosophical refinements, and metaphysical theories lay by me in the hour of anguish, as toys by the bedside of a child deadly sick. May God continue his visitations to my soul, bowing it down, till the pride and Laodicean self-confidence of human reason be utterly done away; and I cry with deeper and yet deeper feelings, O my Soul! thou art wretched and miserable, and poor, and blind, and naked! [92]

One is reminded of the penitent letters to George at the close of the cavalry episode. Throughout Coleridge's career such language is always the symptom of a crisis.

As an edifying attitude this piety was all very well, but the closer he came to actual belief in it the more uncomfortable it made him. Just as he sinks to his knees and faces the truth about himself, the romantic Hamlet cries "About, my brain!" and begins to philosophize. What he increasingly needs, however, is a philosophy which will release him from the bondage of sense and subordinate matter to mind—something more in line with Plato's "dear, gorgeous nonsense." In December he declares himself "a Berkeleyan" in a context which suggests that he now values Berkeley as a Platonist rather than as an empirical psychologist.[93] A month

---

[90] *Unpublished Letters*, I, 49.   [91] *Letters*, p. 167.
[92] *Unpublished Letters*, I, 64.
[93] *Letters*, p. 195. But this change is foretokened by lines in *Religious Musings* which declare that "Life is a vision shadowy of Truth." Coleridge refers to Berkeley in a note on the passage. (*Poems*, p. 124 and note 2.)

earlier, he had asked Thelwall to procure for him Ficino's anthology of excerpts from Iamblichus, Proclus, Plotinus, and other Neoplatonic writers.[94]

But the importance of these facts should not be overemphasized: such reading had fascinated Coleridge ever since Christ's Hospital days. The most that can be said is that he is now in a fair way to take these and similar mystics more seriously. When he settles at Nether Stowey at the close of 1796 he is still loyal to such aspects of Hartley's thought as serve to validate his transcendental impulses. One can discern, however, that the necessitarian faith is wavering slightly under the pressure of unpleasant circumstances, and that he has begun the attempt to escape from reality by means of three anodynes—opium, prayer, and Neoplatonism.

3

During 1797 and most of 1798 Coleridge's psychological curve, which had descended alarmingly toward the end of 1796, took a sharp upward turn. Removal to Nether Stowey gave him the sense of making a fresh start. Before this wholesome impetus had slackened, William and Dorothy Wordsworth did more for him than Hartley or Proclus or Kant or Bishop Leighton were ever able to do: they made him almost a happy man and almost a great poet.

Dorothy—so blessedly different from Sara—gave him womanly companionship, tenderness, adoration of his genius. From William he received not only the admiring friendship of a fellow-poet but the example of a happy, stable character from which his weakness could imbibe strength. The secret of Wordsworth's happiness lay in his ability to live in "the light of *things*," reverently enjoying a world of beautiful concrete objects to which at the same time he masterfully imparted spiritual values by means of his imaginative power.[95] This spectacle of "a sensitive being, a creative soul" enabled Coleridge to lay hold upon reality and thus inspired him to write genuine poetry.

Hitherto his poems had been mawkish flights of an evasive fancy, or callow bits of propaganda, or more substantial attempts to versify philo-

[94] *Ibid.*, p. 182; but the bibliographical point is explained by J. D. Rea, "Coleridge's Intimations of Immortality from Proclus," *Modern Philology*, XXVI, 206.

[95] To say this is to credit Coleridge with the ability to see, in the spring of 1797, what Wordsworth was soon to become in addition to what he already was, but such perceptiveness is characteristic of Coleridge.

sophical abstractions. Only the last group has been of much interest to us. *The Eolian Harp, Religious Musings, The Destiny of Nations,* and *Ode to the Departing Year* display a turgidly rhetorical elevation but almost no ability to respond to philosophical ideas poetically—that is, as if they were beautiful and exciting objects of sense-perception. The example of Wordsworth, whom he regards as a great philosophical poet, now impels him toward a genuinely poetic interweaving—some critics would say an identification—of seeing, feeling, and thinking.

On the other hand, while Coleridge regarded true poetry as the play of imagination upon actuality, he soon came to recognize that metaphysical speculation was one of his avenues of escape from fear. What he says in *Biographia Literaria* is typical:

But if in after time I have sought a refuge from bodily pain and mis-managed sensibility in abstruse research, which exercised the strength and subtlety of the understanding without awakening the feelings of the heart; still there was a long and blessed interval, during which my natural faculties were allowed to expand, and my original tendencies to develope themselves; my fancy, and the love of nature, and the sense of beauty in forms and sounds.[96]

He was a poet when he was happy and self-confident enough to confront the real world, and a metaphysician when he was afraid. Hence although his best poetry is remarkable for its power to realize the strange in images both vivid and hauntingly suggestive and in delicately subtle rhythms, it is of small importance as *philosophical* poetry. There are ideas to which we may, if we insist, attach labels reading "Hartley," "Plotinus," and so on, but they are usually commonplaces of eighteenth-century sentimental naturalism.

Although Coleridge is less deeply saturated in preromantic poetry than Wordsworth, he has learned much from it. At the beginning of this period his admiration for Bowles has not yet been recanted. Thomson is "the honor, yea, the redeemer of Scotland," [97] and his *Castle of Indolence* is a "most lovely poem." [98] Coleridge takes quite seriously the story that Pope advised Young to study St. Thomas in preparation for his chief work:

[96] *Biographia Literaria,* I, 10.
[97] *Coleridge's Miscellaneous Criticism* (ed. T. M. Raysor), p. 301.
[98] *Unpublished Letters,* I, 33.

It is plain . . . from Young's writings that he really formed his mind on the scholastic writers. An edition of the *Night Thoughts* with a running commentary from Aquinas and his followers, would perhaps surprise such of our critics as can construe Latin.[99]

In any discussion of our poet's theory of creative imagination his enthusiasm for Collins should be noted:

Collins's "Ode on the Poetical Character"—that part of it, I should say, beginning with "The band, as faery legends say, Was wove on that creating day," —has inspired and whirled *me* along with greater agitations of enthusiasm than any the most *impassioned* scene in Schiller or Shakespeare." [100]

Like Wordsworth, he valued Akenside highly as a philosophical poet,[101] and we know that he quoted *Pleasures of Imagination* in concluding one of the Bristol addresses. One of the dream-projects listed in the Gutch Memorandum Book was an edition of Akenside. An elegy of 1794 is "Imitated from One of Akenside's Blank-Verse Inscriptions." [102] As we examine the chief works of the Stowey period let us give due weight to the influence of this eighteenth-century background, remembering that poets like to get their ideas from poetry.

In *This Lime-Tree Bower My Prison,* "gentle-hearted Charles" will enjoy the wide prospect of the ocean beneath the setting sun, gazing

> . . . till all doth seem
> Less gross than bodily; and of such hues
> As veil the Almighty Spirit, when yet he makes
> Spirits perceive his presence.[103]

But the poet, confined to Poole's garden by his scalded ankle, must use his senses as William and Dorothy use theirs. Not the grandiose misty view, almost a transcendental idea in itself, but the shadow of one leaf upon another convinces him

> That Nature ne'er deserts the wise and pure;
> No plot so narrow, be but Nature there,
> No waste so vacant, but may well employ

---

[99] *Miscellaneous Criticism*, p. 301.   [100] *Letters*, p. 196.   [101] *Ibid.*, p. 163.
[102] *Poems*, pp. 69–70. See also *Letters*, p. 218, where Akenside's odes provide a criterion of praise. C. T. Houpt, *Mark Akenside*, pp. 146n–147n, gives further evidence of Coleridge's interest in this poet.   [103] *Ibid.*, p. 180.

Each faculty of sense, and keep the heart
Awake to Love and Beauty.[104]

In both passages, Nature is the revelation of the Almighty Spirit whose essence is Love and Beauty; but the former, Coleridge tells Southey, is Berkeleyan,[105] while the latter is Wordsworthian in its religious devotion to *things*.

Frost at Midnight deals with one of Wordsworth's favorite themes, the spiritually educative influence of nature upon the child.[106] Religiously interpreted associationism is implicit in the poem, but no technicalities are introduced. Little Hartley's spirit will be molded by

The lovely shapes and sounds intelligible
Of that eternal language which thy God
Utters, who from eternity doth teach
Himself in all, and all things in himself.[107]

The "Great universal Teacher" who uses natural objects for pedagogical materials would seem to be a personal and transcendent deity; but what this God will teach the child is clearly a mixture of pantheism and panentheism. A much more sophisticated thinker than Wordsworth, Coleridge technically disapproves of pantheism because it implies the existence of evil within the godhead. As we have seen, he is worried by this flaw in Priestley's theology toward the close of 1796. On the other hand he is strongly moved by the usual romantic desire to behold a numinous One, and in later years he will make elaborate efforts to reconcile this experience with orthodox Christianity. In poems written while he is attempting to share Wordsworth's religion of nature the pantheistic element is strongly marked, but such phrases as "adoration of the God in nature" [108] would provide no clear evidence in a heresy trial. On this subject his mind is pure quicksilver.

In *France: An Ode* Coleridge adjusts the politico-religious ideas of the preceding period to the Wordsworthian gospel.[109] Revulsion against the Revolution, insistence that liberty is not to be found in "forms of human power," the importance of finding a *via media* between priestcraft and atheism—all this he had been preaching since 1795. But now we are told

---

[104] *Ibid.*, p. 181.   [105] *Ibid.*, p. 180n.
[106] *The Nightingale* is another treatment of the same theme.
[107] *Poems*, p. 242.   [108] *Ibid.*, p. 262.
[109] The same interpretation could be applied to *Fears in Solitude*.

that the young Coleridge was prepared to greet the dawning Revolution with enthusiasm by associations derived from the liberty of waves and clouds and forests. As *The Prelude* shows, this is Wordsworth's experience; it is not Coleridge's. No such notion appears in *Destruction of the Bastile* or in *To a Young Lady, with a Poem on the French Revolution.* Coleridge explicitly states in *Frost at Midnight* that as a schoolboy he was *deprived* of those benign influences of nature which are to educate his child.[110]

The ode ends, as it begins, with external nature, where alone true liberty can be found. But the last four lines grant more autonomy to the shaping spirit of imagination than Wordsworth would have been likely to grant at the beginning of 1798:

> Yes, while I stood and gazed, my temples bare,
> And shot my being through earth, sea, and air,
> Possessing all things with intensest love,
> O Liberty! my spirit felt thee there.[111]

The reader must make his own guess as to the source of this passage, not forgetting that Hartley is as strong a candidate as Spinoza or Boehme.[112] As a matter of fact nothing in the thought of these lines would startle Thomson, Young, Byrom, or Akenside.[113]

These poems are extremely Wordsworthian in that, although rich in images derived from immediate perceptions of external nature, they are primarily concerned with the writer's inward response to those perceptions. But in the three poems for which Coleridge is chiefly remembered he departs widely from Wordsworth without forgetting the lessons which his friend has taught him. *Kubla Khan, Christabel,* and *The Rime of the Ancient Mariner* are stylistically impersonal to a degree which Wordsworth seldom attained, but they avoid the pain of confronting here-and-now actuality by imposing upon the old and strange and far away the vividness of the real and present world. "Most interesting is it," said the poet in later years, "to consider the effect when the feelings are wrought above the natural pitch by the belief of something mysterious, while all

---

[110] *Poems*, p. 242.　　　[111] *Ibid.*, p. 247.

[112] Theopathy, once attained, impregnates and governs all the lower levels of the associative scale. Hence he who has experienced a God of love "possesses all things" in the light of that experience.

[113] Such statements depend upon evidence provided in the two preceding volumes of *Religious Trends.*

the images are purely natural. Then it is that religion and poetry strike deepest." [114] This naturalizing of the preternatural briefly enabled him to rise above his fear-haunted personality. The three poems are not philosophical, but in a sense they *are* his philosophy: they embody in art that experience of interfusion—Novalis' "Die Welt wird Traum, der Traum wird Welt"—which he vainly tried to *prove* through metaphysics and theology. It is significant that these works draw their deepest inspiration not from systematic treatises[115] but from old legends and superstitions, travelers' tales, medieval romances and ballads, approached partly directly and partly through eighteenth-century medievalists like Chatterton and the German purveyors of Gothic gooseflesh.

Coleridge's triumph was evanescent and fragmentary. Only one of the three poems was completed, and one of the other two owes part of its prestige to a lie. *Kubla Khan* is not an unfinished transcript of a poem of at least two hundred lines composed in an opium dream: it was written like any other poem while the author was awake, but "in a sort of reverie brought on by two grains of opium." [116] The influence of opium upon the poems of this group has been exaggerated and misunderstood. Coleridge did not write poems like *Kubla Khan* because he was a drug-addict: he was a drug-addict because he was the sort of person who writes poems like *Kubla Khan*. Professor Schneider adduces abundant evidence for her assertion that opiates do not give stable persons mental pleasure except as a consequence of relief from pain or worry. "On the other hand, in most unstable persons the drug does produce pleasure during the early stages of addiction; and the intensity of the pleasure . . . is in direct proportion to the degree of instability." The mental pleasure described by such neurotics is usually a sense of relaxation, freedom from troubles, euphoria.[117] Such is the pleasure described by Coleridge to his brother George in April, 1798, *à propos* an illness caused by infected teeth: "Laudanum gave me repose, not sleep; but you, I believe, know how divine that repose is, what a spot of enchantment, a green spot of fountain and flowers and trees in the very heart of a waste of sands!" [118] At this early carefree stage of addiction he muffled his dread long enough to become

---

[114] *Poems*, p. 306n.
[115] Except as quarries from which to dig flavorsome bits of strangeness.
[116] A. D. Snyder, "The MS of *Kubla Khan*," *London Times Literary Supplement*, August 2, 1934, p. 541.
[117] Elisabeth Schneider, "The 'Dream' of *Kubla Khan*," *PMLA*, LX, 789.
[118] *Letters*, p. 240.

a poet. The joy of Wordsworth and the peace of laudanum worked in the same direction.

Of course *Kubla Khan* conveys not the ghost of an idea, religious or otherwise. The same may be said of *Christabel,* which I prefer to read simply as the marvellous tale which it purports to be.[119] Professor Gingerich, although on the whole he agrees with this judgment, finds that the concluding lines of Part I repeat what he takes to be the essential message of *The Ancient Mariner*:

> But this she knows, in joys and woes,
> That saints will aid if men will call:
> For the blue sky bends over all! [120]

It is at least interesting to see how the romantic medievalist translates the language of Catholic piety into the language of the religion of nature.

The numerous divergent interpretations of *The Ancient Mariner*[121] at least agree in suggesting a curious paradox: in his one completed masterpiece Coleridge escapes from self-consciousness into "pure" poetry less fully than in the two magical fragments.[122] In my opinion the poem was conceived and written on two levels which are satisfyingly though perhaps not quite perfectly harmonized. It is a yarn of macabre adventure based upon superstitions no more deliberately edifying than those of *Christabel;* it is *also* an allegorical tract on universal benevolism and the religion of nature. Coleridge lived to regret the obtrusiveness of the latter element, but in 1797 the moral was the poem and the poem was the moral.

The allegory is clear enough to anyone who has saturated himself in the poetry of eighteenth-century sentimentalism. For Coleridge as for

---

[119] Only Part I (1797) pertains to this section of the chapter, but my remarks are also applicable to Part II up to the point where Coleridge abandoned it in 1800.

[120] *Poems*, p. 226; S. F. Gingerich, *Essays in the Romantic Poets*, pp. 38–39.

[121] The following list is adequately representative but not exhaustive: E. K. Chambers, *Samuel Taylor Coleridge*, p. 99; H. I. Fausset, *Samuel Taylor Coleridge*, pp. 165–166; J. L. Lowes, *The Road to Xanadu*, pp. 299–300; Elizabeth Nitchie, "The Moral of the *Ancient Mariner* Reconsidered," *PMLA*, XLVIII, 867–876; N. P. Stallknecht, "The Moral of the *Ancient Mariner*," *PMLA*, XLVII, 559–569, an article which reappears with a few changes in his *Strange Seas of Thought;* Dorothy Waples, "David Hartley in *The Ancient Mariner*," *JEGP*, XXXV, 337–351; R. P. Warren, "A Poem of Pure Imagination," pp. 59–148 of the edn. of *Ancient Mariner* published by Reynal and Hitchcock, New York, 1946. The text and notes of Professor Warren's valuable essay glance at still other interpretations.

[122] Since most significant poetry is extremely "impure" this by no means implies that *The Ancient Mariner* is inferior to *Kubla Khan* and *Christabel.* But considering his personal psychological predicament the other poems would have given him more of what he needed if he had been able to finish them.

Wordsworth, the idea that the universe was a system of universal benevolence was axiomatic. It was common to the traditions descending from
Newton, from Shaftesbury, and from Hartley. The poets did not need to
find "sources" for it: it was in the air they breathed. Symbolically, the
killing of the albatross is a sin against the great sentimental principle that
the universe is one loving Whole. At the climax of the poem the mariner's
blessing of the watersnakes reaffirms the benevolistic Unity and makes
possible his salvation in the religion of nature. Finally, the mariner sums
it up for the wedding-guest in plainest English.

As Professor Warren has suggested, this obvious foreground interpretation does not exclude the possibility that the mariner's sin is a denial
of the beneficent power of imagination, while his redemption results from
his reassertion of that power.[123] The imagination which is love, the love
which is imagination, restores the vision of wholeness which the killing
of the albatross has blasphemed. We cannot be sure how consciously
Coleridge had thought out this important secondary theme at a time when
his doctrine of imagination had not yet fully taken form and when he
had not yet abjured his allegiance to Hartley. Nevertheless the thought
is implicit in the poem, and Coleridge would applaud the ingenuity which
has unearthed it.

A loose popularized Neoplatonism enters into the background of the
cult of universal benevolence, but the scholar who insists upon finding
specific philosophical sources for *The Ancient Mariner* should be chary
of invoking the shades of Proclus, Spinoza, Berkeley, or Boehme. That
the concept of loving unity is more probably derived from Hartley and
Priestley is suggested by the necessitarian atmosphere of the poem.[124]
Although for the sake of the story the sailor must be granted sufficient
free will for the commission of a sin, he is mainly a passive character. The
redemptive blessing of the watersnakes is induced by the fact that the
"slimy things," now beheld in the moonlight, acquire a beauty which
becomes associated in the mariner's mind with love. "I blessed them *un-
aware.*" One can observe this fact without supposing like Miss Waples
that the entire poem was intended to be an allegorical version of *Observations on Man,* and without wholly rejecting Warren's emphasis on the
saving power of creative imagination. The poem represents a transitional

---

[123] R. P. Warren, "A Poem of Pure Imagination," pp. 86–100.
[124] This has been emphasized by S. F. Gingerich, *Essays in the Romantic Poets,* pp. 29–36.
Gingerich's views are controverted, not quite convincingly, by Warren, *op. cit.,* pp. 79–80.

stage in Coleridge's thought, and inconsistencies are to be expected. We have neglected the thesis that the poem is a concealed autobiography. But although Mr. Fausset may be overingenious on this point, one can see a great deal of Coleridge in the mariner, so loving and so much in need of love, and yet "alone on a wide, wide sea," haunted by a sense of guilt which he must relieve by teaching others through his "strange power of speech."[125]

At this time the benevolistic unity-necessity religion expresses Coleridge's conception of Christianity. The mariner's more specifically Catholic piety is merely dramatic—part of the ballad rather than of the allegory. As a romantic medievalist Coleridge somewhat wistfully enjoys the atmosphere of "Mary Queen" and "my kind saint," but he no more believes in them than Chatterton shared the faith of Rowley. The good hermit who will "shrieve my soul" stands on a slightly different footing: hermits usually fare better than monks in eighteenth-century poetry because they can be associated with rural retirement and *Il Penseroso* contemplation. Has any excessively subtle commentator suggested that the hermit is William Wordsworth, who "singeth loud his godly hymns/That he makes in the wood"?[126]

But where, all this while, is the Coleridge whose mind, according to the biographers, was moving steadily away from Hartley toward Kant? The consensus of opinion is that between the autumn of 1796 and the autumn of 1798 Hartley gives place to Berkeley, and Berkeley to Spinoza, whose mixture of mechanistic and Platonic elements forms a bridge over which Coleridge soon passes to Plato, Plotinus, Proclus, Ficino, Bruno, Boehme, Fox, and Law. This view implies a more rapid and neatly arranged progression toward an intuitively apprehended goal than can possibly be inferred from Coleridge's poems and letters. It is based upon the well-known account in *Biographia Literaria*,[127] written in 1815 under a strong urge to prove that he was no mere imitator of the Germans and to place his rejection of the unbelieving and Jacobinical eighteenth century as early in his career as possible.

During the period in question, Coleridge was too nearly at peace with the physical universe to indulge very deeply in metaphysics. It would be absurd to suppose, however, that his passion for abstract speculation was

[125] H. I. Fausset, *Samuel Taylor Coleridge*, pp. 165–167.
[126] *Poems*, p. 206. See also the next stanza.
[127] *Biographia Literaria*, I, 93–98: 132–137.

wholly in abeyance. His own desire for "energic reason and a shaping mind" caused him to interpret Wordsworth's solemn joy in terms of creative imagination. But Hartley had placed the imagination very low in his hierarchy of pleasures and had declared that "Most kinds of Music, Painting, and Poetry, have close connexions with Vice, particularly with the Vices of Intemperance and Lewdness." [128] Furthermore the doctrine of necessity, however qualified by feeble distinctions between "practical" and "philosophical" free will, did not suffice to explain the lofty autonomous power which Coleridge saw in Wordsworth and wanted for himself. As Coleridge knew very well, an essentially transcendental view of creative imagination had been expressed by Watts, Dennis, Aaron Hill, Young, Akenside, Byrom, and Collins.[129] More than most of his contemporaries, however, Coleridge was equipped to interpret the eighteenth-century cult of genius in the light of Neoplatonic and other more or less mystical ideas which had fertilized its roots. Hence without completely abandoning Hartley he turned more and more toward thinkers who had long fascinated him but had left him unconvinced. When he thought of creative genius he thought of Spinoza's *amor intellectualis,*[130] of Plotinus' association of the divine *Nous* with the mind of man, and of Boehme's identification of imagination with a godlike creative will. Such ideas are very imperfectly integrated with the poetry of this period because Coleridge's trend as a metaphysician was toward the abstract, while the influence of Wordsworth pulled him toward the concrete. In any case he probably did not think much about these matters until rather late in 1798, when flagging creativity gives place to a more analytical temper.

According to *Biographia Literaria,* his growing Platonism caused him to take a more friendly attitude toward Pauline and Johannine Christology, but only as a topic in metaphysics:

These principles I held, *philosophically,* while in respect to revealed religion I remained a zealous Unitarian. I considered the *idea* of the Trinity a fair scholastic inference from the being of God, as a creative intelligence; and that it was therefore entitled to the rank of an *esoteric* doctrine of natural religion. But seeing in the same no practical or moral bearing, I confined it to the schools of philosophy.

[128] *Observations on Man,* II, 253.
[129] Again I regret the necessity of referring the reader to my earlier volumes.
[130] See N. P. Stallknecht, *Strange Seas of Thought,* p. 176, for the fact that Coleridge romanticized Spinoza into something like a Renaissance Neoplatonist, largely ignoring his mechanism and determinism.

He believed in the Logos, but not in its hypostasis through the Incarnation; and, as in the preceding period, he could not stomach the Atonement. "Nevertheless," he adds, "I cannot doubt, that the difference of my metaphysical notions from those of Unitarians in general contributed to my final reconversion to the whole truth in Christ." [131] Probably these reminiscences are heavily colored by the moods and motives of 1815. We may infer, however, that he was trying to combine Unitarianism with Platonism rather than with associationism and necessitarianism. But no complete transformation has occurred: as 1798 opens he regards Hartley and Priestley as great religious teachers,[132] and he will not repudiate them decisively until 1801.

Just as he is too happy to be very metaphysical, so he is too happy to be very pious. The Evangelical-sounding emphasis on prayer and penitence which characterizes the autumn of 1796 almost disappears from the letters of 1797. Yet when he thought of the family budget he sighed, "I suppose that at last I must become a Unitarian minister to keep from starving." [133] On the other hand he disapproved of preaching for money "because it gives the teacher an improper bias in favor of particular opinions" [134]—also, according to Thelwall, because of "his repugnance to all regular routine and application." [135] He feels that as a minister he could not conscientiously offer the Lord's Supper to his congregation. Although this is not for him a matter of fundamental importance, "I cannot, I must not play the hypocrite." [136] Such scruples were easily quieted, and on January 5, 1798, he returns the Wedgwoods' original gift with a definite statement of his intention to accept the call of the Shrewsbury congregation. After all, "The *necessary* creed in our sect is but short—it will be necessary for me, in order to my continuance as a Unitarian Minister, to believe that Jesus Christ was the Messiah—in all other points I may play off my intellect *ad libitum*." [137] He would be quite free to preach his view of Christianity as a religion in which "the Feelings are worked upon by Hopes and Fears purely individual, and the Imagination is kept barren in definite Forms and only in cooperation with the Understanding labours after an obscure and indefinite Vastness." [138]

As late as 1803, Coleridge will thank his old Bristol friend Matthew

---

[131] *Biographia Literaria*, I, 136–137.　　　[132] *Unpublished Letters*, I, 94.
[133] *Letters*, p. 228.　　　[134] *Poems*, p. 117n.
[135] Quoted by Lawrence Hanson, *The Life of S. T. Coleridge. The Early Years*, pp. 241–242.
[136] *Unpublished Letters*, I, 79.　　　[137] *Ibid.*, p. 88.　　　[138] *Ibid.*, p. 117.

Coates for having been the first to express to him "that article of faith . . . which is nearest to my heart—the pure fountain of all my moral and religious feelings and comforts,—I mean the absolute Impersonality of the Deity."[139] Coleridge's theology, like his metaphysics, fought against his poetry, for this belief in a quasi-Platonic God of "obscure and indefinite Vastness" imparted an unaesthetic abstractness to his view of the physical world. To Thelwall's praises of the beauties of external nature he responds:

I can at times feel strongly the beauties you describe, in themselves and for themselves; but more frequently all things appear little, all the knowledge that can be acquired child's play; the universe itself—what but an immense heap of *little* things? I can contemplate nothing but *parts,* and parts are all *little!* My mind feels as if it ached to behold something *great,* something one and indivisible. And it is only in the faith of *that,* that rocks or waterfalls, mountains or caverns, give me the sense of sublimity or majesty! But in that faith *all things* counterfeit infinity.[140]

This letter was written in October, 1797, at the high tide of his admiration for Wordsworth. Coleridge's career as a poet was doomed almost as soon as it began.

The Wedgwoods' revised offer gave him a more attractive means of playing off his intellect than the duties of a dissenting parson, and he joyfully returned to Wordsworth and Dorothy and poetry. Very soon, however, one detects undercurrents of distress. The birth of little Berkeley in May was the sort of event which always made him want to run away: at such times his wife was even more than usually unpleasant. There were quarrels with Lloyd, Lamb, and Southey, and savage attacks in *The Anti-Jacobin.* Harried nerves and infected teeth brought on neuralgic pains which he quieted with the familiar remedy. Another anodyne reappears in prayerful and "practical" religion. In April he assures George Coleridge that his opinions are "utterly untainted with French metaphysics, French politics, French ethics, and French theology." Here, I believe for the first time, he proclaims a firm belief in original sin. He continues, however: "And for this inherent depravity I believe that the *spirit* of the Gospel is the sole cure; but permit me to add, that I look for the

---

[139] *Letters,* p. 444. One gathers from Coleridge's correspondence that the Reverend *William* Coates was a Unitarian minister in or near Bristol. *Matthew* was either his son or a considerably younger brother. The family were friends of Southey, who brought Coleridge into contact with them in 1795 or 1796. See *Unpublished Letters,* I, 36, 41, 47, 144.

[140] *Letters,* p. 228.

spirit of the Gospel 'neither in the mountain, nor at Jerusalem.' " [141] He looks for it, we may infer, within himself. More humility appears in a letter written in May to the Unitarian minister, John Estlin:

I have been too neglectful of practical religion—I mean, actual and stated prayer, and a regular perusal of scripture as a morning and evening duty. May God grant me grace to amend this error, for it is a grievous one! Conscious of frailty I almost wish . . . that I had become a stated minister, for indeed I find true joy after a sincere prayer; but for want of habit my mind wanders, and I cannot *pray* as often as I ought. Thanksgiving is pleasant in the performance; but prayer and distinct confession I find most serviceable to my spiritual health when I can do it. But though all my doubts are done away, though Christianity is my *passion*, it is too much my *intellectual* passion, and therefore will do me but little good in the hour of temptation and calamity.[142]

One can see the difficulty of praying to "an obscure and indefinite Vastness."

Consciousness of frailty was not a state which he could long endure. As a pensioner of the Wedgwoods he felt that he should make full use of his talents. "But unfortunately," as Chambers observes, "the longer Coleridge looked at a moral obligation the more he became inclined in practice to shy away from it." [143] The realization that he *must* do something always aroused the dread in his heart and set him in search of some means of evasion which would enhance rather than diminish his self-approval. The German tour, dreamed about since the spring of 1796 and now made possible by his benefactors, was the perfect solution. To go to Germany was certainly to do something—and something which postponed the necessity of doing anything in particular.

Change of scene, with freedom from financial worry and domestic strife, was good for him: on the whole the foreign sojourn was happy and wholesome. There is no evidence that he plunged into the depths of German metaphysics. Much of his time was devoted to studying the language. The twenty-one books which he borrowed from the Goettingen library were chiefly linguistic and literary, and none was technically philosophical. [144]

His most nearly systematic studies consisted of attending the lectures

[141] *Ibid.*, pp. 240–242.   [142] *Ibid.*, p. 247.
[143] E. K. Chambers, *Samuel Taylor Coleridge*, p. 90.
[144] A. D. Snyder, "Books Borrowed by Coleridge from the Library of the University of Göttingen, 1799," *Modern Philology*, XXV, 377–380.

on physiology and natural history offered by Blumenbach, an anti-materialistic scientist who combatted "the identification of man with the brute."[145] Even before crossing the Channel, Coleridge had accepted some of Boehme's physico-mystical notions,[146] and he was now ripe for a vitalistic conception of science which taught that life was the independent *prius* of organization and structure. Blumenbach's lectures, later reinforced by Herder's conception of spiritual power as the basic principle of physical nature and by the more technically romanticized science of Schelling and Steffens, would enable him to argue that "in some way or other the Will is the obscure *Radical* of the Vital Power."[147] He was to sympathize warmly with the vitalistic theories of John Hunter and his disciple Abernethy. It is not surprising, then, that in letters written from Germany he expresses discontent with Priestley and admiration for Leibnitz.[148] At this time he thought of writing a life of Bruno. Indeed, his correspondence with Humphry Davy after his return to England suggests that these anti-materialistic scientific speculations formed the most important immediate influence of the German sojourn.

Here we may pause to observe that of recent years Coleridge and his fellows, especially Wordsworth and Shelley, have been credited with furthering a more modern conception of science than the crudely materialistic and mechanistic one which dominated their own day. Such praise is not undeserved, but it should perhaps be tempered by doubts as to whether romantic transcendentalism is consistent with any tenable conception of science, however "vitalistic" or "organic." In itself, the thesis that intellectual energy is the *prius* of the physical universe is favorable alike to mature science and mature religion, and a valuable means of harmonizing the two. But when this intellectual energy is identified with the imagination of the romantic poet, science is stripped of its most important religious function—that of enforcing belief in a real world which imposes limits upon human self-will. A thoroughly romanticized science becomes merely one more means of flattering that lust for independent spiritual power which genuine science inevitably denies. Rather than regard these poets as harbingers of the atomic bomb I prefer to think of

---

[145] *Works,* II, 143*n*–144*n.* Blumenbach, whom Coleridge knew personally, was an Anglophile and a benevolist who had trained his poodle to hatch hen's eggs and to care for the resultant chickens. (*Ibid.,* p. 145*n.*)

[146] *Unpublished Letters,* II, 201–202.

[147] *Ibid.,* p. 335. See A. G. F. Gode-von Aesch, *Natural Science in German Romanticism.*

[148] *Letters,* pp. 280, 286.

them as extremely unscientific men despite their eagerness to transform science into the stuff of romantic illusion.

If Goettingen science had a believing tinge, Goettingen theology was distinctly rationalistic. In a conversation reported by Mr. Justice Coleridge in 1811, the poet recalled that the state of religion in Germany during his travels

was really shocking. He had never met one clergyman a Christian; and he found professors in the universities lecturing against the most material points in the Gospel. He instanced, I think, Paulus, whose lectures he had attended. The object was to resolve the miracles into material operations.[149]

Doubtless he was less shocked in 1799. If the natural operations into which miracles were to be resolved were those of Blumenbach's life-directed nature, such bold speculations might lead to a harmony of science and faith. He did not attend the theological lectures of the rationalist Eichhorn, but he had access to a student's notes and is said to have clashed with the professor in private argument.[150] He seems, however, to have valued Lessing, whose biography he dreamed of writing, chiefly as a religious liberal.[151] He reveals no great passion for orthodoxy, even of the Unitarian variety, when he tells his wife that "although the *Man* Jesus had never appeared in the world, yet I am Quaker enough to believe, that in the heart of every man the Christ would have revealed himself, the Power of the Word, that was even in the wilderness." [152] He seems to be adding to his old belief in an impersonal God a new belief in an impersonal Messiah—Jesus merely as symbol of the Inner Light.

Though he probably read some Kant before leaving Germany, he did not become deeply versed in the "Sage of Koenigsberg." Three series of lectures on the Kantian philosophy were given at Goettingen in 1799, but he seems not to have attended them. He returned to England, however, with £30-worth of German books, most of them metaphysical. Soon he would begin to read them in earnest.

The poems written during the sojourn in Germany, apart from a few occasional pieces, consisted almost wholly of translations or adaptations from rather inferior German models. The creative urge of 1797 and 1798 has slackened.[153] The free translation of Stolberg's *Hymne an die Erde*

[149] *Table Talk*, p. 297.   [150] Chambers, *op. cit.*, p. 106.   [151] *Works*, VI, 98n.
[152] *Letters*, p. 286.
[153] Of course his mind was full of other things at this time, but the ease with which he abandons serious poetic work is ominous.

suggests some interest in the Neo-Hellenic brand of pantheism then popular in Germany. An original poem, *Lines Written in the Album at Elbingerode,* in the Hartz Forest, contains lines which Professor Gingerich regards as evidence of Coleridge's growing transcendentalism:

> ...I moved on
> In low and languid mood: for I had found
> That outward forms, the loftiest, still receive
> Their finer influence from the life within.[154]

But as the subsequent lines show, this is a poem of homesickness for England. Coleridge is saying that no scene, however fair, is significant unless the beholder can link it to some personal or patriotic association. At the close he apologizes for such narrowness and pays tribute to

> That man's sublimer spirit, who can feel
> That God is everywhere! the God who framed
> Mankind to be one mighty family,
> Himself our Father, and the World our Home.[155]

4

Soon after he settled at Keswick in July, 1800, Coleridge began his descent into the depths. Considering the greatness of his powers, there is no sadder spectacle in English literature. To rehearse the details is needless: we have all looked into that witch's brew of domestic strife, psychosomatic and purely physical illness, the curse of opium without its enchantment, fruitless longing for Sara Hutchinson, growing estrangement from Wordsworth. One cannot arrange the ingredients in a neat causal sequence, for each of them infected, and was infected by, all the others.

Just when creative imagination was becoming the cornerstone of his thought he found, "with a deeper dejection than I am willing to remember," that he could not complete *Christabel.* "I tried and tried, and nothing would come of it." [156] How far below Wordsworth he had fallen! "He is a great, a true Poet—I am only a kind of a Metaphysician. . . . I hope, Phi-

---

[154] *Poems,* pp. 315–316; S. F. Gingerich, *Essays in the Romantic Poets,* pp. 42–43.
[155] *Ibid.,* p. 316.
[156] *Unpublished Letters,* I, 158. He ascribes his failure to "the Disgust which I had suffered in the translation of that accursed Wallenstein," but the real reason was not to be disclosed to Josiah Wedgwood.

losophy and Poetry will not neutralize each other and leave me an inert mass." [157] The death of poetry became an important element in his misery. We might expect him to use the turn toward metaphysics as a means of bolstering his self-esteem, but this he is unable to do for several years because he so closely associates poetry with health, happiness, and firm, dominant will. Thus in May, 1802, during a brief improvement in health and spirits,[158] he promises Poole "that by the end of the year I shall have disburthened myself of all my metaphysics, etc.,—and that the next year I shall devote to a long poem." [159]

The psychological barometer soon dropped again, but during 1802 he composed two poems which deserve attention. In the *Hymn Before Sun-Rise, in the Vale of Chamouni,* the desire to convince himself that he was still a poet caused him to pretend that a deliberate theft from Frederike Brun was an outburst of inspired improvisation.[160] "Earth, with her thousand voices, praises God" is an eighteenth-century theme which descends from the Psalms through Milton to Thomson and through Thomson's German imitators to Frederike, who declares her own verses to be "nach Klopstock." [161] Coleridge expands and greatly improves upon the German poem. The first twenty-three lines, furthermore, are a wholly original description of the technique of worshipping Nature's God through, and finally *in,* a lovely natural form,

> Till the dilating Soul, enrapt, transfused,
> Into the mighty vision passing—there
> As in her natural forms, swelled vast to Heaven! [162]

Here again is that highly self-expansive kind of self-annihilation which characterizes romantic religion. The soul submerges itself in the beautiful object, but only as a means of achieving a mountainous dilation which ultimately swells into a heavenly vastness.

Dejection: An Ode is Coleridge's lament, in words too familiar for extensive quotation, over the loss of that shaping imaginative power which

---

[157] *Ibid.,* pp. 165, 170; see also pp. 173, 232, and *Letters,* p. 378.

[158] At this time he was making a partly successful attempt to get on better with his wife. The recording angel must have noted on Coleridge's *dossier* the intermittent occasions when he fought his weakness with all his enfeebled will-power.

[159] *Unpublished Letters,* I, 193.

[160] Adrien Bonjour, in *Coleridge's "Hymn Before Sunrise,"* has presented evidence which forbids a more charitable judgment.

[161] *Poems,* p. 1131.   [162] *Ibid.,* p. 378.

is the essence of the Wordsworthian joy. Contrary to several other authorities, Professor Lovejoy denies that the "We receive but what we give" doctrine is Kantian:

Coleridge is not expressing the thesis of "transcendental" idealism that the mind gives form to the world of objects that it perceives; he is expressing, out of a painful personal experience, the psychological fact that the power of natural beauty to give us pleasure is conditioned by our subjective states. . . . "Joy" was *not* one of the *a priori* categories of Kant.[163]

Perhaps the technical knowledge of Kant which Coleridge frequently displays has caused Professor Lovejoy to underestimate the facility with which the poet can sentimentalize the Kantian philosophy into a pseudo-Platonic mind-over-matterism. And the pertinent passages go further than Lovejoy's description of them, for they give the soul an active power to *impose* value upon nature by sending forth "a sweet and potent voice" which is "the life and element" of all beauty; and the poet's concluding wish for Sara is that the life of all things may be "the eddying of her living soul." [164] The poem certainly expresses the loose creative-imagination sort of transcendentalism which alone is significant for the interpretation of romantic poetry and which Coleridge is quite capable of imputing to Kant.

It would be even more clearly erroneous, however, to insist that the source of *Dejection must* be a misinterpreted Kant. A striking passage from John Byrom's *Enthusiasm* (1752) will show the rashness of such an assertion:

> 'Tis will, imagination, and desire
> Of thinking life, that constitute the fire,
> The force, by which the strong volitions drive,
> And form the scenes to which we are alive.
>
> . . .
>
> Mind governs matter, and it must obey:
> To all its opening forms desire is key.
>
> . . .
>
> Imagination, trifling as it seems,
> Big with effects, its own creation teems.
> We think our wishes and desires a play,

---

[163] A. O. Lovejoy, "Coleridge and Kant's Two Worlds," *ELH*, VII, 348.
[164] *Poems*, pp. 367, 368.

> And sport important faculties away:
> Edg'd are the tools with which we trifle thus,
> And carve out deep realities for us.[165]

Byrom's ideas are derived from Boehme, partly directly but mainly through William Law, one of whose polemic treatises is closely paraphrased in this poem. Coleridge lists Boehme and Law among those "mystics" who prepared him for the Kantian gospel, and he may well have known the curious poems of Law's enthusiastic disciple. But far from attempting to establish a specific source, I am suggesting that the transcendentalism of *Dejection* may have entered Coleridge's mind from any one of several directions.

Thanks to Professor De Selincourt we know that the original version of the poem was an intimate love-epistle to Sara Hutchinson. Coleridge's feelings toward her have been the equivalent of poetry, for even the knowledge that he cannot possess her has had a vividness which he has never felt in the "coarse domestic life" where there are "No griefs but such as dull and deaden me." On the contrary,

> ... when I mourn'd for you, my Heart might borrow
> Fair forms and living Motions for its Sorrow;
> For not to think of what I needs must feel,
> But to be still and patient all I can;
> And haply by abstruse research to steal
> From my own Nature, all the Natural man—
> This was my sole Resource, my wisest plan! [166]

Here is conclusive evidence that Coleridge used metaphysics as an anodyne which might deaden the pain of actuality. Before 1797, poetry could sometimes be used for the same purpose; but Wordsworth had shown him that true poetry is written with blood. Coleridge attributes the loss of his poetic genius to "my long and exceedingly severe metaphysical investigations," and these he attributes "partly to ill-health, and partly to private afflictions, which rendered any subjects, immediately connected with feeling, a source of pain and disquiet to me." [167]

Yet we do him grave injustice if we fail to grant that while his philosophizing was the flight of a man in deadly fear of pain, it was also a

---

[165] *Religious Trends*, II, 160–161.
[166] Ernest de Selincourt, "Coleridge's *Dejection: An Ode*," *Essays and Studies by Members of the English Association*, XXII, 23.   [167] *Letters*, p. 378.

sincere attempt to solve life's most fundamental problems. It is clinically interesting that a man afflicted with extreme infirmity of will-power should have become so eloquent a preacher of the sovereignty of the moral will, but Coleridge is not the only neurotic who has edified others from the depths of his own weakness.

His repudiation of Hartley was the inevitable result of the psychological crisis which arose in the autumn of 1800. On January 7, 1801, he confides in Thomas Poole:

O me, my dear fellow! The notion of a Soul is a comfortable one to a poor fellow, who is beginning to be ashamed of his Body! For the last four months I have not had a fortnight of continuous health.[168]

To base the *amor intellectualis dei* on the operations of the flesh is intolerable to one whose flesh has become a source of disgust and dread. This letter rings the knell of Hartleyism and of the whole empirical school.

In February, Coleridge informs Humphry Davy that despite his illness he has been "thinking vigorously" about "the relation of thoughts to things; in the language of Hume, of ideas to impressions." [169] One can predict that Hartley's view of this relationship will soon be reversed. Two years before his death, Coleridge expressed in plain English the gist of hundreds of pages of misty verbiage when he declared, "The pith of my system is to make the senses out of the mind—not the mind out of the senses, as Locke did." [170]

We are prepared, then, for the triumphant announcement to Poole on March 16, 1801:

If I do not greatly delude myself, I have not only *completely extricated the notions of time and space,* but have overthrown the doctrine of association, as taught by Hartley, and with it all the irreligious metaphysics of modern infidels—especially the doctrine of necessity. This I have *done;* but I trust that I am about to do more—namely, that I shall be able to evolve all the five senses, that is, to deduce them from one sense, and to state their growth and the causes of their difference, and in the evolvement to solve the process of life and consciousness.[171]

What were the "abstruse researches" which led him to these remarkable results and justified these still more remarkable promises? Rather than

---

[168] *Unpublished Letters,* I, 166–167.   [169] *Letters,* p. 347.
[170] *Table Talk,* p. 173.   [171] *Letters,* p. 348.

engage in an endless series of duels with other scholars I shall simply state my own opinions.

Coleridge was at heart a "Platonist" in the most loosely romantic sense of the term: that is, he wanted to believe that his imaginative power was identical with the Divine Mind, and that its creations represented a higher, more enduring reality than the disappointing world of phenomena which he shrank from confronting. Hence he derived deep satisfaction from the Neoplatonists and from more irregular mystics such as Boehme. But this dreamer was also an acute and subtle thinker whose reason was always a little sceptical of his reveries. His whole career as a philosopher might be interpreted as an endeavor to find a rationalization which would permit him to be "Platonic" without feeling that he was a mere enthusiast. Hartley, Berkeley, Spinoza, the scholastic realists, Kant, Fichte, Schelling, the "Platonizing divines" of the seventeenth century—the masks change, but the craving for "energic reason and a shaping mind" remains constant.

Neoplatonism will of course not provide a sufficient explanation of the letter to Poole. But Coleridge was rereading Bruno and Proclus in 1801, and the latter suggested an entry in *Anima Poetae*:

The whole question of religion seems to me to rest on and in the question: The One and the Good—are these words or realities? I long to read the schoolmen on the subject.[172]

The longing is soon satisfied, for in July he is at work on Duns Scotus in the library of Durham Cathedral:

I mean to set the poor old Gemman on his feet again; and in order to wake him out of his present lethargy, I am burning Locke, Hume, and Hobbes under his nose. They stink worse than feather or assafoetida.[173]

By November of 1803 he can write to Thelwall:

God bless the old Schoolmen! they have been my best comforts, and most instructive companions, for the last 2 years. Could you have believed, that I could have come to *this?* [174]

Platonic schoolmen such as Erigena would help him to believe that the One and the Good *are* realities, and the same reality. The letters cited

---

[172] *Anima Poetae*, pp. 16–17, 63.   [173] *Letters*, p. 358.
[174] *Unpublished Letters*, I, 298.

above are too late to be used in interpreting the letter to Poole, but Coleridge was certainly familiar with the general position of the schoolmen well before July, 1801. Probably their attempt to reconcile Plato with Christian orthodoxy did not greatly impress him at this time. That element in his thought appears considerably later and depends mainly on the Cambridge Platonists. In 1803, indeed, he seems to value Scotus chiefly as "the modern founder of the school of Pantheism." [175] He merely drew from Scotus the weapons against Hartley that he wanted—the reality and primacy of ideas, and a non-associational basis for the sense of divine Oneness.

That the letter to Poole is basically Kantian has been warmly asserted and as warmly denied. The thesis gains no support from a letter sent to Poole in the preceding month which illustrates Coleridge's absorption in metaphysics by the fact that "I turn at times half reluctantly from Leibnitz or Kant even, to read a smoking new newspaper." [176] The "even" suggests that it is a little easier to turn from Kant than from Leibnitz. Leslie Stephen read the lost letters sent to Josiah Wedgwood on February 18 and 24 and reported that far from showing any signs of German influence Coleridge "still sticks to Hartley and to the Association doctrine. . . . Thus he is dissatisfied with Locke, but has not broken with the philosophy generally supposed to be on the Locke line." [177] If Stephen interpreted these letters correctly, the *conscious* decision to abandon Hartley must have been formed more suddenly than is generally supposed. The full effect of Kant upon Coleridge's mind does not find expression before the appearance of *The Friend,* and Shawcross is probably right in saying that his first deeply intensive study of Kant took place at Malta. On the other hand it is inconceivable that a romantic interpretation of Kantian ideas played no part in the repudiation of necessitarianism. René Wellek asserts that "Time and space could not have been extricated by Coleridge without the reading of Kant." [178]

But what is the "one sense" from which the five senses are to be deduced in such a way as to "solve the process of life and consciousness"? Of course it is not a sense at all; but Coleridge, despite his rejection of Hartley, still wishes to sound like a psychologist. Fundamentally, as Mr. Shawcross observes, it is the imaginative faculty.[179] It is also the One of Plotinus, rationalized with the help of the schoolmen. It is also the moral sense

---

[175] *Letters,* p. 424.   [176] *Unpublished Letters,* I, 173.   [177] *Letters,* p. 351n.
[178] René Wellek, *Kant in England,* p. 72.   [179] *Biographia Literaria,* I, xix.

(now more like Shaftesbury's than Hartley's) interpreted in terms of the Kantian moral will. It is also, therefore, a romanticized version of Kant's practical reason. Much later, Coleridge will write in *Aids to Reflection*:

Reason [is the faculty] of Contemplation. Reason indeed is much nearer to Sense than to Understanding; for Reason (says our great Hooker) is a direct aspect of Truth, an inward Beholding, having a similar relation to the Intelligible or Spiritual, as Sense has to the Material or Phenomenal.[180]

This analogy between direct sense-perception and something like mystical contemplation quite possibly owes something to Jacobi. "I should have no objection," says Coleridge in *The Friend*, "to defining reason with Jacobi, and with his friend Hemsterhuis, as an organ bearing the same relation to spiritual objects . . . as the eye bears to material and contingent phenomena."[181]

In deducing the five senses from this sense of intuitive contemplation he would probably have relied upon the device of making mental power the *prius* of all organic life. Schelling will later be helpful in this connection, but at present other authorities will do well enough. Miss Snyder quotes a marginal note in a copy of Boehme's *Aurora*:

That not Heat but Light is the Heart of Nature is one of those truly profound and pregnant Thoughts that ever and anon astonish me in Boehme's writings. That the Heat is not generated by the Blood but by the Nerves has been proved experimentally within the last ten years—But the affinity of the Arterio-muscular system, and of the Flesh and Blood generally to Light I trust I shall make evident in my commentaries on the first and sixth chapters of the Gospel of John. Hence in the Logos (distinctive energy) is *Light*, and the Light became the *Life* of Man—Now [that] the Blood is the Life is affirmed by Moses, and has been forcibly maintained by John Hunter.[182]

These astonishing words were written about 1809, but Coleridge tells us elsewhere that he had "conjured over" the *Aurora* at Christ's Hospital.[183] This kind of thinking lies behind the "one sense." The reason-sense is the Logos; the Logos is that light which is the life of man and the animating principle of all nature. Thanks to Jacobi, Plato, St. John, Boehme, Moses, and Dr. Hunter, nothing could be simpler.

[180] *Aids to Reflection*, p. 148. Observe the characteristic Platonizing of Kant, in this case with the help of Hooker.   [181] *Works*, II, 144.
[182] Quoted by A. D. Snyder, "Coleridge on Böhme," *PMLA*, XLV, 618.
[183] *Unpublished Letters*, II, 201.

Perhaps we may conclude that the background of the letter to Poole and more generally of Coleridge's thought from 1801 to the beginning of the Malta sojourn in 1804 is a medley of Neoplatonism and other kinds of mysticism, Platonic scholasticism, wishfully interpreted Kant, Jacobi, and pseudo-science. The underlying motive of the whole ferment is religious. From now to the end of his days Coleridge will be asking: "What shall I do to be saved? How can I, so weak, so deeply tainted with evil, get away from this hateful body and the hateful world in which it moves and find some higher ground for my conviction that I am *really* good, wise, and creative?"

For some time it will be difficult for him to harmonize his practical religion with his metaphysics. In March, 1800, he is still proud of the title "Dissenter" and scornful of those Unitarians who snobbishly send their sons "to Established and Idolatrous Universities." [184] But by 1802, in the depths of his misery, he begins to waver. He informs his brother George that the inferiority of the French Concordat has made him think so highly of the English conception of an Established Church that his "scruples . . . as to the effects and scriptural propriety of the (supposed) alliance of Church and State were wholly removed." [185] But when George delightedly leaps to the conclusion that his erring brother has become an Anglican, Samuel explains that he meant no such thing. The point of his previous letter was simply that the Church of England is a genuine third estate,

an elementary part of our constitution, not created by our legislature. . . . Now this is indeed an Establishment—res stabilita. It has its own foundation; whereas the present Church of France has no foundation of its own.[186]

Here, as a result of his growing political conservatism, he expresses the root idea of his treatise *On the Constitution of Church and State* (1830), which was to influence so strongly the ecclesiastical theories of the Broad Church school.

Coleridge goes on to explain, however, that so far as Christian doctrines are concerned he is in a state of groping incertitude:

I . . . have convinced myself that the Socinian and Arian hypotheses are utterly untenable; but what to put in their places I found nowhere distinctly revealed that I should dare to impose my opinion as an article of Faith on others: on the contrary, I hold it probable that the Nature of the Being of

[184] *Ibid.*, I, 135–137.   [185] *Ibid.*, p. 198.   [186] *Ibid.*, pp. 200–201.

Christ is left in obscurity, and that it behoves us to think with deep humility on the subject, and when we express ourselves, to be especially careful . . . to use the very words of Scripture. . . . My Faith is simply this—that there is an original corruption in our nature, from which . . . we may be redeemed by Christ—not, as the Socinians say, by his pure morals, or excellent example merely—but in a mysterious manner as an effect of his Crucifixion. And this I believe, not because I *understand* it, but because I *feel* that it is not only suitable to, but needful for my nature, and because I find it clearly revealed. Whatever the New Testament says I believe—according to my best judgment of the meaning of the sacred writer.[187]

As before, he accepts every word of the New Testament—provided that he may interpret it to suit himself. His Inner Light, however, seems to be changing its opinions as regards the nature of Christ and the doctrine of the Atonement.

A few months later, however, in writing to his old Unitarian friend Estlin, he offers no criticism of Socinianism. Instead, he decries an anthropomorphic conception of God wherever it may be found:

Surely, religious Deism is infinitely nearer the religion of our Saviour than the *gross* idolatry of Popery, or the more decorous, but not less genuine idolatry of a vast majority of Protestants. If there be meaning in words, it appears to me that the Quakers and Unitarians are the only Christians altogether pure from Idolatry.

But even Unitarians become idolaters when they conceive of their God as

a distinct Jehovah, tricked out in the *anthropomorphic* attributes of Time and *successive* Thoughts, and think of him as a *Person*, from whom we *had* our Being. . . . God is a Spirit, and must be worshipped in spirit.

In this letter to the Unitarian minister his creed differs from that which he had described to the Anglican clergyman:

My creed is very simple—my confession of Faith very brief. I approve altogether and embrace entirely the *Religion* of the Quakers, but exceedingly dislike the *sect*, and their own notions of their own Religion. By Quakerism I understand the opinions of George Fox rather than those of Barclay—who was the St. Paul of Quakerism.[188]

---

[187] *Ibid.*, pp. 202–203.   [188] *Letters*, pp. 414–415.

The reader will remember that as early as 1799 Coleridge had declared himself "Quaker enough to believe" in an inward revelation of the Word quite independent of the historical Jesus.[189] He now feels more strongly than ever that the only religion reconcilable with his philosophy is a mysticism of the Inner Light. In 1803 he is still grateful to Matthew Coates for having taught him "the absolute Impersonality of the Deity." [190]

On the other hand, he has told his brother that belief in the sinfulness of man and in redemption through the Crucified is "needful to my nature." Since such beliefs imply a personal God and a personal Saviour, he cannot satisfy his needs without cultivating a kind of Christianity which his philosophy forces him to regard as "idolatrous." How is the chasm to be bridged? The answer is to be found in the power of the moral will to establish as absolute truth any of the promptings of conscience. I see no evidence, however, that this solution was arrived at before he molded Kant nearer to his heart's desire during his stay at Malta.

When he returned to England his moral will was at almost its lowest ebb—and he regarded himself as a perfectly orthodox Anglican Christian. In 1807 he answers a letter from Poole "urging him to exert himself" in the distich:

> Let Eagle bid the Tortoise upward soar—
> As vainly Strength speaks to a broken Mind.[191]

But to Joseph Cottle he

stated that he had renounced all his Socinian sentiments, . . . and he further said, that Socinianism was subversive of all that truly constituted Christianity. At this interview he professed his deepest conviction of the truth of Revelation; of the Fall of Man; of the divinity of Christ, and redemption alone through his blood.[192]

His orthodoxy, *The Friend* would soon explain, was perfectly consistent with Kantian metaphysics. There was no longer any chasm.

5

At this point I remind myself, with considerable pleasure, that my theme is the religion of romantic *poets*. After 1807 at the latest,[193]

---

[189] *Vide supra*, p. 300.   [190] *Vide supra*, pp. 296–297.   [191] *Poems*, p. 1001.

[192] Joseph Cottle, *Early Recollections*, II, 76.

[193] It would be fair to use 1802, the year of *Dejection*; but I believe that his final farewell

Coleridge was a romantic critic, metaphysician, theologian, and political theorist, but not a romantic poet. Unwilling to believe or to allow others to believe that poetry had wholly deserted him, he wrote many scraps of verse which occasionally remind us of the gifts which he has squandered. His later thought, however, finds no genuine expression in poetry. In almost none of the late poems which pertain to our subject does he say anything which is not said better in his prose. Throughout this volume I have drawn material from the letters and prose works of the great romantics for the sake of interpreting their poetry; and this I have so far done in the present case, feeling that even the gap between his technical philosophizing and his best poetry is instructive. But now that poetry is no longer even his secondary concern, those who wish to study the remainder of Coleridge's career in any systematic way may seek the aid of scholars who have already given it their expert attention.

One who begins to tell a story, however, is under some obligation to show how it ends. Others have analyzed, with varying degrees of sympathy or repugnance, the metaphysics, theology, and critical theories of the later Coleridge, both in themselves and in their interwoven relationships. They have variously estimated his indebtedness to Kant, Fichte, Schelling, Hegel, Jacobi, Plato, the Neoplatonists, the Cambridge Platonists, Spinoza, Boehme, Bruno, Swedenborg, Vico, Bishop Butler, and so on. They have probed the political aspect of his religious and ecclesiastical ideas and have studied their influence on the thought of the Victorian era. This is not the place to describe or evaluate the results of these investigations. It may still be profitable, however, to discuss certain aspects of the religion of his later years—say from 1816 to the end [194]—which illustrate the way in which the romantic mind of Coleridge refracts and transmutes historic Christianity.

During the Highgate period, Coleridge sailed into the sunset over calm waters. His finances were straitened, but it soon became apparent that the Gillmans thought of him more as an honored guest than as a boarder. Although a sick man, he managed to live on a very moderate "maintenance dose" of opium—occasionally with a bit extra on the sly.[195] He

---

to poetry is expressed in those affecting lines *To William Wordsworth* which he wrote at Coleorton in January, 1807, after hearing his friend read *The Prelude*.

[194] This period is sufficiently homogeneous to be treated as a unit. I shall occasionally draw from earlier years materials which explain or illustrate this final stage in his thought.

[195] L. N. Broughton (ed.), "Some Early Nineteenth-Century Letters Hitherto Unpublished," *Nineteenth-Century Studies*, pp. 66–67.

never completed—one cannot believe that he ever seriously intended to complete—his great metaphysico-theological *summa,* but he published valuable fragments of that dream-synthesis and spouted other fragments to his Thursday-night disciples. But was the relatively peaceful and reputable conclusion of his life the result of a spiritual victory, or mainly the result of the fact that with the Gillmans he found, in addition to a comfortable home and watchful medical care, the conditions which had always soothed his fears: coddling, admiration, and above all freedom from specific obligation? Under these circumstances, at all events, he burgeoned into "the great religious philosopher to whom the mind of our generation in England owes more than to any other man." [196]

The Sage of Highgate taught that there could be no morality without religion and no religion without revelation,[197] and that Christianity is "the only Revelation of permanent and universal validity." [198] The Christian faith comprised "every article of belief and doctrine professed by the first Reformers in common." [199] He was not only a stoutly Protestant Christian but a loyal member of the Church of England, "the defence of whose articles I have most at heart, next to that of the Gospel Truth, which in all but some inessential and comparatively trifling points I sincerely believe consistent with our Articles and Liturgy." [200] Holding "that the Christian Faith . . . is the Perfection of Human Intelligence," [201] he aimed to prove the identity of true religion and true philosophy.

All his old heresies are explicitly rejected. Although his own defense of the Trinity is highly esoteric, he regards Bull and Waterland as "the classical writers" on this mystery.[202] The Triune God, furthermore, is unmistakably personal,

a God that heareth prayers, abundant in forgiveness, and *therefore* to be found, no *fate,* no God as imagined by the Unitarians, a sort of, I know not what *law-giving* Law of Gravitation, to whom prayer would be as idle as to the law of gravity; but . . . a God who *seeketh* that which was lost, who calleth back that which had gone astray; who calleth through His own Name; Word, Son, from everlasting the Way and the *Truth;* and who became man that for poor fallen mankind he might *be* (not merely announced but *be*) the *Resurrection* and the *Life.*[203]

---

[196] Julius Hare as quoted by J. H. Overton, *The English Church in the Nineteenth Century,* p. 209.
[197] *Letters,* p. 676.   [198] *Aids to Reflection,* p. 103.   [199] *Ibid.,* p. xvi.
[200] *Unpublished Letters,* II, 138.   [201] *Aids to Reflection,* p. xvi.
[202] *Table Talk,* pp. 51, 75.   [203] *Letters,* p. 758.

It follows that his objections to the Atonement have disappeared. Needless to say, he is now very stern against any approach to pantheism:

The word Nature, from its extreme familiarity, and in some instances, fitness, as well as from the want of a term, or *other* name, of God, has caused very much confusion. . . . Hence a Nature-God, or God-Nature, not God in Nature.[204]

His own petitions to "a God that heareth prayers" were many and fervent. The *Nightly Prayer* published posthumously in *Literary Remains* is too long to be quoted entire, but an excerpt from the concluding portion will give a touching glimpse of S.T.C. on his knees:

Thy will be done! But if it be according to thy wise and righteous ordinances, O shield me this night from the assaults of disease, grant me refreshment of sleep unvexed by evil and distempered dreams; and . . . O in thy mercy vouchsafe me yet in this life an interval of ease and strength; if so (thy grace disposing and assisting) I may make compensation to thy church for the unused talents which thou hast entrusted to me. . . . To thee, great omnipresent Spirit, whose mercy is over all thy works, who now beholdest me, who hearest me, who hast framed my heart to seek and to trust in thee, in the name of my Lord and Saviour Christ Jesus, I humbly commit and commend my body, soul, and spirit. Glory be to thee, O God![205]

This exemplifies his definition of prayer as "the effort to connect the misery of the self with the blessedness of God."[206]

Only twelve days before his passing he addressed his godson, Adam Steinmetz Kennard:

I now, on the eve of my departure, declare to you . . . that the greatest of all blessings, as it is the most ennobling of all privileges, is to be indeed a Christian. . . . And I thus, on the brink of the grave, solemnly bear witness to you that the Almighty Redeemer, most gracious in his promises to them that truly seek Him, is faithful to perform what he has promised.[207]

On his deathbed "he said he wished to evince in the manner of his death the depth and sincerity of his faith in Christ," and according to his daugh-

---

[204] Thomas Allsop, *Letters, Conversations and Recollections of S. T. Coleridge*, I, 199. See also p. 107, where he glances at Wordsworth in this connection.
[205] *Aids to Reflection*, pp. 361–362.
[206] Quoted from one of the unpublished MSS by J. H. Muirhead, *Coleridge as Philosopher*, p. 220.   [207] *Letters*, pp. 575–576.

ter he succeeded in doing so;[208] but Crabb Robinson reports that "He died with a strong expression of his sense of the unkindness with which he had been treated by his brothers." [209] However this may be, he left behind him a pious epitaph expressing hope for Christ's forgiveness and a wish for the reader's prayers.[210]

So far everything, barring Crabb Robinson's discordant note, indicates that Coleridge became an earnestly believing, prayerful, penitent, verbose Christian. A more searching examination of the evidence, however, inclines one to the opinion that his faith, though usually expressed in more orthodox terms, is almost as private and peculiar as Blake's. For a religion supposed to be in perfect agreement with eternal metaphysical principles, his Christianity is strangely pharmacological—a prescription specifically compounded for a personal disease.

Far from being a Calvinist, he

affirms . . . that there is a distinctly spiritual principle in man, much distorted yet not essentially destroyed, capable of coöperating with the supreme Power towards its own re-establishment as the guiding force of life.[211]

Since Coleridge would add that this capability depends upon the gift of grace, he seems to be an Arminian in the best Anglican tradition. As such Arminianism implies, however, the starting-point of his movement toward God is not human strength but human weakness. Man is "a fallen creature," independently capable of evil but not capable of good without God's help. "I am born a child of wrath." This is a mystery incomprehensible to him, but "my conscience, the sole fountain of certainty, commands me to believe it." [212] Conscience does not, however, command him to interpret original sin in terms of hereditary transmission from Adam. The determinism implied by that conception would destroy the moral freedom and accountability without which man cannot be regarded as a sinner at all. For Coleridge, as Professor Lovejoy explains, sin is "original" in that it belongs, together with moral freedom, in that noumenal world which is the only home of intrinsic and independent truth. Thus Kant's

[208] E. L. Griggs (ed.), "The Death of Coleridge. Being an unpublished letter from Mrs. Henry Nelson Coleridge (Sara) to her brother, Hartley," *Coleridge*, p. 226.

[209] *Henry Crabb Robinson on Books and Their Writers* (ed. Edith J. Morley), p. 446.

[210] *Poems*, p. 492.

[211] H. L. Stewart, "The Place of Coleridge in English Theology," *Harvard Theological Review*, XI, 23.

[212] *Table Talk*, pp. 430–431. See also *Aids to Reflection*, p. 92, and *Anima Poetae*, p. 276.

distinction between the phenomenal realm of Understanding and the noumenal world of Reason, strongly colored by light derived from Jacobi and Schelling, "opened for him a gate back into the emotionally congenial fields of evangelical faith and piety." [213] This solution, however, was not altogether satisfactory. Even Mr. Muirhead, whose admiration for Coleridge's thought is seldom ruffled by doubts, finds it "legitimate to ask whether the difficulty of moral evil is not one which is raised rather than solved by the identification of the supreme reality with Will." [214]

But of course the taproot of Coleridge's belief in original sin was his awareness of his own sinfulness. The following letter, written in 1814, is one of several that might be cited:

Never was I led to this wicked direful practice of taking Opium or Laudanum by any desire or expectation of exciting *pleasurable* sensations; but purely by *terror,* by cowardice of pain, first of mental pain, and afterwards as my system became weakened, even of bodily pain. My Prayers have been fervent, in agony of Spirit, and for hours together, incessant! still ending, O! only for the merits, for the agonies, for the cross of my blessed Redeemer! For I am nothing but evil! Help, Help!—I believe! help thou my unbelief.[215]

It does not seem to me, as it doubtless will to others,[216] that this turning to God in pain and guilt and fear necessarily invalidates Coleridge's religion. I am troubled, however, by the fact that he approaches God *both* as a miserable sinner and as an immensely self-confident transcendental philosopher, full of proud words about intuition and the autonomy of the will. The two roads never joined despite his best efforts to prove them identical.

Crabb Robinson relates that in 1812 Coleridge

walked with me to Anthony Robinson's for *Spinoza,* which I lent him. In the course of a few minutes, while standing in the room, Coleridge kissed Spinoza's face at the title-page, said his book was his gospel, and in less than a minute added that his philosophy was, after all, false. Spinoza's system [Coleridge said] has been demonstrated to be false, but only by the philosophy which has at the same time demonstrated the falsehood of all other philosophies. Did philosophy commence with an IT IS instead of an I AM, Spinoza would be altogether true; and without allowing a breathing-time he parenthetically as-

[213] A. O. Lovejoy, "Coleridge and Kant's Two Worlds," *ELH,* VII, 341, 355–356, 361–362.
[214] J. H. Muirhead, *Coleridge as Philosopher,* p. 243.
[215] *Unpublished Letters,* II, 112–113.
[216] See for example H. I. Fausset, *Samuel Taylor Coleridge,* p. 248.

serted, "I, however, believe in all the doctrines of Christianity, even of the Trinity."[217]

After 1816 he would probably not have praised Spinoza so highly, but the intellectual irresponsibility revealed by this anecdote was never to disappear. Especially significant, however, is Coleridge's strong preference for I AM over IT IS. What he had needed since childhood, what he needed more than ever in the depths of misery and remorse, was a faith which proclaimed, in other tones than Spinoza's, "IT IS"; but all he ever found was the echo of his own declaration, "I AM."

Even when he turns to God as a suffering penitent his religion is deeply tinged with egotism. His sin is not an ugly little nuisance to be confessed and put away, but a boundlessly fascinating psychological peculiarity to be analyzed and discussed and exhibited to his friends with a certain complacency. It makes him proud to feel so penitent. Anyone who has tried to pray for more than five minutes will appreciate the satisfaction with which he declares, "My Prayers have been fervent, in agony of Spirit, and for hours together, incessant!" His private devotions were much too public. In Mr. Wilde's opinion his religion

was not deep enough to regenerate his will and build up his character. He remained to the end a disorganized genius, enthusiastic for virtue but at the mercy of his impulses and feelings: enjoying his Christian experience, but incapable of turning it into action. And not merely is there this lack of self-control but also a, perhaps unconscious, sense of justification through confession, and making a merit of self-abasement.[218]

The last sentence is severe, but certainly one feels at times that Coleridge has found in the sense of sin a satisfying equivalent for the sentimentalist's sense of virtue. His craving for self-approbation is still at work.

Let us turn to aspects of Coleridge's religion which seem at first glance to be more abstract and impersonal. His metaphysical system might provide the groundwork for a Platonic sort of natural religion, but it bears no logical relation to the specifically Christian beliefs which he so warmly professes. Few if any modern scholars would be unwilling to say, with Crabb Robinson,

---

[217] *Henry Crabb Robinson on Books and Their Writers*, p. 112.
[218] Norman Wilde, "The Development of Coleridge's Thought," *Philosophical Review*, XXVIII, 62.

I certainly am altogether unable to reconcile plausibly his metaphysical and empirico-religious opinions. . . . That he is grossly insincere in any of his assertions, I do not believe; but I believe there is in him much self-deception.[219]

This self-deception was partly motivated by the political and social pressures which played so large a rôle in the nominal orthodoxy of Wordsworth. But except as regards Coleridge's Church-and-State opinions, a much stronger factor was the need to rationalize his deepest personal desires. He admits that "The *peculiar* doctrines of the Christian Faith . . . are indeed Mysteries, in evidence of which no reasons can be brought." But precisely because of this fact it is necessary for him "to show . . . that these Mysteries *are* Reason, Reason in its highest form of Self-affirmation." [220]

In considering Coleridge's conception of reason, it is important to recognize that although ostensibly a metaphysical absolutist, he was at bottom an extreme sentimental pragmatist. "But what are 'my metaphysics?" he reassures the uneasy subscribers to *The Friend*. "Merely the referring of the mind to its own consciousness for truths indispensible for its own happiness!" [221] It was in 1796 that he declared to Thelwall, "My philosophical opinions are blended with or deduced from my feelings," [222] but the remark is applicable throughout his life. He will always "find it wise to believe, even on slight evidence, opinions, the contrary of which cannot be proved, and which promote our happiness without hampering our intellect." [223] "Believe me, Southey!" he writes in 1803, "a metaphysical solution that does not instantly *tell* you something in the heart is grievously to be suspected as apocryphal." Hartley's theory is

how flat, how wretched! . . . I almost think that ideas *never* recall ideas, . . . any more than leaves in a forest create each other's motion. The breeze it is that runs through them—it is the soul, the state of feeling.[224]

Transcendental philosophy and Christianity are easily reconciled if one defines the former as "an affectionate seeking after the truth," [225] and the

---

[219] Robinson, *op. cit.*, pp. 55, 108.   [220] *Aids to Reflection*, p. xviii.
[221] *Works*, II, 103.   [222] *Letters*, p. 197.   [223] *Ibid.*, p. 283.
[224] *Ibid.*, p. 428.
[225] *Biographia Literaria*, I, 94. Although this work contains much that is characteristic of Coleridge's later thought I use it rather sparingly in this concluding section because Coleridge came to regard its metaphysics as "informed and immature." (*Table Talk* for June 28, 1834.) In other words it said too much about imagination and not enough about faith, which came to mean the same thing; also it contained too much Schelling and not enough pious Platonism.

latter as "the will in the reason, and love in the will." [226] There is no arguing with a metaphysician who tells you that "Christianity is within a man, even as he is a being gifted with reason; it is associated with your mother's chair, and with the first-remembered tones of her blessed voice." [227] In true pragmatic fashion, *Aids to Reflection* declares that the validity of an idea is to be judged according to its fruits:

Let the believer never be alarmed by objections wholly speculative, however plausible on speculative grounds such objections may appear, if he can but satisfy himself, that the result is repugnant to the dictates of conscience, and irreconcilable with the interests of morality.[228]

It is not difficult for Coleridge to decide such problems, since "Whatever *finds* me bears witness for itself that it has proceeded from a Holy Spirit." [229] That indefinite article casts light upon his Trinitarianism, which for him is chiefly a means of thinking about God "platonically."

In *Aids to Reflection,* after all his subtle theorizing, he falls back upon the purest empiricism: "Christianity is not a Theory, or a Speculation; but a *Life;*—not a *Philosophy* of Life, but a Life and a living Process. . . . TRY IT." The obvious objection is met in the obvious way:

I fear that the Unbelief, which prejudges and prevents the experiment, has its source elsewhere than in the uncorrupted judgment; that not the strong free mind, but the enslaved will, is the true original infidel in this instance.[230]

To say that the experiment always works except for those who are sinfully determined that it won't is one of the least attractive devices of Christian apologetics; and it falls with especially bad grace from the lips of Coleridge, who desires a strong free mind but frequently confesses the enslavement of his will.

Such was the man who undertook to deduce the whole body of Christian faith from the Kantian distinction between Reason and Understanding. How from the first he perverted Kant with the help of Schelling, the Neoplatonists, and other intuitionalists has already been shown by several scholars.[231] Suffice it to say that in the final stage represented by *Aids to*

[226] *Miscellaneous Criticism*, p. 163.   [227] *Table Talk*, p. 23.
[228] *Aids to Reflection*, p. 111.   [229] *Confessions of an Enquiring Spirit*, p. 295.
[230] *Aids to Reflection*, p. 134.
[231] It will be obvious that I agree with Wellek's *Kant in England* and disagree with Muirhead's *Coleridge as Philosopher* except when his knowledge of the real Coleridge undermines his own apologetics. I also greatly esteem Elizabeth Winkelmann's *Coleridge und die*

Reflection and the posthumous *Essay on Faith,* Kantian terminology and some Kantian ideas are still employed, but Reason is granted rights and powers never dreamed of by Kant himself. It "affirms truths which no sense could perceive, nor experiment verify, nor experience confirm." [232] Not only is it autonomous within its own noumenal realm, but it wields lordly sway over the subservient though often rebellious realm of the Understanding:

> The reason as the irradiative power, and the representation of the infinite, judges the understanding as the faculty of the finite, and cannot without error be judged by it. When this is attempted, or when the understanding in its *synthesis* with the personal will usurps the supremacy of the reason, it is then what St. Paul calls the mind of the flesh (φρόνημα σαρκός) or the wisdom of the world. The result is, that the reason is super-finite; and in this relation, its antagonist is the insubordinate understanding, or mind of the flesh.[233]

Such reason might less confusingly be called direct intuition of truth, or faith, or creative imagination, or mystical contemplation. Essentially, it is the Beatific Vision of the One:

> Whene'er the mist, that stands 'twixt God and thee,
> Defecates to a pure transparency,
> That intercepts no light and adds no stain—
> There Reason is, and then begins her reign! [234]

Coleridge still follows Kant in emphasizing the moral basis of religion, but he colors this idea with his peculiar mysticism. Thus he elevates the Practical Reason so far above the Speculative Reason that he reduces the latter almost to the level of Understanding. "All Revealed Truths," he declares with characteristic pragmatism, "are to be judged by us, as far as they are possible objects of human conception, on grounds of practice, or in some way connected with our moral and spiritual interests." Hence although nothing in religion should contradict the Speculative Reason, religion does not *depend* on this faculty, but on

---

Kantische Philosophie, though it is easier to prove that Coleridge's mind was very similar to Jacobi's than that he was strongly influenced by the apostle of *Gefühl.* Muirhead's rejoinder to Wellek and Winkelmann in "Metaphysician or Mystic?", *Coleridge,* pp. 177–197, does not seem to me at all convincing, but the reader must judge for himself.

[232] *Aids to Reflection,* p. 154n.
[233] *Essay on Faith* in *Aids to Reflection,* p. 346.
[234] *Poems,* p. 487.

the *practical* reason of man, comprehending the Will, the Conscience, the Moral Being with its inseparable Interests and Affections—that Reason, namely, which is the Organ of *Wisdom,* and (so far as man is concerned) the source of living and actual Truths." [235]

As if still further to free his shaping spirit of imagination from cold Kantian restrictions, he adds to the second edition of *Aids to Reflection* a footnote asserting that

The Practical Reason alone *is* Reason in the full and substantive sense. It is reason in its own sphere of *perfect freedom;* as the source of IDEAS, which Ideas, in their conversion to the responsible Will, become Ultimate Ends. On the other hand, Theoretic [*i.e.,* Pure or Speculative] Reason, as the ground of the Universal and Absolute in all logical *conclusion,* is rather the *Light* of Reason in the Understanding.[236]

Did he shrink from inserting this important statement into the body of his text because he knew that it meant the complete abdication of philosophy?

At all events the Practical Reason establishes "a law of right and wrong, which, uniting with my sense of moral responsibility, constitutes the voice of conscience." [237] Conscience, or the moral will, justifies belief not only in God, free will, and immortality, but in all the doctrines of revealed Christianity and in the Thirty-Nine Articles of the Church of England. The "perfect freedom" which it confers, since it necessarily implies moral responsibility, is the basis of Coleridge's sense of sin. The same freedom, however, equally authenticates his sense of boundlessly expansive intellectual power, which makes penitence a mere luxury.

His thought on this subject is circular. In the revised *Friend* he avers that God, by adding to our reason "the mysterious faculty of free will and consequent personal amenability, . . . gave us conscience." [238] Whence does conscience derive its authority? From God. But how do we know that there *is* a God? Because conscience tells us to believe in one. Similarly free will is to be established by an assertion of the will. The attempt to combine complete absolutism with complete subjectivism is doomed to failure. Conscience is the voice of perfect, eternal, irresistible truth, "the sole fountain of certainty." [239] But what about the consciences of Spinoza,

---

[235] *Aids to Reflection,* pp. 114–115.   [236] *Ibid.,* p. 277n.
[237] *Confessio Fidei* as given by H. N. Coleridge in *Table Talk,* p. 429.
[238] *Works,* II, 106.   [239] *Confessio Fidei* in *Table Talk,* p. 431.

Hartley, Priestley, Tom Paine, whose certainties were so different from those of the Sage of Highgate? It will not do to say that they were blinded by moral deficiencies, for they were better men than Coleridge. And what about Coleridge's own conscience during his years of open heresy? Was his Practical Reason then in abeyance?   ,

Probably no believer, and certainly no unbeliever, will deny that a personal and subjective sort of pragmatism is an important element in the faith of any individual Christian. One may object, however, to the way in which Coleridge disguises a religion of almost pure inwardness in the trappings of a critical theology. Furthermore, granting that the Christian faith is desirable, there is danger that overemphasis on the subjective and the intuitive will produce a hazy enthusiasm which subjects Christianity to the individual instead of uniting him with Christianity. Coleridge was sometimes aware of this danger,[240] but he did not succeed in eluding it. His Inner Light was never sufficiently allied to any definable Outer Light. He has been warmly praised for anticipating the best elements in modern apologetics:

> The insistence upon internal rather than external evidence, the abandonment of cold rationalistic "proofs," the discernment that man's moral nature rather than his logical dexterity is the key to the position—in a word all that transformed statement of the appeal for the faith which deals in "values" rather than in "facts," found in him one of its first and most lucid exponents.[241]

One can appreciate the importance of Coleridge's contribution to this trend without regarding it as an unmixed blessing. Some of the less desirable consequences may be gathered from his own words.

For Coleridge, as we have seen, morality is nothing without religion, and religion is nothing without revelation. But the only revelation to which he attaches any real importance is the inward or moral revelation. In 1812 he describes his son Hartley, who has recently been confirmed, as

> very religious, and quite orthodox—he says his creed and his Father's are the same. He fully believes in the Christian *Revelation* and more than believes the Christian *Religion,* but the former for the sake of the latter, not the latter for the sake of the former.[242]

[240] *Unpublished Letters*, II, 394–398.
[241] H. L. Stewart, "The Place of Coleridge in English Theology," *Harvard Theological Review*, XI, 28. But see *Religious Trends*, II, 10–13, for indications that the appeal to internal evidence becomes quite common in the second half of the eighteenth century as an aspect of the decay of rationalism.
[242] *Unpublished Letters*, II, 76. See also *Letters*, p. 708.

Mr. Stewart says that in *Confessions of an Enquiring Spirit* "He lays down the great principle that the Bible is to be looked upon as the Word of God because it is true and holy, not as true and holy because it is somehow antecedently known to be the word of God."[243] Coleridge's criticism of a crudely literalistic view of the plenary inspiration of the Scriptures would be admirable were it not based upon the complete subjectivism of the previously quoted statement, "Whatever *finds* me bears witness for itself that it has proceeded from a Holy Spirit." At least those parts of Scripture which "find" him *are* "somehow antecedently known to be the Word of God"—on the authority of his personal desires in the guise of "conscience." This subjectivism clashes bewilderingly with a letter of 1817 in which he informs Poole

that religion is not revealed unless the sacred books containing it are interpreted in the obvious and literal sense of the word, and that, thus interpreted, the doctrines of the Bible are in strict harmony with the Liturgy and Articles of our Established Church.[244]

He was not a liar in the ordinary sense of the term: he had simply fled so far from reality that he no longer possessed any IT IS to use in testing the truth of his own words.

On both the Established and the Universal Church, Coleridge expressed ideas which strongly influenced his own generation and the next.[245] It is impossible to believe, however, that the Church provided any inspiring force, much less any guidance or objectifying control, in his personal religion. Of the Eucharist, except when he is cracking jokes about the Real Presence,[246] he speaks with profound though elusive reverence:

The sacrament of the eucharist is a symbol of *all* our religion; it is the life of man. It is commensurate with our will, and we must, therefore, want it continually.[247]

But since he hardly ever attended church except to hear some particular preacher, his liturgical enthusiasm must have been mainly theoretical. He died without priest or Sacrament. And the words "commensurate with

[243] Stewart, *op. cit.*, p. 20.   [244] *Letters*, p. 676.

[245] See C. R. Sanders, *Coleridge and the Broad Church Movement*, and C. K. Gloyn, *The Church in the Social Order. A Study of Anglican Social Theory from Coleridge to Maurice.*

[246] Thomas Allsop, *Letters, Conversations, and Recollections*, II, 33, 46, 191.

[247] *Table Talk*, p. 79. See also pp. 223, 272.

our will" suggest that even the Eucharist is absorbed into the religion of I AM.

The Church was the creation, in no sense the creator, of his religious philosophy. In 1825 A.D. he can inform an Anglican clergyman that "Almost everything remains to be said about Christian theology" [248]—the implication being that S.T.C. will say it in his *magnum opus*. Still more revealing is a letter to Derwent:

> It does seem to me a very mean and false view of Christianity to suppose that even the Apostles themselves had the degree of clearness and enlargement which a philosophic Believer of the present day may enjoy. . . . Think only of the vast inferiority of the other Apostles to John and Paul—and the distinct marks in the writings of the latter that he was becoming more and more doubtful of the Jewish Literarity in which he as well as the rest had understood the Second Coming of our Lord. What is Christianity at any period? The Ideal of the Human Soul at that period.[249]

Part of this passage might be used in illustrating Newman's views on the development of doctrine. The concluding question and answer, however, point in a wholly different direction. Christianity does not shape the soul: the "Human Soul" of the "philosophic Believer" shapes Christianity without any assistance from Holy Church.

In the Highgate period, then, Coleridge was quite as free to interpret Christianity to suit himself as in any earlier stage of his career. "Father! in Christ we live, and Christ in Thee," [250] he exclaims in the lines on *My Baptismal Birthday* (1833). He has, however, by no means abandoned his old idea of a purely inward Christ-spirit operating quite independently of the historical Incarnation. Thus he assures Allsop that "The law of God and the great principles of the Christian religion would have been the same had Christ never assumed humanity." [251] Perhaps Christ is essentially the World Soul, not so much the Son as the *Sun* of God, or a pious personification of the numinousness of the Universal Whole:

> Why not then an influence of influences from the Sun [*sic*] of God, with the Spirit of God acting directly on the *homo noumenon*, as well as through the *homo phaenomenon*? This would make a just distinction between grace and redemption and providential aids: the direct action on the noumenon would be the grace—the call—the influence on the *noumenon* through the

---

[248] *Unpublished Letters*, II, 335.   [249] *Ibid.*, p. 369.
[250] *Poems*, p. 490.   [251] Allsop, *op. cit.*, I, 88.

homo phaenomenon by the prearrangement of outward or bodily circumstances could be, as they are commonly called in pious language, providences. Finally, on such a view might not Christ be the World as revealed to human knowledge—a kind of common sensorium, the idea of the whole that modifies all our thoughts? And might not numerical differences be an exclusive property of phenomena so that he who puts on the likeness of Christ becomes Christ?[252]

This passage reminds Muirhead, to whom I owe my knowledge of it, "of Blake's identification of Christ with the Imagination, from which perhaps it is not very remote."[253] It is certainly not at all remote from the self-deification through pantheism which Coleridge elsewhere so firmly abjures. Indeed, it goes far toward justifying the judgment of A. W. Benn, who will hardly be accused of bigotry, that Coleridge's religion was

a revival of neo-Platonism, reconstructed on the lines of Kant's criticism as developed into the absolutism of Schelling. The new "reason" ostentatiously distinguishes itself from the old, but it exercises the same distinctive action on religious belief; and the thing called faith, which is put in place of that belief, is simply obedience to the moral law conceived as deriving a mystical authority from the fundamental oneness of nature.[254]

Anyone in the modern world may apply the term "Christianity" to this religion, but whatever its merits or defects may be it is a trifle inconsistent with Coleridge's declared adherence to "every article of belief and doctrine professed by the first Reformers in common."[255]

His attempts to infuse his transcendentalism with an atmosphere of Christian humility by distinctions between the mind of man and the mind of God are unconvincing. In the *Essay on Faith,* to be sure, we are told that

Reason, as one with the absolute will (*In the beginning was the Logos, and the Logos was with God, and the Logos was God*), and therefore for man the certain representative of the will of God, is above the will of man as an individual will.[256]

[252] The Huntington Library fragment *On the Divine Ideas,* quoted, with translation of Greek and Latin terms, by Muirhead, *Coleridge as Philosopher,* p. 250. Observe the similarity of the latter part of the passage to Newton's suggestion that the universe may be thought of as God's sensorium.   [253] Muirhead, *op. cit.,* p. 250n.
[254] A. W. Benn, *The History of English Rationalism in the Nineteenth Century,* I, 270; see also p. 243.
[255] *Vide supra,* p. 313.   [256] *Essay on Faith* in *Aids to Reflection,* p. 346.

According to *Aids to Reflection,* however, there is no such thing as *"human* reason," since

There neither is nor can be but one reason, one and the same: even the light that lighteth every man's individual Understanding (*Discursus*), and thus maketh it a reasonable understanding, discourse of reason.[257]

Hence he is not inconsistent when he tells Allsop of "the inexpressible comfort and inward strength which I experience myself to derive as often as I contemplate truth realised into Being by a human Will";[258] for this will can be no other than the Logos. What in *Aids to Reflection* he calls the Practical Reason had been described in *Biographia Literaria* as the primary imagination, "a repetition in the finite mind of the eternal act of creation in the infinite I AM."[259] But the relationship is even closer than these words would indicate. As we know from an epigram previously quoted, reason is that state of pure contemplation in which nothing stands between man and God.[260] The experience is elsewhere likened to immediate sense-perception.[261] Now the chief aim of Coleridge's trichotomic logic is to establish the identity of subject and object in every act of knowing.[262] Hence no matter whether we think of God as beholding man or of man as beholding God, the experience simply asserts the divine Oneness of all being. This is "Reason in its highest form of Self-affirmation."[263]

Since in the religion of I AM to know oneself is to know God, "The postulate of philosophy . . . is no other than the heaven-descended KNOW THYSELF! (*E cœlo descendit,* Γνῶδι σεαυτόν)."[264] In 1814, to be sure, he tells Daniel Stuart that "We know nothing even of ourselves, till we know *ourselves* to be as nothing;" but this is the language which might be expected of Coleridge in the lowest depths of enslavement to opium. He adds that from this truth he has learned "to counteract calumny by self-reproach,"[265] which suggests that his penitence was sometimes a means of escape from the bad opinion of others.

[257] *Aids to Reflection,* p. 144.   [258] Allsop, *op. cit.,* II, 137.
[259] *Biographia Literaria,* I, 202.   [260] *Vide supra,* p. 320.
[261] *Vide supra,* p. 308.
[262] Elucidation of this highly technical point would lead us far afield. Readers to whom the fact is not familiar should see A. D. Snyder, *Coleridge on Logic and Learning;* also *Biographia Literaria,* I, 183, 185; Muirhead, *op. cit.,* pp. 93–94; I. A. Richards, *Coleridge on Imagination,* pp. 51, 56.   [263] *Aids to Reflection,* p. xviii.
[264] *Biographia Literaria,* I, 173. But the thought is echoed in *Aids to Reflection,* p. xix.
[265] *Letters,* p. 627.

But in *Self-Knowledge,* a poem of 1832, he repudiates Juvenal in tones which should perhaps be taken more seriously:

> Γνῶθι σεαυτόν!—and is this the prime
> And heaven-sprung adage of the olden time!—
> Say, canst thou make thyself?—Learn first that trade;—
> Haply thou mayst know what thyself had made.
> What hast thou, Man, that thou dar'st call thine own?—
> What is there in thee, Man, that can be known?—
> Dark fluxion, all unfixable by thought,
> A phantom dim of past and future wrought,
> Vain sister of the worm,—life, death, soul, clod—
> Ignore thyself, and strive to know thy God! [266]

Here at last is the religion of IT IS, eternally opposed to the religion of I AM. We do not know to what extent he was able to make fruitful use of this glimpse of Christian objectivity. Very little time was left in which to extricate himself from the trap of self, and there is no other indication that he succeeded in doing so. He had formed so close an identification of self-surrender with self-assertion that even the God striven toward in these lines would probably bear a close resemblance to S.T.C. We can only echo the question which Lamb, irritated by his friend's pose of omniscience, asked in his "Theses Quædam Theologicae":

Whether the Vision Beatific be anything more or less than a perpetual representation to each individual Angel of his own present attainments and future capabilities, somehow in the manner of mortal looking-glasses, reflecting a perpetual complacency of self-satisfaction? [267]

---

[266] *Poems,* p. 487.
[267] *The Letters of Charles and Mary Lamb* (ed. E. V. Lucas), I, 124.

Chapter VI

SHELLEY

I

SHELLEY MUST BE THE CLIMACTIC FIGURE IN ANY STUDY OF THE RELIGIOUS AS-
pect of English romanticism.[1] With varying degrees of perversity one critic
or another has denied the title of "romantic poet" to Burns, Blake, Wordsworth, and Keats. Byron's mind is of course a battlefield where romance
and anti-romance contend for mastery. But everyone seems to agree that
if Shelley is not a romantic poet no such phoenix is anywhere to be found.
Although he must share with Coleridge the distinction of an unchallenged
romanticism, he furnishes a body of poetry not only ampler than Coleridge's but more fully revelatory of his religious thought and feeling.

Any attempt to distinguish between Christianity and the religion of
Burns, Blake, Wordsworth, and Coleridge may offend readers who associate precise theological conceptions with bigotry. But Shelley differs
from these poets in explicitly denying that he is a Christian. When
Elizabeth Hitchener claims the right to call herself a Christian because
she believes in universal benevolence he pounces on the fallacy:

A Christian is a follower of the religion which has constantly gone by the
name of Christianity, as a Mahometan is of Mahometanism. Each of these
professors cease to belong to the sect which either word means when they set
up a doctrine of their own, irreconcilable with that of either religion, except in
a few instances in which common and self-evident morality coincides with its
tenets.[2]

Let us remember this intelligent statement when some of his modern interpreters hail him as a great Christian poet. Shelley would repudiate any

---

[1] For me, the arch-romantic is Blake; but his eccentricities are so rampant that it might
be misleading to regard him as the norm of romantic religion or of anything else.

[2] *Complete Works. The Julian Edition,* edd. Roger Ingpen and Walter E. Peck, VIII, 107.
All Shelley references in this chapter are to volume and page of this edition, which will be
referred to as *Works.*

such falsification of his beliefs. Although too much inclined to identify Christianity with the conduct of its most unworthy professors, he knows quite enough about real Christianity to be taken seriously when he asserts that he is not a Christian. Here then is an opportunity to study romantic belief *per se* in the poems of a warmly religious but avowedly non-Christian artist. Here also, with the possible exception of Blake, is the prime example of romantic sainthood—a life which uncompromisingly expresses the man's deepest, most passionate beliefs.

The significance of Shelley for our subject has long been recognized. His religion is so pervasive in his life and art that it not only provides the topic of a doctoral dissertation[3] but looms large in all the biographical and critical studies. In this brief discussion much may therefore be taken for granted, especially as regards the well-worn theme of his sources. I shall also avoid bemusing the reader with a discussion of Shelley's views on immortality, which seem to me too vague, inconsistent, and half-hearted for fruitful analysis.[4] Shelley's beliefs, furthermore, have so often been correlated with his biography that some departure from the method of the preceding chapters is advisable. Hence various aspects of his religion, rather than phases of his life, will furnish the primary basis for classifying our material, although within each section the chronology of the topic will receive as much attention as seems necessary.

2

Before coming to grips with the more positive side of Shelley's religion it may be well to consider his attitude toward Christianity and its Founder. On this subject everything that deserves serious attention in his early thought is summed up in *Queen Mab*. Although in several respects the poem foretokens the maturer Shelley, its views on Christianity are those of his Oxford days. They are now, to be sure, embodied in verse. Discouraged by the failure of the Irish expedition and further chilled by the wet blanket of Godwin's cautious advice, Shelley has begun his campaign

[3] Ellsworth Barnard, *Shelley's Religion*. Warmly as I disagree with Barnard on many points I no less warmly admire his courageous insistence that his subject is meaningful not only for "research" but for the life of man.

[4] Usually he regards the Christian conception of personal immortality as a gross popular superstition, but occasionally he recognizes it as a touching though vain expression of a natural human longing. *Adonais* incongruously combines this longing with the Platonic notion of the soul's return to a reservoir of impersonal spirit. Whatever the values of Shelley's religion may be, they pertain to our life in this world.

to remake the minds of men not through argument, but through the con-tagion of noble thoughts and spectacles of goodness expressed in beautiful images and rhythms. To the end of his days, however, Shelley's poetry contained a considerable amount of direct propaganda, and that element remains uppermost in *Mab*. While at work upon it he told Elizabeth Hitchener that "If every day takes from the fervor of my opposition to Christianity, it adds to its system and determinedness, it adds to the per-fect and full conviction I feel of its falsehood and mischief." [5] Much re-liance was to be placed upon the "long, philosophical, and AntiChristian" notes: "I shall take that opportunity which I judge to be a safe one of propagating my principles, which I decline to do syllogistically in a poem. A poem very didactic is I think very stupid." [6] But even the text of the poem, though naturally less syllogistic than the notes, is quite didactic enough.

Shelley drew his more explicitly anti-Christian ammunition chiefly from British empiricism as interpreted by the most radical *philosophes* (es-pecially Holbach), from Spinoza and Hume, and of course from the adored Godwin. Lucretius and Erasmus Darwin, on their very different levels, showed him that scepticism and science could be combined in poetry. The Roman poet represented that great classical civilization which Christian bigotry destroyed. About a year before the publication of *Mab* he wrote Godwin:

The first doubts, which arose in my boyish mind concerning the genuineness of the Christian religion . . . was excited by a contemplation of the virtues and genius of Greece and Rome. Shall Socrates and Cicero perish whilst the meanest hind of modern England inherits eternal life? [7]

Thus the omniscient Fairy shows the Spirit of Ianthe that "a moral desart" now stretches over that great Mediterranean world once consecrate to political and intellectual liberty:

> Where Socrates expired, a tyrant's slave,
> A coward and a fool, spreads death around—
>   Then, shuddering, meets his own.
> Where Cicero and Antoninus lived,
> A cowled and hypocritical monk
> Prays, curses, and deceives. [8]

[5] *Works*, VIII, 328.   [6] *Ibid.*, IX, 57, 42.   [7] *Ibid.*, VIII, 337.
[8] *Ibid.*, I, 80.

This Neo-Hellenic opposition to Christianity tinges only faintly the callow Jacobinism of *Queen Mab,* but the germ of a tendency which will later assume great importance is worth noting.

More fundamental in this poem, of course, is the assumption that the natural goodness of man has been corrupted by the machinations of "kings, priests, and statesmen." How the law of necessity could have permitted this violation of universal benevolence is a mystery which the Godwinian poet can explain only in terms of educational malpractice. The child is deliberately stuffed with "sophisms" which obscure the light of reason:

> Let priest-led slaves cease to proclaim that man
> Inherits vice and misery, when force
> And falsehood hang even o'er the cradled babe,
> Stifling with rudest grasp all natural good.[9]

Religion is in the forefront of those institutions which interfere not only with necessity but with perfectibility. Reason would speedily triumph

> ...but for thy aid,
> Religion! but for thee, prolific fiend,
> Who peoplest earth with demons, hell with men,
> And heaven with slaves.[10]

As we should expect, Shelley is hot against Christianity for sanctioning the bondage of wedlock. But this is merely a striking instance of the generally corrupting effect of organized religion and of the moral system which it enjoins:

In fact, religion and morality, as they now stand, compose a practical code of misery and servitude; the genius of human happiness must tear every leaf from the accursed book of God, ere man can read the inscription on his heart.[11]

The description of Christian dogma as the imposture of priestcraft was growing a little stale in the days of Toland and Tindal, but for Shelley it is fresh as the sunrise. The doctrine of the Trinity, he says, was devised merely in order that inquisitors might satisfy their lust for persecution. The chief instrument for releasing man from the chains of dogma is physical science in general and astronomy in particular:

[9] *Ibid.,* p. 93. [10] *Ibid.,* p. 107. [11] *Ibid.,* p. 142.

All that miserable tale of the Devil, and Eve, and an Intercessor, with the childish mummeries of the God of the Jews, is irreconcilable with the knowledge of the stars. The works of his fingers have borne witness against him.[12]

Shelley will have none of Paley, his father's favorite theologian. He prefers eighteenth-century authorities for whom the hyphen in "physico-theology" has become a sign of division rather than of union. "The consistent Newtonian is necessarily an atheist." [13]

Shelley was never precisely an atheist. In later years he explained to Trelawny that he used the term "to express my abhorrence of superstition; I took up the word, as a knight took up a gauntlet, in defiance of injustice." [14] It was a means of challenging the God of Christianity, whose name, says Mab, "Has fenced about all crime with holiness." [15] The notes reprint *The Necessity of Atheism* with unimportant changes. Anyone who supposes that Shelley and Hogg wrote this pamphlet with a candid desire to have their doubts removed by some more learned theologian must possess exceptional innocence of mind.[16] Since the authors laid down the axioms that "no testimony can be admitted which is contrary to reason," and that "reason is founded on the evidence of our senses," [17] it is difficult to imagine what proofs they could have hoped to elicit from their episcopal victims. A request for further light does not end with "Q.E.D." Mab's "There is no God" speech, to be sure, is qualified by the statement: "This negation must be understood solely to affect a creative Deity. The hypothesis of a pervading Spirit coeternal with the universe remains unshaken." [18] This pantheistic reservation, however, does not conflict with "atheism" in Shelley's sense of the term.

But if "there is no God" it is necessary to invent one in order to establish an image through which Christianity may be attacked. Shelley's desire to use a favorite legend creates an inconsistency. The Wandering Jew, contrary to Mab, testifies that there is indeed a God—a celestial tyrant whose malice was incarnate in Jesus Christ. If *Queen Mab* were *Prometheus Unbound*, we might interpret this deity as a figment of the perverted human mind; but to read any such subtlety into the earlier poem would

---

[12] *Ibid.*, p. 135.   [13] *Ibid.*, p. 150.

[14] E. J. Trelawny, *Recollections of the Last Days of Shelley and Byron*, II, 190.

[15] *Works*, I, 113.

[16] For examples of this virtue see Carl Grabo, *The Magic Plant*, p. 30, and Ellsworth Barnard, *Shelley's Religion*, p. 241. I accept the view that Shelley and Hogg were about equally responsible for the pamphlet. See F. L. Jones, "Hogg and *The Necessity of Atheism*," *PMLA*, LII, 423–426.   [17] *Works*, I, 147.   [18] *Ibid.*, p. 146.

make nonsense of the far from illusory curse imposed upon Ahasuerus.

For this and for other reasons the Christology of *Queen Mab* is bewildering. Shelley never had the slightest tincture of belief in the divinity of Jesus. Ahasuerus, however, depicts Him as a God who descended to earth in mock humility,

> Veiling his horrible Godhead in the shape
> Of man, scorned by the world, his name unheard,
> Save by the rabble of his native town,
> Even as a parish demagogue. He led
> The crowd; he taught them justice, truth, and peace,
> In semblance; but he lit within their souls
> The quenchless flames of zeal, and blest the sword
> He brought to earth to satiate with the blood
> Of truth and freedom his malignant soul.

On the Cross He only pretends to suffer, for "his unterrestrial sense" could feel no pain. When Ahasuerus indignantly derides His hypocrisy, He curses the Jew with "a smile of godlike malice." [19] But the note intended to illuminate these lines is utterly inconsistent with them. It describes Jesus as a purely human reformer "who desired to rescue his countrymen from the tyranny of their barbarous and degrading superstitions" and who "was sacrificed to the honour of that God with whom he was afterwards confounded." Jesus the false God is the monstrous creation of priestcraft, but Jesus the benevolent rebel "stands in the foremost list of those true heroes who have died in the glorious martyrdom of liberty." Then, to cap the climax, Shelley appends a sub-note: "Since writing this note, I have seen reason to suspect that Jesus was an ambitious man, who aspired to the throne of Judea." [20]

The real question was what conception of Jesus would work most damage to traditional Christianity. Should He appear as a divine villain disguised in the mock-humility of our flesh? As a human martyr to freedom whose benevolent precepts have been perverted by priestly imposture? As a human demagogue? Uncertain of his choice of weapons, the young propagandist employs all three.

Setting aside for the moment Shelley's view of Christ, let us ask whether his attitude toward the Christian religion grows more favorable in later stages of his career. On the whole he becomes gentler, less sophomoric,

---

[19] *Ibid.*, p. 117.   [20] *Ibid.*, pp. 152–153.

more concerned with the positive side of his beliefs. His maturest poems do not directly storm the citadel of bigotry but attempt, as he says in the Preface of *Prometheus Unbound*, "to familiarize the highly refined imagination of the more select class of poetical readers with beautiful idealisms of moral excellence." [21] For some aspects of the cultural influence of Christianity he develops a qualified respect. To the end of his days, however, he detested the doctrines and practices of organized Christianity.

As late as November 22, 1817, he considers *Queen Mab* immature only as a work of art. As for its ideas,

It is the Author's boast that it constitutes no small portion of his happiness that, after six years of added experience and reflection, the doctrines of equality and liberty and disinterestedness, and entire unbelief in religion of any sort, to which the Poem is devoted, have gained rather than lost that beauty and that grandeur which first determined him to devote his life to the inculcation of them.[22]

Shelley is almost always so uncompromisingly honest that this statement may be accepted at its face value—granting that "religion of any sort" does not include *his* sort. *The Revolt of Islam,* contemporary with this letter, abundantly confirms his declaration. Conversing with Horace Smith in the same year, "he attributed all the present evils of mankind to those erroneous views of religion in which had originated . . . the innumerable public and private miseries that made history a revolting record of suffering and crime." [23]

The following year introduces complications. In Italy he simultaneously immersed himself in Plato and in Dante, Petrarch, Ariosto, and Tasso—great Christian poets of Italy who in varying degree had combined the Catholic spirit of chivalry with Platonic love-doctrine. Much as he adored his personal caricature of Plato, he was made uneasy by certain actualities of Greek life, especially its social callousness and its contempt for womanhood. At the very core of the *Symposium* he found a shocking perversion. In the preface to his translation of this dialogue and in the *Discourse on the Manners of the Ancients, Relative to the Subject of Love* he grants that in these matters much good resulted, not of course from Christian beliefs, but from Christian social ideals as embodied in the institutions of chivalry.[24] Fortunately the pure core of these ideals is after

---

[21] *Ibid.,* II, 174.   [22] *Ibid.,* VII, 310.
[23] Quoted by Ellsworth Barnard, *Shelley's Religion,* p. 129n.
[24] *Works,* VII, 223–229.

all Platonic. From Plato "have proceeded those emanations of moral and metaphysical knowledge, on which a long series and an incalculable variety of popular superstitions have sheltered their absurdities from the slow contempt of mankind." [25] To the extent that chivalric Christianity preserves and applies the ideals of Plato there is something to be said for it, but toward the "popular superstitions" he remains adamant. The madman in *Julian and Maddalo* surely speaks for Shelley here: "Believe that I am ever still the same/In creed as in resolve." [26]

In the summer of 1819, Shelley began to study Calderón with the help of Maria Gisborne. His admiration for this rigidly Catholic dramatist was mainly aesthetic: one of the pleasantest qualities of the mature Shelley is his ability to admire good writing which expresses uncongenial ideas. He may also, as Madariaga suggests, have responded with subconscious wistfulness to the unquestioning certitude with which Calderón confronts the mysteries of life.[27] In the *Defense of Poetry*, however, any such temptation is rejected: the Spaniard is said to lose more than he gains "by a substitution of the rigidly-defined and ever-repeated idealisms of a distorted superstition for the living impersonations of the truth of human passion." [28]

Certainly neither the prose nor the verse of 1819 suggests increasing sympathy with "that superstition which has disguised itself under the name of the religion of Jesus." Catholicism as always represents the most hideous form of that superstition, but the Protestant Reformation can be praised only as "that imperfect emancipation of mankind from the yoke of priests and kings." [29] At the close of this year he is praising Hunt's *Examiner* articles on religion: "Added days and years and hours add to my disapprobation of this odious superstition, and to my gratitude to anyone who like you break for ever its ever-gathering bubble." [30] *Prometheus Unbound*, the climax of his career, depicts the revolt of the human mind against the false God it has created. Jupiter embraces all that threatens romantic desire, but this Urizenic symbol certainly includes the God of Christianity.

Shelley's favorable attitude toward the ideals of chivalry was often cancelled out by the anti-Christian implications of his Neo-Hellenism. Although Alcibiades shocks him a little, he has nothing but admiration for

[25] *Ibid.*, p. 161.   [26] *Ibid.*, III, 189.
[27] Salvador de Madariaga, *Shelley and Calderon*, p. 32.   [28] *Works*, VII, 120.
[29] *Ibid.*, pp. 6, 7. (*A Philosophical View of Reform.*)   [30] *Ibid.*, X, 137.

the interfusion of art and nature in Greek life as represented by the ruins of Pompeii. The Greeks, he writes Peacock in January, 1819,

> lived in a perpetual commerce with external nature, and nourished themselves upon the spirit of its forms. . . . O, but for that series of wretched wars which terminated in the Roman conquest of the world; but for the Christian religion which put a finishing stroke to the antient system; but for those changes which have conducted Athens to its ruin—to what an eminence might not humanity have arrived.[31]

As he later informs Mary, "It seems to have been one of the first effects of the Christian religion to destroy the power of producing beauty in art." [32]

In 1820 the *Ode to Liberty* expresses his longing

> That the pale name of PRIEST might shrink and dwindle
> Into the hell from which it first was hurled.[33]

Whenever he deals with contemporary affairs, as in this poem, he resumes the *Queen Mab* vein. The essay *On the Devil, and Devils,* written either in this or the following year, is unusual only for its employment of Voltairean mockery as a polemic technique.

In 1821, however, Shelley revives the more charitable idea that "the Christian and Chivalric systems of manners and religion" furnished necessary leadership to minds which otherwise would have been whirled into chaos upon the collapse of the ancient world. "The evil produced by these systems" must not "be imputed to the poetry they contain." For chivalric Christianity was beneficent, not because it was Christian in the base popular sense of the term, but because it was poetic. In other words, it was Platonic. Everything of real value in the gospel of Christ had been taught by Plato, so that "Christianity in its abstract purity," not wholly defaced by superstition in the works of the greatest Christian poets, "became the exoteric expression of the esoteric doctrines of the poetry and wisdom of antiquity." [34]

The comparatively sympathetic treatment of Christianity in *Hellas* rests partly upon this pseudo-Platonic basis and partly upon dramatic

---

[31] *Ibid.,* p. 26.   [32] *Ibid.,* p. 302.   [33] *Ibid.,* II, 313.

[34] *Ibid.,* VII, 118, 125, 126, 127. Observe that Shelley is not pointing out the Platonic influence on Christian theology: he is associating Christian benevolism, as embodied in chivalry, with a romanticized version of the Platonic love-doctrine and with a Jacobin interpretation of Platonic politics.

necessity. The subject demanded a Cross-versus-Crescent treatment. The Chorus's praise of Christ[35] is explained in a note:

The popular notions of Christianity are represented in this Chorus as true in relation to the worship they superseded, and that which in all probability they will supersede, without considering their merits in a relation more universal.

Another note shows what Shelley thinks of those merits from the latter point of view: "The sublime human character of Jesus Christ was deformed by an imputed identification with a power, who tempted, betrayed, and punished the innocent who were called into existence by his sole will." [36]

Hellas, in fact, is much less exceptional than two lines in *The Boat on the Serchio* (1821):

> All rose to do the task He set to each,
> Who shaped us to His ends and not our own.[37]

The unromantically submissive quality of this passage is, I believe, unique in Shelley. It supported Robert Browning in his belief that "had Shelley lived he would finally have ranged himself with the Christians." [38] Possibly, however, Shelley is here personifying with unprecedented sharpness a sense of all-controlling destiny which haunted him toward the end of his life. The point must be reverted to later.

At all events nothing that Shelley wrote in 1822 fulfills the dim promise of these lines. The abortive *Charles the First* tells us nothing new. The tyrannous popery of Henrietta and Laud, and to a less extent that of Charles, is duly emphasized; but although the rebels are all very noble Shelley's principles forbid him to glorify the specifically religious aspects of their Protestantism. *The Triumph of Life* may, as some critics have suggested, represent a lapse of faith in his personal philosophy; but it is hard to believe with Cherubini that the finished poem would have ended on a definitely Christian note.[39] Death was not far off on April 11, 1822, when Shelley, in a letter to Horace Smith, denied Moore's notion that he was responsible for the heresies of Byron's *Cain:*

---

[35] *Ibid.,* III, 26.   [36] *Ibid.,* pp. 56, 57.   [37] *Ibid.,* IV, 113.
[38] Robert Browning, "An Essay on Shelley," *Complete Poetic and Dramatic Works,* p. 1013.
[39] William Cherubini, "Shelley's Own Symposium: *The Triumph of Life,*" *Studies in Philology,* XXXIX, p. 568.

Pray assure him [Moore] that I have not the smallest influence over Lord Byron, in this particular, and if I had, I certainly should employ it to eradicate from his great mind the delusions of Christianity, which, in spite of his reason, seem perpetually to recur. . . . I differ with Moore in thinking Christianity useful to the world; no man of sense can think it true; and the alliance of the monstrous superstitions of the popular worship with the pure doctrines of the Theism of such a man as Moore, turns to the profit of the former, and makes the latter the fountain of its own pollution. I agree with him, that the doctrines of the French, and Material Philosophy, are as false as they are pernicious; but still they are better than Christianity, inasmuch as anarchy is better than despotism.[40]

This will serve for a final statement. Only a small portion of the available evidence has been presented, but it has been drawn from every year in the life of the mature Shelley. He cannot be said to have developed a more favorable view of "the religion which has constantly gone by the name of Christianity" except in so far as from 1818 onward he sometimes approved of its "poetic" elements as an exoteric popularization of Platonism.

Shelley's opinions of Christ subsequent to the publication of *Queen Mab* deserve separate attention. Such remarks as Mr. Strong's allusion to the "ever-increasing sympathy and respect for His personality which are evident in his later writings" [41] are neither wholly true nor wholly false. The sympathy and respect, in the first place, were directed solely toward a great human rebel, reformer, and martyr to the cause of love and liberty. They do not imply a growing affection for the historic faith.

On April 26, 1811, Shelley wrote Hogg: "I once could tolerate Christ; he then merely injured me once; he merely deprived me of all that I cared for, touching myself, on earth; but now he has done more, and I cannot forgive." [42] Although with Shelley as with his contemporaries the child was rather too completely the father of the man, he certainly matured not only as an artist but as a thinker. This infantile spleen against the Christ who has broken off his engagement to Harriet Grove and expelled him from Oxford is transitory. It survives in *Queen Mab,* but even there the "real" Jesus begins to be Shelley's ally in the warfare against Christianity rather than the personification of bigotry. The change was to be expected. Throughout the eighteenth century, Jesus as a benevolist who rebuked all "mystery" and priestcraft and taught only the universal

[40] *Works,* X, 378.   [41] A. T. Strong, *Three Studies in Shelley,* p. 16.
[42] *Works,* VIII, 75.

principles of morality was a favorite weapon of deism—and even of atheism, for Godwin himself regarded Christ as a perfect embodiment of his ideal of universal benevolence. After *Queen Mab* this conception of Christ becomes a useful part of Shelley's polemic equipment.[43] It was probably the main theme of the lost *Biblical Extracts* contemporary with *Mab* and of the mysterious *Life of Christ* shown to Medwin at Pisa.[44] Even in the famous *Prometheus* passage, the emphasis is on the horrible futility of the Crucifixion and the evils perpetrated in the name of Christ, whose "mild and gentle ghost" is heard "wailing for the faith he kindled." The only consoling feature of the tormenting vision is the admission of the Furies that the flames of this faith will dwindle "almost/To a glow-worm's lamp." [45]

One cannot assert, however, that the Shelleyan Jesus was no more than a cudgel for traditional Christianity. The poet's thought transcended, though it never excluded, that conception. The whole Italian period is characterized by a sincere admiration for the moral teachings, the "extraordinary genius," and the "invincible gentleness and benignity" [46] of Christ—an admiration, needless to say, which the poet shares with millions of other non-Christians. But in Shelley's case a special motive was at work: the fellow-feeling of one martyr for another. Tending more and more to picture himself not as a triumphant reformer but as a "companionless" victim of the world's hatred, he came to imagine a similarity between his fate and that of Jesus. A mourner at the bier of Keats, he "made bare his branded and ensanguined brow,/Which was like Cain's, or Christ's." [47] As an admirer of Byron's drama Shelley would not repudiate the former comparison, but he doubtless regarded the latter as more appropriate.

Shelley could transmute the most alien substances into the stuff of his personal vision. Very early he begins to create a Jesus who is Shelleyan not merely in character but in opinions. Writing Miss Hitchener on June 11, 1811, he insists that the term "God" should be used "merely as a

---

[43] But Christ is so used as early as the *Address to the Irish People* (*Works*, V, 221). For typical later instances, see *Works*, II, 196–198; V, 289–290; VI, 232ff., 255ff.; VII, 145–146.

[44] Thomas Medwin, *The Life of Percy Bysshe Shelley*, p. 270: "Shelley showed me a treatise he had written, of some length, on the Life of Christ. . . . In this work he differs little from Paulus, Strauss, and the Rationalists of Germany. . . . He indeed treats the subject with more respect than either, and although he may reduce Christianity to a code of morals, how does he differ in so doing from the Unitarians?"

[45] *Works*, II, 196–198.   [46] *Ibid.*, VI, 227.   [47] *Ibid.*, II, 399.

synonime for *the existing power of existence.* . . . It is another *word for* the essence of the universe." After more to the same effect the letter concludes: "Adieu. A Picture of Christ hangs opposite in my room. It is well done, and has met my look at the conclusion of this." [48] The implication is that Shelley and Jesus understand each other on these matters.

The *Essay on Christianity,* written probably in 1817, is described by Symonds as "one of the most valuable extant contributions to a sound theology." Here we may see "what reverent admiration he felt for Jesus, and how profoundly he understood the true character of his teaching." [49] Others may prefer to regard the *Essay* as a striking instance of the Shelleyan Jesus's willingness to agree with the poet's thought. Christ is still a pantheist and a necessitarian of the *Queen Mab* type. Scorning "the gross imaginations of the vulgar," He conceived of God as "something "mysteriously and illimitably pervading the frame of things, . . . the overruling Spirit of the collective energy of the moral and material world." Any impreciseness in this conception is not a defect but a virtue, for "where indefiniteness ends idolatry and anthropomorphism begin." As foe of superstition and critic of social evils, Jesus invites comparison with "the more connected and systematic enthusiasm of Rousseau." "Blessed are the pure in heart, for they shall see God" cannot refer to beholding a personal King of Heaven in a realm of bliss beyond the grave. In these words "Jesus Christ has said no more than what the most excellent philosophers have felt and expressed—that virtue is its own reward." The self-approving benevolist sees God within his own "internal sanctity of soul." [50] Professor Weaver suggests that "in the Sermon on the Mount Shelley must have contemplated the Beatitudes until his mind became that which it contemplated." [51] It might be more accurate to say that Shelley contemplated the Beatitudes until they became identified with his own favorite ideas.

Dutifully keeping in step with the movement of Shelley's mind, Jesus next becomes a popularizer of Platonism. This stage, as we have seen, had probably been reached by 1818 but achieves its most explicit expression in the *Defense of Poetry:*

Plato . . . taught also [in addition to human equality] a moral and intellectual system of doctrine, comprehending at once the past, the present, and the

---

[48] *Ibid.,* VIII, 102, 104.   [49] J. A. Symonds, *Shelley,* pp. 100–101.
[50] *Works,* VI, 230, 232, 236, 247.
[51] Bennett Weaver, *Toward the Understanding of Shelley,* p. 157.

future condition of man. Jesus Christ divulged the sacred and eternal truths contained in these views to mankind.[52]

This is the Christ of *Hellas,* who speaks of "Plato's sacred light,/Of which my spirit was a burning morrow." He is "A power from the unknown God"[53] only in the sense that all great and good men are reflections of that higher Imagination which is hailed in the Preface to *The Cenci* as "the immortal God which should assume flesh for the redemption of mortal man."[54]

Jesus, then, is merely one of the numerous mediators of Intellectual Beauty, or the divine Spirit of Love. A cancelled passage of *Epipsychidion* declares that

> ... Socrates, the Jesus Christ of Greece,
> And Jesus Christ Himself, did never cease
> To urge all living things to love each other.[55]

But *Epipsychidion* and *Love's Philosophy* hardly express the gospel of love as taught by Jesus—or for that matter by Socrates. These pantheistic, Rousseauistic, Platonic-love Christs seem as far removed from the Nazarene Carpenter as from the Second Person of the Trinity. And is not the modern habit of coupling the names of Jesus and Socrates characteristic of those who have little understanding of either?

3

It is fortunate that Shelley's attempts to remould Christianity nearer to his heart's desire did not play an important part in his personal religious philosophy. One greatly prefers his downright hostility to Christian doctrines and institutions. So far as the latter are concerned it is wholesome for professors of the faith to be reminded of the ill success with which, both individually and collectively, they have followed the teachings of their Lord, and of how largely the sins of the Church are responsible for the unwillingness of men like Shelley to subscribe to the Christian creed. Particularly at a time when organized Christianity—not of course wholly without provocation—was even more than usually reactionary in matters political, social, and intellectual, it needed to be stung by such a gadfly.

---

[52] *Works,* VII, 127.   [53] *Ibid.,* III, 13–14, 26.   [54] *Ibid.,* II, 72.
[55] *Ibid.,* p. 378.

Both within and without her borders, of course, the Church has had more profound critics than Shelley. Singularly lacking in historical imagination, "he never understood that all the institutions which he hated had been made by men of the same nature as those he wished to deliver from such institutions." [56] His assaults on Christianity are vague, shrill, extravagant, full of the callow cocksureness of a sophomore who has just read *The Golden Bough.* Confronted by the most delicate and many-sided of human problems, he lays about him with the eighteenth-century weapons which the good Dr. Lind had given him at Eton, crying out "tyranny . . . imposture . . . priestcraft . . . vulgar superstition . . . Inquisition . . . reason . . . No man of sense can believe." He is a little too bigoted to be a satisfying foe of bigotry.

It has often been argued, however, that the Christlike beauty of Shelley's character was itself a strong and legitimate rebuke to those who have made the temple a den of thieves. In 1894 the Reverend Stopford Brooke assured the Shelley Society that there is "no tenderer song of the loveliness and duty of absolute and unrevenging forgiveness than is heard throughout Shelley's poetry," that he was a pioneer of the modern social gospel, and that "the method Shelley laid down for attaining the perfect state is that of Jesus Christ." [57] As a reward for this service to the poet's memory, Lady Shelley sent Brooke one of the few copies of *A Refutation of Deism.*[58] Since despite its intentionally misleading title this pamphlet attacks Christianity, the gift was more appropriate than Lady Shelley probably realized.[59]

Brooke's praise is echoed more emphatically by other Shelleyans. Mrs. Campbell, some of whose opinions were cited in the introductory chapter, insists that Shelley not merely professed but lived "a faith which really embodied the simplest and central doctrines of Christianity—Hope all things; love thy fellow as thyself." [60] Mr. Barnard cordially seconds Gilbert Murray's statement that "almost the only great English poet who

[56] Arthur Clutton-Brock, *Shelley, the Man and the Poet,* p. 67.
[57] *The Shelley Society's Papers,* Part I, p. 8.
[58] R. M. Smith and others, *The Shelley Legend,* p. 137.
[59] I warmly agree with N. I. White's view (*Shelley,* I, 295–296) that the *Refutation* is a typical piece of eighteenth-century polemic irony. But F. L. Jones, in "Shelley's 'On Life,' " *PMLA,* LXII, 774–783, regards the pamphlet as a serious defense of Christianity. He groups it with *Essay on Christianity* and *On Life* as evidence that in 1814–1815 Shelley was heading straight toward Christianity but was deflected from the path by rereading Wordsworth. This chapter will, I hope, suggest grounds for rejecting Professor Jones's thesis.
[60] O. W. Campbell, *Shelley and the Unromantics,* p. 183.

was really inspired by the ideals commonly called Christian, and built his poetry out of them, was Shelley." [61] But perhaps the prize in the contest of canonization should be awarded H. B. Forman's entry: "Shelley in other circumstances might have been the Saviour of the World." [62]

As Hamlet says, "That would be scanned." More often than not Shelley was a brave, gentle, generous, forgiving man, whole-heartedly devoting not only his art but his daily life to lofty ideals of thought and conduct. The familiar tributes of Mrs. Shelley, Byron, Trelawny, De Quincey, and others can be substantiated by a judicious selection from the biographical evidence. And of course those for whom the poet is "Christlike" do not expect us to draw a detailed comparison between the earthly lives of Percy Bysshe Shelley and of Jesus Christ. Without committing any such absurdity, however, one may act the Devil's Advocate for a few pages in the hope of suggesting some of the limitations of romantic sainthood.

It would be a waste of time to blame Shelley for refusing to play the game of life according to rules which he never accepted. Plenty of allowance should also be made for his ill health, sometimes imaginary but frequently real enough, and still more for the neurotic, hysterical, and morbid elements in his personality. Some of his interpreters find psychiatric charity helpful in explaining many of his actions but quickly abandon the pathological approach when they turn to his beautiful thoughts. We shall do no injustice to Shelley if we proceed on the assumption that he was a sane but neurotic person who at times, under severe external pressure, thought and acted hysterically.

"O! I burn with impatience for the moment of Christianity's dissolution; it has injured me." [63] This is Shelley's reaction to the separation from Harriet Grove, but it expresses a permanent trait. His biographers have often observed that in large measure his political and religious radicalism was motivated by anger against circumstances which resisted his craving for personal liberty—the bullying at Syon House and Eton, the breaking off of his puppy-engagement to Harriet Grove, the expulsion from Oxford, his father's bungling attempts to control him, the Chancery case, the abuse of the reviewers, and the general sense of being hated and persecuted. The evil institutions from which he longed to free mankind were his personal enemies. They had injured *him*. There is nothing particularly damaging in this: to a considerable extent everyone forms his

[61] Quoted by Ellsworth Barnard, *Shelley's Religion*, p. 294.
[62] Quoted by R. M. Smith, *The Shelley Legend*, p. 255. [63] *Works*, VIII, 24.

general opinions in the same way. It is curious, however, that this personal motivation should be unusually strong and obvious in a man who makes so much of complete disinterestedness and forgetfulness of self.

Professor Grabo disarmingly remarks that Shelley's conduct in matters of sex "already seems less scandalous to an age which is accustomed to easy divorce and extramarital sex relationships." [64] At all events it is a mere tautology to bring charges of adultery against a champion of free love. One may fairly object, however, that Shelley was both too "Platonic" to be happily sensual and too sensual to be genuinely Platonic. In *Epipsychidion*, which Professor Kurtz terms "Shelley's holiest poem on love," [65] he reaches toward the heights of Intellectual Beauty but ends by proposing to Emilia a dreamy but by no means supersensuous or "holy" elopement in which

> Our breath shall intermix, our bosoms bound,
> And our veins beat together; and our lips,
> With other eloquence than words, eclipse
> The soul that burns between them.[66]

One word is too often profaned offers something ineffably higher than "what men call love," but in *Love's Philosophy* the interminglings of nature are worthless "If thou kiss not me." [67]

Shelley's eroticism, though persistent and volatile, was probably not very strong. What chiefly drives him onward from one woman to another is the fact that his mind, like the nympholept's in *Alastor*, "thirsts for intercourse with an intelligence similar to itself." [68] Only by finding his female duplicate, a sort of spiritual *Doppelgängerin,* could he satisfy his desire to love another without violating his love of himself. This largely explains his fondness for incest as a poetic theme. In the early days at Field Place the plastic adoration of his sisters Elizabeth and Hellen satisfied his narcissism in a way which he was never quite able to forget. When other women proved less malleable, as of course they invariably did, he found it hard to forgive them.

"Every one who knows me," said Shelley to Peacock, "must know that the partner of my life should be one who can feel poetry and understand philosophy. Harriet is a noble animal, but she can do neither." [69] She

[64] Carl Grabo, *The Magic Plant*, p. vi.
[65] B. P. Kurtz, *The Pursuit of Death: A Study of Shelley's Poetry*, p. 240.
[66] *Works*, II, 373.　　　　[67] *Ibid.*, p. 89; III, 299.　　　　[68] *Ibid*, I, 173.
[69] T. L. Peacock, *Memoirs of Percy Bysshe Shelley*, II, 336.

was not the ideal wife for Shelley, but no such paragon ever existed. She loved him and needed the support of his best qualities. The slight difficulties which had recently arisen between them could easily have been adjusted. Harriet had borne him a child and was pregnant with another, but Mary Wollstonecraft Godwin could feel poetry and understand philosophy. Shelley could not see why Harriet should dislike being deserted, or why she rejected his high-minded suggestion that she live with him and Mary in triangular bliss. The fault was entirely hers, of course:

I was an Idiot to expect greatness or generosity from you, that when an occasion of the sublimest virtue occurred, you would fail to play a part of the meanest and most despicable selfishness. . . . In your heart it seems you were always enslaved to the vilest superstitions.

A month later, the bailiffs have made him take a quite different tone. Harriet must raise money for him and Mary:

I depend wholly on you. . . . If once in prison, confined in a damp cell, without a sixpence, without a friend, . . . I must inevitably be starved to death. . . . My dear Harriet send quick supplies.[70]

At last the noble animal went to her death in the Serpentine, and Shelley married the Intellectual Beauty.

With all her limitations Godwin's daughter suited Shelley much better than most women could have done, but as a love-relationship the marriage fell short of the poet's ideal—and doubtless of Mary's. Shortly before his death, Shelley told John Gisborne that the only flaw in his happiness at Casa Magni was "the want of those who can feel, and understand me. Whether from proximity and the continuity of domestic intercourse, Mary does not." [71] This almost repeats his words to Peacock about Harriet, for the substitution of "feel and understand me" for "feel poetry and understand philosophy" is really no change at all. What was the trouble? Mary's jealousy of Claire suggests that her natural feelings were

---

[70] *Works*, VII, 296, 297, 300, 306–309. It is only fair to state that Shelley's principal creditor was Charters the coachmaker, from whom his wife had insisted on ordering an equipage. Such expenditures, however, would have been less disastrous if Shelley had not permitted Godwin to drain his purse. In any case gentlemen do not sponge on their wives after deserting them.

[71] Quoted by Newman I. White, *Shelley*, II, 362.

stronger than her Godwinian principles.[72] On the other hand perhaps Mary was frigid, or Shelley too frequently absent-minded. Perhaps, as Professor Grabo suggests, the cause is to be sought in "the deaths of her children and too constant a state of pregnancy."[73]

At all events Shelley blamed her for not being the veiled maiden of *Alastor*. Always the gentlest of men, he took it out on her, so far as we know, entirely through his poetry. *Epipsychidion* may be an extremely "holy" poem so far as Emilia Viviani is concerned; but could not the gentle Shelley have imaged Emilia as the Sun without so plainly stigmatizing Mary as "the cold chaste Moon" and alluding to her jealousy of Claire, the much more interesting Comet of the piece? At first he seems to want one cozy family including Sun, Moon, and Comet; but the concluding Aegean elopement is only for Emilia and Percy, blissfully far away from Mary's "chaste cold bed."[74] A little less obviously, but quite obviously enough for Mary and for most modern scholars, Shelley as the maniac in *Julian and Maddalo* addresses the woman for whom he had deserted Harriet:

> Didst thou not seek me for thine own content?
> Did not thy love awaken mine? . . .
>
> . . .
>
> That you had never seen me, never heard
> My voice, and more than all had ne'er endured
> The deep pollution of my loathed embrace—
> That your eyes ne'er had lied love in my face—
> That, like some maniac monk, I had torn out
> The nerves of manhood by their bleeding root
> With mine own quivering fingers, so that ne'er
> Our hearts had for a moment mingled there
> To disunite in horror.[75]

One of his hysterical moments, of course, but in anyone but the benevolent Shelley such conduct toward even the least congenial of faithful wives would be thought contemptible.

---

[72] As regards Claire and perhaps other women of the Italian period, we simply do not know to what extent Shelley's obvious unfaithfulness to Mary found physical as well as verbal expression. But are his devotees really doing him a favor when they assume that his philandering was purely "ideal"? He was a very peculiar man, but since he begot children on both of his wives it seems gratuitously uncharitable to suppose that he was no man at all.   [73] Carl Grabo, *The Magic Plant*, p. 416.   [74] *Works*, II, 364–368.   [75] *Ibid.*, III, 190–191.

Let us turn to other aspects of Shelley's life. A republican and a champion of the poor and oppressed, he had an unexpectedly large tincture of aristocratic pride. For his time he showed an unusually keen sense of the mass power of the proletariat. Toward individual lowly sufferers he could display all the tenderness of a Mackenzie hero—though it is curious how largely the instances of such conduct group themselves within the Marlow period. He was completely the eighteenth-century person of quality, however, in his distaste for the vulgarity of common folk. Not realizing that the fashion had begun to change, he rejected Christianity partly because he thought it was a mob-superstition which had been rejected by all cultivated gentlemen. He was a genuine romantic humanitarian, but such phrases as "meanest hind," "gross imaginations of the vulgar,"[76] and "the polluting multitude,"[77] come to his lips with disappointing frequency.

An adherent of Godwin's doctrine of absolute sincerity, Shelley was quixotically frank and truthful; but he did not hesitate to abandon this principle when he felt that a higher principle was at stake. Perhaps Mary would not have approved his desertion of Harriet had he not untruthfully assured her that his wife no longer loved him. The end justified the means. In responding to the Bill of Complaint in the Chancery case he falsely declared that after the birth of Ianthe he and Harriet had agreed to separate. To what extent he slandered Harriet's moral character is still a matter of dispute, but there seems to be no doubt that she had been entirely faithful to him and that he tried to suggest the contrary.

In *The Cenci,* Count Francesco appears as a pervertedly pious Catholic, and the priest Orsino as a lustful rogue. Shelley was entitled to tell the story in his own way, but since he gives a good deal of information about his source might he not have told us that the actual Count was a notorious atheist, and that despite his tonsure the actual Orsino helped Beatrice from thoroughly decent motives?[78] The author's failure to do so is on the same ethical plane as the conduct of his heroine in the last act, where rather than admit her guilt she permits her tool Marzio to be tortured to death. Her reason is that there is no guilt for her to confess: the righteous extermination of her monstrous father does not constitute parricide, the crime of which she is accused. The pure white light of truth is upheld by

---

[76] *Vide supra,* pp. 330, 340.   [77] *Works,* II, 59.
[78] *Ibid.,* p. 159. See also N. I. White, *Shelley,* II, 143.

a doctrinaire quibble while Marzio, keeping Beatrice's secret to the end, dies on the rack like an honest murderer.

And yet the sight of human suffering, the mere thought of it, was unbearable to Shelley. Rightly does he describe himself as "a nerve o'er which do creep/The else unfelt oppressions of the earth."[79] A humanitarian who can be so inhuman, a benevolist at times so utterly self-centered, presents a strange paradox. Crane Brinton points the way toward a solution:

Shelley hated Christianity and its priests, not so much because the Church was actually in alliance with Legitimacy and every kind of reaction, but because it held back the flow of human sensation and prevented that complete projection of self into all things which was to him happiness.[80]

His fundamental desire was for limitless self-expansion, but his natural kindliness and his intense nervous sensibility made it impossible for him even to dream of being free and happy in a world where other men were enslaved and miserable. Their freedom and happiness, however, must be *his* freedom and happiness, the reduplication of his personality, the redemptive exploit of his creative imagination. Benevolism hardened into selfishness when another mind checked his craving for boundlessness by failing to mirror his beautiful thoughts. He was extremely charitable, but since he lacked the ability to enter into thoughts and feelings which were different from his own he had little charity. Mrs. Campbell is probably right in saying that "his immense *faith in man* . . . seemed to spring in the first place from that sense of his own divinity with which all geniuses are endowed."[81] Love of mankind which arises from that source is inevitably love of self.

Examining his own heart, Shelley found nothing but pure goodness. It was with him as with Prince Athanase:

> Not his the load of any secret crime,
> For nought of ill his heart could understand
> But pity and wild sorrow for the same.[82]

Frequently he doubted his power to do all the good that he longed to do; but he blamed the blindness of other men, not himself, for this weakness. The sense of sin was foreign to his nature. "There is hardly any evidence,"

[79] *Ibid.*, III, 191.
[80] Crane Brinton, *The Political Ideas of the English Romanticists*, p. 166.
[81] *Vide supra*, p. 11.   [82] *Works*, III, 133.

Mr. Barnard writes, "that Shelley felt any inner discord, any doubt as to what he ought to do, any difficulty in doing what he believed to be right, any remorse at anything he had ever done." [83] This is a dreadful thing to say of a human being, but on the whole it is true. In expanding on this observation Barnard very nearly says that Shelley felt sinless because he *was* sinless. Less enthusiastically, Clutton-Brock remarks that Shelley "was born too good ever to become a saint. He had a facility in virtue like the facility of Raphael in art; and there were moral dangers in that facility." [84] So pellucid a conscience at least incurred the danger of smugness. "I am ardent in the cause of philanthropy and truth" [85]—the self-righteous tone of the first letter to Godwin is sounded again and again. It is easy to understand how Byron could regard Shelley as the best of men and yet refer to him in private as "Shiloh," the Messianic infant whom Joanna Southcott had promised to bring into the world.

Byron's mania for heightened self-portraiture is a classroom commonplace. Shelley's indulgence in the same habit is less frequently noted but almost equally obvious. He not only speaks with self-pity and self-approval in many lyrics but makes an idealized image of himself the hero of several narrative poems. Mary reports that "the subject he loved best to dwell on was the image of One warring with the Evil Principle, oppressed not only by it, but by all, even the good, who were deluded into considering evil a necessary portion of humanity." [86] His favorite subject is his own virtue and his own suffering; he himself is the central figure of his personal gospel. He is the poet in *Alastor;* he is Laon, Athanase, Lionel, Prometheus, and the Christ whom the light-bringer prefigures. And the Shelleyan hero is so pure, gentle, loving, brave, and selfless, so beautiful and swift and yet so pathetically weak and lonely in his martyrdom, so ineffably superior to the humanity which he aspires to redeem, that the palate becomes cloyed with nobility and we think of the narcissi in *The Sensitive Plant,*

> Who gaze on their eyes in the stream's recess,
> Till they die of their own dear loveliness.[87]

Shelley's lack of the sense of sin was not only a matter of temperament but a matter of principle. He refused to regard with fear or reverence

[83] Ellsworth Barnard, *Shelley's Religion*, p. 146.
[84] Arthur Clutton-Brock, *Shelley, the Man and the Poet*, p. 23.
[85] *Works*, VIII, 233.   [86] *Ibid.*, II, 269.   [87] *Ibid.*, p. 275.

any outward law which threatened to curb the outrush of his imagination. "I always go on until I am stopped, and I never am stopped." [88] His ideal was "love calm, steadfast, invincible/By mortal fear or supernatural awe" [89] and hence utterly opposed to the delusions of Christianity, which, as he told Trelawny, "are fatal to genius and originality; they limit thought." [90]

To say that it was difficult for Shelley to be humble would merely be to say that he was human; but failure to attain a virtue and deliberate rejection of that virtue are two quite different things. Like Blake, Shelley passionately spurned humility, obedience, repentance, any sort of control emanating from a source external to his own mind. In *Queen Mab* he asserts that "submissive abjectness" is chiefly to blame for the corruption of man's natural goodness.[91] Cythna tells the sailors who have rescued her not to repent of their past misdeeds, since remorse is a hatred of self which inevitably turns into hatred of others.[92] Flying about at night, the Witch of Atlas finds that the sleep of many mortals is needlessly troubled by

> Distortions foul of supernatural awe,
> And pale imaginings of visioned wrong,
> And all the code of custom's lawless law.[93]

In the *Ode to Liberty,* Shelley longs for the abolition of priestcraft so that

> ... human thoughts might kneel alone
> Each before the judgment-throne
> Of its own aweless soul, or of the Power unknown.[94]

That there is no real difference between these two deities may be inferred from *Prometheus Unbound,* where, beneath the Platonic trappings of the poem, the mind of man is liberated from its dark delusions solely by the mind of man. Professor Bush refuses to equate this cult of pride with Christianity:

Granted that Shelley, like Abou Ben Adhem, loved his neighbor, one looks in vain in a poet exempt from awe for any recognition of Christ's first and great

---

[88] E. J. Trelawny, *Recollections of the Last Days of Shelley and Byron,* II, 194.
[89] *Works,* III, 136.   [90] Trelawny, *op. cit.,* II, 190.   [91] *Works,* I, 88.
[92] *Ibid.,* pp. 361–362.   [93] *Ibid.,* IV, 33.   [94] *Ibid.,* II, 312.

commandment. The God of Christianity, a primitive projection of man's mind, Prometheus destroys when he learns the lesson of love, and the new God of evolving humanity is humanity itself; this is not quite equivalent to "the kingdom of God is within you." Shelley does certainly glorify a Spirit of Good, but there is a difference between being the father and being the child of one's deity.[95]

According to his own lights Shelley was very nearly perfect. According to more generally accepted standards he was less impeccable, but much better than many men who call themselves Christians. He does not, however, very strongly remind me of Jesus Christ.

4

If we may now assume that Shelley was not a Christian and not a fulfilment of the promise of the Second Coming we shall be free to devote our undivided attention to the positive aspects of his religion. The impossibility of studying the subject exhaustively in so brief an essay need not be lamented, since so much first-rate scholarly work has been devoted to it by others. But although students have reached something like a consensus of opinion as to the bare facts they often differ so widely in their interpretation of those facts that a modest contribution to the critical Babel may not be superfluous. Let us consider Shelley's religion as an attempt to satisfy his desire for unlimited self-expansion in the face of obstacles presented by social institutions, by individual human beings, and by his own personality. That other obstacles were imbedded in the very fibres of the universe he sometimes dimly felt but never fully acknowledged.

Although his thought changed with the passing years, too sharp a contrast between an "early" and a "mature" Shelley does injustice to the fact that the former clearly predicts the latter while the latter retains much of the former. His mind never threw away anything that it had gathered, though it might transmute the material almost beyond recognition. The young Jacobin rationalist is already a romantic; the "mystic" of the Italian period remains a *philosophe*.

Did Shelley's aggressiveness arise from authentic feelings of power or from an impulse to compensate for feelings of inferiority? His assertions of strength so often invert themselves into admissions of weakness that

[95] D. N. Bush, *Mythology and the Romantic Tradition in English Poetry*, p. 158.

the latter interpretation is tempting, but more expert psychiatrists must decide the question. At all events the earliest days at Field Place were favorable to his self-will. The first serious obstacles were the bullies of Syon House and Eton. One solution was to dramatize himself as the hero of a novel of terror, or, a bit later, a novel of sensibility. In maturer years his literary taste improved but the habit remained. Another solution lay in the sense of power to be derived from regarding science as magic and magic as science. From the fearsome explosions and smells of his school and college days grew the scientific imagery of *Prometheus Unbound* and other poems of his best period. Since he never became either truly scientific or truly Platonic it is hard to believe that he finally attained a philosophic synthesis of natural science and Platonic idealism, but for an impressive defense of that position the reader should consult the various contributions of Carl Grabo.[96]

The tyranny of Eton was more systematic and institutionalized than that of Syon House. With the help of Dr. Lind and *Political Justice* Shelley added scope and dignity to his personal situation by viewing the schoolboy world as a microcosm. The voices of his tormentors

> Were but one echo from a world of woes—
> The harsh and grating strife of tyrants and of foes.[97]

Not merely at Eton was man's natural goodness thwarted by oppressive institutions. Very soon it was clear to him that organized religion was the direst of these enemies of the free spirit. French philosophism in general and Godwinism in particular seemed to provide the sharpest, brightest, most uncompromisingly defiant weapons for the struggle to which he now dedicated himself. Hence throughout the early period which ends with the publication of *Queen Mab* he is primarily an adherent of the then somewhat old-fashioned creed of Jacobin rationalism.

From the very beginning, however, the process of transmutation is at work. Godwinism for Shelley, even more than for Wordsworth, expressed romance rather than anti-romance. In anything like its orthodox form, however, it could not satisfy Shelley's deepest desires. When with

---

[96] See also A. N. Whitehead, *Science and the Modern World*, pp. 123–126, where Shelley figures as an outstanding example of this philosopher's opinion that the romantic poets were harbingers of the present-day "organic" conception of science. In science and philosophy Whitehead is a most formidable authority; as a student of the romantic he is perhaps less impregnable.　　　[97] *Works*, I, 251.

its aid the fortress of superstition had been stormed, the fruits of victory tasted flat and dry. That bright sword of reason was double-edged: it might pierce one's own illusions as sharply as those of the enemy. Hogg reports of his Oxford comrade:

One thing at least is certain, the denial of the existence of gods, and devils, and spirits, if it was to be found in him at all, was only to be found in his words and arguments; practically, his turn of mind was toward superstition, and by no means toward irreligion and materialism.[98]

And Medwin, speaking of the effect of Shelley's expulsion from Oxford, says:

He now, rankling with the sense of wrong, and hardened by persecution . . . applied himself more closely than ever to that Sceptical philosophy, which he had begun to discard for Plato, and would, but for his expulsion, have soon entirely abandoned.[99]

These authorities are not impeccable, but on this point they are substantiated by the letters of 1811–1813. This devotee of calm, disinterested, uncompromising reason can write to Elizabeth Hitchener:

Certainly *reason* can never account for, or prove, the truth of feeling. I have considered it in every possible light; and reason tells me that death is the boundary of the life of man, yet I feel, I believe the direct contrary.

His next sentence manages both to affirm and to deny the conception of reason advanced in *The Necessity of Atheism:* "The senses are the only inlets of knowledge, and there is an inward sense that has convinced me of this."[100] A few days later he expresses his natural transcendentalism as boldly as at any time in his subsequent career: "I have long been convinced of the eventual omnipotence of mind over matter."[101] Soon he tells Elizabeth that as regards the central problem of religion he clings to reason merely because he lacks the higher certitude of emotional conviction:

But it does not prove the non-existence of a thing that it is not discoverable by reason. . . . Those who *really feel* the being of a God have the best right to

[98] T. J. Hogg, *Life of Shelley*, I, 93. [99] Thomas Medwin, *Life of Shelley*, p. 91.
[100] *Works*, VIII, 158. [101] *Ibid.*, p. 160.

believe it. They may indeed pity those who do not; they may pity me, but *until* I feel it I must be content with the substitute, reason.[102]

To set feeling and reason at loggerheads, however, is less satisfying than to redefine reason in such a way as to make it authenticate the demands of feeling. Shelley has reached this characteristically romantic position by February, 1813, when he writes Hogg: "Now do not tell me that Reason is a cold and insensible arbiter. Reason is only an assemblage of our better feelings—passion considered under a peculiar mode of its operation." [103] Hogg is not told what this mode of operation may be, but probably the doctrine of creative imagination—Wordsworth's "reason in her most exalted mood"—is in the offing. The inward sense (one thinks of Coleridge), mind over matter, the truth of feeling, reason as creative passion—here, beneath the veneer of Godwinism, is the truly Shelleyan way of achieving boundlessness.

This kind of reason will provide a God into which the human spirit may pour itself with enhancement rather than diminution of liberty. The "soul of the universe" frequently appears in letters of 1811. "Some vast intellect animates infinity." [104] It is "as the soul of man to his body, as the vegetative power to vegetables, as the stony power to stones." [105] Shelley believes in a deistic First Cause, but he wants much more than that: "Oh, that this deity were the soul of the universe, the spirit of universal, imperishable love! Indeed I believe it is." [106] When he wrote these words to Hogg on January 12, 1811, he had found the only God he would ever acknowledge. There would be increasingly subtle and beautiful rationalization, but no fundamental change.

The background of his "world soul" pantheism was mainly Platonic or Neoplatonic. Although Shelley made no close study of Plato in the original before the Italian period, at Oxford he had read several dialogues in Dacier's French translation and in the English version of Thomas Taylor and Floyer Sydenham. He may also have come upon Taylor's *Concerning the Beautiful, or a paraphrased translation from the Greek of Plotinus* (1787) or his translation of *Five Books of Plotinus* (1794). Even in his translations from Plato, however, Taylor's commentaries were much more Neoplatonic than Platonic. Perhaps Taylor's influence is partly responsible for the fact that Shelley always tended to see Plato through a

[102] *Ibid.*, p. 170.   [103] *Ibid.*, IX, 45.   [104] *Ibid.*, VIII, 33.
[105] *Ibid.*, p. 102; see also pp. 201, 213, 227.   [106] *Ibid.*, p. 44.

Plotinian haze, but in any case he was *anima naturaliter Neoplatonica*. In preparing to write *Queen Mab*, however, Shelley seems to have been more deeply impressed by Spinoza's restatement of the ancient view of nature as the life of a divine intellect. Excitingly associated with unbelief and yet deeply believing, severely rationalistic and yet satisfying to the emotions, Spinoza was a bridge over which Shelley could pass from Holbach to Plotinus.

In *Queen Mab* he is only halfway across the bridge. But if the notes usually point backward, the text more frequently points forward, transforming Godwinism into a philosophy more idealistic and transcendental than that of *Political Justice*. In some passages, to be sure, nature is the Newtonian universe seen through French spectacles—a completely soulless machine. In later years Shelley's emphasis on cosmic unity may, as Brett believes, have been encouraged not only by Plato and Spinoza but by Berkeley's interpretation of Newton's theory of light "to support the view that all individual forms *may* be contained in the Primal Unity, the apparent plurality of life being a kind of refractive separation." [107] The Newton of *Queen Mab*, however, seems to be all on the side of "atheism" [108] except in one respect: the universe of "circling systems" is "a wilderness of harmony";[109] it has the goodness which the human mind inevitably associates with order and shapeliness. Here, as so often in the eighteenth century, the currents flowing from Newton and from Shaftesbury converge. But the paradoxical phrase "*wilderness* of harmony" suggests that order must not be allowed to curb the sallies of spontaneity. At times the mechanistic theory is inconsistently warmed and softened by a more or less Rousseauistic conception of "simple" nature. The vegetarian fad adds a thin coating of pseudo-science to this sentimental primitivism.[110]

These Arcadian hankerings, however, do not prevent Shelley from affirming the doctrine of necessity in its most uncompromising form:

Every human being is irresistibly impelled to act precisely as he does act: in the eternity which preceded his birth a chain of causes was generated, which, operating under the name of motives, make it impossible that any thought of his mind, or any action of his life, should be otherwise than it is.[111]

[107] G. S. Brett, "Shelley's Relation to Berkeley and Drummond," *Studies in English by Members of University College*, Toronto, p. 184. Does not this article make Shelley a little too much the professor of philosophy?

[108] *Vide supra*, p. 332.   [109] *Works*, I, 77.   [110] *Ibid.*, pp. 157–165.

[111] *Ibid.*, p. 144; see also pp. 110–111 for the passage which Shelley's note illustrates.

But in *Queen Mab* necessity is more than an abstract idea: it is identical
with the all-pervasive animating "Spirit of Nature." [112] This Spirit constitutes the reality underlying all phenomena:

> Throughout this varied and eternal world
> Soul is the only element, the block
> That for uncounted ages has remained.
> The moveless pillar of a mountain's weight
> Is active, living spirit.[113]

Thanks to this device Shelley will henceforth be free to use scientific
language and imagery without subjecting himself to the bondage of
mechanism. When matter grows oppressive he can turn it into spirit,
or when spirit seems too abstract for imaginative treatment he can turn it
into matter. In *Prometheus Unbound,* love can be electricity or electricity
can be love; the difference is merely verbal.

Godwinian perfectibility also suffers a sea-change into something much
richer and stranger. According to *Queen Mab,* it is to be attained not
through progressive improvement of man's reasoning powers but through
return to nature in a great regenerative awakening of love:

> How sweet a scene will earth become!
> Of purest spirits, a pure dwelling-place,
> When man, with changeless nature coalescing
> Will undertake regeneration's work.[114]

Here is foretokened the union of Prometheus and Asia.

But under even so spiritualized a necessity man's voluntary desertion of
nature and his voluntary return to it are alike inconceivable. Shelley comes
very close to describing the Spirit of Nature as a Spirit of Universal Love,
but he is not fully prepared for so bold a departure from authorities who
are valuable allies in his assaults upon oppressive institutions. The most
eloquently necessitarian passage in *Queen Mab* hails the Spirit of Nature
as completely indifferent to human ideas of good and evil:

> No love, no hate thou cherishest; revenge
> And favouritism, and worst desire of fame
> Thou know'st not; all that the wide world contains
> Are but thy passive instruments, and thou

[112] *Ibid.,* pp. 75, 111.   [113] *Ibid.,* p. 94.   [114] *Ibid.,* p. 106.

Regard'st them all with an impartial eye,
Whose joy or pain thy nature cannot feel,
Because thou hast not human sense,
Because thou art not human mind.[115]

Superior to "the God of human error" as this Spinozan deity may be, it plainly takes no interest in the regeneration of society or in the demands of Shelley's ego. Necessity will remain a restrictive rather than an expansive force unless Shelley can place it under the sway of a cosmic Love which is by no means alien to "human mind." Thus although *Queen Mab* shows where Shelley is going it also shows that he has much further to go.

Without attempting to trace the development of his thought from poem to poem, we pass on to the religion of the "mature" Shelley. His God is the One—the all-pervasive but nonetheless transcendent Spirit which comprises all values and interfuses them in a divine cosmic wholeness. Since spirit or mind is the only reality, this Divine Mind is the sum-total of everything real in man and in what man mistakenly calls "external" nature, but it can most fittingly be described in terms of Creative Intellect, Freedom, Beauty, and Love. The last is its highest and most inclusive attribute. The real and eternal world is simply the thought of the Divine Mind, perfectly wise, free, beautiful, beneficent, loving. Love, then, is the law of the universe. Love is Necessity, and Necessity is Love.

This God is not *personal* in the usual sense of that term, but it is sometimes *personified* when Shelley attempts to be metaphysically abstract and poetically concrete at the same time.[116] But although Universal Mind is not a person, it includes the attributes of a perfect human personality —those of the Shelleyan hero, in fact. The relations between Divine Mind and human mind are curiously circular. On the one hand, every human mind must be included within the divine totality of Spirit. On the other hand Shelley, despite inevitable inconsistencies, has become a subjective idealist. Hence although man is within God, God is equally within man. It is hard to say where human mind ends and Divine Mind begins. Which

---

[115] *Ibid.*, p. 110.

[116] I hope this is not too casual a dismissal of Ellsworth Barnard's contention that Shelley believed in a personal God. (*Shelley's Religion,* pp. 62, 66, 79, 88–95.) Barnard also asserts that Shelley's Spirit of Good is limited by "some inscrutable principle" (pp. 55, 73, 79). This in my opinion is not so much a part of his religion as a fear that sometimes shadowed his faith. It is not what he *wants* to believe. The point will receive some attention in the last section of this chapter.

is the Creator, and which the creature? This difficulty must be reverted to after other aspects of Shelley's religion have been considered.

We have been speaking of what Blake calls "Eternity," the true world which is shaped by the Divine Mind of poetic imagination. Most men, however, are content to live in a world of false appearances which they perversely identify with reality. This phenomenal world is not real at all. Its relation to reality is that of shadow to substance, of the refracted image to the object, of fain memory to direct contemplation, of error to truth, of the imperfect Many to the perfect One. When hard pressed by experience, Shelley can fall back on this Platonic method of explaining the immense difference between what apparently is and what ought to be. But the sharpness of the distinction between phenomenal and nou-menal varies with Shelley's mood. Those critics who see him as a complete optimist and those who credit him with a realistic sense of life's difficulties and imperfections are both perfectly right, but they are not thinking about the same passages. As Professor White observes, Shelley displays "what modern psychologists would undoubtedly call a manic-depressive psychology." [117] His mind oscillates between poles of excessive rapture and excessive despair. The despairing Shelley accepts a more or less orthodox Platonic conception of the chasm which separates appear-ance from reality; the rapturous Shelley ignores the chasm and combines the two realms of being in a romantic interfusion. We must distinguish between his total religious experience, in which crests of belief alternate with troughs of doubt, and his declared faith, which is all-confident gladness. At the moment we are considering what he wanted to believe; the collapse of his faith is a different matter.

In its context,

> Life, like a dome of many-coloured glass,
> Stains the white radiance of eternity[118]

expresses a bondage from which death provides the only means of es-cape. But in relation to Shelley's general system there is much to be said for the many-coloured glass. Without it, how in this life could we know aught of the white radiance? The imperfect but delightful beauty of the refraction bears witness to the perfect Beauty of the refracted ideal. Thus the shadow-beauty of women and, when women inevitably disappoint,

[117] N. I. White, *Shelley*, II, 371.   [118] *Works*, II, 404.

the shadow-beauty of nature are so precious as reflections of the Eternal that it is impossible not to think of them as precious in themselves—as real because they raise our minds to reality. They may also be thought of Neoplatonically, not as rungs of a ladder reaching up but as agents of the Spirit of Love reaching down in beneficent revelation. The Platonic Socrates and the Platonic Jesus, all great poets, electrical energy, Emilia Viviani, Mont Blanc, the whole "beloved brotherhood" of west wind and skylark and cloud, are thus mediators of the divine reality to man. Their message, if only mankind would heed it, is that our life is itself, here and now, the eternal world of love and beauty and delight. No chasm, but only the thinnest pearly film of mist on a summer morning, separates us from the full sunlight of Intellectual Beauty.

This is Shelley's faith—"How sweet! did any heart now share in my emotion." [119] But no one else will accept the vision, and so long as he must think of himself as "the companionless sensitive plant" the desire for infinite expansion of his goodness in a good universe is thwarted. To this lonely dreamer the phenomenal and the noumenal seem not interfused but widely sundered. All other men are living in a world of appearances which, deprived of the eternal radiance by their own blindness, is a realm of darkness and error.

In a sense, then, man is a fallen being. How could such a tragedy have occurred in a world where Necessity and Love are identical? The fact that Shelley no longer, as in *Queen Mab,* lays the blame upon external institutions but upon imperfections existing within the mind of man is regarded by most authorities as a prime example of his increasing intellectual maturity. Our admiration of his progress in this respect is tempered, though not destroyed, when we remember that the change was the inevitable consequence of his subjective idealism. Evil *must* exist within the mind of man, for there is no other conceivable location for it to occupy. To be forced into so repugnant a conclusion was more a disaster than a triumph. How did the mind of man, which in the real and eternal world is governed by a necessity of pure love, generate these monstrous illusions of hatred, vice, cruelty, oppression? Even Demogorgon can give no answer—"a voice/Is wanting, the deep truth is imageless." "Eternal Love" is supreme, but man has chosen to live beneath the sway of "Fate, Time, Occasion, Chance, and Change." [120] Relying upon his senses rather than upon his higher intuitive powers, he has placed his neck beneath

[119] *Ibid.,* III, 206.   [120] *Ibid.,* II, 221.

the yoke of a lower necessity of soulless mechanism. And out of his own fear and hatred he has created Jupiter, the false god who enslaves only the self-enslaved.

However paradise has been lost, that it can and must be regained is an essential part of Shelley's creed. One way of regaining paradise is to pass from the phenomenal into the noumenal through the gates of death— "Die,/If thou wouldst be with that which thou dost seek." [121] But why *Adonais* should be regarded as a triumphant assertion of Shelley's religion[122] is hard to understand. This falling back upon an immortality in which he never had any genuine belief represents an abandonment of his highest hope. What he had always wanted was a life on this side of the grave in which the apparent would be redeemed by the ideal while the ideal took on the warmth and color of the apparent—Novalis's "Die Welt wird Traum, der Traum wird Welt." And this interfusion-experience would always be marred by some taint of restriction unless all men shared it with him. Prometheus does not fade away all by himself into a pseudo-Platonic heaven, leaving his fellow-men to "decay/Like corpses in a charnel": in this very world he unites himself with nature through the almighty power of Love, and he imparts that power to others.

Sometimes the Spirit of the Universe is personified and invoked as a deity who might, as in the *Hymn to Intellectual Beauty*, "Free/This world from its dark slavery." [123] Similarly in *Ode to Naples*, "the Great Spirit, deepest Love" is asked to intervene on behalf of the Neapolitan revolutionists.[124] But this is a rhetorical device: the divine energy required for the answer to such a prayer can originate only within the mind of man. He himself must make the Love which is to redeem him.

Like an atrophied muscle, the mind may be restored to Love by exercise in loving acts; that is, by admiration of increasingly generalized higher degrees of beauty in nature, art, and woman, ascending through the Many to the One until at last the loving soul of man and the loving Soul of the Universe are reunited. As Diotima said to Socrates, if the love of phenomenal beauty is so delightful,

what must be the life of him who dwells with and gazes on that which it becomes us all to seek. Think you not that to him alone is accorded the prerogative of bringing forth, not images and shadows of virtue, for he is in contact

[121] *Ibid.*, p. 404.
[122] For an expression of this view see B. P. Kurtz, *The Pursuit of Death*, pp. 266ff.
[123] *Works*, II, 61.   [124] *Ibid.*, IV, 55–56.

not with a shadow, but with reality; with virtue itself, in the production and
nourishment of which he becomes dear to the Gods; and if such a privilege
is conceded to any human being, himself immortal.[125]

Aspiring toward such an apotheosis, Shelley devotes several of his poems
to the cult of Platonic love.

But individual contemplation of the Spirit of Love is not enough. The
vision must be promulgated, shared, brought down into the phenomenal
world and made a redemptive force in nature and in society. This can be
accomplished only when humanity lays hold upon its rightful divinity
by a great assertion of the will to believe that Love is the law of the
world. "It is our will," cries Julian to Maddalo,

> ... that thus enchains us to permitted ill—
> We might be otherwise—we might be all
> We dream of happy, high, majestical.
> Where is the love, beauty and truth we seek
> But in our mind? and if we were not weak
> Should we be less in deed than in desire? [126]

In *Prometheus Unbound* there is no Byron to retort:

> Ay, if we were not weak, and we aspire
> How vainly to be strong!

This greatest of Shelley's poems is also the climactic expression of his
belief

that mankind had only to will that there should be no evil, and there would
be none. . . . That man could be so perfectionized as to be able to expel evil
from his own nature, and from the greater part of the creation, was the cardinal
point of his system.[127]

These famous words of Mrs. Shelley's were not intended to give the impression that Jupiter is destroyed by a facile outgush of sentimental benevolism. The word "only" is rather misleading, but it is balanced by
"could be so perfectionized." It is not easy for Prometheus to revoke his
curse and thus purge his mind of everything but love. The power to do

---

[125] Plato's *Symposium* in Shelley's translation, *Works*, VII, 207.
[126] *Works*, III, 183.   [127] *Ibid.*, II. 269.

so is the slowly matured fruit of struggle and suffering. Only a mind self-disciplined in "gentleness, virtue, wisdom, and endurance" is entitled to destroy evil by denying its existence.

This perfectionizing of man, however, is achieved entirely by man himself. The supremacy of Eternal Love is recognized, but merely as the total energy of human love, not as a superhuman power which man invokes in his insufficiency. The Platonic ideals are not above man, but within him. It is "human love . . . /Which makes all it gazes on Paradise." Even Jupiter acknowledges that Prometheus, "gentle, and just, and dreadless," is "the monarch of the world." In the final liberation man is revealed as a being "Whose nature is its own divine control,"

> Equal, unclassed, tribeless and nationless,
> Exempt from awe, worship, degree, the King
> Over himself.[128]

Here are Blake's "Thine own humanity learn to adore" and Coleridge's "religion of I AM." Man, in short, is God. With this inversion of Platonism into naturalism the religion of human self-assertion once more emerges from one of its familiar disguises.

Prometheus is not *a* man, but a symbol of Man in general. The Titan's victory therefore implies the regeneration of all mankind through one collective affirmation of the law of love. In actual life the process would be immeasurably slower, since Jupiter could not be loved out of existence until every man in the world had perfected his own mind. But although the millennium must arrive gradually, its coming could be hastened by poetry. The mature Shelley was no less a propagandist than the lad who wrote *The Necessity of Atheism,* but he had come to feel that he should work upon society not like a pamphleteer in verse or prose, but

> Like a poet hidden
> In the light of thought,
> Singing hymns unbidden,
> Till the world is wrought
> To sympathy with hopes and fears it heeded not.[129]

---

[128] *Ibid.,* pp. 247, 229, 256.
[129] *Ibid.,* p. 305. *The Mask of Anarchy, Swellfoot the Tyrant,* and several other poems of the Italian period show that Shelley's interest in current affairs did not always permit him to be true to this principle. In general, however, he moved from the propaganda of rhetoric to the propaganda of beauty.

Consequently the *Defense of Poetry* is a precious document for the interpretation of Shelley's religion.

In a way which reminds us of Coleridge, Shelley opens the *Defense* by distinguishing between restrictive and expansive types of intellectual activity and elevating the latter above the former. The lower faculty is reason; the higher, imagination. Reason is logical and analytical; it concerns itself with the relationships of particulars without imposing unity upon them. Imagination is creative and synthetic. It "has for its objects those forms which are common to universal nature and to existence itself." Reason is quantitative; Imagination, qualitative. In Platonic terms we might say that Reason is phenomenal and Imagination is noumenal. "Reason is to imagination as the instrument to the agent, as the body to the spirit, as the shadow to the substance." [130]

"Poetry, in a general sense, may be defined as 'the expression of the imagination,'" and "A poem is the image of life expressed in its eternal truth." To write poetry is therefore to convey eternal truth to mankind. "A poet participates in the eternal, the infinite, and the one." He is a teacher, and even a prophet in the sense that he reveals to mankind the spiritual reality which underlies "that partial apprehension of the agencies of the invisible world which is called religion." [131] Since "All things exist as they are perceived, at least in relation to the percipient," the love, beauty, and truth which the poet perceives so vividly constitute *his* reality. In reading his poems, we share his experience and make it *our* reality. When this benign contagion spreads until love, beauty, and truth become *everyone's* reality, there will be no room for Jupiter in the perfected mind of man. In this way "poetry defeats the curse which binds us to be subjected to the accident of surrounding impressions." [132]

Releasing us from the bondage of the senses, poetry sets free all our higher spiritual faculties. Since imagination is the perception of eternal truth it is "the great instrument of moral good, . . . and poetry administers to the effect by acting upon the cause"—that is, by stimulating the imagination of the reader.[133] In poetry, then, lies the hope of a better revolution than one of hatred and bloodshed:

The most unfailing herald, companion, and follower of the awakening of a great people to work a beneficial change in opinion or institution, is Poetry. . . . Poets are the hierophants of an unapprehended inspiration; the mirrors

---

[130] *Ibid.,* VII, 109.   [131] *Ibid.,* pp. 109, 115, 112.
[132] *Ibid.,* p. 137.   [133] *Ibid.,* p. 118.

of the gigantic shadows which futurity casts upon the present; the words which express what they understand not; the trumpets which sing to battle, and feel not what they inspire; the influence which is moved not, but moves. Poets are the unacknowledged legislators of the world.[134]

Fundamentally, then, Shelley's religion seems to be an assertion of the poet's power to create real and eternal truth. But when we reread the famous peroration we are struck by phrases which imply that the poet is merely the involuntary agent of a higher power. As Shelley says earlier in the essay, "Poetry is not like reasoning, a power to be exerted according to the determination of the will, . . . and the conscious portions of our natures are unprophetic either of its approach or of its departure." [135] In reading the *Ion* he has not perceived that Socrates is fooling the pompous rhapsode to the top of his bent when he concludes:

The God seems purposely to have deprived all poets, prophets, and soothsayers of every particle of reason and understanding, the better to adapt them to their employment as his ministers and interpreters; and that we, their auditors, may acknowledge that those who write so beautifully, are possessed, and address us, inspired by the God.[136]

More is here involved, however, than the fact that Shelley was utterly humorless on serious topics. Does not his view of imagination as controlled by some force external to the poet's consciousness imperil the main thesis of this study and support Barnard's contention that the very core of Shelley's religion was selflessness? [137] Uncomfortably pertinent also is Guérard's remark that this essay "is the classic defense of automatic writing. . . . For Shelley as for Blake, the poet was a passive medium through whom the divine afflatus worked." [138]

The apt comparison between Shelley and Blake reminds us that in an earlier chapter Blake's "casting off of selfhood" was interpreted to mean the casting off of everything that hinders the limitless expansion of self.[139] The same line of argument may be applied to Shelley. Before Prometheus revokes his curse against Jupiter, the Titan's selfhood might be described

[134] *Ibid.*, p. 140.   [135] *Ibid.*, p. 135.

[136] Plato's *Ion* in Shelley's translation, *Works*, VII, 239.

[137] Ellsworth Barnard, *Shelley's Religion*, pp. 197, 221, 266.

[138] Albert Guérard, jr., "Prometheus and the Aeolian Lyre," *Yale Review*, XXXIII, 492. S. F. Gingerich goes so far as to assert that Shelley had no sense of personality or voluntary will, and that the *Defense* is not transcendental but necessitarian. (*Essays in the Romantic Poets*, pp. 223–225, 232–233.)   [139] *Vide supra*, pp. 121, 124.

as the lower, unredeemed selfhood of the phenomenal world. His infinitude is compressed into a hard, tight, constricted mass of suffering
vengefulness by the oppressions which his own mind has conceived. This
selfhood must indeed be cast off, but only in favor of a higher selfhood of
boundless freedom and imaginative energy. To describe such a release
from bondage as a heavenly gift rather than as a personal exploit is
psychologically quite natural. It is a cheap price to pay for so shining a
reward, and it even enhances the dignity of the experience. A poet's claim
to divine inspiration is not usually a proof of his humility.

Commenting on Shelley's conception of immortality, Mr. Barnard
writes:

> The Spirit in which the soul continues to exist after death is not conceived by
> Shelley as a mechanical and blindly working impersonal force, but as an in-
> telligent, benevolent, and purposive Power, including in its nature all that
> man calls good; so that complete union with it would involve not the extinc-
> tion of being but the immeasurable expansion of it. . . . Man's immortality
> must come from union with something greater than himself; and this union
> involves not the extinction of his true self but its complete and perfect realiza-
> tion.[140]

Most of this I accept with pleasure, for since it applies to man's union
with the Spirit of Love in this world as well as in the next it seems to
support my view of Shelley's self-annihilation rather than Barnard's. I
question, however, whether "union with something greater than himself"
can be applied to Shelley without qualification. No more than any other
romantic poet did he consciously set out to deify his genius. Like his contemporaries he wanted to believe in some sort of cosmic imaginative
energy that would say "Yes" to the outgoings of his imagination. This
need would increase as he came more and more to think of himself as
"A Power/Girt round with weakness." [141] Why not a weakness girt round
with Power? If we watch closely, however, we can see the religious aspiration of the romantic poets moving reverently outward toward suprapersonal divinity but circling back in triumph to their own creative spirit.
This circularity is especially obvious in Shelley because his subjective
idealism made it technically impossible for him to conceive of any truth
beyond the walls of his mind.

---

[140] Ellsworth Barnard, *Shelley's Religion*, pp. 217–218.
[141] *Works*, II, 398.

Love is the law of the real and eternal world, and even in this mortal life Shelley would rise toward union with this Power by loving its least imperfect human reflections. But in the essay *On Love* the subject is defined as

that powerful attraction towards all that we conceive, or fear, or hope beyond ourselves, when we find within our own thoughts the chasm of an insufficient void, and seek to awaken in all things that are, a community with what we experience within ourselves. If we reason, we would be understood; if we imagine, we would that the airy children of our brain were born anew within another's; if we feel, we would that another's nerves should vibrate to our own, that the beams of their eyes should kindle at once and mix and melt into our own, that lips of motionless ice should not reply to lips quivering and burning with the heart's best blood. This is Love. This is the bond and the sanction which connects not only man with men, but with every thing which exists. We are born into the world, and there is something within us which, from the instant that we live, more and more thirsts after its likeness.[142]

Love, then, is the insatiable craving to enrich and expand emotional experience by discovering our likeness in individual men and women, in society, in nature, in "every thing which exists." This is hardly the sort of ladder for Shelley to use in ascending toward "union with something greater than himself." He believes in the divine Spirit of Love as a man standing before a magnifying shaving-glass believes in his own enlarged reflection.

5

To say that Shelley was an extremely unorthodox Platonist and not even a very orthodox Neoplatonist is not to condemn his religion. Considered on its own merits, it has been admired by many critics. Mr. Barnard devotes an entire book to the thesis that Shelley's beliefs are not only historically interesting but permanently valuable. According to F. C. Prescott, the poet "gives us what amounts to a new and independent revelation of religious truth. . . . Shelley's religion was the product of a fresh im-

---

[142] *Ibid.*, VI, 201, but the entire essay is pertinent to our inquiry. The date of composition is unknown. It was first published in *The Keepsake* in 1829, and no manuscript exists. I cannot believe that an essay so characteristic of the thought and feeling of the Italian period was written before 1818 at the very earliest. "Lips of motionless ice" seems to refer to the estrangement from Mary in language similar to that of passages in *Julian and Maddalo* and *Epipsychidion*.

aginative apprehension of man's relation to the world of spirit." [143] "He annunciated," says Alfred Noyes, "the most vital belief in God that had been held by any of the masters of our literature, with the sole exception, perhaps, of Milton." [144] It is fruitless to argue about such matters, but one may observe the paradox that Shelley found his religion considerably less satisfying than do some of his interpreters. It has often been noted that his longer, more formal works, despite some important exceptions, are predominantly optimistic, while the lyrics are usually in a minor key. Let us regard the gap between his philosophy and his personal moods with the least possible cynicism. Considering the sadness of his life it is quite natural that the feeling of the moment should often be expressed in a cry of pain, but that on thinking more deeply and largely he should find courage to reassert the faith which looks beyond the transitory to the eternal. Shelley's purpose, however, was not merely to work out a system but to transform the life of men, his own life very emphatically included. If he had truly been lifted up by his faith, would not his responses to daily circumstances have been more brightly colored by the joy of it? Shelley's melancholy, to be sure, was not a constant pall of gloom. To his friends he was usually able to show a cheerful face. His temperament was always up-and-down; we must recognize the heights as well as the depths.

> Many a green isle needs must be
> In the deep wide sea of misery,[145]

and to the end he took delight in them. But he owed his joyous moments less to the mystic's contemplation of the white radiance of eternity than to the poet's ability to enjoy bright fragments of the many-coloured glass. What really enabled him to forget his unhappiness was not Platonic ideas but boats and pretty women with good voices. Yet although such pleasures never lost their power to transport him, the general curve of his deeper feelings throughout the last three or four years of his life tended downward. The waves still rise in crests, but the troughs grow deeper. Much of Shelley's hardest thinking went into his short unhappy lyrics. Frequently they express not merely a momentary sadness but a deliberate questioning of his faith. Sometimes, perhaps, they are brief and fragmentary because he could not bear a longer confrontation of their bitter

[143] *Poetry and Myth*, p. 185. So far as the independence and novelty of Shelley's beliefs are concerned this is demonstrably erroneous.

[144] Quoted by Barnard, *op. cit.*, p. 81*n*.   [145] *Works*, II, 49.

truth. And toward the end the despair of the short lyrics begins to suffuse the longer poems, as if life were breaking down the walls of the system.

Shelley had committed himself to the redemption of society through poetry, "the expression of the imagination," which in turn is described as the faculty that "has for its objects those forms which are common to universal nature and to existence itself." [146] This sounds almost like a paraphrase of Imlac's dictum concerning the streaks of the tulip. It would be difficult to frame a definition of imagination more hostile to the writing of poetry. Shelley was too good a poet to follow his own theory very closely, but the conflict between precept and practice forces him to make a stultifying distinction between what a poet actually writes and his original inspiration:

Could this influence [that of inspiration] be durable in its original purity and force, it is impossible to predict the greatness of the results; but when composition begins inspiration is already on the decline, and the most glorious poetry that has ever been committed to the world is probably a feeble shadow of the original conception of the poet.[147]

But if *true* poetry never gets itself written, what becomes of poetry as the vehicle of eternal truth, and what becomes of the poet as the redeemer of mankind? Perhaps rather too much has been made of the abstractness of Shelley's mind. "Abstract" and "vague" are anything but exact synonyms. He loved large vague ideas because he dreaded the control exerted by precisely formulated conceptions. Nevertheless, being a considerable artist, he could never spurn his images as whole-heartedly as his system demanded. Sometimes his Platonism gave his images the insubstantiality of fabricated symbols, but quite as often his aesthetic naturalism drew his Platonism down to earth with results favorable to his poetry though damaging to his philosophy. In *The Zucca* (1822) he addresses the nameless, intangible object of his love:

> In winds, and trees, and streams, and all things common,
>   In music, and the sweet unconscious tone
> Of animals, and voices which are human,
>   Meant to express some feelings of their own;
> In the soft motions and rare smile of woman,
>   In flowers and leaves, and in the grass fresh shown,

[146] *Vide supra*, p. 363.
[147] *Works*, VII, 135.

Or dying in the autumn, I the most
Adore thee present or lament thee lost.[148]

Thus in Shelley's actual experience, though not in his system, the noumenal is often subordinated to the phenomenal. His official creed is a kind of mysticism, but he is by no means a mystic.

On September 6, 1819, he writes to the Olliers:

The ill account you give of the success of my poetical attempts sufficiently accounts for your silence; but I believe that the truth is, I write less for the public than for myself.[149]

He is making the best of it, but we cannot believe him without disbelieving his whole conception of the poet's prophetic function. If nobody reads him, or reads him only in derision and hatred,[150] what becomes of "my words among mankind?"[151] In 1819 he had high hopes for *Prometheus Unbound*, "the most perfect of my productions"; but three years later he is trying to convince himself that "Prometheus was never intended for more than 5 or 6 persons."[152] At that rate Jupiter would be long adying. Shelley was ready to lay aside the prophetic trumpet as early as the summer of 1820, when in a letter to Peacock he wonders "why I write verses, for nobody reads them."[153] Perhaps his message will be better received by posterity, but "The seeking of a sympathy with the unborn and the unknown is a feeble mood [mode?] of allaying the love within us, and even that is beyond the grasp of so feeble an aspirant as I."[154]

"I have no spirits for serious composition," he informs Claire toward the end of 1821. "I have no confidence, and to write in solitude or put forth thoughts without sympathy is unprofitable vanity."[155] This, as he tells Peacock, means that he has lost his life's battle:

I write nothing, and probably shall write no more. It offends me to see my name classed among those who have no name. If I cannot be something better, I had rather be nothing, and the accursed cause to the downfall of which I dedicate [dedicated?] what powers I may have had—it flourishes like a cedar and covers England with its boughs.[156]

[148] *Ibid.*, IV, 187–188.   [149] *Ibid.*, X, 78–79.
[150] This exaggerates the actual situation, but it represents Shelley's feeling.
[151] *Works*, II, 297.   [152] *Ibid.*, X, 95, 354.
[153] *Ibid.*, p. 187; see also p. 285 for the same thought in a letter to Byron.
[154] *Ibid.*, p. 179. (To John and Maria Gisborne, June 30, 1820.)
[155] *Ibid.*, p. 338.   [156] *Ibid.*, p. 308.

January, 1822, finds him in the lowest depths. To Peacock: "I wish I had something better to do than furnish this jingling food for the hunger of oblivion, called verse." To Leigh Hunt: "My faculties are shaken to pieces, and torpid."[157] Sometimes the thwarted benevolist hopes for a physical withdrawal to match his spiritual isolation. On August 15, 1821, he had written Mary:

My greatest content would be to desert all human society. I would retire with you and our child to a solitary island in the sea. . . . If I dared trust my imagination it would tell me that there were two or three other chosen companions besides yourself whom I should desire. But to this I would not listen— where two or three are gathered together the devil is among them.[158]

Of that fact Shelley's domestic life had provided ample experience. A few months before, in *Epipsychidion,* Emilia Viviani had received the same invitation to a *solitude à deux.*

In short, "Our Adonais has drunk poison." The great elegy is essentially a poem about Shelley, "Who in another's fate now wept his own." But the tragedy of the "herd-abandoned deer"[159] is less ambiguously revealed in the essay *On Love:*

I know not the internal constitution of other men, nor even thine, whom I now address.[160] I see that in some external attributes they resemble me, but when, misled by that appearance, I have sought to appeal to something in common, and unburthen my inmost soul to them, I have found my language misunderstood, like one in a distant and savage land. The more opportunities they have afforded me for experience, the greater has appeared the interval between us, and to a greater distance have the points of sympathy been withdrawn. With a spirit ill fitted to sustain such proof, trembling and feeble through its tenderness, I have everywhere sought sympathy, and have found only repulse and disappointment.[161]

I have quoted very profusely in the hope of establishing the fact that Shelley's growing sense of being "companionless" and "a phantom among men"[162] was more than a mood which occasionally clouded the bright

---

[157] *Ibid.,* pp. 342, 351.   [158] *Ibid.,* p. 315.

[159] *Ibid.,* II, 398, 399; see also pp. 407–408 for cancelled drafts of the Preface which show even more clearly than the printed version the personal motivation of the poem.

[160] Apparently, then, *On Love* was addressed to a particular person. Perhaps to Mary, as an attempt to show her what she had failed to give him?

[161] *Works,* VI, 201.   [162] *Ibid.,* II, 398.

sky of his vision: it meant the total collapse of his scheme of redemption through poetry. "Alas!" he cries in a fragment of 1820, "this is not what I thought life was." [163] His biographers have rightly dwelt upon the close relationship between his melancholy and the specific woes of his life—the death of his children, disillusionment about Godwin, revulsion against specific instances of tyranny, the Hoppner scandal, the Claire-Allegra-Byron problem, and so on. Professor White has especially emphasized the influence of his strained relations with Mary, not only on the "maniac" section of *Julian and Maddalo* and on *Epipsychidion* but on many of the mournful short lyrics. But underlying all these day-to-day troubles, and enhancing their misery, brooded the general awareness of loneliness, weakness, failure. So far as Mary is concerned, it is quite possible that he unconsciously made her the scapegoat of his frustration. At all events no optimist has ever written a larger number of pessimistic poems. In his last year, love becomes almost more a curse than a blessing, since it tortures his frail spirit with longings which can never be satisfied:

> Its passions will rock thee
> As the storms rock the ravens on high;
> Bright reason will mock thee,
> Like the sun from a wintry sky.
> From thy nest every rafter
> Will rot, and thine eagle home
> Leave thee naked to laughter,
> When leaves fall and cold winds come.[164]

These withered leaves will not quicken a new birth.

The mature Shelley has qualified but not abandoned the doctrine of man's natural goodness. In the real and eternal world of Intellectual Beauty man is a perfectly virtuous being. For some inexplicable reason man in the world of appearances denies his birthright of perfection, but it abides within him when he knows it not and he can regain it by affirming the law of love. Shelley also retains much of the Godwinian faith in education: man even at his worst has benevolent impulses which burst through the obscuring film of error in response to the exhortations of the wise and good. But want of human sympathy made it increasingly difficult to maintain this belief. "My firm persuasion," he tells Hunt on January 25, 1822,

[163] *Ibid.*, IV, 76.   [164] *Ibid.*, p. 192.

is that the mass of mankind as things are arranged at present, are cruel, deceitful, and selfish, and always on the watch to surprize those who are not—and therefore I have taken suspicion to me as a cloak, and scorn as an impenetrable shield.[165]

This, be it noted, applies to man only "as things are arranged at present"; but if he retained much hope that Yahoos could be transformed into Houyhnhnms he would not take refuge in suspicion and scorn. Where is now the divine-human love that "throws over the world its healing wings"? [166]

If Shelley's disillusioned view of mankind had included himself, this chapter might have told a different story. But it was only the goodness of others that he doubted, never his own. Inevitably, however, he was forced to imagine himself, not as the Promethean conqueror of evil, but as its pathetically lonely and suffering victim. Far from being sinful, he is too good for this cruel and unfeeling world—too pure, gentle, sensitive, and beautiful to stand up against the rude Eton boys of this life. His spirit, "trembling and feeble through its tenderness," [167] bends beneath the weight of its virtuous sensibility. "Oh lift me from the grass! I die, I faint! I fail!" [168] "I fall upon the thorns of life! I bleed!" [169]

> O Love! that bewailest
> The frailty of all things here,
> Why choose you the frailest
> For your cradle, your home, and your bier? [170]

His self-pity reaches its climax in stanzas xxxi–xxxiv of *Adonais*. That Shelley distinctly relishes himself in this unattractive rôle almost stifles in us the compassion which his tragedy amply merits.

According to Shelley's theology, he could rise above this weakness and turn defeat into victory by laying hold upon the unlimited power of Eternal Love. But he could conceive of no divine force sufficiently distinct from his own personality to exert the necessary upward pull. Platonic love proved a vain reliance, for where actual women were concerned he thought less of Intellectual Beauty than of its fair shadows. The spiritualizing of flesh and the carnalizing of spirit were in conflict, each depriving the other of its proper values. The former was an essential article of his

[165] *Ibid.*, X, 351.   [166] *Ibid.*, II, 261.   [167] *Vide supra*, p. 370.
[168] *Works*, III, 294.   [169] *Ibid.*, II, 296.   [170] *Ibid.*, IV, 192.

creed; the latter dominated his experience of life. Thus Laon gazes upon Cythna, who is not merely the sister of his soul but quite literally, in the original version, the sister of his flesh:

> Her white arms lifted thro' the shadowy stream
> Of her loose hair—oh, excellently great
> Seemed to me then my purpose, the vast theme
> Of those impassioned songs.[171]

The irony here is completely unconscious. As early as the autumn of 1815, however, he was aware of his deficiencies as a Platonic lover. Of the poet in *Alastor* he says: "So long as it is possible for his desires to point toward objects thus infinite and unmeasured, he is joyous, and tranquil, and self-possessed." But the poet loses this peace when he

thirsts for intercourse with an intelligence similar to itself. . . . He seeks in vain for a prototype of his conception. Blasted by his disappointment, he descends into an untimely grave.[172]

Despite the self-knowledge which these words reveal, Shelley continued his search for the veiled maiden:

> In many mortal forms I rashly sought
> The shadow of that idol of my thought.[173]

But *Epipsychidion,* from which this couplet is drawn, proved to be an extreme example of this very rashness. On June 18, 1822, he almost paraphrases the *Alastor* preface in a letter to John Gisborne:

The "Epipsychidion" l cannot look at; the person whom it celebrates was a cloud instead of a Juno. . . . It is an idealized history of my life and feelings. I think one is always in love with something or other; the error, and I confess it is not easy for spirits cased in flesh and blood to avoid it, consists in seeking in a mortal image the likeness of what is perhaps eternal.[174]

That "perhaps" is worth noting. He did not fully realize that the search was rendered fruitless by his insistence that the perfect mortal image of the eternal must be a perfect reflection of his own mind. He could only report in the *Hymn of Pan* that

[171] *Ibid.,* I, 282.   [172] *Ibid.,* p. 173.   [173] *Ibid.,* II, 364.
[174] *Ibid.,* X, 401.

I sang of the dancing stars,
    I sang of the daedal Earth,
And of Heaven—and the giant wars,
    And Love, and Death, and Birth,—
        And then I changed my pipings,—
Singing how down the vale of Mænalus
    I pursued a maiden and clasped a reed:
Gods and men, we are all deluded thus!
It breaks in our bosom and then we bleed.[175]

Nothing much was to be expected, then, of the desire of the moth for the star.

In its broadest sense, however, the Platonic love-cult implies ascent toward Intellectual Beauty through contemplation of *all* fair forms—not merely those of women but those of objects in external nature. Shelley's response to both the physical beauty and the spiritual significance of nature was fundamentally authentic. Between 1815 and 1817 he was strongly and wholesomely influenced by Wordsworth. As late as the autumn of 1818, indeed, *Lines Written Among the Euganean Hills* expresses the Wordsworthian type of interfusion. Wordsworth, however, usually enlarges his personality by absorbing nature into himself, while Shelley prefers to achieve the same end by projecting his mind outward into nature in order to share, with enhancement rather than with loss of selfhood, the benign energy of west wind and skylark and cloud. Shelley is also much more inclined to interpret the spiritual element in nature in terms of an animism derived from Greek mythology sophisticated by Neoplatonism.

Unquestionably the enjoyment of nature was for Shelley a deep source of consolation. But when the nature-experience was genuine it was not very Platonic, and when it was Platonic it was not very genuine. The immense though beautiful verbosity of his imagery suggests that nature became for him largely an anodyne, a means of lulling his mind with manifoldness rather than of sharpening its apprehension of the One. When Shelley is unhappy, furthermore, nature becomes too obviously a wistful substitute for human sympathy. Once more *On Love* proves valuable:

---

[175] *Ibid.,* IV, 44. *Hymn of Pan* was intended for insertion in a drama on the Midas story which Mrs. Shelley had some notion of writing. A strange gift to his wife, who would know how Percy wished her to interpret this stanza.

Hence in solitude, or in that deserted state when we are surrounded by human beings, and yet they sympathize not with us, we love the flowers, the grass, and the waters, and the sky. In the motion of the very leaves of spring, in the blue air, there is then found a secret correspondence with our heart. There is eloquence in the tongueless wind, and a melody in the flowing brooks . . . which by their inconceivable relation to something within the soul, awaken the spirits to a dance of breathless rapture, and bring tears of mysterious tenderness to the eyes, like the enthusiasm of patriotic genius, or the voice of one beloved singing to you alone.[176]

This rapture, however, can provide no lastingly satisfactory equivalent of either the victory of Prometheus or the voice of Jane Williams. Sooner or later he wants another personality upon whom he may project the joy which he derives from nature. This condition is fulfilled in *To Jane: The Recollection*:

> There seemed from the remotest seat
>   Of the wild mountain waste,
> To the soft flower beneath our feet,
>   A magic circle traced,—
> A spirit interfused around
>   A thrilling silent life,—
> To momentary peace it bound
>   Our mortal nature's strife;—
> And still I felt the centre of
>   The magic circle there,
> Was one fair form that filled with love
>   The lifeless atmosphere.[177]

If Jane's form were removed the charm would be broken, and Shelley would relapse to the mood of *Stanzas Written in Dejection Near Naples,* where the beauty of the scene is meaningless because no one will share it with him—"for I am one/Whom men love not." [178] Nature is a substitute for human sympathy, but without human sympathy nature can be enjoyed only superficially.

Ode to the West Wind is the most impressive of Shelley's responses to stimuli derived from nature.[179] It combines the hope of infinite self-expansion through the regeneration of mankind with the sense of frailty which we have more recently considered. Professor White urges that the latter element

---

[176] *Ibid.,* VI, 202.   [177] *Ibid.,* IV, 196.   [178] *Ibid.,* III, 206, 207.
[179] *Ibid.,* II, 295–297, includes all my quotations from this poem.

loses much of its appearance of sentimental self-pity when seen as a deep realization of the disparity between the tremendous things that must somehow
be done and the inadequacy of one mind and body to such a task. The poem
is in fact a reaffirmation of faith in spite of discouragement, and a sustained
prayer for power and opportunity to carry out the purposes that he had resolved upon in childhood.[180]

But what is the basis of this reaffirmation of faith? To what does Shelley
address his prayer? The autumn wind, "destroyer and preserver," is a
benignly revolutionary force, a "Wild Spirit" functioning more or less
Neoplatonically as the mediator of that universal love-energy which alone
can redeem the world. Before this sub-symbol of the One, Shelley appears
to bend the knee. He is weak, the Wind is mighty. He prays that he may
be lifted up by this power and made its Aeolian harp, that the withered
leaves of his poetry may become the instruments of Love in quickening a
new birth. Surely, one is inclined to say, this is a heartfelt confession of
inadequacy and dependence, a genuinely humble prayer for the aid of a
suprapersonal divine reality.

But look again at the fourth section:

> If I were a dead leaf thou mightest bear;
> If I were a swift cloud to fly with thee;
> A wave to pant beneath thy power, and share
>
> The impulse of thy strength, only less free
> Than thou, O uncontrollable!

The leaf-cloud-wave sequence moves from self-submission to self-assertion.
Unlike the *dead* leaf, the *swift* cloud is the partner, not the instrument, of
the wind—"The comrade of thy wanderings over Heaven," as line 49
says. (This desire is fulfilled in *The Cloud,* where the poet speaks in the
first person as one of the beneficent nature-forces.) The wave at first
sounds meek enough, but the slightly masochistic delight of submission to
strength immediately inverts itself into the aggressive delight not of being
used by, but of sharing, an "uncontrollable" energy. "Only less free" represents the usual attempt to have it both ways—to enjoy the dignity of
inspiration without undergoing its discipline. Like Wordsworth, Shelley
longs to regain the naive Promethean illusion of childhood—unlimited
freedom with no Jupiter, no rock, no vultures:

[180] N. I. White, Shelley, II, 193.

> ...If even
> I were as in my boyhood, and could be
>
> The comrade of thy wanderings over Heaven,
> As then, when to outstrip thy skiey speed
> Scarce seemed a vision.

Far from renouncing this rivalry with the present object of his devotion, Shelley yearns to recapture the childish pride. He is now weak merely be- cause of his undeserved sufferings, not because of any essential inferiority to the animating power of nature. He addresses the Wind as one "Wild Spirit" to another—"One too like thee: tameless, and swift, and proud." The "too" is a touch of Byronism.

The final section recalls our earlier discussion of the apparent selflessness of Shelley's theory of poetry. "Make me thy lyre, even as the forest is." Here is the desire for self-expansion through self-annihilation. But in the next tercet the situation is reversed, for the West Wind is urged to iden- tify itself with its worshipper:

> ...Be thou, Spirit fierce,
> My spirit! Be thou me, impetuous one!

Literally speaking, the West Wind was merely a tempest which tossed the branches of an Italian forest on a particular autumn day. It owes its prophetic power as a symbol of regeneration solely to "the incantation of this verse"; that is, to the fact that Shelley has written a poem about it. At the beginning of the section Shelley is the lyre of the wind; at the end, the wind is *his* instrument:

> Be through my lips to unawakened earth
> The trumpet of a prophecy!

Trumpets do not use lips as the wind uses the Aeolian lyre: lips use trumpets. There could be no clearer example of the circularity of ro- mantic religion. Moved by an instinctively religious desire for help, Shelley has addressed his prayer to his own poetic imagination. There is nothing to lift him up but himself, and he lacks the strength for such a feat.

In his less illusioned moments Shelley is fully aware of the futility of this position. He likes to use the stripping away of a veil to symbolize the process by which the loving will pierces through phenomenal error to noumenal truth. Thus Cythna, flushed with victory, cries: "I tore the veil that hid/Nature, and Truth, and Liberty, and Love." [181] But one of his sonnets uses the veil for a quite different symbolic purpose. It deserves to be quoted entire, for although it was written as early as 1818 it is Shelley's self-epitaph:

> Lift not the painted veil which those who live
> Call Life: though unreal shapes be pictured there,
> And it but mimic all we would believe
> With colours idly spread,—behind, lurk Fear
> And Hope, twin Destinies; who ever weave
> Their shadows o'er the chasm, sightless and drear.
> I knew one who had lifted it—he sought,
> For his lost heart was tender, things to love,
> But found them not, alas! nor was there aught
> The world contains, the which he could approve.
> Through the unheeding many he did move,
> A splendour among shadows, a bright blot
> Upon this gloomy scene, a Spirit that strove
> For truth, and like the Preacher found it not.[182]

A fundamental principle of Shelley's religion is that evil, though a terribly potent illusion of the self-darkened mind, has no status in the world of real and eternal truth. But of course Shelley is keenly aware of the actuality of evil—that is why he so passionately asserts its non-existence. Even in terms of his own idealism it was difficult for him to deny the reality of the horrors that lived so vividly in his mental images. If "all things exist as they are perceived," evil is as real as good. Again, as so often in studying Shelley, we think of Blake. Is Innocence truth and Experience illusion, or are both equally existential, their opposition weaving the whole fabric of life?[183] Not infrequently Shelley is forced to adopt the latter view, which in relation to his theology is heretical. The mysterious woman's explanation of the eagle-serpent combat in *The Revolt of Islam* is the clearest example:

> Know, then, that from the depth of ages old,
> Two powers o'er mortal things dominion hold,
> Ruling the world with a divided lot,
> Immortal, all-pervading, manifold,

---

[181] *Works*, I, 366.   [182] *Ibid.*, III, 216–217.   [183] *Vide supra*, pp. 78–80.

Twin Genii, equal Gods—when life and thought
Sprang forth, they burst the womb of inessential nought.[184]

On this Manichaean principle, Jupiter and Prometheus would be "equal Gods," and the latter could not love the former out of existence.

Perhaps *The Revolt of Islam* is too early a poem for the interpretation of the mature Shelley, but his Manichaeanism appears also in the Italian period. In the essay *On the Devil, and Devils,* written probably in 1820 or 1821, Shelley declares that "The Manichaean philosophy, if not true, is at least an hypothesis conformable to the experience of actual facts." [185] The delightful wanderings of the Witch of Atlas occurred long ago,

> Before those cruel Twins, whom at one birth
>   Incestuous Change bore to her father Time,
> Error and Truth, had hunted from the earth
>   All those bright natures which adorned its prime,
> And left us nothing to believe in, worth
>   The pains of putting into learned rhyme.[186]

Apparently the Neoplatonic fancies of this poem were once perfectly true, but they have given way before the harsher dispensation of the struggle between Error and Truth, twins neither of which can be regarded as an illusion. And so we have "nothing to believe in." But we can still, as in *The Witch of Atlas,* treat the old vision with a wistful-playful aestheticism; or we can let the clear voice of Jane Williams convey to our aimlessly erotic idealism

> A tone
> Of some world far from ours,
> Where music and moonlight and feeling are one.[187]

Manichaeanism accords with Shelley's rather naively black-and-white mode of regarding experience. He recognizes, however, not merely the opposition of error and truth, but their inextricable confusion:

> And Good and Ill like vines entangled are,
>   So that their grapes may oft be plucked together.[188]

Could this entanglement of good and evil imply something still more disastrous to Shelley's faith than the concept of Manichaean strife? Could

---

[184] *Works,* I, 264.   [185] *Ibid.,* VII, 87.   [186] *Ibid.,* IV, 17.
[187] *Ibid.,* p. 204.   [188] *Ibid.,* III, 212.

it mean that his God, the Spirit of Good, was limited by some inscrutable Necessity which transcended even the necessity of Love?[189] Admiring the mountains at the entrance to Demogorgon's cave, Asia exclaims:

> Fit throne for such a Power! Magnificent!
> How glorious art thou, Earth! And if thou be
> The shadow of some spirit lovelier still,
> Though evil stain its work, and it should be
> Like its creation, weak yet beautiful,
> I could fall down and worship that and thee.[190]

It is astonishing that the God of *Prometheus Unbound*, Shelley's most confident declaration of faith, should be "weak yet beautiful"—precisely like the poet himself in one of his self-pitying moods.

In this poem the triumph of divinized humanity is not quite complete, for man is not

> . . . exempt, though ruling them like slaves,
> From chance, and death, and mutability.[191]

The difference between ruling over these evils and being exempt from them is far from clear; but this sense of an undefinable threat to human expansion appears not only in Demogorgon's interview with Asia but in his final speech, which suggests that at some future time the Promethean struggle may have to be repeated

> . . . if, with infirm hand, Eternity,
> Mother of many acts and hours, should free
> The serpent that would clasp her with his length.[192]

This conception of a loving but palsied Eternity is puzzling to us and must have been disquieting to Shelley. "Eternity" is the name which Demogorgon assumed when he dethroned Jupiter. Is he now speaking of himself, or of some other power? In any case a similar feeling of a fate beyond even the sway of love broods over the whole of *Hellas*.

I am not at all satisfied with the preceding paragraph, but I despair of extracting any coherent meaning from the confusion which it has tried to

---

[189] In genuine Platonism the power of the Divine Mind is limited by the necessity of copying the eternal forms; but this is not what disturbed Shelley, for like most romantic Platonists he supposed that the forms were themselves created by the Divine Mind.

[190] *Works*, II, 215.   [191] *Ibid.*, p. 242   [192] *Ibid.*, p. 262.

describe. The most that can be said, it seems to me, is that Shelley desires to identify his spirit with an all-powerful Spirit of Love. His hopes for himself and for mankind could rest upon no other basis. It is the very core of his religion. But looking in a less confident mood upon the God that he has created, he fears that the Spirit of Love may reflect not merely the beauty but the weakness of his own nature. Some readers may be gratified by this foretokening of the "limited God" of modernist theology, but it was not what Shelley wanted to believe: a limited God implied a limitation of his own power. Was there Something even mightier than the Spirit of Love, and did it include what man calls evil as well as what man calls good? To answer the question affirmatively would be to deny the central message of *Prometheus Unbound*, returning to the Spinozan necessity of *Queen Mab* with its complete indifference to human cravings. To answer it negatively would be to deny his growing awareness of the reality and power of evil.

Shelley did not answer the question at all. Writing to Medwin on August 22, 1821, he asks:

What were the speculations which you say disturbed you? My mind is at peace respecting nothing so much as the constitution and mysteries of the great system of things;—my curiosity on the point never amounts to solicitude.[193]

Surely he cannot mean that he has solved the mysteries of existence to his complete satisfaction. He is saying that the only way to attain peace is to let these problems alone. Cynicism, however, would give a mind like his no permanent resting-place. The poems of 1821 and 1822 present abundant evidence that his curiosity and solicitude about the great system of things continued in their usual state of inconclusive intensity.

In these last two years, the aspect of evil which particularly oppressed him was the transitoriness of values which according to his declared faith were eternal and unchanging. It seemed no longer possible to resolve this dilemma by turning from the phenomenal to the noumenal. He had always been more eager to interfuse than to distinguish the two realms of being; and now there was no way, on this side of the grave, of rising above the very unsatisfactory world of his actual experience.

> Summer was dead, but I yet lived to weep
> The instability of all but weeping.[194]

[193] *Ibid.*, X, 316–317.   [194] *Ibid.*, IV, 187.

These lines from *The Zucca* (1822) reverse the conclusion of *The Sensitive Plant* (early 1820):

> That garden sweet, that lady fair,
> And all sweet shapes and odours there,
> In truth have never passed away:
> 'Tis we, 'tis ours, are changed, not they.
>
> For love, and beauty, and delight,
> There is no death nor change: their might
> Exceeds our organs, which endure
> No light, being themselves obscure.[195]

That is the true Shelleyan gospel, but not only in *The Zucca* does he seem to have forsworn it. A late lyric entitled *Mutability* begins:

> The flower that smiles today,
> Tomorrow dies;
> All that we wish to stay
> Tempts and then flies.[196]

And there is no changelessness to which we may appeal from these changes, for

> When the lamp is shattered
> The light in the dust lies dead—
> When the cloud is scattered
> The rainbow's glory is shed.
> When the lute is broken,
> Sweet tones are remembered not;
> When the lips have spoken,
> Loved accents are soon forgot.[197]

There could be no more explicit denial of his Platonism. He may well be paraphrasing the argument against immortality advanced by an interlocutor in the *Phaedo*, who urges that man's soul is to his body as music to the lute: break the instrument, and where is the melody?

Since the flux includes no element of permanence, life has been drained of all value:

[195] *Ibid.*, II, 285.
[196] *Ibid.*, IV, 94. The other poem of this title (I, 203) is of 1814 or 1815.
[197] *Ibid.*, p. 191.

Out of the day and night
A joy has taken flight;
Fresh spring, and summer, and winter hoar
Move my faint heart with grief, but with delight
No more—Oh, never more! [198]

Deprived of any abiding love, beauty, or joy, existence becomes a tomb
reeking with decay:

Death is here and death is there,
Death is busy everywhere,
All around, within, beneath,
Above is death—and we are death.

. . .

First our pleasures die—and then
Our hopes, and then our fears—and when
These are dead, the debt is due,
Dust claims dust—and we die too.[199]

But should we dwell upon these morbid little jingles when the spring of
1821 gives us *Adonais,* with its conception of death as the spirit's triumphant release from transitory imperfection into eternal perfection? No one
will wish to deny the beauty of the famous passages, though Miss Bald
becomes almost too fervent when she says that "there is probably nothing
greater in human speech." [200] It is necessary to repeat, however, that in
placing the eternal values on the far side of the grave Shelley completely
abjures the Promethean hope and the whole theory of the redemptive
mission of poetry in our mortal life. Could this retreat—one might almost
say this apostasy—have given him much satisfaction? Furthermore, as the
author himself was glad to acknowledge, *Adonais* is an elaborate, highly
self-conscious work of art in a traditional form. A pastoral monody which
offered no intimations of immortality would be anomalous. Shelley could
hardly have satisfied the demands of the tradition so well had he not been
swept into brief but genuine enthusiasm by his own eloquence. He had
always been responsive to the auto-intoxication of beautiful words and
rhythms. It is impossible to believe, however, that in June, 1821, Shelley
confronted death with a glad confident hope of life in "the abode where

[198] *Ibid.,* p. 97.   [199] *Ibid.,* IV, 59.
[200] M. A. Bald, "Shelley's Mental Progress," *Essays and Studies by Members of the English
Association,* XIII, 136.

the Eternal are." [201] There is more of his real feeling in the self-portrait
of the "frail Form" who had once possessed a great vision,

> Had gazed on Nature's naked loveliness
> Actaeon-like, and now he fled astray
> With feeble steps o'er the world's wilderness,
> And his own thoughts, along that rugged way,
> Pursued, like raging hounds, their father and their prey.[202]

He indeed desired death, but for oblivion rather than for attainment
of the ideal. He could see little use "in keeping up the unnatural connection between this feeble mass of diseases and infirmities and the vapid
and weary spirit doomed to drag it through the world." [203] *The Magnetic
Lady to Her Patient* originated in the fact that in 1822 Jane Williams was
easing his nephritic pains by means of hypnotism—Medwin had shown
her the technique. Shelley imagines the last of the veiled maidens as singing to her "withered flower":

> Sleep, sleep, and with the slumber of
> The dead and the unborn
> Forget thy life and love;
> Forget that thou must wake forever;
> Forget the world's dull scorn;
> Forget lost health, and the divine
> Feelings which died in youth's brief morn;
> And forget me, for I can never
> Be thine.

The patient emerges from his trance feeling "Quite well." But what, Jane
wonders, would relieve his sufferings in the waking state? Shelley replies:

> What would cure, that would kill me, Jane:
> And as on earth I must abide
> Awhile, yet tempt me not to break
> My chain.[204]

[201] Joyfully to anticipate death is not easy for the professor of *any* religion, no matter
what he may feel obligated to say about it; but the vagueness and incertitude of Shelley's
ideas on immortality make it especially unlikely that he could have entertained such a
feeling.
[202] *Works,* II, 398.
[203] *Ibid.,* X, 230. (To Claire, January 16, 1821.)
[204] *Ibid.,* IV, 190–191. Shelley is not, as Trelawny absurdly suggests (*Ibid.,* p. 419n),
"probably alluding to lithotomy," but to death.

The temptation, however, was strong. On June 18, 1822, he asked Trelawny to get him a supply of prussic acid: "I need not tell you that I have no intention of suicide at present, but I confess it would be a comfort to me to hold in my possession that golden key to the chamber of perpetual rest." [205] To use the key proved unnecessary. Soon the door opened of itself—but not quite, for on that stormy day it was pushed a little by the reckless hand of one who desired surcease.

We must conclude that Shelley's religion failed to give him what he wanted. His lust for personal infinitude hurled itself against the walls of reality and was shattered by what it sought to deny. Some authorities believe, however, that at the time of his death Shelley had begun to erect a more mature faith on the ruins of the old. Let us glance at the supposed evidence for this opinion.

Hellas is heavy with a sense of the complexity of life which makes it less cocksure than *Prometheus Unbound* despite its aesthetic inferiority to the earlier work. Professor Bush rightly observes:

The contrast between good and evil, white and black, is not so complete as it is in Shelley's other long poems. Mahmud is not merely an unthinking barbarous despot. . . . Under the influence of Ahasuerus, he passes from fatalistic despair to something like acquiescence in the rightness of his own defeat.[206]

One cannot see, however, that the work points toward any solution of the problems which it raises. The dramatic personification of God and the half dramatic, half pseudo-Platonic Christianity have already been observed. They do not imply that the author was about to join a confirmation class. Ahasuerus delivers one of Shelley's most eloquent assertions of belief in Thought as "that which cannot change—the One,/The unborn and the undying." [207] Perhaps, however, the obvious indebtedness of parts of the speech to Prospero's "Our revels now are ended" indicates aesthetic rather than religious motivation. Mahmud seems deeply impressed by the Wandering Jew's teaching, but when he hears his Turks crying "Victory! Victory!" he reluctantly emerges from the Platonic spell to summarize Shelley's career in the words, "What sound of this importunate earth has broken/My mighty trance?" [208] The concluding Chorus, so often cited in evidence of Shelley's indomitable optimism, ends in utter despair:

[205] *Ibid.*, X, 405.
[206] D. N. Bush, *Mythology and the Romantic Tradition in English Poetry*, p. 164.
[207] *Works*, III, 43–44.   [208] *Ibid.*, p. 47.

> Oh, cease! must hate and death return?
> Cease! must men kill and die?
> Cease! drain not to its dregs the urn
> Of bitter prophecy.
> The world is weary of the past,
> Oh, might it die or rest at last! [209]

If the wheel of destiny brings back the great days of Greece it must also, as it continues to revolve, repeat all the horrors of history down to the present, so that once again Ahasuerus will be preaching Platonism to Mahmud in a world of hate and death. It would be better, says Shelley, to liquidate the whole ghastly business.

The Triumph of Life is Shelley's *Edwin Drood;* the temptation to finish it has proved irresistible to more than one critic. The unusually ascetic theme—the tyranny of the lower fleshly desires over the higher spiritual desires in all men but a few saints and sages—has sometimes been taken to indicate a radical change in the direction of Shelley's thought. As Miss Bald reminds us, however, the poem "should not be taken as Shelley's last word on the final mystery. *The Triumph of Life* was the natural outcome of a reaction from the emotional experience which had occasioned *Epipsychidion.*" [210] Once again he had "pursued a maiden and clasped a reed." This time, however, he had so crushingly revealed to himself the spuriousness of his "Platonic love" that he trembled on the verge of self-reproach. With the help of Petrarch he tries to evade this deathblow to his pride by generalizing the personal situation—"Gods and men, we are all deluded thus!"

Mr. Hughes plausibly conjectures that if Shelley had shaped his conclusion in agreement with the first of Petrarch's *Trionfi*

The Shape or Spirit, the messenger of ideal love, who accompanies the pageant all the way, half-seen to the side of it, would have stepped in glory on to the road, and the horses would have bolted, to the overthrow of rider and driver, and a surcease of the spell, and a rejuvenation somehow of the men and women of the crowd. . .. . But this prophecy, if it was intended, would have convinced us—and Shelley himself, perhaps—less than others before it of the same tenor. The effect of the agony would have cancelled the relief. Who would take it

---

[209] *Ibid.,* p. 53.

[210] M. A. Bald, "Shelley's Mental Progress," *Essays and Studies by Members of the English Association,* XIII, 129. The poem, though not actually begun until late in the spring of 1822, had probably been conceived soon after the completion of *Epipsychidion* in the winter of the preceding year.

that evil so over-mastering could be scouted away? And what merit should there be in souls that, in the grip equally of evil and of good, are leaves in a wind? [211]

To these perceptive comments one need only add that it is unlikely, in any poem written later than *Adonais,* that even the hollowest victory of the Spirit of Love would be hoped for in this mortal life. Probably, therefore, Shelley would have ended with some variant of "Die,/If thou wouldst be with that which thou dost seek." But this would have provided no explanation of

> ...how power and will
> In opposition rule our mortal day,
>
> And why God made irreconcilable
> Good and the means of good.

Even had the poem been completed, it could not have answered Shelley's last bewildered cry, "Then, what is life?" [212]

Before his premature death, Shelley had perceived and had often acknowledged the inadequacy of his religion. He realized his weakness, and *The Triumph of Life* very faintly suggests that he might have learned to blame his own nature instead of the unsympathetic world. Dimly and reluctantly he sensed a terrible Power beyond his creativity which said "No" when his self-projected Spirit of Love said "Yes." To a hopeful eye, those strangely submissive lines in *The Boat on the Serchio*[213] hint that he might some day have recognized this Power as a just and merciful God. But this is the merest guesswork. For us the importance of Shelley lies not in what he might have become but in what he was. More strikingly than any of his contemporaries he combines ecstatically confident assertion of the romantic faith with bitter realization of its futility.

[211] A. M. D. Hughes, "The Theology of Shelley," *Proceedings of the British Academy,* XXIV, 202.   [212] *Works,* IV, 174, 185.   [213] *Vide supra,* p. 337.

Chapter VII

BYRON

I

> This should have been a noble creature: he
> Hath all the energy which would have made
> A goodly frame of glorious elements,
> Had they been wisely mingled; as it is,
> It is an awful chaos—Light and Darkness—
> And mind and dust—and passions and pure thoughts
> Mixed, and contending without end or order,
> All dormant or destructive.[1]

This applies both to Byron's splendid potentialities and to the lack of integration which vitiated them. The chaos is so complete, however, that one despairs of unravelling a mystery which sometimes gave Byron himself as much satisfaction as pain. In 1814 he informs Miss Milbanke that his bumps have recently been examined by Spurzheim. The phrenologist found all the faculties "strongly marked, but very antithetical, for every thing developed in or on this same scull of mine has its opposite in great force, so that, to believe him, my good and evil are at perpetual war." [2] Almost at the end of his career Lady Blessington finds him still fascinated by the puzzle. Presciently he speculates as to what "my future biographers" will make of it:

One will represent me as a sort of sublime misanthrope, with moments of kind feeling. This, *par exemple,* is my favorite rôle. Another will portray me as a

---

[1] Manfred, III, i, 160–167. Throughout this chapter dramatic works, are referred to by act, scene, and line; longer non-dramatic works by Canto and stanza; short poems, by volume and page of the *Works* as edited by E. H. Coleridge.

[2] *Letters and Journals,* ed. R. E. Prothero, III, 137. Henceforward this book will be referred to as *Letters.*

modern Don Juan; and a third . . . will, it is to be hoped, if only for opposi-
tions's sake, represent me as an *amiable,* ill-used gentleman, "more sinned
against than sinning." Now, if I know myself, I should say, that I have no
character at all.[3]

The buried allusion to Pope's "Most women have no characters at all"
suggests that he is thinking in terms of eighteenth-century psychology: he
cannot discern his "ruling passion."

Nor can we discover it. When the Archangel Michael appears in *A
Vision of Judgment,* the first half of the stanza might have been written
by a lesser Dante and the second by Voltaire:

> And from the gate thrown open issued beaming
>   A beautiful and mighty Thing of Light,
> Radiant with glory, like a banner streaming
>   Victorious from some world-o'erthrowing fight:
> My poor comparisons must needs be teeming
>   With earthly likenesses, for here the night
> Of clay obscures our best conceptions, saving
> Johanna Southcott, or Bob Southey raving.[4]

Here, as in *Don Juan,* is a deeper cleavage than can be explained by the
influence of Italian burlesque romance: that form is its means of expression, not its cause. No one can say on which side of the chasm the "real"
Byron is to be found.[5] There is no reason to suppose that he is not equally
sincere in each of his shifting moods; he has rightly been praised for the
complete honesty with which he refuses to paint a more simplified picture of his nature and of the world than he is able to perceive.[6] It may
be said that there is genuine integrity in the frankness with which he
reveals his disintegration.

But although Lady Blessington believes Byron to be sincere both as
sentimentalist and cynic, she adds that "He talks for effect, likes to excite
astonishment, and certainly destroys in the mind of his auditors all confidence in the stability of his character." [7] Let us say that he was a sincere

---

[3] *Conversations of Lord Byron with the Countess of Blessington,* pp. 171–172.

[4] *Works,* IV, 496. The same bewildering oscillation is repeated in the next stanza but one.

[5] The real Byron of *A Vision of Judgment* is to be found in the poem's witty satire, but
this is not the real Byron of *Childe Harold,* or *The Prisoner of Chillon,* or *Fare Thee Well.*

[6] See Peter Quennell, *Byron in Italy,* pp. 61–62, and E. W. Marjarum, *Byron as Skeptic
and Believer,* pp. vii–viii. Although Dr. Marjarum's valuable dissertation may leave something to be desired as an interpretation of Byron's religion it should be consulted for many
specific facts which thanks to him I need not attempt to cram into this brief study.

[7] *Op. cit.,* p. 24.

poseur, an actor who threw himself passionately into all of his rôles while
he kept one eye on his audience and consciously played upon their emotions. The heavier the make-up, the realer he looked and felt in the glare
of the lights which he had so carefully arranged to play upon him. No
one ever caught him behind the scenes and without greasepaint. This includes even himself, for the image in his dressing-room mirror reflected
him only in one or another of his parts.

As a performer in romantic tragedy, however, Byron relates himself to
the general pattern of our study. Of all his contemporaries, he is the most
unabashedly egotistical. Even more obviously than in the others, the
human energies which he glorifies are *his* energies. He differs from his
fellows, however, in that he much more frequently doubts whether those
energies are strong enough to satisfy his craving for unlimited personal
liberty and even whether they are essentially good. This realistic sense of
human limitation and human evil, combined with the superstitious strain
in his character, prevented him from denying that Christianity which he
was never able to accept. But since he lacked any centre from which to
interpret experience he could make no fruitful use of his realism. When
his expansive impulses are thwarted he can take refuge in hollow laughter.
At other times he seeks consolation not in mockery but in melodrama,
deriving from his awareness of insufficiency a complacent feeling of
blighted distinction which converts what might have been humility into
pride. Trying to believe that thwarted insatiability is a sure sign of greatness, he can claim kinship with the fallen Napoleon:

> But Quiet in such bosoms is a Hell,
> And *there* hath been thy bane; there is a fire
> And motion of the soul which will not dwell
> In its own narrow being, but aspire
> Beyond the fitting medium of desire.[8]

Passages of this sort, substantiated as they sometimes are by his actual
conduct, seem to justify the common opinion that Byron's emotions were
overmasteringly powerful. To some ears, however, the most volcanic out-
bursts of his Titanism, as for example in *Manfred,* sound like a weak man
trying to find strength through extravagance. From these pinnacles of
overstrained feeling he contentedly descends to a worldly, cynical, and
even rather sluggish common sense. For Charles du Bos,

[8] *Childe Harold,* III, xlii.

Le fonds Byronien est bien cette mélancholie innée due peut-être à un coeur, si
je puis ainsi m'exprimer, en soi statique qui, pour percevoir ses battements, a
besoin que ceux-ci s'accelèrent jusqu'à la folie.[9]

This theory is accepted by Mario Praz: "His blood had to boil like lava
for him to feel it beating in his pulses. . . . Paroxysm became his natural
atmosphere." [10]

Perhaps these French and Italian authorities are too much inclined to
interpret Byron in terms of a decadent romanticism which even at the
close of the nineteenth century was far rarer in England than on the continent. It seems very probable, however, that Byron combined an aggressively energetic imagination with a comparatively torpid body and a disorganized nervous system. In 1821 he asks his Diary, "What is the reason
that I have been, all my lifetime, more or less ennuyé?" [11] The answer
may be that since his emotions were too chaotic to be interpreted rationally
or turned in any consistent direction they could contribute to his pride
only by being represented as more grandiose and passionate than they
actually were. Thus exploited, the muddle of thought and feeling in which
he lived might impart to himself and to others an illusion of tragic dignity.
If he could not have a character, he could display a personality. Hence the
histrionic exaggeration of feelings which, though by no means wholly
factitious, lacked solid physical support, and hence the revulsion from
rant and strut into an apathy which perhaps equally belied his real nature.

The poet's biographers have analyzed the factors which contributed to
the early disorganization of his character: his ominous heredity, his unhappy relations with his mother, his deformed foot, his loneliness, his demoralizing transformation into a proud young aristocrat who lacked the
purse, the breeding, and the temperament of a gentleman. He himself was
ascribing all his faults to his mother's evil influence as early as 1805, when
he wrote Hanson from Cambridge:

What can be expected of that Man's heart and understanding who has continually (from Childhood to Maturity) beheld so pernicious an Example? His
nearest relation is the first person he is taught to revere as his Guide and In-
structor; the perversion of Temper before him leads to a corruption of his own,
and when that is depraved, vice quickly becomes habitual, and, though timely
Severity may sometimes be necessary and justifiable, surely a peevish harassing
System of Torment is by no means commendable, and when that is interrupted

---

[9] *Byron et le besoin de la fatalité*, p. 84.   [10] *The Romantic Agony*, p. 71.
[11] *Letters*, V, 155.

by ridiculous Indulgence, the only purpose answered is to soften the feelings for a moment which are soon after to be doubly wounded by the recal [sic] of accustomed harshness.[12]

Even granting that Mrs. Byron was sorely tried there can be no doubt that she was an extremely bad mother; but her son's psychologizing falls so trippingly from his tongue that the search for a scapegoat is patent.

The deformed foot was also a scapegoat besides being a genuine cause of the cleavage in his nature. Walter Scott's more serious infirmity developed only in his second year; his mother did not deride him as a "lame brat"; he did not suffer the physical tortures which were visited upon the little Aberdeen cripple. Nevertheless the contrast is not wholly unfair, and it indicates that Byron was a man who could make the most of his afflictions. The deformity may, however, have had deeper roots in Byron's nervous system than he himself realized. Mr. Quennell cites an article in *The Lancet* which suggests that Byron's lameness originated in Little's Disease —hemorrhage on the surface of the infant's brain caused by delay in getting the newborn baby to breathe. The epilepsy-like attack at Missolonghi is said to be symptomatic of this malady.[13] So also, the layman may conjecture, were Byron's "thunder headaches (you know how my head acts like a barometer when there is electricity in the air)." [14]

The clues which Byron has obligingly presented to his biographers are doubtless important, but they all smell a little of subconscious red herring. They explain much and at the same time conceal a more significant cause from us and from the poet himself. The almost certain fact that Byron was sexually ambivalent has been approached with averted eyes by several critics, but so far as I know only Mr. Quennell has treated it with the necessary clarity and firmness.[15] Naturally Byron's homosexuality is less overwhelmingly obvious than his heterosexuality, but the sum-total of the evidence for the less normal tendency is convincing. Consider the mysterious quarrel with Lord Gray de Ruthyn; the circle of handsome little boys who were his favorite companions at Harrow, especially the never-to-be-forgotten Clare, and the similar group of adolescents at the Athenian monastery; the almost overtly revealed passion for Edelston, the fair-haired Cambridge chorister; young Nicolo Giraud, the companion of the Greek travels, whose intimacy with Byron probably explains why Hobhouse re-

[12] *Ibid.*, I, 89–90; see also II, 13.
[13] Peter Quennell, *Byron: The Years of Fame*, p. 62.
[14] *Letters*, VI, 261.   [15] *Op. cit.*, pp. 17, 30–34, 96, 99, 209–210.

turned home and to whom the poet bequeathed £7,000; and even in the closing scenes at Missolonghi, the much-favored Levantine page.

What Byron truly loved was neither man nor woman, but himself. To an unusual extent, however, his self-esteem depended upon the esteem of others. Fame, deeply as he desired it, was not enough: he must have admiring affection. But the chasm in his nature made genuine human relationships impossible except on the most superficial plane. He was imprisoned within a selfhood whose true nature he did not dare confront and whose limitations he sought to transcend by means of fantasies in which he could only fitfully believe. Probably his homosexual tendencies very rarely if ever rose to the level of perverted action. They were suppressed in favor of a heterosexuality which he was forced to exaggerate in order to convince himself and the world that his passions were abnormal only in their excessive strength. This overstrained rôle was one of which he periodically sickened. Another possible reaction to the situation was more complex: it consisted in relieving his suppressed feelings of guilt by thinking and writing as if he had been guilty of something mysterious and terrible. Unfortunately this fantasy was so satisfying that it became more than a novel-of-terror pose. Why not *really* be guilty of a sin monstrous but not unmanly, something that would muffle the nameless guilt-feeling and yet externalize it in a form flattering to a demonic sort of pride? Hence the incest with Augusta,[16] the sadistic treatment of Lady Byron, and all the subsequent masquerading as melodramatic sinner, abused husband, lonely idealist, Titanic rebel, mocking satirist, Regency dandy, and exhausted amorist in search of peace and quiet.

To pride himself on being a fascinating phrenological puzzle was not enough to give him peace. The ministrations of psychoanalysis were not available to him. Another source of help was available, but to that Healer Byron was never able to entrust the fragments of his being.

2

In considering the period of Byron's life which ends with his return from his travels in July, 1811, we are handicapped by inadequate knowledge of his earliest religious training. It has often been supposed that a

---

[16] Is there any respectable authority who does not now regard the incest as an established fact? Since Augusta was only a half-sister it was second-rate sort of incest, but Byron made the most of it as he did of his lameness.

principal cause of his disintegrated personality was the conflict between his hatred of all restraint and the Calvinistic sense of doom which had been impressed upon his mind in childhood. The romantic belief in human goodness and power was constantly thwarted by the Calvinistic insistence upon human corruption. The importance of this influence has perhaps been exaggerated. At all events we may ask how far Calvinism was a genuinely formative factor and how far it was seized upon by Byron as an after-the-fact explanation of his mystery.

Byron himself describes Calvinism as a wholly negative influence in his religious development: his reaction against its rigors, he declares, was so violent that it distorted his attitude toward Christianity in general. He begins an answer to Miss Milbanke's anxious queries about his beliefs by saying, "I was bred in Scotland among Calvinists in the first part of my life which gave me a dislike to that persuasion." [17] Writing Gifford in 1813 he ascribes his scepticism to an early feeling of "the comparative insignificance of ourselves and *our world,* when placed in competition with the mighty whole, of which it is an atom," but also to "being early disgusted with a Calvinistic Scotch school, where I was cudgelled to Church for the first ten years of my life." [18] Byron seems to perceive no relationship between the two causes which he mentions; indeed the words "our world" imply that the feeling of insignificance had a Newtonian rather than a Calvinistic origin.

Byron's remarks about Calvinism, however, would eagerly be seized upon by cheerful believers as a means of showing the awful consequences of enthusiastic gloom. In her girlhood Lady Byron had been a conventional Anglican; but when in later years she became a sentimental liberal with marked Unitarian and Universalist leanings she remembered her husband not as an infidel but as the victim of fanatical religious education. In retrospect she "could not but conclude" from his words and actions during the hideous honeymoon that "he was a believer in the inspiration of the Bible, and had the gloomiest Calvinistic tenets. To that unhappy view of the relation of the creation to the Creator, I have always ascribed the misery of his life." [19] This became almost the official interpretation among contemporaries who were charitably disposed toward Byron. William Harness, who had discussed religious questions with Byron and Francis

[17] *Letters,* III, 402.
[18] *Ibid.,* II, 222.
[19] Quoted by Richard Edgcumbe, *Byron: The Last Phase,* p. 77.

Hodgson at Newstead in December, 1811, later wrote in his biography of Hodgson:

Byron, from his early education in Scotland, had been taught to identify the principles of Christianity with the extreme dogmas of Calvinism. His mind had thus imbibed a most miserable prejudice, which appeared to be the only obstacle to his hearty acceptance of the Gospel.[20]

Surely, however, the entire blame cannot be laid at the door of the Kirk. In *Don Juan* Byron says that his fondness for thinking about the ultimate problems of existence implies no polemic bitterness:

> I always knock my head against some angle
>> About the present, past, or future state:
> Yet I wish well to Trojan and to Tyrian,
> For I was bred a moderate Presbyterian.[21]

Here his early religious training is associated not with bigotry, but with tolerance. "Moderate," we recall from the chapter on Burns, is a technical term which covers various degrees of latitudinarian belief but which is never applied to strict Calvinism. Perhaps he is using the epithet sarcastically; but in the Ravenna diary, written only for himself, his memories of Aberdeen are not particularly painful. At the age of five or a bit earlier he was sent to the school of a Mr. Bowers, where he "learned little . . . except to repeat by rote the first lesson of Monosyllables—'God made man, let us love him,'—by hearing it often repeated, without acquiring a letter." Whatever its pedagogical futility, such a lesson could hardly have filled his mind with gloomy fears. After a year of this he was placed under "a very decent, clever little clergyman, named Ross. . . . Under *him* I made astonishing progress, and I recollect to this day his mild manners and good-natured pains-taking." Still later he had as tutor "a very serious, saturnine, but kind young man, named Paterson. . . . He was a rigid Presbyterian also." From Paterson he went to Grammar School, "where I threaded all the Classes to the *fourth,* when I was re-called to England . . . by the death of my Uncle." [22] Unlike the letter to Gifford, the diary says nothing about "being early disgusted with a Calvinistic Scotch school, where I was cudgelled to Church." Even if the implications of "moderate" are discounted, the doctrinal rigidity of his teachers seems to have been

[20] *Letters*, I, 179n.   [21] *Don Juan*, XV, xci.   [22] *Letters*, V, 406–407.

tempered with plenty of human kindness. He remembers keenly enjoying the Old Testament stories; the New Testament, significantly, seems to have meant little to him.

His mother wished him to believe what other folk believed, but nothing indicates that she was an extreme theological precisian. Byron was probably correct in supposing that her abundant superstitions were the source of his own. There is nothing peculiarly Calvinistic, however, about belief in cheiromancy and astrology. Perhaps May Gray, his nurse, was not only harsh and neglectful but a bad religious influence. Miss Mayne, however, seems unduly shocked by the fact that the woman taught her charge to repeat the First and Twenty-third Psalms each morning while she was squeezing his foot into the cruel appliance.[23] "He shall be as a tree planted by the rivers of water. . . . The Lord is my shepherd." The attempt to raise him above his pain was a failure, but it might have worked better with a different boy. May Gray was using the only antidote of which she knew.

As an element in the domestic, educational, and social pressures of the first ten years, the Kirk doubtless played some part in the formation of Byron's character. But modern critics are excessively prone to cry "How Calvinistic!" whenever a poet uses the word "sin," which was not invented in Geneva. Any form of religion which imposed outward control upon his passions would have been repugnant to Byron, but his unwillingness to deny the faith which he could never accept arose from his interwoven scepticism and superstition rather than from whatever systematic teachings Aberdeen vainly tried to impress upon him. The resistless doom which pursues the Byronic hero is sometimes described in terms which suggest the doctrine of predestination, but its ultimate source is probably not the *Institutions* but the novel of terror. Perhaps Calvinism was less important in shaping his character than in providing materials which could later be used for expressing his deeper feelings in a simplified form. When he desired to protect his unbelief he could employ images derived partly from Aberdeen to depict a Christianity which no enlightened person could accept. Or when his sense of guilt clashed with his romantic aspirations he could lash out against God "in passionate denial of the justice of the decree which makes man the victim of inherited passions and unto-

---

[23] Ethel C. Mayne, *Byron*, I, 24–25. The First Psalm, to be sure, threatens the ungodly with destruction, but its main emphasis is on the rewards of belief. It could not damage the mind of any child.

ward circumstances and then condemns him as solely and entirely responsible." [24]

Yet in the *Epistle to Augusta* he admits that if he has suffered from

> . . . worldly shocks,
> The fault was mine; nor do I seek to screen
> My errors with defensive paradox;
> I have been cunning in mine overthrow,
> The careful pilot of my proper woe.[25]

Still more explicitly, in the transparent disguise of Lara, Byron declares:

> But haughty still, and loth himself to blame,
> He called on Nature's self to share the shame,
> And charged all faults upon the fleshly form
> She gave to clog the soul, and feast the worm;
> Till he at last confounded good and ill,
> And half mistook for fate the acts of will.[26]

As a scapegoat, then, Calvinism was not always satisfactory.

The Aberdeen child is completely hidden from us. The young lord of Newstead Abbey wears a mask, but at least the mask is visible. His first volume of verse—to distinguish its bibliographical phases is not important for us—represents what he wished to think of himself toward the close of the Harrow days and in the first year or two at Cambridge. The reader's first impulse is to describe *Hours of Idleness* as a mass of adolescent affectations, but gradually he comes to the more disquieting conclusion that Byron means exactly what he says in such lines as

> For me, how dull the vacant moments rise,
> To no fond bosom linked by kindred ties!

or

> Fain would I fly the haunts of men—
> I seek to shun, not hate mankind;
> My heart requires the sullen glen,
> Whose gloom may suit a darken'd mind.[27]

Fundamentally these are the moods of *Childe Harold* III and of *Manfred;* he will simply learn to express them better.

[24] H. J. C. Grierson, *The Background of English Literature*, p. 183.
[25] *Works*, IV, 58.   [26] *Lara*, XVIII.   [27] *Works*, I, 95, 206.

"Lord Calthorpe," the poet told Dr. Kennedy, "was the first who called me an atheist when we were at school at Harrow, for which I gave him as good a drubbing as ever he got in his life." [28] These early verses, far from justifying Calthorpe's accusation, mingle with their sentimental melancholy such bits of conventional piety as "I'll ne'er submission to my God refuse." [29] But the only poem which gives a clear picture of the lad's religious position is *The Prayer of Nature*. After praying the "Father of Light" to "Avert from me the death of sin," Byron continues:

> No shrine I seek, to sects unknown;
>   Oh, point to me the path of truth!
> Thy dread Omnipotence I own;
>   Spare, yet amend, the faults of youth.
>
> Let bigots rear a gloomy fane,
>   Let Superstition hail the pile,
> Let priests, to spread their sable reign,
>   With tales of mystic rites beguile.
>
> Shall man confine his Maker's sway
>   To Gothic domes of mouldering stone?
> Thy temple is the face of day;
>   Earth, Ocean, Heaven, thy boundless throne.
>
> Shall man condemn his race to Hell,
>   Unless they bend in pompous form?
> Tell us that all, for one who fell,
>   Must perish in the mingling storm?
>   . . .
> Father! no prophet's laws I seek,—
>   *Thy* laws in Nature's works appear;—
> I own myself corrupt and weak,
>   Yet will I *pray*, for thou wilt hear! [30]

Here the influence of Pope is obvious, but the poem is both more positive and more negative than *The Universal Prayer*. It interestingly jumbles vestiges of Christianity, destructive deism of the anti-priestcraft sort, and

---

[28] James Kennedy, *Conversations on Religion with Lord Byron and Others*, p. 49.
[29] *Works*, I, 6; see also pp. 24, 241, 242.
[30] *Ibid.*, pp. 224–228. *The Prayer of Nature* was first published by Moore in 1830. It certainly belongs to the *Hours of Idleness* period, and Byron's trend toward more negative views under the influence of Matthews suggests that 1807, the date conjecturally assigned it by E. H. Coleridge, is the latest year in which it could have been written.

sentimental, preromantic, more or less pantheistic deism. In the next-to-last stanza quoted, the theme of *Cain* already appears, and in the preceding stanza is foretokened the nature-religion of *Childe Harold* III.

The Christian element, however, is obviously fading out. It will never completely disappear, but henceforward the other two elements, unbelief and romantic belief, sometimes alternately and sometimes in combination, will be dominant. In the remainder of the period under discussion, however, Byron's pride will attempt to satisfy itself almost wholly through negation. In 1807, when the early poems reached their final form in *Hours of Idleness,* Byron had already begun to turn from the rôle of melancholy young sentimentalist to that of witty young libertine. Ten years later, in exactly the same spirit, he would turn from *Manfred* to *Beppo.*

It was in 1807 that he first became acquainted with Charles Skinner Matthews, whom he had met some time before through Hobhouse. Matthews was a lazy, learned, witty, dissipated eccentric whom Byron perhaps correctly considered "a man of the most astonishing powers." He was also "a most decided atheist, indeed noxiously so, for he proclaimed his principles in all societies." [31] In Matthews, Byron could see in full bloom a side of his own character which was just beginning to develop. It was an unaccustomed delight for the lonely, shy young nobleman to play host to his friend and seven or eight other cronies at Newstead Abbey, where, as Byron later told Murray,

I had got a famous cellar, and *Monks'* dresses from a masquerade warehouse. We . . . used to sit up late in our friars' dresses, drinking burgundy, claret, champagne, and what not, out of the *skull-cup,* and all sorts of glasses, and buffooning all round the house, in our conventual garments. Matthews always denominated me "the Abbot." [32]

Byron's emphasis on the rented monastic costumes implies that the zest of profanation was an important feature of these revels. They were not at all serious about it, of course. The poet does not remind his publisher that this playacting was a feeble imitation of the orgies at Medmenham Abbey, where Sir Francis Dashwood had been the Abbot.

If time permitted one could make out a good case for the assertion that

---

[31] *Letters,* I, 338. This letter was written in 1811, when Byron's mood had undergone a partial change; hence the mingling of admiration with disapproval. It is not, however, to Matthews' atheism that Byron objects but to his neglect of the aristocratic principle that gentlemen do not discuss religion in public.

[32] *Ibid.,* pp. 153–154.

Byron's favorite model at this time was not Matthews or any other living man, but Charles Churchill—satirist, Medmenhamite, foe of conventional cant, and infidel. Churchill was particularly attractive as a prime example of that mixed eighteenth-century type which I have called the "libertine sentimentalist." [33] He was more than a mocking roysterer. He had a passionate heart as well as a witty brain. His enmity toward all control arose from belief in the rightness of unchecked human impulse. Violently Whiggish in politics, he championed the ideals of his boon companion Wilkes. Man-about-town and thwarted genius, doomed victim of his own freedom, he flaunted a shattered but striking personality before the eyes of the canting world. Byron was to visit his neglected grave with a deep sense of kinship. Both in general conception and in style, *English Bards and Scotch Reviewers* closely resembles Churchill's *Rosciad*. It should be remembered that Byron's satire was merely a revision and enlargement of a 380-line assault upon *British Bards* which had been finished over two months before Brougham's slashing review of *Hours of Idleness*. The *Edinburgh* for January, 1808, merely confirmed a choice of rôles which had already been made.

Apart from its anti-romantic implications, *English Bards and Scotch Reviewers* has nothing of interest to us except for flings at the pious "mangled prose" of Grahame, the Evangelical bard, and at the snoopery of the Society for the Suppression of Vice:

> Whet not your scythe, suppressors of our vice!
> Reforming saints! too delicately nice!
> By whose decrees, our sinful souls to save,
> No Sunday tankards foam, no barbers shave! [34]

Byron has begun his long campaign against pietistic cant. There is no need to think of Aberdeen at this point: Churchill had adopted precisely the same tone toward the Methodist "saints" of his day.

Letters of 1807 and 1808 help to round out the picture. To Ensign Long he declares:

Of Religion I know nothing, at least in its *favour*. We have *fools* in all sects and Impostors in most; why should I believe mysteries no one understands,

---

[33] See "Sentimentalism, libertine," in the topical indexes of *Religious Trends*, I and II; and for a sketch of Churchill in relation to our general subject see II, 35–41.

[34] *English Bards and Scotch Reviewers*, ll. 319–326, 633–637. For the fact that the second passage specifically alludes to the Society for the Suppression of Vice I am indebted to M. J. Quinlan, *Victorian Prelude*, p. 202.

because written by some who chose to mistake madness for Inspiration, and style themselves *Evangelicals?* . . . . This much I will venture to affirm, that all the virtuous and pious *Deeds* performed on Earth can never entitle a man to Everlasting happiness in a future State; nor on the other hand can such a Scene as a Seat of eternal punishment exist, it is incompatible with the benign attributes of a Deity to suppose so. I am surrounded here [Southwell] by parsons and methodists, but, as you will see, not infected with the mania. I have lived a *Deist,* what I shall die I know not; however, come what may, *ridens moriar.*[35]

Perhaps not wholly without a desire to shock, he tells Dallas that he has recently turned from Stoicism to Epicureanism.

In morality, I perfer Confucius to the Ten Commandments, and Socrates to St. Paul (though the two latter agree in their opinion of marriage). In religion, I favor the Catholic emancipation, but do not acknowledge the Pope; and I have refused to take the sacrament, because I do not think eating bread or drinking wine from the hand of an earthly vicar will make me the inheritor of heaven. I hold virtue, in general, or the virtues generally, to be only in the disposition, each a *feeling,* not a principle. I believe truth the prime attribute of the Deity, and death an eternal sleep, at least of the body.[36]

At Cephallonia Byron gave Kennedy to believe that during his school and college days he read rather deeply in Barrow and other English theologians.[37] His letters hardly substantiate this claim, but they show what light spiritual luggage he took with him when he embarked in June, 1809. On March 17, however, he had assumed his seat in the House of Lords without the sponsorship of his kinsman the Earl of Carlisle and in his mortification had received the Lord Chancellor's welcome with ungracious coldness. His utter loneliness at a moment which should have been richly satisfying to his pride shook his swaggering confidence and brought to the surface the sentimental and melancholy side of his libertinism. Wavering and uncertain, then, are the moods of his travels. Byron the wit produced *Hints from Horace;* Byron the sated and disillusioned but fitfully passionate Man of Feeling produced *Childe Harold* I and II.

Miss Mayne is captivated by the "heavenly-foolish" qualities of these early cantos of *Childe Harold:*

He did not so much write poetry as *be* a great poet; indeed, one might almost say that one of his functions was to show us what bad poetry a great poet can write. It is like a convulsion of nature—the volcano flinging lava.[38]

[35] *Letters,* II, 19n. [36] *Ibid.,* I, 173.
[37] James Kennedy, *Conversations,* p. 35. [38] Ethel C. Mayne, *Byron,* I, 156.

From this we see that the ladies still find Byron "dangerous to know."
Whatever merits or faults the poem may possess in other respects, there
is nothing at all volcanic about the religion of Byron in the guise of "a
modern Timon, perhaps a poetical Zeluco." [39]

Spain and Portugal provide many opportunities for purely conventional abuse of the "Babylonian Whore." [40] The wanderer addresses personified Cadiz:

> Soon as the Matin bell proclaimeth nine,
> Thy Saint-adorers count the Rosary:
> Much is the VIRGIN teased to shrive them free
> (Well do I ween the only virgin there)
> From crimes as numerous as her beadsmen be;
> Then to the crowded circus forth they fare,

and honor the Sabbath by enjoying the bullfight. [41] But even a corrupted
piety lends zest to love: a lyrical by-product of the tour describes *The
Girl of Cadiz* as equally bewitching when she dances the bolero, sings
traditional lays while strumming her guitar,

> Or counts her beads with fairy hand
>   Beneath the twinkling rays of Hesper,
> Or joins Devotion's choral band,
>   To chant the sweet and hallowed vesper. [42]

Byron's disapproval of Catholicism does not, of course, imply any devotion to Protestantism. He is a Whiggish milord in the land of the Inquisition. To some extent, also, like many of the eighteenth-century
sceptical wits who have recently been his models, he finds reprobation of
Catholic abuses a safe means of expressing his dislike of all organized
and authoritative religion. In Canto II he sometimes generalizes more
boldly against

> Foul Superstition! howso'er disguised,
> Idol—Saint—Virgin—Prophet—Crescent—Cross—
> For whatsoever symbol thou art prized,
> Thou sacerdotal gain, but general loss!
> Who from true Worship's gold can separate thy dross? [43]

[39] *Works*, II, 3.   [40] *Childe Harold*, I, xxix. See also xx and lxvi–lxvii.
[41] *Ibid.*, lxxi.   [42] *Works*, III, 3.   [43] *Childe Harold*, II, xliv.

Certainly not Byron, whose superstitions were a standing joke among his acquaintances.

For us the only important passage is the meditation on the Parthenon in the first eight stanzas of Canto II. Utterly futile, the ruins seem to say, are all the proud aspirations of man, that "Poor child of Doubt and Death, whose hope is built on reeds." The temple once sacred to Zeus is now in Mohammedan hands: "Even gods must yield—religions take their turn." Is there, then, any enduring power to which man may appeal in his weakness? Socrates was right: "All that we know is, nothing can be known." The only lasting peace we can hope for is the final oblivion. In the original version of the poem, stanza viii flatly denied any hope of a future life:

> Frown not upon me, churlish Priest! that I
> Look not for Life, where life may never be:
> I am no sneerer at thy phantasy;
> Thou pitiest me, alas! I envy thee,
> Thou bold Discoverer in an unknown sea
> Of happy Isles and happier Tenants there.[44]

Under pressure from Dallas and Murray, Byron replaced these lines with a feeble but slightly more hopeful stanza saying that it would be very nice

> . . . if, as holiest men have deemed, there be
> A land of souls beyond that sable shore,
> To shame the doctrine of the Sadducee
> And sophists, madly vain of dubious lore.

Childe Harold's only substitute for the beliefs which he has spurned is vaguely rhetorical praise of Nature. At this time the term has for Byron no deep religious or philosophical meaning. It implies a cynical primitivism, the cult of melancholy retirement, and admiration for the Salvator Rosa sort of scenery—three familiar eighteenth-century traditions:

> Dear Nature is the kindest mother still!
> Though always changing, in her aspect mild;
> From her bare bosom let me take my fill,
> Her never-weaned, though not her favoured child.
> Oh! she is fairest in her features wild,
> Where nothing polished dares pollute her path:

[44] *Works*, II, 103n–104n.

To me by day or night she ever smiled,
Though I have marked her when none other hath,
And sought her more and more, and loved her best in wrath.[45]

We may call the preference typically Byronic if we remember that it was also the preference of Edwin in Beattie's *Minstrel*.

To his flesh-and-blood mother, whom he did *not* love best in wrath, he sends polite, objectively descriptive letters. But when she attempts to pry into his beliefs he irritatedly shrugs her off:

Nobody but yourself asks me about my creed,—what I am, am not, etc., etc. If I were to begin *explaining*, God knows where I should leave off; so we will say no more about that, if you please. I am no "good soul," and not an atheist, but an English gentleman, I hope, who loves his mother, mankind, and his country.[46]

This invocation of the English gentleman's Trinity is particularly amusing in view of the fact that the young traveller was busily acquiring that cosmopolitanism which was to make him the most broadly European of English romanticists.

Byron was later to remember that only in Greece had he ever been truly happy. He revelled in the relaxed moral atmosphere of the Near East. But the slackening of tension brought to the surface of his mind, and perhaps even into the sphere of action, the buried side of his bi-sexual nature. He saw himself very nearly if not quite as he really was, and ultimately the spectacle revolted him. If only it were true that to understand ourselves is to be relieved of our psychic burdens! When he returned to England in July, 1811, he was in a morbid and agitated state of mind. At all costs he must pull himself together and restore his self-esteem by a great display of energy—literary, political, sexual. All of us know what happened during the next five years, but we must examine Byron's religion in that period of his highest fame and deepest degradation.

3

The remaining months of 1811 seemed to lead nowhere. In his rooms at the Albany there hung a crucifix which he had brought from Greece; but it could have been no more than a decorative souvenir, for at this

---

[45] *Childe Harold*, II, xxxvii.   [46] *Letters*, I, 259.

time he seems more seriously and bitterly anti-Christian than during the Cambridge days of witty libertinism. With a perfectly natural inconsistency, he was saddened by the death of his mother; but her passing stirred in him no hopes for her soul or his own.[47] Soon he directed his shocked solicitors to draw up a will one clause of which specified that he should be buried in the garden of Newstead in the same vault where he had already placed the carcass of Boatswain, his Newfoundland dog.[48] Just at the site of the high altar of the ancient monastery,[49] Byron and his only faithful friend were to share oblivion.

In the autumn he lost Matthews, "my 'guide, philosopher, and friend,' " and the fair youth Edleston, "one very dear to me in happier times." [50] But when Hodgson offers the Christian remedy for melancholy, Byron lashes out at his pious friend: "The basis of your religion is *injustice;* the *Son of God,* the *pure,* the *immaculate,* the *innocent,* is sacrificed for the Guilty." He grants that Christ's death was heroic, but how could it possibly remove the guilt of other men? "You degrade the Creator, in the first place, by making Him a begetter of children; and in the next place you convert Him into a Tyrant over an immaculate and injured Being." As for miracles, surely Hume has said the last word on their absurdity. With a sneer he continues:

Besides, I trust that God is not a Jew, but the God of all Mankind; and as you allow that a virtuous Gentile may be saved, you do away with the necessity of being a Jew or a Christian. I do not believe in any revealed religion, because no religion is revealed: and if it pleases the Church to damn me for not allowing a *nonentity,* I throw myself on the mercy of the "Great First Cause, least understood."

After recommending Malthus as the best antidote for the illusion of Pangloss he concludes: "I will write, read, and think no more; indeed, I do not wish to shock your prejudices by saying all I do think. Let us make the most of life, and leave dreams to Emmanuel Swedenborg." [51] If even this highly explicit letter withholds his boldest thoughts on Christianity we may conclude, to put it very mildly, that the negative side of his deism is in the ascendant.

[47] *Lord Byron's Correspondence* (ed. John Murray), I, 44.   [48] *Letters,* I, 329–330.
[49] I owe this significant detail to Peter Quennell, *Byron: The Years of Fame,* p. 38.
[50] *Letters,* II, 29, 52.
[51] *Ibid.,* pp. 35–36. For other letters of the same tenor written in the autumn of 1811 see pp. 18–21, 48, 72–73.

In the following year he made the most of life with a vengeance. On February 27, 1812, his speech against the Framebreaking Bill delighted the Whigs, and in March *Childe Harold* delighted everybody who mattered. Political and literary fame, enhanced by his "beautiful pale face" and the mystery of his personality, paved the way for social and sexual triumphs which only gradually became wearisome.

Byron's opposition to the Framebreaking Bill was motivated partly by his sympathy with all manifestations of rebellious energy but largely by his anxiously fostered aristocratic pride. To the lord of Newstead it was intolerable that Nottingham should be ruled by Plugson of Undershot. Byron would be astonished at the notion that his support of the saboteurs had any connection with religion, but out of deference to those who would emphasize such a relationship I shall briefly discuss the general question of Byron's liberalism in the next section of this chapter. His later speech in behalf of the Catholic Emancipation Bill touches upon a religious issue merely in order to show the absurdity of deliberating

how far a difference in the ceremonials of worship, how far believing not too little, but too much (the worst that can be said for the Catholics), how far too much devotion to their God may incapacitate our fellow-subjects from effectually serving their king.

Apparently the Scarlet Woman is a purely continental harlot. English Catholics are simply eccentric Englishmen; if they wish to believe more than people of common sense, let them do so. They should be tolerated not because religious questions are important but because they are trivial: "It is indeed time that we should leave off . . . these Lilliputian sophistries, whether our 'eggs are best broken at the broad or narrow end.'" [52]

In the early days of her acquaintance with Byron, Miss Milbanke noted in her diary that she had been assured by mutual friends that "Lord Byron never suffers the slightest hint in disrespect to Religion to *pass at* his table." [53] Though his conduct in this matter may have varied with the nature of the company, the report is probably correct. He was too superstitious and too sceptical to be sure of his unbelief. Also, as a part of his aristocratic rôle, Byron had acquired the Chesterfieldian view that open attacks upon pious flummery disrupt the urbanity of dinner-parties and

[52] *Ibid.*, pp. 431–432.
[53] Ethel C. Mayne, *Life and Letters of Lady Byron*, p. 55.

even imperil the stability of a civilization in which most lives are supported by edifying fictions.

Byron was not fitted for a sustained performance in the part of Don Giovanni. He took pride in his collection of long, glossy locks of hair, but he was never a rapacious sensualist. As it became increasingly clear that poor mad Caro was after his scalp rather than he after hers, the advantages of respectable married life became increasingly attractive; and there could be no more impeccable symbol of upper-class British propriety than the Princess of Parallelograms. Miss Milbanke's rejection of him on October 12, 1812, was the immediate cause of his downfall. As a sort of compromise he turned to Lady Oxford: an affair with so matronly a mistress might almost provide an equivalent of domesticity. It was probably in June of the following year, when the futility of this gesture toward integration had become patent, that he commenced the incestuous relationship with Augusta. If he could not bury his guilty feelings in marriage, he must achieve a sin that would account for them.

The psychological motivation of this disastrous choice pervades the long series of adventure-poems which begins in May, 1813, with *The Giaour* and ends in the spring of 1815 with *The Siege of Corinth* and *Parisina*. In his attitude toward his writing as in everything else, Byron is inconsistent. He tells Annabella that

The great object of life is sensation—to feel that we exist, even though in pain. It is this "craving void" which drives us to gaming—to battle—to travel, to intemperate, but keenly felt pursuits of every description, whose principal attraction is the agitation inseparable from their accomplishment.[54]

The lust for sensation drives him also to poetry, which he conceives of as the boiling over of personal agitation. But in his Journal for November, 1813, he writes:

To withdraw *myself* from *myself* (oh that cursed selfishness!) has ever been my sole, my entire, my sincere motive in scribbling at all; and publishing is also the continuance of the same object, by the action it affords to the mind, which else recoils upon itself.[55]

Thus Byron, struggling to escape from introspection, creates characters in which he may recognize his own lineaments—one more example of romantic circularity.

[54] *Letters*, III, 400.　　[55] *Ibid.*, II, 351.

The Byronic hero as he appears in these poems has been amply discussed both in himself and in relation to his literary ancestry. He is not
by nature a monster of wickedness. The Giaour's sneering mirth is
ghastly enough,

> But sadder still it were to trace
> What once were feelings in that face:
> Time hath not yet the features fixed,
> But brighter traits with evil mixed;
> And there are hues not always faded,
> Which speak a mind not all degraded
> Even by the crimes through which it waded:
> The common crowd but see the gloom
> Of wayward deeds, and fitting doom;
> The close observer can espy
> The noble soul, a lineage high.[56]

By what overmastering fatality, or by what strange perversity of will, did
so good-hearted a child of nature and so fine a gentleman become so
very wicked? That is the mystery which fascinated Byron no less than
his readers.

These poems assume the existence of a God in order that the hero may
defy him. At the point of death, Lara rejects with a disdainful smile "the
absolving Cross" and "the holy bead." [57] The Giaour tells the Abbot his
story not in penitence but in a bitter, joyless pride. His crime originated
in resistless passion, and even such imperfect love as his is "light from
heaven":

> Devotion wafts the mind above,
> But Heaven itself descends in Love;
> A feeling from the Godhead caught,
> To wean from self each sordid thought;
> A ray of Him who formed the whole;
> A Glory circling round the soul! [58]

To kill the slayer of Leila was therefore quite in the spirit of the God of
Love. Granting that this argument is a little over-ingenious, it is not for
a bloodless dotard like the Abbot to offer reproof or pity to a Byronic hero:

> But talk no more of penitence;
> Thou seest I soon shall part from hence:

[56] *The Giaour*, ll. 859–869.   [57] *Lara*, XIX.   [58] *The Giaour*, ll. 1131ff.

And if the holy tale were true,
The deed that's done canst *thou* undo?
Think me not thankless—but this grief
Looks not to priesthood for relief.
My soul's estate in secret guess:
But wouldst thou pity more, say less.
When thou canst bid my Leila live,
Then will I sue thee to forgive;
Then plead my cause in that high place
Where purchased masses proffer grace.
Go, where the hunter's hand hath wrung
From forest-cave her shrieking young,
And calm the lonely lioness:
But soothe not—mock not *my* distress! [59]

Byron fully realizes the futility of such bluster. He knows that the passions of his heroes are not self-justifying, but self-destructive:

The Mind, that broods o'er guilty woes,
Is like the Scorpion girt by fire:

. . .

One sad and sole relief she knows—
The sting she nourished for her foes,
Whose venom never yet was vain,
Gives but one pang, and cures all pain,
And darts into her desperate brain:
So do the dark in soul expire,
Or live like Scorpion girt by fire;
So writhes the mind Remorse hath riven,
Unfit for earth, undoomed for heaven,
Darkness above, despair beneath,
Around it flame, within it death! [60]

Was it with some hope of escaping from this fiery circle that Byron resumed his courtship of Annabella after committing incest with Augusta, or did he desire the morbid thrill of piling desecration upon desecration? However we may choose to answer this unanswerable question, his replies to Miss Milbanke's inquiries about his beliefs give her fair warning that she will find him a very sceptical husband. He cannot share her enthusiasm for the certainties of mathematics. As a schoolboy he enjoyed only

[59] *Ibid.*, ll. 1202ff.   [60] *Ibid.*, ll. 422ff.

those theorems (is that the word), in which, after ringing the changes upon AB and CD, etc., I at last came to "which is absurd"—"which is impossible," and at this point I have always arrived and I fear always shall through life— very fortunate if I can continue to stop there.[61]

For "mathematics," read "religion."

Other letters to her are more explicit. From religion "I never did, and believe never can, derive comfort." He approaches belief only when he receives some undeserved kindness which, men being what they are, seems to come from an other than human source. Adversity he simply bears as well as he can "without any glimpses of the future."

Why I came here, I know not. Where I shall go, it is useless to inquire. In the midst of myriads of the living and the dead worlds—stars—systems—infinity— why should I be anxious about an atom?[62]

This is the Newtonian universe with which Lucifer bewilders Cain. Despite all the Boyle Lectures and Bridgewater Treatises, physico-theology was going over to the enemy. Attempting to account for his scepticism, he tells Annabella that his childhood experience of Calvinism

gave me a dislike to that persuasion. Since that period I have visited the most bigotted and credulous countries—Spain, Greece, Turkey. As a spectacle, the Catholic is more fascinating than the Greek or the Moslem; but the last is the only believer who practises the precepts of his Prophet to the last chapter of his creed.

Since among Christians he has observed nothing but bigotry, superstition, and hypocrisy,

My opinions are quite undecided. . . . I believe doubtless in God, and should be happy to be convinced of much more. If I do not at present place implicit faith in tradition and revelation of any human creed, I hope it is not from want of reverence for the Creator but the created.

Christian morality is "beautiful" and "sublime" but not unique, for "we find some of its finer precepts in the earlier axioms of the Greeks." [63]

In lyric verse, however, he could make more concessions to the pious tastes of his fiancée. Soon after they became engaged he began to write the *Hebrew Melodies,* which do not, of course, reflect his genuine be-

---

[61] *Letters,* III, 404.   [62] *Ibid.,* p. 408.   [63] *Ibid.,* pp. 402–403.

liefs or those of anyone else. They were tossed off too carelessly to justify a charge of deliberate hypocrisy, but it is not pleasant to remember that the most definitely Biblical of these lyrics were composed during his sadistic honeymoon.

They were married on January 2, 1815. Poor Annabella must have been astonished to discover that her husband was not only a worse man than she had dreamed but a more orthodox Calvinist. In interpreting her later recollections of married life some allowance should be made for the change in her own religious views and for the possibility that she may too hastily have identified the fatalism of Zeluco with the predestination of John Knox. Probably, however, her memory did not wholly play her false. Blasphemy is the spice of sadism, and religion must be asserted if it is to be profaned. Unfortunately the believing moments of an unbeliever do not invariably represent his highest spiritual state.

Bryon's great sin had been a sad fiasco. As a partner in diabolism Augusta Leigh was inadequate, for she could never get it into her muddled head that she had done anything wrong. What can you do with a half-sister who commits incest with you and then presents you with a Bible? And how, we may interject, can we hope to understand the man who inscribed on the flyleaf of that Bible some extremely devout verses by Sir Walter Scott? [64]

Augusta was a moral moron, but she was a lady. After her brother's marriage she refused to continue the incestuous relationship, and she was very kind to Annabella. It was still possible for Byron to torture his wife with brutal scorn, melodramatic threats, and broad hints of his passion for Augusta. But his sadism was essentially ideal; his attempts to drag it into the sphere of action did violence to the real goodness which he perversely sought to suppress. Hence his cruelty was mingled with genuine as well as with histrionic penitence, and with pathetic outreachings of tenderness which tortured his wife all the more by giving her some hope. But by the middle of January, 1816, Lady Byron had abandoned all hoping. In Byron's fantasy, she had been his helpless victim. In actuality, she simply left him when she could bear no more. Then separation, open scandal, ostracism. In a whirl of fury, remorse, and injured innocence, Childe Harold once more set forth on his travels.

[64] Richard Edgcumbe, *Byron: The Last Phase*, p. 73; James Kennedy, *Conversations*, p. 79; *Letters*, V, 391.

4

Switzerland, Shelley, the first summer of exile—these produce the climactic phase of Byron's romanticism. Thanking Moore for his praise of *Childe Harold* III, Byron calls the poem

a fine indistinct piece of poetical desolation, and my favorite. I was half mad during the time of its composition, between metaphysics, mountains, lakes, love inextinguishable, thoughts unutterable, and the nightmare of my own delinquencies. I should, many a good day, have blown my brains out, but for the recollection that it would have given pleasure to my mother-in-law.[65]

But these half-mocking words were written at Venice in 1817, at the beginning of the anticlimax. The actual mood of 1816 is expressed in *The Dream*:

> He fed on poisons, and they had no power,
> But were a kind of nutriment; he lived
> Through that which had been death to many men,
> And made him friends of mountains; with the stars
> And the quick Spirit of the Universe
> He held his dialogues; and they did teach
> To him the magic of their mysteries;
> To him the book of Night was opened wide,
> And voices from the deep abyss revealed
> A marvel and a secret—Be it so.[66]

All the tendencies of this period are latent in his earlier poems, even in *Hours of Idleness;* but they are now deepened by a stronger and less factitious turmoil of emotion, heightened and sweetened by Shelley's influence, and treated with a maturer though always slipshod artistry. Byron now tries to cultivate a romanticism of pantheistic nature-feeling, a romanticism of the Promethean mind, and a romanticism of social liberty. In examining them we shall draw not only upon *Childe Harold* III and its satellites but upon *Childe Harold* IV and *Manfred*. Subsequently we shall observe the respects in which the two later poems betoken a descent from the Alps.

None of the poets discussed in this book maintains the illusion of infinite self-expansion for more than occasional fleeting moments. Byron's ro-

[65] *Letters*, IV, 49.   [66] *Works*, IV, 41.

mantic desire, however, is frustrated not only by external reality but by inward division. On the one hand his egotism, much cruder than that of his contemporaries, constantly bursts through its rationalizing garments of benevolism, pantheism, transcendentalism, and revolutionary idealism, and betrays itself in stark nakedness. On the other hand his ego was not a concentrated drive but a ferment of conflicts. In his craving for self-deification he is almost a caricature of the romantic type, but not even in this period can he believe in himself firmly enough to achieve the desired end.

Beginning as early as 1807, when he wrote *The Prayer of Nature,* Byron had occasionally paid his respects to the natural religion of the eighteenth century. It had given him no real spiritual satisfaction, but it represented the almost obligatory position of a young deist in his more affirmative moods. In *Childe Harold* III there is still mention of "Fit speculation . . . found in wonder-works of God and Nature's hand." [67] On this rather old-fashioned deistic basis he could easily, like his contemporaries, erect the familiar structure of romantic nature-mysticism. In the land of Rousseau, whom he deemed a kindred spirit, surrounded by scenes whose beauty and terror reflected his own passions, and accompanied by Shelley, who at this time was only beginning to Platonize the nature-doctrine of Wordsworth, Byron inevitably seeks enlargement through pantheistic interfusion:

> I live not in myself, but I become
> Portion of that around me; and to me
> High mountains are a feeling, and the hum
> Of human cities torture: I can see
> Nothing to loathe in nature, save to be
> A link reluctant in a fleshly chain,
> Classed among creatures, when the soul can flee,
> And with the sky, the peak, the heaving plain
> Of ocean, or the stars, mingle, and not in vain.[68]

This intermingling implies not only the projection of himself into nature, but the absorption of nature into himself:

> Are not the mountains, waves, and skies, a part
> Of me and of my soul, as I of them?
> Is not the love of these deep in my heart
> With a pure passion?[69]

---

[67] *Childe Harold,* III, x.   [68] *Ibid.,* lxxii.   [69] *Ibid.,* lxxv.

The motive which impels him thus to "mingle with the Universe" becomes transparent when he apostrophizes "Ye Elements!—in whose ennobling stir/I feel myself exalted." [70]

"The feeling infinite" includes a vague awareness that

> All is concentered in a life intense,
> Where not a beam, nor air, nor leaf is lost,
> But hath a part of being, and a sense
> Of that which is of all Creator and defense.

This sense of boundless being constitutes true worship, whereas Grecian or Gothic temples—another highly symptomatic phrase—"circumscribe thy prayer." [71] Elsewhere in *Childe Harold* III this pantheism points toward a kind of immortality. When mind is free from the degradations of the body,

> And dust is as it should be, shall I not
> Feel all I see, less dazzling, but more warm?
> The bodiless thought? the Spirit of each spot?
> Of which, even now, I share at times the immortal lot? [72]

But probably there is more of Shelley in this than of Byron.

Byron's nature-religion is vitiated by his rampant egocentricity. Alluding to *Manfred*, Miss Mayne admiringly says of the author that "His personality dominated even the Alps." [73] So fervent a tribute might be staggering even to Byron, but unintentionally it shows why he is unable to complete the circle of romantic nature-worship. He resents making the gesture of reverence which is the price that the romantic poet must pay for the privilege of dealing masterfully with his surroundings. His talk of mingling with the universe is eloquent rhetoric, but he is too egotistic to derive much real satisfaction from mingling with anything. So completely isolated a man cannot be a successful pantheist.

Wordsworth's "love of nature leading to love of man"—the traditional romantic justification for solitary enjoyment of scenery—is meaningless to Byron. Even in childhood, as Dr. Marjarum observes, nature had often "provided him a ready means of escape from social intercourse with other persons." [74] Now Harold flees to his only friends, the mountains, because

---

[70] *Ibid.*, IV, clxxvii–clxxviii.   [71] *Ibid.*, III, lxxxix–xci.   [72] *Ibid.*, lxxiv.
[73] Ethel C. Mayne, *Byron*, II, iii.
[74] E. W. Marjarum, *Byron as Skeptic and Believer*, p. 52.

> ...he knew himself the most unfit
> Of men to herd with Man, with whom he held
> Little in common;[75]

and Manfred speaks from the very depths of Byron's divided character
when he says that

> ...From my youth upwards
> My spirit walked not with the souls of men,
> Nor looked upon the earth with human eyes;
> The thirst of their ambition was not mine,
> The aim of their existence was not mine;
> My joys, my griefs, my passions, and my powers,
> Made me a stranger; though I wore the form,
> I had no sympathy with breathing flesh,
>
> . . .
>
> ...but instead
> My joy was in the Wilderness.[76]

Sometimes—one guesses that he has been talking with Shelley—he
qualifies his misanthropy: "To fly from, need not be to hate, mankind." [77]
But at the close of *Childe Harold* IV, immediately after saying "I love
not Man the less, but Nature more," he hails the ocean as the aspect of
nature most completely exempt from man's control, most savagely indifferent to his pettiness.[87] His relations with nature, then ,are strictly private; he enjoys them not as being human, but as being alien to the rest
of mankind. Mother Nature and her unique lover stand apart in gloomy
scorn of the herd. Thus to share the "ennobling stir" of the elements is
not to attain a religious experience of the romantic or of any other kind.

To full-fledged romanticism, as preceding chapters have reminded us,
the religion of nature is less important in itself than as an aspect of a
wider faith in the creative powers of mind, especially the mind of the poet.
At this time transcendentalism offers Byron an attractive means of re-
pairing his shattered pride:

> ...The mind can make
> Substance, and people planets of its own
> With beings brighter than have been, and give
> A breath to forms which can outlive all flesh.[79]

---

[75] *Childe Harold*, III, xii.   [76] *Manfred*, II, ii, 50ff.
[77] *Childe Harold*, III, lxix.   [78]*Childe Harold*, IV, clxxviii–clxxx.
[79] *Works*, IV, 33–34.

This is the very tabernacle of the romantic faith. It demands, however, the will to affirm that despite all appearances there exists a continuity, a kinship, a mutual responsiveness between the spirit of man and the spiritual reality of the universe. There can be no infinite expansion of selfhood in a cosmos which is indifferent or hostile to the self. Here again Byron's romantic impulses are thwarted from within as well as from without. He conceives of life, not in terms of confident assertion echoed back to man by nature, but in terms of despairing though defiant rebellion against fate. This doom is usually assigned to the non-ego; but when Byron delves deepest he grants that he "half mistook for fate the acts of will." [80]

Professor Chew speaks of "that philosophic defiance and trust in the self-sufficiency of the human intellect which is the central theme of *Manfred* and of *Cain*." [81] The defiance is obvious, though I see nothing philosophic about it except in the sense that it forms a consistent element of the romantic side of the poet's thought. Byron's intellectual self-sufficiency, however, is not the triumphantly outreaching self-sufficiency of the true romantic spirit: it is a retreat to the Alps of the proud and lonely mind. These mountain fortresses are impregnable, but they are not the home of peace. The mind looks outward from them into the world and "vainly pants/For some celestial fruit forbidden to our wants." [82]

Byron longs to bridge the gap between the world reported by the senses and the world shaped by the aspiring imagination, but his scepticism forbids any Shelleyan transformation of what apparently is into what apparently is not. For him the romantic experience is merely an internal secretion, like a pearl in an oyster:

> Of its own beauty is the mind diseased,
> And fevers into false creation:—where,
> Where are the forms the sculptor's soul hath seized?—
> In him alone. Can Nature show so fair?

Prompted by Shelley, he can at times struggle to transfer illusion from the mind to the phenomenal world:

> Our life is a false nature—'tis not in
> The harmony of things,—this hard decree,
> This uneradicable taint of sin,

[80] *Vide supra*, p. 397.   [81] S. C. Chew, *The Dramas of Lord Byron*, p. 27.
[82] *Childe Harold*, IV, cxx.

This boundless upas, this all-blasting tree
Whose root is earth, whose leaves and branches be
The skies which rain their plagues on men like dew.

But the next stanza is an inconclusive mixture of Shelley's hope and Byron's despair:

Yet let us ponder boldly; 'tis a base
Abandonment of reason to resign
Our right of thought—our last and only place
Of refuge; this at least, shall still be mine:
Though from its birth the faculty divine
Is chained and tortured, cabined, cribbed, confined,
And bred in darkness, lest the truth should shine
Too brightly on the unprepared mind,
The beam pours in, for time and skill will couch the blind.[83]

The perfectibilitarianism of these lines may be heavily discounted. What is genuinely Byronic is the conception of mind as man's last and only refuge. Hence while Shelley's Prometheus can love Jupiter into nothingness, Byron's can only defy and endure:

Like thee [Prometheus] Man is in part divine,
  A troubled stream from a pure source;
And Man in portions can foresee
His own funereal destiny;
His wretchedness, and his resistance,
And his sad unallied existence:
To which his Spirit may oppose
Itself—an equal to all woes—
  And a firm will, and a deep sense,
Which even in torture can descry
  Its own concentred recompense,
Triumphant where it dares defy,
And making Death a Victory.[84]

This passage from *Prometheus* epitomizes everything in *Manfred* that rises above mere Gothicism and histrionic exploitation of his private affairs. Though doomed by destiny, the hero somehow possesses enough freedom to defy the spirits of nature, Arimanes and his cohorts, and finally death itself. Professor Chew has noted that Manfred differs from

[83] *Ibid.*, cxxii, cxxvi–cxxvii.   [84] *Works*, IV, 51.

Faust in his refusal to make any pact with the evil forces of the universe: for better or worse he will preserve his independence in the very teeth of fate. As the same authority rightly observes, "Manfred breathes no defiance against 'the overruling Infinite,' the 'other powers' who guard and govern the blessed and to whom he bids even Arimanes bow." [85] Unlike Astarte, however, Manfred does not "belong to the other powers": he lives in the unique isolation of his proud remorse, owning allegiance neither to extrapersonal evil nor to extrapersonal good. The only salvation or damnation which can apply to him must be shaped by his own mind. Haughtily he spurns the consolations and warnings of traditional belief as represented by the Chamois Hunter and the Abbot:

> ... That word was made
> For brutes of burthen, not for birds of prey!
> Preach it to mortals of a dust like thine,—
> I am not of thine order.[86]

And when at last the demons come to claim his soul their powers are even more vigorously repudiated:

> ... I stand
> Upon my strength—I do defy—deny—
> Spurn back, and scorn ye! . . .
>
>   . . .
>
> ... Back to thy hell!
> Thou hast no power upon me, *that* I feel;
> Thou never shalt possess me, *that* I know:
> What I have done is done; I bear within
> A torture which could nothing gain from thine:
> The mind which is immortal makes itself
> Requital for its good or evil thoughts,
> Is its own origin of ill and end,
> And its own place and time—its innate sense,
> When stripped of this mortality, derives
> No colour from the fleeting things without,
> But is absorbed in sufferance or in joy,
> Born from the knowledge of its own desert.[87]

---

[85] S. C. Chew, *The Dramas of Lord Byron* pp. 76, 80. His references are to *Manfred,* II, iv, 46–49, 114–115.

[86] *Manfred,* II, i, 34ff.; see also 87ff. and III, i, 66–78.

[87] *Ibid.,* III, iv, 109ff. Observe the reminiscence of Milton's Satan.

Quite possibly Shelley has been expounding to Byron his solipsistic interpretation of Berkeley's idealism. Here at all events self-sufficiency reaches heights which some readers will think sublime and others absurd. There is no suggestion, however, that the mind has any transcendental power to shape or transform experience: it is merely a fortress with no entrance and no exit.

A moment later this completely uncontrolled puppet of fate expires, saying to the Abbot, "Old man! 'tis not so difficult to die." [88] Byron was furious with Murray for omitting this line from the first edition: "You have destroyed the whole effect and moral of the poem." [89] Even when the line is restored, however, the moral remains elusive. According to Professor Chew, Manfred's master passion is the craving for universal knowledge. In relation to the philosophy of the drama, Astarte gives specific form to the melancholy engendered by the inevitable frustration of this ambition in mortal life. "But Manfred does not rest in mere negation; in spite of failure he refuses to abandon the *right to know*." Hence he seeks the ultimate wisdom beyond the grave, for "In death alone is there realization of definite ends." This onward striving into the unknown is by no means the message of the serenely limited Goethe:

Here is the fundamental distinction between classicism and romanticism. And Byron, in *Manfred* and throughout his poetry, points to an ideal truer and nobler than Goethe's just because it is impossible of accomplishment. Such a doctrine is indeterminate, enormous; but it is full of inspiration.[90]

The Byron of 1816 would like all this very much, especially the identification of the true and the noble with the impossible. But has Professor Chew described the drama that Byron actually wrote? The quest-of-knowledge theme is lifted from *Faust:* it corresponds to nothing fundamental in Byron's own experience. In Act II, Manfred tells the Witch of the Alps that his solitary researches gave him keen delight until his sin with Astarte, but that since that disaster he has desired only "forgetfulness." Hamlet-like, he doubts whether death will confer the meed of Lethe, but he is desperate enough to make the experiment. His attempts to die, however, have been thwarted by a Wandering-Jew sort of curse which seemingly compels him to live forever.[91] In the preceding act the

---

[88] *Ibid.*, l. 151.   [89] *Letters*, IV, 157.
[90] S. C. Chew, *op. cit.*, pp. 78–84. It is only fair to observe that this esteemed scholar's dissertation was published as early as 1915.   [91] *Manfred*, II, ii, 79–163.

Spirits of Nature have mockingly declared their inability to grant him "Oblivion—self-oblivion." [92] Later, when he visits the Hall of Arimanes, the First Destiny describes him not as a passionate seeker after knowledge, but as one who has learned

> That knowledge is not happiness, and science
> But an exchange of ignorance for that
> Which is another kind of ignorance.[93]

We must conclude that Manfred does not think of death as the culmination of his yearning for truth: all he wants is escape from his tortured self into eternal sleep. How he finally discovers that " 'tis not so difficult to die" is puzzling, but probably we are to infer that he gains the privilege through resolute defiance of all the forces which have been holding him back from the precipice. To speak bluntly, Manfred is a frustrated and disillusioned egotist who wishes to die because he has committed a dreadful sin and who, after a great deal of mouthing and posturing, finally manages to do so. This may be "indeterminate and enormous," but it is hard to see that it is "full of inspiration." [94]

The most amiable aspect of the romantic desire for self-expansion is the advocacy not merely of personal liberty but of social and political liberty in general. In the period now under discussion Byron strongly manifests this tendency in many passages of *Childe Harold* and in *The Prisoner of Chillon* and its prefatory sonnet. These and later expressions of liberalism were a potent force in European thought, especially after Missolonghi had stamped them with the seal of martyrdom. They would have been more influential if the hopes which they express had not so often been denied in his melancholy or cynical moods. De Musset regards Byron as a chief inspirer of the nerveless despair which afflicted young Frenchmen after the fall of Napoleon,[95] and Carlyle's advice to the seeker of the Everlasting Yea is "Close thy Byron; open thy Goethe." [96] Here, however, is perhaps the fitting place for a brief estimate of Byron as a champion of liberalism.

---

[92] *Ibid.*, I, i, 135ff.   [93] *Ibid.*, II, iv, 61–63.

[94] The more realistic interpretation of *Manfred* which has here been offered derives considerable support from Bertrand Evans, "Manfred's Remorse and Dramatic Tradition," *PMLA*, LXII, 752–773. The article shows that the hero's remorse, while undoubtedly Byron's, is also a familiar element in Gothic drama.

[95] Alfred de Musset, *La Confession d'un Enfant du Siècle*, p. 17.

[96] Thomas Carlyle, *Sartor Resartus*, p. 145.

In many respects he was a fairly typical Holland House Whig, but his early travels and his later ostracism had given him a continental orientation and an unusually broad panorama of recent European history. In matters not too closely related to his basic conflicts he was kind and generous in a lazily good-natured way. He hated cant, hypocrisy, and obscurantism, which in his day as always were prime agents of reaction. The atmosphere of revolution—secret plotting, adventure, defiance, upheaval—was deeply fascinating to one side of his nature, and he liked to picture himself as a man of action in the forefront of such movements. His egotism included a wistful desire to emulate the benevolistic hero who completely externalizes himself in sacrificial devotion to a noble cause. He had the English schoolboy's love of fair play, and the aristocrat's horror at seeing a fine horse beaten by a groom—the horse being the nobler animal of the two. He confused the rebellion of the suffering many against the oppressive few and the rebellion of the distinguished few against the oppressive many. Without any positive program of reform he seems to say, as Crane Brinton expresses it, that "Our sympathies must always be with the will that is beating against restraint, since our own wills would know no master." He was "the poet of the nihilism that is simply the new faith in natural impulse stripped of religious, moral, social, aesthetic control." [97] This equipment was quite sufficient to make him an important figure in the nineteenth-century liberal movement, but not sufficient to make him a lover of his fellow-men. A terrific snob as well as a complete individualist, he despised the mob quite as much as he hated the tyrant. He detested reformers like Colonel Stanhope, who, heaven knows, have a cant of their own, and he felt that Hobhouse had lost caste by associating with the radical members of Parliament. His devotion to the popular cause constantly lapsed into gloom or mockery, for it rested upon an antisocial aversion to control rather than upon any genuine human sympathy. Completely involved in self, he was a rebel of pride and scorn, not a rebel of love. In this spirit he struck many a good blow for freedom, but the most ardent advocate of the social gospel would find it hard to detect an authentically religious quality in Byronic liberalism.

We have seen that pantheistic naturalism, transcendentalism, and liberalism failed to give Byron spiritual satisfaction because his egotism was too blatant to be enwrapped in apparent self-abnegation. He was the betrayer of romanticism, however, in an even more important respect.

[97] *The Political Ideas of the English Romanticists,* pp. 160, 186.

His ego was not merely rampant, but divided against itself. Hence when his romantic bubble expands to the extreme limit of tension, his fingers itch to prick it with the needle of irony. Not long can he breathe the thin, clear, Shelleyan air of the Alps. In October, 1816, he begins his spiritual as well as physical descent to Venice. *Childe Harold* III is the true climax of his serious romantic poetry. *Manfred* foretokens anticlimax in its imitativeness, its overstrained extravagance, its Gothicism, and especially in its thinly concealed exploitation of Byron's personal tragedy.[98] There is hardly the slightest pretense of a benevolistic regard for mankind, and the relation between the hero and his physical surroundings has relapsed into a melancholy dualism. Byron recognized that *Manfred* was "too much in my old style" [99]—more like *Lara* than like *Childe Harold* III. The third act, written in Venice, was originally a piece of only half-serious Gothic claptrap hardly worthy of Monk Lewis. During his visit to Rome he forced himself to revise it into its present "inspiring" state. To Murray, however, he admitted that *Manfred* as a whole was a drama "of a very wild, metaphysical, and inexplicable kind," and that "I have no great opinion of this piece of fantasy." [100] Thus does Venice deflate the illusions of Switzerland.

Childe Harold IV, though written almost wholly in Venice, originated in Rome and has a Roman rather than a Venetian atmosphere. "It treats more of works of art than of nature," the poet assures his publisher.

There are no metaphysics in it—at least, I think not. . . . The Fourth Canto is not a continuation of the Third. I have parted company with Shelley and Wordsworth. Subject-matter and treatment are alike new.[101]

As we have seen, the fourth canto is not so utterly different from the third as these remarks would imply, but Byron's description is substantially accurate. On the whole it is a piece of Holland House Whiggish classicism agitated by the subsiding waves of the romanticism of the preceding year. Highly sensitive in all matters concerning his literary repu-

---

[98] It is a little puzzling that the history of Mary Chaworth, as related in *The Dream* (1816), is made to resemble that of Astarte, who is almost certainly Augusta Leigh. But this difficulty justifies no doubt of the incest hypothesis. Byron wants to hint darkly at his secret without revealing it. He introduces Augusta into *Manfred,* but in *The Dream* and elsewhere he resurrects his early affection for Mary Chaworth in an attempt to convince the public—and perhaps himself—that it was the great love-tragedy of his life. Mary is one of the numerous red herrings of Byron's complicated psychology.

[99] *Letters,* IV, 71.   [100] *Ibid.,* p. 54.   [101] *Ibid.,* p. 155.

tation, Byron has learned from the reviewers, as well as from his own veering nature, to sneer at Wordsworth and Shelley as hopelessly "metaphysical."

But the shift toward a serious classicism was delayed by the dissipations of Venice—at first politely amoral, but increasingly bestial, as Byron, seeking self-forgetfulness through self-desecration, plunged deeper and deeper into the mire. From a strictly literary point of view the results were excellent: Byron as wit, cynic, and satirist writes much better than when he strains to be romantic. What concerns us, however, is his recantation of all that had claimed his allegiance in Switzerland. He must be sneering at Shelley in *Beppo:*

> Oh, Mirth and Innocence! Oh, Milk and Water!
> Ye happy mixtures of more happy days!
>
>   . . .
>
> Oh, for old Saturn's reign of sugar-candy!—
> Meantime I drink to your return in brandy.[102]

In *Don Juan*,[103] Plato as an authority on love is described as more demoralizing than all the poets and novelists put together:

>   . . . You're a bore,
> A charlatan, a coxcomb—and have been,
> At best, no better than a go-between.[104]

A still more striking passage shows young Juan, in the throes of his first love-affair, attempting to achieve spiritual union with nature when what he really wants is physical union with Donna Julia:

> In thoughts like these true wisdom may discern
>   Longings sublime, and aspirations high,
> Which some are born with, but the most part learn
>   To plague themselves withal, they know not why:
> 'Twas strange that one so young should thus concern
>   His brain about the action of the sky;
> If *you* think 'twas philosophy that this did,
> I can't help thinking puberty assisted.

---

[102] *Beppo,* lxxx.

[103] Since only two cantos of *Don Juan* were composed in the Venetian period I shall postpone any general discussion of Byron's masterpiece.

[104] *Don Juan,* I, cxvi.

In the preceding stanzas Byron thrusts at Wordsworth as "unintelligible" and at Coleridge as a "metaphysician." [105] So much for the pantheism of *Childe Harold* III.

We need not suppose that during the Venetian period Byron gave much serious thought to religious questions either pro or con. The gap between Christian theory and Christian practice provides excellent opportunities of which he takes legitimate advantage in *Don Juan:*

> Christians have burnt each other, quite persuaded
> That all the Apostles would have done as they did.[106]

Pious hysteria adds a peculiar hideousness to the shipwreck in Canto II:

> There's nought, no doubt, so much the spirit calms
> As rum and true religion: thus it was,
> Some plundered, some drank spirits, some sung psalms,
>
> . . .
>
> Strange sounds of wailing, blasphemy, devotion,
> Clamoured in chorus to the roaring Ocean.[107]

Both in the Venetian portions of *Don Juan* and in *Beppo,* however, Byron's gibes are directed primarily at Roman Catholicism. He no longer seriously rebukes the Whore of Babylon as in *Childe Harold* I. His tone, on the contrary, is that of a very broad-minded cosmopolitan who derives a sophisticated pleasure from the intermingled piety and corruption of Latin society. Not unlike Pope in *The Rape of the Lock,* he enjoys what he satirizes and is glad to be a part of it. Remembering these days at Cephallonia he told Dr. Kennedy: "I have known a person engaged in sin, and when the vesper-bell has rung, stop and repeat the Ave Maria, and then proceed in the sin: absolution cured all." [108] This is the spirit of the carnival in *Beppo,* when

> The People take their fill of recreation,
> And buy repentance, ere they grow devout.[109]

Wrestling with temptation, Donna Julia

---

[105] *Ibid.,* xc–xciv. In the Dedication, of course, he had derided the Lake poets, especially Southey, as political turncoats and middle-class professional scribblers.
[106] *Ibid.,* lxxxiii.   [107] *Ibid.,* II, xxxiv.
[108] James Kennedy, *Conversations,* p. 86.   [109] *Beppo,* i.

> ... prayed the Virgin Mary for her grace,
> As being the best judge of a lady's case—[110]

and straightway proceeded to commit adultery with Juan. Being Catholics, those who perished in the shipwreck were doubly unfortunate, since

> They must wait several weeks before a mass
> Takes off one peck of purgatorial coals,
> Because, till people know what's come to pass,
> They won't lay out their money on the dead—
> It costs three francs for every mass that's said.[111]

But Fletcher testifies that at this time his master began the practice—faithfully continued thenceforward—of Friday abstinence, and that he was frequently seen to dismount and kneel when a religious procession passed.[112] To a considerable extent, no doubt, he regarded these practices as local superstitions which it might be "good luck" to observe. Friday was a day of ill omen; being in Italy, he would try the Italian way of averting its menace. Medwin, who observed him a few years later, reports: "Lord Byron even formed good and evil auguries from the flight of birds and when he met a *single* magpie in his rides, I have seen him seriously take off his hat—as a propitiation." [113] In no very different spirit did he doff his hat and bend his knee when the Blessed Sacrament went by. Probably it was all nonsense, but one could never be sure.

On a less trivial but still superficial level, Byron was responsive to the magnificence of Catholic worship. On April 9, 1817, he tells Murray that he will not be ready to die until he has paid off some old scores. "Besides," he adds, "when I turn thirty, I will turn devout; I feel a great vocation that way in Catholic churches, and when I hear the organ." [114] Translate this into the poetry of *Childe Harold* IV, and you have the passage on St. Peter's, "this eternal Ark of worship undefiled":

> Enter: its grandeur overwhelms thee not;
> And why? it is not lessened—but thy mind,
> Expanded by the Genius of the spot,
> Has grown colossal, and can only find

---

[110] *Don Juan*, I, lxxv. A discarded MS variant of the second line reads, "Thinking God might not understand the case." (*Works*, VI. 35n.)

[111] *Ibid.*, II, lv.   [112] Kennedy, *op. cit.*, p. 200.

[113] Thomas Medwin, *Life of Shelley*, p. 40n.   [114] *Letters*, IV, 99.

A fit abode wherein appear enshrined
The hopes of Immortality—and thou
Shalt one day, if found worthy, so defined
See thy God face to face, as thou dost now
His Holy of Holies—nor be blasted by his brow.[115]

This passage is very exceptional. Swept along on the torrent of Byron's rhetoric, one hardly notices that he values the cathedral because its bigness, by a sort of empathy, makes him feel "colossal" and fit to confront God. We shall see later what becomes of Byron's Catholic sympathies at Ravenna and Pisa. During the Venetian period they amount to very little.

Neither in body nor in spirit was Byron long able to maintain the mad pace that he set himself at the Palazzo Mocenigo. *So We'll Go No More A-Roving,* probably the best of his lyrics, voices a temporary weariness after the carnival of February, 1817, but the mood gradually becomes chronic:

For the sword outwears its sheath,
And the soul wears out the breast,
And the heart must pause to breathe,
And Love itself have rest.[116]

Before he has finished Canto I of *Don Juan* in September of the following year he admits that he feels played out. His curls are streaked with gray. He no longer thinks his soul "invincible," and he has lost that "freshness of the heart" which doubles the sweetness of actual experience. His own spirit is no longer the whole universe to him: "The illusion's gone for ever." "My days of love are over," and the doctor has cut down his wine. He must take up avarice as "a good old-gentlemanly vice." He has learned too much about the futility of human hopes to be any longer ambitious for fame. But he has had his fling,

So thank your stars that matters are no worse,
And read your Bible, sir, and mind your purse.[117]

But this prematurely middle-aged renunciation of romance and of romanticism is not made without a struggle. Witness the stanza that he scribbled on the back of the manuscript of Canto I:

[115] *Childe Harold,* IV, cliv–clv.   [116] *Works,* IV, 538.
[117] *Don Juan,* I, ccxii–ccxx.

I would to heaven that I were so much clay
  As I am blood, bone, marrow, passion, feeling—
Because at least the past were past away—
  And for the future—(but I write this reeling,
Having got drunk exceedingly today,
  So that I seem to stand upon the ceiling)
I say—the future is a serious matter—
And so—for God's sake—hock and soda-water! [118]

He did not intend to print this stanza: the mask had slipped a little too completely.

At the opening of 1819 Byron fell seriously ill as a result of his dissipations. Thanks largely to Hoppner's influence, La Fornarina and her gang were sent packing. Knowing that Byron could bear anything more easily than ridicule, his wily friend told him that Venetian gossip was depicting him not as an awesome diabolist but quite simply as a fool. On recovering, the poet resumed his visits to such discreetly sophisticated salons as had welcomed him when he first came to Venice. In April he met Teresa Guiccioli, and in December he followed her to Ravenna as her official *cavaliere servente*.

5

It will be convenient to treat as a single period the years spent at Ravenna (December, 1819–October, 1821) and at Pisa (November, 1821– September, 1822). Although during this phase Byron does not achieve integration he comes closer than before to finding an outward *modus vivendi,* a working compromise between the clashing elements of his character. He wants peace and quiet, and he is willing to sacrifice a good deal of romantic illusion in order to be comfortable. Still avid of distinction, he now desires to win it as a poet rather than as a lurid personality. For the time being the Countess Guiccioli was extremely good for him. She was a soothing, sentimental blend of wife, mother, and feminine adorer of genius, rather than a mistress. Satisfying his anxious need of heterosexual dominance without being exhaustingly rapacious in the manner of La Fornarina, she helped to submerge his inner conflict. Through her brother, Count Pietro Gamba, he became associated with the Carbonari. These revolutionists were gentlemen or respectable bour-

[118] *Works,* VI, 2.

geois of gentlemanly behavior whose acquaintance an English nobleman

geois of gentlemanly behavior whose acquaintance an English nobleman might cultivate without soiling his hands. The *opéra bouffe* quality of their secret-society activities sometimes amused him, but they gave a tinge of adventurous idealism to an existence which otherwise might have seemed a little ignoble in its external placidity.

The influence of La Guiccioli on Byron's poetry was less benign: the third and fourth cantos of *Don Juan,* composed during the winter of 1819–1820, were no more to her taste than those written in Venice. Their raciness shocked her prudery; their cynicism offended her sentimentality. Yielding to her entreaties, Byron laid his best poem aside and undertook to be idealistic, patriotic, and classical. Teresa should not, however, bear the whole blame for *Marino Faliero, The Two Foscari,* and *Sardanapalus.* Not only she but Murray had been unenthusiastic about *Don Juan.* As early as 1817, also, Byron had shown in *Childe Harold* IV some tendency to cultivate classicism as a reaction from the overstrained romanticism of the preceding year. After the wild irregularities of Venice, this motive arose again with redoubled force. When introspection became unbearable he recognized his need of outwardness. From embodying the ideals of Italian liberalism in classical tragedies like those of Alfieri (but Otway had shown how to do it in English) he might derive a healing objectivity. This also explains his controversy with Bowles. When Byron sickens of the *élan vital* he turns, almost like a "new humanist," to the *frein vital.*

But when he abjures romanticism he does no less violence to his nature than when he abandons himself to it. He is better as a wit than as a serious romantic poet, but he is better as a serious romantic poet than as a classical dramatist. It is not necessary to show how he defeats his aim of impersonality by projecting obviously personal feelings and situations through the dramatic mask. The three tragedies are of slight importance for us, since other works of the period reveal his religious gropings more directly and richly. Still less need we pause over two plays in which he throws classicism overboard: the cheaply Gothic *Werner,* and *The Deformed Transformed,* which is noteworthy only for the autobiographical interest of its opening scene.

Cain must not be treated so cavalierly. Its importance as a clue to Byron's thought will vary with our belief in his repeated protestations that the utterances of Cain and Lucifer are merely the appropriate speeches of dramatic characters.[119] If these disclaimers are to be credited,

---

[119] *Works,* V, 207–208; *Letters,* VI, 70, 72; Kennedy, *Conversations,* p. 90.

the work is the most astonishing piece of unintentional self-revelation on record. Consciously or unconsciously (but need we hesitate to choose the former adverb?), *Cain* is a faithful reflection of Byron's spiritual predicament. He denies responsibility for his thoughts partly as a defense against the reviewers but largely because he does not like to admit even to himself the full extent of his unbelief. The Preface is a smoke-screen: in Genesis nothing is said about Satan—the serpent is Eve's only tempter; the Old Testament gives no hint of a future life—hence the idea would be new to Cain; Cuvier's theory of pre-Genesis worlds and pre-Adamite men does not conflict with Moses. This emphasis on the relatively superficial combined with complete omission of the essential is not fully explained by Byron's awareness that many of his readers would attach supreme importance to the former. He is not a profound thinker, but he is not as shallow as this. He knew that his real theme was man's hopeless defiance of God, and he shrank from that knowledge.

Other scholars have said all that needs to be said about the intellectual and literary background of the drama—its Manichaeanism, its indebtedness to Bayle and other sceptics, its enlistment of science against orthodoxy, its relationship to *Faust,* and so on. Let us rather focus our attention on Cain's personal tragedy:

> It is not with the earth, though I must till it,
> I feel at war—but that I may not profit
> By what it bears of beautiful, untoiling,
> Nor gratify my thousand swelling thoughts
> With knowledge, nor allay my thousand fears
> Of Death and Life.[120]

It is important to observe that his passion for knowledge implies no delight in the quest for truth or in the free play of speculation. For Byron as for his hero, knowledge is not the goal of thought, but the result of being released from the necessity of thinking. Just as Cain would enjoy the bounties of nature "untoiling," so he would be granted, without painful effort, the answers to all the unanswerable questions. Pending such omniscience he will not worship the inexplicable God of Zillah's prayer,

> ...who, loving, making, blessing all,
> Yet didst permit the Serpent to creep in,
> And drive my father forth from Paradise.[121]

[120] *Cain,* II, ii, 125–130.   [121] *Ibid.,* I, i, 18–20.

Neither the humility nor the adventure of faith holds any meaning for him. He can see no reason for gratitude or for contrition. Why should he be subject to the curse of death merely because his parents have erred?

> ...What is that
> To us? They sinned, then *let them* die! [122]

Beneath all his turbulent questionings and denials lies the flinty rock of pride. When Adah begs him to find happiness in submission to God he retorts:

> I will have nought to do with happiness
> Which humbles me and mine. [123]

As Professor Chew has noted,

The chief flaw in the poem from the technical point of view is that Lucifer is but a glorified Cain. . . . There is no dramatic contrast, no struggle between good and evil. Lucifer does not have to win Cain over to his side. [124]

They are both

> Souls who dare use their immortality—
> Souls who dare look the Omnipotent tyrant in
> His everlasting face, and tell him that
> His evil is not good! [125]

Cain, to be sure, refuses to bow before Lucifer just as he has always refused to bow before God, but he is answered:

> ...Ne'er the less,
> Thou art my worshipper; not worshipping
> Him makes thee mine the same. [126]

This is so obviously true that it is ungrateful of Lucifer to encompass the destruction of so loyal a disciple. It is also inconsistent; for Byron, as Dr. Marjarum observes, has made "a complete break with historic Christianity" by identifying Lucifer not with evil but with knowledge. [127]

---

[122] *Ibid.*, III, i, 75–76.   [123] *Ibid.*, I, i, 465–466.
[124] S. C. Chew, *The Dramas of Lord Byron*, pp. 130–131.
[125] *Cain*, I, i, 137–140.   [126] *Ibid.*, ll. 301–319.
[127] E. W. Marjarum, *Byron as Skeptic and Believer*, p. 35.

Herein lies the only important difference between the rebellious angel and his pupil. The former, in the expressive slang of our students, "knows all the answers." Foreseeing the incest of Byron and Augusta he warns Cain and his sister that in future ages such love as theirs will be prohibited.[128] Much more importantly he suggests that God, "so restless in his wretchedness," may some day create a Son of His own—"and if he doth,/Mark me! that Son will be a sacrifice!" [129] Here we recall a letter of 1811 in which Byron tells Hodgson that "The basis of your religion is *injustice; the Son of God,* the *pure,* the *immaculate,* the *innocent,* is sacrificed for the Guilty." [130] Apparently he was never able to think of the Atonement otherwise than as a particularly repulsive example of divine unfairness. I cannot agree with Marjarum in ascribing to Byron's early religious training his rejection of the whole redemptive aspect of Christianity.[131] There is more of egotism than Calvinism in his attitude. He feels that he would have been highly indignant if God had crucified *him* for the sins of other men. Unable to conceive of divine self-sacrifice, he cannot see in Genesis the first stages of a redemptive plan: it is merely an ugly tale of obscurantism and malice.

But let us return to Lucifer. He demoralizes Cain by making him feel at the same time excessively big and excessively little. By means of the universal tour he satisfies his victim's pride with huge draughts of knowledge, but he crushes that pride by demonstrating Cain's insignificance in relation to infinite space and time, the fleshly degradations of earthly existence, and the inevitable doom of death. How Act II prepares for the catastrophe of Act III is clearly explained to Murray:

Cain is a proud man; if Lucifer promised him kingdoms, etc., it would *elate* him: the object of the Demon is to *depress* him still further in his own estimation than he was before, by showing him infinite things and his own abasement, till he falls into the frame of mind that leads to the Catastrophe, from mere *internal* irritation, *not* premeditation, or envy of Abel, . . . but from the rage and fury against the inadequacy of his state to his conceptions, and which discharges itself rather against Life, and the Author of Life, than the mere living.[132]

Professor Chew objects that in Act III Cain is, after all, angered because Abel's sacrifices prove more acceptable than his own, and that

---

[128] *Cain,* I, i, 363–367.   [129] *Ibid.,* ll. 137ff.   [130] *Vide supra,* p. 405.
[131] *Op. cit.,* p. 21.   [132] *Letters,* V, 470.

Byron's faithfulness to the Biblical narrative at this point clashes with his depiction of the first murderer as a noble man who desires nothing but good.[133] Perhaps, however, Cain is not so much personally envious of his brother as irritated beyond endurance by the submissiveness of those

> ...burnt offerings, which he daily brings
> With a meek brow, whose base humility
> Shows more of fear than worship—as a bribe
> To the Creator.[134]

The humility of others is hard for frustrated pride to bear.

Byron's only serious and substantial attempt to grapple with basic religious problems ends in a stalemate between his mind, which, as Lucifer says, was "made/To sway," [135] and the checks which God imposes upon its ambitions. His pride forbids him to believe in an extrapersonal curb, but his sense of limitation forces that belief upon him. "The inadequacy of his state to his conceptions" does not express the tragedy of a character in a play: it expresses the personal tragedy of Lord Byron. The only hint of a solution appears in Lucifer's parting words:

> Think and endure,—and form an inner world
> In your own bosom—where the outward fails;
> So shall you nearer be the spiritual
> Nature, and war triumphant with your own.[136]

Here is the *Manfred* conception of mind as a stronghold against life. But the inner world of Byron's bosom was a chaos which, as he well knew, did not include the power to transform itself into a cosmos.

Cain deserves the sympathetic respect of all readers, whatever they may believe or disbelieve. *Heaven and Earth* deserves no respect at all. Byron was not the man to base a sacred drama upon Genesis vi,1,2: "And it came to pass that the sons of God saw the daughters of men that they were fair." [137] "The new Mystery," he eagerly assures Moore, "is less speculative than *Cain,* and very pious; besides, it is chiefly lyrical." [138] Surely the reviewers would not fall upon so edifying a work. As for the lyricism, the unrhymed strophes owe far too much to Southey's *Thalaba:* one should

---

[133] *Op. cit.,* p. 130.   [134] *Cain,* III, i, 100–103.   [135] *Ibid.,* I, i, 215–216.
[136] *Ibid.,* II, ii, 463–466.
[137] Actually the poem draws more from the Book of Enoch than from Genesis.
[138] *Letters,* VI, 31.

not borrow from an enemy. The piety is pervasive but factitious. Byron's real sympathies are clearly with the fiery Aholibamah, a descendant of Cain who preserves much of her ancestor's rebellious spirit. The human-angelic love-affairs would be distasteful if they were not so absurd. The angel Samiasa, scolded by Noah as he emerges from the cave where he (Samiasa, not Noah) has been enjoying an assignation with Aholibamah, ingeniously justifies his conduct:

> Was not man made in high Jehovah's image?
> Did God not love what he had made? And what
> Do we but imitate and emulate
> His love unto created love?[139]

With the possible exception of *Hebrew Melodies, Heaven and Earth* is the sole work in which Byron is consciously dishonest. He deserves credit only for having been unable to finish it.

The relatively stable equilibrium of the Ravenna-Pisa period, lost on the tragic level in *Cain,* is at least outwardly regained on the level of satiric comedy in *Don Juan.*[140] Although Byron was never further from achieving integration than in this masterpiece, the Italian tradition of mock-romance, now inflating and now pricking the romantic bubble, enabled him to juxtapose the discordant elements of his nature in an aesthetic illusion of unity. In resuming *Don Juan* he was not exactly breaking his promise to the Countess, for he made of it something rather different from the *Beppo*-like poem to which she had objected. Canto V, which belongs to the autumn of 1820, is mainly in the old frivolously racy manner; but Cantos VI–XVI, written between June, 1822, and the end of March, 1823,[141] are considerably more penetrating in their social satire and more serious in their fundamental thinking.

But we probably exaggerate this change if we assert that *Don Juan* "turned gradually into a battle standard of revolt."[142] There is still much

---

[139] *Heaven and Earth,* iii, 477–480.

[140] The same remark would apply to *The Vision of Judgment.* Despite the amusing irreverence of its "machinery" that magnificent satire moves on a high ethical plane, but it tells us little or nothing about Byron's religion. See the opening of this chapter, however, for the satirist's unexpectedly warm response to the glory of the Archangel Michael.

[141] The poem therefore runs beyond the close of the Ravenna-Pisa period, but this section is the most appropriate place for our discussion of it.

[142] Elizabeth F. Boyd, *Byron's Don Juan,* p. 16. The same overemphasis on the serious purposiveness of the poem appears in P. G. Trueblood, *The Flowering of Byron's Genius: Studies in Byron's Don Juan.*

to be said for Fuess's old-fashioned view that although Byron is wonderfully effective in attacking specific evils and absurdities he becomes "essentially shallow and cynical" when he touches upon general ideas and that he "took no positive attitude toward any of the great problems of existence."[143] Attempts to discover a single consistent theme in *Don Juan* are not convincing. Sir Herbert Grierson rightly rejects E. H. Coleridge's influential interpretation when he says:

Byron is not concerned to vindicate the natural man or life. He is content to describe with a blend of Fielding's sympathy with youth, Voltaire's mocking gaiety, and Swift's sombre reflection on human nature, life in the class that ruled Europe, from Britain to Turkey.[144]

In a manner traditional with satirists, Byron frequently appeals from the vices and follies of corrupt civilization to a standard called "nature." The contrast is blurred, however, because on the one hand he does not firmly believe in nature, either external or internal; while on the other hand upper-class European society "possessed for Byron an attraction and authority it never possessed for Shelley."[145]

> It is not that I adulate the people:
>   Without *me,* there are demagogues enough,
> And infidels, to pull down every steeple,
>   And set up in their place some proper stuff.
> Whether they may sow scepticism to reap Hell,
>   As is the Christian dogma rather tough,
> I do not know;—I wish men to be free
> As much from mobs as kings—from you as me.[146]

As always, Byron wants liberty. But anyone enlisting under this "battle standard of revolt" would find it hard to say what he was fighting *for.*

Since criticism of *Don Juan* is not our prime concern, let us freely blend the text of the poem with Byron's letters and journals of the period and with reports of contemporary observers. Byron has a fine hatred of pious cant and pretense:

> Oh for a *forty-parson power* to chant
>   Thy praise, Hypocrisy! Oh for a hymn

[143] C. M. Fuess, *Lord Byron as a Satirist in Verse,* pp. 179, 215.
[144] *The Background of English Literature,* p. 195.
[145] *Ibid.,* p. 168.   [146] *Don Juan,* IX, xxv.

> Loud as the virtues thou dost loudly vaunt,
> Not practise! [147]

Any sort of bigotry and intolerance is detestable to him. The clerical guest at the Amundeville house-party, "Who did not hate so much the sin as sinner," [148] might have been one of those parsons who enraged him by preaching against *Cain*—"the scoundrels of priests, who do more harm to religion than all the infidels that ever forgot their catechisms!" [149] For him the Athanasian Creed is a prime example of the facility with which Christians consign one another to damnation:

> 'Tis so sententious, positive, and terse,
> And decorates the Book of Common Prayer,
> As doth a rainbow the just clearing air.[150]

On the whole subject of Hell, as Dr. Marjarum points out, he is naturally a little uneasy;[151] but in the Ravenna Diary he spurns the doctrine of *eternal* punishment as a bullying threat which is inconsistent with belief in a loving God.[152] Pietro Gamba remembered that he preferred no one Christian denomination over another but always expressed deep respect for the fundamental teachings of Christ.[153] In *Don Juan* Jesus is addressed as one whose "pure creed" men have distorted into a "sanction of all ill," and a note adds: "If ever God was man—or man God—he was *both*. I never arraigned his creed, but the use—or abuse—made of it." [154]

Although *Don Juan* is not to be recommended for Lenten reading it does not expressly deny any essential doctrine of historic Christianity. But if Byron were asked to be more specific as to the "creed" of Jesus he would probably have fallen back upon a sentimentally benevolistic interpretation of Christian ethics. "As for the incomprehensible mysteries of religion," says Gamba, "his mind floated in doubts which he wished most earnestly to dispel, as they oppressed him." He was a doubter who found no satisfaction in his doubts: arguments overtly hostile to religion, like those of Helvétius, "gave him pain." [155] Medwin also testifies that even in private conversation Byron "never scoffed at religion. . . . In fact he was always afraid to confess to himself his own infidelity." [156] There is some evidence

---

[147] *Ibid.*, X, xxxiv. The first line alludes to a quip by Sydney Smith. (*Works*, VI, 410n.)
[148] *Ibid.*, lxxxvii. [149] *Letters*, VI, 24. [150] *Don Juan*, VI, xxiii.
[151] *Op. cit.*, p. 36. [152] *Letters*, VI, 457.
[153] Richard Edgcumbe, *Byron: The Last Phase*, p. 16.
[154] *Don Juan*, XV, xviii; *Works*, VI, 548n. [155] Edgcumbe, *op. cit.*, p. 5.
[156] *Life of Shelley*, p. 331.

that he read his Bible rather diligently,[157] but none that it solved any of his difficulties.

In 1821 he was deeply affected on receiving from one John Shepard, a pious clothier of Frome, a courteous letter enclosing a prayer on Byron's behalf which he had found among the papers of his dead wife.[158] Two years later the poet still cherishes this tender charitable intercession, so free from pharisaical spleen and so full of admiration of his misused genius. "Before I had read this prayer," he told Lady Blessington,

I never rightly understood the expression, so often used, "The beauty of holiness." This prayer and letter has done more to give me a good Opinion of religion, and its professors, than all the religious books I ever read in my life.

"Mrs. Shepard," he said to the Countess on another occasion, "is mixed up with all my religious aspirations: nothing ever so excited my imagination, and touched my heart, as her prayer." He imagines her alone in her chamber, praying for *him*. "I would give anything to have her portrait"— Shepard's description of his wife as "lovely" enhanced Byron's appreciation of the beauty of holiness.[159] But not many Evangelical women possessed this qualification, and when they prayed for Byron at all it was usually with a confident hope that their prayers were in vain. If Evangelicalism had not been an increasingly dominant force in the Church of England at this time, Byron might have found it easier to accept Christianity. He greatly disliked the religious temper of that middle class from which he had escaped in boyhood.

On the other hand—for these paragraphs must waver with the waverings of Byron's mind—the Regency man-about-town tradition to which he remained somewhat anachronistically loyal gave him an equal dislike for radical system-mongers and doctrinaire infidels. Even toward one unusually admirable example of the type he was growing cooler. "Shelley appears to me to be mad with his metaphysics," he said to Gamba. "What trash in all these systems! Say what they will, mystery for mystery, I still find that of the Creation the most reasonable of any." [160]

But one could never be *certain,* and he was unwilling to take a single step in the dark. An entry in the Ravenna Diary reads:

[157] *Letters,* V, 391; Kennedy, *Conversations,* p. 201.
[158] *Letters,* V, 489–490. Mrs. Shepard had written the prayer in 1814.
[159] *Conversations of Lord Byron with the Countess of Blessington,* pp. 47–50.
[160] Edgcumbe, *op. cit.,* p. 15.

According to the Christian dispensation, no one can know whether he is *sure* of salvation. . . . Now therefore, whatever the certainty of faith in the facts may be, the certainty of the individual as to his happiness or misery is no greater than it was under Jupiter.

And yet, although the immortality of the soul may be only a *grand peut-être*. "still it is a grand one. Every body clings to it—the stupidest, and dullest, and wickedest of human bipeds is still persuaded that he is immortal." [161] But this proved nothing, and without proof he could not believe.

Perhaps change of locale is the chief reason why Byron's confidential gibes at the Church of Rome and its adherents become less frequent in the later cantos of *Don Juan*. There is external evidence, however, that during the Ravenna-Pisa period he feels a rather strong attraction toward Catholicism. It is certainly the best religion for little Allegra, who will grow up in Italy and will probably marry an Italian. She must be sent to a convent rather than remain with those vegetarian infidels, the Shelleys, "to perish of Starvation, and green fruit, or to be taught to believe that there is no Deity." [162] In discussing her rearing, furthermore, Byron sometimes intimates that Catholicism would also be the best religion for him if he could believe anything at all. To Moore, who has been alarmed by the impieties of *Cain,* he makes his usual disclaimer of responsibility for the opinions of his characters and adds:

I am no enemy of religion, but the contrary. As a proof, I am educating my natural daughter a strict Catholic in a convent of Romagna; for I think people can never have *enough* of religion if they are to have any. I incline, myself, very much to the Catholic doctrines.[163]

Four days later he explains to the same correspondent that the Catholic Church appeals to him because it is so "tangible":

It is by far the most elegant worship, hardly excepting the Greek mythology. What with incense, pictures, statues, altars, shrines, relics, and the real presence, confession, absolution,—there is something sensible to grasp at. Besides, it leaves no possibility of doubt; for those who swallow their Deity, really and truly, in transubstantiation, can hardly find anything else otherwise than easy of digestion. I am afraid that this sounds flippant, but I don't mean it to be so;

---

[161] *Letters*, V, 186–187.   [162] *Ibid.*, p. 15; see also p. 264 and IV, 123–124.
[163] *Ibid.*, VI, 32.

only my turn of mind is so given to taking things in the absurd point of view, that it breaks out in spite of me every now and then. Still, I do assure you that I am a very good Christian.[164]

This jumble of essentials and non-essentials, of desire for certitude and mockery, is the very essence of Byron.

Dr. Marjarum finds it surprising that the poet was friendliest to Catholicism in his most sceptical period.[165] But is not the unhappy doubter with no faith in reason one of the types most likely to be attracted by an authoritative religion which gives "something sensible to grasp at" and "leaves no possibility of doubt"? The sceptical road to Rome has been followed by many a pilgrim. It seldom leads to the very centre, but it will get one within the city limits. In Canto XI of *Don Juan* Byron says that he would like to accept the philosophy of Berkeley, which he wrongly associates with a "universal egotism," but he suspects that the theory is absurd. He has decided that all metaphysical problems are hopeless. With each bout of illness he grows more and more orthodox. Now he wishes that there were *four* Persons in the Godhead, "On purpose to believe so much the more." [166] In this mood he might easily have submitted to the Church. He was held back by his British prejudices, by his romantic aversion to control, and by the honesty which never quite deserted him.

In *Don Juan* these Catholic hankerings are only faintly discernible. For the most familiar example we must go back as far as the "Ave Maria" lines in stanzas cii–ciii in Canto III. But this passage, after all, merely adds a spice of mock-spirituality to the scene in which

> The lady and her lover, all alone,
> The rosy flood of twilight's sky admired.

The identification of "the hour of prayer" with "the hour of love" is ambiguous. Having used the Virgin for a stage effect he dismisses her completely in stanza civ:

> Some kinder casuists are pleased to say,
> In nameless print—that I have no devotion;
> But set those persons down with me to pray,

---

[164] *Ibid.*, p. 38.   [165] *Op. cit.*, p. 82.
[166] *Don Juan*, XI, i–vi. The reference to Berkeley suggests that a misinterpretation of his philosophy may have provided the basis for Byron's conception of the mind as an impregnable personal refuge.

And you shall see who has the properest notion
Of getting into Heaven the shortest way;
   My altars are the mountains and the Ocean,
Earth—air—stars,—all that springs from the great Whole,
Who hath produced, and will receive the Soul.

Dr. Marjarum, who seems inclined to take Byron's Catholicism too seriously, defends the "Ave Maria" passage:

The admixture of pantheism and natural religion which follows it by no means proves that Byron's reverence was shallow. He very probably felt nothing incongruous between nature-mysticism and the adoration of a religious personage.[167]

But one cannot attribute much profundity of religious emotion to a man who can be a Catholic in one stanza and a nature-worshipper in the next. The incongruity is not only one of doctrine, but of feeling; that Byron fails to perceive it is precisely what convicts him of shallowness. Stanza civ in itself is a muddle: when he calls "the great Whole" a creative "Who," he is neither a pantheist nor a believer in a personal God.

Even disregarding this inconsistency, the pantheism of the stanza is that of Pope rather than that of Shelley. The latter's nature-mysticism had been abandoned before the close of 1816 and it was never seriously revived. According to Countess Guiccioli, in the period now under discussion pantheism was "odious to him," and she shows unusual acuteness in suggesting that the main reason was his unwillingness to make any surrender of his individuality.[168] In his occasional reliance on the eighteenth-century sort of natural revelation he is exactly where he was in 1807 when he wrote *The Prayer of Nature*. At Ravenna he demanded of Pietro Gamba, "How, raising our eyes to heaven, or directing them to the earth, can we doubt of the existence of a God?"[169] As early as 1813, however, he had told Gifford that one of the two chief sources of his unbelief was his sense of "the comparative insignificance of ourselves and *our world,* when placed in competition with the mighty whole";[170] and it is largely by arousing the same feeling that Lucifer works the destruction of *Cain*. Nature was not for Byron a consistently satisfying object of devotion: she spelt affirmation or negation according to his mood.

[167] *Op. cit.*, p. 80.   [168] Richard Edgcumbe, *Byron: The Last Phase*, p. 15.
[169] James Kennedy, *Conversations*, p. 204.   [170] *Vide supra*, p. 394.

Returning for a moment to the question of Byron's Catholic sympathies, we recall that in Canto XIII the Gothic glories of Norman Abbey (Newstead, of course) include a crowned statue of

> The Virgin-Mother of the God-born Child,
> With her Son in her blessed arms . . .
>
> . . .
>
> She made the earth below seem holy ground.
> This may be superstition, weak or wild,
> But even the faintest relics of a shrine
> Of any worship wake some thoughts divine.[171]

This more than merely descriptive stanza rings truer than the "Ave Maria" passage. It suggests, however, that Byron wants Catholic worship without Catholic belief, and that he is wistfully aware of the futility of deriving "thoughts divine" from the former while rejecting the "superstition" of the latter. Emotionally, he often wishes that he could believe; intellectually, he will accept no creed which cannot be "proved" in an almost childishly literal sense.

Nothing remains for him, then, but the scepticism which is all-pervasive in *Don Juan* and which vitiates the constructive elements of the great satire. If we knew the real truth about anything, he says, a great deal of excellent philosophizing would be spoiled. No question can be answered. We cannot trust our senses, but what else *can* we trust? He neither affirms nor denies anything. The only certitude is that man is mortal. We long for rest, but we dread death—and yet we are almost ready to destroy ourselves in order to solve the mystery.[172] Something impels him, however, to keep asking unanswerable questions:

> My tendency is to philosophize
>   On most things, from a tyrant to a tree;
> But still the spouseless virgin *Knowledge* flies.
>   What are we? and whence came we? what shall be
> Our *ultimate* existence? what's our present?
> Are questions answerless, and yet incessant.[173]

In reading such passages do we reach the very rock-bottom of Byron? Or are we to say that he believes much more than this, but wishes to

---

[171] *Don Juan,* XIII, lxi.   [172] *Ibid.,* XIV, i–vi.

[173] *Ibid.,* VI, lxiii. Passages of the same tenor are numerous; see for example V, xxxviii–xxxix; IX, xvii; X, xx.

evade the curb imposed by definite conclusions? Or is he trying to conceal from himself a deeper, more defiant negation which is more boldly expressed in *Cain?* I do not know, and I shall not attempt to guess. What seems certain is that the witty Pyrrhonism of *Don Juan* gives him no genuine peace:

> Ecclesiastes said, "that all is vanity"—
>   Most modern preachers say the same, or show it
> By their examples of true Christianity:
>   In short, all know, or very soon may know it;
> And in this scene of all-confessed inanity,
>   By Saint, by Sage, by Preacher, and by Poet,
> Must I restrain me, through the fear of strife,
> From holding up the nothingness of Life?[174]

There is the real theme of *Don Juan.* Burlesque has supplanted romance; but often the laughter of the poem is merely a cynical substitute for tears,

>   ...and if I weep,
>   'Tis that our nature cannot always bring
>   Itself to apathy, for we must steep
> Our hearts first in the depths of Lethe's spring,
>   Ere what we least wish to behold will sleep:
> Thetis baptized her mortal son in Styx;
> A mortal mother would on Lethe fix.[175]

In 1821 he confided to his Diary:

If I had to live over again, I do not know what I would change in my life, unless it were *for not to have lived at all.* . . . What can it [life] give us but *years?* and those have little good but their ending.[176]

6

It was a confused and unhappy man who established himself at Genoa in September, 1822. His inward conflicts had continued to seethe beneath the apparent stability of the preceding period, and even the outward circumstances of those years had gradually deteriorated. In varying degrees his spirits had been depressed by the increasing wearisomeness of Teresa Guiccioli, the collapse of the Italian revolutionary movement, the impor-

[174] *Ibid.,* VII, vi.   [175] *Ibid.,* IV, iii–iv.   [176] *Letters,* V, 456.

tunities of Claire, the deaths of Allegra and of Shelley, and the strained relations with Leigh Hunt after Shelley's passing.

Worst of all, by the end of 1822 it was clear to Byron that his literary reputation was declining. Once he had been "the grand Napoleon of the realms of rhyme,"

> But Juan was my Moscow, and Faliero
> My Leipsic, and my Mont Saint Jean seems Cain.[177]

His three classical tragedies, written as penance for the literary sins of his youth, were severely attacked in the *Edinburgh Review* and won no favor elsewhere. Yet when he revived and matured his romantic manner in *Cain* or offered high comedy in *Don Juan* he was assailed as a monster of immorality and impiety. Mr. Johnson has shown that Byron exaggerated the element of canting hypocrisy in the public reaction to *Cain* and *Don Juan* because he did not realize the extent to which the Evangelical temper, if not the Evangelical creed, had permeated all levels of British society. Even before his exile he had led a curiously isolated existence, and since the spring of 1816 he had been entirely shut off from developments which had made the standards of a Regency buck increasingly unfashionable.[178] His association with vulgar Cockney radicals in the *Liberal* scheme had aggravated his politico-literary unpopularity and had caused him to lose face even with his London friends and advisers.

If he could no longer expand his personality through poetry, it was time to adopt a new rôle—that of the man of action. Perhaps in the land where once he had been happy he could escape his thoughts in an assertion of vital power:

> The sword, the banner, and the field,
> Glory and Greece, around me see!

And perhaps he might find, like Manfred, that " 'tis not so difficult to die":

> If thou regret'st thy youth, *why live?*
> The land of honourable death

---

[177] *Don Juan*, XI, lv–lvi.

[178] E. D. H. Johnson, "Don Juan in England," *ELH*, XI, 135–153. See also M. J. Quinlan, *Victorian Prelude*, for evidence of the degree to which "Victorianism" had become dominant in English culture long before the accession of Victoria.

Is here:—up to the field and give
Away thy breath! [179]

Lady Blessington puts it more coolly:

The end and aim of his life is to render himself celebrated: hitherto his pen has
been the instrument to cut his road to renown; . . . this, he thinks, has lost
some of its point, and he is now about to change it for the sword.[180]

Since Byron's motives were never unmixed, it would be no less rash than
unfair to assert that a genuine enthusiasm for human liberty played no
part in his decision; but there can be little doubt that the Greek expedition
was almost wholly a personal remedy for a personal predicament.

Unfortunately, by the time Lady Blessington cast her shrewd eyes upon
him in Genoa he greatly regretted that he had ever entangled himself
with the Greek Committee. The officiousness of Trelawny, that parody of
the Byronic hero, had pushed a luxurious fantasy into the uncomfortable
sphere of action. If ever he had been fitted to lead a politico-military expedition, the time for such exertions had passed. The whole thing was "a
fool's errand." [181] As for "a soldier's grave," he felt a presentiment that
"as I have not been famous for my luck in life, most probably I shall . . .
draw my last sigh, not on the field of glory, but on the bed of disease." [182]
To Lady Blessington it seemed

extraordinary to see a man about to engage in a chivalrous, and according to
the opinion of many, a Utopian undertaking, for which his habits peculiarly
unfit him, without any indication of the enthusiasm that leads men to embark
in such careers.[183]

With ominously rapid oscillation, he appeared before her now as the
cynical wit, now as the extinct volcano of blighted passion; uneasily histrionic, living more in the past than in the present, mulling over his "domestic misfortunes" with an "incontinency of speech" which to her more
genuinely aristocratic taste betrayed "want of delicacy of mind." [184]

Byron would not, however, be likely to obtrude the defiant infidelity of
Cain upon a lady of quality. Furthermore, this was a time when he should

---

[179] *Works*, VII, 87–88. *On This Day I Complete My Thirty-Sixth Year* was of course
written at Missolonghi, but as an attempt to revive the mood in which he had first conceived of the Greek expedition.   [180] *Op. cit.*, p. 63.   [181] *Letters*, VI, 257.
[182] Blessington, *op. cit.*, p. 173.   [183] *Ibid.*, p. 63.   [184] *Ibid.*, pp. 24, 36.

try to believe as much as possible: if the Greek expedition was not to be a complete spiritual disaster he must emphasize all the positive and constructive fragments of his divided thought. Hence Lady Blessington found him *"sceptical,* but not unbelieving," a firm believer in immortality and "a sworn foe to Materialism, tracing every defect to which we are subject, to the infirmities of clay in which the heavenly spark is confined." Matter, we may remind ourselves, was always one of Byron's favorite scapegoats; his determinism was more pseudo-scientific than Calvinistic. His observer continues:

Conscience, he says, is to him another proof of the Divine Origin of Man, as is also his natural tendency to the love of good. A fine day, a moonlight night, or any other fine object in the phenomena of nature excites (said Byron) strong feelings of religion in all elevated minds, and an outpouring of the spirit to the Creator, that, call it what we may, is the essence of innate love and gratitude to the Divinity.[185]

Sentimental deism was the only positive form of belief to which he could lay claim, and at this time he was apparently making the most of it.

Since *Don Juan* was considered in the preceding section, little need be said about the poetry of this short and mainly non-literary final period. *The Age of Bronze* briefly thrusts at a Church of England which is more concerned with tithes and pluralities than with religion. It also includes an angry sneer at the growing influence of the Jews in Europe and especially in England; Byron's tolerance was only theoretically unlimited.[186] Just as this ineffective satire looks back to *English Bards and Scotch Reviewers,* *The Island* looks back to the early tales of Mediterranean adventure. It is rather disconcerting to see how easily Byron can turn his different veins of poetry on and off like taps of hot and cold water. Here is the Byronic hero in all his blighted pride:

> But Christian, of a higher order, stood
> Like an extinct volcano in his mood;
> Silent, and sad, and savage—with the trace
> Of passion reeking from his clouded face.[187]

Or shall we have a little of the pantheism which he has described to Teresa as "odious"?

---

[185] *Ibid.,* pp. 49–50.   [186] *The Age of Bronze,* ll. 642ff., 673ff.
[187] *The Island,* III, 139–142.

> Live not the Stars and Mountains? Are the waves
> Without a spirit? Are the dropping caves
> Without a feeling in their silent tears?
> No, no; they woo and clasp us to their spheres,
> Dissolve this clog and clod of clay before
> Its hour, and merge our soul in the great shore.
> Strip off this fond and false identity!
> Who thinks of self when gazing on the sky?[188]

Byron, for one, most assuredly does. The more-than-Turkish rapture of love in the South Seas gives promise of immortality,

> ... for earthly life has nought
> Matched with that burst of Nature, even in thought;
> And all our dreams of better life above
> But close in one eternal gush of love.[189]

As he had said to Lady Blessington,

> Whatever creed be taught, or land be trod,
> Man's conscience is the Oracle of God.[190]

But the real meaning of this elevating statement is revealed by another couplet in praise of

> The wish, which ages have not yet subdued
> In man, to have no master save his mood.[191]

Byron's activities in Greece do not pertain to our subject. In my opinion Nicolson is amply justified in refusing to believe

the legend that Byron went to Greece inspired solely by Philhellenic enthusiasms, or that his sojourn in Missolonghi was anything but a succession of humiliating failures. . . . Lord Byron accomplished nothing at Missolonghi except his own suicide; but by that single act of heroism he secured the liberation of Greece.[192]

More important for us, however, are the attempts of Dr. Kennedy to convert him before he left Cephallonia for the mainland.

James Kennedy was a Scottish medical officer attached to the garrison

---

[188] *Ibid.*, II, 386–393.   [189] *Ibid.*, ll. 119–122.   [190] *Ibid.*, I, 123–124.
[191] *Ibid.*, ll. 37–38.   [192] H. G. Nicolson, *Byron: the Last Journey*, p. ix.

of the island. Nicolson calls him a Methodist.[193] The pious doctor himself disclaims this title, though he adds: "I have a high respect for this zealous body. . . . Wesley, I think, was much inferior to Whitefield." [194] Close inspection of his book reveals him as a Presbyterian sufficiently strict to regard Boston's *Fourfold State of Man,* that rock-ribbed epitome of free-grace Calvinism,[195] as the most useful systematic sketch of Christian fundamentals. ("I shall read it with pleasure," Byron gravely promised.)[196] Kennedy had also, however, been strongly influenced by English Evangelicalism: the writings of John Newton and Scott's *Commentary* were treasured weapons in his apologetic armory. It is natural that as a Calvinist he should have preferred Whitefield to Wesley. Although he innocently fancied himself a theologian he was really very simple both in mind and heart. The spirit if not the letter of his creed was mild and charitable, and his enthusiasm was completely honest. "You have saved my life. Saint Kennedy has been boring me to distraction," said Byron to a noble caller who had interrupted one of their colloquies.[197] But in reasonably small doses he respected and liked the doctor, finding in his appearance and way of speaking a similarity to Shelley. The medico admired Byron's poems although he disapproved of them. Needless to say, however, his favorite poet was William Cowper—a preference which Byron did not share.[198]

Despite what seems to us an excessively literalistic view of the Scriptures, Kennedy was so warm an admirer of Thomas Erskine, the Scottish liberal theologian, that he valued the internal evidences of Christianity even more than the external. But being extremely systematic, he thought it more logical to begin with the external evidences as a sort of prolegomenon. Being also extremely long-winded, and meeting plenty of opposition from his lordship, he had not reached the internal evidences when Byron left Metaxata.[199] This was perhaps an error in tactics, for the poet was more responsive to religious feelings than to alleged religious facts. On the other hand one wonders whether any amount of self-scrutiny would have led Byron into the Christian fold. At all events Kennedy was the man to set Byron talking about religion, but not the man to convert him. Nicolson suggests that if the doctor had been a Catholic "the result might well have been a dramatic and emotional conversion. Which, I suppose, would have

---

[193] *Ibid.,* p. 152.   [194] James Kennedy, *Conversations,* p. 144.
[195] *Vide supra,* p. 33.   [196] Kennedy, *op. cit.,* p. 113.
[197] Nicolson, *op. cit.,* p. 150.   [198] Kennedy, *op. cit.,* pp. 88–89.
[199] Kennedy (*op. cit.,* p. 139) did give Byron a French translation—the only copy available —of Erskine's *Internal Evidences of Religion,* but we cannot suppose that Byron read it.

proved of considerable subsequent assistance." [200] Let us lay heavy stress on "dramatic and emotional," and let us conjecture that the assistance thus gained might not have been very solid or lasting.

Even as an Evangelical Protestant, however, Dr. Kennedy had some reason to think that his task was not utterly hopeless. Byron assured him that he not only approached the subject with an open mind but was "very desirous of believing, for I have no happiness in my present unsettled notions on religion." He had had a strict religious upbringing. "I have a Bible which my sister gave me, who is an excellent woman, and I read in it very often." He believes in predestination, "and in the depravity of the human heart in general, and of my own in particular." He has always respected the conscientious believer as deeply as he has detested the hypocrite. He grants "that if the mild and benignant spirit of this religion were believed and acted upon by all, there would be a wonderful change in this wicked world." He demands "only sufficient proofs of it to take up the profession in earnest," and he thinks himself as good a Christian as many of those who have abused him with such un-Christian fury.[201]

But when Kennedy insists that all these favorable beliefs and dispositions will be of no avail unless he acknowledges his need of a Saviour and throws himself on the mercy of Christ, Byron wavers like a horse refusing a high fence: "This is going too fast. There are many points and difficulties to be cleared up; when that is done, I will consider what you say." [202] With these "points and difficulties" poor Kennedy wrestles in vain. A brief summary of them may be helpful to us.

Byron is obsessed by the idea that almost all professors of Christianity are hypocrites. In Catholic Italy, hypocrisy is allied with superstition; in Evangelical England, with cant and lack of charity—qualities which have been displayed by his critics. He insists that *Cain* should be judged as a drama, and that *Don Juan* satirizes only pretenders to religion, not religion itself. Sectarian bickering is incongruous with the ideal of brotherly love: Christians are intolerant not only of the heathen, who are often worthier of salvation than they, but of one another. He doubts whether "there had been fewer wars and persecutions, and less slaughter, misery and wretchedness in the world since the introduction of Christianity than before." Kennedy urges him to distinguish between true Christianity and

---

[200] *Op. cit.*, p. 152.
[201] Kennedy, *op. cit.*, pp. 35, 78, 79, 86, 95, 96.
[202] *Ibid.*, p. 96.

the failure of its professors to behave like Christians, but Byron is too empirical to be impressed by this argument.[203]

He thinks it noteworthy that "the diffusion of knowledge has diminished . . . the number of believers in Christianity." Nowadays learned and cultivated men are seldom devout. On the other hand he suspects that when pious women of a certain age direct their love toward the Saviour they are rightly "accused of retaining a mixture of their earthly love, blended with purer feelings, in their devotion." [204] Byron's sensitiveness to prestige and his scorn of women strengthen these objections.

Like the hero of *Cain,* Byron demands natural knowledge of supernatural mysteries; and he conceives of knowledge not as the crown of reason but as release from the pains of speculation. His naive insistence on proof is an expression of his divided nature. On the one hand, he would gladly accept Christianity because he longs for the peace of certitude. On the other hand, his romantic pride, though sadly battered by experience and frequently denied and mocked by Byron himself, remains too strong to permit him to pay the price of self-submission. So far as his conscious thought is concerned his "points and difficulties" are sincere, and by no means all of them are trivial; but they could easily have been swept away if reason and will had been united by a strong desire to find an extrapersonal God. He feels this desire only faintly, and he protects himself against it by demanding a sort of proof which he could not possibly hope to obtain. "But why are these difficulties so great?" he plaintively asks. "It is not necessary to mention more, when I find sufficient already: there is, for instance, the doctrine of the Trinity, which is alone quite appalling." He has seen too much of other men and of himself to doubt "the wickedness and depravity of human nature," but he balks at translating this experience into "doctrines . . . which lead us back into all the difficulties of original sin, and to the stories in the Old Testament, which many who call themselves Christians reject." And even granting that men are sinners, eternal punishment in Hell "is certainly not a humane doctrine, and appears very inconsistent with the mild and benevolent doctrines of Christ." [205]

With bibliolatrous rashness, Kennedy urges his lordship to ignore all theological quibbling and cleave to the inspired simplicity of Holy Writ. But on this ground Byron makes the most of his rich opportunities. Chris-

[203] *Ibid.,* pp. 35, 41, 44, 85–86, 104.   [204] *Ibid.,* pp. 37, 44, 86.
[205] *Ibid.,* pp. 81, 98–99, 119–120, 123.

tians—witness the swarm of wrangling sects—cannot agree as to what the Bible means. A man of sense is justified in saying: "Let it alone, and let these people fight among themselves, and when they have settled what religion is, then we can begin to study it." Prophecy, a specialty of Kennedy's, leaves him cold: contrary to the New Testament, the world did *not* come to an end before the generation of the Apostles had passed away. As for miracles, "it is easy to persuade people of the truth of any thing if it comes in a religious shape, as they were then willing to give up both their senses and their reason." He brings forth bits of negative criticism, most of them drawn from second-rate authorities, which he must have been treasuring up through the years. He is greatly impressed by Warburton's contention in *The Divine Legation of Moses* that the Jews had no notion of a future life. "The apostles are accused of not having written in good Greek." Even John Scott, Kennedy's favorite exegist, "does not venture to say that it was the devil who spoke to Eve by means of the serpent." Kennedy says that Byron had a copy of Gibbon in the Metaxata cottage and seemed to be deeply saturated in his views. His lordship cites the historian's coupling of women and priests as "ready to believe in the grossest superstition and follies." [206] Certainly not all of Byron's difficulties would have been removed if a more mature interpretation of Scripture had been available to him, but the literalistic view of plenary inspiration was a major obstacle. As employed by him, however, it was also a valuable defense against the claims of Christianity.

Kennedy confronts Byron with the inevitable hurdle. If, as the poet asserts, he sincerely desires the gift of faith, he "must pray humbly to God to grant you, by his Holy Spirit, a sense of your own iniquity, and a proper view of the necessity of a Saviour." Byron's answer reveals the futility of poor Kennedy's efforts:

But I do not see very much the need of a Saviour, nor the utility of prayer. Prayer does not consist in the act of kneeling, nor in repeating certain words in a solemn manner. Devotion is the affection of the heart, and this I feel; for when I view the wonders of creation, I bow to the Majesty of Heaven; and when I feel the enjoyments of life, health, and happiness, I am grateful to God for having bestowed these upon me.[207]

When hard pressed, then, he takes refuge from Christianity in sentimental deism.

---

[206] *Ibid.*, pp. 35–36, 39, 43, 44, 47, 81, 82, 104.   [207] *Ibid.*, pp. 78–79.

Byron left for the mainland with many promises to think further on these matters and to read the books and tracts which Kennedy had given him. Even supposing that he had some intention of doing so, the confusions of Missolonghi would probably have prevented him. He often told Stanhope that he was "a confirmed deist"; but once, referring to both political and religious problems, he said, "The more I think the more I doubt; I am a perfect sceptic."[208] Interpreting his last illness as a curse which had been laid upon him, he seriously begged Dr. Millingen to find a witch who could exorcise the evil spirit.[209] None of these anecdotes suggests that the colloquies at Metaxata had affected him in any way.

The reports of his deathbed vary with the wishes of the observer, with the fluctuations of the patient's sufferings, and to some extent, no doubt, with the impression which he desired to make upon this or that visitor. At least once in his delirium he was the courageous, dominant, man of action, shouting, "Forward! Forward—courage, follow my example, don't be afraid."[210] Perhaps he was picturing himself as scaling the walls of Lepanto, which the venal Turkish garrison had agreed in advance to surrender after a token resistance.

To the lovable Parry he expressed a confident hope of immortality, adding:

Christianity is the purest and most liberal religion in the world; but the numerous teachers who are eternally worrying mankind with their denunciations and their doctrines are the greatest enemies of religion. I have read, with more attention than half of them, the Book of Christianity, and I admire the liberal and truly charitable principles which Christ has laid down. There are questions connected with this subject which none but Almighty God can solve. Time and space, who can conceive? None but God: on him I rely.[211]

Here a deist takes to himself the title of Christian as a result of having identified deism with Christianity. The device is at least as old as Pope's defense of the orthodoxy of the *Essay on Man,* nor was Byron the last person to employ it.

As death drew nearer, however, Dr. Millingen

did not hear him make any, even the smallest, mention of religion. At one moment I heard him say: "Shall I sue for mercy?" After a long pause he added: "Come, come, no weakness! Let's be a man to the last."[212]

[208] Edgcumbe, *op. cit.,* pp. 207, 208.   [209] Nicolson, *op. cit.,* p. 254.
[210] Edgcumbe, *op. cit.,* p. 71.   [211] *Ibid.,* p. 79.
[212] Nicolson, *op. cit.,* p. 263.

Even those who regret that Byron maintained his self-sufficiency to the very end must honor him for refusing to be frightened into what would have been a mere affectation of submissiveness.

Who should have been with him in his parting moments but his grumbling, bungling, invincibly loving manservant? Fletcher's report is tenderer than Millingen's but not radically inconsistent with it. He says that his master frequently repeated, " 'I am not afraid to die,' and,—in as composed a way as a child, without moving head or foot, or even a gasp— went as if he were going into the finest sleep." [213] We shall never know the message that he tried to send Lady Byron through the valet, who could not understand his master's broken words.

Miss Mayne's final estimate of Byron is that his vocation was more than merely literary:

It was to be the most splendid example we have of the struggling, winning and losing, enjoying and scorning, aspiring and falling, loving and hating, human spirit.
"Es irrt der Mensch
So lang er strebt:"—
no other human being has incarnated that saying as Byron has.[214]

In other words, Byron shows that human greatness lies in the outrush of confused, aimless, uncontrolled, insatiable energy. But he so frequently sickened of this notion and repudiated its absurdity that he cannot wholly be summed up in terms of Faustian rant. In parting from him it seems more charitable to remember a letter of 1819 in which he tells Hoppner of two epitaphs in a cemetery near Bologna:

Martini Luigi
Implora pace

Lucrezia Picini
Implora eterna quiete

Although Byron does not understand these epitaphs in their full Christian sense, he feels in them something better than "Es irrt der Mensch." These simple words, he says, "comprise and compress all that can be said on the subject. Pray, if I am shovelled into the Lido churchyard in your time, let me have the *implora pace,* and nothing else, for an epitaph." [215]

---

[213] Kennedy, *op. cit.,* pp. 201–202.   [214] Ethel C. Mayne, *Byron,* II, 315.
[215] *Letters,* IV, 310.

Chapter VIII

KEATS

I

LIKE SHELLEY, FROM WHOM IN MOST OTHER RESPECTS HE DIFFERED PROFOUNDLY, Keats was an avowed non-Christian. Whether he also resembled Shelley in formulating a romantic religion of his own is a disputed point. He is by no means barren of ideas, but his best thinking is concerned with a sort of poetry in which ideas are not of great importance. With Professor Garrod I regard him primarily as a poet of sensuous delight and of emotions and thoughts very closely related to such delight, a poet who reveals his peculiar greatness "only when the senses capture him, when he finds truth in beauty, that is to say, when he does not trouble to find truth at all." [1] In their best work Keats's great contemporaries are less explicitly rhetorical, more "simple, sensuous, and passionate," more inclined to speak in and through the image, than even the least pseudo-classical of their precursors. Nevertheless one must say of their poetry as a whole that it represents a deliberate campaign to express philosophical and religious truths for the benefit of their fellow-men. They glorify their art not on aesthetic but on moral and spiritual grounds, exalting creative imagination as the key which unlocks the secrets of the universe. Keats's best work, on the contrary, implies a conception of poetry so much "purer" than the dominant romantic view that Amy Lowell regards him as "an almost completely modern man," [2] while Professor Bush asserts that "Keats speaks to us directly, almost as one of ourselves; we do not need to approach him through elaborate reconstructions of dead philosophies or dead poetical fashions." [3] Similarly "A. E. Powell" finds that

His poetic work was never bent, as was that of the others, into unpoetic channels, by the imposition of intellectual and moral aims. . . . There is no

[1] H. W. Garrod, *Keats,* pp. 30–34, 63.   [2] Amy Lowell, *John Keats,* I, 33.
[3] Douglas Bush, *Mythology and the Romantic Tradition in English Poetry,* p. 81.

sign of the romantic reaction from materialism, no fear of the physcial, no desire to transcend the beauty of bodily things and through it reach a world of spirit which it imperfectly expresses.[4]

With the reservation that the poetry of the present decade shows signs of returning to a rather un-Keatsian interest in purposive conceptual thinking, one accepts these remarks as a description of what Keats wanted to be, and of what, in his happiest moments, he actually was. But he was quite sufficiently a man of his time to be haunted by the notion that he should make his poetry the vehicle of a helpful, elevating philosophy. Within the walls of an accepted religious tradition he could have written his poetry of delicious sensation in happy innocence, but since for him no such walls existed he was compelled to undertake the usual romantic task of creating for himself the world which he desired to enjoy.

Although in my opinion he had small talent for such construction, others have regarded his philosophy very highly. According to one authority,

Any thorough study of the poems and letters must end in the conviction that Keats was at core a thinker. . . . He took a keen interest in, and showed profound insight into, the life about him; . . . he had a philosophy of life, balanced, sane, and in many respects profound; and finally, he had an aesthetic philosophy—into which all his thinking gradually converged.[5]

This is hardly what Mr. Clutton-Brock means by saying that Keats was a philosophic poet because he knew better than to confuse poetry "with other things such as morals or science." [6] Those who credit Keats with a philosophy seldom agree as to what the philosophy was. For most of them his thought is aesthetic or ethical (or sometimes both) rather than religious, but even here there are exceptions. Miss Lowell insists that

His was a strongly religious nature, but the religion he harboured was a highly individualized form of satisfaction in ignorance. He believed in the "principle of beauty" and the wisdom of virtue, but beyond these shadowy outlines of truth he was content not to go. He was the type of man who holds to a visionary clue flung out from himself and projected into the unknown. To such a man, the ideal is a magnified essence of his own finest qualities.[7]

[4] "A. E. Powell" (Mrs. E. R. Dodds), *The Romantic Theory of Poetry*, pp. 222, 223.
[5] C. D. Thorpe, *The Mind of John Keats*, p. 24.
[6] Arthur Clutton-Brock, "Keats and Shelley—A Contrast," *Keats Memorial Volume*, p. 63.
[7] *Op. cit.*, I, 498.

An even more amusing glimpse of what it is to have "a strongly religious nature" is revealed in Mr. Arthur Lynch's contribution to the *Keats Memorial Volume:*

Endymion is a book of religion . . . as Kant's *Kritik,* or Spencer's *Data of Ethics,* or Byron's *Manfred* are books of religion. In all of these writings I find a spiritual affinity. . . . Keats was in this sphere a great soul untrammeled by dogma, sending his "Herald thought into the wilderness," and searching for guidance in the march of the Universe itself. . . . He seems the mind the most finely touched, the most deeply inspired by the celestial meaning, of all in the range of literature. He sitteth on the right hand of God.[8]

Mr. Lynch has been quoted merely to provide a little comic relief for students of spiritual pathology. No such frivolous use should be made of John Middleton Murry's *Keats and Shakespeare.* Without attempting to revise the Apostles' Creed, he describes Keats as a "hero of humanity" toward whom "the proper attitude of criticism . . . is one of complete humility."[9] According to Mr. Murry, Keats is gifted with profound religious insight not at all because he is a philosopher in Professor Thorpe's sense, but because he is a master of "pure" poetry, which is "one of the few roads that remain open to the eternal reality that is less directly and less fully expressed in religion."[10] The famous letter on "soul-making" is interpreted to mean that

Mind must be utterly loyal to immediate and unintellectual experience—to the passions, to the affections, to the intuitions. . . . By this loyalty, by this submission of consciousness to unconsciousness is slowly created—the Soul. . . . The achievement of this condition of soul-knowledge results immediately in a knowledge of the harmony and necessity of the universe.[11]

To know this harmony is to know God, for

God *is* that harmony of the universe which flowers into a consciousness of its own nature through the human being who can make his Heart his Mind's Bible, and thereby achieve his soul.

"Knowledge of God is acceptance of life," and such acceptance becomes for Keats the essence of poetry. He is one of those "religious rebels" who

---

[8] Arthur Lynch, "John Keats," *Keats Memorial Volume,* pp. 128, 129, 132.
[9] J. M. Murry, *Keats and Shakespeare,* p. 5.
[10] *Ibid.,* pp. 11, 144.   [11] *Ibid.,* pp. 139, 140.

rediscover the truth of religion by the path of loyalty to their complete human-ity. . . . The reality which the Church has lost . . . is a knowledge of the unity and harmony of the universe which can be reached only through the in-dividual's knowledge of unity and harmony in himself.[12]

Inward unity and harmony are precisely the qualities which Keats vainly struggled to attain. Mr. Murry has given us, however, a statement of romantic religion which, in content if not in expression, deserves a place beside the most revealing utterances of Blake or Shelley. If this is truly Keats's creed and not merely Mr. Murry's, a study of the poet's re-ligion may be more rewarding than one had expected. Even if we find no such wisdom, the negative result will be of some interest for the historian of ideas. These introductory pages have cited secondary authorities pro-fusely to remind the reader of the bewilderingly diverse views which a student of Keats must weigh in forming his own opinions. It is time to meet the man himself.

2

Adopting the broadest and loosest conception of religion, let us inquire into the reliances and commitments of the youth whom Charles Cowden Clarke introduced to Leigh Hunt in the autumn of 1816. He was a duly baptized and confirmed Anglican whose faith had gradually become so meaningless to him that he probably saw no need of consciously repudiat-ing it. A few of the earliest poems imply a background of conventional Christianity, and *As from the darkening gloom,* the sonnet on the death of his grandmother Jennings, consists wholly of the pious *clichés* appropri-ate to the occasion.[13] In *The Fall of Hyperion* he will show familiarity with both the Old and New Testaments,[14] and we shall see that he remem-bered or relearned enough elementary theology to help his sister Fanny in preparing for confirmation. In 1815, however, George Felton Matthew found him "of the sceptical and republican school. An advocate for the

---

[12] *Ibid.,* pp. 142, 147.

[13] *The Poetical Works of John Keats* (ed. H. W. Garrod, 1939), p. 529; referred to here-after as *Works.* As Garrod's headnote shows, Woodhouse dates this sonnet 1816 but quotes Keats's statement that it was written "about five days after" the death of Mrs. Jennings, which occurred in December, 1814. Both internal and external evidence indicate that Keats composed it at the close of 1814 or the beginning of 1815, though he may have polished it later without altering its sentiments.

[14] J. L. Lowes, "Moneta's Temple," *PMLA,* LI, 1098–1113.

innovations which were making progress in his time. A faultfinder with everything established." [15] Making allowances for Matthew's timid respectability, we may accept this picture as overdrawn but not basically false. So far as the scepticism is concerned, it should be remembered that Keats at this time was a medical student living in an atmosphere not particularly conducive to piety. With an adolescent swagger he scribbled in his hospital notebook:

> Give me women, wine and snuff
> Until I cry out "hold, enough!"
> You may do so sans objection
> Till the day of resurrection;
> For bless my beard they aye shall be
> My beloved Trinity.[16]

There is no reason to suppose that his parents were devout; what we know of his impulsive and perhaps oversexed mother points in the opposite direction. Economically and socially ambitious, they wished their son to be associated with the church of prosperous, genteel folk. They themselves had been married at ultra-fashionable St. George's, not in their own shabby parish. If their finances had permitted, they would have sent John to Harrow. The best available substitute, Mr. Clarke's school at Enfield, was faithful to the external observances of the Church of England. The headmaster, however, was a political and religious liberal who took in *The Examiner*. Through the younger Clarke, Leigh Hunt's views on art, politics, and religion were already influencing Keats toward the end of his schooldays and during the Edmonton apprenticeship.

When his mother died in February, 1810, the orphan became the ward of Richard Abbey. Keats soon saw in his well-meaning guardian the embodiment of his liveliest detestations. This wholesale tea and coffee merchant was thin-blooded, cautious, conservative, and suspicious of poetry on both economic and moral grounds. The fact that he was also a priggish, nasty-minded, bigoted Evangelical did nothing to increase his ward's enthusiasm for Christianity. Keats already liked the atmosphere of Catholic piety breathed forth by the literature of olden days. He would always be fond of cathedrals and cathedral towns. If the ritualistic phase of the Oxford Movement had begun during his lifetime it is not inconceivable that the beauty of holiness might have worked upon him through the holiness

---

[15] Quoted by Sidney Colvin, *John Keats*, p. 25.   [16] *Works*, p. 552.

of beauty. But during the years when this latest-born of the great romantics was growing to maturity, Evangelicalism was the only element in the Church of England which possessed any vitality. The Evangelicals disliked all poetry which does *not* "have a palpable design upon us." In 1806, Bishop Porteous and William Wilberforce thought Cowper a much better poet than Wordsworth,[17] for it was important that the design should be not only palpable but Evangelical. Richard Abbey was a particularly unpleasant example of that fusion of utilitarianism and puritanism which, through its antagonism toward all non-instrumental beauty, was to stimulate the art-for-art's-sake rebellion among the spiritual heirs of Keats in the Victorian era.

In March, 1805, the painter Westall called upon his colleague Farington.

> He said Thomas Hope had been with him and proposed that the figure of Apollo in one of the pictures which Westall had painted for him, which is now *naked* should be covered in part by a thin drapery as otherways *in the Exhibition* [of the Royal Academy] it may be objected to. Westall proposed to paint this drapery in water colour and to wash it off when it is returned from the Exhibition.[18]

"O Delphic Apollo!" If this was Christianity, Keats preferred Greek paganism and Renaissance naturalism as he had come to know them with the help of Charles Cowden Clarke.[19] It is not for the moral benefits of literature that he thanks his friend in the *Epistle,* but because

> ... you first taught me all the sweets of song:
> The grand, the sweet, the terse, the free, the fine;
> What swell'd with pathos, and what right divine;
> Spenserian vowels that elope with ease,
> And float along like birds o'er summer seas;
> Miltonian storms, and more, Miltonian tenderness;
> Michael in arms, and more, meek Eve's fair slenderness—

a slenderness unmarred by Evangelical drapery.

He is also grateful to Clarke for a quite different reason:

> You too upheld the veil from Clio's beauty,
> And pointed out the patriot's stern duty;
> The might of Alfred, and the shaft of Tell;

---

[17] *The Farington Diary,* III, 249, 291.   [18] *Ibid.,* p. 68.
[19] Consider also what a medical student would think of such prudery.

> The hand of Brutus, that so grandly fell
> Upon a tyrant's head.[20]

We recall Matthew's phrase, "sceptical and republican." At a time when the Church was the bulwark of conservatism, the two radicalisms were interdependent.[21] The same mixture of liberalism and delight in sensuous luxury appears in the epistles *To George Felton Matthew* and *To My Brother George*. "Juxtaposition" might be more accurate than "mixture," for the two elements are never fully integrated either now or later despite the traditional attractiveness of Neo-Hellenism for lovers of freedom. Keats's liberalism, to which some of the shorter early poems are wholly devoted,[22] was not a boyishly imitative pose. It was thoughtful and sincere, and he retained it to the end.[23] But it was by no means the master passion of his life. He was unable to derive from it the luxury on which his art depended or to express it without falling into the didacticism which he hated. Injected into his poetry it becomes aesthetically spurious and reveals the gap between his social conscience and his artistic conscience.

Before meeting Hunt he has begun to find in Greek myth an expression of his joy in the world's loveliness, but not with any feelings that could be called religious. Much more Elizabethan than Greek, he bends the knee only to creative genius. Of Beaumont and Fletcher he writes:

> The thought of this great partnership diffuses
> Over the genius-loving heart, a feeling
> Of all that's high, and great, and good, and healing.

This is not what most readers derive from *Philaster* and *The Maid's Tragedy*. But Keats, endowed with a gift for friendship, loves to think of these writers as partners:

> Sweet are the pleasures that to verse belong,
> And doubly sweet a brotherhood in song.[24]

Above all, however, they wrote excellent verses, and that is what Keats, except in his uneasily philosophical moments, means by "genius."

[20] *Works*, p. 36.
[21] The Evangelicals supported many humanitarian and moderately liberal reforms and even joined forces with Benthamites in order to achieve them; but Keats was not likely to give them credit for this fact.   [22] *Works*, pp. 40, 525.
[23] C. D. Thorpe, "Keats's Interest in Politics and World Affairs," *PMLA*, XLVI, 1228–1245.
[24] *Works*, p. 28.

Being not merely an appreciator of art but an artist, Keats never thought long about beauty without thinking of those who fix its elusive essence in images and rhythm. One might say that his devotion to great poets was essentially religious were it not necessary to add that he seldom thought of great poets without thinking of himself. His former fellow-students at Guy's would remember that during this period his passion for fame was intense.[25] It has been interpreted as "chiefly the result of his being sub-normal in stature and of the early death of his parents."[26] Let us substitute "partly" for "chiefly," and add that this desire was a specialized form of the general ambitiousness of the Keats family. It included the wish to compensate for a sense of social inferiority. There was no better way of getting beyond the sound of Bow Bells. Had not Ben Jonson laid bricks, and Shakespeare held horses for patrons of the theatre? The great Eliza-bethans, too, had made much of the immortality conferred by fame. In *To My Brother George,* after describing the delights of him "Whose head is pregnant with poetic lore," John continues:

> These are the living pleasures of the bard:
> But richer far posterity's award.
> What does he murmur with his latest breath,
> While his proud eye looks through the film of death?
> "What though I leave this dull, and earthly mould,
> Yet shall my spirit lofty converse hold
> With after times."[27]

During his brief career Keat's artist-worship found more and more worthy objects of devotion and contributed greatly to the maturing of his work. But it also gave him feelings of uncertainty, strain, and frustration by forcing him constantly to compare himself with poets whose art was incommensurable with his. After concluding the long passage whose open-ing lines have just been quoted he says:

> ... Ah, my dear friend and brother,
> Could I, at once, my mad ambition smother,
> For tasting joys like these, sure I should be
> Happier, and dearer to society.[28]

---

[25] Sidney Colvin, *John Keats,* p. 28.
[26] H. E. Briggs, "Keats's Conscious and Unconscious Reactions to Criticism of *Endymion,*" *PMLA,* LX, 1108.
[27] *Works,* p. 33.   [28] *Ibid.,* p. 34.

He distrusts his ambition because it is anti-social and because it has begun to give him more pain than pleasure. At Enfield he had been the ideal English schoolboy—handsome, generous, athletic, pugnaciously brave, kind, loyal, humorous, impulsive, sanguine. But beneath these qualities, and sometimes rising to the surface, there was already a hypochondriacal supersensitiveness, a nervously melancholy distrust of himself and the world. Speaking of his brother as he knew him during the Edmonton apprenticeship and at Christ's Hospital, George told Haydon that John was morbidly afraid of falling below the highest greatness in poetry and had declared a determination to destroy himself rather than fail.[29] His otherwise ennobling devotion to genius—the nearest thing to a religion which can be ascribed to him—was cankered at the root.

3

Keats's working career after the beginning of his association with Leigh Hunt may be divided at August, 1818, when he returned from his Scottish tour. The present section is concerned with the first of the two periods which this device provides.

Leigh Hunt combined a would-be Voltairian scepticism toward Christianity with a very soft and optimistic deism. Thanks to his cheerfulness and good nature, the latter element was usually uppermost. Readers of my second volume will see in him a strong resemblance to John Gilbert Cooper—political liberal, smiling sceptic, Neo-Hellenic hedonist, pseudo-Platonic sentimental naturalist in the aesthetic-harmony tradition of Shaftesbury.[30] The mixture was attractive to Keats, and during the winter of 1816–1817 he adopted it enthusiastically. One would give much to have been present on the evening of March 26, when Keats joined Hunt, Clarke, and Novello in warbling Hunt's hymn *To the Spirit Great and Good*. Hunt had composed the music as well as the words, but for us the latter must suffice:

> To the Spirit great and good,
> Felt, although not understood,—
> By whose breath, and in whose eyes,
> The green earth rolls in the blue skies,—
> Who we know, from things that bless,
> Must delight in loveliness;

[29] H. E. Briggs, *op. cit.*, p. 1108.   [30] *Religious Trends*, II, 319–324.

And who, therefore, we believe,
Means us well in things that grieve,—
    Gratitude! Gratitude!
Heav'n be praised as heavenly should—
Not with slavery, or with fears,
But with a face as towards a friend, and with thin sparkling tears.[31]

The tears are demanded by sensibility, but they must be thin and sparkling lest they traduce the benevolence of the singers' divine friend and fellow-artist.

Shelley's hostility to Christianity also influenced Keats at this time, but mainly by bringing into the open the more negative side of Hunt's deism. In the presence of pious guests like Haydon and Severn, the kindly Hunt was inclined to avoid argument on religious questions. Shelley practiced no such restraint, and when he spoke his mind Hunt could not resist entering the fray on his side. Keats seems to have taken little or no part in these debates, but he kept his ears wide open.[32] Singing in Hunt's pantheistic quartet, however, was pleasanter than listening to Shelley's high-pitched fanaticism. A natural sceptic in the strict sense of that abused term, Keats distrusted cocksure propaganda. Also, as Hunt reports, he was "a little too sensitive on the score of his origin" and "felt inclined to see in every man of birth a sort of natural enemy." [33] In this as in several other respects his kinship with Burns is close.

Hunt's political liberalism and his literary aestheticism were never effectively fused, but his religion provided a flimsy link between them. In his double sonnet *To Percy Shelley, On the Degrading Notions of Deity*, freedom is allied with "the Spirit of Beauty" against their common foe, Christianity.[34] Through this alliance Keats briefly strove to reconcile sensuous luxury and "the patriot's stern duty." Very much in his mentor's vein is the sonnet *Written in Disgust of Vulgar Superstition*. This first outright repudiation of Christianity was composed on the evening of Sunday, December 23, 1816, when he heard the "melancholy round" of the churchbells summoning their dupes to gloomy and slavish devotions:

[31] Leigh Hunt, *Poetical Works*, p. 381; John Keats, *Letters* (ed. M. B. Forman, 1935), p. 16.
[32] C. L. Finney, *The Evolution of Keats's Poetry*, pp. 155–158, provides the most thorough treatment of this point, though in my opinion he somewhat overestimates Shelley's influence and underestimates Hunt's.
[33] Quoted by Colvin, *op. cit.*, pp. 71–72. See also Arthur Clutton-Brock, "Keats and Shelley—A Contrast," *Keats Memorial Volume*, p. 61.
[34] Leigh Hunt, *Poetical Works*, p. 242.

> Surely the mind of man is closely bound
>   In some black spell; seeing that each one tears
>   Himself from fireside joys, and Lydian airs,
> And commerce high of those with glory crown'd.
> Still, still, they toll, and I should feel a damp—
>   A chill as from a tomb, did I not know
> That they are dying like an outburnt lamp;
>   That 'tis their sighing, wailing ere they go
> Into oblivion;—that fresh flowers will grow,
> And many glories of immortal stamp.[35]

Despite the characteristic emphasis on Lydian airs and fresh flowers, the glories which will replace the silenced church bells are political as well as aesthetic.[36] Thus he was not consciously deserting the cause of freedom when at about this time he expounded to Severn "the Greek spirit,—the Religion of the Beautiful, the Religion of Joy, as he used to call it." [37]

But in Keats's mind reform was always vague, rhetorical, and didactic, while the world's beauty, as the happy immaturity of *I stood tip-toe* bears witness, was intoxicatingly alive and fresh. From the same "posey/Of luxuries bright, milky, soft and rosy," [38] it is clear that for him the Greek myths were primarily a means of imparting the richness and dignity of a high poetic tradition to his voluptuous enjoyment of nature. Even when most earnest and intense, his paganism is much more aesthetic than religious—unless one applies the latter term to anything associated with keen pleasure. In a sonnet of the period he says that

> To one who has been long in city pent,
>   'Tis very sweet to look into the fair
>   And open face of heaven,—to breathe a prayer
> Full in the face of the blue firmament.

But immediately he adds:

> Who is more happy, when, with heart's content,
>   Fatigued he sinks into some pleasant lair
>   Of wavy grass, and reads some debonair
> And gentle tale of love and languishment? [39]

---

[35] *Works*, p. 530.

[36] See *Ibid.*, p. 527, where similar "glories" are prophesied in the more definitely political sonnet *On Receiving a Laurel Crown from Leigh Hunt.*

[37] William Sharp, *Life and Letters of Joseph Severn*, p. 29.

[38] *Works*, p. 4.   [39] *Ibid.*, p. 44.

The two experiences, if not quite identical, are not significantly different. Nature, whether honored in Greek mythology or English scenery, is the "Maker of sweet poets," [40] the quarry from which they dig the golden ore of fame. Her cult is inseparable from

> ... all the pleasant flow
> Of words at opening a portfolio.[41]

The couplet which has last been quoted, however, appears in *Sleep and Poetry*. This poem, as all readers of Keats are aware, reveals a conflict between the luxury of the senses and a half-reluctant feeling of obligation to serve a more loftily ethical ideal of poetic greatness:

> And can I ever bid these joys farewell?
> Yes, I must pass them for a nobler life,
> Where I may find the agonies, the strife
> Of human hearts.[42]

There is no question here of reform propaganda. The far-off goal is a more diffused and general benevolence, a deeply sympathetic understanding of human nature to be expressed in poetry for the betterment of mankind. Apollo, as Hunt describes him in *The Feast of the Poets*, is a youth of somewhat Endymion-like and effeminate beauty, but

> ... though he was blooming, and oval of cheek,
> And youth down his shoulders went smoothing and sleek,
> Yet his look with the reach of past ages was wise,
> And the soul of eternity thought through his eyes.

Hunt's poet-god rebukes Byron for his misanthropy:

> For poets, earth's heaven-linking spirits, were born,
> What they can, to amend,—what they can't, to adorn;
> And you hide the best proof of your office and right,
> If you make not as I do a contrast with night,
> And help to shed round you a gladness and light.[43]

This is precisely what Keats means when in *Sleep and Poetry* he protests that his contemporaries, though incomparably superior to the school of Pope, are too melancholy,

[40] *Ibid.*, p. 7.   [41] *Ibid.*, p. 59.   [42] *Ibid.*, p. 54.
[43] Leigh Hunt, *Poetical Works*, p. 150.

> . . . forgetting the great end
> Of poesy, that it should be a friend
> To soothe the cares, and lift the thoughts of man.[44]

Nevertheless the vision of the charioteer implies a dark, undefined, unattainable dream of greatness which rises above Hunt's cheery humanitarian prattle. Herein the influence of Haydon is probably at work. The Christian piety of Haydon meant nothing to Keats but this third-rate Blake's solemn glorification of art encouraged the young poet's craving for fame and gave it a quality of self-consciously earnest aspiration. In this mood, Keats saw with increasing clarity that Hunt's rosy-posey, blisses-kisses couplets were inadequate for the ascent of Parnassus. In *Sleep and Poetry* he tried to persuade himself that the antidote for Huntian prettiness was a larger infusion of Huntian benevolism. When he looked at the Elgin Marbles, however, he saw that the vaguely conceived higher ideal had nothing to do with social service. Yet as often happens when he confronts the highest greatness in art, he draws more bewilderment and pain from his overstrained ambition than healing joy from his reverence for beauty:

> My spirit is too weak—mortality
>   Weighs heavily on me like unwilling sleep,
>   And each imagin'd pinnacle and steep
> Of godlike hardship tells me I must die
> Like a sick Eagle looking at the sky.

Ominously, he falls back upon the "gentle luxury" of tears. Of Haydon, who had recently established the authenticity of the Marbles, he asks pardon

> . . . that I cannot speak
> Definitively on these mighty things;
> Forgive me that I have not angel's wings—
> That what I want I know not where to seek.[45]

This frank avowal of incertitude should be a warning to all overconfident interpreters of Keats.

Haydon, however, kept urging him to break away from the shallow prettiness and scepticism of Hunt in order to undertake a substantial work

---

[44] *Works,* p. 57.   [45] *Ibid.,* pp. 477, 478.

of high seriousness. The challenge was both terrifying and irresistible. On March 17, 1817, Keats informs Reynolds:

My Brothers are anxious that I should go by myself into the country—they have always been extremely fond of me, and now that Haydon has pointed out how necessary it is that I should be alone to improve myself, they give up the temporary pleasure of living with me continually for a great good which I hope will follow.[46]

This great good was *Endymion*. In discussing the "philosophy" of the poem it is well to remember Keats's own estimate of it as a piece of adolescent mawkishness which he finds himself unable to revise because "The foundations are too sandy. It is just that this youngster should die away." [47] The original Preface, unlike the manly Dedication which was substituted for it, is feebly apologetic:

I have fought under disadvantages. Before I began I had no inward feel of being able to finish, and as I proceeded my steps were all uncertain. . . . I have written to please myself and in hopes to please others, and for a love of fame.

He concludes, poor fellow, with a nervously whimsical plea for mercy from the two all-powerful reviews.[48] Why did he publish a poem which he regarded as a failure? Probably because with all its faults it contained particular beauties which he longed to see in print, and which he hoped against hope might atone for the larger deficiencies of the work.[49] Long before he had finished it, however, he had lost the feeling that he was contributing to any "great good."

As he himself confesses, his nerve failed him as soon as he had begun. Solitude was less beneficial than he had expected: it brought him face to face with the contrast between what he was and what he aspired to be.[50] On May 10 he confides in Hunt:

---

[46] *Letters*, p. 15.   [47] *Works*, p. 64.   [48] *Ibid.*, pp. lxxxviii–lxxxix.

[49] In *John Keats' Fancy*, J. R. Caldwell argues that Keats, much influenced by Hartley and Alison, wrote by free, more or less dreamlike association. Hence "the dreamy fantasy of *Endymion*" is "the intended and essential quality of the poem" (p. 196). If so, it is strange that Keats should have thought the poem a failure and especially that he should have lamented the fact that "as I proceeded my steps were all uncertain." He was a dreamy poet, but he had hoped to make this poem much more than a blur of reverie.

[50] In May, also, he "received a letter from George by which it appears that Money Troubles are to follow us up for some time to come perhaps for always—these vexations are a great hindrance to one." (*Letters*, p. 30.)

I have asked myself so often why I should be a poet more than other Men,—seeing how great a thing it is,—how great things are to be gained by it—What a thing it is to be in the mouth of Fame—that at last the Idea has grown so monstrously beyond my seeming Power of attainment that the other day I nearly consented with myself to drop into a Phaeton—yet 'tis a disgrace to fail even in a huge attempt, and at this moment I drive the thought from me.[51]

The thought, however, was not to be banished so readily, especially since it was by this time apparent that his first volume of *Poems* had fallen flat.

To a similar letter Haydon responds with advice to shun Hunt's "delusions and sophistications" and to "go on, don't despair, collect incident, study characters, read Shakespeare and trust in Providence."[52] Keats replies that despite "a horrid Morbidity of Temperament" which is "likely to be the cause of my disappointment, . . . I never quite despair and I read Shakspeare—indeed I think I shall never read any other book much. . . . I am very near agreeing with Hazlit [*sic*] that Shakspeare is enough for us." The implied preference of Shakespeare over the Bible parries Haydon's allusion to Providence. The letter closes with genial mockery: "So now in the name of Shakspeare, Raphael, and all our Saints I commend you to the care of Heaven!"[53] Three days before, he had congratulated Hunt for levelling "a battering-ram against Christianity" in the article on intolerance in the *Examiner* for May 4, 1817.[54]   ,

Warned against oversanguine expectations by the author himself, we are ready to ask what *Endymion* means. Its general model is the allegorical-mythological romantic narrative of the Renaissance, and in agreement with several examples of the type its main theme was intended to be the Neoplatonic quest of the soul for ideal beauty and ideal love.[55] Even in Books I and II, however, this theme is not only whirled away in a welter of centrifugal luxuries but sharply refracted by the essential anti-Platonism of Keats's mind. "His habitation," as Professor Bush says, "is the dome of

---

[51] *Letters*, p. 26; see also p. 21.   [52] *Ibid.*, p. 28.   [53] *Ibid.*, pp. 31, 33.
[54] *Ibid.*, p. 23, but the entire letter pertains to our subject.
[55] Here the reader should weigh for himself the thesis of W. W. Beyer in *Keats and the Daemon King* that Wieland's *Oberon* is the most important of all literary influences on *Endymion* and several other major poems of Keats. It seems to me that although many of his parallels are of the "salmon in both rivers" type Beyer succeeds in showing that *Oberon* exerted on Keats's images, scenes, and narrative devices an influence which, if less predominant than the thesis asserts, was nevertheless surprisingly strong. But the attempt to demonstrate Wieland's influence on Keats's *ideas* seems vitiated by a misunderstanding of those ideas, and in general the contention that Wieland was responsible for practically everything that Keats ever thought or felt or wrote is badly overstrained. At most Wieland deserves a place several degrees above Mary Tighe in the hierarchy of Keatsian sources.

many-colored glass, . . . and, in general, the more spiritual parts of the poem are less real than the sensuous." [56] As the opening lines show, he desires not Beauty but "a *thing* of beauty," "some *shape* of beauty," found either directly in nature or through the mediation of great poets.

The first scene in Book I is the festival of Pan, who finally emerges as a symbol of universal nature. In calling the Hymn "a pretty piece of paganism" Wordsworth, besides being a churlish and purblind critic, showed a more surprising inability to recognize his own thought on the lips of another poet. From this eloquent though cloudy praise of divinized Nature, Keats passes on to the interview between Endymion and his sister Peona. The connection between the two scenes is by no means explicit, but we may infer that Endymion's problem is to find not a more ethereal abstraction but a more satisfyingly concrete embodiment of that Pan-spirit which will otherwise remain beyond the reach of imagination.

In his speech to Peona,[57] the hero desires to "slake/My thirst for the world's praises" by devoting himself to some high suprapersonal value which will give the supreme happiness of "A fellowship with essence; till we shine,/Full alchemized, and free of space." The spirit climbs toward this rapture through "the clear religion of heaven" (delight in the blue sky), musical and literary pleasure, and the joys of friendship to the very summit, which is represented by love. So far this aspiration sounds Platonic. But the love which crowns the quest for happiness proves not to be "heavenly" or "intellectual" in the manner of Spenser or even of Shelley. It is "earthly love," "The mere commingling of passionate breath," which "has power to make/Men's being mortal, immortal." The voluptuous dream which he describes to Peona is not worth brooding about unless he may hope that it will come true.[58] In order to shake off the vague tortures of ambition, Endymion (Keats) longs for the most intense and concrete personal achievement—satisfaction of physical desire for the *real* love and *real* beauty of a woman. This circular movement from flesh to pseudo-spirit and back again to flesh is profoundly un-Platonic. The same inversion of the Platonic relationship between earthly and heavenly love runs throughout Book II, with its "naked waist" and "slippery blisses."

[56] Douglas Bush, *Mythology and the Romantic Tradition in English Poetry,* p. 99.

[57] *Endymion,* I, 769–857. Lines 776–781 in the published text are a revision sent to Taylor on January 30, 1818. (*Letters,* p. 91.) But although Keats regarded the change as important, one cannot see that he had done more than achieve a more satisfactory expression of what he had tried to say in his first draft. (*Works,* p. 88n.)

[58] Line 857, "A hope beyond the shadow of a dream," does not mean "a hope even dreamier than a dream," but "a hope much more tangible than a dream."

Book III, however, is given a humanitarian turn by the influence of Benjamin Bailey. The pious and prudish[59] Oxford student, as Garrod says,

> had the design of making this singularly pagan poet, not indeed a clergyman, but a philosophic poet upon what may be called modified clerical lines; with a philosophy, that is, approximating as closely as possible to that of Wordsworth's *Excursion*.[60]

Though unsuccessful in this aim he managed to revive in Keats the *Sleep and Poetry* conflict between sensuousness and service. Since Keats was trying to write a poem of philosophical significance, he half-heartedly injected a good deal of the latter element into this part of the poem. Despite Bailey's enthusiasm for Wordsworth, the indignant liberalism of the opening lines and the benevolism of the Glaucus episode[61] are primarily Huntian. Keats would probably have accepted with relief and gratitude Colvin's explanation that "the soul enamoured of and pursuing Beauty cannot achieve its quest in selfishness and isolation, but to succeed must first be taken out of itself and purified by active sympathy with the lives and sufferings of others." [62] Quite possibly some such idea was floating in the back of Keats's mind, but it clashes with the whole spirit of the first two books and in no way leads into the fourth. After finishing Book III he told Haydon that he was thoroughly disgusted with the poem and that he was already meditating "a new Romance which I have in my eye for next Summer." [63] The thought of Book III associates it less with *Endymion* than with *Hyperion*. He was determined, however, to bring *Endymion* to some sort of conclusion—"so on/I move to the end in lowliness of heart." [64]

In the final book he returns to his inversion of Platonic love. The hero's culminating discovery that the Indian Maid and Cynthia are identical implies, as Finney expresses it, that "The beauty of a particular woman is a manifestation of ideal and essential beauty, . . . and the love of the beauty of a particular woman is the highest means by which man can attain a fellowship with essence." [65] In this way Keats achieves a verbal sort of

---

[59] The later discovery that he was at bottom something of a sensualist helped to darken Keats's view of human nature.　　　[60] H. W. Garrod, *Keats*, p. 37.

[61] Amy Lowell, *op. cit.*, I, 415, insists that the action of the Glaucus story is "that of hundreds of legends in every language. Expiation of some fault or misfortune by the performance of a noble and difficult deed is mere stock in trade with all such tales." This is true, but probably Keats interpreted this familiar *motif* in the light of his personal conflict.

[62] *Op. cit.*, p. 172.　　　[63] *Letters*, p. 51.　　　[64] *Endymion*, IV, 28–29.

[65] C. L. Finney, *The Evolution of Keats's Poetry*, p. 319.

reconciliation between poetry of sensation and poetry of ideal aspiration. This solution, however, is brought about not by an ascent from the delusions of sense to eternal truth, but by a descent from false idealism to delightful realism. The important fact is not that the Indian Maid turns out to be Cynthia, but that Cynthia turns out to be the Indian Maid.[66] When Endymion clasps her in his arms he explicitly renounces the desire of the moth for the star. In seeking "a great dream" he has sinned against love, nature, friendship, human greatness—against mighty Pan:

> There never liv'd a mortal man, who bent
> His appetite beyond his natural sphere,
> But starv'd and died. My sweetest Indian, here
> Here will I kneel, for thou redeemed hast
> My life from too thin breathing: . . .
>   .   .   .
> My river-lily bud! one human kiss!
> One sigh of real breath—one gentle squeeze,
> Warm as a dove's nest among summer trees,
> And warm with dew at ooze from living blood! [67]

This key passage implies a sound aesthetic principle which, had Keats been a Christian, might have been harmonized with a sacramental view of religion. As it stands, however, it simply asserts his unquenchable desire to be a poet of sensation. But this was not what Keats had intended to say when he embarked upon a Neoplatonic allegory of the quest for ideal Beauty. It was not what Haydon, or Bailey, or Hunt even, expected of him. It was a genuine expression of his nature, but for that very reason he distrusted it, since it did not possess that quality of noble nonsense which his intellectual environment impelled him to associate with poetic fame. Hence he finished *Endymion* as he began it, in a mood of uncertainty and tension.

His letters show that he continued to struggle with the problem which *Endymion* had failed to solve, but not that he arrived at any permanently satisfying conclusion. Professor Thorpe upholds the opposite view, but he admits that the poems do not display the progressive intellectual development which despite some wavering he finds in the letters.[68] Since a

---

[66] She is no object of humanitarian sympathy, but simply a beautiful girl. Her previous misfortunes do not serve to unify Books III and IV, and I cannot believe that they were meant to. [67] *Endymion*, IV, 636–667.
[68] C. D. Thorpe, *The Mind of John Keats*, pp. 21–24, 30.

poet—above all such a poet as Keats—must be judged by his poetry, the admission damages the thesis that Keats died on the threshold of high philosophical art. The letters themselves do not support this idea unless they are read with strong determination to find what one is seeking. They reveal, however, a most interesting ferment of thought and feeling.

During the last two months of 1817, in agreement with Book IV of *Endymion,* he seems to be reacting sharply against the moralistic intellectualism which Bailey had been trying to impose upon him. The result is the cluster of related ideas to which he applies the term, "Negative Capability." In order to study this doctrine, which for Miss Lowell constitutes his religion of "satisfaction in ignorance" [69] and which for some other critics is the cornerstone of his matured philosophy, let us regard as a single document the letter of November 22 to Bailey and that of December 21 to his brothers. Here he parries each of the demands made upon him by his environment—demands which he instinctively repudiated although he feared that they were valid.

An optimistic view of man, nature, and society had been impressed upon him ever since his schooldays, and one side of his character inclined him to accept it. But since the spring of this year his "horrid Morbidity of Temperament" has been at work. At the very opening of *Endymion,* shapes of beauty are treasured not because life is normally good, but because it is normally bad:

> Spite of despondence, of the inhuman dearth
> Of noble natures, of the gloomy days,
> Of all the unhealthy and o'er-darkened ways
> Made for our searching: yes, in spite of all,
> Some shape of beauty moves away the pall
> From our dark spirits.[70]

In the November letter he expresses the same feeling:

I scarcely remember counting upon any Happiness—I look not for it if it be not in the present hour—nothing startles me beyond the Moment. The setting sun will always set me to rights—or if a Sparrow come before my Window I take part in its existence.

What then is the use of struggling toward far-off social goals? If Bailey finds him lacking in human sympathy he is "not to put it to the account

[69] *Vide supra,* p. 453.　　　　[70] *Endymion,* I, 8–13.

of heartlessness but abstraction." [71] For Keats, "abstraction" means concentration upon shapes of beauty in defiance of the miseries of life. In his home-made technical vocabulary a close synonym is "intensity," as in the sentence, "The excellence of every art is its intensity, capable of making all disagreeables evaporate, from their being in close relationship with Beauty and Truth." [72]

This rejection of ultimate happiness will protect his conception of art against moralistic and humanitarian claims. But another threat to the poetry of delicious sensation is presented by the idea—axiomatic with men like Bailey—that great poets are great thinkers, men of wisdom nourished by learning, actively philosophical seekers and finders of truth. Here Keats's desire for fame, combined with his tendency to doubt even his own doubts, renders him unsure of himself; but he defends the breach in his walls as best he can:

I have never yet been able to perceive how any thing can be known for truth by consecutive reasoning—and yet it must be. Can it be that even the greatest Philosopher ever arrived at his goal without putting aside numerous objections? However it may be, O for a life of Sensations rather than of thoughts! [73]

Much critical ingenuity has been devoted to that famous exclamation, but the likeliest supposition is that Keats meant exactly what he wrote at the moment when he wrote it.

To Bailey he imparts a "favorite Speculation"

that we shall enjoy ourselves hereafter by having what we call happiness on Earth repeated in a finer tone. And yet such a fate can only befall those who delight in Sensation rather than hunger as you do after Truth.

He sets no great store by this bit of theology—"I am continually running away from the subject." Perhaps after all it is better to have "a complex Mind" like that of Bailey, "who would exist partly on Sensation partly on thought—to whom it is necessary that years should bring the philosophic mind." [74] The allusion to Wordsworth, who in his stodgier moments was placed by Bailey beside Dante and Milton, hints that the conflict has not been resolved.

But there is a loftier than Wordsworth. In the spring, Keats was "very

[71] *Letters*, p. 69. [72] *Ibid.*, p. 71. [73] *Ibid.*, p. 68.
[74] *Ibid.*

near agreeing with Hazlit that Shakespeare is enough for us"; in December, he tells us why. Shakespeare is free from didacticism and subjective self-torture. Full of thoughts, he never appears to be thinking: he
treats ideas, whether pleasant or painful in actual life, as if they were
delightful sensations. Hence he is the supreme example of *"Negative
Capability,* that is, when a man is capable of being in uncertainties, mysteries, doubts, without any irritable reaching after fact and reason." His
genius proves "that with a great poet the sense of Beauty overcomes
every other consideration, or rather obliterates all consideration." [75]

Protected by Shakespeare against the claims of consideration, Keats is
able to declare:

I am certain of nothing but the holiness of the Heart's affections and the
Truth of Imagination—What the imagination seizes as Beauty must be truth—
whether it existed before or not—for I have the same Idea of all our Passions
as of Love; they are all, in their sublime, creative of essential Beauty.[76]

"Holiness of the Heart's affections" is flatly inconsistent with "the inhuman dearth/Of noble natures," but he usually felt better when he read
Shakespeare. The remainder of the passage enunciates the familiar romantic idea that the imagination has power to apprehend and even to create
essential truth. Keats, however, gives this thought a characteristically non-
mystical turn, since for him the only real truth is that of beauty, and the
only real beauty is the warm, physical beauty of the Indian Maid.

Such is the doctrine of Negative Capability. For Mr. Murry, it is Keats's
"true philosophy" and the basis of his religion.[77] To insist that it is rather
a defense *against* philosophy would perhaps be a mere quibble, for the
idea expresses important aspects of his character and art. But since it
excludes reliance upon any sort of supersensuous reality I cannot call it
a religion. Keats himself never regarded it in that light.

Even for his own non-religious purposes, this philosophy or anti-
philosophy fell short of adequacy. "Men of genius," he says in the letter
to Bailey, "are great as certain ethereal Chemicals operating on the Mass
of neutral intellect—but they have not any individuality, any determining
Character." [78] To borrow words which Endymion applies to himself, they
"have no self-passion or identity." [79] But since Keats's longing to be recog-

---

[75] *Ibid.,* p. 72.   [76] *Ibid.,* p. 67.
[77] J. M. Murry, *Keats and Shakespeare,* p. 58.
[78] *Letters,* p. 67.   [79] *Endymion,* IV, 477.

nized as a man of genius was a most intense form of "self-passion," his efforts to achieve impersonality were uneasily personal. Shakespeare was detached; he did not struggle toward detachment. Furthermore, when Keats was happy his approach to life was direct and passionate. Imagination creates beauty-truth with an intensity of feeling which he compares to physical love. I cannot quite agree with G. R. Elliott that "his central instinct was for high poetic repose." [80] He was an Elizabethan, not a Greek. He really wanted "passionate breath"; the "quiet breathing" [81] of Negative Capability was a remedy for fever. *In a drear-nighted December,* written at this time, expresses envy of even the inanimate ataraxy of natural objects.[82] For these reasons Negative Capability was vulnerable to assaults originating not only in his environment but in his own divided spirit.

The letters and poems of January, 1818, exhibit signs of wavering. "I think," he tells his brothers, "a little change has taken place in my intellect lately—I cannot bear to be uninterested or unemployed, I, who for so long a time had been addicted to passiveness"—a state which he would have defended a short while before. To show that he is "getting at it, with a sort of determination and strength," [83] he encloses the sonnet *On Sitting Down to Read King Lear Once Again.* The poem is a convincing illustration of how great art simultaneously kindles and tortures his ambition, clarifies his aims and enshrouds them in perplexity. The spirit of *King Lear* is not that of Romance, the "Queen of far-away" by whose charms Keats has been enthralled. Yet how is the difference to be defined? This supreme tragedy has not the cool detachment of Negative Capability: it is a "fierce dispute/Betwixt damnation and impassioned clay." The genius of Shakespeare now seems to be utterly dissimilar, not merely in degree but in kind, from his worshipper's delight in sensuous luxury. Keats can only pray that he may be "consumed in the fire" to soar with the "Phoenix wings" of an utterly new greatness.[84]

Perhaps, then, Shakespeare was after all a philosophical poet in Bailey's sense of the term, a sort of dramatic Milton. To the same month belong the *Lines on Seeing a Lock of Milton's Hair,* where Keats confesses himself unworthy to sing of Milton until he has grown, like him, a philosopher and seer.[85] But in *When I have fears* he wonders if there will be

[80] G. R. Elliott, *The Cycle of Modern Poetry,* p. 38.   [81] *Endymion,* I, 833, 5.
[82] *Works,* pp. 549–550.   [83] *Letters,* pp. 88, 89.   [84] *Works,* p. 482.
[85] *Ibid.,* p. 479.

time for the attainment of such gigantic hopes. In the darkness of this paralyzing doubt, "love and fame to nothingness do sink." [86] Well may he pray to Apollo:

> . . . God of Song,
> Thou bearest me along
> Through sights I scarce can bear:
> O let me, let me share
> With the hot lyre and thee,
> The staid Philosophy.
> Temper my lonely hours,
> And let me see thy bowers
> More unalarmed! [87]

In these lines, which Woodhouse assigns to February, the "philosophy" is probably that of Negative Capability, though "staid" is a queer and ominous epithet. On the whole, however, February and March bring so vigorous a reassertion of Keats's natural sensuousness, scepticism, and dislike of versified preachment that even Negative Capability seems rather too theoretical and systematic a term for it. He openly falls back upon the feelings which that doctrine was intended to protect, refusing

to be bullied into a certain Philosophy engendered in the Whims of an Egotist. . . . We hate poetry which has a palpable design upon us. . . . I will have no more of Wordsworth or Hunt in particular. . . . Let us have the old Poets, and Robin Hood.[88]

In return for Reynolds' sonnets on the outlaw hero he encloses his own *Robin Hood*, pleasantly free from all "design" except that of restoring a merrily unreflective past. "The old Poets" are similarly honored in *Lines on the Mermaid Tavern*, where Keats doubts if their departed spirits have found an Elysium "choicer" than Elizabethan reality.[89]

In another letter to Reynolds, who was sympathetic with this side of Keats's character, he claims the right to think, not with the vain hope of reaching a logical conclusion, but as a personal aesthetic pleasure. The attempt to argue that such enjoyment is not anti-social is unconvincing, but it shows that even at this time the benevolistic principle has not been forgotten.[90] Keats reveals more of his real self when he encloses the charm-

---

[86] *Ibid.*, p. 462.   [87] *Ibid.*, p. 481.   [88] *Letters*, pp. 96–97.
[89] *Works*, pp. 269–270.   [90] *Letters*, pp. 103–104.

ing lines in which the thrush sings him a message very different from that of Benjamin Bailey:

> O fret not after knowledge—I have none,
> And yet my song comes native with the warmth.
> O fret not after knowledge—I have none,
> And yet the Evening listens.[91]

A little ashamed of himself, he concludes in prose: "Now I am sensible all this is a mere sophistication (however it may neighbour to any truths) to excuse my own indolence." [92] The parenthesis is sincerer than the main clause. Two days later, however, he describes himself to George and Tom as reading Voltaire and Gibbon while "the thrushes are singing now as if they would speak to the winds, because their big brother Jack, the Spring, is not far off . . . although I wrote to Reynolds the other day to prove reading of no use." [93] One thinks of Wordsworth's Solitary, poring over *Candide* in the Lake Country.

Such reading may have helped to nourish the utter scepticism of the letter written to Bailey on March 13. Keats is trying to explain, as kindly as possible, why he cannot discuss a sermon of Bailey's which Mrs. Dilke has lent him:

You know my ideas about Religion. I do not think myself more in the right than other people, and that nothing in this world is proveable. . . . I am sometimes so very sceptical as to think Poetry itself a mere Jack a lanthen to amuse whoever may be struck by its brilliance. As Tradesmen say every thing is worth what it will fetch, so probably every mental pursuit takes its reality and worth from the ardour of the pursuer—being in itself a nothing.[94]

This suggests a sort of aesthetic pragmatism: ideas are true in proportion to the pleasure of chasing them. The application of this principle even to poetry makes it difficult to regard Keats as a worshipper of eternal and absolute Beauty. But as usual he refuses to be taken seriously:

Now my dear fellow I must once for all tell you I have not one Idea of the truth of any of my speculations—I shall never be a Reasoner because I care not to be in the right, when retired from bickering and in a proper philosophical temper.[95]

For "philosophical," read "indifferent to philosophy."

[91] *Works*, p. 482. [92] *Letters*, p. 105. [93] *Ibid.*, p. 107.
[94] *Ibid.*, pp. 111-112. [95] *Ibid.*, pp. 112-113.

According to the verse-epistle sent *To J. H. Reynolds* on March 25, Keats is not yet ready to philosophize, fears that he will never be able to do so, and does not really wish to do so. The following lines hark back to Book IV of *Endymion* and point forward to one of the great odes:

> ...It is a flaw
> In happiness to see beyond our bourn—
> It forces us in Summer skies to mourn:
> It spoils the singing of the Nightingale.

Keats prefers "something of material sublime" to any abstract concept.[96]

In this poem the escapist element in Negative Capability is particularly clear. He has had a glimpse of nature as "an eternal fierce destruction" exemplified not only by sharks and hawks, but by "The gentle Robin, like a pard or ounce/Ravening a worm." One sees no suggestion here of that "harmony of the universe" which for Mr. Murry is implied by Negative Capability.[97] In this mood Keats repudiates the universe of sentimental pantheism, but he has cut himself off from any more rationally hopeful interpretation of the struggle for existence. The only escape lies in the enjoyment of art, since actual thrushes and nightingales are no more benevolent than robins. And so

> ...I'll dance.
> And from detested moods in new Romance
> Take refuge.[98]

In this case the new romance is probably not *Hyperion* but *Isabella,* begun in February and completed in first draft in April. In style and tone it stands halfway between the adolescent luxuriance of *Endymion* and the more chastened and centripetal sensuousness of the masterpieces of 1819. No critic, I believe, has extracted from this beautifully morbid tale any high intellectual or spiritual significance. Professor Finney, commenting on the speech of Lorenzo's ghost in stanzas 38–40, rightly observes: "The state of departed souls which this passage suggests is more Greek than Christian. It reminds one of the thin, shadowy existence of the souls whom Odysseus called up out of Hades." [99] The outburst of humanitarian indignation against Isabella's wicked merchant brothers is incon-

---

[96] *Works,* p. 485. *Vide supra,* p. 469, for the *Endymion* passage echoed here.
[97] *Vide supra,* p. 454.   [98] *Works,* p. 486.   [99] *Op. cit.,* p. 375.

gruous and forced.[100] Bernard Shaw is not at his best when he infers from it that Keats was a precursor of Marx, and that "had he lived, [he] would no doubt have come down from *Hyperions* and *Endymions* to tin tacks as a very full-blooded modern revolutionist." [101]

This unfortunate passage in *Isabella* prepares us, however, for the fact that in April the pendulum swings away from sensation toward "philosophy" and social service. At first the movement is hesitant: "I have not the slightest feel of humility towards the Public—or to anything in existence,—but the Eternal Being, the Principle of Beauty, and the Memory of great Men." Despite his recent observations on nature red in tooth and claw, the "Eternal Being" is Leigh Hunt's "Spirit Great and Good." "Principle of Beauty" simply means "all beautiful things." "Memory of great Men" is that bitter-sweet mixture of reverence and tortured ambition aroused in him by works of genius. He explains his defiance of the public by adding: "I would jump down Ætna for any great Public Good —but I hate a mawkish popularity." [102]

Here is some sort of God, and here are men—not readers to be placated, but human beings to be helped. The letter of April 24 to Taylor declares that as men grow up they abandon "the idea that such a thing as happiness is to be had, . . . and instead of striving from Uneasiness greet it as an habitual sensation, a pannier which is to weigh upon them through Life." Unexpectedly, however, a solution very different from Negative Capability is proposed:

I find cavalier days are gone by. I find that I can have no enjoyment in the world but continual drinking of Knowledge—I find there is no worthy pursuit but the idea of doing some good for the world—some do it with their society— some with their wit—some with their benevolence—. . . there is but one way for me—the road lies through application, study, and thought. I will pursue it and to that end purpose retiring for some years. I have been hovering for some time between an exquisite sense of the luxurious and a love for Philosophy—were I calculated for the former I should be glad—but as I am not I shall turn all my soul to the latter.[103]

Here is *Sleep and Poetry* again—delight in sensuous luxury reluctantly put aside in favor of the poetry of helpful wisdom. The composition of

---

[100] *Works*, pp. 219–220. Sidney Colvin, *op. cit.*, p. 392, reminds us that the source is a passage in Dryden's *Annus Mirabilis* on the Dutch merchants in the East Indies.

[101] G. B. Shaw, "Keats," *Keats Memorial Volume*, pp. 175–176.

[102] *Letters*, pp. 130, 131.   [103] *Ibid.*, pp. 134–135.

such poetry, being deeply repugnant to Keats, will be postponed "for some years" while he devotes himself less unpleasantly to reading and musing. His psychology at this point is rather Coleridgian.

On May 3 we find him saying to Reynolds that "an extensive knowledge is needful to thinking people—it takes away the heat and fever; and helps, by widening speculation, to ease the Burthen of the Mystery." [104] This knowledge is not that which in April was to implement his aim of "doing some good for the world," but a slightly intellectualized variant of Negative Capability. Keats is saying that for those who have read widely the pain of life is never merely personal. It is cooled, objectified, diffused through a world of fellow-sufferers, and expressed in graceful forms, so that at last it becomes a source of aesthetic pleasure. Such is the knowledge implied by the *Ode to May,* Keats's most authentically Greek poem, which he sent to Reynolds with this letter. He would hymn Maia with the serene and noble sensuousness of the ancients:

> O, give me their old vigour, and unheard
> Save of the quiet Primrose, and the span
> Of heaven and few ears,
> Rounded by thee, my song should die away
> Content as theirs,
> Rich in the simple worship of a day.[105]

The poem is unfinished, perhaps because Keats knows that this untroubled acceptance of life and of oblivion is not for modern men, least of all for him. The same letter includes the famous comparison of human life to "a large Mansion of Many Apartments." Here some readers have been misled by the temptation to impute peculiar profundity to a truism expressed in pleasantly imaginative language. The passage says merely that Keats has reached that stage of human development in which we realize that life is extremely difficult without knowing how to solve the difficulties.[106]

Wordsworth and Milton—it is noteworthy that Shakespeare is not mentioned—are skilled in exploring the dark corridors of life's mansion. Spurned with Leigh Hunt in February, Wordsworth now appears as "deeper than Milton—though I think it has depended more upon the general and gregarious advance of intellect, than individual greatness of

---

[104] *Ibid.,* p. 140. Observe the reminiscence of *Tintern Abbey.*
[105] *Works,* p. 487.   [106] *Letters,* pp. 143–144.

mind." Milton, with the rest of his generation, relied too unquestioningly on the "Dogmas and superstitions" which Protestantism, despite its immense superiority to Popery, continued to regard as axiomatic.

He did not think into the human heart as Wordsworth has done—Yet Milton had sure as great powers as Wordsworth—What then is to be inferr'd? O many things—It proves there is really a grand march of intellect—, It proves that a mighty providence subdues the mightiest Minds to the service of the time being, whether it be in human Knowledge or Religion. . . . After all there is certainly something real in the world.

The "something real" is apparently a beneficent spirit revealed through a law of progressive human enlightenment. This perfectibilitarianism is part of the eighteenth-century heritage, though "march of intellect" has a Tennysonian ring. Perhaps Keats has been talking with Dilke, who carried the banner of Godwin into the Victorian period. But the letter, after rising to this confident climax, ends with an unconscious hint of doom: "Tom has spit a leetle blood this afternoon, and that is rather a damper." [107]

Another "damper" is imparted to Bailey toward the end of May: the beloved George is to marry and emigrate to America. "I am now so depressed that I have not an Idea to put to paper—my hand feels like lead—and yet it is an unpleasant numbness—it does not take away the pain of existence." [108] He announces his intention of touring Scotland with Brown. A subsequent letter explains that

I thought it would give me more experience, rub off more Prejudice, use me to more hardship, identify finer scenes, load me with grander Mountains, and strengthen more my reach in Poetry, than would stopping at home among Books even though I should reach Homer.[109]

So much for the "continual drinking of Knowledge," his ideal of April.

In writing the Jeffrey sisters on June 4 he combines his earlier horror at the struggle for existence with a fling at clerical hypocrisy:

Are the little Robins weaned yet? Do they walk alone? You have had a christening a top o' the tiles and a Hawk has stood God father and taken the little

[107] *Ibid.*, pp. 144–145.

[108] *Ibid.*, p. 147. See also p. 151, where he associates the misfortunes of George and Tom with a world in which "women have Cancers," and says that "now I am never alone without rejoicing that there is such a thing as death."   [109] *Ibid.*, p. 193.

Brood under the shadow of its Wings much in the way of Mother Church—
a Cat too has very tender bowels in such pathetic cases.[110]

He is angry at the oily priests of the God who permits Tom to suffer so.
Even more than with most men, Keats's view of the universe veered from
optimism to pessimism and back again according to his personal circumstances.

As the tour begins, however, the scenery about Wordsworth's Win-
andermere reveals a wholly different God—the God of Nature approached
aesthetically. The mountains "make one forget the divisions of life . . .
and refine one's sensual vision into a sort of north star which can never
cease to be open lidded and stedfast over the wonders of the great
Power." [111]

The Scots, he found, had a less unctuous Deity than the English, but
an even more detestable one. He remarks severely upon the tyrannous
bigotry of the Kirk, quite possibly with Burns in mind: "I would sooner
be a wild deer than a Girl under the dominion of the Kirk, and I would
sooner be a wild hog than be the occasion of a Poor Creature's penance
before those execrable elders." [112] It was a pleasant surprise to meet a
Scottish deist, although the man expressed his opinions very cautiously
even after "he had received several encouraging hints from us." [113] Perhaps because of Keats's dislike of the Kirk, perhaps because of the companionship of the libertine scoffer Brown, some of the trivial verses
composed on the tour give frivolous expression to his heterodoxy. He
joins Brown in a feeble satire on monkish superstitions and smiles at

> . . . a pious spouse
> Who seven times a day
> Scolds as King David pray'd, to chouse
> And have her holy way.[114]

There is no prayer at all in the sonnet, *Read me a lesson, Muse*. The
mist which enshrouds him on the summit of Ben Nevis symbolizes man's
utter ignorance of heaven, of hell, and of his own nature:

> Here are the craggy stones beneath my feet,—
> Thus much I know that, a poor witless elf,

[110] *Ibid.*, p. 150.   [111] *Ibid.*, p. 155. Compare the *Bright Star* sonnet.
[112] *Ibid.*, p. 173.   [113] *Ibid.*, p. 160.
[114] *Works*, pp. 547, 559. Brown was soon to write a life of David in the vein of Voltaire.

I tread on them,—that all my eye doth meet
Is mist and crag, not only on this height,
But in the world of thought and mental might! [115]

This statement of Keats's philosophical and religious position as of August 3, 1818, should be accepted as meaning exactly what it says. It does not express the "satisfaction in ignorance" which Miss Lowell attributes to him.

Not only the metaphorical but the actual mists of Ben Nevis played a part in his tragedy. The ascent and still more the descent of the mountain fatigued him and aggravated the "throat condition" which had troubled him for some time.[116] At Inverness he became feverish, and the local physician had just warned him to abandon his travels when the news came that Tom's condition was alarming. John left Scotland at once and reached Hampstead on August 18.

4

Keats loved his slowly dying brother, but he was not made to be a nurse. On September 21 he tells Dilke that Tom's

identity presses upon me so all day that I am obliged to go out—and although I intended to have given some time to study alone I am obliged to write, and plunge into abstract images to ease myself of his countenance, his voice and feebleness—so that I live now in a continual fever. . . . Imagine "the hateful siege of contraries"—if I think of fame or poetry it seems a crime to me, and yet I must do so or suffer.[117]

Observe the synonymous relationship of "fame" and "poetry," and the rapid shift from Tom's sufferings to his own. Although the principle of human service now has a specific and personal claim upon him, on the following day he addresses Reynolds:

This morning Poetry has conquered—I have relapsed into those abstractions which are my only life—I feel escaped from a new strange and threatening

[115] *Ibid.*, p. 494.
[116] Amy Lowell, *op. cit.*, I, 512–516, argues rather cogently that the first "faint indications" of his tuberculosis can be traced back to the autumn of 1817. The point is unimportant for us. It would not be surprising that the spiritual feverishness which he manifests then and even earlier should have been related to his physical condition.
[117] *Letters*, p. 216.

sorrow—and I am thankful for it.—There is an awful warmth about my heart like a load of Immortality.[118]

These letters set forth the main though not the only trend of Keats's thought during this period. Negative Capability henceforth is clearly a means of escaping from life into art. The more intolerable his own feelings become, the more necessary it is for him to transcend identity through concentration upon that beauty which "obliterates all consideration."

In this light should be interpreted the well-known letter of October 27 to Woodhouse, with its contrast between "the poetical Character" and "the Wordsworthian or egotistical sublime":

A Poet is the most unpoetical of any thing in existence; because he has no Identity—he is continually informing and filling some other Body. . . . It is a wretched thing to confess; but it is a very fact that not one word I ever utter can be taken for granted as an opinion growing out of my identical nature—how can it, when I have no nature?

The humanitarian obligation is recognized; but, as in the preceding spring, it is indefinitely postponed:

I am ambitious of doing the world some good: if I should be spared that may be the work of maturer years—in the interval I will assay to reach to as high a summit in Poetry as the nerve bestowed upon me will suffer.

He returns, however, to the surest bulwark against misery—the denial of identity: "But even now I am perhaps not speaking from myself: but from some character in which I now live." [119] Such words imply more than a wholesome repudiation of Wordsworth's didactic egotism: they suggest a morbid desire to "fade far away, dissolve, and quite forget" the world in which Tom "grows pale, and spectre-thin, and dies."

Much more importantly, as Keats had discovered in September, this is also the world in which Lockharts and Crokers blight the aspirations of young poets. "The only thing that can ever affect me personally for more than one short passing day, is any doubt about my powers for poetry." [120] But such doubts often plagued him, and now they arose in a cloud. He had written not merely for creative pleasure but for glory. The fear that

---

[118] *Ibid.*, p. 217. "Abstractions," be it remembered, are intense depersonalizing acts of concentration upon shapes of beauty.

[119] *Ibid.*, pp. 227–229.   [120] *Ibid.*, p. 241.

he was "one whose name was writ in water" was the bitterest ingredient in the porridge about which Browning inquires. Let us return to the letters of September 21 and 22 and observe the importance of "fame or poetry" and "load of Immortality." Perhaps, as is generally supposed, Keats's ruling passion was love of beauty; but he never thought long about beauty without thinking about fame. Unromantic as he is in several respects, this craving is his special form of romantic self-trust and self-expansion. His gods are the great poets, and he would be hailed as one of them. But his 1817 volume had been a failure, he himself had condemned *Endymion,* and now the all-powerful reviews had made him a laughing-stock. Shelley's account of Adonais' death is obviously incomplete and exaggerated; but it is more nearly correct than the notion that Keats cared nothing about the critics, or was troubled only when he realized their effect upon his finances. Woodhouse reports that at Hessey's dinner party in October "Keats declared that there was now nothing original to be written in poetry, . . . and that he should, consequently, write no more." [121] He would never have uttered such nonsense if he had not been deeply wounded. Dilke, in a letter of 1841 to Severn, speaks of the harsh criticism "that had poisoned his [Keats's] living existence." [122] In 1829, responding to Charles Brown's request for cooperation in his life of Keats, Fanny Brawne grants "that as he was so much calumniated and suffered so much from it, it is perhaps the duty of those who loved and valued him to vindicate him also." She and Fanny Keats told Gerald Griffin that they had

oft found him on suddenly entering the room, with that review in his hand, reading as if he would devour it—completely absorbed—absent and drinking it in like mortal poison. The instant he observed anyone near him, however, he would throw it by, and begin to talk of some indifferent matter.[123]

Truly, "Our Adonais has drunk poison."

Although to assert that "a Poet . . . has no identity" was to deny his

---

[121] Quoted by C. L. Finney, *The Evolution of Keats's Poetry,* p. 446.

[122] William Sharp, *Life and Letters of Joseph Severn,* p. 199.

[123] *Letters,* pp. lx, lxiii. "That review" was probably Lockhart's, but Croker's may have been even more painful because it condemned *Endymion* on more definitely literary grounds. With Fanny Brawne's letter to Brown compare the one to Medwin quoted by Amy Lowell, *op. cit.,* II, 456. See also H. E. Briggs, "Keats's Conscious and Unconscious Reactions to Criticism of *Endymion,*" *PMLA,* LX, 1106–1129. His psychiatric approach is perhaps too ingenious, but he gives convincing evidence that Keats's self-esteem was shaken by the reviews.

romantic aspiration, Keats's own gradually increasing illness and the financial difficulties which were soon aggravated by those of Haydon and George drew him further toward this vain endeavor to surrender his creative selfhood. In September, too, he had met Fanny Brawne. Perhaps tuberculosis, poverty, and thwarted ambition are largely to blame for the fact that love soon brought him more misery than happiness. It is idle to complain that she was unworthy of him: whatever her shortcomings, she was ready and able to give him higher values than he ever sought in her. His passion was morbid, jealous, selfish, and fleshly. At best, Fanny for him was simply the Indian Maid; he never even tried to identify her with Cynthia. At worst, she was *La Belle Dame Sans Merci.*

Tom died on December first. "I will not," writes Keats to George and his wife, "enter into any parsonic comments on death. . . . I have scarce a doubt of immortality of some nature or other—neither had Tom." We had better not lean too heavily on this statement. At such a time he was not the man to add to the sorrow of far-away mourners whose beliefs, though unorthodox, were more conventional than his; and the Huntian deism, which could still be appealed to in these emergencies, did not preclude a non-parsonic hope of eternal life. What is more to the point, his "studies . . . have been greatly interrupted lately," and he is now eager to return to them. There is also mention of Fanny Brawne, "beautiful and elegant, graceful, silly, fashionable and strange." [124] On the eighteenth of this month he refuses Woodhouse's invitation to meet the Porter sisters: "I have a new leaf to turn over—I must work—I must read—I must write." [125] Bravely gathering up all his energies, he threw himself upon *Hyperion.*

For reasons which need not be explained here, I accept Mr. Ridley's orthodox view that *Hyperion: A Fragment* was begun about the middle of December and abandoned about the middle of the next month; and that although *The Fall of Hyperion: A Dream* received some attention later in the winter, it was composed chiefly in July, August, and September of 1819.[126] At present we are concerned only with the first version.

In writing *Hyperion* Keats was desperately eager to show that the ignorant and sentimental cockney whose *Endymion* had been so cruelly de-

---

[124] *Ibid.,* pp. 246, 249.   [125] *Ibid.,* p. 270.
[126] M. R. Ridley, *Keats's Craftsmanship,* p. 58. For alternative views neither of which would affect the main contentions of this chapter, see Amy Lowell, *op. cit.,* II, 339–346, and Finney, *op. cit.,* pp. 448, 458–459.

rided could produce a long poem in the high epic tradition—objective, learned, severe, majestic. In order to rise above the human bewilderment which had vitiated the earlier poem, he would sing of gods. But because he was saturated in the poetry of the English Renaissance and also knew something about contemporary theories of myth, he could not conceive of a mythological epic which was not allegorical. Nor could he conceive of an allegory which did not pertain to his own struggles to achieve the heights of poetic fame. Thus Apollo became confused with John Keats, epic impersonality collapsed into subjectivity, and the result was a stalemate.

Had the work been completed according to his original plan, it would probably have been a "progress of poetry" in epic form, identifying England with the Isles of the Blest as the final and happiest home of the Muse.[127] In his more optimistic moments, as we know, Keats believed in "the march of intellect." Oceanus asserts this perfectibilitarianism when he recognizes "the eternal law/That first in beauty should be first in might." [128] How is this principle of progress to be applied to poetry? In significant violation of the original myth, the Titans themselves are gentle, serene, beautiful. One might say that they possess Negative Capability. But when Keats is robust and confident—and he is trying hard to seem so in this poem—the escapism of Negative Capability is too calm and passive for his Elizabethan love of personal vigor and excitement. Apollo, then, represents a higher ideal in what Mr. Caldwell terms "his capacity for passionate experience." [129] In this respect the conquering poet-god is genuinely Keatsian.

But Caldwell errs, I believe, in saying that "There appears to be no warrant for reading any further meaning into the poem as it stands." [130] Let us see what Apollo, once he attains full stature with the help of Mnemosyne, is passionate *about:*

> Knowledge enormous makes a God of me.
> Names, deeds, gray legends, dire events, rebellions,

[127] I adopt this much of E. B. Hungerford's interpretation in *Shores of Darkness,* pp. 137–162, without accepting all of his hypothetical details. The story as he reconstructs it would glorify the Saturnian line, whereas it seems clear that Keats is forcing himself to associate great poetry with Apollo. Even Hungerford's general idea may seem highly dubious to those who have not studied, with his help, the strange theories of the "speculative mythologists."

[128] *Hyperion,* II, 228–229.

[129] J. R. Caldwell, "The Meaning of *Hyperion,*" *PMLA,* LI, 1096.

[130] *Ibid.*

> Majesties, sovran voices, agonies,
> Creations and destroyings, all at once
> Pour into the wide hollows of my brain,
> And deify me.[131]

This eloquent jumble is by no means self-explanatory, but a general familiarity with Keats's thought suggests the likeliest interpretation. To possess and utter philosophic wisdom concerning the thoughts and actions and destinies of man is to be truly a god and a poet. But although poetic deification was Keats's deepest desire, he did not want it on these terms. Such wisdom is so far above Keats, and so alien to his natural temper, that as always he associates it with learning, which unweaves the rainbow; with consecutive thinking, which is powerless to attain beauty-truth; with generalized concepts, which spoil the singing of the nightingale; with the edifying didacticism of the Wordsworthian or egotistical sublime, which has too palpable a design upon us. Once Keats realized that if he continued this attempt to write a philosophical allegory Apollo would symbolize the sort of poetry which at heart he detested, there was nothing to do but break off.

He does so gladly. Instead of grappling with the dark mysteries of human souls, he finds in *Fancy* the power to shape delightful images of nature and of woman's beauty which are more enduring and less marred by pain than those provided by actual experience. This conception of art as a refuge from life rather than as a fulfilment of life's potentialities will soon become the theme of his most serious poems, but at present he expresses it lightly and whimsically.

Like a boy released from school he turns from the Miltonic and Wordsworthian Apollo to his old friends Beaumont and Fletcher. They are *Bards of Passion and of Mirth,* not of "knowledge enormous." Their spirits dwell in a fancy-created Elysium which is, after all, "Choicer than the Mermaid Tavern," [132] for there

> ...the Nightingale doth sing
> Not a senseless, tranced thing,
> But divine, melodious truth;
> Philosophic numbers smooth;
> Tales and golden histories
> Of heaven and its mysteries.[133]

[131] *Hyperion*, III, 113–118.   [132] *Works*, p. 269.   [133] *Ibid.*, p. 268.

For the moment, fancy resolves the strife between philosophy and the nightingale by transforming the bird into a better philosopher than Mnemosyne or Benjamin Bailey.

Delightedly also he renews his allegiance to the superficies of Spenser in *The Eve of St. Agnes,* which is thoroughly characteristic of his happiest work in its entranced absorption in the pleasures of the five senses. These pleasures, however, are not unalloyed. The warm, bright, tender story is buried deep in the past and framed in darkness, cold, fear, hate, and the feebleness of old age. At the close, the lovers go out "into the storm." Having briefly experienced beauty-truth, they must experience life.

As the undercurrent of melancholy in the lovely tale prepares us to expect, this spurt of creative activity soon ceased. During February, March, and the first week or so of April, 1819, he wrote almost no verse, and his correspondence suggests a low state of morale. Haydon must have been shocked to receive the letter of March 8:

I have experienced the satisfaction of having great conceptions without the trouble of sonnetteering. . . . I am three and twenty, with little knowledge and middling intellect. It is true that in the height of enthusiasm I have been cheated into some fine passages; but that is not the thing.[134]

Only a poet whose pride had been grievously hurt would thus protect himself through silence. His inactivity provides no real solace. On the thirteenth of April, when Haydon complains of not having received the loan which Keats had promised him, Keats explains his own difficult circumstances and adds: "Now you have maimed me again—when your note came I was engaged in a Book—I dread as much as a Plague the idle fever of two months more without any fruit." [135]

But the indestructible sweetness and rightness of Keats is seen when he addresses his sister Fanny on March 31. She is preparing for confirmation and has sent him a list of questions, such as are now covered by the "Offices of Instruction" in the revised Book of Common Prayer, on the Creed, the Sacraments, and other points of doctrine. Her brother has sent her "a little book," but meanwhile coaches her himself with an accuracy implying considerable knowledge of the beliefs which he rejected. He may of course have refreshed his memory for the occasion. There is not the slightest hint of opposition or sarcasm except in the whimsical signa-

---

[134] *Letters,* p. 285.
[135] *Ibid.,* p. 294. The "book" was probably *The Fall of Hyperion.*

ture, "Your affectionate Parson, John." [136] A fortnight later, however, when Fanny has passed her examination, he lets himself go a little but not in a way to distress her:

I am glad you got on so well with Monsr. le Curè [*sic*]—is he a nice Clergyman—a great deal depends upon a cock'd hat and powder—not gun powder, lord love us, but lady-meal, violet-smooth, dainty-scented, lilly-white, feather-soft, wigsby-dressing, coat-collar-spoiling, whisker-reaching, pig-tail loving, swan's down-puffing, parson-sweetening powder.[137]

The girl would think that her jolly brother was at his jokes again.

At about the same time he imparts to George and Georgiana a more grown-up version of his anticlericalism:

A Parson is a Lamb in a drawing-room and a lion in a Vestry. The notions of Society will not permit a Parson to give way to his temper in any shape—so he festers in himself—his features get a peculiar diabolical self-sufficient iron stupid expression. He is continually acting. His mind is against every Man and every Man's mind is against him. He is an Hippocrite to the Believer and a Coward to the Unbeliever. He must be either a Knave or an Ideot. . . . Parsons will always keep up their character, but as it is said there are some animals the ancients knew which we do not, let us hope that posterity will miss the black badger with the tri-cornered hat.[138]

True to the concretizing quality of his imagination, he could seldom think about Christianity without thinking about parsons. There could be no greater obstacle to belief.

The foregoing passage is drawn from the huge journal-letter to George and Georgiana which concerns his life between February 14 and May 3. We must consider that portion which runs to the end of March. He goes about in society "very little now, . . . being almost tired of men and things. . . . A Dance would injure my throat very much." [139] Perhaps need of money will force him to become a physician—"it's not worse than writing poems, and hanging them up to be fly-blown in the Review shambles." [140] At present, however, he is in a state of laziness—it is really a sort of anaesthetic numbness—in which

pleasure has no show of enticement and pain no unbearable frown. Neither Poetry, nor Ambition, nor Love have any alertness of countenance as they pass by me. . . . This is the only happiness; and it is a rare instance of advantage in the body overpowering the Mind.[141]

These remarks parallel so closely not only the thought but the structure and even the language (see stanzas ii and iii) of the *Ode on Indolence* that Miss Lowell and Professor Finney must be wrong in placing the poem last in the great series of odes. It had certainly been conceived in some detail, and probably written, about the end of March.[142] In the ode, Keats will not even raise his head from the grass to bid farewell to those "three Ghosts"—the great passions of his life—Love, Ambition, and "my demon Poesy,"

> For I would not be dieted with praise,
>   A pet-lamb in a sentimental farce!
> Fade softly from my eyes, and be once more
>   In masque-like figures on the dreamy urn;
>   Farewell! I yet have visions for the night,
>   And for the day faint visions there is store;
>   Vanish, ye Phantoms! from my idle spright
> Into the clouds, and never more return![143]

Back to the letter. An important passage declares that "Complete disinterestedness" is very rare; if it were universal, it would "injure society." (Has he perhaps heard of Bernard Mandeville's thesis?) Men are as selfishly rapacious as hawks. "This is what makes the Amusement of Life—to a speculative Mind." (Negative Capability is now not merely detached but cynical.) Nevertheless—the inconsistency is no less bewildering than characteristic—there is goodness in the human heart:

I have no doubt that thousands of people I never heard of have had hearts completely disinterested: I can remember but two—Socrates and Jesus—their histories evince it. . . . It is to be lamented that the history of the latter was written and revised by Men interested in the pious frauds of Religion. Yet through all this I see his splendour.[144]

---

[141] *Ibid.*, p. 315.

[142] The obvious difficulty is the allusion to "the sweet tears of May" in stanza v (*Works*, p. 449). But both March and April are awkward for rhymesters; also Keats would wish to present Love, Ambition, and Poesy at the season in which their enticements are most potent. Of course it is possible that he revised the poem in May.

[143] *Works*, p. 449. As for the urn, see an unquoted portion of the letter under discussion for exactly the same image. The *Ode on a Grecian Urn* is already fermenting in his mind. (*Letters*, p. 315.)   [144] *Letters*, pp. 316–317.

Returning to the subject of indolently speculative pleasure, he asks: "May there not be superior beings amused with any graceful though instinctive attitude my mind may fall into, as I am entertained with the alertness of a Stoat or the anxiety of a Deer?" If our attitudes of mind are as graceful as a deer with raised forefoot in the lily-pads at dawn, that is as close an approximation of truth as the gods expect of us on earth. Whatever wisdom may be expressed here is hardly of the kind imputed to Keats by critics like Professor Thorpe. Even this idea is prefaced by the admission that he is "writing at random—straining at particles of light in the midst of a great darkness—with knowing the bearing of any one assertion of any one opinion." [145]

At this point he inserts the sonnet *Why did I laugh tonight*, which clearly shows that his attempt to view life with the detachment of a Lucretian god is an inadequate protection against despair:

> O Darkness! Darkness! ever must I moan,
> To question Heaven and Hell and Heart in vain.

Despite all the joys of fancy,

> Yet would I on this very midnight cease,
> And the world's gaudy ensigns see in shreds;
> Verse, Fame, and Beauty are intense indeed,
> But Death intenser—Death is Life's high meed.[146]

Indolence will not, after all, suffice to allay the tortures of Love, Ambition, and Poesy; not beauty, but death alone, will "obliterate all consideration."

As the letter to George and Georgiana moves on into April, there is at first no marked change. "I am still at a stand in versifying." Perhaps he will become a journalist in London rather than a physician.[147] The dream of perfectibility, he says, seems futile when one remembers the savage strife which pervades all of nature below the human level. Even the inanimate world is hostile to man's hopes: "Look at the Poles and at the Sands of Africa, Whirlpools and volcanoes—Let men exterminate them and I will say that they may arrive at earthly happiness." [148]

Nevertheless he insists that the world should not be called a "vale of tears," but "the vale of Soul-making." He goes on to present a theory

---

[145] *Ibid.*, p. 317.
[146] *Works*, p. 470. Observe the anticipation of *Ode to a Nightingale*.
[147] *Letters*, p. 320.   [148] *Ibid.*, pp. 334–335.

which several critics have regarded with admiring solemnity. On the day when he propounded it, Keats himself thought it "a grander system of salvation than the Christian religion," and probably "the Parent of all the more palpable and personal Schemes of Redemption." The theory is, as he says, "a system of Spirit-creation" rather than of salvation in the ordinary sense. "There may be intelligences or sparks of divinity in millions, but they are not souls till they acquire identity, till each one is personally itself." The world is the "school" in which intelligences become individual souls. In this school "the human heart (as distinguished from intelligence or Mind)" is the "hornbook" in which Mind learns to read. But this metaphor does not express the full importance of the heart: "Not merely is the Heart a Hornbook, It is the Mind's Bible, it is the Mind's experience, it is the teat from which the Mind or intelligence sucks its identity." [149]

Mr. James remarks that this theory, which Keats regards as "grander" than Christianity, "is virtually a restatement of the true Christian view." [150] The observation is valid as regards the general idea that the world is the place for making individual souls which are worthy of salvation, but not as regards the nature of the process. G. R. Elliott observes that the struggle between good and evil in the human soul is ignored. [151] One might add that grace plays no part in the process, and that there is no recognition of the corporate element in Christian soul-making.

It is therefore more profitable to ask whether the scheme provided Keats with a satisfying explanation of the bitterness of life. Thorpe infers from it that he "had finally arrived at comparative peace with the world, in spite of all its horrid incongruities, and had found a justification for its suffering and misery." [152] To say this is to express a low estimate of Keats's mental powers. The exceptional earnestness with which the theory is enunciated is an ominous rather than a hopeful sign. According to Finney, who sides with Thorpe on this point, "The heart is the seat of sensuous experience and of the passions which are stimulated by sensuous experience." [153] But the mind-heart dichotomy is thoroughly immature. And is the heart, as "hornbook" would imply, merely the elementary foundation on which the mind must build; or is it, as "Bible" would imply and as Mr. Murry wishes to believe, [154] the supreme standard by which the

[149] *Ibid.*, pp. 335–337.   [150] D. G. James, *Scepticism and Poetry*, p. 202.
[151] G. R. Elliott, *The Cycle of Modern Poetry*, p. 52.
[152] C. D. Thorpe, *The Mind of John Keats*, p. 88.
[153] *Op. cit.*, p. 601.   [154] *Vide supra*, p. 454.

mind must be guided in its efforts to achieve individuality? Keats leans toward the latter view, but his old conflict between sensuousness and "philosophy" forbids a decisive answer. Another difficulty is that individual mind, that which is to be produced, is a factor in its own production. Furthermore, the end and aim of the soul-making process is the acquisition of personal identity. Since denial that the poet possesses any such identity has become Keats's most nearly consistent aesthetic opinion, this is a strange idea for him to advance. The remainder of his career indicates that "soul-making" is by no means his philosophical or religious terminus but merely one of the momentary products of his endless groping. It influences none of the great poems which he is about to write, and he never returns to it in his letters as he repeatedly returns to more congenial ideas.

On April 30 Keats included in his journal-letter the *Ode to Psyche*. His climactic period of creative activity had begun toward the close of this month, and it would continue through the next. Besides the poem already mentioned, it includes *La Belle Dame Sans Merci, Ode on Melancholy, Ode to a Nightingale,* and *Ode on a Grecian Urn.* I have given reasons for placing *Ode on Indolence* a little earlier; it indicates the psychological background against which the others were written. This sudden outburst of great poetry is not the result of his having reached a triumphant solution of life's problems. It shows, on the contrary, that he has found no solution whatever; that his failure to do so has generated powerful feelings which have piled up until they demand release; and that out of his unhappiness has at last arisen the determination to write his own poetry in his own way, heedless of obligations and models and reviewers. "New Phoenix wings" have not been granted him. He has become, not a philosophical or humanitarian Apollo, but simply a more accomplished artist of his own kind. As sensuous as ever, he has outgrown his adolescent mawkishness and developed a surer, more restrained taste. He has known sickness, sorrow, love, poverty, and scorn. He has read and thought earnestly, though inconclusively; and his deep awareness of the painful mystery of life has given his yearning for delight a tragic dignity.

The keenest pleasure which these poems offer is almost independent of conceptual thinking, but our subject compels us to consider ideas rather than images. Keats's theme throughout the whole group is that, despite his longing to find joy in a real world of human warmth, art is better than life and death is better than art. Though the "happy pieties" of

Greece can no longer be cultivated as objective truths, the artist may still erect a fane for Psyche "In some untrodden region of my mind." [155] But the cult of Psyche, as Garrod has observed, is not fresh and joyous, but "melancholy and languorous." [156] *La Belle Dame Sans Merci* has already hinted at the awakening which must follow such enchantment. After the "rosy sanctuary," the "cold hillside."

Like *La Belle Dame, Ode on Melancholy* is heavy with the morbidity of his feelings toward Fanny Brawne. The greater the capacity for joy, the greater the capacity for sadness. The deepest melancholy is to be found not in scenes of horror but in scenes of beauty: "She dwells with Beauty—Beauty that must die." [157] Since the beauty glimpsed in firsthand experience of life is thus doomed, Keats turns in *Ode on a Grecian Urn* to the beauty of art, where delight never fades because it is never consummated—the blessed opiate which teases us out of thought by making it unnecessary for us to think at all.

Let us not bemuse ourselves over "Beauty is truth, truth Beauty." The famous statement includes, no doubt, a remnant of the transcendentalism earlier expressed to Bailey: "What the Imagination seizes as Beauty must be truth." But for Keats truth is now anything that will make life seem endurable; and beauty, as always, pertains to lovely shapes. His thought here is no more Platonic than in Book IV of *Endymion*. Professor Bush is surely right: "Neither beauty nor truth is for Keats a real abstraction, a Platonic Idea; beauty is something beautiful, the 'material sublime.'" [158] The only truth known to Keats on this earth is that things like the urn are lovely, and he vainly tries to persuade himself that he needs no other knowledge. But it is sad to think of art as precious because life is worthless. Keats has too lusty an appetite for joyous experience to be satisfied with "unheard" melodies or with a kiss which through all the centuries is only just about to happen. His real sympathies are with the deserted "little town" whose "breathing human passion" is *not* forever frozen on the urn.

This deeply sad poem is the essence of optimism compared to the *Ode to a Nightingale*. The bird is immortal not as this one melodious creature but as symbolizing an enduring tradition of poetic beauty and poetic fame,

[155] *Works*, pp. 263, 264.

[156] H. W. Garrod, *Keats*, p. 98. See also pp. 99–101 for remarks on the close relationship between *Ode to Psyche* and *Ode on Melancholy*.

[157] *Works*, p. 275.

[158] Douglas Bush, *Mythology and the Romantic Tradition in English Poetry*, p. 108.

> An endless fountain of immortal drink,
> Pouring unto us from the heaven's brink.[159]

Keats can participate in the "full-throated ease" of the poet-bird only through a dissolution in which he will

> ...quite forget
> What thou among the leaves hast never known,
> The weariness, the fever, and the fret
> Here, where men sit and hear each other groan;
> Where palsy shakes a few, sad, last, grey hairs,
> Where youth grows pale, and spectre-thin, and dies;
> Where but to think is to be full of sorrow
> And leaden-eyed despairs,
> Where Beauty cannot keep her lustrous eyes,
> Or new Love pine at them beyond tomorrow.[160]

The aid of wine is rejected: only the exercise of art will give him the artist's exemption from life's pain. But hardly have "the viewless wings of Poesy" wafted him into the odorous darkness than he thinks of "easeful Death" as a richer and more complete means of forgetting the transitoriness of human joy. Even in this thought, however, there is no absolute peace, for now his unquenchable ambition arises and he contrasts himself as "a sod" with the enduring fame of the nightingale. The jar of conflict between the desire to die as a man and the desire to live forever as a poet shatters his trance. Thrown back upon reality, he closes by denying all that he has said about the healing power of imagination:

> Adieu! the fancy cannot cheat so well
> As she is famed to do, deceiving elf.[161]

"Fled is that music." By the end of May, the wonderful outpouring of luxury and pain has subsided, leaving him precisely what he had been before. His correspondence throughout the rest of 1819 displays the medley of moods with which we are now familiar. Absence from London during the summer, however, causes him to begin the distressing series of letters to Fanny Brawne. By July 25 he has identified his desire for her body with his desire for annihilation:

[159] *Endymion*, I, 23–24.
[160] *Works*, p. 258.
[161] *Ibid.*, p. 260.

I have two luxuries to brood over in my walks, your Loveliness and the hour of my death. O that I could have possession of them both in the same minute. I hate the world: it batters too much the wings of my self-will, and would I could take a sweet poison from your lips to send me out of it.

The same letter, however, informs her that he is at work on "a very abstract Poem" [162]—he has determined to finish the *Fall* version of *Hyperion*.

Most of the poems composed during the brief remainder of his career must be read with four facts in mind: he had shot his bolt in May; by July he was a very sick man; his artistic integrity was threatened by the feeling that he must write for money; his natural scepticism was sometimes given a cheaply cynical turn by his association with Charles Brown and his awareness of the reasons for Byron's success. Even the beauty of *Lamia* is marred by knowing winks and leers. So far as Keats's thought is concerned, however, this poem marks a revival of the old struggle between sensuous luxury and "philosophy." Who is the real villain of the piece, the wise Apollonius or the lovely witch? Burton's tale is meant to show how youth may be rescued from sensual passion by philosophy, and the same moral may be drawn from the poem if one reads it very hastily. On the other hand, the disenchantment of Lycius kills him, for it destroys those illusions which are more precious than actuality. Nor is this an exceptional case:

> ...Do not all charms fly
> At the mere touch of cold philosophy?
> There was an awful rainbow once in heaven:
> We know her woof, her texture; she is given
> In the dull catalogue of common things.
> Philosophy will clip an angel's wings,
> Conquer all mysteries by rule and line,
> Empty the haunted air, and gnomed mine—
> Unweave a rainbow, as it erewhile made
> The tender-person'd Lamia melt into a shade.[163]

Keats had not, however, abandoned his hope of writing a great serious work which would redeem his name in the eyes of the public; and by some strange perversity of judgment he was never able to dissociate this aim from the distasteful notion that a true poet must express wisdom

[162] *Letters*, pp. 361–362.   [163] *Works*, pp. 211-212.

grounded upon systematic knowledge and implemented by benevolence. Hence in *The Fall of Hyperion* he bends the knee to Apollonius, demanding of Moneta:

> Majestic shadow, tell me: sure not all
> Those melodies sung into the world's ear
> Are useless: sure a poet is a sage;
> A humanist, physician to all men.
> That I am none I feel, as vultures feel
> They are no birds when Eagles are abroad.
> What am I then?

And Moneta echoes his deepest fears when she responds:

> ...Art thou not of the dreamer tribe?
> The poet and the dreamer are distinct,
> Diverse, sheer opposite, antipodes.
> The one pours out a balm upon the world,
> The other vexes it.[164]

It is no wonder that before the end of September Keats wearied of nagging himself, dropped this last attempt to be a "philosophical" poet, and veered with relief to Negative Capability: "The only means of strengthening one's intellect is to make up one's mind about nothing—to let the mind be a thoroughfare for all thoughts." [165] Perhaps only a sharp reaction against Moneta's egotistical sublimity could have enabled him to achieve, in the teeth of despair, the completely objective and impersonal sensuous beauty of *To Autumn*. Let those who regard him as a profound thinker say whether the true Keats is to be found in this poem, or in *The Fall of Hyperion*.

Thereafter, however, the descent is steep, and a close study of the disintegration of this fine spirit would not be fruitful for our purposes. The association between love and death continues. On October 13 he tells Fanny:

You have absorb'd me. I have a sensation at the present moment as though I was dissolving. . . . I have been astonished that Men could be martyr'd for religion—I have shuddered at it. I shudder no more—I could be martyr'd for

---

[164] *The Fall of Hyperion*, I, 187–202. See also ll. 147–159, which declare that only those who "Labour for mortal good" may occupy the heights of poetry.
[165] *Letters*, p. 426.

my Religion—Love is my religion—I could die for that. I could die for you. My Creed is love and you are its only tenet.[166]

But no reader of the letters to Fanny can dwell with much satisfaction upon the Keatsian religion of love. It includes no ideal aspiration—merely, as in the sonnet *I cry your mercy,* a frustrated appetite for

> That shape, that fairness, that sweet minor zest
> Of love, your kiss,—those hands, those eyes divine,
> That warm, white, lucent, million-pleasured breast—
> Yourself—your soul—in pity give me all.[167]

Her soul is mentioned, to be sure, but it seems to be no more than a means of summing up her physical charms. Nor does the last stanza of *Ode to Fanny* imply any turning toward the altar:

> Let none profane my Holy See of love,
> Or with a rude hand break
> The sacramental cake.[168]

This is the metaphor of a poet who has had no Christian experience whatever.

January, 1820, finds him still fighting against his doom. He tells Georgiana that he is tempted to sail with George, who is now in England, for a visit to America,

but then I ought to be diligent or at least keep myself within the reach of materials for diligence. Diligence! that I do not mean to say, I should say dreaming over my Books, or rather other people's Books.

His frankness helps us to interpret the phrase, "my studies," which he had used so often throughout 1819. He adds one of many denials of "the holiness of the heart's affections":

Upon the whole I dislike Mankind: whatever people on the other side of the question may advance they cannot deny that they are always surprised at hearing of a good action and never of a bad one.

So much for this wholesome vale of soul-making. He concludes by parodying the Athanasian Creed in a bit of nonsense about "three witty peo-

---

[166] *Ibid.,* p. 436.   [167] *Works,* p. 474.   [168] *Ibid.,* p. 456.

ple"—Rice, Reynolds, and Richards: "The first is Swiftian, the second Tom Cribean, and third Shandean—and yet these three Eans are not three Eans but one Ean." [169]

On the third of February the pillow was stained with his blood.

5

During the remnant of his life Keats wrote no poems, or none which has been preserved. It should now be evident that his literary career presents only a few fleeting, inconsistent, and uncertain indications of thoughts or feelings which the haziest mind could describe as religious. No one can say what would have happened had his life been prolonged, but there is nothing to suggest a movement in the direction of any spiritual goal. It is possible to select from his writings the materials of a philosophy much like Walter Pater's—a thoroughly non-religious, pessimistic, and materialistic hedonism grounded upon scepticism, love of art, and dread of life; but whether he would ever have worked out such a philosophy more systematically is doubtful.

The conclusion of our story may therefore be brief. We must not forget that he was sick in mind as well as in body. "Obvious lie" is Miss Lowell's estimate of Haydon's report that Keats took refuge in liquor and laudanum during this winter.[170] It is more probably an exaggeration, but clear evidence is lacking. No such anodynes, in any case, could suffice to calm an agony of spirit which often expressed itself in jealous suspicions of Fanny Brawne. Tortured love became the chief medium for voicing a more general bitterness which would otherwise have remained unfocussed:

I appeal to you by the blood of that Christ you believe in: Do not write to me if you have done anything this month which it would have pained me to have seen. . . . I cannot live without you, and not only you but *chaste* you, *virtuous you.*[171]

As regards his own beliefs the blood of Christ was merely a metaphor in the religion of love. In one of numerous tenderer moments he says of a ring which Fanny has given him: "The power of your benediction is of not so weak a nature as to pass from the ring in four and twenty hours—

---

[169] *Letters*, pp. 448, 452, 454.   [170] *Op. cit.*, II, 375.   [171] *Letters*, p. 497.

it is like a sacred Chalice once consecrated and forever consecrate." [172]
Subconsciously, perhaps, these Christian allusions are wistful glances in
the direction of faith; but so far as his conscious thought is concerned Miss
Lowell rightly states that "He had lost every vestige of religious belief;
even the consoling doctrine of immortality, which had given him some
small measure of comfort after Tom's death, had gone." [173]

He had not, however, wholly lost his stubborn courage, his dignity, or
his love of fame:

"If I should die," said I to myself, "I have left no immortal work behind me—
nothing to make my friends proud of my memory—but I have loved the principle of beauty in all things, and if I had had time I would have made myself
remembered." [174]

"Principle of beauty in all things" is the sort of phrase which leads some
critics to ascribe to Keats a religion of ideal beauty. They should observe
that the "principle" is not the supersensuous *prius,* but merely the inductive sum-total, of the "things." Separate from the latter, the former
would be as unreal and worthless as the moon-goddess without the Indian
Maid.

During the last year of his life, indeed, the learned and benevolently
purposive kind of thinking to which he had uneasily applied the term
"philosophy" is strikingly absent. In May, Fanny Brawne is told that

For this week I have been employed in marking the most beautiful passages in
Spenser, intending it for you, and comforting myself in being somehow occupied to give you however small a pleasure. It has lightened my time very
much.[175]

Not Dante, Shakespeare, Milton, or Wordsworth, but Spenser—and surely
not the "sage and serious" passages. It is his early love, the sensuously
luxurious Spenser, whom he remembers when in August he left-handedly
thanks Shelley for *The Cenci:*

There is only one part of it I can judge of—the poetry and dramatic effect,
which by many spirits nowadays is considered the Mammon. A modern work,
it is said, must have a purpose, which may be the God. An artist must serve
Mammon; he must have "self-concentration"—selfishness, perhaps. You, I am

---

[172] *Ibid.,* p. 473.   [173] *Op. cit.,* II, 440.   [174] *Letters,* p. 468.
[175] *Ibid.,* p. 489.

sure, will forgive me for sincerely remarking that you might curb your magnanimity a little, and be more of an artist, and load every rift of your subject
with ore.[176]

The side of Spenser which disapproves of Mammon is meaningless to
Keats: he knows only that the treasure-cave is rich with the truth of
beauty. "What shocks the virtuous philosopher delights the chameleon
poet."

The letter to Shelley is Keats's last utterance on the nature of poetry.
It vigorously spurns the sense of ethical obligation which had been the
chief nuisance of his career. The identification of artistic "selfishness"
with "self-concentration," however, seems equally to deny Negative Capability, which had been largely a factitious defense-mechanism. On the
other hand, the letter gives no inkling of that pseudo-mystical "submission
of consciousness to unconsciousness" [177] which for Mr. Murry is the essence of Keats's religion. Nothing remains but the fact that the man was
an artist who loved beautiful things for their own sake.

Shortly before sailing for Italy, Keats persuaded Severn to get him a
bottle of laudanum so that he might resort to an overdose whenever it
became quite certain that he must die. In Rome, however, Severn took
the drug from the patient's room and gave it to Dr. Clarke—an action
which Miss Lowell views with indignation:

Nothing could more certainly have prevented Keats from accepting the religion
offered him than this attitude prompted by the same religion. . . . The mercy
accorded to a dog was denied to Keats in the name of religion.[178]

Was Keats, in his last days, comforted by any glimpse of the mercy
accorded to a *man?* An army chaplain once told me that he regarded as
a sign of grace the words of a wounded soldier who called to him, "For
Christ's sake give me a cigarette!" According to Joseph Severn, who was
afflicted with this sort of mentality, as the end drew near Keats said

that he now felt convinced how much every human being required the support of religion that he might die decently. . . . "Now my dear Severn, I am
sure if you could get some of the works of Jeremy Taylor to read to me, I
might become *really* a Christian, and leave this world in peace.". . . . I read

---

[176] *Ibid.*, p. 507. The whole passage alludes to the Mammon episode in Book II of the
Faerie Queene, and the last clause is drawn from II, vii, 28, ll. 4–5.

[177] *Vide supra,* p. 454.   [178] *Op. cit.,* II, 467, 522–523.

some passages to him, and prayed with him, and I could tell by the grasp of his dear hand that his mind was reviving. . . . At last I had the consolation of finding him calm, trusting, and more prepared for his end than I was. . . . In all he uttered he breathed a simple Christian spirit; indeed, I always think that he died a Christian, that "Mercy" was trembling on his dying lips, and that his tortured soul was received by those Blessed Hands which could alone welcome it.[179]

Colvin tries to accept this report, but Miss Lowell is probably right in discounting it heavily.[180] Unlike Shelley, Keats had never been a doctrinaire foe of Christianity: his scepticism had included his own unbelief. It is by no means inconceivable that in his pain and despair he paid some tribute to the pragmatic value of Christianity for one who wished to accept the final luxury "decently." His noble courtesy might also have inclined him to relieve the pious distress of his friend. Anything like a deathbed conversion, however, is unsupported by evidence and utterly foreign to Keats's nature.

Another of Severn's reminiscences is so completely characteristic of Keats that it may be accepted without question. As the end drew near the sufferer's weakness made him appear more calm.

He kept continually in his hand a polished, oval, white cornelian, the gift of his widowing love, and at times it seemed his only consolation, the only thing left him in this world clearly tangible.[181]

It was "something of material sublime," a fragment of the only truth he had ever clearly apprehended.

[179] Quoted by C. D. Thorpe, *The Mind of John Keats*, p. 80. Benjamin Bailey had been a warm admirer of Taylor.

[180] Colvin, *op. cit.*, p. 509; Lowell, *op. cit.*, II, 521–522. My remarks on this point do not pertain to the last clause of Severn's statement.

[181] William Sharpe, *Life and Letters of Joseph Severn*, p. 91.

Chapter IX

EVALUATIONS

EACH OF THESE POETS, IN HIS OWN WAY, EXEMPLIFIES THE GENERAL DESCRIPtion of romantic religion which was offered in the introductory chapter. Readers who are unwilling to accept this conclusion would hardly be convinced by a last-minute peroration. They may also protest that any attempt to assess the merits and defects of a body of religious ideas will inevitably be too subjective to possess general validity. They may well be right. Certainly the critical historian, whatever his personal commitments may be, must refrain from measuring the faith of the romantics against a fixed dogmatic norm. A more empirical criterion is demanded. Romantic religion should be judged by its ultimate fruits in art, in the life of the individual, and in social life as a whole. Although such an evaluation must await the completion of this series of studies, the urgent importance of the problem for our own day perhaps justifies a tentative expression of opinion.

From many points of view romanticism today seems to be on its last legs—ignored by servants of the machine, derided by cynical futilitarians, earnestly repudiated both by naturalists and by supernaturalists. Nevertheless it would be rash to characterize the 1940's as completely unromantic. Much of our literature expresses romantic aspirations either directly or through a very unrealistic realism which thinly disguises the agony of romantic spirits who fear that they have been deprived of the last justification for being romantic. The religion preached from the pulpits of liberal Christianity and liberal Judaism, and from those of innumerable miscellaneous cults, is often barely distinguishable from the religion of the romantic poets. The current revival of historic Christianity among intellectuals is paralleled by, and sometimes confused with, a revival of non-Christian, anti-rationalistic mysticism. The new science has opened up chasms of mystery which the romantic spirit has eagerly exploited. That spirit is also at work in political philosophy. It is quite true that democracy is grounded upon Christianity, but this statement is often interpreted to mean that democracy is grounded not upon humility and brotherhood but upon pride and individualistic aggressiveness.

The romantic faith is preserved and fostered by the study of English literature in schools and colleges.[1] The child is usually placed in the hands of schoolma'ams who have no religion in particular but who have plenty of "ideals" which are richly satisfied by Wordsworth and Shelley. Since their concern with literature is primarily moralistic they use romantic poetry as material for "character-building." Some students react so sharply against such indoctrination that they grow up with a distrust not only of poetry but of all supersensuous values. The more docile, however, are likely to acquire the notion that Shelley is a profound master of the spiritual life. Even in colleges and universities the "Romantic Poets" course is often entrusted to a hortatory and prophetic personality who does not hesitate to reveal the kinship between his own insights and those of the great romantics. Since professors of English have frequently abandoned the Christian creed but retain an amorphous religiosity, they are likely to base their faith upon the rock of transcendentalism. Some of these teachers are also productive scholars whose writings combine the expert investigator's passion for facts with a desire to show that the romantic poets were not only great artists but great philosophers, mystics, and spiritual guides. Their efforts are often seconded by non-academic critics who, less cramped by the obligations of research, are freer to be "creative."

There is little evidence that romantic apologetics is on the wane. The extravagant and falsely-grounded assaults of the "new humanists" only impelled pro-romantic critics and scholars to defend their cause with redoubled vigor. More recently the solemn superciliousness of certain neometaphysical poet-critics has made even unromantic students think more kindly of Shelley than ever before.[2] The "save the humanities" movement is motivated largely by the hope that liberal education will provide a substitute-religion for young people who are growing up without spiritual resources in an age of doubt and confusion. It is Matthew Arnold's old remedy for "this strange disease of modern life," but with an important difference. Arnold's prescription was compounded of classical ingredients:

[1] The following observations pertain more particularly to the United States, but *mutatis mutandis* they are also applicable to British education.
[2] See R. H. Fogle, "Romantic Bards and Metaphysical Reviewers," *ELH*, XII, 221–250.

Homer's high seriousness, Epictetus' calm rejection of painful desire, Sophocles' steady and integrated contemplation of life. Today, except for a few die-hards, the basic humanistic discipline is not ancient but modern literature. And despite the present attempt to achieve "global consciousness" through study of foreign cultures, the young men and women of English-speaking countries must be expected to derive "spiritual values" chiefly from English literature. Furthermore, there is much to be said for the thesis that of all periods of English literature the Romantic Period is richest in such values. In this present age of bewildered brains, dry hearts, and nerveless hands, is not the romantic confidence in human goodness and power precisely what the doctor ordered? Has not the loss of this confidence brought modern civilization to the verge of collapse? May not these poets help us to reaffirm our shaken faith in the dignity and worth of the individual?

Those who advocate a revival of romanticism will assert that although our poets were not orthodox Christians they preserved the essentials of Christianity and of all pure religion at a time not unlike our own in that those essentials were in danger of being abandoned along with the outworn creeds which had obscured them. They resisted external dogmas and oppressive ecclesiastical institutions only because they believed so ardently in the free faith of the heart. In the same spirit they championed the rights of the human soul against the crudely mechanistic conception of science and the dehumanizing effects of the Industrial Revolution. Their passionate individualism was not a thing of selfish pride: on the contrary, their highest aspiration was submergence of selfhood in devotion to extrapersonal ideals.

The romantic poets believed in love as the divine creative principle of the universe. They sang of brotherhood, freedom, democracy. They were great liberals and humanitarians. Often, too, they elevated sexual love to a religious level. They believed in nature—not as a mass of matter operating like a soulless machine, but as a beneficent force uniting in a cosmic wholeness of being the divine spirit of love, the love-begotten world of sense-perception, and the loving heart of man. They believed in the creativity of the imagination as the repetition within the human mind of the divine creative act of self-assertion. They believed in the beauty of truth and the truth of beauty. For them poetry was not an elegant amusement, but a prophetic force, a revelation of mystical insight. In a word, they believed in man—in his natural goodness, his spiritual and intellectual energies, his power to see into the life of things, his kinship with divinity.

This, the twentieth-century champion of romanticism will conclude, is the creed of a genuine religion, a religion still available for the reintegration of the modern ego. Romantic religion seems to offer a means of rising above a merely animal or mechanical existence. It promises, furthermore, that in accepting it we shall obtain the higher spiritual values without paying the stiff price exacted by Christianity: discipline, humility, self-surrender, awareness of sin, penitence and penance, the way of the Cross. The romantic faith offers Easter without Good Friday. But if we prefer to identify it with Christianity—Christianity without tears—there is nothing to hinder us from doing so. Coleridge himself has declared that "Christianity at any period" is "the ideal of the Human Soul at that period." [3]

It seems to me, however, that my deliberately flattering sketch has described not what these poets actually believed, but what they vainly longed and struggled to believe. From the utterances of some of our contemporaries we might infer that in shifting our minds backward into the Romantic Period we should be moving from an atmosphere of stultifying doubt into one of vigorous confidence. On the contrary, the final impression made upon us by these poets is that they are desperately striving to retain prerogatives which the three preceding centuries had transferred from God to man but which they now feel to be slipping from their grasp. The extravagance of their most confident moments often sounds overstrained and shrill, and one of their persistent themes is the impossibility of achieving the romantic experience. Sooner or later they all acknowledge the barrenness of their illusions. That Byron does so is obvious. A possible exception is Blake: partly because of his deeper mental eccentricity and partly because he works with his hands as well as with his brain, he holds the vision more firmly and happily than his fellows. Even he, however, is unable to forget the "little curtain of flesh on the bed of our desire." The devotion to "pure" art which characterizes the final phase of his career is in some measure a retreat from the mental fight to which he had originally devoted himself. Burns, after all his glorification of impulse, admits man's weakness and insufficiency. "I have been a fool all my life" is his final judgment of "the religion of the bosom." Wordsworth

___

[3] In this chapter all quotations from the romantic poets are drawn from earlier pages of this book. It seems useless to plague the reader with frequent repetition of *vide supra*.

soon begins to lament the fading of the visionary gleam, and Coleridge the loss of his shaping spirit of imagination. Both poets formally abjure the romantic faith in favor of a religion which remains too romantic to be Christian although it has become too Christian to be romantic. Shelley's iridescent hopes go on and off like a firefly's light, but at the end negation has almost completely triumphed over affirmation. Keats acknowledges that the transforming power of fancy has been overrated, and he is forced to think of death as an "intenser" luxury than beauty or fame. If we wish to draw inspiration from the spectacle of a firm, consistent, sustaining faith in man's intellectual and spiritual potencies, the romantic poets will disappoint us.

Or do we hope to pull ourselves together through the contemplation not of great ideas but of great personalities, models of what the good human life has been in the past and therefore may be again in the future? Coleridge and Byron are not to be recommended for this purpose. Burns is lovable but not admirable; Wordsworth on the whole is admirable but not lovable. According to their own lights Blake and Shelley are great and good men, but they are hardly practicable patterns. Keats is in many respects a noble person, but he is united with the others by his weakest, not by his strongest qualities. So wonderfully gifted are these men, so rich in potentialities of wisdom and goodness, that to scold at their shortcomings would be to expose one's own immeasurable inferiority. And yet one must recognize the tragic paradox that these great personalities never quite surmount the hurdle of adolescence. Unable to transcend the egocentric universes of their childhood, they do not establish a thoroughly mature relationship between the *me* and the *not-me*. Far from helping them to solve this problem, their religion merely enshrouds it in a flattering haze of illusion which prevents them from coping with it.

It may be urged that just as the sacramental functions of a priest are independent of his personal character, so one may demand of a poet only that he be duly ordained by the Muses to confer grace through the liturgy of art. The imperfect analogy may be accepted for the sake of the argument. Since all serious poems directly or indirectly express a man's fundamental beliefs, our subject is pertinent to literary criticism; and criticism, conversely, is rich in implications for the study of our subject. Without regard to absolute standards of true or untrue, lofty or base, any thought or feeling which is important in the life of any man deserves to be expressed in art. In this sense the men whom we have studied are admirable poets. The beautiful externalization of the glory and the futility of their aspirations will continue to move us long after we have forgotten the arid little conundrums of those who now regard them with such ineffable scorn.

Romantic religion deserves much of the credit for the best qualities of romantic poetry. Deprived of their faith, these poets would have had nothing of large human significance to affirm or to deny. Possessing that faith, or struggling to possess it, they had a high hope and a deep sorrow, a style, a cause, a philosophy, and a cult. Obeying the urge toward infinite expansiveness, they "shot their being through earth, sea, and air,/Possessing all things with intensest love." To the great benefit of English poetry, they enriched the resources of imagery and rhythm, united man's feelings with external nature and with the glamorous past, revealed the beauty of neglected areas of life, gave a sweet and potent voice to the inmost depths of the human mind.

And yet the religion of the romantics is equally responsible for the deficiencies of their art. The primary business of the poet is not to make a world, but to fashion works of art out of positive or negative responses to the qualities of a world which already exists. The romantic faith in imaginative power, however, can be satisfied only by the creation of a universe. The poems themselves are but confessedly inadequate blueprints of the cosmic mansion. For those who insist with Browning that a man's reach should exceed his grasp the hugeness of the romantics' ambition establishes the greatness of their poetry, but others will object that all this straining to make poetry do the work of metaphysics and theology is damaging not only to religion but to art.

At their best these dreamers are also artists, masters of the technique of their instrument; but too often the joy of the craftsman is hampered by an excessively self-conscious awareness of the priesthood of genius. On the whole they think too much about being poets and not enough about writing poems. They are overly impressed by the powers and duties of the prophetic function. The urgency of their didactic obligation frequently impels them toward symbolism or even toward emotionalized rhetorical discussion. Artists are happier, and they give more happiness to mankind, when they take art a little less solemnly.

Neo-romantic scholars who describe these poets as great mystics unwittingly expose one of their most serious shortcomings. Since the religious implications of poetry are not mystical but sacramental, poetry and mysticism represent opposite poles of spiritual life.[4] Admittedly the pinnacle of the romantic faith is a sense of cosmic interfusion. But so far as this experience is genuinely mystical it transcends the utmost powers of speech, while so far as it is laden with the sensuousness of genuine poetry it vitiates the mystical aspiration. Hence the feverish struggle to express the inexpressible through a mixture of concreteness and vagueness which stirs our emotions without completely satisfying the demands either of religion or of art.[5]

There is a large tincture of traditional snobbery in the habit of regarding the lyric as an essentially inferior type. It is significant, however, that the longing for a vast spiritual synthesis does not enable these writers to build a long poem which is more than a loosely strung succession of short ones, while on the other hand it is much more encouraging to the expression of fleeting moods. Even the admirable lyrics, moreover, move us through the part rather than through the whole. Since the romantic faith is evanescent, uncertain, and fragmentary it prohibits the very ambition which it inspires. The cosmic model shifts her pose too bewilderingly to permit the artist to create a unity.

But in romantic art, of course, there is no model at all other than that provided by inward feeling. Since poetry of any type is basically subjective, these poets should not be reproached for being almost exclusively concerned with their personal emotions. It is fair to say, however, that if inwardness is to be fruitful for religion or philosophy or art it must achieve harmonious relationship with a limiting outwardness, and that the romantic spirit denies this obligation.[6] But just on the point of describing the subjectivity of the romantic poet as solipsistic, we remember the paradox which has plagued us throughout this study. Why does the romantic, at the very summit of his egotism, seem to desire the dissolution of his personal identity?

More than once I have tried to answer this question by saying that

[4] The Abbé Brémond's *Prière et poésie* is probably the most formidable expression of a view precisely contrary to mine. The reader must judge for himself.

[5] Keats must be regarded as an illustrious exception to these remarks on the limitations of romantic poetry; but even he, as we have observed, often plagues himself with the notion that he *should* resemble his contemporaries in these respects. The romanticism of Burns is so rudimentary that he also should be absolved from these strictures.

[6] Wordsworth endeavors to establish such a relationship, but his unusual respect for objective reality cannot be regarded as a typically romantic trait. Romantic poets are not embodiments of romanticism with no admixture of other tendencies. To the extent that they are romantic, however, they live and write by the Inner Light.

romantic self-annihilation, implying the removal of all boundaries and restrictions, represents the extremest form of romantic self-expansion. If my explanation is valid—and the poets themselves appear to accept it— the apparent anomaly becomes a clue to the whole problem of romantic belief. From the pragmatic point of view which this chapter has adopted, the only motive for a man's cultivation of any religion is his desire to obtain more peace, sureness, goodness, and strength than he now possesses by uniting himself with some extrapersonal being or cosmic force which has power to confer those qualities or from which they may be drawn.[7] Even more strongly than most men the romantic poets are moved by this desire. But their genuinely religious aspirations are frustrated by their reluctance to believe in any force superior to the force of their own genius. The divine universal interfusion which they attempt to worship is merely the goal of their personal creativity. Nature, love, brotherhood, liberty, beauty—all the objects of their devotion—become so many ways of expressing the spiritual sufficiency and independence of man. And deified romantic man is the self-portrait of the poet, for what any individual asserts of humanity he asserts primarily of himself. My students are sometimes inclined to attach lofty spiritual significance to Swinburne's "Glory to man in the highest, for man is the master of things"; but when I invite them to delete "man" from this stirring line and substitute "Swinburne" or their own names, they laugh at the absurdity. With the exception of Byron, the romanticists do not laugh. The failure of their attempt to glorify their egotism by means of reverential disguises brings them nothing but despair.

For the last time let us remind ourselves of what we have termed the "circularity" of the romantic religious experience. Burns is a warm-hearted soul, but he uses the benevolism enjoined by his "religion of the bosom" as a means of obtaining membership in a select circle of exceptionally sensitive and enlightened spirits. Hence it becomes an expression of egotism rather than of brotherhood. As a lover of women he is even more obviously self-centered.

Blake, who seems at first glance the most ardently religious of the group, provides the most extreme example of self-deification. "Man can have no idea of anything greater than man. . . . All deities reside in the human

---

[7] Perhaps this is broad enough to include even the contemporary non-theistic view of religion as the sum-total of beneficent human activity. Unless those who hold this position conceive of the totality of men's upward endeavors as somehow higher and more potent than the strivings of the individual, they are pushing the term "religion" beyond its furthest limits.

breast. . . . Thine own humanity learn to adore." With the deepest reverence he worships a Jesus who is no more than a symbol of his own creative energy. God is man, man in Eternity is imagination, and imagination is the genius of William Blake.

Wordsworth is set somewhat apart from his fellows by his more genuine objectivity and his desire for the security provided by extrapersonal law. It is all the more significant, therefore, that in the last analysis his interfusion-experience should prove to be the exploit of the "absolute power" of the imaginative will, a *fiat* of "the Godhead which is ours." When in revising *The Prelude* he substituted "man's power" for "my power" he made no essential change. Even after he had renounced

> That licentious craving of the mind
> To act the God amongst external things,

he hoped to derive from Christianity a sense of "Submission constituting strength and power." Even his warmest contemporary admirers granted that he was utterly self-willed. Had his reverence always been a subconscious means of obtaining a safe harbor within which his mind could sail about under the illusion of perfect liberty?

There is no need to retrace Coleridge's "religion of I AM" through the mazes of his thought: it is obvious that from Ottery to Highgate he never contemplated anything but the ego which he simultaneously adored and loathed. Always he yearns to behold the ultimate reality as

> The whole one Self! Self that no alien knows!
> Self, far diffused as Fancy's wing can travel!
> Self, spreading still! Oblivious of its own,
> Yet all of all possessing!

A finished virtuoso of self-esteem, at the last he can transform even penitence into a source of pride.

The narcissistic quality of Shelley's aspiration was, I believe, sufficiently set forth in the chapter devoted to him. With all his loving soul he sought a reflection of his self-centered goodness in nature, in society, in the heart of woman, and in the Spirit of the Universe. For him as for Blake his imagination is God, and a man precisely like himself is the only conceivable redeemer. In more discouraged moments he can draw almost equal satisfaction from admiration of his blameless sufferings.

In Byron the arc of romantic religion is short-circuited by the very blatancy of his egotism. Because of his special psychological situation he both asserts and denies the impulse which dominates his fellows. He seeks inflation by means of liberalism, pantheism, and the cult of genius; but he is at once too lonely and too cynical to have any strong belief in these disguises of self-regard. He betrays romanticism in deriding his own bluster.

The romantic aspiration of Keats is specialized but intense. Much more of an artist than the others, he tries to elevate sensuous beauty to the level of an object of devotion. But when he thinks of beauty he thinks of the great poets who create it; when he thinks of great poets he thinks of fame; and when he thinks of fame he thinks of his own baffled ambition.

Whatever a romantic poet appears to be devoted to, closer examination reveals that his worship curves backward upon himself. The same may be said of innumerable professors of other religions, but there remains a vast difference between remorsefully failing to surmount a human weakness and making a cult of that weakness. By nature Saint Paul is hardly less egotistic than Blake, but he does not identify his self-esteem with the law of the universe. In his worst moments he says, "I speak as a fool," not "I speak as a genius."

Hence the beginning and the end of romantic religion is what old-fashioned folk call pride. All the loveliness that lies between results from the endeavor to impart some sort of numinous sanction to the craving for independent power. Thus romanticism originates in the deepest primordial subsoil of human nature. Historically speaking, however, the so-called Romantic Movement represents the turning-point of a Titanic assertion of human self-sufficiency which had begun to manifest itself as a dominant movement of mind in the sixteenth century.

The romantic poets show us the crest of the wave just as it shatters itself against the cliffs of reality. But the futility of pride is a lesson that each man must learn for himself, and the devices for evading the repugnant truth are legion. In many respects the major romantic poets were so far ahead of their times that it was necessary for the Victorians to repeat in their own lives the hope and the despair of these precursors. The recession of the wave of human self-trust was also retarded by science-worship and the cult of material progress. Gradually, however, the experience of Western man has caught up with the experience of the great romantics. At last the tide seems to have reached its lowest ebb. Probably there has never been a time when so many men were so desperately aware of their inadequacy, and so uncertain of how to pull themselves together.

This crisis offers the opportunity for a revival of the doctrines of sin and salvation, and such a revival is clearly at work. But the claims of historic Christianity will be resisted so long as there remains the slightest hope of devising a substitute-religion which will proclaim man's ability to redeem himself. It is quite possible that the whole tragedy of modern history, the inflation and collapse of hybris, will be repeated despite the danger that in the next performance the catastrophe will be final. Already we hear it said that reliance on man as man, which would seem to have been stripped of the last tatters of pseudo-spirituality, must be restored as the religion of democracy.

On the other hand there are true lovers of democracy who insist that the cult of human self-sufficiency can never provide a solid foundation for the ideals of freedom and world brotherhood. They hold that pride is ultimately suicidal unless its selfish and anarchic impulses are chastened, sublimated, and guided into beneficent channels. Then indeed, like the scientifically controlled waters of a mighty river, it may become a constructive force in the life of the individual and in society. But the unaided nature of man, as modern history has shown, includes no Tennessee Valley Authority for the flood-control of his passions.

Perilously unstable in romantic religion are the relations between the hard core of self-will and the "idealistic" garments—nature-loving, man-loving, transcendental, pseudo-mystical, aesthetic—in which it is enwrapped. In the younger days of romanticism the latter contributed so richly to the well-being and happiness of man, and provided so useful a bulwark against the encroachments of mechanism, that one is tempted to ignore or condone the former. But since in the long run the idealistic rationalizations cannot save from disillusionment the craving for self-expansion, romantic pride is liable to invert itself into cynicism or despair—a collapse of faith not only in the actualities but in the potentialities of human nature. In less passionate spirits, however, the normal result is nothing so flavorsome as cynicism or so violent as despair, but simply a dull indifference to all that lies beyond the machine, the purse, and the belly.

As the twentieth century knows too well, there is an even more disastrous possibility: not an abandonment of romantic illusion but an exaggerated and hysterical assertion of the fundamental lust for power. In that case the idealism is thrown aside, or kept merely for propaganda, and only the stark cult of energy remains. Aggressive self-trust cannot long masquerade as a religion because in reality there is nothing religious about it. On the animal plane to which it easily relapses it shows its fangs and claws. As poet, the Carlylean hero may seem to be an inspired revealer of the spiritual reality of the universe; but as a political dictator who proclaims that "the strong thing is the just thing" he is not exactly the redeemer of mankind. His "intuitions" become particularly dangerous when more disillusioned, less masterful romantics use him to restore their damaged pride by submerging their identity in his and drawing vicarious strength from his Titanism—the old device of self-expansion through bogus self-annihilation. With consequences hardly less destructive this slave-romanticism may be directed not toward a person but toward some collectivist concept of nation, race, or economic theory. But since these abstractions are too vague for potency, in the long run a Fuehrer generally emerges from them. Masochism is nothing without sadism. All such devotions include a delusively religious impulse, but they never constitute a religion because they look toward nothing above the naturalistic plane.

Romantic totalitarianism is stronger than romantic democracy because it has more boldly and consistently moved onward to the ultimate conclusion of the cult of power: it knows precisely what it wants and refuses to debilitate itself with chatter about "ideals." Those liberals who possess no religion other than sentimental humanitarianism are confronted by a dilemma. Unsupported by the force of pride, the "ideals" which once provided romanticism with a benevolistic façade are merely a clutter of *Schwärmerei,* too feeble and futile to serve as a weapon or even as a refuge. On the other hand, if the battered gospel of human self-sufficiency is restored to something like its original degree of strength it will eventually smash through the amiable "ideals" and reveal itself as the same force which actuates the foes of democracy. I believe that the non-romantic democracy of the Christian tradition, if it became sufficiently widespread, organized, and militant, would be infinitely stronger than any form of Fascism.[8] At present, however, the most popular antidote seems to be a diluted form of the poison which we dread.

Let us end, as we began, with Emerson:

[8] A further proviso must reluctantly be made: it would be necessary for the largest and most powerful branch of Catholic Christendom to develop more fully the ability to distinguish between the order which oppresses and the order which liberates.

Nothing great was ever achieved without enthusiasm. The way of life is wonderful; it is by abandonment. The great moments of history are the facilities of performance through the strength of ideas, as the works of genius and religion. "A man," said Oliver Cromwell, "never rises so high as when he knows not whither he is going."

If this is true, our present elevation must be unrivalled. But the next two sentences, which conclude the aptly named essay on *Circles,* admit that the true romantic abandonment is difficult to maintain, and that ordinary folk must have recourse to substitutes:

Dreams and drunkenness, the use of opium and alcohol, are the semblance and counterfeit of this oracular genius, and hence their dangerous attraction for men. For the like reason they ask the aid of wild passions, as in gaming and war, to ape in some manner these flames and generosities of the heart.[9]

Here at least is fair warning.

[9] R. W. Emerson, *Essays: First Series,* p. 300.

LIST OF SOURCES

My original intention was to give a separate list of sources for each chapter, but I found that so many items pertained to more than one poet that the device would only be a nuisance to the reader. Accordingly I present here a single list of all books and articles cited in this study. To these I have added, chiefly for the benefit of students, a considerable amount of material which, though not expressly cited, has been useful in the composition of my book.

Adams, M. R. Studies in the Literary Backgrounds of English Radicalism. Lancaster (Pa.), 1947.

Aldridge, A. O. Akenside and Imagination. Studies in Philology, XLII, 769–792.

—— The Eclecticism of Mark Akenside's "The Pleasures of Imagination." Journal of the History of Ideas, V, 292–314.

Alison, Archibald. Essays on the Nature and Principles of Taste. From the Edinburgh Edition of 1811. Boston, 1812.

Allen, B. S. The Reaction against William Godwin. Modern Philology, XVI, 225–243.

—— William Godwin as a Sentimentalist. PMLA, XXXIII, 1–29.

Allsop, Thomas. Letters, Conversations and Recollections of S. T. Coleridge. London, 1836.

Angellier, Auguste. Robert Burns. Paris, 1893.

Aubin, R. A. Topographical Poetry in Eighteenth-Century England. New York, 1936.

Babbitt, Irving. Rousseau and Romanticism. Boston and New York, 1919.

Babenroth, A. C. English Childhood: Wordsworth's Treatment of Childhood in the Light of English Poetry from Prior to Crabbe. New York, 1922.

Bald, M. A. Shelley's Mental Progress. Essays and Studies by Members of the English Association, XIII, 112–137.

Bald, R. C. Coleridge and The Ancient Mariner: Addenda to The Road to Xanadu. In Nineteenth-Century Studies, Ithaca (N.Y.), 1940, pp. 1–45.

Barnard, Ellsworth. Shelley's Religion. Minneapolis, 1937.

Barrell, Joseph. Shelley and the Thought of His Time. New Haven, 1947.

Barzun, Jacques. Romanticism and the Modern Ego. Boston, 1943.

Batho, Edith C. The Later Wordsworth. New York, 1933.

Beach, J. W. The Concept of Nature in Nineteenth-Century English Poetry. New York, 1936.

—— Expostulation and Reply. PMLA, XL, 346–361.

—— Reason and Nature in Wordsworth. Journal of the History of Ideas, I, 335–351.

—— A Romantic View of Poetry. Minneapolis, 1944.

Beatty, Arthur. Joseph Fawcett: The Art of War. Its Relation to the Early Development of William Wordsworth. University of Wisconsin Studies in Language and Literature, No. 2. Madison (Wis.), 1918.

—— William Wordsworth: His Doctrine and Art in Their Historical Relations. Madison (Wis.), 1922.

Beatty, Frederika. William Wordsworth of Rydal Mount. New York, 1939.

Beeley, Harold. The Political Thought of Coleridge. In Coleridge, London, 1934, pp. 149–175.

Benn, A. W. The History of English Rationalism in the Nineteenth Century. London, 1906.

Berger, Pierre. William Blake, Poet and Mystic. Tr. Daniel H. Conner. New York, 1915.

Beyer, W. W. Keats and the Daemon King. New York, 1947.

Blake, William. Poetry and Prose. Ed. Geoffrey Keynes. London, 1927.

—— The Prophetic Writings. Ed. D. J. Sloss and J. P. R. Wallis. Oxford, 1926.

Blessington, Countess of. Conversations of Lord Byron with the Countess of Blessington. Philadelphia, 1836.

Blunden, Edmund. Coleridge and Christ's Hospital. In Coleridge, London, 1934, pp. 53–69.

—— Shelley: a Life-Story. London, 1946.

Bonjour, Adrien. Coleridge's "Hymn Before Sunrise." Lausanne, 1942.

Boyd, Elizabeth F. Byron's Don Juan: A Critical Study. New Brunswick (N.J.), 1945.

Bradley, A. C. Keats and "Philosophy." In Keats Memorial Volume, London, 1921, pp. 45–54.

—— Notes on Shelley's Triumph of Life. Modern Language Review, IX, 441–456.

Brailsford, H. N. Shelley, Godwin, and Their Circle. New York, n.d. [1913.]

Brandes, George. Main Currents in Nineteenth Century Literature. Vol. IV: Naturalism in England. New York, 1924.

Brandl, Alois. Coleridge und die Englische Romantik. Berlin, 1886.

Brémond, Henri. Prière et poésie. Paris, 1926.

Brett, G. S. Shelley's Relation to Berkeley and Drummond. In Studies in English by Members of University College, Toronto, Toronto, 1931, pp. 170–202.

Briggs, H. E. Keats's Conscious and Unconscious Reactions to Criticism of Endymion. PMLA, LX, 1106–1129.

Brilioth, Y. T. The Anglican Revival. London, 1933.

Brinton, Crane. The Political Ideas of the English Romanticists. Oxford, 1926.

Bronowski, J. William Blake: A Man Without a Mask. London, 1944.

Broughton, L. N. (ed.). Some Early Nineteenth-Century Letters Hitherto Unpublished. *In* Nineteenth-Century Studies, Ithaca (N.Y.), 1940, pp. 47–88.

Brown, F. K. The Life of William Godwin. London, 1926.

Brown, Leonard. The Genesis, Growth, and Meaning of *Endymion*. Studies in Philology, XXX, 618–653.

Browning, Robert. Complete Poetic and Dramatic Works. Boston and New York, 1895.

Bruce, H. L. William Blake and Gilchrist's Remarkable Coterie of Advanced Thinkers. Modern Philology, XXIII, 285–292.

—— William Blake in This World. London, 1925.

Burke, Edmund. Select Works. Oxford, 1898.

Burns, Robert. Common Place Book. Edinburgh, 1872.

—— Complete Poetical Works. Boston, 1897.

—— Letters. Ed. J. D. Ferguson. Oxford, 1931.

—— The Life and Works of Robert Burns. Ed. Robert Chambers. Revised by William Wallace. New York, 1896.

Bush, Douglas. Mythology and the Romantic Tradition in English Poetry. Cambridge (Mass.), 1937.

Byron, G. G. Childe Harold's Pilgrimage and Other Romantic Poems. Ed. S. C. Chew. New York, 1936.

—— Don Juan and Other Satirical Poems. Ed. L. I. Bredvold. New York, 1935.

—— Lord Byron's Correspondence, Chiefly with Lady Melbourne, etc. Ed. John Murray. New York, 1922.

—— Works. Ed. E. H. Coleridge (Poems) and R. E. Prothero (Letters and Journals). London and New York, 1898–1904.

Caldwell, J. R. John Keats' Fancy. Ithaca (N.Y.), 1945.

—— The Meaning of *Hyperion*. PMLA, LI, 1080–1097.

Cameron, K. N. A Major Source of *The Revolt of Islam*. PMLA, LVI, 175–206.

—— The Political Symbolism of *Prometheus Unbound*. PMLA, LVIII, 728–753.

—— Shelley and the Reformers. ELH, XII, 62–86.

Campbell, O. J. Sentimental Morality in Wordsworth's Narrative Poetry. University of Wisconsin Studies in Language and Literature, XI, 21–51. Madison (Wis.), 1920.

—— Wordsworth's Conception of the Esthetic Experience. *In* Wordsworth and Coleridge, Princeton, 1939, pp. 26–46.

Campbell, Mrs. O. W. Shelley and the Unromantics. London, 1924.

Carlyle, Thomas. Sartor Resartus. On Heroes, Hero-Worship, and the Heroic in History. London, 1926.

Carswell, Catherine. The Life of Robert Burns. New York, 1931.

Cazamian, Louis. L'Évolution psychologique et la littérature en Angleterre, 1660–1914. Paris, 1920.

Cerf, Barry. Wordsworth's Gospel of Nature. PMLA, XXXVII, 615–638.

Chambers, E. K. Samuel Taylor Coleridge: A Biographical Study. Oxford, 1938.

Chapman, E. M. English Literature and Religion, 1800–1900. London, 1910.

Cherubini, William. Shelley's Own Symposium: *The Triumph of Life*. Studies in Philology, XXXIX, 559–570.

Chew, S. C. Byron in England: His Fame and After-Fame. New York, 1924.

—— The Dramas of Lord Byron. Göttingen, 1915.

Christensen, Francis. Creative Sensibility in Wordsworth. Journal of English and Germanic Philology, XLV, 361–368.

Clark, H. W. History of English Nonconformity. Vol. II: From the Restoration to the Close of the Nineteenth Century. London, 1913.

Clutton-Brock, Arthur. Keats and Shelley—a Contrast. *In* The John Keats Memorial Volume, London, 1921, pp. 61–64.

—— Shelley, the Man and the Poet. New York, 1922.

Cobban, Alfred. Edmund Burke and the Revolt against the Eighteenth Century. New York, 1929.

Coleridge, E. H. Biographical Notes. Contributed with introductory remarks by the Rev. G. H. B. Coleridge. *In* Coleridge, London, 1934, pp. 3–52.

Coleridge, S. T. Aids to Reflection and Confessions of an Enquiring Spirit. To which are added his Essay on Faith and Notes on the Book of Common Prayer. London, 1913.

—— Anima Poetae. Ed. E. H. Coleridge. London, 1895.

—— Biographia Literaria. Ed. John Shawcross. London, 1939.

—— Complete Poetical Works. Ed. E. H. Coleridge. Oxford, 1912.

—— Complete Works. Ed. W. G. T. Shedd. New York, 1878.

—— Confessions of an Enquiring Spirit. See Aids to Reflection.

—— Essay on Faith. See Aids to Reflection.

—— Letters. Ed. E. H. Coleridge. Boston and New York, 1895.

—— Miscellaneous Criticism. Ed. T. M. Raysor. London, 1936.

—— The Rime of the Ancient Mariner. With an essay by R. P. Warren. New York, 1946.

—— Table Talk and Omniana. Ed. Thomas Ashe. London, 1923.

—— Unpublished Letters. Ed. E. L. Griggs. London, 1932.

Coleridge, Sara (Mrs. H. N.). The Death of Coleridge. Being an unpublished letter from Mrs. Henry Nelson Coleridge (Sara) to her brother, Hartley. Contributed by E. L. Griggs; *in* Coleridge, London, 1934, pp. 223–232.

Colvin, Sidney. John Keats. London, 1920.

Confessions of Faith, Catechisms, Directories, Form of Church-Government, Discipline, etc., of Public Authority in the Church of Scotland. Glasgow, 1771.

Cottle, Joseph. Early Recollections. London, 1837.

Cunningham, John. The Church History of Scotland. Edinburgh, 1882.

Damon, S. F. William Blake, His Philosophy and Symbols. Boston and New York, 1924.

De Quincey, Thomas. Collected Writings. Ed. David Masson. Edinburgh, 1889–1890.

De Selincourt, Basil. William Blake. London, 1909.

De Selincourt, Ernest. Coleridge's Dejection: An Ode. Essays and Studies by Members of the English Association, XXII, 7–25.

—— Dorothy Wordsworth. Oxford, 1933.

—— The Warton Lecture on Keats. In The John Keats Memorial Volume, London, 1921, pp. 1–21.

—— Wordsworthian and Other Studies. Oxford, 1947.

De Vere, Aubrey. Essays Chiefly on Poetry. London, 1887.

Dicey, A. V. The Statesmanship of Wordsworth. Oxford, 1917.

Dodds, Mrs. E. R. ("A. E. Powell"). The Romantic Theory of Poetry. London, 1926.

Donner, J. O. E. Lord Byrons Weltanschauung. Helsingfors, 1897.

Dowden, Edward. The Life of Percy Bysshe Shelley. London, 1886.

Draper, J. W. The Funeral Elegy and the Rise of English Romanticism. New York, 1929.

Du Bos, Charles. Byron et le besoin de la fatalité. Paris, 1929.

Dunn, S. G. A Note on Wordsworth's Metaphysical System. Essays and Studies by Members of the English Association, XVIII, 74–109.

Edgcumbe, Richard. Byron: The Last Phase. New York, 1909.

Eimer, Manfred. Byron und der Kosmos. Anglistische Forschungen, XXXIV. Heidelberg, 1912.

Eliot, T. S. Blake. In The Sacred Wood, London, 1920, pp. 137–143.

Elliott, G. R. The Cycle of Modern Poetry. Princeton, 1929.

Ellis, E. J. The Real Blake. London, 1907.

Emerson, R. W. Essays. First Series. Boston, 1885.

Estlin, J. P. A Unitarian Christian's Statement and Defence of His Principles. Bristol, 1815.

Evans, Bertrand. Manfred's Remorse and Dramatic Tradition. PMLA, LXII, 752–773.

Evans, F. B. III. Shelley, Godwin, Hume, and the Doctrine of Necessity. Studies in Philology, XXXVII, 632–640.

Fairchild, H. N. Additional Notes on John Johnson's Diary. PMLA, XLIII, 571–572.

——Hartley, Pistorius, and Coleridge. PMLA, LXI, 1010–1021.

—— The Noble Savage. New York, 1928.

—— Religious Trends in English Poetry. Vol. I: 1700–1740, Protestantism and the Cult of Sentiment. Vol. II: 1740–1780, Religious Sentimentalism in the Age of Johnson. New York, 1939, 1942.

—— The Romantic Quest. New York, 1931.

—— Unpublished References to Blake by Hayley and Lady Hesketh. Studies in Philology, XXV, 1–10.

—— Wordsworth's Doctrine of Creative Delusion. South Atlantic Quarterly, XLVI, 545-555.

Farington, Joseph. The Farington Diary. Ed. James Greig. New York, 1923, 1924.

Fausset, H. I. Samuel Taylor Coleridge. London, 1926.

Ferguson, De Lancey. Pride and Passion: Robert Burns. New York, 1939.

—— The Suppressed Poems of Burns. Modern Philology, XXX, 53-60.

Finney, C. L. The Evolution of Keats's Poetry. Cambridge (Mass.), 1936.

Firkins, O. W. Power and Elusiveness in Shelley. Minneapolis, 1937.

Fisch, M. H. The Coleridges, Dr. Prati, and Vico. Modern Philology, XLI, 111-122.

Fitzhugh, R. T. Robert Burns, His Associates and Contemporaries. With the Journal of the Border Tour, edited by De Lancey Ferguson. Chapel Hill (N.C.), 1943.

Fogle, R. H. Romantic Bards and Metaphysical Reviewers. ELH, XII, 221-250.

Fox, Sir John C. The Byron Mystery. London, 1924.

Frend, William. An Account of Some Late Proceedings of the Society for Promoting Christian Knowledge. London, 1789.

—— An Address to the Members of the Church of England, and to Protestant Trinitarians in General, Exhorting Them to Turn from the False Worship of Three Persons, to the Worship of the One True God. London, 1788.

—— A Proposal for Forming a Society for the Extension of Religious Liberty. [London, 1791].

—— Thoughts on Subscription to Religious Tests, Particularly That Required by the University of Cambridge, of Candidates for the Degree of Bachelor of Arts. St. Ives, 1788.

Frye, Northrop. Fearful Symmetry: A Study of William Blake. Princeton, 1947.

Fuess, C. M. Lord Byron as a Satirist in Verse. New York, 1912.

Gairdner, John. Robert Burns and the Ayrshire Moderates. Edinburgh, 1883.

Gardner, Charles. Blake the Man. London, 1919.

Garrod, H. W. Keats. Oxford, 1926.

—— Wordsworth. Oxford, 1927.

Geen, Elizabeth. The Concept of Grace in Wordsworth's Poetry. PMLA, LVIII, 689-715.

Gilchrist, Alexander. The Life of William Blake. Ed. W. G. Robertson. London, 1907.

Gill, F. C. The Romantic Movement and Methodism. London, 1937.

Gingerich, S. F. Essays in the Romantic Poets. New York, 1924.

Gloyn, C. K. The Church in the Social Order. A Study of Anglican Social Theory from Coleridge to Maurice. Forest Grove (Oregon), 1942.

Gode-von Aesch, A. G. F. Natural Science in German Romanticism. New York, 1941.

Godwin, William. An Enquiry Concerning Political Justice and Its Influence on General Virtue and Happiness. Ed. R. A. Preston. New York, 1926.

Grabo, C. H. The Magic Plant: The Growth of Shelley's Thought. Chapel Hill (N.C.), 1936.

—— The Meaning of the Witch of Atlas. Chapel Hill (N.C.), 1935.

—— A Newton among Poets: Shelley's Use of Science in Prometheus Unbound. Chapel Hill (N.C.), 1930.

—— Prometheus Unbound: An Interpretation. Chapel Hill (N.C.), 1935.

Graham, H. G. Scottish Men of Letters in the Eighteenth Century. London, 1901.

—— The Social Life of Scotland in the Eighteenth Century. London, 1901.

Grierson, Sir Herbert J. C. The Background of English Literature. London, 1925.

Griggs, E. L. Hartley Coleridge on His Father. PMLA, XLVI, 1246–1252.

Guérard, Albert, Jr. Prometheus and the Aeolian Lyre. Yale Review, XXXIII, 482–497.

Halévy, Elie. A History of the English People, 1815–1830. Tr. E. I. Watkin. New York, n.d.

—— A History of the English People in 1815. With an introduction by Graham Wallas. Tr. E. I. Watkin and D. A. Barber. New York, 1924.

Haller, William. The Rise of Puritanism. New York, 1938.

—— Tracts on Liberty in the Puritan Revolution, 1638–1647. Records of Civilization, No. XVIII. New York, 1934.

Hamblen, Emily S. On the Minor Prophecies of William Blake. London, 1930.

Hanson, Lawrence. The Life of S. T. Coleridge. The Early Years. New York, 1939.

Harper, G. M. William Wordsworth, His Life, Works, and Influence. New York, 1916.

Hartley, David. Observations on Man. London, 1749.

Havens, R. D. The Mind of a Poet. Baltimore, 1941.

—— Shelley's Alastor. PMLA, XLV, 1098–1115.

—— Unreconciled Opposites in Keats. Philological Quarterly, XIV, 289–300.

Hayley, William. Poetical Works. Dublin, 1785.

Hazlitt, William. Collected Works. Edd. A. R. Waller and Arnold Glover. London, 1902–1904.

Henderson, T. F. Scottish Vernacular Literature. London, 1898.

Herford, Brooke. Unitarianism in England. Unitarianism, pp. 78–96. Boston, 1888–1889.

Herford, C. H. William Blake. Hibbert Journal, XXXVI, 15–30.

—— Wordsworth. London, 1930.

Hoffman, H. L. An Odyssey of the Soul: Shelley's Alastor. New York, 1933.

Hogg, T. J. The Life of Percy Bysshe Shelley as Comprised in The Life of Shelley by Thomas Jefferson Hogg. The Recollections of Shelley and Byron by Edward John Trelawny. Memoirs of Shelley by Thomas Love Peacock. Ed. Humbert Wolfe. London, 1933.

Holcroft, Thomas. The Life of Thomas Holcroft. Written by Himself. Continued to the Time of His Death . . . by William Hazlitt. Ed. Elbridge Colby. London, 1925.

Houpt, C. T. Mark Akenside: A Biographical and Critical Study. Philadelphia, 1945.

Howard, Claud. Coleridge's Idealism: A Study of Its Relationship to Kant and to the Cambridge Platonists. Boston, 1924.

Hughes, A. M. D. The Nascent Mind of Shelley. Oxford, 1947.

—— The Theology of Shelley. Proceedings of the British Academy, XXIV, 191–203.

Hulme, T. E. Speculations. London, 1936.

Hungerford, E. B. Shores of Darkness. New York, 1941.

Hunt, John. Pantheism and Christianity. London, 1884.

—— Religious Thought in England in the Nineteenth Century. London, 1896.

Hunt, Leigh. Poetical Works. Ed. H. S. Milford. London, 1923.

Hutcheson, Francis. An Inquiry into the Original of our Ideas of Beauty and Virtue. Glasgow, 1772.

Inge, W. R. The Platonic Tradition in English Religious Thought. London, 1926.

—— Studies in English Mystics. London, 1907.

Ingpen, Roger. Shelley in England. London, 1917.

James, D. G. Scepticism and Poetry. London, 1937.

Jamieson, A. B. Burns and Religion. Cambridge, 1931.

Johnson, E. D. H. Don Juan in England. ELH, XI, 135–153.

Jones, F. L. Hogg and The Necessity of Atheism. PMLA, LII, 423–426.

—— The Shelley Legend. PMLA, LXI, 848–890.

—— Shelley's On Life. PMLA, LXII, 774–783.

Kaufman, Paul. The Reading of Southey and Coleridge. Modern Philology, XXI, 317–320.

Keats, John. Letters. Ed. M. B. Forman. 2nd ed. New York, 1935. [My chapter on Keats was written before the third edition appeared in 1947. The changes and additions are not important for my purposes.]

—— Poetical Works. Ed. H. W. Garrod. Oxford, 1939.

Kellner, L. Shelley's Queen Mab and Volney's Les Ruines. Englische Studien, XXII, 9–40.

Kennedy, James. Conversations on Religion with Lord Byron and Others. Philadelphia, 1833.

Kennedy, W. L. The English Heritage of Coleridge of Bristol. New Haven, 1947.

Kurtz, B. P. Coleridge on Swedenborg, with Unpublished Marginalia on the

"Prodromus." University of California Publications in English, XIV, 199–214.

—— The Pursuit of Death: A Study of Shelley's Poetry. New York, 1933.

Lamb, Charles. Letters. Ed. E. V. Lucas. New Haven, 1935.

Larrabee, S. A. English Bards and Grecian Marbles. New York, 1943.

Lee, Umphrey. The Historical Backgrounds of Early Methodist Enthusiasm. New York, 1931.

Legg, J. Wickham. English Church Life from the Restoration to the Tractarian Movement. London, 1914.

Legouis, Emile. The Early Life of William Wordsworth. Tr. J. W. Matthews. London, 1921.

—— Some Remarks on the Composition of the Lyrical Ballads of 1798. In Wordsworth and Coleridge, Princeton, 1939, pp. 3–11.

Levin, Harry. The Broken Column: A Study in Romantic Hellenism. Cambridge (Mass.), 1931.

Lewis, C. S. Rehabilitations and Other Essays. London, 1939.

Lindsey, Theophilus. An Historical View of the State of the Unitarian Doctrine and Worship from the Reformation to Our Own Times. London, 1783.

Lotspeich, H. G. Shelley's "Eternity" and Demogorgon. Philological Quarterly, XIII, 309–311.

Lovejoy, A. O. Coleridge and Kant's Two Worlds. ELH, VII, 341–362.

—— Kant and the English Platonists. In Essays Philosophical and Psychological in Honor of William James, New York, 1908, pp. 265–302.

Lowell, Amy. John Keats. Boston and New York, 1925.

Lowery, Margaret R. Windows of the Morning. New Haven, 1940.

Lowes, J. L. Moneta's Temple. PMLA, LI, 1098–1113.

—— The Road to Xanadu. Boston and New York, 1927.

Lucas, F. L. The Decline and Fall of the Romantic Ideal. New York, 1936.

Lynch, Arthur. John Keats. In The John Keats Memorial Volume, London, 1921, pp. 127–132.

Madariaga, Salvador de. Shelley and Calderon. New York, n.d.

Marjarum, E. W. Byron as Skeptic and Believer. Princeton, 1938.

Martin, A. D. The Religion of Wordsworth. London, 1936.

Martineau, Harriet. Autobiography. Ed. Maria W. Chapman. Boston, 1881.

Mayne, Ethel C. Byron. London, 1912.

—— Life and Letters of . . . Lady Byron. New York, 1929.

McGiffert, A. C. Protestant Thought before Kant. New York, 1911.

McNulty, J. B. Autobiographical Vagaries in Tintern Abbey. Studies in Philology, XLII, 81–86.

Medwin, Thomas. The Life of Percy Bysshe Shelley. Ed. H. B. Forman. London, 1913.

Meyer, G. W. Wordsworth's Formative Years. Ann Arbor (Mich.), 1943.

Millar, J. H. A Literary History of Scotland. New York, 1903.

More, P. E. The Drift of Romanticism. Shelburne Essays. Eighth Series. Boston, 1913.

Morley, Edith J. Coleridge in Germany (1799). *In* Wordsworth and Coleridge, Princeton, 1939, pp. 220–236.

Mossner, E. C. Coleridge and Bishop Butler. Philosophical Review, XLV, 206–208.

Muirhead, J. H. Coleridge as Philosopher. London, 1930.

—— Metaphysician or Mystic? Coleridge, pp. 177–197. London, 1934.

Mumford, Lewis. Technics and Civilization. New York, 1934.

Munk, Elias. William Wordsworth. Ein Beitrag zur Erforschung seiner religiösen Entwicklung. Germanische Studien, LII. Berlin, 1927.

Murry, J. M. Heroes of Thought. New York, 1938.

—— Keats and Shakespeare. London, 1925.

Musset, Alfred de. La Confession d'un enfant du siècle. Paris, 1936.

Myers, F. W. H. Wordsworth. London, 1881.

Neff, Emery. A Revolution in European Poetry, 1660–1900. New York, 1940.

Newman, J. H. Loss and Gain. London, 1874.

Nicolson, H. G. Byron: The Last Journey, 1823–1824. London, 1940.

Nitchie, Elizabeth. The Moral of the *Ancient Mariner* Reconsidered. PMLA, XLVIII, 867–876.

Notopoulos, J. A. The Dating of Shelley's Prose. PMLA, LVIII, 477–498.

—— The Platonic Sources of Shelley's "Hymn to Intellectual Beauty." PMLA, LVIII, 582–584.

—— Shelley and Thomas Taylor. PMLA, LI, 502–517.

Overton, J. H. The English Church in the Nineteenth Century (1800–1833). London, 1894.

Paine, Thomas. The Age of Reason. Ed. M. D. Conway. New York, 1910.

Park, Mary C. Joseph Priestley and the Problem of Pantisocracy. Proceedings of the Delaware County Institute of Science. Media (Pa.), July, 1947.

Peacock, T. L. Memoirs of Percy Bysshe Shelley. *See* Hogg, T. J.

Peck, W. E. Shelley: His Life and Work. New York, 1927.

—— Shelley, Mary Shelley, and Rinaldo Rinaldini. PMLA, XL, 165–171.

Percival, M. O. William Blake's Circle of Destiny. New York, 1938.

Perdeck, A. A. Theology in Augustan Literature. Groningen, 1928.

Pierce, F. E. Blake and Thomas Taylor. PMLA, XLIII, 1121–1141.

—— The Genesis and General Meaning of Blake's *Milton*. Modern Philology, XXV, 165–178.

—— Wordsworth and Thomas Taylor. Philological Quarterly, VII, 61–64.

Plowman, Max. An Introduction to the Study of Blake. New York, 1927.

"Powell, A. E." *See* Dodds, Mrs. E. R.

Praz, Mario. The Romantic Agony. Tr. Angus Davidson. London, 1933.

Prescott, F. C. Poetry and Myth. New York, 1927.

Priestley, Joseph. Defences of Unitarianism for the Year 1787. Birmingham, 1788.
—— and Richard Price. A Free Discussion of the Doctrines of Materialism, and Philosophical Necessity. London, 1778.
—— Letters to the Philosophers and Politicians of France, on the Subject of Religion. London, 1793.
—— Memoirs of Dr. Joseph Priestley to the Year 1795, Written by Himself: With a Continuation, to the Time of His Decease, by His Son, Joseph Priestley. Northumberland (Pa.), 1806.

Quennell, Peter. Byron: The Years of Fame. New York, 1935.
—— Byron in Italy. New York, 1941.
Quinlan, M. J. Victorian Prelude. New York, 1941.

Rader, M. M. Presiding Ideas in Wordsworth's Poetry. University of Washington Publications in Language and Literature, VIII. Seattle, 1931.
—— The Transcendentalism of William Wordsworth. Modern Philology, XXVI, 169–190.
Railo, Eino. The Haunted Castle: A Study of the Elements of English Romanticism. London, 1927.
Raleigh, Walter. Wordsworth. London, 1903.
Rawnsley, H. D. Reminiscences of Wordsworth among the Peasantry of Westmoreland. Transactions of the Wordsworth Society, VI, 159–194.
Rea, J. D. Coleridge's Health. Modern Language Notes, XLV, 16–17.
—— Coleridge's Intimations of Immortality from Proclus. Modern Philology, XXVI, 201–213.
Read, Herbert. Wordsworth. New York, 1931.
Reid, Thomas. Essays on the Intellectual Powers of Man. Ed. James Walker. Philadelphia, 1878.
Richards, I. A. Coleridge on Imagination. New York, 1935.
Richter, Helene. Lord Byron: Persönlichkeit und Werk. Halle, 1929.
—— Die philosophische Weltanschauung von S. T. Coleridge und ihr Verhältnis zur deutschen Philosophie. Anglia, XLIV (Neue Folge, XXXII), 261–290, 297, 424.
—— Zu Shelleys philosophischer Weltanschauung. Englische Studien, XXX, 224–265, 383–435.
Ridley, M. R. Keats' Craftsmanship. Oxford, 1933.
Roberts, J. H. Poetry of Sensation or of Thought? PMLA, XLV, 1129–1139.
—— The Significance of Lamia. PMLA, L, 550–561.
Roberts, R. E. Samuel Rogers and His Circle. London, n.d. [1910]
Robinson, H. C. The Correspondence of Henry Crabb Robinson with the Wordsworth Circle. Ed. Edith J. Morley. Oxford, 1927.
—— Henry Crabb Robinson on Books and Their Writers. Ed. Edith J. Morley. London, 1938.

Routh, H. V. Towards the Twentieth Century: Essays in the Spiritual History of the Nineteenth. New York, 1937.

Russell, G. W. E. A Short History of the Evangelical Movement. London, 1915.

Rydal Mount Library Catalogue, The. Transactions of the Wordsworth Society, VI, 195–257.

Sanders, C. R. Coleridge and the Broad Church Movement. Durham (N.C.), 1942.

Santayana, George. Character and Opinion in the United States. New York, 1920.

—— Little Essays Drawn from the Writings of George Santayana. Ed. L. P. Smith. New York, 1920.

Saurat, Denis. Blake and Milton. London, 1935.

—— Blake and Modern Thought. London, 1929.

Schneider, Elisabeth. The "Dream" of *Kubla Khan*. PMLA, LX, 784–801.

Schöffler, Herbert. Protestantismus und Literatur. Leipzig, 1922.

Schorer, Mark. Swedenborg and Blake. Modern Philology, XXXVI, 157–178.

—— William Blake: The Politics of Vision. New York, 1946.

Scott, W. R. Francis Hutcheson. Cambridge, 1900.

Seth, Andrew. Scottish Philosophy. Edinburgh, 1885.

Shafer, Robert. Christianity and Naturalism. New Haven, 1926.

Sharp, William. The Life and Letters of Joseph Severn. London, 1892.

Shaw, G. B. Keats. *In* The John Keats Memorial Volume, London, 1921, pp. 173–176.

Shelley Society's Papers, The. Part I. London, 1888.

Shelley, Mary. Journal. Ed. F. L. Jones. Norman (Okla.), 1947.

—— Letters. Ed. F. L. Jones. Norman (Okla.), 1944.

Shelley, P. B. Complete Works. Julian Edition. Edd. Roger Ingpen and W. E. Peck. London and New York, 1927–1930.

Smith, Adam. Works. Vol. I: The Theory of Moral Sentiments. London, 1812.

Smith, Elsie (ed.). An Estimate of William Wordsworth by his Contemporaries. Oxford, 1932.

Smith, J. C. A Study of Wordsworth. Edinburgh, 1944.

Smith, R. M., and Others. The Shelley Legend. New York, 1945.

Snyder, A. D. Books Borrowed by Coleridge from the Library of the University of Göttingen, 1799. Modern Philology, XXV, 377–380.

—— Coleridge on Böhme. PMLA, XLV, 616–618.

—— Coleridge on Giordano Bruno. Modern Language Notes, XLII, 427–436.

—— Coleridge on Logic and Learning. New Haven, 1929.

—— The MS of *Kubla Khan*. London Times Literary Supplement, August 2, 1934, p. 541.

Snyder, F. B. The Life of Robert Burns. New York, 1932.

Solve, M. T. Shelley: His Theory of Poetry. Chicago, 1927.

Sperry, W. L. Wordsworth's Anti-Climax. Cambridge (Mass.), 1935.

Stallknecht, N. P. The Doctrine of Coleridge's *Dejection* and Its Relation to Wordsworth's Philosophy. PMLA, XLIX, 196–207.

—— The Moral of the *Ancient Mariner*. PMLA, XLVII, 559–569.

—— Nature and Imagination in Wordsworth's Meditation upon Mt. Snowdon. PMLA, LII, 835–847.

—— Strange Seas of Thought. Durham (N.C.), 1945.

—— The Tragic Flaw in Wordsworth's Philosophy. *In* Wordsworth and Coleridge, Princeton, 1939, pp. 47–61.

—— Wordsworth and Philosophy. PMLA, XLIV, 1116–1143.

—— Wordsworth's *Ode to Duty* and the Schöne Seele. PMLA, LII, 230–243.

Stawell, F. M. On Shelley's *The Triumph of Life*. Essays and Studies by Members of the English Association, V, 104–131.

Stern, B. H. The Rise of Hellenism in English Literature, 1732–1786. Menasha (Wis.), 1940.

Stewart, H. L. The Place of Coleridge in English Theology. Harvard Theological Review, XI, 1–31.

Storr, V. F. The Development of English Theology in the Nineteenth Century. 1800–1860. London, 1913.

Stoughton, John. Religion in England from 1800 to 1850. London, 1884.

Stovall, Floyd. Desire and Restraint in Shelley. Durham (N.C.), 1931.

Strachey, Lytton. The Poetry of Blake. *In* Books and Characters, New York, 1922, pp. 210–233.

Strong, A. T. Three Studies in Shelley. London, 1921.

Strout, A. L. (ed.). John Bull's Letter to Lord Byron. Norman (Okla.), 1947.

Symonds, J. A. Shelley. New York, 1879.

Symons, Arthur. William Blake. New York, 1907.

[Taylor, John]. A Narrative of Mr. Joseph Rawson's Case. London, 1737.

Thompson, H. W. A Scottish Man of Feeling. London and New York, 1931.

Thorpe, C. D. Coleridge on the Sublime. *In* Wordsworth and Coleridge, Princeton, 1939, pp. 192–219.

—— The Imagination: Coleridge *versus* Wordsworth. Philological Quarterly, XVIII, 1–18

—— Keats's Interest in Politics and World Affairs. PMLA, XLVI, 1228–1245.

—— The Mind of John Keats. New York, 1926.

Trelawny, E. J. Recollections of the Last Days of Shelley and Byron. *See* Hogg, T. J.

Trueblood, P. G. The Flowering of Byron's Genius: Studies in Byron's Don Juan. Stanford University, 1945.

Tulloch, John. Movements of Religious Thought in Britain During the Nineteenth Century. New York, 1885.

Waples, Dorothy. David Hartley in *The Ancient Mariner*. Journal of English and Germanic Philology, XXXV, 337–351.

Ward, W. S. Some Aspects of the Conservative Attitude toward Poetry in English Criticism, 1798–1820. PMLA, LX, 386–398.

Warre Cornish, Francis. The English Church in the Nineteenth Century. Part I. London, 1933.

Warren, R. P. A Poem of Pure Imagination. Appended to S. T. Coleridge, The Rime of the Ancient Mariner. New York, 1946.

Watters, R. E. Wordsworth's "Amaranthine Flower of Faith." Modern Language Quarterly, V, 339–356.

Weaver, Bennett. Toward the Understanding of Shelley. Ann Arbor (Mich.), 1932.

Welch, Livingston. Imagination and Human Nature. Psyche Monographs, No. 3. London, 1935.

Wellek, René. Immanuel Kant in England, 1793–1838. Princeton, 1931.

Whelan, Sister M. Kevin, S. S. J. Enthusiasm in English Poetry of the Eighteenth Century, 1700–1774. Washington, 1935.

White, Helen C. The Mysticism of William Blake. University of Wisconsin Studies in Language and Literature, No. 23. Madison (Wis.), 1927.

White, N. I. Shelley. New York, 1940.

—— Shelley's *Prometheus Unbound,* or Every Man His Own Allegorist. PMLA, XL, 172–184.

Whitehead, A. N. Science and the Modern World. New York, 1939.

Wicksteed, J. H. Blake's Innocence and Experience. London, 1928.

—— Blake's Vision of the Book of Job. London, 1910.

Wilberforce, William. A Practical View of the Prevailing Religious System of Professed Christians in the Higher and Middle Classes of Society, Contrasted with Real Christianity. New York, 1851.

Wilde, H. O. Der Gottesgedanke in der englischen Literatur. Das Problem der Entwicklung von puritanischer zu romantischer Literatur. Breslau, 1930.

Wilde, Norman. The Development of Coleridge's Thought. Philosophical Review, XXVIII, 147–163.

Willey, Basil. The Eighteenth Century Background. New York, 1941.

Wilson, Mona. The Life of William Blake, London, 1932.

Winkelmann, Elizabeth. Coleridge und die Kantische Philosophie. Leipzig, 1933.

Winstanley, D. A. Unreformed Cambridge. Cambridge, 1935.

Winstanley, Lillian. Platonism in Shelley. Essays and Studies by Members of the English Association, IV, 72–100.

Witcutt, W. P. Blake: A Psychological Study. London, 1947.

Wordsworth, Christopher. Memoirs of William Wordsworth. London, 1851.

—— Scholae Academicae, Cambridge, 1877.

Wordsworth, Dorothy. Journals. Ed. Ernest de Selincourt. New York, 1941.

Wordsworth, G. G. The Boyhood of Wordsworth. Cornhill Magazine, XLVIII, 410–420.

Wordsworth, William. The Convention of Cintra. Ed. A. V. Dicey. London, 1915.

—— Ecclesiastical Sonnets. Ed. Abbie F. Potts. New Haven, 1922.

—— A Guide to the District of the Lakes in the North of England. Kendal, 1835.

—— Poetical Works. Edd. Ernest de Selincourt (Vols. I and II) and Helen Darbishire (Vol. III). Oxford, 1940, 1944, 1946.

—— Poetical Works. Ed. Thomas Hutchinson. New edition, revised by Ernest de Selincourt. London, 1942.

—— The Prelude. Ed. Ernest de Selincourt. Oxford, 1926.

—— Prose Works. Ed. William Knight. London, 1896.

—— The Recluse. London, 1888.

—— The White Doe of Rylstone. A Critical Edition by Alice Pattee Comparetti. Cornell Studies in English, XXIX. Ithaca (N.Y.), 1940.

Wordsworth, William, and Dorothy Wordsworth. The Early Letters. Ed. Ernest de Selincourt. Oxford, 1935.

—— Letters. The Middle Years. Ed. Ernest de Selincourt. Oxford, 1937.

—— Letters. The Later Years. Ed. Ernest de Selincourt. Oxford, 1939.

Worthington, Jane. Wordsworth's Reading of Roman Prose. New Haven, 1946.

Wright, Dudley. Robert Burns and Freemasonry. Paisley, n.d.

Yarnall, Ellis. Wordsworth and the Coleridges. New York, 1899.

INDEX OF NAMES

INDEX OF TOPICS

Child labor, 237

Children, effects of Industrial Revolution on, 217 f.; spiritually educative influence of nature, 289

Chivalry, 334, 335, 336

Christianity, see also Catholicism; Deism; Faith; God; Jesus Christ; Protestantism; Reformation; Religion; and under names of Christian churches, e.g., Kirk of Scotland; romantic conception, vii–ix, 3–18; Blake's version, 75, 99, 124; chivalric, 334 ff.; Coleridge's conception, 294, 298, 319, 324; effect of overemphasis on subjective and intuitive, 322; gospel of Shaftesbury consistent with, 27; ideal of the human soul, 505; identification of benevolism with, 41, 203; identity of art and, 121, 127; only Revelation of permanent validity, 313; purification of, 11; reactionary, 341; reduced to a code of morals, 339n; a religion of self-trust, 10; Shelley's attempts to remould, 329 ff.; spirit of, torn from its doctrinal setting, 130; transcendental philosophy and, reconciled, 318; vestiges of, in Byron's verse, 398

Christians, hypocrisy, 447

Church, Christian, 323; medieval, abused her forms, 238; sins of, responsible for agnosticism, 341; see also Kirk of Scotland

Church and State, 217, 219, 227, 255, 309, 318

Church of England, 154, 156, 221 ff., 225, 309, 436, 457; Byron's thrusts at, 444; Catholic attributes, 248; Coleridge a member of, 313; more churches needed, 223; promotion through patronage, 222; Wordsworth's praise of, 219

Church of France, 309

"Circle of Destiny," 104–8 passim, 125, 133

Circularity, romantic, 377, 407, 509

Civilization, modern, 504

Classicism, 419

Clergy, appointment by democratic call, 32; appointment by parochial patronage, 34; dependence of New Light, upon upper class, 34; heresy among, of Ayrshire, 30; promotion through patronage, 222; secular literary interests, 16; symbol of oppressive authority, 67, 88; training at University of Glasgow, 25 ff.

Common sense, intuitive principles of, 30

Common Sense school of philosophy, 29, 58

Communion with invisible world, 211

Concubinage, 86n

Conscience, 311, 321, 444; see also Inner Light; Moral sense

Consciousness, 500; taproot of romanticism, 3

Conservativism, 204, 225

Contemplation, 131, 147, 175, 308

Contraries, 80

Conversion, moral, 172

Corruption, total, 24, 27

Cosmic man, 106, 110

Cosmic unity, 355

Creation, 3, 436

Creative power, see Over-Soul

Creativity, human, 7

Creed and dogma, 225, 227, 260, 310, 331, 435

Crucifixion, see Atonement

Day of Judgment, see Judgment Day

Death, 108, 198, 383, 384n, 506

Deism, 8, 16, 18, 24, 31, 60, 113, 170, 171, 198, 274, 310, 339, 413; see also Atheism; Christianity; God; Rationalism; decline of overt, 203; identified with Christianity, 450; revival encouraged by French Revolution, 203; sentimental, 147, 170, 177, 261, 449

Democracy, Catholic, 238; Christian, 503, 513; of Calvinism, 34; religion of, 512

Denial, 80

Destiny, 105

Determinism, see Necessitarianism

Devil, see Satan

Dissent, see Nonconformity

Divine Humanity, 68, 73, 110

Divine Mind, 357

Divine Spirit, 7

Divine Vision, 6, 66, 107, 109, 110, 128, 133

Divinity, universal, 180

Doctrine, pragmatic justification of, 260

Dogma, see Creed and dogma

Drug addiction, 291

Drunkenness, 52

Earth, 201

Education, Dr. Bell's scheme of, 218; rate-supported, 236; religious and secular, in Scotland, 19; Wordsworth's plea for universal elementary, 218

Ego, 4; creative, 24

Egotism, 508, 509 ff., 121, 135; Absolute, 13

Eighteenth century, indebtedness of romantic poets to, 187, 479